Publius Vergilius Maro

The Works of Virgil Literally

Traslated Into English Prose with Notes by Davidson

Publius Vergilius Maro

The Works of Virgil Literally
Traslated Into English Prose with Notes by Davidson

ISBN/EAN: 9783741139697

Manufactured in Europe, USA, Canada, Australia, Japa

Cover: Foto ©Thomas Meinert / pixelio.de

Manufactured and distributed by brebook publishing software
(www.brebook.com)

Publius Vergilius Maro

The Works of Virgil Literally

A CATALOGUE OF
BOHN'S VARIOUS LIBRARIES.

PUBLISHED BY
GEORGE BELL AND SONS,
4, 5, & 6, YORK STREET, COVENT GARDEN, LONDON.
1873.

I.

A SERIES OF
POST

TIONS, PRINTED IN
A VOLUME
18E).

Bacon's Essays
dom of the An
Henry VII., wi
Portrait.

Beaumont and
Selection from.

Beckmann's H
Discoveries, an
enlarged. Part

Bremer's (Miss
Mary Howitt.
Vol. 1. The P
Vol. 2. The P
Vol. 3. The P
Vol. 4. A Dia

Butler's (Bp.)
and Sermons, w

Carafas (The) of Maddaloni: and
Naples under Spanish Dominion. Trans-
lated from the German of Alfred de
Reumont.

Carrel's Counter Revolution in England. Fox's History and Lonsdale's
Memoir of James II. Portrait.

Cellini (Benvenuto), Memoirs of.
Translated by Roscoe. Portrait.

Coleridge's (S. T.) Friend. A Series of
Essays on Morals, Politics, and Religion.

Coleridge's (S. T.) Biographia Liter-
aria, and two Lay Sermons.

Condé's Dominion of the Arabs in
Spain. Translated by Mrs. Foster. In
3 vols.

late Works. Edited,
the Author, by Southey.
50 Engravings. In 8 vols.
moir and Correspondence.
Poetical Works. Plates.
's Iliad. Plates.
's Odyssey. Plates.

s of the Duke of
artraits. In 3 vols.
re plans of Marlborough's
to. 10s. 6d.

of the House of
tes. In 4 vols.

. Constitution of Eng-
with Notes, by John

plete Works. 2 vols.

Life and Correspond-
ence. Edited by J. E. Ryland. In 2 vols.

—— Lectures at Broadmead
Chapel. Edited by J. E. Ryland. In
2 vols.

—— Critical Essays. Edited by
J. E. Ryland. In 2 vols.

—— Essays—On Decision of Character, &c. &c.

—— Essays—On the Evils of Popular Ignorance, &c.

—— Fosteriana: Thoughts, Reflections, and Criticisms of the late John
Foster, selected from periodical papers,
and Edited by Henry G. Bohn (nearly
400 pages). 5s.

Fuller's (Andrew) Principal Works.
With Memoir. Portrait.

2

WALTER K.
...
slated into
...
ur, and Revolt

' the Revolt
Wallenstein's
u ; the Death
'Brian Tell
' Stuart, Maid
' Measina,
sco, Love and
Secov.
ed by EDGAR

BOWRING, M.P.

Schlegel's Philosophy of Life and of Language, translated by A. J. W. MOR-RISON.

——— History of Literature, Ancient and Modern. Now first completely translated, with General Index.

——— Philosophy of History. Translated by J. B. ROBERTSON. *Portrait.*

——— Dramatic Literature. Translated. *Portrait.*

——— Modern History.

——— Esthetic and Miscellaneous Works.

Sheridan's Dramatic Works and Life *Portrait.*

Sismondi's Literature of the South of Europe. Translated by ROSCOE. *Portraits.* In 2 vols.

Smith's (Adam) Theory of the Moral Sentiments; with his Essay on the First Formation of Languages.

Smyth's (Professor) Lectures on Modern History. In 9 vols.

——— Lectures on the French Revolution. In 2 vols.

Sturm's Morning Communings with God, or Devotional Meditations for Every Day in the Year.

Taylor's (Bishop Jeremy) Holy Living and Dying. *Portrait.*

Thierry's Conquest of England by the Normans. Translated by WILLIAM HAZLITT. *Portrait.* In 2 vols.

——— Tiers Etat, or Third Estate, in France. Translated by F. B. WELLS. 2 vols. in one. 5s.

Vasari's Lives of the Painters, Sculptors, and Architects. Translated by Mrs. FOSTER. 6 vols.

Wesley's (John) Life. By ROBERT SOUTHEY. New and Complete Edition. Double volume. 5s.

Wheatley on the Book of Common Prayer. *Frontispiece.*

II.

Uniform with Bohn's Standard Library.

Bailey's (P. J.) Festus. A Poem. Seventh Edition, revised and enlarged. 5s.; with Portrait, 6s.

British Poets, from Milton to Kirke White. Cabinet Edition. In 4 vols. 14s.

Cary's Translation of Dante's Heaven, Hell, and Purgatory. 7s. 6d.

Cervantes' Galatea. Translated by GORDON GYLL.

Chillingworth's Religion of Protestants. 3s. 6d.

Classic Tales. Comprising in One volume the most esteemed works of the imagination. 3s. 6d.

Demosthenes and Æschines, the Orations of. Translated by LELAND. 3s.

Dickson and Mowbray on Poultry. Edited by Mrs. LOUDON. *Illustrations by Harvey.* 5s.

Hawthorne's Tales. In 2 vols., 3s. 6d. each.

    Vol. I. Twice Told Tales, and the Snow Image.

    Vol. 2. Scarlet Letter, and the House with the seven Gables.

Henry's (Matthew) Commentary on the Psalms. *Numerous Illustrations.* 4s. 6d.

Holland's British Angler's Manual. Improved and enlarged, by EDWARD JESSE, Esq. *Illustrated with 60 Engravings.* 7s. 6d.

Horace's Odes and Epodes. Translated by the Rev. W. SEWELL. 3s. 6d.

Irving's (Washington) Life of Washington. *Portrait.* In 4 vols. 3s. 6d. each.

——— (Washington) Life and Letters. By his Nephew, PIERRE E. IRVING. In 2 vols. 3s. 6d. each.

Irving's (Washington) Complete
Works. In 11 vols. 3s. 6d. each.
  Vol. 1. Salmagundi and Knickerbocker.
  Portrait of the Author.
  Vol. 2. Sketch Book and Life of Gold-
  smith.
  Vol. 3. Bracebridge Hall and Abbots-
  ford and Newstead.
  Vol. 4. Tales of a Traveller and the
  Alhambra.
  Vol. 5. Conquest of Granada and Con-
  quest of Spain.
  Vols. 6 and 7. Life of Columbus and
  Companions of Columbus, with a new
  Index. *Fine Portrait.*
  Vol. 8. Astoria and Tour in the Prairies.
  Vol. 9. Mahomet and his Successors.
  Vol. 10. Conquest of Florida and Ad-
  ventures of Captain Bonneville.
  Vol. 11. Biographies and Miscellanies.
For separate Works, see Cheap Series, p.15.

Joyce's Introduction to the Arts and
Sciences. With Examination Questions.
3s. 6d.

Lawrence's Lectures on Compara-
tive Anatomy, Physiology, Zoology, and the
Natural History of Man. *Illustrated.* 5s.

Lilly's Introduction to Astrology.
With numerous Emendations, by ZADKIEL.
5s.

Miller's (Professor) History Philoso-
phically considered. In 4 vols. 3s. 6d.
each.

Political Cyclopædia. In 4 vols.
3s. 6d. each.

——— Also bound in 2 vols, with
leather backs. 15s.

Uncle Tom's Cabin. With Introductory Remarks by the Rev. J. SHERMAN.
*Printed in a large clear type. Illustra-
tions.* 3s. 6d.

Wide, Wide World. By ELIZABETH
WETHERALL. *Illustrated with 10 highly-
finished Steel Engravings.* 3s. 6d.

III.
Bohn's Historical Library.
UNIFORM WITH THE STANDARD LIBRARY, AT 5s. PER VOLUME.

Evelyn's Diary and Correspondence.
Illustrated with numerous Portraits, &c.
In 4 vols.

Pepys' Diary and Correspondence.
Edited by Lord Braybrooke. With im-
portant Additions, including numerous
Letters. *Illustrated with many Portraits.*
In 4 vols.

James's Memoirs of the Reign of the
Stuarts, including the Protectorate. With
General Index. *Upwards of 40 Portraits.*
In 3 vols.

James's Memoirs of the Pretenders
and their Adherents. 6 *Portraits.*

Nugent's (Lord) Memorials of
Hampden, his Party, and Times. 12
Portraits.

Strickland's (Agnes) Lives of the
Queens of England, from the Norman
Conquest. From official records and
authentic documents, private and public.
Revised Edition. In 6 vols.

——— Life of Mary Queen of Scots.
2 vols.

IV.
Bohn's Library of French Memoirs.
UNIFORM WITH THE STANDARD LIBRARY AT 3s. 6d. PER VOLUME.

Memoirs of Philip de Commines,
containing the Histories of Louis XI. and
Charles VIII. and of Charles the Bold,
Duke of Burgundy. To which is added,
The Scandalous Chronicle, or Secret

History of Louis XI. *Portraits.* In
2 vols.

Memoirs of the Duke of Sully, Prime
Minister to Henry the Great. *Portraits.*
In 4 vols.

V.
Bohn's School and College Series.
UNIFORM WITH THE STANDARD LIBRARY.

Bass's Complete Greek and English
Lexicon to the New Testament. 2s.

New Testament (The) in Greek.
Griesbach's Text, with the various readings of Mill and Scholz at foot of page, and

Parallel References in the margin; also a
Critical Introduction and Chronological
Tables. Two fac-similes of Greek Manu-
scripts. (650 pages.) 3s. 6d.; or with the
Lexicon, 5s.

VI.

Bohn's Philological and Philosophical Library.

UNIFORM WITH THE STANDARD LIBRARY, AT 5s. PER VOLUME (EXCEPTING THOSE MARKED OTHERWISE).

Hegel's Lectures on the Philosophy of History. Translated by J. Sibree, M.A.

Herodotus, Turner's (Dawson W.) Notes to. With Map, &c.

—— Wheeler's Analysis and Summary of.

Kant's Critique of Pure Reason. Translated by J. M. D. Meiklejohn.

Logic; or, the Science of Inference. A Popular Manual. By J. Devey.

Lowndes' Bibliographer's Manual of English Literature. New Edition, enlarged, by H. G. Bohn. Parts I. to X. (A

to X). 3s. 6d. each. Part XI. (the Appendix Volume). 5s. Or the 11 parts in 4 vols. half morocco, 2l. 2s.

Smith's (Archdeacon) Complete Collection of Synonyms and Antonyms.

Tennemann's Manual of the History of Philosophy. Continued by J. R. Morell.

Thucydides, Wheeler's Analysis of.

Wheeler's (M.A.) W. A., Dictionary of Names of Fictitious Persons and Places.

Wright's (T.) Dictionary of Obsolete and Provincial English. In 2 vols. 5s. each; or half-bound in 1 vol. 10s. 6d.

VII.

Bohn's British Classics.4

UNIFORM WITH THE STANDARD LIBRARY, AT 3s. 6d. PER VOLUME.

Addison's Works. With the Notes of Bishop Hurd, much additional matter, and upwards of 100 Unpublished Letters. Edited by H. G. Bohn. Portrait and 8 Engravings on Steel. In 6 vols.

Burke's Works. In 8 Volumes.
Vol. I. Vindication of Natural Society, On the Sublime and Beautiful, and Political Miscellanies.
Vol. 2. French Revolution, &c.
Vol. 3. Appeal from the New to the Old Whigs; the Catholic Claims, &c.
Vol. 4. On the Affairs of India, and Charge against Warren Hastings.
Vol. 5. Conclusion of Charge against Hastings; on a Regicide Peace, &c.
Vol. 6. Miscellaneous Speeches, &c. With a General Index.

Burke's Speeches on Warren Hastings; and Letters. With Index. In 2 vols. (forming vols. 7 and 8 of the works).

—— Life. By Prior. New and revised Edition. Portrait.

Defoe's Works. Edited by Sir Walter Scott. In 7 vols.

Gibbon's Roman Empire. Complete and Unabridged, with Notes; including, in addition to the Author's own, those of Guizot, Wenck, Niebuhr, Hugo, Neander, and other foreign scholars; and an elaborate Index. Edited by an English Churchman. In 7 vols.

VIII.

Bohn's Ecclesiastical Library.

UNIFORM WITH THE STANDARD LIBRARY, AT 5s. PER VOLUME.

Eusebius' Ecclesiastical History. With Notes.

Philo Judæus, Works of; the contemporary of Josephus. Translated by C. D. Yonge. In 4 vols.

Socrates' Ecclesiastical History, in continuation of Eusebius. With the Notes of Valesius.

Sozomen's Ecclesiastical History, from A.D. 324-440; and the Ecclesiastical History of Philostorgius.

Theodoret and Evagrius. Ecclesiastical Histories, from A.D. 332 to A.D. 427, and from A.D. 431 to A.D. 544.

II.

Bohn's Antiquarian Library.

UNIFORM WITH THE STANDARD LIBRARY, AT 5s. PER VOLUME.

I.

Bohn's Illustrated Library.

UNIFORM WITH THE STANDARD LIBRARY, AT 5s. PER VOLUME
(EXCEPTING THOSE MARKED OTHERWISE).

Allen's Battles of the British Navy.
Revised and enlarged. *Numerous fine Portraits.* In 2 vols.

Andersen's Danish Legends and Fairy Tales. With many Tales not in any other edition. Translated by CAROLINE PEACHEY. 120 *Wood Engravings.*

Ariosto's Orlando Furioso. In English Verse. By W. S. ROSE. *Twelve fine Engravings.* In 2 vols.

Bechstein's Cage and Chamber Birds. Including Sweet's Warblers. Enlarged edition. *Numerous plates.*
.°. All other editions are abridged.
With the plates coloured. 7s. 6d.

Bonomi's Nineveh and its Palaces. New Edition, revised and considerably enlarged, both in matter and Plates, including a Full Account of the Assyrian Sculptures recently added to the National Collection. *Upwards of 300 Engravings.*

Butler's Hudibras. With Various Notes, a Biography, and a General Index. Edited by HENRY G. BOHN. *Thirty beautiful Illustrations.*

—— ; or, *further illustrated with* 62 *Outline Portraits.* In 2 vols. 10s.

Cattermole's Evenings at Haddon Hall. 24 exquisite *Engravings on Steel, from designs by himself,* the Letterpress by the BARONESS DE CARABELLA.

China, Pictorial, Descriptive, and Historical, with a now Account of Ava and the Burmese, Siam, and Anam. *Nearly 100 Illustrations.*

Craik's (G. L) Pursuit of Knowledge under Difficulties, illustrated by Anecdotes and Memoirs. Revised Edition. *With numerous Portraits.*

Cruikshank's Three Courses and a Dessert. A Series of Tales, with 50 humorous Illustrations by Cruikshank.

Dante. Translated by I. C. WRIGHT, M.A. New Edition, carefully revised. *Portrait and 34 Illustrations on Steel, after Flaxman.*

Didron's History of Christian Art; or, Christian Iconography. From the French. *Upwards of 150 beautiful outline Engravings.* Vol. I. (Mons. Didron has not yet written the second volume.)

Flaxman's Lectures on Sculpture. *Numerous Illustrations.* 6s.

Gil Blas, The Adventures of. 24 *Engravings on Steel, after Smirke, and* 10 *Etchings by George Cruikshank.* (612 pages.) 6s.

Grimm's Gammer Grethel; or, German Fairy Tales and Popular Stories. Translated by EDGAR TAYLOR. *Numerous Woodcuts by Cruikshank.* 3s. 6d.

Holbein's Dance of Death, and Bible Cuts. *Upwards of 150 subjects, beautifully engraved in fac-simile,* with Introduction and Descriptions by the late FRANCIS DOUCE and Dr. T. F. DIBDIN. 2 vols. in 1. 7s. 6d.

Howitt's (Mary) Pictorial Calendar of the Seasons. Embodying the whole of Aiken's Calendar of Nature. *Upwards of 100 Engravings.*

—— **(Mary and William) Stories of** English and Foreign Life. *Twenty beautiful Engravings.*

India, Pictorial, Descriptive, and Historical, from the Earliest Times to the Present. *Upwards of 100 fine Engravings on Wood, and a Map.*

Jesse's Anecdotes of Dogs. New Edition, with large additions. *Numerous fine Woodcuts after Harvey, Bewick, and others.*

—— ; or, *with the addition of 34 highly-finished Steel Engravings.* 7s. 6d.

King's Natural History of Precious Stones, and of the Precious Metals. *With numerous Illustrations.* Price 6s.

Kitto's Scripture Lands and Biblical Atlas. 24 *Maps, beautifully engraved on Steel,* with a Consulting Index.

—— ; *with the maps coloured,* 7s. 6d.

Krummacher's Parables. Translated from the German. *Forty Illustrations by Clayton, engraved by Dalziel.*

Lindsay's (Lord) Letters on Egypt, Edom, and the Holy Land. New Edition, enlarged. *Thirty-six beautiful Engravings, and 2 Maps.*

Lodge's Portraits of Illustrious Personages of Great Britain, with Memoirs. *Two Hundred and Forty Portraits, beautifully engraved on Steel.* 8 vols.

B

BOHN'S CLASSICAL LIBRARY.

THE WORKS OF VIRGIL,

LITERALLY TRANSLATED.

THE

WORKS OF VIRGIL.

LITERALLY TRANSLATED INTO ENGLISH PROSE,

WITH NOTES,

BY DAVIDSON.

A NEW EDITION, REVISED, WITH ADDITIONAL NOTES,

BY

THEODORE ALOIS BUCKLEY,

OF CHRIST CHURCH.

LONDON:

BELL & DALDY, YORK STREET, COVENT GARDEN.

1873.

PREFACE.

THE object of the publisher in issuing the present volume was not so much to produce a new book, as to render an old and, in many respects, a good one, more suited to the present state of scholarship, and the exigencies of the student.

With this view the translation has been carefully compared with Wagner's text, and with the principal commentaries; many thousand alterations, involving either closer accuracy in translation or a stricter adherence to the construction, have been introduced; and, while the brief historical and mythological notes of the original work have been retained for the use of the tyro, attention has also been paid in the editor's further illustrations to the requirements of the more advanced scholar.

The brief Memoir of Virgil contains every fact necessary to be known by the general student and nothing more. In criticising a poet, whose taste, rather than his invention, is to be commended, it is easy to offend many, and please none; to draw comparisons, but fail of conviction.

THEODORE ALOIS BUCKLEY,

CHRIST CHURCH.

MEMOIR.

PUBLIUS VIRGILIUS MARO was born on the 15th of October, B. c. 70, at Andes, a little village near Mantua. His mother's name was Maia, and his father was probably a small landowner. Great attention must have been bestowed upon the education of our poet, as he appears to have been thoroughly imbued with the spirit of ancient philosophy by his master, Syron. Delicacy of health, and the probable want of influence arising from his not being a Roman citizen by birth, no doubt prevented his attention to the more rising professions of war and oratory, and contributed to strengthen his natural inclination for a retirement sacred to poetry and agriculture.

The fatal issue of the battle of Philippi, in B. c. 42, placed Mark Antony and Octavianus at the head of affairs, and the latter quickly began, on his return, to reward his soldiers with allotments of land. To make way for these new occupants, the old possessors had to give up their own estates, and amongst these sufferers

was Virgil. The particulars of the case are insufficiently
known to us, but Virgil probably owed the subsequent
restitution of his estate (between b. c. 42 and 40) to the
advice and intercession of Asinius Pollio. The first
Eclogue is commonly regarded as a thank-offering of
the poet to Augustus.

About the same time Virgil became acquainted with
the proverbial patron of men of genius, Mæcenas, at
whose mansion his friendship with Horace probably
commenced. The writings of the latter show that the
most cordial intimacy must have subsisted between these
distinguished poets and their liberal entertainer.

Critics seem to agree in placing the completion of the
Georgics in b. c. 31, while his Eclogues were no doubt
of an earlier date. As Theocritus formed the model of
these brief pastorals, so the Greek agricultural and
astronomical poems of Hesiod, Aratus, Nicander, and
others, whose works are only known to us in fragments,
furnished the materials, and often the language, of the
Georgics of Virgil.

The Æneid must have occupied our poet's thoughts
for a long time, although we have no certain data of its
commencement and progress.[1] At whatever time, however, it was begun, the poet appears to have regarded
it·as an unfinished production at the time of his death,

---

[1] A summary of some of the principal suppositions on this head will
be found in Mr. George Long's article " Virgilius," in Smith's Biographical Dictionary.

an opinion in which modern critics have unanimously coincided.

On the return of Augustus from Samos in the year B. c. 20, he met Virgil at Athens. An intended tour through Greece was prevented by his failing health, and Virgil died soon after his arrival at Brundusium, on the 2nd of September, B. c. 19. His remains were carried to Naples, which had been his favourite place of residence, and, if we may believe Donatus, the following inscription, from the poet's own hand, was placed on the tomb.

> " Mantua me genuit, Calabri rapuere, tenet nunc
> Parthenope. Cecini pascua, rura, duces."

Although Virgil had lived with the greatest liberality, and had been studiously mindful of the fulfilment of filial duty, he left considerable property, accumulated by the liberality of his friends. His manners were modest and retiring; his disposition distinguished by amiable urbanity and unassuming gentleness. Nor was his fortune inferior to his merits. He lived in the best age of Rome, among the best spirits of that age, and enjoyed the delights of fame without the persecutions of envy and the sacrifice of character. If not possessed of the mighty inventive genius of a Homer or Æschylus, he was beyond all others in the true perception of elegance, in the unaffected love of his subject, and in the exquisite finish and sublimity of his episodes.

VIRGIL'S BUCOLICS.

ECLOGUE I.

Virgil, in this Eclogue, celebrates the praises of Augustus, for restoring to him his lands, of which he had been dispossessed, having been bestowed upon the veteran soldiers who had fought in the cause of Augustus, at the battle of Philippi, B. C. 42. *Tityrus* personates Virgil, or probably his father, and *Meliboeus*, his less fortunate neighbours, the Mantuans.

MELIBŒUS, TITYRUS.

M. You, Tityrus, reclined under the covert of a full-spread beech, practise a woodland lay on a slender oaten pipe: We leave the bounds of our country, and our pleasant fields; we fly our country; you, Tityrus, stretched at ease in the shade, teach the woods to re-echo beauteous Amaryllis.[1]

T. O Meliboeus, a god hath vouchsafed us this tranquillity; for to me he shall always be a god; a tender lamb from our folds shall often stain his altar [with its blood]. He permitted my heifers to range at large, as you see, and myself to play what I wished on my rural reed.

M. I envy you not indeed; I rather marvel; to such an extent is there confusion in the lands. Lo, myself, sick at heart, am driving forth my tender she-goats: this, too, O Tityrus, I drag along with difficulty: for here just now among the thick hazels having yeaned twins, the hope of a flock, she left them, alas! on the naked flinty rock. This calamity, I remember, my oaks stricken from heaven often presaged to me, had not my mind been infatuated: [often the ill-boding crow from a hollow oak presaged.[2]] But tell me, Tityrus, who is this god of yours?

---

[1] Amaryllis, the name of a country girl. Some have supposed that the poet spoke of Rome under that name.

[2] This line properly belongs to Ecl. ix. 15. "Memini" is elegantly used with respect to ill omens. Cf. Ter. Phorm. i. 2, 24. B.

T. The city, Melibœus, which they call Rome, I foolish imagined to be like this our [Mantua[3]], whither[4] we shepherds oft are wont to drive down[5] the tender offspring of our ewes. So I had known whelps like dogs, so kids [like] their dams: thus was I wont to compare great things with small. But that city hath raised its head as far above others, as the cypresses are wont among the limber shrubs.[6]

M. And what so great a reason had you to visit Rome?

T. Liberty; which, though late, yet kindly looked upon me although indolent, after my beard began to fall off with a whitish hue when I shaved; yet [on me] she looked, and after a long time came, when Amaryllis began to sway me, and Galatea had cast me off. For I will not disown it, while Galatea ruled me, I had neither hopes of liberty, nor concern about my stock. Though many a victim went from my folds, and fat cheese was pressed for the ungrateful city,[7] my right hand never returned home heavy with money.

M. I used to wonder, Amaryllis, why disconsolate you were invoking the gods; and for whom you suffered the apples to hang on the tree. Your Tityrus hence was absent. The very pines, O Tityrus, the fountains, these very copses called for thee.

T. What could I do? It was neither in my power, while I staid here, to deliver myself from servitude, nor elsewhere to experience gods so propitious. Here, Melibœus, I saw that youth, to whom for twice six days our altars yearly smoke [with incense]. Here first he gave this entreating answer to me: "Swains, feed your heifers as formerly, and yoke your steers."

M. Happy old man, your lands then will remain [still in your possession], and large enough for you. Though the naked flint, and marsh with slimy rush, overspread all the pasture-grounds; yet no unaccustomed fodder shall harm thy languid

---

[3] Mantua, a city in the north of Italy on the Mincio, in the neighbour-hood of which Virgil was born.

[4] "Quo "="ad quam." This is a common usage in poetry, but is scarcely to be imitated in prose. See Muncker on Hyginus, Fab. 3. B.

[5] "Depellere." It must be remembered, that Virgil's village, Andes, stood on high ground, and hence the road to the city lay downwards. B.

[6] "Viburnum" is properly the "wayfaring tree." B.

[7] Urbs is emphatically applied to Rome. So Tibull. i. 9, 61, "To canet agricola, e magna cum venerit urbs." B.

pregnant ewes; nor noxious diseases of the neighbouring flock shall hurt them. Happy old man! here, among well-known streams and sacred fountains, you will enjoy the cool shade. On this side, a hedge planted at the adjoining boundary, whose willow blossoms are ever fed on by Hyblæan bees,[8] shall often court you by its gentle hummings to indulge repose. On the other side, the pruner beneath a lofty rock shall sing to the breezes: nor meanwhile shall either the hoarse wood-pigeons, thy delight, or the turtle from his lofty elm, cease to coo.

T. Sooner therefore shall the fleet stags pasture high in the air, and the seas leave the fish naked on the shore; sooner, the bounds of each being traversed, shall the Parthian[9] exile drink the Arar, or Germany the Tigris, than his countenance be effaced from my breast.

M. But we must go hence; some to the parched Africans,[10] some of us shall visit Scythia, and Oaxes the rapid [river] of Crete, and the Britons totally separated from all the world. Ah! shall I ever hereafter, after a length of time, with wonder behold my native territories, and the roof of my poor cot, piled up with turf; some ears of corn,[11] my [only] kingdom? Shall a ruffian soldier possess these well-cultivated fields?—a barbarian, these my fields of standing corn? See! to what extremity discord hath reduced us wretched citizens. See! for whom we have sown our fields. Now, Melibœus, graft your pear trees; in order range your vines. Begone, my

[8] Hyblæan bees, from Hybla, a mountain of Sicily, celebrated for its excellent honey.

[9] Parthian, &c. Parthia, now part of Persia, a country of Asia. The Arar, or Saone, a river of France, which falls into the Rhone at Lyons. Germany, a large country of Europe, to the north of Italy. The Tigris, a river of Asia, forming a junction with the Euphrates.

[10] Africans, &c. Africa, one of the three divisions of the ancient world. Scythia, a general name given by the ancients to the extreme northern parts of Europe and Asia. Oaxes, a river in the southern part of the island of Crete. The Britons, the inhabitants of Britain, which some of the ancients believed was once joined to the continent of Europe.

[11] So the later commentators; but I am still inclined to follow Servius in interpreting *aristas* "corn seasons." He observes, "quasi rusticus per aristas numerat annos." See my note on Soph. Ant. 340. Dind. So Silius It. viii. 61, "Dum flavas bis tondet messor aristas." Ausonius, however, probably understood it the other way, if we may judge from his imitation, Id. 3, "Salve hærediolum majorum regna meorum." B.

goats, once a happy flock, begone: no more shall I, stretched
out in my verdant grot, henceforth behold you hanging far
above me from a rock with bushes overgrown. No carols
shall I sing; no more, my goats, as I feed you, shall you
browse the flowery cytisus and bitter willows.

T. Yet here this night you may take up your rest with
me on green leaves. We have mellow apples, soft chestnuts,
and plenty of fresh-pressed curd. And now the high tops of
the villages afar smoke, and larger shadows fall from the lofty
mountains. .

ECLOGUE II.

The subject of this Eclogue is copied from Theocritus. The shepherd Corydon is deeply enamoured of Alexis, an ungrateful youth of great beauty.

ALEXIS.

THE shepherd Corydon burned[1] for beauteous Alexis, the
darling of his master; nor had he any thing to hope. Only
among the thick beeches, high embowering tops, he continually came: there, in solitude, with unavailing fondness, he
cast forth to the mountains and the woods these undigested
[complaints]:

Ah, cruel Alexis, for my songs hast thou no care? on me
hast thou no pity? thou wilt surely at last[2] compel me to die.
Even the cattle now pant after shades and cool retreats; now
the thorny brakes shelter even the green lizards; and Thestylis pounds the garlic and wild thyme, strong-scented herbs,
for the reapers spent with the violent heat. But to the hoarse
grasshoppers in company with me the thickets resound, while
under the scorching sun I trace thy steps. Was it not better
to endure the rueful spite and proud disdain of Amaryllis?
Would it not [have been better to endure] Menalcas, though
he was black, though thou wast fair? Ah, comely boy, trust
not too much to complexion. White privets fall neglected;
the purple hyacinths are gathered. By thee, Alexis, I am
neglected; nor dost thou inquire who I am; how rich in

---

[1] For this Grecism compare Hermesianax, 37, ειιιro μιν Ναννοις.
Nemes. Ecl. ii. 1, " Formosam Donacen puer Idas et puer Alcon arde-
bant." B.
[2] The full force of " denique" seems to be, "What then? will you
force me," &c. B.

flocks, how abounding in snow-white milk.[3] A thousand
ewes of mine stray on the mountains of Sicily. I want not
milk in summer; I have it new even in the cold weather. I
warble the same airs which Theban Amphion[4] was wont,
when on Attic Aracynthus[5] he called his herds together. Nor
am I so deformed: upon the shore I lately viewed myself,
when the sea stood unruffled by the winds. I will not fear
Daphnis, thyself being judge, if my image never deceives me.
O would it but please thee to inhabit with me our mean rural
retreats and humble cots, and to pierce the deer, and to drive
together a flock of kids to the green mallow! In the woods
along with me thou shalt rival Pan in singing. Pan[6] first
taught [men] to join several reeds with wax; Pan guards
both the sheep and the shepherds. Nor let it displease thee
to rub thy lip with a shepherd's reed. What did Amyntas
not do to learn this same art? I have a pipe of seven unequal
reeds compactly joined, of which Damœtas some time ago
made me a present, and dying, said, Thou art now its second
master. Damœtas said: the foolish Amyntas envied. Besides [I have] two young he-goats I found in a valley not
safe, whose skins even now are speckled with white; each
day they drain both the udders of an ewe; these I reserve
for thee. Long Thestylis has begged to have them from
me; and she shall do so, since my presents are disdained
by you.

Come hither, O lovely boy; behold the nymphs bring thee
lilies in full baskets. For thee, fair Näis, cropping the pale
violets[7] and heads of poppies, joins the daffodil and flower of

[3] I follow Anthon's punctuation. But Servius defends " nivei peco-
ria." There seems little difference. B.

[4] Amphion, the famous king of Thebes who built the walls of that
city ; the stones whereof he is said to have made to dance into their places
by the music of his lyre. He is called Dircæus, either from Dirce, his
step-mother, whom he put to death for the injuries she had done to his
mother, Antiope; or from a fountain in Bœotia of that name.

[5] Aracynthus was a town on the confines of Attica and Bœotia,
where was the fountain Dirce: it is called Acteo. Attic, from Acta or
Acte, the country about Attica, Ovid. Met. lib. ii. 720, "Sic super
Actæas agilis Cyllenius arces inclinat cursus."

[6] Pan, the god of shepherds, chiefly worshipped in Arcadia. B.

[7] i. e. gilliflowers or wall-flowers. The term "pale" is here applied
to denote a pale, tawny hue, not mere whiteness, as Anthon has observed. B.

sweet-smelling dill. Then, interweaving them with cassia,[8] and other fragrant herbs, sets off the soft hyacinths with saffron marigold. Myself will gather for thee quinces hoary with tender down and chestnuts which my Amaryllis loved. Plums I will add of waxen hue. On this fruit[9] too shall honour be conferred. And you, O laurels, I will crop; and thee, O myrtle, next: for, thus arranged, you mingle sweet perfumes.

Corydon, thou art a clown. Alexis neither minds thy presents; nor, if by presents thou shouldst contend, would Iolas yield. Alas, alas, what was the bent of my wretched mind? Undone, I have let the south wind loose among my flowers, and the boars in my crystal springs. Ah, madman, whom dost thou fly? The gods themselves have dwelt in woods, and the Trojan Paris. Let Pallas herself inhabit the citadels she has erected. Let woods above all things delight us. The grim lioness pursues the wolf, the wolf on his part the goat; the wanton goat pursues the flowery cytisus; Corydon thee, O Alexis. His own peculiar pleasure draws on each one.

See, the steers bring home the plough hung upon the yoke, and the retreating sun doubles the growing shadows; but me love still consumes. For what bounds can be set to love? Ah, Corydon, Corydon, what frenzy hath possessed thee? Half-pruned is thy vine on the leafy elm.[10] Why rather triest[11] thou not to weave, of osiers and pliant rush, some one at least of those implements which thy work requires. Thou wilt find another Alexis, if this disdains thee.

---

[8] The "spurge plant," or "mountain widow-waile," not the aromatic plant of the same name. ANTHON.

[9] "Pomum" is literally "an apple," but it is also used as a general term for all kinds of fruit.

[10] Vines were trained to elms. So Hor. Ep. i. 16, 3, "amicta vitibus ulmo." B.

[11] Literally, "but do you rather," i. e. "than go on in this mad way." B.

ECLOGUE III.

This Eclogue exhibits a trial of skill in singing, between Damœtas and Menalcas. Palæmon, who is chosen judge, after hearing them, declares his
inability to decide such an important controversy.

MENALCAS, DAMŒTAS, PALÆMON.

M. TELL me, Damœtas, whose[1] is that flock? Is it that of
Melibœus?

D. No; but Ægon's. Ægon lately intrusted it to my care.

M. Ah sheep, ever a luckless flock; while he himself caresses Neæra, and fears that she may prefer me to him, this
hireling shepherd milks his ewes twice in an hour; and the
juice[2] is filched from the flock, and the milk from the lambs.

D. Remember, however, that these scandals should with
more reserve be charged on men. We know both who [cor-
rupted] you, and in what sacred grot, while the goats looked
askance; but the good-natured nymphs smiled.

M. Then, I suppose, when they saw me with a felonious
bill hack Mycon's elm-grove and tender vines.

D. Or here by these old beeches, when you broke the bow
and arrows of Daphnis: which when you, cross-grained Menalcas, saw given to the boy, you both repined, and had you
not, by some means or other, done him a mischief, you had burst
[for envy].

M. What can masters do, when pilfering slaves are so audacious? Miscreant! did I not see thee entrap that goat of
Damon, while his mongrel barked with fury? And when I
cried out, Whither is he now sneaking off? Tityrus, assemble
your flock; you skulked away behind the sedges.

D. Ought he not, when vanquished in singing, to give me
the goat which my flute by its music won? If you know it
not, that same goat was my own: and Damon himself owned
it to me, but alleged that he was not able to pay.

M. You [vanquish] him in piping? Or was there ever a
wax-jointed pipe in your possession? Wast thou not wont,
thou dunce, in the cross-ways to murder a pitiful tune on a
squeaking straw?

[1] "Cujum," from the obsolete " cujus, -a, -um." B.
[2] I. e. animal lymph, as Edwards observes. Cicero Tusc. Q. II. 17,
" Subduc cibum unum diem athletæ, ferre non posse exclamabit." B.

D. Are you willing, then, that each of us try by turns what we can do? This young heifer I stake; and lest you should possibly reject it, she comes twice a day to the milking pail: two calves she suckles with her udder: say for what stake you will contend against me.

M. I dare not stake any thing with thee from the flock: for I have a sire at home, I have a harsh step-dame: and twice a-day both of them number the cattle, and one the kids. But what thou thyself shalt own of far greater value, since thou choosest to be mad, I will stake my beechen bowls, the carved work of divine Alcimedon,[3] round which a curling vine, superadded by the skilful carver's art, mantles the clustering berries diffusely spread by the pale ivy. In the midst are two figures, Conon; and, who was the other? He who with his wand distributed among the nations the whole globe; [who taught] what seasons the reaper, what the bent ploughman, should observe. Nor have I yet applied my lips to them, but I keep them carefully laid up

D. For me too the same Alcimedon made two bowls, and with soft acanthus[4] wreathed their handles: Orpheus in the midst he placed, and the woods following. Nor have I yet applied my lips to them, but keep them carefully laid up. If you consider the heifer, you have no reason to extol your bowls.

M. By no means shalt thou this day escape: I will come to any terms you challenge. Let but that very person who comes (lo, it is Palæmon) listen to this strain: I will take care that you shall not challenge any henceforth at singing.

D. Come on, then, if thou hast aught [to sing]; in me there shall be no delay: nor do I shun any one. Only, neighbour Palæmon, weigh this with the deepest attention; it is a matter of no small importance.

P. Sing, since we are seated on the soft grass; and now every field, now every tree, is budding forth: now the woods look green; now the year is most beauteous. Begin, Damœtas: then you, Menalcas, follow. Ye shall sing in alternate verses: the Muses love alternate verses.

---

[3] Alcimedon, an excellent carver, but of what country is uncertain Conon, a Greek astronomer of Samos, the contemporary and friend of Archimedes, who, probably, was the other figure mentioned by the poet.
[4] Plin. Ep. v. 6, "Acanthus in plano mollis, et, pene dixerim, liquidus." It is the modern "Brankursine." B

D. From Jove, ye Muses,[5] let us begin: all things are full of Jove: he cherishes the earth; by him are my songs esteemed.

M. And me Phœbus loves: for Phœbus[6] are still with me his appropriate gifts, the laurel and sweet-blushing hyacinth.

D. Galatea, wanton girl, pelts me with apples,[7] and flies to the willows, but wishes first to be seen.

M. But my flame Amyntas voluntarily offers himself to me; so that now not Delia's[8] self is more familiar to our dogs.

D. A present is provided for my love: for I myself marked the place where the airy wood-pigeons have built.

M. What I could, I sent to my boy, ten golden apples gathered from a tree in the wood: to-morrow I will send him ten others.

D. O how often, and what things Galatea spoke to me! Some part, ye winds, waft to the ears of the gods.

M. What avails it, O Amyntas, that you despise me not in your heart, if, while you hunt the boars, I watch the toils.

D. Iolas, send to me Phyllis: it is my birthday. When for the fruits I sacrifice a heifer, come thyself.

M. Iolas, I love Phyllis above others: for at my departure she wept, and said, Adieu, fair youth, a long adieu.

D. The wolf is fatal to the flocks; showers to ripened corn; winds to the trees; to me the anger of Amaryllis.

M. Moisture is grateful to the sown corn; the arbute to weaned kids; the limber willow to the teeming cattle; to me, Amyntas alone.

---

[5] Musæ, goddesses who presided over poetry, music, &c. The nine Muses were called the *Pierian* Sisters, from Pieria in Macedonia, where they were born. Virgil also calls them *Sicilian* Muses, because Theocritus, the celebrated pastoral poet, was a native of Sicily; and *Libethrian* nymphs, from Libethra, a mountain of Bœotia, in Greece.

[6] Phœbus, a name given to Apollo. The "laurel" refers to his mistress Daphne, who was changed into that tree, whilst flying from her lover. B.

[7] The apple, under the Latin name of which (*malum*) the Romans comprehended also the quince, the pomegranate, the citron, the peach, &c., was sacred to Venus, whose statues sometimes bore a poppy in one hand and an apple in the other. A present of an apple, or a partaking of an apple with another, was a mark of affection; and so, also, to throw an apple at one. To dream of apples was also deemed by lovers a good omen. ANTHON.

[8] Delia. Diana was so called, because she was born in the island of Delos.

D. Pollio loves my muse, though rustic: ye Pierian Sisters, feed a heifer for your reader.

M. Pollio himself too composes unrivalled verses: feed [for him] the bull which already butts with the horn, and spurns the sand with his feet.

D. Let him who loves thee, Pollio, rise to the same state to which he rejoices that thou [hast risen]; for him let honey flow, and the prickly bramble bring forth amomum.

M. Who hates not Bavius'[9] verse, may love thine, O Mævius; and the same may yoke foxes, and milk he-goats.

D. Ye swains who gather flowers, and strawberries that grow on the ground, oh fly hence; a cold snake lurks in the grass.[10]

M. Forbear, sheep, to advance too far; it is not safe trusting to the bank; the ram himself is but now drying his fleece.

D. Tityrus, from the river remove your browsing goats; I myself, when it is time, will wash them all in the pool.

M. Pen up the sheep, ye swains: if the heat should dry up the milk as of late, in vain shall we squeeze the teats with our hands.

D. Alas, how lean is my bull amid the fattening vetch! the same love is the bane of the herd and of the herdsman.

M. Surely love is not the cause with these: they scarcely stick to their bones. Some evil eye or other bewitches my tender lambs.

D. Tell me, (and you shall be my great Apollo,) where heaven's circuit extends no farther than three ells.[11]

---

* Bavius and Mævius, two contemptible poets in the age of Augustus, contemporary with Virgil.

[10] The Greek proverb is, ὑπὸ παντὶ λίθῳ σκόρπιος, ["under every stone a scorpion,"] in Carcinus apud Athen. xv. 15. With regard to the epithet, "frigidus," Kiessling, on Theocr. xv. 58, quotes a remark of the Scholiast on Nicander Th. 291, to the effect that the epithet ψυχρὸς is applied to all reptiles in a similar manner. B.

[11] Numerous explanations have been given to the enigma here stated, some making the reference to be to a well; others, to a pit in the centre of Rome, in the Comitium, &c. The best solution, however, is that of Asconius Pedianus, who heard Virgil himself say, that he meant to allude to a certain Cœlius, a spendthrift at Mantua, who, having run through all that he possessed, retained mere.y enough ground for a sepulchre; and that this very sepulchre, embracing about three ells in extent, is what Dammetas refers to in the text, the whole enigma turning upon the similarity in form and sound between cœli, "of heaven," and Cœli, (i. e. Cœlii,) "of Cœlius." ANTHON.

M. Tell me in what land flowers grow, inscribed with the names of kings;[12] and have Phillis to thyself alone.

P. It is not for us to determine so great a controversy between you; both you and he deserve the heifer; and whoever [so well] shall sing the fears of sweet [successful] love, and experimentally describe the bitterness of [disappointment].[13] Now, swains, shut up your streams; the meads have imbibed enough.

ECLOGUE. IV.

Virgil, in this Eclogue, is supposed by some to refer to the birth of Marcellus, the son of Octavia, the sister of Augustus; or to a son of his patron, the consul Pollio, to whom the Eclogue is inscribed. Others consider it to be founded on ancient predictions respecting the Messiah, and apply it to our blessed Saviour.

POLLIO.

YE Sicilian Muses, let us sing somewhat higher strains. Vineyards and lowly tamarisks delight not all. If rural lays we sing, let those lays be worthy of a consul's ear. The last era, of Cumæan[1] song, is now arrived: The great series of ages begins anew. Now, too, returns the virgin Astræa,[2] returns the reign of Saturn; now a new progeny is sent down from high heaven. Be thou but propitious to the infant boy, under whom first the iron age shall cease, and the golden age over all the world arise, O chaste Lucina; now thy own Apollo reigns. While thou too, Pollio, while thou art consul, this glory of our age shall make his entrance; and the great months begin to roll. Under thy conduct, whatever vestiges of our guilt remain, shall, being done away, release the earth from fear for ever. He shall partake the life of gods,

[11] The allusion is to the hyacinth, which has, according to a poetic legend, the letters AI marked on its petals, not only as a note of sorrow for the death of Hyacinthus, but also as constituting half the name of Ajax, i. e: Αἴας. ANTHON.

[12] There is much uncertainty respecting the reading of this passage Anthon ingeniously transposes "amores" and "amaros." But I cannot help thinking that there is no occasion to alter the common reading. B.

[1] Cumæan song, from Cumæ, a city of Italy, north-west of Naples, in the vicinity of which resided the celebrated Cumæan Sibyl.

[2] Astræa, in the mythology of the ancients, was the goddess of Justice, who resided on earth during the reign of Saturn, or the golden age. Being shocked by the impiety of mankind, she returned to heaven, and became one of the twelve signs of the zodiac, under the name of Virgo.

shall see heroes mingled in society with gods, himself be seen by them, and rule the peaceful world with his father's virtues. Meanwhile the earth, O boy, as her first offerings, shall pour thee forth every where, without culture, creeping ivy with lady's glove, and Egyptian beans with smiling acanthus intermixed. The goats of themselves shall homeward convey their udders distended with milk; nor shall the herds dread huge overgrown lions. The very cradle shall pour thee forth attractive flowers. The serpent also shall die; and the poison's fallacious plant shall die: the Assyrian spikenard shall grow in every soil. But soon as thou shalt be able to read the praises of heroes, and the achievements of thy sire, and to understand what virtue is,[3] the field shall by degrees grow yellow with soft ears of corn; blushing grapes shall hang on the rude brambles and hard oaks shall distil the dewy honey. Yet some few footsteps of ancient vice shall remain, to prompt [men] to brave the sea in ships, to enclose cities with walls, and cleave furrows in the earth. There will then be another Tiphys, and another Argo[4] to waft chosen heroes: there shall be likewise other wars: and great Achilles[5] shall once more be sent to Troy. After this, when confirmed age shall have ripened thee into man, the sailor shall of himself renounce the sea; nor shall the naval pine barter commodities: all lands shall all things produce. The ground shall not endure the harrow, nor the vineyard the pruning-hook; the sturdy ploughman, too, shall now release his bulls from the yoke. Nor shall the wool learn to counterfeit various colours: but the ram himself shall in the meadows tinge his fleece, now with sweet-blushing purple, now with saffron dye. Scarlet shall spontaneously clothe the lambs as they feed. The Destinies, harmonious in the established order of the Fates, sung to their spindles: "Ye ages, run on thus." Dear offspring of the gods, illustrious increase of Jove, set forward on thy

[3] Servius rightly understands the successive studies of poetry and philosophy, as they are enumerated in Plato Protag. § 43. - B.

[4] Argo, the name of the ship which carried Jason and his fifty-four companions to Colchis, to recover the golden fleece. Tiphys, who was pilot of the ship, died before reaching Colchis. The Argonautic expedition happened about 1263 B. C.

[5] Achilles, the bravest of all the Greeks in the Trojan war, where he performed prodigies of valour. He slew Hector, but was himself at last slain by Paris.

way to signal honours; the time is now at hand. See the
world with its convex weight nodding to thee, the earth, the
regions of the sea, and heavens sublime: See how all things
rejoice at the approach of this age. Oh that my last stage of
life may continue so long, and so much breath as shall suffice
to sing thy deeds! Neither Thracian Orpheus,[6] nor Linus,
shall surpass me in song, though his mother aid the one, and
his sire the other, Calliopea Orpheus, and fair Apollo Linus.
Should even Pan with me contend, Arcadia's self being judge,
even Pan should own himself overcome, Arcadia's self being
judge. Begin, sweet babe, to distinguish thy mother by thy
smiles;[7] ten months brought on thy mother tedious qualms. Begin, young boy; that child on whom his parents never smiled,
nor god ever honoured with his table, nor goddess with her bed.

ECLOGUE V.

In this Eclogue, the shepherds Menalcas and Mopsus celebrate the funeral
eulogium of Daphnis.

MENALCAS, MOPSUS.

ME. SINCE, Mopsus, we are met, both skilful swains, you
in piping on the slender reed, I in singing verses, why have
we not sat down here among the elms intermixed with hazels?

Mo. You, Menalcas, are my superior; it is just that I be
ruled by you; whether under the shades that waver by the
fanning zephyrs, or rather into this grotto we repair: see how
the wild vine with scattered clusters hath spread the grotto.

ME. Amyntas alone in our mountains may vie with thee.

Mo. What if the same should vie with Phœbus' self in
song?

ME. Begin you, Mopsus, first; whether you are disposed
to sing the passion of Phyllis,[1] or the praises of Alcon, or the
strife of Codrus; begin: Tityrus will tend the browsing kids.

---

[6] Orpheus, the son of Œagrus, king of Thrace, and the muse Calliope,
celebrated for his masterly skill in music.
[7] Heyne wrongly refers "risu" to the mother's smile. B.
[1] The names here introduced, namely, Phyllis, Alcon, and Codrus, belong not to real characters, but to fictitious pastoral personages. Phyllis,
therefore, must not be confounded with the daughter of Lycurgus, king of
Thrace, who was abandoned by Demophoon, nor Codrus with the early
king of Athens. ANTHON.

Mo. Nay, I will rather try those strains which lately I
inscribed on the green bark of the beech tree, and sang and
noted them by turns: then bid Amyntas vie with me.

Me. As far as the limber willow is inferior to the pale
olive, and humble lavender to crimson beds of roses; so far
is Amyntas, in my judgment, inferior to you.

Mo. But, shepherds, cease further words: we have reached
the grot. The nymphs wept Daphnis cut off by cruel death;
ye hazels and ye streams witnessed [the mourning of] the
nymphs, when the mother, embracing the hapless corpse of
her son, reproached both gods and stars with cruelty. The
swains, O Daphnis, then forgot to drive their fed cattle to the
cooling streams: no quadruped either tasted of the brook, or
touched a blade of grass. The savage mountains, Daphnis,
and the woods, can tell that even the African lions mourned
thy death. Daphnis taught to yoke Armenian tigers in the
chariot; Daphnis, to lead up the dances in honour of Bacchus,
and wreathe the pliant wands with soft leaves. As the vine
is the glory of the trees,.as grapes are of the vine, as the bull
is of the flock, as standing corn of fertile fields; so thou wast
all the glory of thy fellow-swains. Ever since the Fates
snatched thee away, Pales [2] herself, and Apollo too, have left
the fields. Luckless darnel, and the barren oats, spring up in
these furrows, where we were wont to sow the plump barley.
Instead of the soft violet, instead of the purple narcissus, the
thistle springs up, and the thorn with its sharp prickles.
Strew the ground with leaves, ye shepherds, form a shade
over the fountains: these rites Daphnis for himself ordains.
And form a tomb; and on that tomb inscribe this epitaph: I
am Daphnis of the groves, hence even to the stars renowned,
the shepherd of a fair flock, fairer myself.

Me. Such, matchless poet, is thy song to me, as slumbers
to the weary on the grass; as in scorching heat to quench
thirst from a salient rivulet of fresh water. Nor equal you
your master in the pipe only, but also [3] in the voice. Happy
swain, you shall now be the next to him. Yet, I will sing
in my turn these verses of mine, such as they are, and exalt

----

[2] Pales, the goddess of sheepfolds and of pastures, was worshipped with
great solemnity among the Romans.
[3] I have supplied the ellipse of "et," with Burm. on Phædr. Prol
l. 6. B.

your Daphnis to the stars: Daphnis I will raise to the stars:
me too Daphnis loved.

Mo. Can aught be more acceptable to me than such a present? The swain himself was most worthy to be sung, and
Stimichon hath long since praised to me that song of thine.

Me. Daphnis, robed in white, admires the courts of heaven,
to which he is a stranger, and under his feet beholds the clouds
and stars. Hence mirthful pleasure fills the woods and every
field, Pan and the shepherds, and the virgin Dryads.[4] The
wolf doth neither meditate plots against the sheep, nor are
any toils set to insnare the deer; good Daphnis delights in
rest. For joy, even the unshorn mountains raise their voices
to the stars: now the very rocks, the very groves, resound
these notes: a god, a god, he is, Menalcas. O be propitious
and indulgent to thy own! Behold four altars; lo, Daphnis,
two for thee,[5] and two for Phœbus. Two bowls foaming with
new milk, and two goblets of fat oil, will I present to thee
each year: and chiefly, enlivening the feast with plenty of
the joys of Bacchus,[6] before the fire if it be winter; if harvest, in the shade,[7] I will pour thee forth Ariusian wine, a
new kind of nectar. Damœtas and Lyctian Ægon shall sing
to me: Alphesibœus shall mimic the frisking satyrs. These
rites shall be ever thine, both when we pay our solemn anniversary vows to the nymphs, and when we make the circuit
of the fields. While the boar shall love the tops of mountains;
while fishes love the floods; while bees on thyme shall feed,
and grasshoppers on dew; thy honour, name, and praise shall
still remain. As to Bacchus and Ceres,[8] so to thee the

[4] Dryads, nymphs who presided over the woods.

[5] "Lo! two (altars) for thee, O Daphnis, two larger ones for Phœbus." Observe that *altaria* is here in opposition with *aras* understood.
This passage shows plainly that the distinctive difference between *ara* and
altars is here meant to be observed. *Ara* is an altar of smaller size, on
which incense, fruits of the earth, and similar oblations are offered up;
altars is an altar of larger size, on which victims are burned. This serves
to explain, also, what immediately follows. To Daphnis, as to a deified
hero, no bloody offerings are to be made; the oblations are to consist
merely of milk, oil, and wine. Anthon.

[6] Bacchus first taught the use of the vine, &c., and was therefore called the God of wine. Ariusia, i. e. Chios, now Scio, an island in the
Archipelago, celebrated for its excellent wine.

[7] Cicero de Senect. 14, "Me vero delectant et pocula minuta atque
rorulia, et refrigeratio æstate, et vicissim aut Sol aut ignis hibernus." R.

[8] Ceres, the goddess of corn and of harvests.

swains shall yearly perform their vows: thou too slight bind
them by their vows.

Mo. What, what returns shall I make to thee for so excellent a song? For neither the whispers of the rising south
wind, nor shores lashed by the wave, nor rivers that glide
down among the stony vales, please me so much.

Mr. First I will present you with this brittle reed. This
taught me, "Corydon for fair Alexis burned." This same
hath taught me, "Whose is this flock? is it that of Melibœus?"

Mo. But do you, Menalcas, accept this sheep-hook, beautiful for its uniform knobs and brass, which Antigenes never
could obtain, though he often begged it of me; and at that
time he was worthy to be loved.

ECLOGUE VI.

Silenus, a demi-god and companion of Bacchus, was noted for his love of
wine and skill in music: here he relates concerning the formation of the
world, and the nature of things, according to the doctrine of the Epicureans.

SILENUS.

My Thalia is the first who deigned to sport in Syracusian
strain, nor blushed to inhabit the woods. When I offered to
sing of kings and battles, Apollo twitched my ear, and warned
me thus: A shepherd, Tityrus, should feed his fattening
sheep, and sing in humble strain.[1] Now will I, O Varus,[2]
(for there will be many who will desire to celebrate thy
praises, and record disastrous wars,) exercise my rural muse
on the slender reed. I sing not unbidden strains: yet whoso
enamoured [with my strains], whoso shall read even these, to
him, O Varus, our tamarisks, each grove shall sing of thee:
nor is any page more acceptable to Phœbus, than on whose
front the name of Varus is inscribed. Proceed, O Muses.

Deductum dicere carmen, a humble or slender song; a metaphor
taken from wool spun out till it becomes fine and slender. So Hor. lib.
ii. 1, 225, Tenui deducta poemata filo.   And Tibul. lib. i. 3. 86, Deducat
plena stamina longa colo.
[2] Varus, Quintilius Varus, a Roman proconsul, who commanded an
army in Germany, where he lost his life, with three whole legions
A. D. 10.

Chromis and Mnasylus, the youthful swains, saw Silenus lying
asleep in his cave, his veins, as usual, swoln with yesterday's
debauch. His garlands just[3] fallen from his head, lay at some
distance, and his heavy flagon hung by its worn handle.
Taking hold of him, (for often the sire had amused them both
with the promise of a song,) they bind him with his own
wreaths. Ægle associates herself with them, and comes unexpectedly upon the timorous swains; Ægle, fairest of the
Naiads; and just as he is opening his eyes, she paints his
forehead and temples with blood-red mulberries. He, smiling
at the trick, says, Why do ye fasten these bonds? Loose me,
swains: it is enough that I have suffered myself to be seen.
Hear the song which you desire: the song for you; for her,
I shall find another reward. At the same time he begins.
Then you might have seen the Fauns and savages frisking in
measured dance, then the stiff oaks waving their tops. Nor
rejoices the Parnassian rock so much in Phœbus:[4] nor do
Rhodope and Ismarus[5] so much admire Orpheus. For he
sang how, through the mighty void,[6] the seeds of earth, and
air, and sea, and pure fire, had been together ranged; how
from these principles all the elements, and the world's tender[7]
globe itself, combined into a system: then how the soil began
to harden, to shut up the waters apart[8] within the sea, and by

[3] Tantum capti delapsa, "Having fallen to such a distance from his
head." It is very hard to say what is here the true meaning of *tantum*.
If we join it with *procul*, it makes a most harsh construction; if we render it "only," it clashes with *procul*, unless this stand for *justa*, which
is too forced; if, with Voss., we make it equivalent to *modo*, "just," it
appears frigid and tame. We have ventured, therefore, to regard it as
standing for *in tantum*. ANTHON.

[4] Parnassian rock. Parnassus, a celebrated mountain of Phocis in
Greece, sacred to Apollo and the Muses, remarkable for its two summits.

[5] Rhodope and Ismarus, two high mountains in Thrace.

[6] Magnum per inane. The Epicureans, whose philosophy is here
sung, taught that incorporeal space, here called *magnum inane*, and corporeal atoms were the first principles of all things: their void space they
considered as the womb, in which the seeds of all the elements were
ripened into their distinct forms.

[7] "Tener," Anthon says, "because just created." But I prefer under-
standing it of the plastic nature of the materials, with Pliny, Hist. Nat.
li. 3. B.

[8] Et discludere Nerea ponto. Literally, "to shut up Nereus apart in
the sea," i. e. to separate the waters into their channel: Nereus the sea-
god being here put for the waters in general.

c

degrees to assume the forms of things: and how anon the
earth was astonished to see the new-born sun shine forth; and
how from the clouds, suspended high, the showers descend:
when first the woods began to rise, and when the animals, yet
few, began to range the unknown mountains. He next tells
of the stones which Pyrrha[9] threw, the reign of Saturn, the
fowls of Caucasus,[10] and the theft of Prometheus. To these
he adds the fountain where the sailors had invoked aloud
Hylas[11] lost; how the whole shore resounded Hylas, Hylas.
And he soothes Pasiphaë[12] in her passion for the snow-white
bull: happy woman if herds had never been! Ah, ill-fated
maid, what madness seized thee? The daughters of Prœtus[13]
with imaginary lowings filled the fields: yet none of them
pursued such vile embraces of a beast, however they might
dread the plough about their necks, and often feel for horns on
their smooth foreheads. 'Ah, ill-fated maid, thou now art
roaming on the mountains! He, resting his snowy side on the
soft hyacinth, ruminates the blenched herbs under some
gloomy oak, or courts some female in the numerous herd. Ye
nymphs, shut up now, ye Dictæan[14] nymphs, shut up the
avenues of the forests, if any where by chance my bullock's
wandering footsteps may offer to my sight. Perhaps some
heifers may lead him on to the Gortynian stalls,[15] either

* Pyrrha, the wife of Deucalion, in whose age all mankind was destroyed by a deluge, these two excepted. On consulting the oracle, they
were directed to repair the loss, by throwing stones behind their backs;
those which Pyrrha threw were changed into women, and those of
Deucalion into men.

[10] Caucasus, a lofty mountain of Asia, between the Euxine and Caspian
Seas. Prometheus, having made a man of clay, which he animated with
fire stolen from heaven, was, for the impiety, chained to a rock on the top
of Caucasus, where a vulture continually preyed upon his liver.

[11] Hylas, a youth, the favourite of Hercules, who accompanied the
Argonautic expedition, but was drowned in the Ascanius, a river of
Bithynia, which afterwards received his name.

[12] Pasiphaë, the wife of Minos, king of Crete, who disgraced herself by
her unnatural passion.

[13] Prœtus, king of Argolis, whose three daughters became insane for
neglecting the worship of Bacchus, or, according to some, for preferring
themselves to Juno.

[14] Dictæan nymphs, Cretan nymphs from Dicte, a mountain in the
island of Crete, where Jupiter was worshipped.

[15] Gortynian stalls. Gortyna, an ancient city of Crete, the country
around which produced excellent pastures.

enticed by the verdant pasture, or in pursuit of the herd.
Then he sings the virgin,[16] charmed with the apples of the
Hesperides: then he surrounds the sisters of Phaeton[17] with
the moss of bitter bark, and raises the stately alders from the
ground.   Then he sings how one of the Sister Muses led
Gallus, wandering by the streams of Permessus,[18] to the
Aonian mountains; and how the whole choir of Phœbus
rose up to do him honour: how Linus, the shepherd of song
divine, his locks adorned with flowers and bitter parsley,
thus addressed him: Here, take these pipes the Muses give
thee, which before [they gave] to the Ascræan[19] sage; by
which he was wont to draw down the rigid wild ashes from
the mountains.   On these let the origin of Grynium's grove[20]
be sung by you; that there may be no grove in which Apollo
may glory more.   Why, should I tell how [he sang] of
Scylla[21] the daughter of Nisus? or of her whom, round the
snowy waist, begirt with barking monsters, fame records to
have vexed[22] the Dulichian ships, and in the deep abyss, alas,
to have torn in pieces the trembling sailors with sea-dogs?

[16] i. e. Atalanta, daughter of Schœneus, king of Scyros, or, according
to others, of Iasius, king of Arcadia, who was famed for her beauty,
which gained her many admirers. She consented to bestow her hand on
him that could outrun her, though he was to die if he lost the race.
Many of her suitors had perished in the contest, when Hippomenes offered
himself; during the race, he dropped, at intervals, three golden apples
from the garden of the Hesperides, which Atalanta stopping to pick up, he
arrived first at the goal, and obtained her in marriage.
[17] The sisters of Phaeton, according to the mythologists, bewailing his
unhappy end, were changed into poplars by Jupiter.
[18] Permessus, a river issuing from Mount Helicon in Aonia, (Bœotia,)
sacred to the Muses.
[19] Ascræan sage. Hesiod, so named from Ascra, a village of Bœotia
in Greece, where he was born.
[20] Grynium's grove. Grynium, a town on the coast of Æolia in Asia
Minor, where Apollo had a temple with a sacred grove.
[21] Scylla, a daughter of Nisus, king of Megara, feigned to have been
changed into a lark. Dulichian ships, those of Ulysses, who was king
of the island of Dulichium. After the fall of Troy, Ulysses, in his return
home, encountered incredible hardships, and with difficulty escaped the
rocks of Scylla, so named from a daughter of Typhon, who was changed
by Circe into a frightful monster, when, throwing herself into the sea between Italy and Sicily, she became the dangerous rocks which continued
to bear her name.
[22] Virgil's use of "vexare" is discussed by Gellius, ii. 6, and Macrob.
Sat. vi. 7. From their remarks, the word *harass* best appears to express
its meaning. B

or how he described the limbs of Tereus[22] transformed?
what banquets and what presents Philomela for him prepared? with what speed he sought the deserts, and with what
wings, ill-fated one, he fluttered over the palace once his own?
All those [airs] he sings, which happy Eurotas[24] heard, and
bade its laurels learn, when Phœbus played of old. The valleys, stricken [with the sound], re-echo to the stars; till
Vesper[25] warned [the shepherds] to pen their sheep in the
folds, and recount their number; and came forth from reluctant Olympus.

ECLOGUE VII.

In this Eclogue, Virgil, as Melibœus, gives an account of a poetical contest
between Thyrsis and Corydon.

Melibœus, Corydon, Thyrsis.

M. DAPHNIS by chance sat down under a whispering[1]
holm-oak, and Corydon and Thyrsis had driven their flocks
together; Thyrsis his sheep, Corydon his goats distended
with milk: both in the flower of their age, Arcadians both,[2]
equally matched at singing, and ready to answer. To this
quarter, while I was fencing my tender myrtles from the cold,
the he-goat himself, the husband[3] of the flock, from me had
strayed away: and I espy Daphnis: when he in turn saw me,
he cried out, Come hither quickly, Melibœus; your goat and

---

[22] Tereus, a king of Thrace. He married Progne, a daughter of Pan-
dion, king of Athens, who, in revenge for his having violated her sister
Philomela, and cut out her tongue, killed his son Itys, and served him
up at a banquet. According to the poets, they were all changed into different kinds of birds.

[24] Eurotas, (Vasili Potamo,) a river of Laconia, washing ancient Sparta,
and falling into the Mediterranean.

[25] Vesper, the planet Venus, or the evening star.

[1] The rustling of the breeze in the leaves is thus said ψιθυρίζειν in
Greek. B.

[2] i. e. both skilled in music, which was greatly cultivated among the
Arcadians. No reference to their country is intended, but merely to
their musical excellence. B.

[3] Vir gregis ipse caper. "The he-goat himself, the husband of my
flock." (Compare Theocritus, viii. 49: Ὁ τράγε, τᾶν λευκᾶν αἰγῶν
ἀνήρ.) Observe the force of ipse here, implying that he was followed by
the rest of the flock; (Wagner, Quæst. Virg. xviii. 2, b.;) and hence we
have, in verse 9th, "caper tibi salvus et hœdi." ANTHON. So Martial,
Ep. ix. 31, "pecorisque maritus tanigeri." B.

kids are safe; and, if you can stay a while, rest under this
shade.   Hither thy bullocks of themselves will come across
the meads to drink.   Here Mincius [4] hath fringed the verdant
banks with tender reed, and from the sacred oak swarms of
bees resound.   What could I do?   I had neither Alcippe, nor
Phyllis, to shut up at home my weaned lambs : but there was
a great match proposed, Corydon against Thyrsis.   After all,
I postponed my serious business to their play.   In alternate
verses therefore the two began to contend : alternate verses
the Muses would have me record.   These Corydon, those
Thyrsis, each in his turn recited.

C. Ye Libethrian nymphs, my delight, either favour me
with such a song as ye did my Codrus [5] (he makes verses next
to those of Phœbus) ; or, if we cannot all attain to this, here
on this sacred pine my tuneful pipe shall hang.

T. Ye Arcadian shepherds, deck with ivy your rising poet,
that Codrus' sides may burst with envy.   Or, if he praise me
beyond what I desire, bind my brow with lady's glove, lest his
evil tongue should hurt your future poet.

C. To thee, Delia, young Mycon [for me presents] this
head of a bristly boar, and the branching horns of a long-lived
stag.   If this success be lasting, thou shalt stand at thy full
length in polished marble, thy legs with scarlet buskin bound.

T. A pail of milk and these cakes, Priapus, [6] are enough
for you to expect [from me] ; you are the keeper of a poor ill-
furnished garden.   Now we have raised thee of marble such
as the times admit ; but, if the breed recruit my flock, thou
shalt be of gold.

C. Galatea, daughter of Nereus, sweeter to me than Hybla's
thyme, whiter than swans, fairer than white ivy ; soon as the
well-fed steers shall return to their stalls, come, if thou hast
any regard for Corydon.

T. May I even appear to thee more bitter than Sardinian
herbs, [7] more rugged than the furze, more worthless than sea-

---

[4] Mincius, the Mincio, a river in the north of Italy, falling into the
Po below Mantua.

[5] Codrus, a Latin poet, contemporary with Virgil.

[6] Priapus, a deity among the ancients, who presided over gardens. He
was the son of Bacchus and Venus, and was chiefly worshipped at
Lampsacus on the Hellespont.

[7] Sardinian herbs, a bitter herb which grew in the island of Sardinia,
said to cause convulsions and death.

weed cast upon the shore, if this day be not longer to me than a whole year. Go home, my well-fed steers, if you have any shame, go home.

C. Ye mossy fountains, and grass more soft than sleep, and the green arbute-tree that covers you with its thin shade, ward off the midsummer heat from my flock; now scorching summer comes, now the buds swell on the fruitful tendrils.

T. Here is a glowing hearth, and resinous torches; here is always a great fire, and lintels sooted with continual smoke. Here we just as much regard the cold of Boreas,[8] as either the wolf does the number [of sheep], or impetuous rivers their banks.

C. Junipers and prickly chestnuts stand thick;[9] beneath each tree its apples here and there lie strewn; now all things smile; but, were fair Alexis to go from these hills, you would see even the rivers dry.

T. The field is parched; by the intemperature of the air the dying herbage thirsts; Bacchus has envied our hills the shadow of his vine; [but,] at the approach of our Phyllis, every grove shall look green, and Jove abundantly descend in joyous showers.

C. The poplar is most grateful to Hercules,[10] the vine to Bacchus, to lovely Venus[11] the myrtle, to Phœbus his own laurel; Phyllis loves the hazels: so long as Phyllis loves them, neither the myrtle nor the laurel of Phœbus shall surpass the hazels.

T. The ash is fairest in the woods, the pine in the gardens, the poplar by the rivers, the fir on lofty mountains: but if, my charming Lycidas, you make me more frequent visits, the ash in the woods shall yield to thee, and the pine in the gardens.

---

[8] Boreas, the name of the north wind. According to the ancient poets, Boreas was the son of Astræus and Aurora.

[9] Anthon rightly observes that this is the force of " stant." So Lutatius Placidus on Stat. Theb. x. 157, interprets " stat furor," by " plenus est," quoting this line as an example. B.

[10] Hercules, the most celebrated hero of fabulous history, the son of Jupiter and Alcmena, was, after a life spent in achieving the most incredible exploits, ranked among the gods, and received divine honours.

[11] Venus, a principal deity among the ancients, the goddess of love and beauty. She was the wife of Vulcan, but passionately loved Adonis and Anchises; by the latter she became the mother of Æneas.

M. These verses I remember, and that vanquished Thyrsis in vain contended. From that time Corydon, Corydon is our man.

ECLOGUE VIII.

This Bucolic contains the strains of Damon for the loss of his mistress; and Alphesibœus records the charms of an enchantress.

DAMON, ALPHESIBŒUS.

THE muse of the shepherds, Damon and Alphesibœus, whom the heifers, unmindful of their pasture, admired contending, and by whose song the lynxes were astonished, and the rivers, having changed their courses, stood still; the muse of Damon and Alphesibœus I sing.

Whether thou art now passing for me[1] over the rocks of broad Timavus,[2] or cruising along the coast of the Illyrian Sea;[3] say, will that day ever come, when I shall be indulged to sing thy deeds? say, shall it come that I may be indulged to diffuse over the world thy verses, which alone merit comparison with Sophocles'[4] lofty style? With thee my muse commenced; with thee shall end. Accept my songs begun by thy command, and permit this ivy to creep around thy temples among thy victorious laurels.

Scarce had the cold shades of night retired from the sky, a time when the dew on the tender grass is most grateful to the cattle, when Damon, leaning against a tapering olive, thus began:—

D. Arise, Lucifer,[5] and preceding usher in the cheerful day; while I, deceived by the feigned passion of my mistress Nisa, complain; and to the gods, now that I die, (though I have availed me nought in taking them to witness,) yet in my last hour appeal. Begin with me, my pipe, Mœnalian strains.

[1] "Mihi" is the dativus ethicus. B.
[2] Timavus, the Timavo, a river of Italy, rising at the foot of the Alps and falling into the gulf of Trieste. At its mouth are several small islands containing hot springs.
[3] Illyrian Sea, the Adriatic Sea between Italy and Dalmatia, &c.
[4] Sophocles, a celebrated tragic poet of Athens, remarkable for sublimity of style. He was contemporary with Pericles and Euripides, and died B. c. 406.
[5] Lucifer, the name of the planet Venus, or morning star; as Hesperus was of the same planet, or evening star.

Mænalus[6] always has a vocal grove and shaking pines; he ever hears the loves of shepherds, and Pan, the first who suffered not the reeds to be[7] neglected. Begin with me, my pipe, Mænalian strains. Nisa is bestowed on Mopsus! what may we lovers not expect? Griffins now shall match with horses, and in the succeeding age the timorous does with dogs shall come to drink. Mopsus, cut your fresh nuptial torches: for thee a wife is on the point of being brought home. Strew the nuts,[8] bridegroom; Hesperus for thee forsakes Œta.[9] Begin with me, my pipe, Mænalian strains. O thou matched to a worthy spouse! while you disdain all others, and while you detest my pipe and goats, my shaggy eye-brows, and my overgrown beard; nor believe that any god regards the affairs of mortals. Begin with me, my pipe, Mænalian strains. When thou wast but a child, I saw thee with thy mother gathering the dewy apples on our hedges; I was your guide; I had then just entered on the year next after eleven, I was then just able to reach the slender boughs from the ground. As soon as I saw thee, how was I undone! O how an evil error bore me away! Begin with me, my pipe, Mænalian strains. Now I know what Love is: Ismarus, or Rhodope, or the remotest Garamantes,[10] produced him on rugged cliffs, a boy not of our race or blood. Begin with me, my pipe, Mænalian strains. Relentless Love taught the mother[11] to stain her hands in her own children's blood; a cruel mother too thou wast: whether more cruel was the mother or more impious the boy? Impious was the boy: thou, mother, too, wast cruel. Begin with me, my pipe, Mænalian strains. Now let

---

[6] Mænalus, now Roino, a mountain of Arcadia in Greece, sacred to Pan. It was covered with pine trees.

[7] "Esse" is elegantly omitted after such words as "pati," "sinere," &c. Nemes. Cyn. 70, "Omnia tentantem passi." Apul. de Deo Socr. "Sejugam veluti debilem passa est." Seneca, Ined. 182, "Quemve securum sinit." Virg. Æn. i. 389, "Nec plura querentem Passa Venus." B.

[8] On this custom compare Catull. Epith. p. 98. Muret. "Da nucis pueris iners Concubine, satis diu Lucisti nucibus." B.

[9] Œta, a celebrated mountain, or, more properly, chain of mountains, between Thessaly and Greece Proper. It was so high, that the poets feigned the sun, moon, and stars rose behind it.

[10] Garamantes, a people in the interior of Africa, now called Zaara.

[11] Matrem. This cruel mother is Medea, who, to be avenged on Jason for preferring another mistress to her, slew her sons whom she bore to him, before his eyes.

the wolf of himself fly from the sheep; the hard oaks bear
golden apples; the alder bloom with narcissus; the tamarisks
distil rich amber from their barks; let owls with swans contend; be Tityrus an Orpheus; an Orpheus in the woods, an
Arion[11] among the dolphins. Begin with me, my pipe, Mænalian strains. Let all things become very mid ocean; ye
woods, farewell. From the summit of yon aërial mountain
will I throw myself headlong into the waves: take this last
present from me dying. Cease, my pipe, now cease Mænalian strains.

Thus Damon: ye Pierian muses, say what Alphesibœus
sung. We cannot all do all things.

A. Bring forth the water, and bind these altars with a soft
fillet: burn thereon oily vervain and male[13] frankincense,
that I may try, by sacred magic spells, to dispossess my love
of a sound mind. Only charms are here wanting. My charms,
bring Daphnis from the town, bring him home. Charms
can even draw down the moon from heaven; by charms
Circe[14] transformed the companions of Ulysses: the cold snake
is in the meads by incantation burst. My charms, bring
Daphnis from the town, bring him home. First, these
three threads, with threefold colours varied, I round thee
twine; and thrice lead thy image round these altars. The
gods delight in the uneven number. My charms, bring
Daphnis from the town, bring him home. Bind, Amaryllis,
three colours in three knots; bind them. Amaryllis, now;
and say, I bind the chains of Venus. My charms, bring
Daphnis from the town, bring him home. As this clay
hardens, and as this wax dissolves with one and the same fire;
so may Daphnis by my love. Sprinkle the salt cake, and
burn the crackling laurels in bitumen. Me cruel Daphnis
burns; I on Daphnis burn this laurel. My charms, bring
Daphnis from the town, bring him home. May such love

---

[11] Arion, a famous lyric poet and musician of the isle of Lesbos. On
his return to Corinth from Italy, the mariners formed a plot to murder him
for his riches, when he threw himself into the sea, and was carried on the
back of a dolphin to Tænarus in the Morea.

[13] i. e. frankincense of the best sort.

[14] Circe, a daughter of Sol and Perseis, celebrated for her knowledge
of magic and poisonous herbs. She changed the companions of Ulysses
into swine; but afterwards, at his solicitation, restored them to their former state.

[scize] Daphnis as when a beifer, tired with ranging after the
bull through lawns and lofty groves, distracted, lies down on
the green sedge by a rivulet, nor is mindful to withdraw from
the late hour of night: let such love seize Daphnis; nor let
his cure be my concern.   My charms, bring Daphnis from the
town, bring him home.   These garments the faithless one left
with me some time ago, the dear pledges of himself; which
to thee, O earth, on the very entrance, I now commit: these
pledges owe me Daphnis.   My charms, bring Daphnis from
the town, bring him home.   These herbs, and these baneful
plants, in Pontus[15] gathered, Mœris himself gave me: in Pontus numerous they grow.   By these have I seen Mœris transform himself into a wolf, and skulk into the woods, often from
the deep graves call forth the ghosts, and transfer the springing harvests to another ground.   My charms, bring Daphnis
from the town, bring him home.   Bring forth the ashes,
Amaryllis; throw them into a flowing brook,[16] and over thy
head; look not back.   Daphnis with these I will assail:
nought he regards the gods, nought my charms.   My charms,
bring Daphnis from the town, bring him home.   See the very
ashes have spontaneously seized the altars with quivering
flames, while I delay to remove them may it be a happy omen.
'Tis certainly something or other; and Hylax[17] in the entrance
barks.   Can I believe? or do those in love form to themselves fantastic dreams?   Cease; for Daphnis comes from the
town ; now cease, my charms.

ECLOGUE IX.

Virgil, having recovered his patrimony through the favour of Augustus,
devotes this pastoral to complain against Arius the centurion, who had
possession of his lands, and laid a plan for his assassination.

LYCIDAS, MŒRIS.

L. WHITHER, Mœris, do thy feet [lead][1] thee? are you for
the town, whither the way leads?

15 Pontus, a country of Asia Minor, bordering on the Euxine: it was
the kingdom of Mithridates the Great.
16 Rivoque fluenti, the same as in rivum fluentem, of which construction many examples occur in Virgil. See Æn. i. 293; ii. 250; v. 451;
vi. 191; viii. 591; ix. 664; xii. 263.
17 Hylax, the name of a dog.
1 Supply "ducunt" from the following "ducit." B.

M. Ah, Lycidas, we have lived to see the day when an
alien possessor of my little farm (what we never apprehend-
ed) may say: These are mine; old tenants, begone. Now
vanquished and disconsolate, since fortune confounds all
things, to him I convey these kids, of which I wish him little
good.

L. Surely, I heard that your Menalcas had saved by his
verse all that ground where the hills begin to decline, and by
an easy declension to sink down their ridges as far as the
stream and now broken tops of the old beech.

M. Thou heardst it, Lycidas, and it was reported;[2] but
our verse just as much avails amid martial arms, as they say
the Chaonian[3] pigeons do, when the eagle comes upon them.
But had not the ill-boding raven, from a hollow holm-oak,
warned me by any means to cut short the rising dispute,
neither your Mœris here, nor Menalcas himself, had been
alive.

L. Alas, is any one capable of so great wickedness? Alas,
Menalcas, the charms of thy poetry were almost snatched from
us with thyself! Who [then] had sung the nymphs? who
with flowering herbs had strewn the ground, or covered with
verdant shade the springs? or who [had sung] those songs
which lately I .secretly stole from you, when you used to resort to our darling Amaryllis? "Feed, Tityrus, my goats till
I return, short is the way; and when they are fed, drive
them, Tityrus, to watering; and while you are so doing, beware of meeting the he-goat: he butts with the horn."

M. Nay, rather these, which to Varus, and yet unfinished,
he sung: "Varus, the tuneful swans shall raise thy name
aloft to the stars, if Mantua remain. But in our possession;
Mantua, alas, too near unfortunate Cremona!"[4]

L. If thou retainest any, begin; so may thy swarms avoid
Cyrnean yews:[5] so may thy heifers, fed with cytisus, dis-

---

[2] I, however, prefer putting a note of interrogation after "audieras,"
with Wagner. B.

[3] Chaonian pigeons. Chaonia was a mountainous part of Epirus, in
which was the sacred grove of Dodona, where pigeons were said to deliver oracles.

[4] Cremona, a city of Italy on the northern bank of the Po. Its lands
were divided among the veteran soldiers of Augustus.

[5] Cyrnean yews. Cyrnus, now Corsica, an island in the Mediterranean, near the coast of Italy. The honey produced here had a bitter

tend their dugs. The Muses have also made me a poet: I too have my verses; and the shepherds call me bard: but to them I give no credit: for as yet methinks I sing nothing worthy of a Varus or a Cinna,[6] but only gabble like[7] a goose among sonorous swans.

M. That very thing, Lycidas, is what I am about; and now con it over in silence with myself, if I can recollect it: nor is it a vulgar song. "Come hither, Galatea: for what pleasure have you among the waves? Here is blooming spring; here, about the rivers, earth pours forth her various flowers; here the white poplar overhangs the grotto, and the limber vines weave shady bowers. Come hither: leave the mad billows to buffet the shores."

L. [But] what were those which I heard you singing in a clear night alone? I remember the air, if I could recollect the words.

M. Daphnis, why gaze you on the risings of the signs of ancient date? Lo, Dionæan Cæsar's[8] star hath entered on its course; the star by which the fields were to rejoice with corn, and by which the grapes on sunny hills were to take their hue. Daphnis, plant thy pear-trees. Posterity shall pluck the fruit of thy plantations. Age bears away all things, even the mind itself. Often, I remember, when a boy, I spent long summer-days in song. Now all these songs I have forgotten; now the voice itself has left Mœris; the wolves have seen Mœris first.[9] But these Menalcas himself will often recite to you.

L. By framing excuses thou puttest off for a long time my fond desire. And now the whole main for thee lies smooth and still; and mark how every whispering breeze of wind hath died away. Besides, half of our journey still remains: for

---

taste, in consequence of the bees feeding on the yew trees, with which the island abounded.

[6] Cinna, a grandson of Pompey, the intimate friend of Augustus, and patron of Virgil.

[7] The poet puns upon the name of Anser, a contemporary poet. The saying seems proverbial; as in Symmachus, Ep. i. 1, " Licet inter olores canoros anserem strepere." B.

[8] Dionæi Cæsaris. Cæsar of the Julian family, which sprung from Æneas the son of Venus, whom Mythology makes the daughter of Jupiter and Dione.

[9] Lupi Mœrim videre priores. Alluding to a superstitious notion, that, if a wolf saw a man before it was seen by him, it made him lose his voice

Hianor's[18] tomb begins to appear. Here, where the swains are
stripping off the thick leaves, here, Mœris, let us sing. Here
lay down your kids ; yet we shall reach the town. Or if we
are afraid that the night may gather rain before [we arrive],
yet we may still go on singing ; the way will be less tedious.
That we may go on singing, I will ease you of this burden.

M. Shepherd, urge me no more ; and let us mind the business now in hand. We shall sing those tunes to more advantage when [Menalcas] himself arrives.

ECLOGUE X.

Gallus, to whom this Eclogue is inscribed, was the patron of Virgil, a soldier
and a poet. He was greatly enamoured of Cytheris, whom he calls Lycoris, celebrated for her beauty and intrigues; but she forsook him for
Mark Antony, by whom she was in turn abandoned for Cleopatra.

GALLUS.

GRANT unto me, O Arethusa,[1] this last essay. A few
verses, but such as Lycoris herself may read, I must sing to
my Gallus. Who can deny a verse to Gallus? So, when
thou glidest beneath the Sicilian wave, may the salt Doris[2]
not intermingle her streams [with thine]. Begin : let us sing
the anxious loves of Gallus, while the flat-nosed goats browse
the tender shrubs. We sing not to the deaf ; the woods reply to all. What groves, ye virgin Naiads, or what lawns
detained you, while Gallus pined[3] with ill-requited love? for
neither any of the tops of Parnassus, nor those of Pindus,[4]
nor Aonian Aganippe, did retard you. The very laurels, the
very tamarisks bemoaned him : even pine-topped Mænalus
[bemoaned] him as he lay beneath a lonely rock, and over

---

[18] "The same as Ocnus, of whom Virgil says in the tenth Eclogue, *Fa-
tidica Mantus, et Thusci filius Amnis.* He was the founder of Mantua."
SERVIUS. B.

[1] Arethusa, the nymph who presided over the fountain of the same
name in Sicily.

[2] Doris, a sea nymph, the mother of the Nereids ; here used to express
the sea itself. Naiads, nymphs,—goddesses who presided over rivers
and fountains.

[3] Observe that "periret" is used to express the ἰράχετο, i. e. "wasted
away," of Theocr. i. 66. B.

[4] Pindus, a mountain between Thessaly and Epirus, sacred to Apollo
and the Muses. Aonian Aganippe, a celebrated fountain of Bœotia, of
which Aonia was a district.

him the stones of cold Lycæus[5] wept. His sheep too stand
around him, nor are they ashamed of us; nor, divine poet, be
thou ashamed of thy flock; even fair Adonis[6] tended sheep
by the streams. The shepherd too came up; the slow-paced
herdsmen came; Menalcas came wet from winter-mast. All
question whence this thy love? Apollo came: Gallus, he
says, why ravest thou thy care?[7] Lycoris is following another
through snows and horrid camps. Silvanus[8] too came up
with rural honours on his head, waving the flowering fennels
and big lilies. Pan, the god of Arcadia, came; whom we
ourselves beheld stained with the elder's purple berries and
vermilion. What bounds, he says, will you set [to mourning]?
Love regards not such matters. Nor cruel love with tears,
nor grassy meads with streams, nor bees with cytisus, nor
goats with leaves, are satisfied. But he, overwhelmed with
grief, said, Yet[9] you, Arcadians, shall sing these my woes on
your mountains; ye Arcadians, alone skilled in song. Oh how
softly then may my bones rest, if your pipe in future times
shall sing my loves! And would to heaven I had been one
of you, and either keeper of your flock, or vintager of the
ripe grape! Sure whether Phyllis or Amyntas, or whoever
else, had been my love, (what though Amyntas be swarthy?
the violet is black, and hyacinths are black,) they would have
reposed-with me among the willows under the limber vine;
Phyllis had gathered garlands for me, Amyntas would have
sung. Here are cool fountains; here, Lycoris, soft meads,
here a grove: here with thee I could consume my whole life
away. Now frantic love detains me in the service of rigid
Mars, in the midst of darts, and adverse foes. Thou, far from
thy native land, (let me not believe it,) beholdest nothing
but Alpine snows,[10] and the colds of the Rhine, ah, hard-

---

[5] Lycæus, a mountain of Arcadia, sacred to Jupiter, and also to Pan.
[6] Adonis, a youth, the favourite of Venus: having lost his life by the
bite of a wild boar, he was changed into the flower Anemone.
[7] Æsch. Choeph. 233, ὦ φίλατον μέλημα (i. e. "cura") δώμασιν πα-
τρός. B.
[8] Silvanus, a rural deity among the Romans, who presided over woods.
[9] But Nonius Marcell. i. s. v. triste est mœstum, connects "tamen"
with "ille," which I should almost prefer, the sense being, "But he
(despite all that even Pan could say) yet replied," &c. B.
[10] Alpine snows. The Alps are a chain of mountains, the highest in
Europe, separating Italy from France, Switzerland, and Austria. The

hearted one! alone, without me. Ah, may neither these colds
hurt thee! ah, may not the sharp ice wound thy tender feet!
I will go, and warble on the Sicilian shepherd's reed those
songs which are by me composed in Chalcidian strain." I
am resolved, rather to endure [my passion] in the woods,
among the dens of wild beasts, and to inscribe my loves upon
the tender trees: as they grow up, so you, my loves, will grow.
Meanwhile, in company with the nymphs, over Mœnalus will
I range, or hunt the fierce boars. No colds shall hinder me
from traversing with my hounds the Parthenian lawns[13] around.
Now over rocks and resounding groves methinks I roam:
pleased I am to shoot Cydonian shafts from the Parthian bow:
[Fool that I am!] as if these were a cure for the rage of love;
or as if that god could learn to be softened by human woes.
Now, neither the nymphs of the groves, nor songs themselves,
charm me any more: even ye woods, once more farewell. No
suffering can change him, though amidst frosts we drink of
Hebrus,[13] and undergo the Sithonian snows[14] of rainy winter;
or even if we should tend our flocks in Ethiopia,[15] beneath the
sign of Cancer, when the dying rind withers on the stately elm.
Love conquers all;[16] and let us yield to love. These strains,
ye divine Muses, it shall suffice your poet to have sung, while
he sat and wove his little basket of slender osiers: these you
will make acceptable to Gallus; to Gallus, for whom my love
grows as much every hour, as the green alder shoots up in the
infancy of spring. Let us arise: the shade is wont to prove
noxious to singers; the juniper's shade now grows noxious;
the shades are hurtful even to the corn. Go home, the evening star arises, my full-fed goats, go home.

Rhine, a celebrated river which rises in the Alps, and, after a course of
600 miles, discharges itself into the German Ocean.

[11] Chalcidian strain, that is, in the elegiac strain of Euphorion, a Greek
poet of Chalcis in Eubœa.

[12] Parthenian lawns. Parthenius was a mountain of Arcadia, for
which it is here used; as Cydonian shafts is used for Cretan darts,—Cydon being a city of Crete.

[13] The cold of the Hebrus in Thrace was celebrated, as we find from
Philippus in Anthol. p. 47, Ἕβρον θρηΐκιον κρυμῷ πεπιδημένον ὕδωρ. B.

[14] Sithonian snows, from Sithonia, a part of Thrace.

[15] Ethiopia, an extensive country of Africa: by the ancients, this name
was applied to modern Abyssinia, and the southern regions of Africa.

[16] Heyne finds fault with the abruptness of this passage, but Ambon
well remarks, that "this line is meant to express a return to a sounder
mind." H.

VIRGIL'S GEORGICS.

BOOK I.

This admirable Poem was undertaken at the particular request of that great patron of poetry, Mæcenas, to whom it is dedicated, and has justly been esteemed the most perfect and finished of Virgil's works. Of the Four Books of which it consists, the First treats of ploughing and preparing the ground; the Second, of sowing and planting; the Third, of the management of cattle, &c.; and the Fourth gives an account of bees, and of the manner of keeping them among the Romans.

WHAT makes the harvests joyous; under what sign, Mæcenas, it is proper to turn the earth and join the vines to elms; what is the care for kine, the nurture for breeding sheep;[1] and how much experience for managing the frugal bees; hence will I begin to sing. Ye brightest lights[2] of the world, that lead the year gliding along the sky; Bacchus and fostering Ceres, if by your gift mortals exchanged the Chaonian acorn for fattening ears of corn, and mingled draughts of Achelous[3] with the invented juice of the grape; and ye Fauns propitious to swains, ye Fauns and Virgin Dryads, advance your foot in tune: your bounteous gifts I sing. And thou, O Neptune, to whom the earth, struck with thy mighty trident, first poured forth the neighing steed; and thou, tenant of the groves, for whom three hundred snow-white bullocks crop Cæa's[4] fertile

---

[1] Pecori. Pecus here, as opposed to boves, signifies the lesser cattle, as sheep and goats, but especially sheep; as the word, I think, always signifies in Virgil when it stands by itself. See Ecl. i. 75; iii. 1, 20, 34; v. 87. Georg. ii. 371.

[2] Vos, ò clarissima mundi, &c. Varro, in his seventh book of Agriculture, invocates the sun and moon, then Bacchus and Ceres, as Virgil does here: which sufficiently confutes those who take the words, vos, ò clarissima lumina, to be meant of Bacchus and Ceres.

[3] Achelous, (Aspro Potamo,) a river of Epirus in Greece, said by some to have been the first river that sprung from the earth after the deluge; hence it was frequently put by the ancients, as it is here, for water. DAVIDSON. Servius observes, "Acheloum generaliter, propter antiquitatem fluminis, omnem aquam veteres vocabant." B.

[4] Cæa, (Zea,) an island in the Archipelago, one of the Cyclades.

thickets: thou too, O Pan, guardian of the sheep, O Tegæan[1] god, if thy own Mænalus be thy care, draw nigh propitious, leaving thy native grove, and the dells of Lycæus: and thou Minerva, inventress of the olive; and thou, O boy, teacher of the crooked plough; and thou, Sylvanus, bearing a tender cypress plucked up by the root: both gods and goddesses all, whose province it is to guard the fields; both ye who nourish the infant fruits from no seed, and ye who on the sown fruits send down the abundant shower from heaven.

And thou too, Cæsar, whom it is yet uncertain what councils of the gods are soon to have; whether thou wilt vouchsafe to visit cities, and [undertake] the care of countries, and the widely extended globe receive thee, giver of the fruits, and ruler of the seasons, binding thy temples with thy mother's myrtle: or whether thou comest, god of the unmeasured ocean, and mariners worship thy divinity alone; whether remotest Thule[6] is to be subject to thee, and Tethys[7] to purchase thee for her son-in-law with all her waves; or whether thou wilt join thyself to the slow months, a new constellation, where space lies open between Erigone and the [Scorpion's] pursuing claws: the fiery Scorpion himself already contracts his arms and leaves for thee more than an equal proportion of the sky. Whatever thou wilt be, (for let not Tartarus[8] expect thee for its king, nor let such dire lust of sway once be thine; though Greece admires her Elysian fields, and Proserpina,[9] redemanded, is not inclined to follow her mother,) grant me an easy course, and favour my adventurous enterprise; and pitying with me the swains who are strangers to their way, commence [the god], and accustom thyself even now to be invoked by prayers.

In early spring, when melted snows glide down from the

[1] Tegæan god. Pan is so called, from Tegea, a town of Arcadia, in Greece, which was sacred to him.

[6] Thule, an island in the most northern parts of the German Ocean, to which the ancients gave the epithet of Ultima. Some suppose that it is the island of Iceland, or part of Greenland, while others imagine it to be the Shetland Isles.

[7] Tethys, the chief of the sea-deities, was the wife of Oceanus. The word is often used by the poets to express the sea.

[8] Tartarus, the infernal regions, where, according to the ancients, the most impious and guilty among mankind were punished.

[9] Proserpine, the daughter of Ceres, and wife of Pluto, who stole her away as she was gathering flowers in the plains of Enna in Sicily.

hoary hills, and the crumbling glebe unbinds itself by the
zephyr; then let my steer begin to groan under the deep-
pressed plough, and the share worn by the furrow [begin] to
glitter. That field at last answers the wishes of the covetous
farmer, which twice hath felt the sun, twice the cold,[10] harvests immense are wont to burst his barns.

But, before we cleave an unknown plain with the ploughshare, let it be our care previously to learn the winds, and
various character of the climate, the ways of culture practised
by our forefathers, and the tillage and habits of the soil;
what each country is apt to produce, and what to refuse.
Here grain, there grapes, more happily grow; nurseries of
trees elsewhere, and herbs spontaneous bloom. Do not you
see, how Tmolus[11] sends saffron odours, India ivory, the soft
Sabæans their frankincense? But the naked[12] Chalybes [send]
steel, Pontus strong-scented castor, Epirus[13] the prime of the
Olympic mares. These laws and eternal conditions nature
from the beginning imposed on certain places: what time
Deucalion first cast stones into the unpeopled world, whence
men, a hardy race, sprang up. Come then, let your sturdy
steers forthwith turn up a soil that is rich for the first month
of the year; and let the dusty summer bake the scattered clods
with mature suns. But, if the land be not fertile, it will be

[10] Anthon observes, "The usual custom of the Roman farmers was to
plough the land three times, when it fell under the denomination of hard
land. The first ploughing was in the spring, the second in the summer,
the third in autumn (tertiabatur, Colum. ii. 4). In this way the ground
was exposed twice to the heat of the sun, and once to the frost. If, however, the soil was unusually hard and stubborn, a fourth ploughing took
place at the end of autumn or beginning of winter; and it is to such a
process that the poet here alludes, the land having thus, in the course of
its four upturnings with the plough, twice felt the sun and twice the cold."

[11] Tmolus, a mountain of Lydia, in Asia Minor, abounding in vines,
saffron, &c. Sabæans, the inhabitants of Saba, a town of Arabia, famous
for frankincense, myrrh, and aromatic plants. Chalybes, a people of
Pontus, in Asia Minor; their country abounded in iron mines.

[12] If "nudi" be correct, Virgil must speak of the Chalys only as
lightly clad, (leviter vestiti,) as in his direction to husbandmen "to
plough and sow naked." But although this would be a very proper
way of speaking among people acquainted with this limitation of meaning, yet it seems scarcely an apt epithet for a barbarian tribe, dwelling in
a cold region. Some years since, I proposed to read "duri." See the
supplement to my notes on Apul. de Deo Socr. B.

[13] Epirus, (Albania,) a country of Greece, famous for its fine breed of
horses.

enough to raise it up with a light furrow, even towards the
rising of Arcturus:[14] in the former case, lest weeds obstruct
the joyous corn; in the latter, lest the scanty moisture forsake the barren sandy soil.

You will likewise suffer your lands after reaping to lie fallow every other year, and the exhausted field to harden by
repose. Or, changing the season, you will sow there yellow
wheat, whence before you have taken up the joyful pulse,
with rustling pods, or the vetch's slender offspring and the
bitter lupine's brittle stalks, and rustling grove. For a crop
of flax burns[15] the land: as burn the oats and poppies impregnated with Lethæan sleep.[16] But yet your labour will be
easy [even though you should sow these kinds of grain] every
other year, provided only you be not backward to saturate
the parched soil with rich dung, or to scatter sordid ashes
upon the exhausted lands: thus, too, your land will rest by
changing the grain. Nor, in the mean time, will there be
ungratefulness.

Often, too, it has been of use to set fire to barren lands, and
burn the light stubble in crackling flames: whether the land
thence receives secret strength and rich nourishment from a
field left fallow; or whether every vicious quality is exhaled
by the fire and the superfluous moisture sweats off; or whether the heat opens more passages, and secret pores, through
which the sap may come to the tender blades; or whether it
hardens more, and binds the gaping veins; that the small
showers, or keen influence of the violent sun, or penetrating
cold of Boreas, may not parch it up.

He, too, greatly benefits the land, who breaks the sluggish
clods with harrows, and drags osier hurdles over them, (nor
does yellow Ceres view him from high Olympus,[17] to no

---

[14] Arcturus, a star near the tail of Ursa Major, whose rising and setting was supposed to portend great tempests. In the time of Virgil, it
rose about the middle of September.

[15] i. e. exhausts. Virgil does not forbid the sowing of flax and poppies.
but explains that, from their exhausting nature, they are bad crops in
rotation after wheat. So Anthon. B.

[16] Lethæan sleep. Lethe was one of the rivers of hell, whose waters
had the power of causing forgetfulness.

[17] Olympus, a lofty mountain on the confines of Thessaly and Macedonia, separated from Ossa by the vale of Tempe. The ancients supposed that it touched the heavens with its top, and on that account the
poets made it the residence of the gods.

purpose,) and he also who, after the plain has been torn, again breaks through the land; that raises up its ridges, turning the plough across,[18] and gives it frequent exercise and rules his lands imperiously.

Pray, ye swains, for moist summers and serene winters. In winter's dust most joyful is the corn, joyful is the field. On no culture does Mysia[19] so much pride herself, and [hence] even Gargarus admires his own harvest.

What shall I say of him, who, immediately after sowing the seed, presses on the lands, and levels the heaps of barren sand; then on the sown corn drives the stream and ductile rills? and when the field is scorched with raging heat, the herbs all dying, lo! from the brow of a hilly tract he decoys the torrent; which falling down the smooth rocks, awakes the hoarse murmur, and with gurgling streams allays the thirsty lands.

What of him who, lest the stalk with over-loaded ears bend to the ground, feeds down the luxuriance of the crop in the tender blade, when first the springing corn equals the furrows; and who drains from soaking sand the collected moisture of the marsh, chiefly when, in the changeable months, the swelling river overflows, and overspreads all around with slimy mud, whence the hollow dykes sweat with tepid vapour?

After all, (when the labours of men and oxen have tried these expedients in cultivating the ground,) the voracious goose, the Strymonian[20] cranes, and succory with its bitter roots, and even the shades are in some degree injurious. The Sire himself willed the ways of tillage not to be easy, and first aroused the fields by art, whetting the skill of mortals with care; nor suffered he his reign to lie inactive in heavy sloth. Before Jove, no husbandmen subdued the fields; nor was it even lawful to mark out, or by limits divide the ground. They made all things common gain, and earth of herself produced every thing freely without any one asking. He infused the noxious poison into the horrid serpent, commanded the wolves to prowl, and the sea to be stirred; and he shook the

---

[18] A description of "cross-ploughing." B.

[19] Mysia, a country of Asia Minor, bordering on Troas. Gargarus, a mountain, or rather a part of Mount Ida, in Troas.

[20] Strymonian cranes. Strymon, a river of Macedonia, the ancient boundary between that country and Thrace.

honey from the leaves, removed fire, and restrained the wine that ran commonly in rivulets; that experience, by dint of thought, might gradually hammer out the various arts, in furrows seek the blade of corn, and from the veins of flint strike out the hidden fire. Then first the rivers felt the excavated alders; then the seamen gave the stars their numbers and their names, the Pleiades,[21] Hyades, and the bright bear of Lycaon. Then were invented [the arts of] catching wild beasts in toils, deceiving with birdlime, and encompassing the spacious lawns with hounds. And now one seeking the depths, lashes the broad river with his casting-net; and on the sea another drags his humid lines along. Then [arose] the rigid force of steel, and the flat blade of the grating saw (for the first mortals cleft the splitting wood with wedges); then various arts ensued. Incessant labour and want, in hardships pressing, surmounted every obstacle. Ceres first taught mortals with steel to turn the ground: when now the acorns and arbutes of the sacred wood failed, and Dodona[22] refused sustenance. Soon too was distress inflicted on the corn; when noxious mildew eat the stalks, and the lazy thistle shot up its horrid spikes in the field. The crops of corn die; a prickly wood succeeds, burs and caltrops, and, amidst the shining fields, unhappy darnel and barren wild oats bear sway. But unless you both vex the ground by continual harrowings, fright away the birds with a noise, and with the pruning-knife restrain the shades of the shaded field, and by prayers call down the showers; alas, [while thy labour proves] in vain, thou wilt view another's ample store, and in the woods solace thy hunger by shaking [acorns] from the oak.

We must also describe what are the instruments used by the hardy swains; without which the crops could neither be sown nor spring. First, the share, and the heavy timber of the curved plough, and the slow-rolling wains of the Eleusinian mother, Ceres, and sledges and drags, and harrows of unwieldy weight;

[21] Pleiades, a name given to the seven daughters of Atlas and Plaione, made a constellation in the heavens. Hyades, the five daughters of Atlas, who were also changed into stars, and placed in the constellation Taurus. Bear of Lycaon. Calisto, the daughter of Lycaon, was changed by Juno into a bear, but Jupiter made her the constellation Ursa Major.

[22] Dodona, an ancient city of Epirus, in Greece, where was a sacred grove, with a celebrated oracle and temple of Jupiter.

besides the mean osier furniture of Celeus,[33] arbute hurdles,
and the mystic fan of Bacchus; all which, with mindful care,
you will provide long before-hand, if glory of a blissful country duly awaits thee. In the first place,[34] in the woods an elm
bent with vast force is subdued into the plough tail, and receives the form of the crooked plough. To this, at the lower
end, are fitted a beam extended to eight feet, two earth-boards,
and share-beams with a double back. The light linden also
is felled before-hand for the yoke, and the tall beech, and the
plough-staff, to turn the bottom of the carriage behind; and
the smoke seasons[35] the timber hung up in the chimneys.

I can recite to you many precepts of the ancients, unless
you decline them, and think it not worth while to learn these
trifling cares. The threshing-floor chiefly must be levelled
with the huge roller, and wrought with the hand, and con-
solidated with binding chalk, that weeds may not spring up,
and that overpowered with drought it may not chap. Then
various pests baffle us; often the diminutive mouse has built
its cell, and made its granaries; or the moles, deprived of
sight, have dug their lodges under ground; and in the cavities
has the toad been found, and vermin which the earth produces
in abundance; the weevil plunders vast heaps of corn, and
the ant, fearful of helpless old age.

Observe also, when the almond[36] shall clothe itself abundantly with blossom in the woods, and bend its fragrant
boughs: if the rising fruit abound, in like quantity the corn
will follow, and a great threshing with great heat will ensue.
But, if the shady boughs abound with luxuriance of leaves, in
vain the floor shall bruise the stalks, fertile only in chaff.

I have indeed seen many sowers artificially prepare their
seeds, and steep them first in saltpetre and black lees of oil,

[33] Celeus, a king of Eleusis, was the father of Triptolemus, whom
Ceres instructed in husbandry.
[34] The order is, "ulmus flexa in silvis magna vi domatur in burim, et
accipit formam curvi aratri." ANTHON.
[35] Literally, "explores," "searches," i. e. to see if there be any
chinks. B.
[36] The term mas is employed by the Roman writers in an extended
sense, to denote the almond, the walnut, the hazel-nut tree, &c. Most
commonly, however, an epithet is added, to make the meaning more de-
finite; thus, mas juglans, "the walnut;" mas amygdala, "the almond;"
mas avellana, "the hazel-nut or filbert," &c. ANTHON.

that the produce might be larger in the fallacious pods. And though, being hastened, they were soaked over a slow fire, selected long, and proved with much labour, yet have I seen them degenerate, unless human industry with the hand culled out the largest every year. Thus all things, by destiny, hasten to decay,[27] and gliding away, insensibly are driven backward; not otherwise than he who rows his skiff with much ado against the stream, if by chance he slackens his arms, and the tide hurries him headlong down the river.

Further, the stars of Arcturus, and the days of the Kids, and the shining Dragon, must be as much observed by us, as by those who, homeward borne across the main, attempt the [Euxine] Sea,[28] and the straits of oyster-breeding Abydos.

When Libra makes the hours of day and night equal, and now divides the globe in the middle between light and shades, work your steers, ye swains, sow barley in the fields, till toward the last shower of the inclement winter solstice. Then too is the time to hide in the ground a crop of flax, and the poppy of Ceres, and high time to ply your harrows; while the ground yet dry, you may, while the clouds are yet suspended.

In the spring is the sowing of beans: then thee too, O Medic plant![30] the rotten furrows receive, and millet comes, an annual care, when the bright Bull with gilded horns opens the year, and the Dog sets, giving way to the backward star. But if you labour the ground for a wheat-harvest and sturdy grain, and are bent on bearded ears alone; let the Pleiades in the morning be set, and let the Gnosian star[31] of [Ariadne's] blazing Crown depart, before you commit to the furrows the

[27] The infinitive is used absolutely to signify what is wont to happen. B.

[28] The Euxine (or Black) Sea is situated between Europe and Asia, and communicates with the Mediterranean by the Sea of Marmora and the Dardanelles.

[29] Abydos, a city of Asia Minor, on the Hellespont, (Dardanelles,) opposite to Sestos, in Thrace; famous for the bridge of boats which Xerxes made there across the Hellespont, when he invaded Greece; and for the loves of Hero and Leander.

[30] Medic plant, a species of trefoil, so called, because introduced from Media into Greece.

[31] Gnosian star, &c., Ariadne's crown, consisting of seven stars, so called from Gnosus, a city of Crete, where Minos, the father of Ariadne, reigned. Maia, one of the Pleiades. Boötes, a constellation near the Ursa Major, or Great Bear.

seed designed, and before you hasten to trust to the unwilling
earth the hopes of the year. Many have begun before the
setting of Main; but the expected crop hath mocked them
with empty ears. But if you are to sow vetches, and cheap
kidney beans, nor despise the care of the Egyptian lentil; set- -
ting Boötes will afford thee signs not obscure. Begin, and
extend thy sowing to the middle of the frosts.

For this purpose, the golden sun, through the twelve constellations of the world, rules the globe measured out into
certain portions. Five zones embrace the heavens; whereof
one is ever glowing with the bright sun, and scorched for ever
by his fire; round which two furthest ones to the right and
left are extended, stiff with cerulean ice and horrid showers.
Between these and the middle zones, two by the bounty of the
gods are given to weak mortals; and a path is cut through both,
where the series of the signs might revolve obliquely. As
the world rises high towards Scythia and Riphæan [a] hills; so
sloping downward it is depressed towards the south winds of
Libya. [b] The one pole to us is always elevated; but the other,
under our feet, is seen by gloomy Styx [c] and the ghosts below. [d]
Here, after the manner of a river, the huge Dragon glides
away with tortuous windings, around and through between the
Bears; the Bears that fear to be dipped in the ocean. There,
as they report, either dead night for ever reigns in silence,
and, outspread, wraps all things up in darkness; or else Aurora [e] returns thither from us, and brings them back the day:
and when the rising sun first breathes on us with panting
steeds, there ruddy Vesper lights up his late illuminations.

Hence we are able to foreknow the seasons, in the dubious
sky, hence the days of harvest, and the time of sowing; and
when it is proper to sweep the faithless sea with oars, when
to launch the armed fleets, or to fell the pine in the woods in

---

[a] Riphæan hills, in the north of Scythia, near the rivers Tanais and Rha.

[b] Libya, an extensive country of Africa, lying between Egypt and the Syrtis Major; by the ancients it was often applied to Africa in general.

[c] Styx, one of the rivers of hell, round which it was said to flow nine times. The gods held the waters of the Styx in such veneration, that they always swore by them; an oath which was inviolable.

[d] So "profunda Juno," for Proserpine, in Claudian, de Vap. i. 2. B.

[e] Aurora, the goddess of the morning. Vesper, the evening star; often used for the evening, as Aurora is for the morning.

season. Nor in vain do we study the settings and the risings of the signs, and the year equally divided into four different seasons.

If at any time a bleak shower confines the husbandman, then is his time to do many things in season, which, as soon as the sky is serene, would have to be done with expedition.[77] The ploughman sharpens the hard edge of the blunted share, scoops little boats from trees, or stamps the mark on the sheep, or the number on his sacks. Others sharpen stakes and two-horned forks, and prepare Amerine [osier] bands[38] for the limber vine. Now let the pliant basket of bramble twigs be woven; now parch your grain over the fire, now grind it with the stone: for even on holy-days, divine and human laws permit to perform some works. No religion hath forbidden to clear the channels, to raise a fence before the corn, to lay snares for birds, to fire the thorns, and plunge in the wholesome river a flock of bleating sheep. Often the driver of the sluggish ass loads his ribs with oil, or common apples; and, in his return from the town, brings back an indented mill-stone, or a mass of black pitch.

The moon too hath allotted days auspicious to works, some in one order, some in another. Shun the fifth: [on this] pale Pluto[39] and the Furies were born. Then at an unholy birth the earth brought forth Cœus,[40] Iapetus, and savage Typhœus, and the brothers who conspired to tear down the skies. For thrice did they essay to pile Ossa[41] upon Pelion, and to roll woody Olympus upon Ossa: thrice the Sire, with his thun-

---

[77] So this line appears to be explained by Nonius Marc. l. p. 512, and Macrob. Sat. vi. 3. "Maturare" at times is nearly identical with "properare." B.

[38] Amerine bands, from Ameria, a city of Umbria, in Italy, which abounded in osiers.

[39] Pluto, in ancient mythology, was the son of Saturn and Ops, and brother to Jupiter and Neptune; in the division of his father's empire, the kingdom of Hell was allotted to him.

[40] Cœus, Iapetus, &c., famous giants, sons of Cœlus and Terra, who, according to the poets, made war against the gods; but Jupiter at last put them to flight with his thunderbolts, and crushed them under Mount Ætna, in Sicily.

[41] Ossa, Pelion, &c., celebrated mountains of Thessaly, in Greece, which the giants, in their war against the gods, were feigned to have heaped on each other, that they might with more facility scale the walls of heaven.

der, overthrew the piled-up mountains. The seventh, next
to the tenth, is lucky both to plant the vine, and break the
oxen caught, and to add the woof to the warp: the ninth is
better for flight, adverse to thefts.[42] Many works too have
succeeded better in the cool night; or when morning sprinkles the earth with the rising sun. By night the light stubble, by night the parched meadows, are better[43] shorn: the
clammy dews fail not by night. And some by the late fires
of the winter light, watch all night, and with the sharp steel
point torches. Meanwhile, his spouse, cheering by song her
tedious labour, runs over the webs with the shrill shuttle; or
over the fire boils down the liquor of the luscious must, and
skims with leaves the tide of the trembling caldron.

But reddening Ceres is cut down in noontide heat; and in
noontide heat the floor thrashes out the parched grain. Plough
naked,[44] sow naked: winter is an inactive time for the hind.
In the cold weather the farmers mostly enjoy the fruit of their
labour, and, rejoicing with one another, provide mutual enter-
tainments: the genial winter invites them, and relaxes their
cares; as when weather-beaten ships have reached the port,
and the joyous mariners have planted garlands on the sterns.
But it then is the time both to strip the mast of oak, and the
bay-berries, the olive, and the bloody myrtle-berries; then to
set springes for cranes, and nets for stags, and to pursue the
long-eared hares; and whirling the hempen thongs of the
Balearian[45] sling, to pierce the does, when the snow lies deep,
when the rivers hurtle down the ice.

Why should I speak of the storms[46] and constellations of
autumn? and what must be guarded against by swains when
the day is now shorter, and the summer milder? or when the

[42] Anthon remarks, "The ninth day would be favourable for the run-
away, since the moon would then be of sufficient age to give a good light,
and help him on his way. For this very reason, on the other hand, it
would be unfavourable for the thief, who prefers darkness." Voss. ad loc.

[43] I think the harmony of this verse will be increased by transposing,
thus, "Nocte leves stipulæ melius," as it is quoted by Jul. Rufin. Schem.
Lex. 6. p. 31, ed. Ruhnk. B.

[44] i. e. in thin attire. B.

[45] Balearian sling, from the Baleares; a name given to the islands of
Majorca and Minorca, in the Mediterranean, because the inhabitants were
expert slingers.

[46] Nonius, L. s. v. tempestas, limits the sense of this word to "turbo
ventorum," I think, scarcely with reason. B.

showery spring pours down, the spiky harvest bristles in the
fields, and the milky corn swells in the green stalk? Oft have
I seen, when the farmer had just brought the reaper into the
yellow fields, and was binding up the barley with the brittle
straw, all the battles of the winds engage, which far and wide
tore up the full-loaded corn from the lowest roots, and tossed
it up: just so, with blackening whirlwind, a wintry storm
would drive light straw and flying stubble. Often also an
immense march of waters gathers in the sky, and clouds, collected from on high, brew thick an ugly storm of black showers: the lofty sky pours down, and with storms of rain sweeps
away the joyful corn, and toils of steers: the ditches are filled,
and the hollow rivers[47] swell with roaring, and in the steaming friths the sea boils. The Sire himself, amidst a night of
clouds, launches the thunders with his flaming right hand:
with the violence of which mighty earth trembles; the beasts
are fled, and through the nations lowly fear hath sunk the
hearts of men. He with his flaming bolts strikes down or
Athos,[48] or Rhodope, or high Ceraunia:[49] the south winds
redouble, and the shower is more and more condensed; now
woods, now shores, moan 'neath the mighty blast.

This dreading, observe the months and constellations of the
heavens: which way the cold star of Saturn shapes his course,
into what circuits Mercury's fiery planet wanders in heaven.
Above all, venerate the gods; and renew to great Ceres the
sacred annual rites,[50] offering up thy sacrifice upon the joyous
turf, at the expiration of the last days of winter, when the
spring is serene. Then the lambs are fat, and then the wines
most mellow; then slumbers on the hills are sweet, and thick
the shades. For thee let all the rural youths adore Ceres; to
whom, mix thou the honey-comb with milk and gentle wine;
and thrice let the auspicious victim go round the recent grain;
which let the whole chorus of thy companions accompany in

[47] I. e. the mountain streams. Hesych. θάλασσα κοίλη, ἡ χειμέριας. B.
[48] Athos, a lofty mountain of Macedonia, in Greece, on a peninsula:
It is now called Monte Santo, from the number of monasteries erected
upon it. Ceraunia, large mountains of Epirus, in Greece, stretching out
far into the Adriatic.
[49] " Acroceraunia " is more usual. Servius on Æn. iii. B.
[50] The poet here alludes to the Ambarvalia, a festival in honour of
Ceres, and which was so called because the victim was led around the
fields (quod victima ambiret arva) before it was sacrificed. ANTHON.

jovial mood, and with acclamation invite Ceres into their dwellings; nor let any one put the sickle to the ripe corn, till, in honour of Ceres, having his temples bound with wreathed oak, he dance in measure uncouth, and sing hymns.

And that we may learn these things by certain signs, both heats and rains, and cold-bringing winds, the Sire himself has appointed what the monthly moon should betoken; under what sign the south winds should fall; from what common observations the husbandman should learn to keep his herds nearer their stalls.

Straightway, when winds are rising, the friths of the sea with tossings begin to swell, and a dry crashing noise to be heard in the high mountains; or the far-sounding shores to be disturbed, and the murmurs of the grove to increase. Now hardly the billows refrain themselves from the crooked ships, when the cormorants fly swiftly back from the midst of the sea, and send their screams to the shore; and when the sea-coots sport on the dry beach; and the heron forsakes the well-known fens, and soars above the lofty cloud. Often too, when wind threatens, you will see the stars shoot precipitate from the sky, and behind them long trails of flame whiten athwart the shades of night; often the light chaff and fallen leaves flutter about; or feathers swimming on the surface of the water frisk together.

But when it lightens from the quarter of surly Boreas, and when the house of Eurus[11] and Zephyrus thunders, all the fields are floated with full ditches, and every mariner on the sea furls his damp sails. Showers never hurt any unforewarned: either the airy cranes have shunned it in the deep valleys as it rose; or the heifer, looking up to heaven, hath snuffed in the air with wide nostrils; or the chattering swallow hath fluttered about the lakes; and the frogs croaked their old complaint in the mud.[12] And often the ant, drilling her narrow path, hath conveyed her eggs from her secret cell; and the mighty bow hath drunk deep; and an army of ravens, on their return from feeding, have beaten the air and made a noise, with wings close crowded. Now you may observe the various sea-fowls, and those that rummage about the Asian

---

[11] Eurus and Zephyrus, the east and west winds.
[12] Alluding to the metamorphosis of the Lycian peasants into frogs for insulting Latona. Ovid, Met. vi 376. ANTHON. B.

meads, in Cayster's [53] pleasant lakes, keenly lave the copious dews upon their shoulders; now offer their heads to the working tides, now run into the streams, and, sportive, revel vainly in their desire of bathing. Then the impudent crow with full throat invites the rain, and solitary stalks by herself on the dry sand. Nor were even the maids, carding their nightly tasks, ignorant of the approaching storm; when they saw the oil sputter on the heated sherd, and foul fungous clots grow thick.[54]

Nor with less ease may you foresee, and by certain signs discern, sunshine succeeding rain, and open serene skies. For neither are the stars then seen with blunted edge, nor the moon to rise as if indebted to her brother's beams; nor thin fleecy [55] clouds to be borne through the sky. Nor do the halcyons, beloved by Thetis,[56] expand their wings upon the shore to the warm sun: the impure swine are not heedful to toss about with their snouts the loosened wisps. But the mists seek the lower grounds, and rest upon the plain; and the owl, observant of the setting sun from the high house-top, practises her evening songs in vain. Nisus in the clear sky appears aloft, and Scylla pays penalty for the purple lock. Wherever she flying cuts the light air with her wings, lo, hostile, implacable Nisus,[57] with loud screams pursues her through the sky: where Nisus mounts into the sky, she swiftly flying cuts the light air with her wings. Then the ravens, with com-

<hr>

[53] Cayster, a river of Asia Minor, which falls into the Ægean Sea, near Ephesus.

[54] This was a popular superstition, as we learn from Schol. Aristoph. Vesp. 260. B.

[55] Cf. Lucret. vi. 503, "veluti pendentia vellera lanæ." B.

[56] Thetis, one of the sea-deities, daughter of Nereus and Doris and mother of Achilles.

[57] Minos having laid siege to Megara, of which Nisus was king, became master of the place through the treachery of Scylla, the daughter of the latter. Nisus had a purple or golden lock of hair growing on his head, and, as long as it remained uncut, so long was his life to last. Scylla, having seen Minos, fell in love with him, and resolved to give him the victory. She accordingly cut off her father's precious lock as he slept and he immediately died. The town was then taken by the Cretans; but Minos, instead of rewarding the maiden, disgusted with her unnatural treachery, tied her by her feet to the stern of his vessel, and thus dragged her along till she was drowned. Nisus was changed after death into the bird called the sea-eagle, (ἁλιάετος,) and Scylla into that named ciris (κεῖρις); and the father continually pursues the daughter, says the legend, to punish her for her crime. ANTHON.

at the dawn the rays shall break themselves diversely among
the thick clouds; or when Aurora, leaving the saffron bed of
Tithonus,[60] rises pale; ah, the vine-leaf will then but ill defend the mellow grapes; so thick the horrid hail bounds rattling on the roofs. This too it will be more advantageous to
remember, when, having measured the heavens, he is just
setting; for often we see various colours wander over his face.
The azure threatens rain; the fiery, wind. But if the spots
begin to be blended with bright fire, then you will see all
things embroiled together with wind and storms of rain. Let
none advise me that night to launch into the deep, or to tear
my cable from the land. But if, both when he ushers in, and
when he shuts up, the revolving day, his orb is lucid; in vain
will you be alarmed by the clouds, and you will see woods
waved by the clear north wind.

In fine, the sun will give thee signs what [weather] late
Vesper brings, from what quarter the wind will roll the
clouds serene, what wet Auster[61] meditates. Who dares to
call the sun deceiver? He even forewarns often that hidden
tumults are at hand, and that treachery and secret wars are
swelling to a head. He also pitied Rome at Cæsar's death,
when he covered his bright head with murky iron hue,[62] and
the impious age feared eternal night; though at that time the
earth too, and ocean's plains, ill-omened dogs, and presaging
birds, gave ominous signs. How often have we seen Ætna[63]

[60] Tithonus, a son of Laomedon, king of Troy, was so beautiful that
Aurora became enamoured of him, and carried him away to Ethiopia.

[61] Auster, the south wind.

[62] "When he shrouded his bright head with a dark ferruginous hue."
According to Plutarch, (Vit. Cæs. c. 90,) Pliny, (II. N. ii. 30,) and Dio
Cassius, (xlv. 17,) the sun appeared of a dim and pallid hue after the
assassination of Julius Cæsar, and continued so during the whole of the
year. It is said, too, that, for want of the natural heat of that luminary,
the fruits rotted without coming to maturity. What Plutarch calls paleness, Virgil, it will be perceived, denominates by a stronger term, *ferrugo*.
This, of course, is the licence of poetry. The phenomenon mentioned by
the ancient writers is thought by some modern inquirers to have been oc-
casioned by spots on the sun; and this is the more probable opinion.
There appears, however, to have been an actual eclipse of the sun that
same year, in the month of November. Anthon.

[63] Ætna, (Gibello,) a celebrated volcanic mountain of Sicily. This
immense mountain is of a conical form; it is two miles in perpendicular
height, 100 miles round the base, with an ascent, in some places, of 30
miles, and its crater is a circle of about 3½ miles in circumference.

from its burst furnaces boil over in waves on the lands of the
Cyclops,[64] and shoot up globes of flame, and molten rocks!
Germany heard a clashing of arms over all the sky; the Alps
trembled with unwonted earthquakes. A mighty voice too
was commonly heard through the silent groves, and spectres
strangely pale were seen under cloud of night; and the very
cattle (O horrid!) spoke; rivers stopped their courses, the
earth yawned wide; the mourning ivory weeps in the temples, and the brazen statues sweat. Eridanus,[65] king of rivers,
overflowed, whirling in mad eddy whole woods along, and
bore away the herds with their stalls over all the plain.
Nor at the same time did either the fibres fail to appear
threatening in the baleful entrails, or blood to flow from the
wells, and cities to resound aloud with wolves howling by
night. Never did more lightnings fall from a serene sky, or
direful comets so often blaze. For this Philippi[66] twice saw
the Roman armies in intestine war[67] engage; nor seemed it
unbecoming to the gods, that Emathia[68] and the extensive
plains of Hæmus should twice be fattened with our blood.
Ay, and the time will come, when in those regions the husbandman, labouring the ground with the crooked plough,
shall find javelins all-eaten with corrosive rust, or with his
cumbrous harrows shall clash on empty helmets, and marvel
at the huge bones in dug-up graves.

Ye guardian deities of my country, ye Indigetes,[69] and thou,

---

[64] Cyclops, a gigantic race of men, sons of Cœlus and Terra: they
were Vulcan's workmen in fabricating the thunderbolts of Jupiter, and
were represented having only one eye in the middle of their forehead.

[65] Eridanus, called afterwards Padus, (the Po,) the largest river of
Italy, rises in the Alps, and, after a course of nearly 400 miles, falls into
the Adriatic, to the south of the city of Venice.

[66] Philippi, a city of Macedonia, on the confines of Thrace, famous
for the defeat of Brutus and Cassius by Antony and Augustus, B. C. 42.
By the other battle at Philippi, mentioned here, Virgil is supposed to
allude to that between Cæsar and Pompey on the plains of Pharsalia,
in Thessaly, which was fought near a town also called Philippi,
B. C. 48.

[67] The force of "paribus telis" is well expressed by Lucan, L. 7,
"pares aquilas, et pila minantia pilis," as remarked by Servius. B.

[68] Emathia, an ancient name of Macedonia and Thessaly. Hæmus, an
extensive chain of mountains through Thrace, &c., in length about 400
miles.

[69] Indigetes, a name given to those deities who were worshipped in
particular places, or to such heroes as were deified.

O Romulus,[70] and mother Vesta,[71] who guardest the Tuscan Tiber,[72] and the palaces of Rome; forbid not that this youthful hero at least repair the ruins of the age. Long since enough have we with our blood atoned for the perjuries of Laomedon's Troy.[73] Long since, O Cæsar, the courts of heaven envy us thee, and complain that thou art concerned about the triumphs of mortals; since among them the distinctions of right and wrong are perverted; so many wars, so many aspects of crimes, are throughout the world; the plough has none of its due honours; the fields lie waste, their owners being drawn for service; and the crooked scythes are forged into rigid swords. Here Euphrates,[74] there Germany, raises war; neighbouring cities, having broken their mutual leagues, take arms; impious Mars[75] rages through all the world. As when the four-horsed chariots have burst forth from the goal, they add speed to speed, and the charioteer, stretching in vain the bridle, is hurried away by the steeds, nor is the chariot heedful of the reins.

[70] Romulus, a son of Mars and Rhea, grandson of Numitor, king of Alba, and twin-brother of Remus. He was the founder and first king of Rome, which he built on Mount Palatine, B. c. 753. By the triumphs of their arms, and the terror of their name, the Romans gradually rose, during a succession of ages, to universal empire, and Rome became, for a time, mistress of the world. After his death, Romulus was ranked among the gods, and received divine honours under the name of Quirinus.

[71] Vesta, daughter of Rhea and Saturn, called the mother of the gods, was the goddess of fire, and the patroness of the vestal virgins, among the Romans.

[72] Tiber, a celebrated river of Italy, rises in the Apennines, and falls into the Mediterranean Sea, sixteen miles below the city of Rome.

[73] Laomedon, king of Troy, and the father of Priam. He built the walls of Troy, with the assistance of Apollo and Neptune; but, on the work being finished, he refused to reward them for their labours, and, in consequence, incurred the displeasure of the gods.

[74] Euphrates, a celebrated river of Asia, which rises in the mountains of Armenia, and discharges itself into the Persian Gulf.

[75] Mars, the god of war. Among the Romans, this deity received the most unbounded honours.

BOOK II.

Virgil, having, in the First Book, treated of tillage, proceeds in the Second to the subject of planting; describes the varieties of trees, with the best methods of raising them; gives rules for the management of the vine and olive, and for judging of the nature of soils; and, in a strain of exalted poetry, celebrates the praises of Italy, and the pleasures of a country life.

THUS far of the culture of fields, and of the constellations of the heavens; now, Bacchus, will I sing of thee, and with thee of woodland trees, and of the slow-growing olive's offspring. Hither, O father[1] Lenæus[2] (here is all full of thy bounties: for thee the field, laden with the viny harvest, flourishes; [for thee] the vintage foams in the full vats): hither, O father Lenæus, come; and, having thy buskins stripped off, stain thy legs, bared of the sandals, with me in new wine.

First, nature is various in producing trees: for some, without any cogent means applied by men, come freely of their own accord, and widely overspread the plains and winding rivers; as the soft osier and limber broom, the poplar and the whitening willows, with sea-green leaves. But some arise from deposited seed; as the lofty chestnuts, and the æsculus, which, in honour of Jove, shoots forth its leaves, the most majestic of the groves, and the oaks reputed oracular by the Greeks. To others a most luxuriant wood [of suckers] springs from the roots; as the cherries and the elms: thus, too, the little bay of Parnassus raises itself under its mother's mighty shade. Nature at first ordained these means [for the production of trees]: by these every species blooms, of woods, and shrubs, and sacred groves. Others there are, which experience has found out for itself on the way.[3] One, cutting off the tender suckers from the body of their mother, sets them in the furrows; another buries the stocks in the ground, and stakes split in four, and poles with the wood sharpened to a point; and some trees expect the bent-down arches of a layer,

---

[1] The term " pater " is here applied to Bacchus, not with any reference to advanced years, for the god is always represented by the ancient artists with the attributes of youth, (compare Muller, Archæolog. der Kunst, p. 566,) but merely as indicative of his being the beneficent author of so many good gifts unto men. ANTHON.

[2] Lenæus, a surname of Bacchus, the god of wine, from ληνός, a winepress.

[3] " Via " here denotes the " march of intellect." B.

and living nurseries in their native soil. Others have no need
of any root; and the planter makes no scruple to commit to
earth the topmost shoots, restoring them [to their parent soil].
Even (what is wondrous to relate) after the trunk is cut in
pieces, the olive-tree shoots forth roots from the dry wood.
Often we see the boughs of one tree transformed, with no
disadvantage, into those of another, and a pear-tree, being
changed, bear ingrafted apples, and stony cornels grow upon
plum stocks.[1]

Wherefore come on, O husbandmen, learn the culture proper to each kind, and soften the wild fruits by cultivation:
nor let any lands lie idle: it is worth while to plant Ismarus
with vines, and clothe vast Taburnus[2] with olives.

And thou, O glory mine, O thou deservedly the greatest
portion of my fame, be present, Mæcenas, pursue with me this
task begun, and flying set sail on this sea, now opening wide.
I choose not to comprise all matters in my verse, even if I
had a hundred tongues, a hundred mouths, and an iron voice;
be present, and coast along the nearest shore. The earth is
near at hand; I will not here detain thee with fictitious song,
or with circumlocution and tedious preamble.

Those which spring up spontaneously into the regions of
light are unfruitful indeed; but they rise luxuriant and strong:
for in the soil lies a native quality. Yet, if any one ingraft
even these, or deposit them transplanted in trenches well prepared, they will put off their savage nature, and by frequent
culture will not be slow to follow whatever modes of culture
you call them to. And [the sucker] also which sprouts up
barren from the low roots, will do the same,[3] if it be distributed through fields where room: now [in its natural state]
the high shoots and branches of the mother overshadow, and
hinder it from bearing fruit as it grows up, or pinch and
starve it when it bears. The tree, again, that is raised from
fallen seed, grows up slowly, so as to form a shade for late
posterity, and its fruits degenerate, forgetting their former
juices: thus even the vine bears sorry clusters, a prey for
birds. In fact, labour must be bestowed on all, and all must

---

[1] So Martyn. But see Anthon. B.
[2] Taburnus, a mountain of Campania, in Italy, which abounded with olives.
[3] i. e. will lay aside its wild and unproductive nature. ANTHON.

be forced into the trench, and tamed with vast pains. But olives answer better [when propagated] by truncheons, vines by layers, the myrtles of the Paphian [goddess' by settings] from the solid wood. From suckers the hard hazels grow, the mighty ash, and the shady poplar-tree, a crown for Hercules, and the oaks of the Chaonian Sire: thus also the lofty palm is propagated, and the fir-tree doomed to visit the dangers of the main.

But the rugged arbute is ingrafted on the offspring of the walnut, and barren planes have borne stout apple-trees. Chestnut-trees [have borne] beeches, and the mountain ash hath whitened with* the snowy blossoms of the pear: and swine have crunched acorns under elms. Nor is the method of ingrafting the same with that of inoculating. For [inoculating is thus]: where the buds thrust themselves forth from the middle of the bark, and burst the slender coats, a small slit is made in the very knot: hither they enclose a bud from another tree, and teach it to unite with the moist rind. Or again, [in ingrafting,] the knotless stocks are cut, and a passage is cloven deep into the solid wood with wedges: then fertile scions are inserted; and in no long time a huge tree shoots up to heaven with prosperous boughs, and admires its new leaves and fruits not its own.

Moreover, the species is not single, either of strong elms, or of willows, of the lote-tree, or of the Idæan cypresses;* nor do the fat olives grow in one form, the orchades, and the radii, and the pausia with bitter berries; nor apples, and the orchards of Alcinous; nor are the shoots the same of the Crustumian and Syrian pears, and of the heavy volemi. The same vintage hangs not on our trees, which Lesbos[10] gathers

---

ʳ Paphian goddess. Venus was so called, from Paphos, (Baffa,) a city of Cyprus, where she was worshipped.

⁸ "Incanuit" is an instance of zeugma, for the chestnut bears no white flower. B.

⁹ Idæan cypresses, from Mount Ida, in the island of Crete. Orchards of Alcinous, king of Phæacia, afterwards called Corcyra, (Corfu,) one of the Ionian Islands: his gardens, which were greatly famed, are beautifully described by Homer. Crustumian and Syrian pears; the first were so called from Crustuminum, a town of Etruria, in Italy; and the latter from Syria, a country of Asia, along the eastern shore of the Mediterranean. Phœnicia and Palestine were generally reckoned provinces of Syria.

¹⁰ Lesbos, (Mytilene,) a large island in the Archipelago, celebrated

from the Methymnæan vine. There are the Thasian vines,
and there are the white Mareotides; these fit for a rich soil,
and those for a lighter one: and the Psythian, more service-
able when dried, and the thin lageos, which will tie the feet
at length, and bind the tongue: the purple and the rath-ripe:
And in what numbers shall I sing of thee, Ó Rhætian grape?
nor therefore vie thou with the Falernian[11] cellars. There
are also Amminean vines, best-bodied wines; which even
Tmolus and Phanæ, king of mountains, honour; and the
smaller Argitia, which none can rival, either in yielding so
much juice, or in lasting so many years. I must not pass thee
over, Rhodian grape, grateful to the gods and second courses,
nor thee, bumastos, with thy swollen clusters. But we neither can recount how numerous the species, nor what are their
names, nor imports it to comprise their number; which whoever would know, the same may seek to learn how numerous
are the sands of the Libyan Sea tossed by the zephyr; or to
know how many waves of the Ionian Sea[12] come to the shores,
when Eurus, more violent, falls upon the ships.

But neither can all soils bear all sorts [of trees]. Willows
grow along the rivers, and elders in miry fens; the barren
wild ashes on rocky mountains; the shores rejoice most in
myrtle groves: Bacchus, in fine, loves open hills; the yews,
the north wind and the cold.

Survey, also, the globe subdued by the most distant culti-
vators, both the eastern habitations of the Arabians,[13] and the
tattooed Geloni. Countries are distinguished by their trees.

particularly the city of Methymna, for its excellent wines. Thasian
vines, those of Thasos, also an island in the Archipelago, near the coast
of Thrace. Mareotides, a vine from Mareotis, a lake in Egypt, near
Alexandria. Psythian, from Psythia, an ancient town of Greece, famous
for its grapes. Rhætian grape, from Rhætia, (the Tyrol, &c.,) a mountainous country to the north of Italy.

[11] Falernian, &c. Falernus, a fertile mountain and plain of Campania,
in Italy. Amminia, a district of Campania. Phanæ, a promontory of
the island of Chios (Scio). Rhodian grape, from Rhodes, a large and
fertile island in the Mediterranean, near the coast of Asia Minor, celebrated for a colossal statue of Apollo.

[12] Ionian Sea, a part of the Mediterranean Sea, at the bottom of the
Adriatic, and between Sicily and Greece.

[13] Arabians, &c., the inhabitants of Arabia, an extensive country of
Asia, forming a peninsula between the Persian and Arabian Gulfs: the
atter separates it from Africa. Geloni, a people of Scythia.

India alone bears black ebony: the frankincense-tree belongs to the Sabæans only. Why should I mention to thee balms distilling from the fragrant woods, and the berries of the evergreen acanthus? why the forests of the Ethiopians whitening with downy wool? and how the Seres[14] comb the slender fleeces from the leaves? or the groves which India, nearer the ocean, the utmost skirts of the globe, produces? where no arrows by their flight have been able to surmount the airy summit of the tree: and yet that nation is not slow at archery. Media bears the bitter juices and the permanent flavour of the happy apple; than which no remedy comes more seasonably, and expels the black venom from the limbs, when cruel stepdames have drugged the cup, and mingled herbs and not innoxious spells. The tree itself is stately, and in form most like a bay; and if it did not widely diffuse a different scent, would be a bay. Its leaves fall not off by any winds; its blossoms are extremely tenacious. With it the Medes correct their breaths and unsavoury mouths, and cure their asthmatic old men.

But neither the land of Media, most rich in woods, nor the beauteous Ganges,[15] and Hermus turbid with golden sands, can match the praises of Italy: not Bactra,[16] nor the Indians, and Panchaia, all enriched with incense-bearing soil. Bulls breathing fire from their nostrils never ploughed these regions, sown with the teeth of a hideous dragon; nor did a crop of men shoot dreadful up with helmets and crowded spears: but teeming corn and Bacchus' Campanian juice have filled [the land], olives and joyous herbs possess it. Hence the warrior-horse with stately port advances into the field; hence, Clitumnus,[17] thy white flocks, and the bull, chief of victims, after

[14] Seres, a nation of Asia, between the Ganges and Eastern Ocean; the modern Tibet, or probably China. Media, a celebrated country of Asia, to the south of the Caspian Sea.

[15] Ganges, a celebrated river of India, which arises in the Himalaya mountains, and, after a course of 1500 miles, falls into the bay of Bengal, below Calcutta. Hermus, (Sarabat,) a river of Lydia, in Asia Minor, whose sands were mingled with gold: it receives the waters of the Pactolos near Sardis, and falls into the Ægean, north-west of Smyrna.

[16] Bactra, (Balkh,) the capital of Bactriana, a country of Asia. Panchaia, a district of Arabia Felix.

[17] Clitumnus, a river of Umbria, in Italy, which falls into the Tiber. It was famous for its milk-white flocks, selected as victims in the celebration of the triumph.

they have been often plunged in thy sacred stream, escort the
Roman triumphs to the temples of the gods. Here is perpetual spring, and summer in months not her own: twice a
year the cattle are big with young, twice the trees productive
in fruit. But here are no ravening tigers, nor the savage
breed of lions; nor wolfsbane deceives the wretched gather-
ers; nor along the ground the scaly serpent sweeps his immense orbs, nor with so vast a train gathers up himself into
coils. And so many magnificent cities, and works of elaborate
art; so many towns upreared with the hand on craggy rocks;
and rivers gliding beneath ancient walls. Or need I mention
the sea which washes it above, and that below? or its lakes
so vast? thee, Larius,[18] of largest extent? and thee, Benacus,
swelling with the waves and roaring of the sea? Or shall I
mention its ports, and the moles raised to dam the Lucrine,[19]
and the sea raging indignant with loud murmurs, where the
Julian wave far resounds, the sea pouring in, and the Tuscan
tide is let into the straits of Avernus? The same land hath
in its veins disclosed rivers of silver and mines of copper, and
copious flowed with gold. The same hath produced a warlike
race of men, the Marsi[20] and the Sabellian youth, and the
Ligurian inured to hardship, and the Volscians armed with
sharp darts; this same the Decii,[21] the Marii, and the great

[18] Larius, (Como,) a beautiful lake of Cisalpine Gaul, through which
the Adua runs in its course to the Po, above Cremona. Benacus, (L. di
Garda,) a large lake, from which the Mincius issues, and flows into
the Po.

[19] Lucrine Lake, near Cumæ, on the coast of Campania. During an
earthquake, A. D. 1538, this lake disappeared, and in its place was formed
a mountain, two miles in circumference, and one thousand feet high, with
a crater in the middle. Avernus, a lake of Campania, whose waters were
so putrid, that the ancients regarded it as the entrance of the infernal regions. Augustus united the Lucrine and Avernian lakes by the famous
Julian harbour, and formed a communication between the latter lake
and the sea.

[20] Marsi were a people of Germany, who emigrated to Italy, and settled near the lake Fucinus. The Sabellians were descended from the
Sabines, or from the Samnites;—the Ligurians inhabited Piedmont;—
the Volscians were a warlike people of Latium (Campagna di Roma).

[21] Decii, a noble family of Rome, who devoted themselves to death for
the safety of their country. Marii, the Marian family, the chief of whom
was Caius Marius, who, from a peasant, became one of the most powerful and cruel tyrants that Rome ever beheld during her consular government.

Camilli,[22] the Scipios[23] invincible in war, and thee, most
mighty Cæsar; who, at this very time victorious in Asia's
remotest limits, art turning away from the Roman towers the
humbled Indian. Hail, Saturnian[24] land, great parent of
fruits, great parent of heroes; for thee I enter on a subject
of ancient renown and art, venturing to disclose the sacred
springs; and I sing an Ascræan strain through Roman cities.
    Now it is time to describe the qualities of soils; what is
the strength of age, what colour, and what its nature is most
apt to produce. First, stubborn lands, and unfruitful hills,
where lean clay [abounds], and pebbles in the bushy fields,
rejoice in Pallas' wood of long-lived olives. The wild olive
rising copious in the same soil is an evidence, and the fields
strewn with woodland berries. But, to the ground that is fat,
and gladdened with sweet moisture, and to the plain that is
luxuriant in grass, and of a fertile soil, (such as we are often
wont to look down upon in the hollow valley of a mountain,)
streams glide from the high rocks, and draw a rich fattening
slime along: and that which is raised to the south, and
nourishes the fern abhorred by the crooked ploughs, will in
time afford vines exceedingly strong, and flowing with abundant wine: this will be prolific of grapes, this of such liquor
as we pour forth in libation from golden bowls, when the sleek
Tuscan has blown the ivory pipe at the altars, and we offer
up the smoking entrails in the bending chargers.
    But if you are rather studious to preserve herds [of kine
and calves, or the offspring of the sheep, or kids that kill the
pastures; seek the lawns and distant fields of fruitful Tarentum,[25] and plains like those which hapless Mantua hath lost,

    [22] Camilli, two celebrated Romans, father and son: the latter was
chosen five times dictator, expelled the Gauls under Brennus from Rome,
and, on account of his services to his country, was called a second Romulus.
    [23] The Scipios. P. Cornelius Scipio, surnamed Africanus, the con-
queror of Hannibal, and his grandson, P. Æmilianus Scipio, called Africanus the younger, on account of his victories over Carthage, B. C. 146.
The two Scipios may justly be ranked among the brightest ornaments of
Roman greatness.
    [24] Saturnian land. Italy was so called, from Saturn, who, on being
dethroned by Jupiter, fled to Italy, where he reigned during the golden
age.
    [25] Tarentum, (Torento,) a maritime city of Calabria in Italy, situated
on a noble bay of the same name.

feeding snow-white swans in the grassy stream. Neither
limpid springs nor pastures will be wanting to the flocks: and
as much as the herds will crop in the long days, so much will
the cold dews in the short night restore.

A soil that is blackish and fat under the deep-pressed share,
and whose mould is loose and crumbling, (for this we aim at
in ploughing,) is generally best for corn; (from no plain will
you see more waggons move homeward with tardy oxen;) or
that from which the angry ploughman has cleared away a
wood, and felled the groves that have been at a stand for
many years, and with their lowest roots grubbed up the ancient dwellings of the birds; they abandoning their nests soar
on high, but the field looks gay when the ploughshare is driven
into it. For the lean hungry gravel of a hilly field scarcely
furnishes humble cassia and rosemary for bees: and no other
lands, they say, yield so sweet food to serpents, or afford them
such winding coverts, as the rough rotten-stone, and chalk
corroded by black water-snakes. That land which exhales
thin mists and flying smoke, and drinks in the moisture, and
emits it at pleasure; and which always clothes itself with its
own fresh grass, nor hurts the ploughshare with scurf and
salt rust; will entwine thine elms with joyous vines; that
also is fertile of olives; that ground you will experience, in
manuring, both to be friendly to cattle and submissive to
the crooked share. Such a soil rich Capua[28] tills, and the
territory neighbouring to Mount Vesuvius,[27] and the Clanius
not kind to depopulated Acerræ.[28]

Now I will tell by what means you may distinguish each.
If you desire to know whether it be loose or unusually stiff
(because the one is fit for corn, the other for wine; the stiff
is best for Ceres, and the most loose for Bacchus): first you

[28] Capua, a famous city of Italy, the capital of Campania.

[27] Vesuvius, a celebrated volcanic mountain of Campania, about six
miles south-east of Naples, and 3780 feet high. The first great eruption
of Vesuvius on record was accompanied by an earthquake, A. D. 79, when
the towns of Herculaneum, Pompeii, and Stabia were overwhelmed
under lava and ashes. The discovery of these towns after having lain
above 1600 years buried and unknown, has furnished the world with
many curious and valuable remains of antiquity.

[28] Acerræ, a town of Campania, near the city of Naples; the river
Clanius almost surrounded the town, and by its inundations frequently
depopulated it.

shall mark out a place with your eye, and order a pit to be sunk deep in solid ground, and again return all the mould into its place, and level with your feet the sands at top. If they prove deficient, the soil is loose, and more fit for cattle and bounteous vines: but, if they deny the possibility of returning to their places, and there be an overplus of mould after the pit is filled up, it is a dense soil; expect reluctant clods, and stiff ridges, and give the first ploughing to the land with sturdy bullocks.

But saltish ground, and what is accounted bitter, where corn can never thrive,[*] (it neither mellows by ploughing, nor preserves to grapes their kind, nor to fruits their qualities,) will give a proof to this effect. Snatch from the smoky roofs baskets of close woven twigs, and the strainers of thy wine-press. Hither let some of that vicious mould, and sweet water from the spring, be pressed brimful: be sure all the water will strain out, and big drops pass through the twigs. But the taste will clearly make discovery; and in its bitterness will distort the wry faces of the tasters with the sensation.

Again, what land is fat we briefly learn thus: When squeezed by the hand, it never crumbles, but, in handling, it sticks to the fingers like pitch. The moist soil produces herbs of a larger size, and is itself luxuriant beyond due measure. Ah, may none of mine be [thus] too fertile, nor show itself too strong at the first springing of the grain!

That which is heavy betrays itself by its very weight, without my telling you; and likewise the light. It is easy to distinguish the black at first sight, and what is the colour of each. But to search out the mischievous cold, is difficult: only pitch-trees, and sometimes noxious yews, or black ivy, disclose its signs.

These rules observed, remember to dry and bake the soil long before, and to encompass the spacious hills with trenches, expose the turned-up clods to the north wind, before you plant the vine's joyous race. Fields of a loose crumbling soil are best; this effect the winds and cold frosts produce, and the sturdy delver, close plying his acres, tossed and turned upside down.

But those men, whom not any vigilance escapes, first seek

[*] This rule is however scarcely universal, as is shown by Van Goes. on the Scriptorr. Rei Agrim. p. 137. B.

out the same sort of soil, where the first nursery may be provided for their trees, and whither it may soon be transplanted
in rows; lest the slips take not kindly to this mother suddenly
changed. They even mark on the bark the quarter of the sky,
that, in whatever manner each stood, in what part it bore the
southern heats, what sides it turned to the northern pole, they
may restore [it to the same position]. Of such avail is custom in tender years.

Examine, first, whether it is better to plant your vines on
hills or on a plain. If you lay out the fields of a rich plain,
plant thick ; Bacchus will not be less productive in a densely-
planted soil: but if a soil rising with a gentle ascent, and
sloping hills, give room to your ranks ; yet so that, your trees
being exactly ranged, each path between may be exactly even,
a line being cut. As often in dread war, when the extended
legion hath ranged its cohorts, the battalions stand marshalled
on the open plain, the armies set in array, and the whole
ground wide waves with gleaming brass; nor yet are they
engaged in horrid battle, but Mars hovers dubious in the
midst of arms: [thus,] let all your vineyards be laid out in
equal proportions, not only that the prospect may idly feed
the mind, but because the earth will not otherwise supply
equal strength to all; nor will the branches be able to extend
themselves at large.

Perhaps, too, you may ask what depth is proper for the
trenches. I could venture to commit my vine even to a slight
furrow. Trees, again, are sunk deeper down, and far into the
ground: especially the æsculus, which shoots downward to
Tartarus with its roots, as far as [it rises] with its top to the
ethereal regions. Therefore, nor wintry storms, nor blasts of
winds, nor showers, can uproot it: it remains unmoved, and,
rolling many ages of men away, outlasts them in surviving ;
then stretching wide its sturdy boughs and arms this way and
that way, itself in the midst sustains a mighty shade.

Nor let the vineyards lie towards the setting sun ; nor plant
the hazel among your vines ; neither seek after the extremities
of the shoots ; nor gather your cuttings from the top of the
tree, so much is their love for the earth: nor hurt your shoots
with blunted steel ; nor plant among them truncheons of wild
olive. For fire is often let fall from the unwary shepherds,
which at first secretly lurking under the unctuous bark,

catches the solid wood, and shooting up into the topmost
leaves, raises a loud crackling to heaven; thence pursuing its
way, reigns victorious among the branches and the lofty tops,
involves the whole grove in flames, and, condensed in pitchy
vapour, darts the black cloud to heaven; especially if a storm
overhead rests on the woods, and the driving wind rolls round
the flames. When this happens, their strength decays from
the root, nor can they recover, though cut, or sprout up from
the deep earth such as they were: the unblest wild olive with·
its bitter leaves [alone] survives.

Let no counsellor be so wise in your eyes as to persuade
you to stir the rigid earth when Boreas breathes. Then winter
shuts up the fields with frost; and when the slip is planted,
suffers not the frozen root to fasten to the earth. The planta-
tion of the vineyard is best, when in blushing spring the white
stork comes in, abhorred by the long snakes; or towards the
first colds of autumn, when the vehement sun does not yet
touch the winter with his steeds, and the summer is just gone.
The spring, too, is beneficial to the foliage of the groves, the
spring is beneficial to the woods: in spring the lands swell,
and demand the genial seeds. Then almighty father Æther [30]
descends in fertilizing showers into the bosom of his joyous
spouse, and great himself, mingling with her great body,
nourishes all her offspring. Then the retired brakes resound
with tuneful birds; and the herds renew their loves on the
stated days. Then bounteous earth is teeming to the birth,
and the fields open their bosoms to the warm breezes of the
Zephyr: in all a gentle moisture abounds; and the herbs dare
safely trust themselves to the infant suns; nor do the vine's
tender shoots fear the rising south winds, or the shower pre-
cipitated from the sky by the violent north winds; but put
forth their buds, and unfold all their leaves. No other day, [31]
I should think, had shone at the first origin of the rising world;
it was spring, the spacious globe enjoyed spring, and the east
winds spared their wintry blasts; when first the cattle drew
in the light, and the earthly race of men upreared their heads

---

[30] Virgil here follows the notions of Chrysippus, as delivered in Æschylus, (Fragm. Danaid. fragm. 38, Dind.,) but especially by Euripides,
(Fragm. Chrysipp. No. vi. Dind.) B.
[31] It was an ancient supposition, that the world was created in the
spring. B.

from the rugged glebe, and the woods were stocked with wild
beasts, and the heavens with stars. Nor could the tender pro-
ductions [of nature] bear this labour, if so great rest did not
intervene between the cold and heat, and if heaven's indulgent
season did not visit the earth in its turn.

For what remains, whatever layers you bend down over all
the fields, overspread them with fat dung, and carefully cover
them with copious earth ; or bury about them spongy stones,
or rough shells: for thus the rains will soak through, and a
subtile vapour penetrate them, and the plants will take courage. Some, too, have been found, who are for pressing them
from above with a stone, and the weight of a great potsherd :
this is a defence against the pouring rains : this [a defence]
when the sultry dog-star cleaves the gaping fields with
drought.

After your layers are planted, it remains to convey earth
often to the roots, and ply the hard drags ; or to work the soil
under the deep-pressed share, and guide your struggling bullocks through the very vineyards ; then to adapt [to the vines]
smooth reeds, and spears of peeled rods, and ashen stakes, and
two-horned forks ; by whose strength they may learn to shoot
up, to contemn the winds, and climb from stage to stage along
the highest elms.

And, while their infant age sprouts with new-born leaves,
you must spare the tender vines ; and while the joyous shoot
raises itself on high, being sent onward through the open air
with loose reins,[33] the edge of the pruning-knife itself must
not be applied ; but the leaves should be plucked with the in-
bent hands, and culled here and there. Thereafter, when they
have shot forth, embracing the elms with firm stems, then cut
their locks, then lop their arms. Before this they dread the
steel ; then, and not till then, exercise severe dominion, and
check the loose straggling boughs.

Fences, too, should be woven, and all cattle be kept out ;
especially while the leaves are tender and unacquainted with

[33] A metaphor taken from horses, in imitation of Lucretius :
    Arboribus datum est variis exinde per auras
    Crescendi magnum immissis certamen habenis.
Per purum in Virgil signifies the same as per auras in Lucretius. Horace
uses it also for the air :
    ————— Per purum tonantes
    Egit equos.

hardships; to which, besides the rigorous winters and vehement sun, the wild bulls[33] and persecuting goats continually do wanton harm; the sheep and greedy heifers browse upon them. Nor do the colds, condensed in hoary frosts, or the severe heat beating upon the scorched rocks, hurt them so much as the flocks, and poison of their hard teeth, and a scar imprinted on the gnawed stem.

For no other offence is the goat sacrificed to Bacchus on every altar, and the ancient plays come upon the stage:[34] and the Athenians proposed for wits prizes about the villages and crossways; and, joyous amidst their cups, danced in the soft meadows on wine-skins smeared with oil. [On the same account,] the Ausonian[35] colonists also, a race sent from Troy, sport in uncouth strains, and unbounded laughter; assuming horrid masks of hollowed barks of trees: and thee, Bacchus, they invoke in jovial songs, and to thee hang up mild images[36] from the tall pine. Hence every vineyard shoots forth with large produce; both the hollow vales and deep lawns are filled with plenty, and wherever the god hath moved around his propitious countenance. Therefore will we solemnly ascribe to Bacchus his due honours in our country's lays, and offer chargers, and the consecrated cakes; and the sacred goat led by the horn shall stand at his altar, and we will roast the fat entrails on hazel spits.

There is also that other toil in dressing the vines; on which you can never bestow pains enough: for the whole soil must be ploughed three or four times every year, and the

[33] These must not be confounded with either the bison or the buffalo. See Anthon. B.

[34] Proscenia. In the Roman theatre there was first the porticus or gallery for the populace, where the seats were formed like wedges, growing narrower as they came near the centre of the theatre, and therefore called cunei, or wedges. 2. The orchestra, in the centre and lowest part of the theatre, where the senators and knights sat, and where the dancers and musicians performed. 3. The proscenium, or space before the scenes which was raised above the orchestra, and where the actors spoke.

[35] Ausonian, &c., the inhabitants of Ausonia, an ancient name of Italy, who were supposed to be descended from Æneas.

[36] Compare Anthon's remark: " And in honour of thee hang up the mild oscilla on the tall pine." Oscillum, a diminutive, through osculum, from os, means, properly, "a little face, and was the term applied to faces or heads of Bacchus, which were suspended in the vineyards to be turned in every direction by the wind. Whichsoever way they looked, they were supposed to make the vines and other things in that quarter fruitful."

clods continually be broken with bended drags; the whole
grove must be disburthened of its leaves. The farmer's past
labour returns in a circle, and the year rolls round on itself on
its own steps. And now, when at length the vineyard has
shed its late leaves, and the cold north wind has shaken from
the groves their honours;[n] even then the active swain extends
his cares to the coming year, and closely plies the forsaken
vine, cutting off [the superfluous roots] with Saturn's crooked
hook, and forms it by pruning. Be the first to trench the
ground, be the first to carry home and burn the shoots, and
the first to return beneath your roof the vine-props: be the
last to reap the vintage. Twice the shade assails the vines;
twice do weeds overrun the field with thick bushes; each a
hard labour. Commend large farms; cultivate a small one.
Besides all this, the rough twigs of butcher's-broom are to be
cut throughout the woods, and the watery reed on the banks:
and the care of the uncultivated willow gives new toil. Now
the vines are tied; now the vineyard lays aside the pruning-
hook; now the exhausted vintager salutes in song his utmost
rows: yet must the earth be vexed anew, and the mould put
in motion; and now Jove is to be dreaded by the ripened
grapes.

On the other hand, the olives require no culture; nor do
they expect the crooked pruning-hook and tenacious harrows,
when once they are rooted in the ground, and have stood the
blasts. Earth of herself supplies the plants with moisture,
when opened by the hooked tooth of the drag, and weighty
fruits, when [opened] by the share. Nurture for thyself with
this the fat and peace-delighting olive. The fruit-trees too,
as soon as they feel their trunks vigorous, and acquire their
strength, quickly shoot up to the stars by their own virtue,
and need not our assistance. At the same time, every grove
is in like manner loaded with offspring, and the uncultivated
haunts of birds glow with blood-red berries: the cytisus is
browsed; the tall wood supplies with torches; and our nocturnal fires are fed, and shed beamy light. And do men hesitate to plant and bestow care?

Why should I insist on greater things? The very willows
and lowly broom supply either browse for cattle, or shade for

---

[n] Hor. Ep. ii. 5. " December—silvis honorem decutit." B.

shepherds, fences for the corn, and materials for honey. It is delightful to behold Cytorus [38] waving with the grove of Narycian pitch: it is delightful to see the fields not indebted to the harrows, or to any care of men. Even the barren woods on the top of Caucasus, which the fierce east winds continually are crushing and tearing, yield each their different produce: they yield pines, an useful wood for ships, and cedars and cypresses for houses. Hence the husbandmen have rounded spokes for wheels; hence they have framed solid orbs for waggons, and bending keels for ships. The willows are fertile in twigs, the elms in leaves for fodder; the myrtle again is useful for sturdy spears, and the cornel for war; the yews are bent into Ityræan bows. [39] In like manner the smooth-grained limes, or box polished by the lathe, receive a shape, and are hollowed with sharp steel. Thus too the light alder, launched on the Po, [40] swims the rapid stream: thus too the bees hide their swarms in the hollow bark, and in the heart of a rotten holm. What have the gifts of Bacchus produced so worthy of record? Bacchus has given occasion to offence and guilt: he quelled by death the furious Centaurs, [41] Rhœtus and Pholus, and Hylæus threatening the Lapithæ with a huge goblet.

Ah! the too happy swains, did they but know their own bliss! to whom, at a distance from discordant arms, earth, of herself most liberal, pours from her bosom their easy sustenance. If the palace, high raised with proud gates, vomits not forth from all its apartments a vast tide of morning visitants;

[38] Cytorus. (Kidros,) a city and mountain of Paphlagonia, on the Euxine. Narycian pitch, from Narycia, a town of the Locrians in Magna Græcia, in the neighbourhood of which were forests of pine, &c.

[39] Ityræan bows, from Ityræa, a province of Syria, whose inhabitants were famous archers.

[40] Po, anciently called also Eridanus, the largest river of Italy, rises in Mount Vesulus, one of the highest mountains of the Alps, and after an easterly course of nearly 400 miles, and receiving numerous tributary streams, discharges its waters into the Adriatic, about 30 miles S. of the city of Venice.

[41] Centaurs, a people of Thessaly, represented as monsters, half men and half horses. The Lapithæ, also a people of Thessaly, who inhabited the country about Mount Pindus and Othrys. The allusion here is to the battle of the Centaurs and Lapithæ, at the celebration of the nuptials of Pirithous, king of the latter, who invited not only the heroes of his age, but also the gods themselves. In the contest that ensued, many of the Centaurs were slain, and the rest saved themselves by flight.

and they gape not at porticoes variegated with beauteous tor-
toise-shell, and on tapestries tricked with gold, and on Corinthian brass; and if the white wool is not stained with the
Assyrian drug, nor the use of the pure oil corrupted with
Cassia's aromatic bark; yet [there is] peace secure, and a life
ignorant of guile, rich in various opulence; yet [theirs are]
peaceful retreats in ample fields, grottoes, and living lakes;
yet [to them] cool vales, the lowings of kine, and soft slumbers under a tree, are not wanting.   There are woodlands and
haunts for beasts of chase, and youth patient of toil, and
inured to thrift; the worship of the gods, and fathers held in
veneration: Justice, when she left the world, took her last
steps among them.

But me may the Muses, sweet above all things else,[41] whose
sacred symbols I bear, smitten with violent love, first receive
into favour; and show me the paths of heaven, and constellations; the various eclipses of the sun, and labours of the
moon; whence the trembling of the earth; from what influence the seas swell high, bursting their barriers, and again
sink back into themselves; why the winter suns make such
haste to dip themselves in the ocean, or what delay retards
the slow-paced [summer] nights.

But if the cold blood about my heart hinders me from
penetrating into these parts of nature; let fields and streams
gliding in the valleys be my delight; inglorious may I court
the rivers and the woods.   O [to be] where are the plains,[42]
and Sperchius, and Taygetus,[43] the scene of Bacchanalian
revels to Spartan maids! O who will place me in the cool valleys of Hæmus, and shelter me with a thick shade of boughs?
Happy is he who has been able to trace out the causes of
things, and who has cast beneath his feet all fears, and inexorable Destiny, and the noise of devouring Acheron?[44]

[41] I have followed Wagner in joining "dulces ante omnia," but I have
some doubts whether the old interpretation is not better. B.
[42] Thessalian plains. Thessaly, a country of Greece, south of Macedonia, in which was the celebrated vale of Tempe. Sperchius, a river of
Thessaly, rises in Mount Œta, and runs into the Maliac Gulf, near the
pass of Thermopylæ.
[43] Taygetus, a mountain of Laconia in Peloponnesus, (Morea,) on
which were celebrated the orgies of Bacchus; it hung over the city of
Sparta, and extended from Tænarus to Arcadia.
[44] Acheron, one of the rivers of hell, according to the ancient poets;

F

Blest too is he who has known the rural deities, Pan and old
Silvanus, and the sister nymphs! him nor the fasces of the
people, nor the purple of·kings; nor discord persecuting faithless brothers, nor the Dacian descending from the conspiring
Danube;[45] nor the revolutions of Rome, or perishing kingdoms, have moved. He neither pined with grief, lamenting
the poor, nor envied the rich. What fruits the boughs, what
the willing fields spontaneously yielded, he gathered; nor saw
the iron-hearted laws, the madly litigious bar, or the public
courts.

Some vex the dangerous seas with oars, some rush into
arms, some work their way into courts, and the palaces of
kings. One destines a city and wretched families to destruction, that he may drink in gems, and sleep on Tyrian purple.[47]
Another hoards up wealth, and broods over buried gold.
One, astonished at the rostrum, grows giddy; another, peals
of applause along the rows, (for it is redoubled both by the
people and the fathers,) have captivated, and set agape; some
rejoice when stained with their brother's blood; and exchange
their homes and sweet thresholds for exile, and seek a country lying under another sun. The husbandman cleaves the
earth with a crooked plough; hence the labours of the year;
hence he sustains the country, and his little offspring; hence
his herds of kine, and deserving steers. Nor is there any intermission, but the year either abounds with apples, or with
the breed of the flocks, or with the sheaf of Ceres' stalk; loads
the furrows with increase, and overstocks the barns. Winter
comes: the Sicyonian[48] berry is pounded in the oil-presses;
the swine come home gladdened with acorns; the woods yield
their arbutes; and the autumn lays down its various produc-

often taken for hell itself. Virgil here follows Lucretius, l. 37, "Et
metus ille foras præceps Acheruntis agendus Funditus, humanam qui
vitam turbat ab imo, Omnia suffundens mortis nigrore." And soon after,
va. 79, "Quare religio pedibus subjecta." B.

   [45] The Danube rises in the black forest of Suabia, and, after a course of
about 1600 miles, discharges itself into the Euxine Sea. The Dacians
inhabited an extensive country, north of the Danube, now called Walla-
chia, Transylvania, and Moldavia.

   [47] Tyrian purple, from Tyre, a city of Phœnicia in Asia, celebrated for
its early commerce and numerous colonies, and for the invention of scarlet and purple colours; its ancient name was Sarra, now Soor.

   [48] Sicyonian berry, the olive, with which Sicyonia, a district of Peloponnesus, in Greece, abounded.

tions; and high on the sunny rocks the mild vintage is ripened. Meanwhile the sweet babes twine round their parents' neck: his chaste family maintain their purity; the cows hang down their udders full of milk; and the fat kids wrestle together with butting horns on the cheerful green. The swain himself celebrates festal days; and, extended on the grass, where a fire is in the middle, and where his companions crown the bowl, invokes thee, O Lenæus, making libation; and on an elm sets forth to the masters of the flock prizes to be contended for with the winged javelin; and they strip their hardy bodies for the rustic ring.

This life of old the ancient Sabines;[48] this Remus and his brother strictly observed; thus Etruria[50] grew in strength; and thus too did Rome become the glory and beauty of the world, and, single, hath encompassed for herself seven hills with a wall. This life, too, golden Saturn led on earth, before the sceptred sway of the Dictæan[51] king, and before an impious race feasted on slain bullocks. Nor yet had mankind heard the warlike trumpets blow; nor yet the swords laid on the hard anvils clatter.

But we have finished this immensely extended field; and now it is time to unloose the smoking necks of our steeds.

BOOK III.

In the third Book, after invoking the rural deities, and eulogising Augustus, Virgil treats of the management of cattle, laying down rules for the choice and breeding of horses, oxen, sheep, &c. The book abounds in admirable descriptions; many passages are inimitably fine.

THEE, too, great Pales, and thee, famed shepherd from Amphrysus,[1] ye woods and Arcadian rivers, will I sing. Other themes, that might have 'entertained minds disengaged from

---

[48] Sabines, an ancient people of Italy, reckoned among the aborigenes, or those inhabitants whose origin was unknown; their country was situated between the rivers Tiber, Nar, and Anio, having the Apennines on the east.

[50] Etruria, (Tuscany,) a country of Italy lying west of the Tiber.

[51] Dictæan king, Jupiter is so called from Mount Dicte in Crete, where he was worshipped.

[1] Amphrysus, a river of Thessaly, on the banks of which Apollo fed the flocks of king Admetus. Arcadian rivers: Arcadia was a pastoral district of Peloponnesus in Greece, of which Pan was the tutelary deity.

song, are now all trite and common. Who is unacquainted
either with severe Eurystheus,[2] or the altars of infamous
Busiris? By whom has not the boy Hylas been recorded, and
Latonian Delos?[3] or Hippodame,[4] and Pelops, conspicuous
for his ivory shoulder, victorious in the race? I, too, must attempt a way, whereby I may raise myself from the ground,
and victorious hover through the lips of men.

I first returning from the Aonian mount, will (provided
life remain) bring along with me the Muses into my country;
for thee, O Mantua, I first will bear off the Idumæan[5] palms,
and on thy verdant plains erect a temple of marble, near the
stream where the great Mincius winds in slow meanders, and
fringes the banks with tender reed. In the middle will I have
Cæsar, and he shall command the temple. In honour of him
will I victorious, and in Tyrian purple conspicuous, drive a
hundred four-horsed chariots along the river. For me all
Greece, leaving Alpheus[6] and the groves of Molorchus, shall
contend in races and the raw-hide cestus. I myself, graced
with leaves of the shorn olive, will bear offerings. Even now
I am well pleased to lead on the solemn pomps to the temple,
and to see the bullocks slain; or how the scene with shifting
front retires; and how the inwoven Britons lift up the purple
curtain. On the doors will I delineate, in gold and solid

[2] Eurystheus, king of Argos and Mycenæ, who, at the instigation of
Juno, imposed upon Hercules the most perilous enterprises, well known
by the name of the twelve labours of Hercules. Busiris, a king of
Egypt, noted for his cruelty in sacrificing all foreigners who entered his
country.

[3] Delos, a small but celebrated island of the Ægean Sea, nearly in
the centre of the Cyclades, in which Latona gave birth to Apollo and
Diana; hence the former is frequently called Delius, and the latter
Delia.

[4] Hippodame, a daughter of Œnomaus, king of Pisa in Elis. Her
father refused to marry her except to him who could overcome him in a
chariot race; thirteen had already been conquered, and forfeited their
lives, when Pelops, the son of Tantalus, entered the lists, and by bribing
Myrtilus, the charioteer of Œnomaus, insured to himself the victory.

[5] Idumæan palms, from Idumæa, a country of Syria, on the south of
Judæa, famed for its palm-trees.

[6] Alpheus, (Rouphia,) a river of Elis in Peloponnesus, where the
Olympic games were celebrated. Molorchus, a shepherd of Argolis, who
kindly received Hercules, and in return the hero slew the Nemæan lion
which laid waste the country; hence the institution of the Nemæan
games.

ivory, the battle of the Gangarides,[7] and the arms of conquering Quirinus; and here the Nile[8] swelling with war, flowing majestic, and columns rising with naval brass. I will add the vanquished cities of Asia, and subdued Niphates,[9] and the Parthian presuming on his flight and arrows shot backward,[10] and two trophies snatched by the hand from two widely-distant foes, and nations twice triumphed over on either shore. Here too shall stand in Parian[11] marble, breathing statues, the offspring of Assaracus,[12] and the chiefs of the Jove-descended race; both Tros, the great ancestor [of Rome], and Cynthian Apollo, founder of Troy. Here baneful envy shall dread the Furies, and the grim river of Cocytus,[13] Ixion's twisted snakes, the enormous wheel, and the insurmountable stone.

Meanwhile, let us pursue the woods of the Dryads, and untrodden lawns; thy commands, Mæcenas, of no easy import. Without thee my mind ventures on nothing sublime; come then, break off idle delays. Cithæron[14] calls with loud halloo, and the hounds of Taygetus, and Epidaurus, the tamer of horses; and the voice, doubled by the assenting groves, re-

[7] Gangarides, a people of Asia, near the mouth of the Ganges.

[8] Nile, a great river of Africa, and one of the most celebrated in the world, is generally supposed to have its sources in that immense chain of mountains in Central Africa, called the Mountains of the Moon. Its course runs in a northerly direction, flowing through Nubia and Egypt; a little below Cairo it divides itself into two great branches, which enclose the Delta, and fall into the Mediterranean, the western branch at Rosetta, and the eastern at Damietta.

[9] Niphates, a mountain of Armenia, part of the range of Taurus, from which the river Tigris takes its rise.

[10] Cf. Plutarch, Crass. p. 558, ὑπέρφυγον γὰρ ἅμα βάλλοντες οἱ Πάρθοι. B.

[11] Parian marble, from Paros, an island of the Ægean Sea, one of the Cyclades, famed for its beautiful white marble.

[12] Assaracus, a Trojan prince, father of Capys, and grandfather of Anchises. Tros, a son of Erichthonius, king of Troy, which was so named after him. Cynthian Apollo: the surname is from Cynthus, a mountain in the island of Delos, where Apollo and Diana were born, and which was sacred to them.

[13] Cocytus, a river of Epirus in Greece, called by the poets one of the rivers of hell. Ixion, a king of Thessaly, whom Jupiter is fain to have struck with his thunder for having attempted to seduce Juno; he was bound with serpents to a wheel in hell, which was perpetually in motion.

[14] Cithæron, a mountain of Bœotia in Greece, sacred to Jupiter and the Muses. Epidaurus, (Pidavra,) a city of Argolis in Peloponnesus, famed for a temple of Æsculapius, and for its fine breed of horses.

echoes. Yet ere long shall I be prepared to sing of Cæsar's ardent battles, and to transmit his name with honour through as many years as Cæsar is distant from the first origin of Tithonus.

Whether any one, aspiring to the praises of the Olympian palm, breeds horses, or whether any one [breeds] sturdy bullocks for the plough, let him choose with special care the bodies of the mothers. The stern-eyed heifer's form is best, whose head is disproportionately large, whose neck is brawny, and whose dew-laps hang from the chin down to the legs. Then there is no measure in her length of side; all her parts are huge, even her foot; and her ears are rough under her crumpled[15] horns. Nor would she displease me if streaked with white spots, or if she refuses the yoke, and sometimes is surly with her horn, and in aspect approaches nearer to a bull, and if she is stately throughout, and sweeps her steps with the extremity of her tail, as she goes along.

The age to undergo breeding and proper union ends before ten, and begins after four years: the other years [cows] are neither fit for breeding, nor strong for the plough. Meantime, while the flocks abound with sprightly youth, let loose the males: be the first to indulge thy cattle in the joys of love: and by generation raise up one race after another. Each best time of life fly fast away from wretched mortals: diseases succeed, and sad old age, and pain; and the inclemency of inexorable death snatches them away. There will always be some whose bodies you would choose to have changed [for better]. Therefore continually repair them; and, that you may not regret them when lost, be beforehand, and yearly provide a new offspring for the herd.

The same discriminating care is also requisite for a breed of horses. But still, on those which you intend to bring up for the hope of the race, bestow your principal diligence immediately from their tender years. The colt of generous breed from the very first walks high throughout the fields, and nimbly moves his pliant legs; he is the first that dares to lead the way, and tempt the threatening floods, and trust himself to an unknown bridge; nor starts affrighted at vain alarms. Lofty is his neck, his head little and slender, his

---

[15] Nonius, Marc. l., explains "camurum by obtortum." Hesiod, Opp 452, Ἕλικας βοάς. B.

belly short, his back plump, and his proud chest swells luxuriant with brawny muscles: (the bright bay and bluish grey
are in most request; the worst colours are the white and sor-
rel.) Then, if he by chance hears the distant sound of arms,
he knows not how to stand still; he pricks up his ears, trembles in every joint, and snorting, rolls the collected fire under
his nostrils. Thick is his mane, and, waving, rests on his right
shoulder. A double spine [16] runs along his loins, his hoof
scoops up the ground, and deep resounds with its solid horn.
Such was Cyllarus, broken by the reins of Amyclæan Pollux,[17]
and such (which the Grecian poets have described) the harnessed brace of Mars, and the chariot-horses [18] of great Achilles. Such Saturn too himself, swift at the coming of his
wife, spread out a full mane on his [assumed] horse's neck,
and flying filled lofty Pelion with shrill neighing.

Him too, when with sickness oppressed, or now enfeebled
with years, he fails, shut up in his lodge, and spare his not inglorious age. An old horse is cold to love, and in vain drags
on the ungrateful task, and if ever he comes to an engagement,
he is impotently furious, as at times a great fire without
strength among stubble. Therefore chiefly mark their spirit
and age; then their other qualities, their parentage, and what
is the sorrow of each when vanquished, what the pride when
victorious.

See you not?[19] when in the rapid race the chariots have
seized the plain, and pouring forth rush along; when the
hopes of the youth are elevated, and palpitating fear heaves
their throbbing hearts: they ply with the twisted lash, and
bending forward give full reins: the axle flies glowing with
the impetuosity. And now low, now high, they seem to be
borne aloft through the open air, and to mount up into the

[16] In a horse that is in good case, the back is broad, and a fulness of
flesh near the spine is indicated, by which two ridges are formed, one at
each side of the bone. This is what the ancients mean by a double spine.
VALPY.

[17] Amyclæan Pollux was the son of Jupiter, by Leda, and the twin
brother of Castor; he was so called from Amiclæ, a city of Lyconia,
where he was born.

[18] With this sense of "currus," compare the similar Greek usage, Eur.
Hipp. 1224, τέτρωρον ἐκμαίνων ὄχον, vs. 1352, ed. Monk, and Ion,
1151. B.

[19] This is a formula used in adducing examples. Comp. Georg. I. 56;
Lucr. ii. 196. HICKIE.

skies.   No stop, no stay: but a thick cloud of yellow sand is
tossed up; the foremost are wet with the foam and breath of
those that follow.   So powerful is the love of praise, so anxious the desire of victory.

First Erichthonius [20] dared to yoke the chariot and four
steeds, and upon the rapid wheels victorious to stand.   The
Pelethronian Lapithæ first mounted on horseback applied the
reins, and turned him in the ring; taught the horsemen under
arms to spurn the plain, and with proud ambling pace to
prance along.   Either toil is equal; with equal care the masters in either case seek after a [steed that is] youthful, of
warm mettle, and eager in the race: [they do not make choice
of an old horse,] though often he may have driven before him
the flying foes, may boast of Epirus, or of warlike Mycenæ [21]
for his country, and derive his pedigree even from Neptune's
breed.

These things observed, they are very careful about the time
[of generation], and bestow all their care to plump him up
with firm fat whom they have chosen leader, and assigned
stallion to the herd: they cut downy herbs, and supply him
with plenty of water and corn, that he may be adequate to [22]
the soothing toil, and lest the puny sons should declare the
meagreness of their sires.   But they purposely attenuate the
brood mares with leanness: and, when now the known pleasure solicits the first enjoyment, they both deny herbs, and
debar them from the springs; often too they shake them in
the race, and tire them in the sun, when beneath the beaten
grain the barn floor deeply groans, and in the rising zephyr
the empty chaff is tossed about.   This they do, that excessive
pampering may not blunt the powers of the genial soil, and
choke up the sluggish passages; but that it may with eagerness drink in the joys of love, and lay them up more deeply
within.

[20] Erichthonius, a son of Vulcan, and king of Athens; the invention
of chariots is ascribed to him.   Pelethronian Lapithæ, so called from
Pelethronium, a town of Thessaly at the foot of Mount Pelion, inhabited
by the Lapithæ, who were excellent horsemen.

[21] Mycenæ, a city of Argolis in Peloponnesus, once the capital of a
kingdom, and the residence of Agamemnon.

[22] "Supreme" is explained "præstantior esse" by the Scholiast on
Avianus, Fab. xiii. 10, but more clearly by Gellius, i. 22, " supra laborem
esse, neque opprimi a labore."   B.

Again the cares of the sires begin to fail, and that of the dams to succeed; when now, their months elapsed, they rove about pregnant: let no one suffer them to drag the yokes of heavy waggons,[22] or to leap across the way, scamper over the meads with sprightly career, and swim the rapid floods. They ought then to feed[24] in spacious lawns, and beside full rivers, where moss, and grassy banks of prime verdure, and caves may shelter them, and over them a shady rock project.

About the groves of Silarus,[25] and Alburnus, verdant with ever-green oaks, abounds a flying thing,[26] which the Romans name asilus, and the Greeks in their language have rendered œstros; of angry sting, humming harshly; with which whole herds affrighted fly dispersed through the woods; the sky is furiously shaken with bellowings, and the woods and banks of dry Tanagrus. With this monster did Juno once exercise her fell revenge, having meditated a plague for the Inachian[27] heifer. This, too, (for in the noontide heat it rages more keenly,) you must keep off from the pregnant cattle; and feed your herds when the sun is newly risen, or when the stars usher in the night.

After the birth, the whole care is transferred to the calves; and from the first they stamp with a hot iron the marks and names of the race; and which they choose to bring up for the increase of the flock, or to keep sacred for the altar, or to cleave the ground, and turn up the soil all rugged with broken clods: the rest of the herd graze amidst the green pastures.

Those which you would form for the design and service of agriculture, train up while calves, and enter on the way to

---

[22] Here waggons stand for any "wheeled vehicle." HICKIE.

[24] Or rather, "scamper over." Heyne remarks, "proprie via carpitur per prata." B.

[25] Silarus, (Sele,) a river of Italy, separating Lucania from the territory of the Picentini: its banks were much infested with the gad-fly. Alburnus, a lofty mountain of Lucania, at the foot of which rises the river Tanagrus, (Negro,) remarkable for its cascades and its beautiful meanderings.

[26] "Volitans," as Anthon remarks, is here used as a kind of substantive. Compare "volucri asilo," Valer. Flacc. iii. 581.

[27] Inachian heifer. Io, daughter of Inachus, and priestess of Juno at Argos, according to the poets, was changed into a heifer by Jupiter, but afterwards restored to her own form, when she married Telegonus or Osiris, king of Egypt, and after death was worshipped under the name of Isis.

tame them, whilst their minds in youth are tractable, while
their age is pliant. And first fasten about their necks loose
collars of slender twigs; next, when they have accustomed
their free necks to servitude, match your bullocks in pairs
joined by those same collars, and make them step together;
and now let empty wheels be dragged by them along the
ground, and let them print their traces in the surface of the
dust. Afterwards let the beechen axle labouring under a
ponderous load creak, and the brass-girt pole draw the joined
wheels. Meanwhile for the young untamed bullocks you will
crop with your hand not only grass, or the tender [25] leaves of
willows, or a marshy sedge, but also springing corn: nor shall
your suckling heifers, as was the custom of our fathers, fill
the snowy milking-pails, but spend all their udders on their
sweet offspring.

But if thy inclination is to war and martial troops, or with
thy wheels to skim along the brink of Pisa's [29] Alphæan
streams, and drive the flying chariot in Jupiter's grove: the
first task of the horse must be to view the fierceness and the
arms of warriors, to be patient of the trumpet, and to bear the
rumbling of the wheels in their career, and in his stall to hear
the rattling bridles; then more and more to rejoice in the
coaxing praises of his master, and to love the sound of his
patted neck. [30] And these let him hear as soon as weaned
from the udder of his dam, and now and then yield his mouth
to the soft halters when weak, and yet trembling, and yet not
confident in his years. But, three full years elapsed, when
his fourth summer has arrived, let him forthwith begin to
wheel in the ring, and with regular steps to prance; and let
him bend the pliant joints of his legs alternately, and seem to
labour. Then let him dare the winds in swiftness, and
through the open plains flying, as loosened from the reins,
scarcely print his steps on the surface of the sand. As when
boisterous Boreas hath rushed forth from the Hyperborean
regions, and drives along the Scythian storms and dry clouds;

---

[25] "Vescas" is interpreted by Servius, "siccas et teneras." See
Gronov. on Liv. xxxiii. 48. intpp. on Lucret. i. 327. B.

[29] Pisa, an ancient city of Elis in Peloponnesus, on the banks of the
Alpheus, and on the ruins of which Olympia is supposed to have been
built.

[30] Silius, iv. 265, " stimulans grato plausæ cervicis honore, Cornipedem
alloquitur." B.

then the high corn and waving fields tremble with the gentle
gusts, the tops of the woods rustle, and the lengthened waves
press towards the shore: he flies, sweeping in his career at
once the fields, at once the seas. Such a courser will either
sweat at the goals and spacious bounds of the Elean plain, and
drive the bloody foam from his mouth, or will better bear the
Belgic cars on his pliant neck. Then at last, when they are
broken, let their ample bodies grow with fattening mash; for,
[if full fed] before breaking them in, they will swell their
mettle high, and when seized, refuse to bear the limber whip,
and to obey the hard curb.

But no industry more confirms their strength than to avert
Venus from them, and the stings of blind love, whether any
one be more fond of a breed of bullocks or of horses. And
therefore they remove the bulls to a distance, and to lonely
pastures, behind an obstructing mountain, and beyond broad
rivers, or keep them shut up within at full cribs; for the female insensibly consumes his vigour, and fires him while in
his eye,[31] nor suffers him to mind his groves and pastures.
Often by her sweet allurements she even impels her haughty
lovers to combat with their horns. The beauteous heifer
feeds in the spacious wood; they by turns with mighty force
engage with repeated wounds; black blood laves their bodies;
and their adverse horns are impelled on the straggling foes
with a vast groan; the woods and spacious skies rebellow.
Nor is it usual for the warriors to dwell together; but the one
vanquished retires, and becomes an exile in unknown distant
coasts; much and often bemoaning his disgrace, and the
wounds of the proud victor, in fine, the loves which un-
avenged he has lost; and, often gazing at the stalls, departs
from his hereditary realms. Therefore with the utmost care
he exercises his strength, and lies all night among the hard
rocks, on an unspread couch, feeding on prickly leaves and
sharp rushes; he tries himself, and learns to collect his rage
into his horns, butting against the trunk of a tree; dares the
winds with blows, and preludes to the fight by spurning the
sand. Afterwards, when his strength is rallied, and his vigour

---

[31] Literally, "by their beholding her." Anthon truly remarks, that it
is a mistake to suppose that the gerund is used for the passive. Cf.
"cantando," Ecl. viii. 71, "legendo," Georg. iii. 454, "habendo,"
Lucret. i. 313. B.

recovered, he begins the march,[32] and is borne headlong on
his unmindful foe; as a wave, when it begins to whiten in
the midst of the sea, at distance and from the deep, draws
out its bosom, and as rolling to the land. it roars dreadful
among the rocks, nor less than very mountain falls; while
with whirlpools the water from the bottom boils, and tosses
up the blackening sand on high.

Indeed every kind on earth, both of men and wild beasts,
the fish, the cattle, and painted birds, rush into maddening
fires; love is in all the same. At no other time does the
lioness, forgetful of her whelps, range the plains more fierce;
nor do the unshapely bears usually spread so numerous ravages
and such havoc in the woods: then ferocious is the boar, then
most fell the tiger. It is then, alas! unhappy wandering in
the desolate fields of Libya. See you not how tremour thrills
through the horse's whole body, if his smell has but sucked
in the well-known gales? And now neither bridles of men,
nor cruel whips, nor cliffs, nor hollow rocks, and opposed rivers
that whirl with the torrent even mountains swept away, can
retard him. Even the Sabellian boar rushes, and whets his
tusks, and with his feet tears up the ground, rubs his flanks
against a tree, and on this side and that side hardens his
shoulders to wounds. What does the youth, in whose vitals
relentless love fans the mighty fire? Why, late in the darksome night he swims the frith boisterous with bursting storms;
over whom the spacious gate of heaven thunders, and the seas
dashing against the rocks remurmur; nor can his distressed
parents recall him, nor the maiden too, about to perish by a
cruel fate. What do the spotted ounces of Bacchus, and the
fierce race of wolves and dogs? what the timorous stags?
what dreadful wars they wage! Yet know, the fury of the
mares is most of all extraordinary: and this spirit Venus
herself inspired, when four Potnian mares tore the limb of
Glaucus[33] to pieces with their jaws. Love drives them across
Gargarus, and roaring Ascanius:[34] they climb the mountains,
swim the rivers; and forthwith, when the flame is secretly

---

[32] Literally, "strikes the tents."   B.

[33] Glaucus, a son of Sisyphus, king of Corinth, who was torn to pieces
at Potnia in Bœotia, by his own mares.

[34] Ascanius, afterwards called the Hylas, a river of Bithynia in Asia
Minor, flowing into the Propontis near Cius.

conveyed into their craving marrow, chiefly in the spring, (for
in the spring the heat returns into their bones,) they all, with
their mouth turned towards the Zephyr, stand on high rocks,
and catch the gentle gales; and often, wondrous to relate!
without any mate, impregnated by the wind, over rocks and
cliffs and hollow vales they scour; not towards thine, O Eurus,
nor the sun's rising, nor towards Boreas and Caurus,[35] or
whence grim Auster arises, and saddens the sky with bleak
rain. Hence at last, what the shepherds call by its true
name, hippomanes, a clammy poison distils from their groins;
hippomanes, which wicked stepdames often have gathered,
and mixed [therewith] herbs, and not innoxious spells. But
time flies meanwhile, flies irretrievable, while we, enamoured
[of the theme], minutely trace particulars.

Thus far of herds. Another part of our care remains, to
manage the fleecy flocks and shaggy goats. A labour this;
hence hope for praise, ye sturdy swains. Nor am I at all
ignorant how difficult it is to raise such subjects by style, and
add this dignity to things so low. But the sweet love [of the
Muses] transports me along the lonely heights of Parnassus:
it delights me to range those mountain-tops, where no path
trodden by the ancients winds down with gentle descent to
Castalia.[36]

Now, adorable Pales, now must I sing in lofty strain. To
begin, I appoint the sheep to be foddered in soft cots, till first
the leafy spring return: and that the hard ground under
them be strewn with plenty of straw, and with bundles of
ferns, lest the cold ice hurt the tender flock, and bring on the
scab, and foul foot-rot. Next, leaving them, I order to provide the goats with leafy arbutes, and to supply them with
fresh streams: and, away from the woods, to oppose their cots
to the winter sun, turned towards the south: when cold
Aquarius[37] now sets at length, and in the extremity of the
year sheds his dews. Nor are these to be tended by us with
less care: nor will their usefulness be less; though Milesian

---

[35] Caurus, the north-west wind; Auster, the south wind.
[36] Castalia, a celebrated fountain of Mount Parnassus, sacred to the
Muses.
[37] Aquarius, one of the signs of the Zodiac, rises in January, and, as its
name imports, frequently accompanied with rain.

fleeces,[35] that have drunk the Tyrian glow, be bartered for a
great price. From these is a more numerous breed, from
these a greater quantity of milk. The more the pail froths
with their exhausted udder, the more will joyous streams flow
from their pressed dugs. Meanwhile [the shepherds] also
shear the beards, and hoary chins, and long waving hair of
the Cinyphian[39] he-goats, for the service of the camp, and for
coverings to the adventurous mariners. And then they find
pasture from the woods, from the summits of Lycæus, from
the rough brambles, and from brakes that love the craggy
rocks. And mindful, the goats of themselves return home,
and bring their young with them, and can scarcely get over
the threshold with their teeming udders. Therefore, the less
they lack the care of mortals, the more careful must you be
to defend them from the ice and snowy winds; and you must
cheerfully bring them food, and browse of tender twigs; nor
shut up from them your stores of hay during the whole
winter.

But when the summer, rejoicing in the inviting Zephyrs,
shall send forth both flocks into the lawns and pastures; at
the first rising of Lucifer, let us take to the cool fields; while
the morning is new, while the grass is hoary, and the dew,
most grateful to the cattle, is on the tender grass. Then, as
soon as the fourth hour of day has brought on thirst, and the
plaintive grasshoppers shall rend the groves with their song;
order the flocks to drink the water running in oaken troughs,
or at the wells, or at the deep pools; but in the noontide heats
seek out a shady vale, wherever Jove's stately oak with ancient strength extends its huge bows, or wherever a grove,
embrowned with thick evergreen oaks, projects its sacred
shade. Then give them once more the translucent streams,
and once more feed them at the setting of the sun, when cool
Vesper tempers the air, and now the dewy moon refreshes the
lawns, and the shores resound with Halcyonè, and the bushes
with the goldfinch.

Why should I trace for thee in song the shepherds and

---

[35] Milesian fleeces, from Miletus, a city of Asia Minor, the ancient
capital of Ionia: it was famous for its excellent wood.

[36] Cinyphian he-goats, from Cinyphus, a river and country of Africa,
near Tripolis.

pastures of Libya, and their huts with few and straggling roofs? Their flocks often graze both day and night, and for a whole month together, and repair into long deserts without any shelter; so wide the plain extends. The African shepherd carries his all with him, his house, and household god, his arms, his Amyclean dog, and Cretan quiver:[40] like the fierce Roman, when armed for his country, he takes his way under the unequal load, and, having pitched his camp, stands in array of battle against the foe, before he is expected.

But not so, where are the Scythian nations, and the Mæotic waves,[41] and the turbid Ister whirling his yellow sand; and where Rhodope returns,[42] stretched out itself under the middle of the pole: there they keep their herds shut up in stalls; nor are either any herbs to be seen in the fields, or leaves on the trees; but the country lies deformed with mounts of snow, and deep ice all around, and rises seven ells in height. It is always winter, always north-west winds, blowing cold. Then the sun never dissipates the pale shades, either when borne on his steeds he climbs the lofty sky, or when he bathes his swift chariot in the ocean's ruddy plain. Crusts of ice suddenly are congealed in the running river: now on its back the wave sustains wheels bound with iron; the wave hospitable to broad ships before, to waggons now. Vases of brass frequently burst asunder, their garments grow stiff when worn, they cut with axes the liquid wine, whole pools turn to solid ice, and the horrid icicle hardens on their uncombed beards. Meanwhile it snows incessantly through all the air; the cattle perish; the large bodies of oxen stand wrapped about with hoar frost; and the deer, crowding all together, lie benumbed under the un-

---

[40] Cretan quiver; Crete, (Candia,) one of the largest Islands in the Mediterranean, at the south of the Cyclades. It was anciently famed for its hundred cities, and for the laws of Minos established there; the Cretans were excellent archers, but infamous for falsehood and other vices. The island was subdued by the Romans, B. C. 66.

[41] Mæotic waves, now the Sea of Asoph, a large lake, or more properly part of the sea between Europe and Asia, north of the Euxine, with which it communicates by the Cimmerian Bosphorus.

[42] Hickie compares Georg. li. 271, "quæ terga obverterit axo," with the following remark: Rhodope is a chain of mountains in Thrace, which extends eastward, and is then joined with Hæmus, and parting from it, *returns* northward." I need hardly remind the reader that Virgil is partial to assigning verbs of motion to phænomena which only *appear* to exercise it. B.

usual load, and scarcely appear with the tips of their horns.
These they pursue not with hounds let loose, nor with any
toils, nor scare them with the terror of the crimson plume; [45]
but as in vain they are shoving with their breasts the opposed
mountain [of snow], they stab them with the sword close at
hand, and put them to death piteously braying, and with loud
acclamation bear them off triumphant. The inhabitants themselves, in caves dug deep under ground, enjoy undisturbed
rest, and roll to their hearths piled oaks, and whole elms,
and give them to the flames. Here they spend the night in
play; and joyous, imitate the juice of the grape with their
beer and acid service. Such is that savage race of men lying
under the northern sign of Ursa Major, buffeted by the
Riphæan east wind, and whose bodies are clothed with the
tawny furs of beasts.

If the woollen manufacture be thy care; first let prickly
woods, and burs, and caltrops, be far away: shun rich pastures: and from the beginning choose flocks that are white
with soft wool. And that ram, though he himself be of the
purest white, under whose moist palate there lurks but a black
tongue, reject, lest he should sully the fleeces of the new-born
lambs; and look out for another over the well-stocked field.
Thus Pan, the god of Arcadia, (if the story be worthy of
credit,) deceived thee, O moon, captivated with a snowy offering of wool, inviting thee into the deep groves: nor didst
thou scorn his invitation.

But let him who is studious of milk, carry to the cribs with
his own hand the cytisus, and plenty of water-lilies, and salt
herbs. Hence [the animals] are both more desirous of the
river, and distend their udders the more, and in their milk
return a faint savour of the salt.

Many restrain the kids as soon as grown up from their
dams, and fasten muzzles with iron spikes about their snouts.
What they milk at the sun-rising and the hour of morn, they
press at night: what they milk now in the evening and at
sun-setting, the shepherd at daybreak carries to town in baskets; or they season it with a small quantity of salt, and lay
it up for winter.

Nor let your care of dogs be the last: but feed at once with

---

[45] On the "formido" here spoken of, see my note on Æn. iv. 121.   B

fattening whey the swift hounds of Sparta,[44] and the fierce
mastiff of Molossis. While these are your guards, you need
never fear the nightly robber to your stalls, the incursions of
the wolves, or the restless Iberians [45] coming upon you by
stealth. Often too in the chase you will pursue the timorous
wild asses, and with hounds you will hunt the hare, with
hounds the hinds. Often, driving on with full cry, you will
give chase to the boar roused from his sylvan soil; and over
the lofty mountains with shouts pursue the stately stag into
the toils.

Learn also to burn fragrant cedar in the folds, and to drive
away the rank water-snakes with the scent of galbanum. Often
under the mangers, when not moved, either the viper of pernicious touch lies concealed, and affrighted flies the light; or
that snake, the direful pest of kine, which is wont to shelter itself under a roof and shade, and shed its venom on the cattle,
keeps close to the ground. Snatch up stones, shepherd, snatch
up clubs; and while he rears his threatening gorge, and swells
his hissing neck, knock him down: and now in fright he has
deeply hidden his dastardly head, while his middle-knots and
the wreaths in his tail's extremity are unfolded, and his last
tortuous joint now drags its slow spires along. There is also
that baneful snake in the Calabrian lawns,[46] winding up his
scaly back, with breast erect, and a long belly speckled with
broad spots; who, while any rivers burst from their fountains,
and while the lands are moist with the dewy spring and rainy
south winds, haunts the pools, and, lodging in the banks, intemperate gorges his horrid maw with fishes and croaking frogs.
When the fen is burned up, and the earth gapes with drought,
he darts forth on dry ground, and, rolling his inflamed eyes,
rages in the fields, exasperated with thirst, and aghast with
heat. Let me not then choose to indulge soft slumbers in the
open air, or to lie along the grass in the slope of a wood, when,

[44] Sparta, called also Lacedæmon, (Misitra,) a famous city of Peloponnesus in Greece, the capital of Laconia, and long the rival of Athens.
Molossis, a district in the south of Epirus, celebrated for its fierce breed
of dogs.

[45] Iberians, the Spaniards were so called, from Iberus, (the Ebro,) a
large river of Spain.

[46] Calabrian lawns. Calabria is a country in the south of Italy, anciently part of Magna Græcia.

E

renewed and sleek with youth by casting his slough, he rolls
along, leaving either his young or eggs in his den, reared to
the sun, and in his mouth quivers a three-forked tongue.

I will also teach thee the causes and the signs of their diseases. The filthy scab infects the sheep, when the raw shower
hath pierced deep into the quick, and winter, rough with hoary
frost; or, when the sweat unwashed away adheres to them
after shearing, and prickly briers have torn their bodies. On
this account, the shepherds drench the whole flock in sweet
streams, and the ram with damp fleece is plunged into the pool,
and sent to float along the stream; or they besmear their bodies
after shearing with bitter lees of oil, and mix with it litharge
of silver, native sulphur, Idæan pitch, and fat unctuous wax, and
the sea-leek, rank hellebore, and black bitumen. But there is
not any more effectual remedy for their sufferings, than to lance
the head of the ulcer with steel: the distemper is nourished
and lives by being covered; while the shepherd refuses to apply the healing hand to the wound, or sits still, praying the
gods for better omens.

Moreover, when the malady, penetrating into the inmost
bones of the bleating sheep, rages, and the parching fever preys
upon their limbs, it has been of use to drive out the kindled
inflammation, and between the under parts of the feet to open
a vein spouting with blood; in such manner as the Bisaltæ [47]
use, and the fierce Gelonian, when he flies to Rhodope, and the
deserts of the Getæ, and drinks milk thickened with the blood
of horses.

Whatever sheep thou seest either creep away at a distance
from the rest, under the mild shade, or listlessly crop the tops
of the grass, and follow in the rear, or lie down as she is feeding in the middle of the plain, and return by herself late in the
evening; forthwith check the evil by the steel, before the dire
contagion spreads among the unwary flock.

The whirlwind, that brings on a wintry storm, rushes not
so frequent from the sea, as the plagues of cattle are numerous.
Nor do diseases only sweep away single bodies, but also whole
folds suddenly, the offspring and the flock at once, and the

---

[47] Bisaltæ, a people of Macedonia or Thrace. Getæ, a people of European Scythia, inhabiting that part of Dacia near the mouths of the Ister
(Danube).

whole stock from the first breed. Whoever views the aërial
Alps, and the Noric castles on the hills, and the fields of Iapi-
dian Timavus, and the realms of the shepherds even now after
so long a time deserted, and the lawns lying waste far and
wide, may then know this. Here, in former times, a doleful
sweeping plague [48] arose from the distemper of the air, and
grew more and more inflamed through the whole heat of au
tumn; and delivered over to death all the race of cattle, all
the savage race; poisoned the lakes, and tainted the pastures
with contagion. Nor was the way of their death simple; [49]
but when the burning fever, revelling in every vein, had
shrunk up their wretched limbs, again the dropsical humour
overflowed, and converted into its substance all the bones
piecemeal consumed by the disease. Often amidst the service
of the gods, the victim standing at the altar, while the woollen
wreath is entwined with snowy fillet, has dropped down gasping to death [50] in the hands of the lingering officiators. Or, if
the priest had stabbed any one before [it fell], neither do its
entrails, when laid on the altars, burn, nor is the augur, when
consulted, able thence to give responses; and the knives applied are scarcely tinged with blood, and the surface of the
sand hardly stained with the meagre gore. Hence the calves
every where expire in the luxuriant pastures, and render up
their sweet lives at the full cribs. Hence the fawning dogs are
seized with madness; and wheezing cough shakes the diseased
swine, and suffocates them with tumours in the throat. The
unfortunate horse, [once] conqueror, forgetful of his exercises
and his pasture, pines away, loathes the springs, and often
paws the ground with his foot; his ears hang down; an in-
termitting sweat [breaks out] about them, and that too cold
at the approach of death; his withered skin feels hard, and
in handling resists the touch. These symptoms they give before death in the first days. But if in process of time the
disease begins to rankle, then are their eyes inflamed, and the

---

[*] It is almost unnecessary to remind the reader that Virgil is indebted
to Thucydides and Lucretius throughout the following description. B.

[49] *Nec* for *et non*: "And various were the forms of death." HICKIE.
"Nor was the path of death one and the same." ANTHON.

[50] "Moribundus," according to Wagner, has three significations in Virgil:
1.—Moriens, Georg. iii. 488. 2.—Moriturus, Æn. iv. 323. 3.—Mortalis,
Æn. vi. 732. B.

breath fetched from the bottom of the breast is sometimes
mixed with a heavy groan; and with a long sob they distend
their lowest flanks: black blood gushes from their nostrils,
and the rough tongue clings to their choked-up jaws. At first
it proved of service to pour the tensean draught down their
throats; this appeared the sole remedy for the dying: soon
after, this very thing proved their destruction; and being re-
cruited, they burned with furious rage, and they themselves,
now in the agonies of death (may the gods award better things
to the good, and such frenzy to our foes!) tore their own mangled limbs with their naked teeth. Lo, the bull too, smoking
under the oppressive share, drops down, and vomits out of his
mouth blood mingled with foam, and fetches his last groans.
The ploughman, unyoking the steer that mourns his brother's
death, goes away sad, and in the midst of his work leaves the
plough fixed in the earth. Neither the shades of the deep
groves, nor the soft meadows, can affect his mind, nor the
river which, rolling over the rocks, glides to the plain more
pure than amber: but his deep sides grow lank, deadness rests
upon his heavy eyes, and his neck drops with unwieldy weight
to the ground. What do their labours or good offices now
avail them? what [avails it] to have turned the heavy lands
with the share? Yet they were never injured by the rich
gifts of Bacchus, or by banquets of many courses. They feed
on leaves and the nourishment of simple herbs; the crystal
springs and running rivers are their drink; and no care breaks
their healthful slumbers. At no other time, they tell us that
kine were wanting in those regions for Juno's sacred rites, and
that the chariots were drawn to her lofty shrine by wild-bulls
ill-matched. Therefore, with difficulty they tear the ground
with harrows, and with their very nails set the corn, and over
the high mountains drag the croaking waggons with their
strained necks. The wolf meditates no ambuscades around
the folds, nor prowls about the flock by night; a sharper care
subdues him. The timorous deer and fugitive stags saunter
among the dogs, and about the houses. Now, too, the waves
wash out upon the extremity of the shore the breed of the
immense ocean, and all the race of swimmers, like shipwrecked
bodies; and the unwonted sea-calves fly to the rivers. The
viper, too, in vain defended by her winding den, expires, and

the astonished water-snakes, erecting their scales. To the very
birds the air becomes pernicious; and falling headlong, they
leave their lives beneath the lofty cloud.

Nor, moreover, avails it now for their pasture to be changed;
the arts to which they had recourse prove noxious: the masters failed, Chiron,[51] the son of Phillyra, and Melampus, the
son of Amythaon. Pale Tisiphone,[52] sent from the Stygian
glooms to light, rages: drives before her diseases and dismay:
and daily rising, higher erects her baleful head. With bleating of the flocks, and frequent lowings, the rivers, the withered
banks, and sloping hills resound; and now by droves and
flocks she deals destruction, and in the very stalls heaps up
carcasses rotting away with foul contagion, till they learn to
bury them in the ground, and hide them in pits. For neither
was there use for their hides, nor could any cleanse their flesh
with water, or purge it by fire; nor durst they so much as
shear the fleeces corrupted with disease and filthy sores, or
touch the infected yarn. But yet, if any one tried the odious
vestments, fiery pustules and filthy sweat overspread his
noisome body; and then, no long time intervening, the sacred
fire preyed upon his infected limbs.

BOOK IV.

The subject of the Fourth Book is the management of bees; their habits,
economy, polity, and government, are described with the utmost fidelity,
and with all the charm of poetry. The Book concludes with the beautiful episode of Aristæus recovering his bees.

NEXT will I set forth the heavenly gift of aërial honey.
Vouchsafe, Mæcenas, thy regard to this part also of my work.[1]
I will sing spectacles to you marvellous of minute things: the
magnanimous leaders, the manners and employments, the
tribes and battles of the whole race in order. My labour is
upon an humble theme, but not mean the praise, if the adverse
deities permit one, and Apollo invocated hear.

[51] Chiron, one of the Centaurs, son of Saturn and Phillyra, was famous
for his skill in music, physic, and shooting. Melampus, a celebrated
soothsayer and physician of Argos.

[52] Tisiphone, one of the Furies, who was the minister of Divine vengeance, and punished the wicked in Tartarus.

[1] Probably in imitation of Aratus. Phæn. 29, μέχθος μὲν τ' ὀλίγος, τὸ
δὶ μέριον αὐτίς' ὄνειαρ.   n.

First, a seat and station must be sought for the bees, where
neither winds may have access, (for the winds hinder them
from carrying home their food,) nor sheep and frisky kids
may trample down the flowers, or heifer, straying in the plain,
spurn off the dews, and bruise the rising herbs.

And let the lizards with speckled scaly backs be far from
the rich hives, and woodpeckers, and other birds; and Progne,[1]
whose breast is stained with her bloody hands. For they lay
all things waste around, and in their mouths bear away the
bees themselves while on the wing, a sweet morsel for their
merciless young. But let clear springs, and pools edged with
green moss, be near, and a gentle rivulet swiftly running
through the meads; and let a palm or stately wild olive over-
shade the entrance: that, when the new kings lead forth the
first swarms in their own spring, and the youth, issuing from
the hives, indulge in sport, the neighbouring bank may invite
them to withdraw from the heat, and the tree just in their
way may receive them with its leafy shelter. Into the midst
of the water, whether it stagnates idle or purling runs, throw
willows across, and huge stones, that they may rest upon
frequent bridges, and spread their wings to the summer sun,
if the impetuous east wind has by chance dispersed those that
lag behind, or immersed them in the flood. Around these
places let green cassia, and far-smelling wild thyme, and
plenty of strong-scented savory, flower; and let beds of
violet drink an irrigating[2] fountain.

But as for your hives themselves, whether they be compacted
of hollow bark, or woven with limber osier, let them have their
inlets narrow; for winter congeals the honey with its cold,
and the heat melts and dissolves the same: either force is
equally dreaded by the bees: nor is it in vain that they smear
with wax[4] the slender crevices in their houses, and fill up the
edges with fucus and flowers, and preserve for those very uses
collected glue, more tenacious than bird-lime, or the pitch of
Phrygian Ida.[5] Often, too, if fame be true, they have

  [1] Progne, the wife of Tereus, king of Thrace, was feigned to have
been changed into a swallow. See note ™ on Ecl. 6.
  [2] Observe the active force of "irriguos." B.
  [4] i. e. propolis. See Anthon.
  [5] Phrygian Ida, a celebrated mountain, or ridge of mountains, in the
vicinity of Troy, covered with pine trees, &c., and commanding an extensive view of the Hellespont and the adjacent countries. From Mount

cherished their families in cells dug under ground, and have been found deep down in hollow pumice-stones, and the cavity of a rotten tree. But do thou, carefully cherishing, daub their chinky chambers round with smooth mud, and strew it thinly over with leaves; and suffer not a yew near their lodges, nor burn in the fire the 'reddening crabs, nor trust them to a deep fen, or where there is a noisome smell of mire, or where the hollow rocks resound on being struck, and the struck image of the voice rebounds.

For what remains, when the golden sun has driven the winter under ground, and opened the heavens with summer light; they forthwith traverse the lawns and woods, crop the bright-hued flowers, and lightly skim the surface of the streams. Hence, gladdened with I know not what agreeable sensation, they grow fond of their offspring and young breed: hence they labour out with art new waxen cells, and form the clammy honey. After this, when now you see the swarm, after emerging from the hives into the open air, swim through the serene summer sky, and marvel at the blackening cloud driven about by the wind, mark well: they always seek the waters and leafy coverts : here sprinkle the juices prescribed, bruised balm and the common herb of honey-wort: awake the tinkling sounds, and beat around the cymbals of the mother.[*] They of themselves will settle on the medicated seats; they of themselves, after their manner, will retreat into the inmost cells.

But if they should go forth to battle, (for often discord with huge commotion seizes two kings,) you may straightway know long before-hand both the animosity of the populace, and their hearts in trepidation for war : for that martial clang of hoarse brass rouses the loiterers, and a voice is heard resembling the broken sounds of trumpets. Then in a hurry they assemble, quiver with their wings, sharpen their stings upon their beaks, prepare their sinews, crowd thick around their king and to his pavilion, and with loud hummings challenge the foe.

As soon, therefore, as they find the spring serene, and the

Ida issued the Simois, Scamander, and other rivers, and here it was that Paris adjudged the prize of beauty to the goddess Venus.
[*] Cybele, called the Mother of the Gods, was the daughter of Cælus and Terra, and wife of Saturn. DAVIDSON.

fields of air open, forth they rush from their gates: they join
battle: buzzing sounds arise in the sky aloft: mingled they
cluster in a mighty round, and fall headlong: hail rains not
thicker from the air, nor such quantities of acorns from the
shaken oak.   The kings themselves amidst the hosts, distinguished by their wings, exert mighty souls in little bodies:
obstinately determined not to yield till the dread victor has
compelled either these or those to turn their backs in flight.
These commotions of their minds, and this so mighty fray,
checked by the throw of a little dust, will cease.

But when you have recalled both leaders from the battle,
put him to death that appears the worse, lest by prodigality
he do hurt; and suffer the braver to reign in the court without a rival.   The one will glow with refulgent spots of gold;
for there are two sorts: this is the better, distinguishable both
by his make, and conspicuous with glittering scales: the
other is horribly deformed with sloth, and ingloriously drags
a large belly.

As the kings are of two figures, so are the bodies of their
people.[7]   For the one looks hideously ugly; as when a
parched traveller comes from a very dusty road, and spits the
dirt out of his dry mouth: the others shine and sparkle with
brightness, glittering with gold, and their bodies spangled
with equal drops.   This is the better breed: from these at
stated season of the sky you will press the luscious honey;
yet not so luscious as pure, and fit to correct the hard relish
of the grape.

But when the roving swarms fly about and sport in the air,
disdain their hives, and leave the cold habitations, you will
restrain their unsettled minds from their vain play.   Nor is
there great difficulty in restraining them: do you but clip the
wings of their kings; not one will dare, while they stay behind, to fly aloft, or pluck up the standard from the camp.

Let gardens fragrant with saffron flowers invite them; and
the protection of Hellespontaic Priapus, the averter of thieves
and birds, with his willow scythe preserve them.   Let him
who makes such things his care, himself bring thyme and
pines from the high mountains, to plant them far and wide

---

* This, like many other of Virgil's statements respecting bees, is er-
roneous.   The reader will find much information in Anthon's entertaining notes. B.

about their hives: let him wear his hands with the hard
labour, set himself the fruitful plants in the ground, and water
them with kindly showers.

And indeed, were I not just furling my sails at the last
period of my labours, and hastening to turn my prow to land,
perhaps I might both sing what method of culture would
adorn rich gardens, and the rose-beds of twice blooming
Pæstum ;[8] and how endive and banks green with parsley delight in drinking the rills ; and how the cucumber winding
along the grass swells into a belly: nor had I passed in silence
the late-flowering daffodil, or the stalks of the flexile acanthus,
or the pale ivy, and the myrtles that love the shores.   For I
remember that, under the lofty turrets of Œbalia,[9] where
black Galæsus[10] moistens the yellow fields, I saw an old
Corycian,[11] to whom belonged a few acres of neglected land ;
nor was that soil rich enough for the plough, proper for flocks,
or commodious for vines. Yet here among the bushes, planting a few pot-herbs, white lilies, vervain, and esculent poppies
all around, he equalled in disposition the wealth of kings ;
and returning late at night, loaded his board with unbought
dainties.   He was the first to gather the rose in spring, and
fruits in autumn ; and, even when sad winter split the rocks
with cold, and bridled up the current of the rivers with ice,
in that very season he was cropping the locks of the soft
acanthus, chiding the late summer, and the lingering zephyrs.

He, therefore, was the first to abound with pregnant bees
and numerous swarms, and to strain the frothing honey from
the pressed combs : he had limes and pines in great abundance ; and as many fruits as the fertile tree had been clothed
with in early blossoms, so many it retained ripe in autumn.
He too transplanted into rows the late [far-grown] elms, and
hard pear-trees, and sloe-trees now bearing damascenes, and
the plane now ministering shade to drinkers. But these I for

    [8] Pæstum, (Pesto,) a town of Lucania, on the Gulf of Salerno, where
the roses blossom twice a year.
    [9] Œbalia, Tarentum, in the south of Italy, was so called because built
by a colony under Phalanthus, who came from Œbalia, or Laconia, in
Greece.   Galæsus, a river of Calabria, flowing into the Bay of Tarentum.
    [10] Cf. "umbrosus Galæsus," Propert. ii. 25, 67. B.
    [11] Corycius, a contented old man of Tarentum, whose time was employed
in taking care of his bees. Some suppose that by Corycius, Virgil meant
a native of Corycus, (a town of Cilicia,) who had settled in Italy.

my past pass over, restrained by the narrow bounds I have prescribed to myself, and leave to others hereafter to record.

Come, now, I will unfold the qualities which Jupiter himself has implanted in the bees; for which reward accompanying the shrill sounds and tinkling brass of the Curetes,[12] they fed the king of heaven under the Dictæan cave. They alone have their offspring in common, share the buildings of a city in common, and pass their lives under powerful laws; and they alone have a country of their own, and a fixed abode. And, mindful of the coming winter, they experience toil in summer, and lay up their acquisitions into the common stock. For some are provident for food, and by fixed compact are employed in the fields; some within the enclosure of their hives lay Narcissus'[13] tears, and clammy gum from bark of trees, for the first foundation of the combs, then build downwards the viscid wax; others bring up to their full growth the young, the hope of the nation; others condense the purest honey, and distend the cells with liquid nectar. Some there are to whose lot has fallen the watching at the gates, and these by turns observe the waters and clouds of heaven; or receive the loads of those who return; or, forming a band, drive from the hives the drones, a sluggish horde. The work is warmly plied, and the honey smells fragrant of thyme.

And as when the Cyclops urge on the thunderbolts from the stubborn masses, some receive and render back, the air in the bull-hide bellows; some dip the sputtering brass in the trough: Ætna groans under the weight of their anvils: they alternately with vast force lift their arms in time, and turn the iron with the griping pincers. Just so, if we may compare small things with great, the innate love of gain prompts the Cecropian bees,[14] each in his proper function. The elder have

---

[12] Curetes, or Corybantes, the priests of Cybele, who inhabited Mount Ida in Crete; they were intrusted with the education of the infant Jupiter, and to prevent his being discovered by his father, who sought to destroy him, they invented a kind of dance, and drowned his cries by the noise of their cymbals.

[13] Narcissus, a beautiful youth, who, on seeing his image reflected in a fountain, became enamoured of it, thinking it to be the nymph of the place. He died of grief, and was changed into a flower, which still bears his name.

[14] Cecropian bees, that is, Attic or Athenian bees, from Cecrops, the founder and first king of Athens.

the care of their towns, and to fortify the combs, and frame
the artificial cells. But the younger return fatigued late at
night, their thighs laden with thyme; they feed at large on
arbutes, and grey willows, on cassia, and glowing crocus, on
the gummy lime, and deep-coloured hyacinths. All have one
rest from work, all one common labour. In the morning they
rush out of the gates without any delay. Again, when the
evening at length has warned them to return from feeding in
the fields, then they seek their habitations, and then refresh
their bodies: the hum arises, and they buzz about the borders
and entrance of their hives. Soon after, when they have
composed themselves in their cells, all is hushed for the night;
and their proper sleep seizes their weary limbs. Nor do they
remove to a great distance from their hive when rain im-
pends, or trust the sky when east winds approach; but in
safety supply themselves with water all around under the
walls of their city, and attempt but short excursions; and
often take up little stones, as unsteady vessels do ballast in a
tossing sea; with these they poise themselves through the
void airy regions.

Chiefly you will marvel at this custom peculiar to the bees,
that they neither indulge in conjugal embrace, nor softly dissolve their bodies in the joys of love, nor bring forth young
with a mother's throes. But they themselves cull their progeny with their mouths from leaves and fragrant herbs: they
themselves raise up a new king and little subjects, and build
new palaces and waxen realms.

Often, too, in wandering among the flinty rocks, have they
torn their wings, and voluntarily yielded up their lives under
their burden: so mighty is their love for flowers, and such
their glory in making honey. Therefore, though a narrow
term of life is their lot, (for it is not prolonged beyond the
seventh summer,) yet the race remains immortal, and through
many years the fortune of the family subsists, and grandsires
of grandsires are numbered.

Besides, not Egypt's self, nor great Lydia,[15] nor the nation
of the Parthians, nor Median Hydaspes, are so observant of
their king. Whilst the king is safe, there is one mind among

[15] Lydia, a country of Asia Minor, south of Mysia, now part of Ana-
tolia. Hydaspes, a river of Persia, supposed to be the Choaspes, or the
Araxes.

all: when he is dead, they sever their allegiance; they themselves tear to pieces the fabric of their honey, and demolish
the structure of their combs. He is the guardian of their
works: him they admire, and all encircle him with thick
humming, and guard him in a numerous body; often they lift
him up on their shoulders, expose their bodies in war, and
through wounds seek a glorious death.

From these appearances, and led by these examples, some
have alleged that a portion of the divine mind, and a heavenly
emanation, may be discovered in bees; for that the Deity
pervades the whole earth, the tracts of sea, and depth of heaven; that hence the flocks, the herds, men, and all the race
of beasts, each at its birth, derive their slender lives. Accordingly, [they affirm] that all of them, when dissolved, return and are brought back thither hereafter; nor is there any
room for death; but that they mount up alive each into his
proper order of star, and take their seat in the high heaven.

When you intend to rifle the narrow mansions [of the
bees], and their honey preserved in their treasures, first,
sprinkled [as to your body],[16] gargle your mouth with a
draught of water, and bear in your hand before you the search-
ing smoke. Twice they press the teeming cells; there are
two seasons of that harvest; one, as soon as the Pleiad Taygete[17] has displayed her comely face to the earth, and spurns
with her foot the despised waters of the ocean; or when the
same star, flying the constellation of the watery Fish, descends
in sadness from the sky into the wintry waves. They are
wrathful above measure, and when provoked, breathe venom
into their stings, and leave their hidden darts fixed in the
veins, and lay down their lives in the wound.

If, however, fearing[18] a hard winter, you both be sparing
for the future, and have pity on their drooping spirits and
shattered state; yet who will hesitate to fumigate [their hives]
with thyme, and cut away the empty wax? for often the
lizard preys unseen upon the combs, and the cells are stuffed
with cockroaches that shun the light; the drone also that sits
exempt from duty at another's repast, or the fierce hornet has

---

[16] See Anthon's note. B.
[17] Taygete, a daughter of Atlas and Pleione, who became one of the
Pleiades after death.
[18] The older editions read "metues." B.

engaged them with unequal arms; or the moth's direful
breed; or the spider, hateful to Minerva, has suspended her
loose nets in their gates.

The more they are exhausted, the more vigorously will
they all labour to repair the ruins of their decayed race, to fill
up the rows of cells, and weave their magazines of flowers.
But since life has on bees too entailed our misfortunes, if
their bodies shall languish with a sore disease, which you may
know by undoubted signs; immediately the sick change
colour; horrid leanness deforms the countenance: then they
carry the bodies of the dead out of their houses, and lead the
mournful funeral processions; or clinging together by the feet,
hang about the entrance, and loiter all within their houses
shut up, both listless through famine, and benumbed with
contracted cold. Then a hoarser sound is heard, and in
drawling hums they buzz; as at times the south wind murmurs through the woods; as the ruffled sea creaks hoarsely
with refluent waves; as rapid fire in the pent furnace roars.
In this case now I would advise to burn gummy odours, and
to put in honey through pipes of reed, kindly tempting and
inviting the enfeebled bees to their known repast. It will be
of service also to mix with it the juice of pounded galls, and
dried roses, or inspissated must[19] thickened over a strong fire,
or raisins from the Psythian vine, Cecropian thyme, and
strong-smelling centaury. There is also in the meadows a
flower, to which the husbandmen have given the name of
amellus; an herb easy to be found; for from one root it
shoots a vast luxuriance of stalks, itself of golden hue; but on
the leaves, which are spread thickly around, the purple of the
dark violet sheds a gloss. The altars of the gods are often
decked with plaited wreaths [of this flower]. Its taste is
bitterish in the mouth: the shepherds gather it in new-shorn
valleys, and near the winding streams of Mella.[20] Boil the
roots thereof in fragrant wine; and present it as food [for the
bees] in full baskets at their door.

But if the whole stock should suddenly fail any one, and
he should have no means to recover a new breed; it is time

[19] "When must was inspissated to one-half, it acquired the name of
defrutum." ANTHON.
[20] Mella, a small river of Cisalpine Gaul, falling into the Ollius, and
with it into the Po.

both to unfold the memorable invention of the Arcadian master, and how the tainted gore of bullocks slain has often produced bees : I will disclose the whole tradition, tracing it high
from its first source. For where the happy nation of Pellæan
Canopus [21] inhabit the banks of the Nile, floating [the plains]
with his overflowing river, and sail around their fields in
painted gondolas ; and where the river, that rolls down as far
as from the swarthy Indians, presses on the borders of quivered
Persia, and fertiles verdant Egypt with black silt, and pouring.
along divides itself into seven different mouths ; all the country grounds infallible relief on this art. First a space of
ground of small dimensions, and contracted for this purpose,
is chosen ; this they strengthen with the tiling of a narrow
roof and confined walls ; and add four windows of slanting
light in the direction of the four winds. Then a bullock, just
bending the horns in his forehead two years old, is sought out:
whilst he struggles exceedingly, they close up both his nostrils,
and the breath of his mouth ; and when they have beaten him
to death, his battered entrails are crushed within the hide that
remains entire. When dead, they leave him pent up, and lay
under his sides fragments of boughs, thyme, and fresh cassia.
This is done when first the zephyrs stir the waves, before the
meadows blush with new colours, before the chattering swallow suspend her nest upon the rafters. Meanwhile the juices,
warmed in the tender veins, ferment : and animals, wonderful
to behold, first short of their feet, and in a little while buzzing
with wings, swarm together, and more and more take to the
thin air : till they burst away like a shower poured down from
summer clouds ; or like an arrow from the whizzing string,
when the swift Parthians first begin the fight.

What god, ye Muses, what god disclosed to us this art ?
whence took this new experience of men its rise ?

The shepherd Aristæus, [22] flying from Peneian Tempe, [23]

---

[21] Canopus, (near Aboukir,) a city of Egypt, 12 miles east from Alexandria. It is here called Pellæan, having been founded by a colony from
Pella, a city of Macedonia, or in allusion to the conquest of the country
by Alexander the Great, who was born at Pella.

[22] Aristæus was the son of Apollo and Cyrene. He became enamoured
of Eurydice, the wife of Orpheus, and was the first who taught mankind
the culture of olives, and the management of bees ; after death he was
worshipped as a god.

[23] Peneian Tempe, a celebrated vale in Thessaly, between Mount Olym-

having lost his bees, as it is said, by disease and famine, stood mournful by the sacred source of the rising river, much and oft complaining : and with these accents addressed his parent: Mother Cyrene, mother, who inhabitest the depth of this flood, why hast thou brought me forth of the illustrious race of gods, (if indeed, as you pretend, Thymbræan Apollo be my sire,) thus abhorred by destiny? or whither is thy love for me banished? why didst thou bid me hope for heaven? Lo, I, though thou art my mother, am even bereft of this very glory of my mortal life, which, amidst my watchful care of flocks and agriculture, I, after infinite essays, with much difficulty achieved. Why then, go on; root up with thine own hands my happy groves; bear the hostile flame into my stalls, and kill my harvests; burn up my plantations, and wield the sturdy bill against my vineyards ; if such strong aversion to my praise hath seized thee.

But his mother heard the sound beneath the chambers of the deep river ; her nymphs around her were carding the Milesian fleeces, dyed with rich glass-green tincture ; Drymo[94] and Xantho, Ligea and Phyllodoce, their comely hair flowing down their snow-white necks ; Nesæe and Spio, Thalia and Cymodoce, Cydippe and golden Lycorias ; the one a virgin, the other just experienced in the first labours of Lucina ; Clio, and her sister Beroe, both daughters of Oceanus, both in gold, both in spotted skins arrayed ; Ephyre and Opis, and Asian Deïopeia ; and swift Arethusa, having at length laid her darts aside : among whom Clymene was relating Vulcan's unavailing care, the tricks and pleasant thefts of Mars, and recounted the frequent amours of the gods down from Chaos. Whilst the nymphs, charmed with this song, wind off their soft task from the spindles, the lamentations of Aristæus again struck his mother's ears, and all were amazed in their crystal beds :

pus and Ossa, through which the river Peneus flows into the Ægean. Tempe was about five miles in length, but very narrow, in few places above a quarter of a mile broad. The ancient poets have described it as one of the most delightful spots in the world ; hence all valleys that are pleasant are by the poets called Tempe. Thymbra, a plain in Troas, through which the river Thymbrius flowed in its course to the Scamander. Apollo had there a temple, and thence it is called Thymbræan.

[94] Drymo, &c. These were sea-nymphs, the attendants of Cyrene, daughter of the river Peneus, who was carried by Apollo to that part of Africa which was called Cyrenaica, where she became the mother of Aristæus.

but Arethusa upreared her golden head before her other sisters, darting her eyes abroad ; and afar [she cried], O sister Cyrene, not in vain alarmed with such piteous moaning, thy own Aristæus, overwhelmed with sorrow, thy darling care, stands weeping by the water of Peneus thy sire, and calls thee cruel by name. To her the mother, her soul seized with unusual concern, cries, Conduct, conduct him quickly to us: to him it is permitted to tread the courts of the gods. At the same time she commands the deep floods to divide on all sides, that the youth might make his approach. And the water, bent into the shape of a mountain, stood round about him, received him into its ample bosom, and let him pass under the river. And now admiring his mother's palace, and humid realms, the lakes pent up in caverns, and the sounding groves, he passed along, and amazed at the vast motion of the waters, surveyed all the rivers gliding under the great earth in different places ; Phasis [25] and Lycus, and the source whence deep Enipeus first bursts forth, whence father Tiberinus,[26] and whence Anio's [27] streams, and Hypanis [28] roaring down the rocks, and Mysian Caicus, and Eridanus, his bull-front decked with two gilt horns, than whom no river pours along the fertile fields with greater violence into the dark, troubled [29] sea.

After he had arrived under the roof of her bed-chamber, hung with pumice-stones, Cyrene was informed of the vain lamentations of her son, the sisters in order serve up the crystal streams for the hands, and bring smooth towels. Some load the board with viands, and plant the full cups. The altars

---

[25] Phasis, (Phas or Rhion,) a river of Colchis, rising in Mount Caucasus, and falling into the Euxine. Lycus, a river of Armenia. Enipeus, a river of Thessaly, falling into the Peneus.

[26] Tiber, a celebrated river of Italy, on whose banks the city of Rome was built. It was originally called Albula, from the whiteness of its waters, and afterwards Tiber, from Tiburinus, king of Alba, who was drowned in it. The Tiber rises in the Apennines, and, after dividing Latium from Etruria, falls into the Mediterranean 16 miles below Rome.

[27] Anio, (Teverone,) a river of Italy which falls into the Tiber.

[28] Hypanis, (Bog,) a river of European Scythia, which runs into the Euxine. Caicus, (Grimakli,) a river of Mysia, falling into the Ægean.

[29] Compare Anthon, who observes, "We have preferred rendering purpureum here by a double epithet. It is analogous to the Greek πορφύρεος, as said of the troubled sea, whence βίος πορφυρεοῦς θαλάσσης, "a seaman's troublous life."

blaze with Panchæan fires. Then the mother thus speaks:
Take bowls of Mæonian wine, let us offer a libation to Ocean.
At the same time she herself addresses Ocean, the parent of
things, and the sister nymphs, a hundred of whom preside over
woods, a hundred over rivers. Thrice she sprinkled glowing
Vesta with the liquid nectar: thrice the flame, mounting to
the top of the roof, brightened: with which omen encouraging
her soul, she thus begins: In Neptune's Carpathian gulf there
dwells a seer, cœrulean Proteus,[30] who measures the great sea
with fishes, and in a chariot yoked with two-legged steeds.
He now revisits the ports of Emathia and his native Pallene:[31] him both we nymphs, and old Nereus [32] himself adore;
for the prophet knows all things that are, that have been, and
what is being drawn on as about to be. For such is the will
of Neptune; whose unwieldy droves, and ugly sea-calves, he
feeds under the deep. He, my son, must first be surprised
with chains, that he may explain to you the whole cause of
the disease, and make the issue prosperous. For no instructions will he give without compulsion, nor can you move him
by entreaty: ply him, when taken, with rigid force and
chains: all his tricks to evade these, proving vain, will at
length be baffled. I myself, as soon as the sun has inflamed
his noon-tide heats; when the herbs thirst, and the shade becomes more grateful to the cattle, will conduct you into the
old god's retreats, whither he retires from the waves when fatigued; that you may easily assail him overpowered with
sleep. But when you shall hold him fast confined within
your arms and chains, then various forms and features of wild
beasts will mock your grasp. For suddenly he will become a
bristly boar, a fell tiger, a scaly dragon, and a lioness with a
tawny mane: or he will emit the roaring of flame, and escape
the chain; or, liquefied into fluid waters, glide away. But the
more he shall transform himself into all shapes, still closer
draw, my son, the hampering chains, till, rechanged, he shall

---

[30] Proteus, a sea-deity, son of Oceanus and Tethys. He is represented
by the poets as usually residing in the Carpathian Sea between Crete and
Rhodes: he possessed the gift of prophecy, and also the power of assuming different shapes.
[31] Pallene, a small peninsula of Macedonia, on the Ægean Sea.
[32] Nereus, a sea-god, son of Oceanus and Terra, and husband of Doris
by whom he had fifty daughters, the Nereids

■

become such as you saw him when he closed his eyes in sleep
commenced. She spoke; and shed around the liquid odour of
ambrosia, wherewith she sprinkled over the whole body of her
son. Now from his trimmed locks a delicious fragrance
breathed, and active vigour was infused into his limbs. In the
side of a hollowed mountain is a spacious cave, whither many
a wave is driven by the wind, and divides itself into receding
curves; at times a station most secure for weather-beaten
mariners. Within Proteus hides himself behind the barrier of
a huge rock. Here the nymph places the youth in ambush remote from view; she herself takes her station at a distance,
shrouded in a misty cloud. Now the sultry dog-star, scorching the thirsty Indians, blazed in the sky, and the fiery sun
had finished half his course: the herbs withered; and the rays
made the shallow over-heated rivers boil, their channels being
drained to their slimy bottom; when Proteus, repairing to his
accustomed den, advanced from the waves. The watery race
of the vast ocean, gamboling around him, scatter the briny
spray far and near. The sea-calves apart lay themselves
down to sleep along the shore. He himself (as at times the
keeper of a fold upon the mountains, when evening brings
home the bullocks from the pasture, and the lambs with noisy
bleatings whet the hunger of the wolves) sits in the centre on
a rock, and counts over their numbers. Of [seizing] whom
since so favourable an opportunity offered itself to Aristæus,
scarcely suffering the aged god to compose his weary limbs, he
rushes upon him with a great shout, and surprises him with
chains reclining. He, on the other hand, not forgetful of his
art, transforms himself into all the wondrous shapes in nature;
fire, and a fierce savage, and flowing river. But when no
shifts could find him an escape, overpowered he returned to
himself, and at length thus spoke in human accent: Who,
most presumptuous youth, enjoined thee (he said) to approach
my habitation? or what demandest thou here? But he [re-
plied], Thou knowest, O Proteus, thou knowest of thyself;
nor is it in any one's power to deceive thee: but do thou cease
to try [to escape me]. In pursuance of divine command, I
come hither to consult thy oracle about my ruined affairs.
Thus much he spoke. Then the prophet at length, with
mighty force, rolled his eyes flashing with azure light, and
gnashing his teeth fiercely, thus opened his mouth to disclose.

the Fates: It is the vengeance of no mean deity that pursues
thee: thou art making atonement for heinous crimes: these
sufferings, by no means proportioned to thy guilt, unhappy
Orpheus entails upon thee, unless the Fates oppose; and he
sorely rages for his ravished queen. She indeed, rushing
headlong along the river's bank, provided she could only
escape thee, the maid doomed to death saw not the hideous
water-snake before her feet, guarding the banks in the tall
grass. But her fellow choir of Dryads filled the highest
mountains with shrieks: the rocks of Rhodope wept; so did
lofty Pangæa,[33] and the martial land of Rhesus, the Getæ, and
Hebrus, and attic Orithyia. Orpheus[34] himself, soothing the
anguish of his love with his concave shell, sang of thee, sweet
spouse, of thee by himself on the lonely shore; thee when the
day arose, thee when the day declined, he sang. He entering
even the jaws of Tænarus, Pluto's gates profound, and the
grove overcast with gloomy horror, visited the Manes, and
their tremendous king, and hearts unknowing to relent at
human prayers. But the airy shades, and phantoms of the
dead, moved at his song, stalked forth from the deep recesses of Erebus,[35] in such throngs, as birds that shelter
themselves by thousands in the woods, when evening, or a
wintry shower, drives them from the mountains; matrons, and
men, and ghosts of gallant heroes deceased, boys and unmarried
virgins, and youths laid on the funeral piles before the faces
of their parents; whom the black mud and unsightly reeds
of Cocytus, and the unlovely lake with sluggish wave, enclose
around, and Styx, nine times poured between, confines. The
very habitations and deepest dungeons of death were astonished, and the Furies, with whose hair blue snakes were interwoven; and yawning Cerberus repressed his three mouths;
and the whirling of Ixion's wheel was suspended by the song.
And now retracing his way, he had overpassed all dangers;

[33] Pangæa, a mountain on the confines of Macedonia and Thrace.
[34] Orpheus was feigned by the poets to have descended into the infernal
regions to recover his wife Eurydice, when he so charmed Pluto and
Proserpine with the music of his lyre, that they consented to restore her,
provided he forbore looking behind until he had gained the upper regions; but he forgot his promise, and his Eurydice instantly vanished.
[35] Erebus, a god of hell; often used to signify hell itself. Cerberus,
represented as a dog with three heads, that watched the entrance into the
infernal regions.

and restored Eurydice was just approaching the regions above,
following him ; for Proserpine had given him that law ; when
a sudden frenzy seized the unwary lover, pardonable, indeed,
if the Manes knew to pardon.   He stopped, and on the very
verge of light, ah! unmindful, and not master of himself,
looked back on his Eurydice: there was all his labour wasted,
and the law of the relentless tyrant broken ; and thrice a dismal groan was heard through the Avernian lake.   Orpheus,
she says, who hath both unhappy me and thee undone: what
so great frenzy is this ? see once more the cruel Fates call me
back, and sleep closes my swimming eyes.   And now farewell : I am snatched away, encompassed with thick night, and
stretching forth to thee my feeble hands! ah, thine no more.
She spoke ; and suddenly fled from his sight a different way,[36]
like smoke blended with the thin air: nor more was seen by
him grasping the shades in vain, and wishing to say a thousand things ; nor did the ferryman of hell suffer him again to
cross the intervening fen.   What should he do? whither
should he turn himself, his love twice snatched away? with
what tears move the Manes, with what words the gods? She
already cold was sailing in the Stygian boat.   For seven whole
months, it is said, he mourned beneath a weather-beaten rock,
by the streams of desert Strymon, and unfolded these his woes
under the cold caves, softening the very tigers, and leading
the oaks with his song : as mourning Philomel under a poplar
shade bemoans her lost young, which the hard-hearted clown
observing in the nest has stolen unfledged ; but she weeps
through the night, and, perched upon a bough, renews her
doleful song, and fills the places all around with piteous wailings.   No loves, no hymeneal joys, could bend his soul.   Alone
he traversed the Hyperborean tracts of ice, the snowy Tanais,
and fields never-free from Riphæan frosts, deploring his ravished Eurydice, and Pluto's useless gifts ; for which despised
rite [37] the Ciconian matrons, amidst the sacred service of the

---

[36] I have always felt dissatisfied with this participle "diversa," although, I believe, Servius and all MSS. support it. I think "dilapsa" is
more Virgilian. Cf. Georg. iv. 410. So Lucan, in an evident imitation of
this passage, iii. 34, " Sic fata, refugit Umbra per amplexus trepidi dilapsa
mariti." So "delapsa," Ovid, Art. Am. i. 43 ; "relapsa," Met. x. 57. B.
[37] The attempts to explain this passage are confessedly hopeless. See
Anthon. "Munere" probably arose from a gloss upon the preceding
"dona." Can "quo nomine " (= on what pretext) be the true reading ? B

gods and nocturnal orgies of Bacchus, having torn the youth
in pieces, scattered his limbs over the wide fields. And even
then, whilst Œagrian Hebrus rolled down the middle of its
tide, his head torn from the alabaster neck, the voice itself,
and his chilling tongue, invoked Eurydice, ah, unfortunate
Eurydice! with his fleeting breath: the banks re-echoed Eurydice all along the river. Thus Proteus sang, and plunged
with a bound into the deep sea; and, where he plunged, he
tossed up the foaming billows under the whirling tide.

But not so Cyrene: for kindly she bespoke the trembling
[Aristeas]: My son, you may ease your mind of vexatious
cares. This is the whole cause of your disaster; hence the
nymphs, with whom she used to celebrate the mingled dances
in the deep groves, have sent this mournful destruction on
your bees: but suppliant bear offerings, beseeching peace, and
venerate the gentle wood-nymphs; for at your supplications
they will grant forgiveness, and mitigate their wrath. But
first will I show you in order what must be your manner of
worship. Single out four choice bulls of beauteous form,
which now graze for you the tops of green Lycæus; and as
many heifers, whose necks are untouched [by the yoke]. For
these erect four altars at the lofty temples of the goddesses:
from their throats emit the sacred blood, and leave the bodies
of the cattle in the leafy grove. Afterwards, when the ninth
morn has displayed her rising beams, you may offer Lethæan
poppies as funeral rites to Orpheus, venerate appeased Eurydice with a slain calf, sacrifice a black ewe, and revisit the
grove.

Without delay, he instantly executes the orders of his
mother; repairs to the temple; raises the altars as directed;
leads up four chosen bulls of surpassing form, and as many
heifers, whose necks were untouched. Thereafter, the ninth
morning having ushered in her rising beams, he offers the
funeral rites to Orpheus, and revisits the grove. But here
they behold a sudden prodigy, and wonderful to relate; bees
through all the belly hum amidst the decomposed bowels of
the cattle; pour forth with the fermenting juices from the
burst sides, and in immense clouds roll along; then swarm
together on the top of a tree, and hang down in a cluster from
the bending boughs.

Thus of the culture of fields, and flocks, and of trees, I

sung; whilst great Cæsar at the deep Euphrates was thundering in war, was victoriously dispensing laws among the
willing nations, and pursuing the path to Olympus. At that
time, me, Virgil, sweet Parthenope[34] nourished, flourishing in
the studies of inglorious ease; who warbled pastoral songs,
and, adventurous through youth, sung thee, O Tityrus, under
the covert of a spreading beech.

[34] Parthenope, afterwards called Neapolis, (Naples,) a celebrated city
of Campania, in Italy, seated on a beautiful bay, from which it rises 'like
an amphitheatre. It received the name of Parthenope from one of the
Sirens who was buried there.

VIRGIL'S ÆNEID

BOOK I.

The subject of the Æneid is the settlement of Æneas in Italy. This noble Poem, on the composition of which Virgil was engaged eleven years, consists of twelve books, and comprehends a period of eight years. In the First Book, the hero is introduced, in the seventh year of his expedition, sailing from Sicily, and shipwrecked upon the coast of Africa, where he is kindly received by Dido, queen of Carthage. The description of the storm in this book is particularly admired.

ARMS I sing,[1] and the hero, who first, exiled by fate, came from the coast of Troy to Italy, and the Lavinian[2] shore: much was he tossed both on sea and land, by the power of those above, on account of the unrelenting rage of cruel Juno: much too he suffered in war till he founded a city, and brought his gods into Latium: from whence the Latin progeny, the Alban fathers, and the walls of lofty Rome.

Declare to me, O Muse! the causes, in what[3] the deity being offended, by what the queen of heaven was provoked to drive a man of distinguished piety to struggle with so many calamities, to encounter so many hardships. Is there such resentment in heavenly minds?

An ancient city there was, Carthage,[4] (inhabited by a colony of Tyrians,) fronting Italy and the mouth of the Tiber, far remote; vast in riches, and extremely hardy in warlike exercises; which [city] Juno is said to have honoured more

[1] Respecting the four verses usually prefixed to the Æneid, see Anthon. B.
[2] Lavinium, (Pratica,) a city of Latium, built by Æneas, and called by that name in honour of Lavinia.
[3] i. e. "quo modo." It is a mistake to suppose that we should join "quo numine," since Juno has been already mentioned. B.
[4] Carthage, a powerful city of ancient Africa, on a peninsula, 12 miles north-east of Tunis, was built by a colony of Tyrians under Dido, about 100 years before the foundation of Rome. After having been long mistress at sea, and the rival of Rome, Carthage was totally destroyed by Scipio Africanus the younger, in the third Punic war, B. C. 146, an event to which the memorable words, "Delenda est Carthago," of the elder Cato, mainly contributed.

than any other place of her residence, Samos[5] being set aside.
Here lay her arms; here was her chariot; here the goddess
even then designs and fondly hopes to establish a seat of
universal empire, would only the Fates permit. But she had
heard of a race to be descended from Trojan blood, that was
one day to overturn the Tyrian towers: that hence a people
of extensive regal sway, and proud in war, would come to the
destruction of Libya: so the destinies ordained. This the
daughter of Saturn dreading, and mindful of the old war
which she had the principal hand in carrying on before Troy,[6]
in behalf of her beloved Argos;[7] nor as yet were the causes
of her rage and keen resentment worn out of her mind; the
judgment of Paris dwells deeply rooted in her soul, the affront
offered to her neglected beauty, the detested [Trojan] race,
and the honours conferred on ravished Ganymede:[8] she, by
these things fired, having tossed on the whole ocean the
Trojans, whom the Greeks and merciless Achilles had left,
drove them far from Latium;[9] and thus, for many years, they,
driven by fate, roamed round every sea: so vast a work it
was to found the Roman state.

[5] Samos, an island in the Ægean Sea, near the coast of Ionia. It is
extremely fertile, producing the most delicious fruits, and is famous as
being the birth-place of Pythagoras. Samos was sacred to Juno, who
had here a most magnificent temple.

[6] Troy, or Ilium, one of the most renowned cities of antiquity, the
capital of Troas in Asia Minor, was built on a small eminence near Mount
Ida, between the Simois and Scamander, a short distance above their
confluence, and about four miles from the Ægean shore. Of all the wars
that have been carried on among the ancients, that of Troy is the most
famous, whether we regard the celebrity of the chiefs engaged in it, or
the deeds in arms which it called forth. According to the generally received account, the Trojan war was undertaken by the Greeks to recover
Helen, the wife of Menelaus, whom Paris, the son of Priam, king of
Troy, had carried away. All Greece united to avenge the cause of Menelaus, and Troy, after a siege of ten years, was taken and burnt, B. C.
1184. No vestige now remains of ancient Troy; and even its site has
become matter of uncertainty.

[7] Argos, the capital of Argolis, a district of Peloponnesus, of which
Juno was the chief deity. During the Trojan war, Agamemnon was king
of the united kingdom of Argos and Mycenæ.

[8] Ganymede, the son of Tros, king of Troy, feigned to have been taken
up to heaven by Jupiter, and there became the cupbearer of the gods in
the place of Juno's daughter Hebe.

[9] Latium, (Campagna di Roma,) a country of Italy, on the east of the
Tiber. The Latins rose into importance when Romulus had founded the
city of Rome in their country.

Scarcely had the Trojans, losing sight of Sicily,[10] with joy launched out into the deep, and were ploughing the foaming billows with their brazen prows, when Juno, harbouring everlasting rancour in her breast, thus with herself:[11] Shall I then, baffled, desist from my purpose, nor have it in my power to turn away the Trojan king from Italy? because I am restrained by fate! Was Pallas able to burn the Grecian ships, and bury themselves in the ocean, for the offence of one, and the frenzy of Ajax,[12] Oileus' son? She herself, hurling from the clouds Jove's rapid fire, both scattered their ships, and upturned the sea with the winds: him too she snatched away in a whirlwind, breathing flames from his transfixed breast, and dashed him against the pointed rock. But I, who move majestic,[13] the queen of heaven, both sister and wife of Jove, must maintain a series of wars with one single race for so many years. And who will henceforth adore Juno's divinity,[14] or humbly offer sacrifice on her altars?

The goddess by herself revolving such thoughts in her inflamed breast, repairs to Æolia,[15] the native land of storms, regions[16] pregnant with boisterous winds. Here, in a vast cave, king Æolus controls with imperial sway the reluctant winds and sounding tempests, and confines them with chains

---

[10] Sicily, the largest and most celebrated island in the Mediterranean Sea, to the south of Italy, and separated from it by the Straits of Messina. It is of a triangular form, and from its three promontories was anciently called Trinacria. Its name Sicily was derived from the Siculi, a people of Italy who settled in it.

[11] Cf. interpp. on Ter. Andr. i. 1, 55, "Egomet continuo mecum." B.

[12] Ajax, the son of Oileus, king of Locris, one of the Grecian chiefs in the Trojan war. He was surnamed Locrian, to distinguish him from Ajax the son of Telamon.

[13] Such is the proper sense of "incedere." Cf. Æn. i. 493. Tibull. ii. 6, 34. Propert. ii. 1, 5. More particularly Seneca, Nat. Q. vii. 31, "non ambulamus, sed incedimus." Propert. ii. 2, 58, "incedit vel Jove digna soror." B.

[14] Some MSS. of Quintilian, ix. 2, p. 772, give "nomen." Cf. Drak. on Sil. i. 93. B.

[15] The Æolian Islands, situated between Italy and Sicily, which were seven in number. Here Æolus, the son of Hippotas, reigned, reputed king of the winds, because, from a course of observations, he had acquired some knowledge of the weather, and was capable of foretelling at times what wind would blow for some days together, as we learn from Diodorus and Pliny.

[16] For the change of number, "patriam .... loca," cf. Æn. vi. "Itur in antiquam silvam, stabula alta ferarum." B.

in prison. They roar indignant round their barriers, filling
the mountain with loud murmurs. Æolus is seated on a lofty
throne, wielding a sceptre, and assuages their fury, and moder-
ates their rage. For, unless he did so, they, in their rapid
career, would bear away sea and earth, and the deep heaven,
and sweep them through the air. But the almighty Sire,
guarding against this, hath pent them in gloomy caves, and
thrown over them the ponderous weight of mountains, and
appointed them a king, who, by fixed laws, and at command,
knows both to curb them, and when to relax their reins;
whom Juno then in suppliant words thus addressed: Æolus,
(for the sire of gods and the king of men hath given thee
power both to smooth the waves, and raise them with the
wind,) a race by me detested sails the Tuscan Sea, transport-
ing Ilium, and its conquered gods, into Italy. Strike force
into thy winds, overset and sink[17] the ships; or drive them
different ways, and strew the ocean with carcasses. I have
twice seven lovely nymphs, the fairest of whom, Deïopeia, I
will join to thee in firm wedlock, and assign to be thine own
for ever,[18] that with thee she may spend all her years for this
service, and make thee father of a beautiful offspring.

To whom Æolus replies: 'Tis thy task, O queen, to consider what you would have done: on me it is incumbent to
execute your commands. You conciliate to me whatever of
power I have, my sceptre, and Jove. You grant me to sit
at the tables of the gods:[19] and you make me lord of storms
and tempests.

Thus having said, whirling the point of his spear, he struck
the hollow mountain's side: and the winds, as in a formed
battalion, rush forth at every vent, and scour over the lands
in a hurricane. They press upon the ocean, and at once, east,
and south, and stormy south-west, plough up the whole deep
from its lowest bottom, and roll vast billows to the shores.
The cries of the seamen succeed, and the cracking of the cord-
age. In an instant clouds snatch the heavens and day from

---

[17] i. e. " obrue, at submergantur." So in Greek, as Soph. Œd. T. 163,
ἠνύσατ' ἱστολίαν φλόγα, ɪ. e. ὥστε εἶναι ἱστολίαν. Eur. Ph. 446, διαλ-
λάξασαν ὁμογενεῖς φίλους.   B.

[18] This is the complete sense of " propriam," expressing the Homeric
ᾗν αἶιν Ἴλδιαι ᾗρατα πάντα (Il. X. cap. 269). Cf. Westerhov. on Ter.
Andr. iv. 3, 1. B.

[19] Festus, " maxima enim fuit honos, Divum epulis accumbere." B

the eyes of the Trojans: sable night sits brooding on the sea,
thunder roars from pole to pole, the sky glares with repeated
flushes, and all nature threatens them with immediate death.
Forthwith Æneas'[20] limbs are relaxed with cold shuddering
fear. He groans, and, spreading out both his hands to heaven,
thus expostulates: O thrice and four times happy they, who
had the good fortune to die before their parents' eyes, under
the high ramparts of Troy! O thou, the bravest of the Grecian race, great Tydeus'[21] son, why was I not destined to fall
on the Trojan plains, and pour out this soul by thy right
hand? where stern Hector[22] lies prostrate by the sword of
Achilles; where mighty Sarpedon[23] [lies]; where Simois[24]
rolls along so many shields, and helmets, and bodies of heroes
snatched away beneath its waters.

While uttering such words a tempest, roaring from the
north, strikes across the sail, and heaves the billows to the
stars. The oars are shattered: then the prow turns away,
and exposes the side to the waves. A steep mountain of
waters follows in a heap. These hang on the towering surge ;
to those the wide-yawning deep discloses the earth between
two waves: the whirling tide rages with [mingled] sand.
Three other ships the south wind, hurrying away, throws on
hidden rocks; rocks in the midst of the ocean, which the
Italians call Altars,[25] a vast ridge rising to the surface of the

[20] Æneas, a Trojan prince, son of Anchises and Venus, who, after the
fall of Troy, came to Italy, where he married Lavinia, the daughter of
Latinus, whom he succeeded in his kingdom.
[21] Tydeus' son, Diomedes, the son of Tydeus and Delphyle, was king
of Ætolia, and one of the most renowned of the Grecian chiefs in the
Trojan war, where he performed many heroic deeds.
[22] Hector, the son of Priam and Hecuba, was the most valiant of all
the Trojan chiefs. For a long time he gloriously sustained the destinies
of Troy, till at last he fell by the hand of Achilles, who dragged the body,
with insulting triumph, thrice times round the tomb of Patrocles and the
walls of Troy.
[23] Sarpedon, a son of Jupiter by Europa, and brother to Minos, went
to the Trojan war to assist Priam, and was slain by Patroclus. According
to some authors, the Sarpedon who assisted Priam was king of Lycia,
and son of Jupiter by Laodamia, the daughter of Bellerophon.
[24] Simois, a river of Troas, which rose in Mount Ida, and fell into the
Scamander below Troy.
[25] Altars ; these were the Ægates, three small islands opposite Carthage, near which the Roman fleet, under L. Catulus, obtained a decisive victory over that of the Carthaginians, which put an end to the

sea. Three from the deep the east wind drives on shoals and
flats, a piteous spectacle! and dashing on the shelves, it encloses them with mounds of sand. Before the eyes of Æneas
himself, a mighty billow, falling from the height, dashes
against the stern of one which bore the Lycian crew, and
faithful Orontes:[76] the pilot is tossed out and rolled headlong, prone [into the waves]; but her the driving surge
thrice whirls around in the same place, and the rapid eddy
swallows up in the deep. Then floating here and there on
the vast abyss, are seen men, their arms and planks, and the
Trojan wealth, among the waves. Now the storm overpowered the stout vessel of Ilioneus,[77] now that of brave
Achates, and that in which Abas sailed, and that in which
old Alethes: all, at their loosened and disjointed sides, receive
the hostile stream, and gape with chinks.

Meanwhile Neptune perceived that the sea was in great
uproar and confusion, a storm sent forth, and the depths overturned from their lowest channels. He, in violent commotion, and looking forth from the deep, reared his serene countenance above the waves; sees Æneas's fleet scattered over
the ocean, the Trojans oppressed with the waves and the ruin
from above. Nor were Juno's wiles and hate unknown to
her brother. He calls to him the east and west winds; then
thus addresses them: And do you thus presume upon your
birth? dare you, winds! without my sovereign leave, to embroil heaven and earth, and raise such mountains. Whom
I——[78] But first it is right to assuage the tumultuous waves.
A chastisement of another nature from me awaits your next
offence. Fly apace, and bear this message to your king: That
not to him the empire of the sea, and the awful trident, but
to me by lot are given: his dominions are the mighty rocks,

---

first Punic war, B. C. 241. DAVIDSON. Heyne would condemn this
line as spurious. It is, however, quoted by Quintil. viii. 2, p. 675. Cf.
Wyttenb. on Plat. Phædon. § 135.　B.

[76] Orontes commanded the Lycian fleet, which, after the fall of Troy,
accompanied Æneas in his voyage to Italy.

[77] Ilioneus, son of Phorbas, was distinguished for his eloquence.
Achates, a friend of Æneas, whose fidelity was so exemplary, that Fidus
Achates became a proverb.

[78] This ἀποσιώπησις, or sudden break in speaking, is remarked by
Donatus on Ter. Eun. i. 1, 20. Aquila Romanus, fig. rhet. p. 147, ed.
Ruhnk. and Quintil. ix. 2, p. 781.　B.

your proper mansions, Eurus: in that palace let king Æolus proudly boast, and reign in the close prison of the winds.

So he speaks, and, more swiftly than his speech,[79] smooths the swelling seas, disperses the collected clouds, and brings back the day. With him Cymothoë,[30] and Triton with exerted might, heave the ships from the pointed rock. He himself raised them with his trident; lays open the vast sandbanks, and calms the sea; and in his light chariot glides along the surface of the waves. And as when a sedition has perchance[31] arisen among a mighty multitude, and the minds of the ignoble vulgar rage; now firebrands, now stones fly; fury supplies them with arms: if then, by chance, they espy a man revered in piety and worth, they are hushed, and stand with ears erect; he, by eloquence, rules their passions, and calms their breasts. Thus all the raging tumult of the ocean subsides, as soon as the sire, surveying the seas, and wafted through the open sky, guides his steeds, and flying, gives the reins to his easy chariot.

The weary Trojans direct their course towards the nearest shores, and make the coast of Libya. In a long recess, a station lies; an island forms it into a harbour by its jutting sides, against which every wave from the ocean is broken, and divides itself into receding curves. On either side vast cliffs, and two twin-like rocks, threaten the sky; under whose summit the waters all around are calm and still. Above is a sylvan scene with waving woods, and a dark grove with awful shade hangs over. Under the opposite front a cave is of pendant rocks,[32] within which are fresh springs, and seats of living stone,[32] the recess of nymphs. Here neither cables hold, nor anchors with crooked fluke moor the weather-beaten ships. To this retreat Æneas brings seven ships, collected from all his fleet; and the Trojans, longing much for land, disembarking, enjoy

---

[79] See Anthon. So λόγου θᾶττον, Heliodor. Eth. L 15. iv. 10. B.

[30] Cymothoë, one of the Nereids. Triton, a powerful sea-deity, son of Neptune and Amphitrite. Many of the sea-gods were called Tritons, but the name was generally applied to those only who were represented half men and half fishes.

[31] "Sæpe," like the Greek πολλάκις, is often used in this sense, as observed by Abresch. Diluc. Thucyd. p. 174, and Heindorf on Plat. Phædon. § 11. B.

[32] My interpretation is justified by Ennius, Scriver. p. 20, "per speluncas saxis structas asperis pendentibus." B.

[33] αὐτόπετρ' ἄντρα, Æsch. Prom. 309. In English, "natural caves." B

the wished-for shore, and stretch their brine-drenched limbs upon the beach. Then first Achates struck spark from a flint, received the fire in leaves, round it applied dry combustible matter, and instantly blew up a flame from the fuel. Then, spent with toil and hunger, they produce their grain, damaged by the sea-water, and the instruments of Ceres; and prepare to dry over the fire, and to grind with stones, their rescued corn. Meanwhile Æneas climbs a rock, and takes a prospect of the wide ocean all around, if, by any means, he can descry any [man like] Antheus tossed by the wind, and the Phrygian galleys, or Capys,[34] or the arms of Caicus, on the lofty deck. He sees no ship in view, but three stags straying on the shore: these the whole herd follow, and are feeding through the valley in a long-extended train. Here he stopped short, and snatching his bow and swift arrows, (weapons which the faithful Achates bore,) first prostrates the leaders, bearing their heads high with branching horns; next the vulgar throng; and disperses the whole herd, driving them with darts through the leafy woods. Nor desists he, till conqueror he stretches seven huge deer on the ground, and equals their number with his ships. Hence he returns to the port, and shares them amongst all his companions. Then the hero divides the wine which the good Acestes[35] had stowed in casks on the Sicilian shore, and given them at parting, and with these words cheers their saddened hearts: O companions, who have sustained severer ills than these, (for we are not strangers to former days of adversity,) to these, too, God will grant a termination. You have approached[36] both Scylla's fury, and those deep roaring rocks; you are unacquainted with the dens of the Cyclops: resume then your courage, and dismiss your desponding fears; perhaps hereafter it may delight you to remember these sufferings. Through various mischances, through so many perilous adventures, we steer to Latium, where the Fates give us the prospect of peaceful settlements. There Troy's kingdom

[34] Capys. This brave Trojan was one of those who, against the advice of Thymœtes, wished to destroy the wooden horse, which proved the destruction of Troy.

[35] Acestes, a king of Sicily, who assisted Priam in the Trojan war, and who afterwards kindly entertained Æneas when he landed upon the coast of Sicily.

[36] "Accedere," — "to encounter," is properly used of any thing dangerous. Cf. Burm B.

is allowed once more to rise. Persevere, and reserve yourselves for prosperous days. So he says in words; and oppressed with heavy cares, wears the looks of hope, buries deep
anguish in his breast.

They address themselves to the spoil and future feast; tear
the skin from the ribs, and lay the flesh bare. Some cut into
parts, and fix on spits the quivering limbs: others place the
brazen caldrons on the shore, and prepare the fires. Then
they repair their strength with food, and, stretched along the
grass, regale themselves with old wine and fat venison. After
hunger was taken away by banquets, and the viands removed,
in long discourse they inquire after their lost companions, in
suspense between hope and fear, whether to believe them yet
alive, or that they have finished their destiny, and no longer
hear when called. Above the rest, the pious Æneas, within
himself, bemoans now the loss of the active Orontes, now of
Amycus, and then the cruel fate of Lycus, with valiant Gyas,
and valiant Cloanthus.

And now there was an end [of discourse]; when Jove,
looking down from the lofty sky upon the sail-flown sea, and
the lands lying at rest, with the shores and the nations dispersed abroad; thus stood on the pinnacle of heaven, and
fixed his eyes on Libya's realms. To him, revolving such
cares in his mind, Venus, in mournful mood, her bright eyes be-
dimmed with tears, addresses herself: O thou, who with eternal sway rulest, and with thy thunder overawest, the affairs of
both gods and men, what so high offence against thee could
my Æneas or the Trojans be guilty of, that, after having suffered so many deaths, they must be shut out from all the world
on account of Italy? Surely you promised, that in some future
age, after circling years, the Romans should descend from
them, powerful leaders spring from the blood of Teucer [77] restored, who should rule the sea, the nations with absolute
sway. Father! why is thy purpose changed? I, indeed, was
solacing myself with this promise under Troy's fall and sad
ruin, with fates balancing contrary fates. Now the same
fortune still pursues them, after they have been driven with
such variety of woes. Great king, what end to their labours wilt

[77] Teucer, a king of Phrygia, son of Scamander. Troy was called
from him Teucria, and the Trojans Teucri.

thou give?[38] Antenor, escaped from amidst the Greeks, could with safety penetrate the Illyrian gulf, and the inmost realms of Liburnia,[39] and overpass the springs of Timavus; whence, through nine mouths, with loud echoing from the mountain, it bursts away a sea impetuous, and sweeps the fields with a roaring deluge. Yet there he built the city of Padua,[40] established a Trojan settlement, gave the nation a name, and set up the arms of Troy. Now in calm peace composed he rests: we, thy own progeny, whom thou by thy nod ordainest the throne of heaven, (oh woe unutterable!) having lost our ships, are betrayed, driven hither and thither far from the Italian coast, to gratify the malice of one. Are these the honours of piety? is it thus thou replacest us on the throne?.

The sire of gods and men, smiling upon her, with that aspect wherewith he clears the tempestuous sky, gently kissed his daughter's lips; then thus replies: Cytherea,[41] cease from fear: immoveable to thee remain the fates of thy people. Thou shalt see the city and promised walls of Lavinium, and shalt raise magnanimous Æneas aloft to the stars of heaven; nor is my purpose changed. In Italy he (for I will tell thee, since this care lies gnawing at thy heart, and tracing farther back, I will reveal the secrets of fate) shall wage a mighty war, crush a stubborn nation, and establish laws and cities to his people, till the third summer shall see him reigning in Latium, and three winters pass after he has subdued the Rutulians.[42] But the boy Ascanius,[43] who has now the surname of Iülus, (Ilus he was, while the empire of Ilium flourished,) shall measure with his reign full thirty great circles of revolving months, transfer the seat of his empire from Lavinium, and strongly

[38] Eur. Alcest. 214, ἰὼ Ζεῦ, τίς ἂν πᾶ πόρος κακῶν Γένοιτο, καὶ λύσις τύχας; B.

[39] Liburnia, (Croatia,) a province of Illyria, at the head of the Adriatic.

[40] Padua, a city of Italy, celebrated as the birth-place of Livy.

[41] Cytherea, a surname of Venus, from Cythera, (Cerigo,) an island on the southern coast of Laconia in Peloponnesus, which was sacred to her.

[42] Rutulians, a people of Latium, anciently known, as well as the Latins, by the name of Aborigines. They supported Turnus their king in the war which he waged against Æneas.

[43] Ascanius, called also Iülus, was the son of Æneas by Creusa; he accompanied his father to Italy, succeeded him in the kingdom of Latinus, and built the city of Alba Longa.

fortify Alba Longa. Here again, for full three hundred years, the sceptre shall be swayed by Hector's line, until Ilia,[44] a royal priestess, impregnated by Mars, shall bear two infants at a birth. Then Romulus, exulting in the tawny hide of the wolf his nurse, shall take upon him the rule of the nation, build a city sacred to Mars, and from his own name call the people Romans. To them I fix neither limits nor duration of empire; dominion have I given them without end. And even sullen Juno, who now, through jealous fear, creates endless disturbance to sea, and earth, and heaven, shall change her counsels for the better, and join with me in befriending the Romans, lords of the world, and the nation of the gown. Such is my pleasure. An age shall come, after a course of years, when the house of Assaracus shall bring under subjection Phthia[45] and renowned Mycenæ, and reign over vanquished Argos. A Trojan shall be born of illustrious race, Cæsar, who shall bound his empire by the ocean, his fame by the stars, Julius his name, from great Iülus derived. Him, loaded with the spoils of the East, you shall receive to heaven at length, having seen an end of all your cares: he too shall be invoked by vows and prayers. Then, wars having ceased, fierce nations shall soften into peace. Hoary Faith, Vesta, and Quirinus,[46] with his brother Remus, shall administer justice. The dreadful gates of war[47] shall be shut with close bolts of iron. Within impious Fury, sitting on horrid arms, and his hands bound behind him with a hundred brazen chains, in hideous rage shall gnash his bloody jaws.

He said, and from on high sent down Maia's son,[48] that the coasts of Libya and the new towers of Carthage might be open hospitably to receive the Trojans; lest Dido,[49] ignorant of heaven's decree, should shut them out from her ports. He, on the

[44] Ilia, or Rhea, priestess of Vesta, was a daughter of Numitor, king of Alba, and the mother of Romulus and Remus by Mars.
[45] Phthia, a city of Thessaly, celebrated as the birth-place of Achilles; it gave name to the surrounding district.
[46] Quirinus, a name given to Romulus, after he was deified.
[47] i. e. of Janus. War is here personified.
[48] Maia's son; Mercury, a celebrated god of antiquity, the son of Jupiter and Maia; he was the messenger of the gods, and of Jupiter in particular.
[49] Dido, called also Elisa, tho daughter of Belus king of Tyre, and the wife of Sichæus, whom her brother Pygmalion murdered for his riches.

I

steerage of his wings, flies through the expanded sky, and speedily alighted on the coasts of Libya. And now he puts his orders in execution; and, at the will of the god, the Carthaginians lay aside the fierceness of their hearts: the queen, especially, entertains thoughts of peace, and a benevolent disposition towards the Trojans.

But pious Æneas, by night revolving many things, resolved, as soon as cheerful day arose, to set out, and to reconnoitre the unknown country, on what coasts he was driven by the wind; who are the inhabitants, whether men or wild beasts, (for he sees nothing but uncultivated grounds,) and inform his friends of his discoveries. Within a winding grove, under a hollow rock, he secretly disposed his fleet, fenced round with trees and gloomy shades: himself marches forth, attended by Achates alone, brandishing in his hand two javelins of broadpointed steel. To whom, in the midst of a wood, his mother presents herself, wearing the mien and attire of a virgin, and the arms of a Spartan maid; or resembling Thracian Harpalyce,[60] when she tires her steeds, and in her course outflies the swift Hebrus: for, huntress-like, she had hung from her shoulders a light bow, and suffered her hair to wanton in the wind; bare to the knee, with her flowing robes gathered in a knot. Then first, Pray, youths, she says, inform me if by chance ye have seen any of my sisters wandering this way, equipped with a quiver, and the skin of a spotted lynx, or with full cry urging the chase of a foaming boar. Thus Venus, and thus Venus' son replied: Of your sisters not one has been heard or seen by me. O virgin, by what name shall I address thee? for thou wearest not the looks of a mortal, nor sounds thy voice human. O thou a goddess surely! Are you the sister of Phœbus, or one of the race of the nymphs? Oh! be propitious, and whoever you are, ease our anxious minds, and inform us under what climate, on what region of the globe, we at length are thrown. We wander strangers both to the country and the inhabitants, driven upon this coast by furious winds and swelling seas. So shall many a victim fall a sacri-

---

Dido was the founder of the city of Carthage, where she hospitably entertained Æneas, who had been shipwrecked upon the coast.

[60] Harpalyce, a daughter of Harpalycus, king of Thrace, a woman of the most undaunted courage

fice at thine altars by our right hand. Then Venus: I, indeed, deem not myself worthy of such honour. It is the custom for the Tyrian virgins to wear a quiver, and bind the leg thus high with a purple buskin. You see the kingdom of Carthage, a Tyrian people, and Agenor's city.[51] But the country is that of Libya, a race invincible in war. The kingdom is ruled by Dido, who fled hither from Tyre, to shun her brother's hate: tedious is the relation of her wrongs, and intricate the circumstances; but I shall trace the principal heads.[52] Her husband was Sichæus, the richest of the Phœnicians in land, and passionately beloved by his unhappy spouse. Her father had given her to him in her virgin bloom, and joined her in wedlock with the first connubial rites: but her brother Pygmalion then possessed the throne of Tyre; atrociously wicked beyond all mortals. Between them hatred arose. He, impious, and blinded with the love of gold, having taken Sichæus by surprise, secretly assassinates him before the altar, regardless of his sister's great affection. Long he kept the deed concealed, and wicked, forging many lies, amused the heart-sick, loving [queen] with vain hope. But the ghost of her unburied husband appeared to her in a dream, lifting up his visage amazingly pale and ghastly: he opened to her view the bloody altars, and his breast transfixed with the sword, and detected all the hidden villany of the house; then exhorts her to hasten flight, and quit her native country; and, to aid her flight, reveals treasures ancient in the earth, an unknown mass of gold and silver. Dido, roused by this awful messenger, provided friends, and prepared to fly. They assemble, who either had mortal hatred or violent dread of the tyrant: what ships by chance are ready, they seize in haste, and load with gold. The wealth of the covetous Pygmalion is conveyed over sea. A woman is guide of the exploit. Thither they came, where now you will see the stately walls and rising towers of a new-built Carthage, and bought as much ground as they could enclose with a bull's hide, called Byrsa,[53] in commemoration of the deed. But [say] now, who

[51] Agenor's city; Carthage is so called, as being built by Dido, who was a descendant of Agenor, king of Phœnicia.
[52] Literally, "the chief footsteps." B.
[53] Byrsa is also a citadel in the middle of Carthage, on which was the temple of Æsculapius.

are you? or from what coasts you came, or whither are you
bending your way? To these her demands, the hero, with
heavy sighs, and slowly raising his words from the bottom of
his breast, [thus replies,] If I, O goddess! tracing from their
first source, shall pursue, and you have leisure to hear, the
annals of our woes, the evening star will first shut heaven's
gates upon the expiring day.[54] Driven over a length of seas
from ancient Troy, (if the name of Troy hath by chance
reached your ears,) a tempest, by its wonted chance, threw
us on this Libyan coast. I am Æneas the pious, renowned
by fame above the skies, who carry with me in my fleet the
gods I snatched away from the enemy. I seek my country,
Italy; and my descendants sprang from Jove supreme. With
twice ten ships I embarked on the Phrygian Sea, having followed the destinies vouchsafed me, my goddess-mother pointing out the way; seven, with much ado, are saved, torn and
shattered by waves and wind. Myself, a stranger, poor and
destitute, wander through the deserts of Africa, banished from
Europe and from Asia. Venus, unable to bear his further
complaints, thus interrupted in the midst of his grief: Whoever you may be, I trust you live[55] not unbefriended by the
powers of heaven, who have arrived at a Tyrian city. But
do you forthwith bend your course directly to the palace of
the queen: for, that your friends are returned, and your ships
saved, and by a turn of the north wind wafted into a secure
harbour, I pronounce to thee with assurance, unless my parents, fond of a lying art, have in vain taught me divination.
See these twelve swans exulting in a body, whom the bird of
Jove,[56] having glided from the ethereal region, was chasing
through the open air: now, in a long train, they seem either
to choose their ground, or to hover over the place they have
already chosen. As they, returning, sportive clap their
rustling wings, wheel about the heavens in a troop, and raise
their melodious notes; just so your ships and youthful crew,
either are possessed of the harbour, or are entering the port

---

[54] See Anthon. Demosth. de Cor. § 91, ἐπιλείψει με λέγοντα ἡ ἡμέρα
τὰ τῶν προδοτῶν ὀνόματα. B.
[55] Huhnk. on Xen. Mem. iv. 3, 8, most appositely illustrates the
phrase, "auras vitales carpere," from a passage of Ælian in Suidas, καὶ
ἀέρος σπᾶν, καὶ ἔχειν τροφὴν ζωῆς τὸ ἐξ αὐτοῦ πνεῦμα.
[56] Bird of Jove, i. e. the eagle.

with full sail. Proceed, then, and pursue your way where
this path directs.

She said, and turning away, shone radiant with her rosy
neck, and from her head ambrosial locks breathed divine fragrance : her robe hung flowing to the ground, and by her gait
the goddess stood confessed. The hero, soon as he knew his
mother, with these accents pursued her as she fled : Why so
oft dost thou too cruelly mock thy son with vain shapes ?
why is it not granted me to join my hand to thine, and to hear
and answer thee by turns in words sincere and undissembled ?
Thus he expostulates with her, and directs his course to the
walls. But Venus screened them on their way with dim
clouds, and the goddess spread around them a thick veil of
mist, that none might see, or touch, or cause them interrup-
tion, or inquire into the reasons of their coming. She herself
wings her way sublime to Paphos, and with joy revisits her
seats ; where, sacred to her honour, is a temple, and a hundred
altars smoke with Sabean incense, and are fragrant with fresh
garlands.

Meanwhile they urged their way where the path directs.
And now they were ascending the hill that hangs over a great
part of the town, and from above surveys its opposite towers,
Æneas admires the mass of buildings, once cottages :[67] he admires the gates, the bustle, and the paved streets. The Tyrians warmly ply the work : some extend the walls, and raise a
tower to push along unwieldy stones ; some choose out the
ground for a private building, and enclose it with a trench.
Some choose [a place for] the courts of justice, for the ma-
gistrates' [halls] and the venerable senate.[68] Here some are
digging ports ; there others are laying the foundations for
lofty theatres, and hewing huge columns from the rocks, the
lofty decorations of future scenes. Such their toil as in summer's prime employs the bees amidst the flowery fields under
the sun, when they lead forth the full-grown swarms of their
race, or when they press close the liquid honey, and distend
the cells with sweet nectar ;[69] or when they disburden those

---

[67] i. e. "moveable huts." See Anthon.
[68] But it is perhaps better to regard "legunt" as joined with "jura,"
by a zeugma, in this sense ; "they [institute] laws, and choose magis-
trates." B.
[69] So μελίσσαν νέκταρι. Eur. Bacch. 143

that come home loaded, or in formed battalion, drive the inactive flock of drones from the hives. The work is hotly
plied, and the fragrant honey smells strongly of thyme. O
happy ye, whose walls now rise! Æneas says, and lifts his
eyes to the turrets of the city. Shrouded in a cloud, (a marvel
to be told!) he passes amidst the multitude, and mingles with
the throng, nor is seen by any.[59] In the centre of the city
was a grove, most delightful in shade, where first the Carthaginians, driven by wind and wave, dug up the head of a
sprightly courser, an omen which royal Juno showed: for
by this [she signified], that the nation was to be renowned
for war, brave and victorious through ages. Here Sidonian
Dido built to Juno a stately temple, enriched with gifts, and
the presence of the goddess; whose brazen threshold rose on
steps, the beams were bound with brass, and the hinge creaked
beneath brazen gates. In this grove the view of an unexpected scene first abated the fear [of the Trojans]: here
Æneas first dared to hope for redress, and to conceive better
hopes of his afflicted state. For while he surveys every object in the spacious temple, waiting the queen's arrival; while
he is musing with wonder on the fortune of the city; and
[compares] the skill of the artists and their elaborate works,
he sees the Trojan battles [delineated] in order, and the war
now known by fame over all the world; the sons of Atreus,[61]
Priam,[62] and Achilles implacable to both. He stood still; and,
with tears in his eyes, What place, Achates, what country on
the globe, is not full of our disaster? See Priam! even here
praiseworthy deeds[63] meet with due reward: here are tears
for misfortunes, and the breasts are touched[64] with human
woes. Dismiss your fears: this fame of ours will bring thee
some relief. Thus he speaks, and feeds his mind with the
empty representations, heaving many a sigh, and bathes his
visage in floods of tears. For he beheld how, on one hand,
the warrior Greeks were flying round the walls of Troy, while
the Trojan youth closely pursued; on the other hand, the

* A Grecism for "ab ullo." Ovid, Trist. v. 10, 38, "non intelligor
ulli." B.
[61] Sons of Atreus, Agamemnon and Menelaus.
[62] Priam, the son of Laomedon, and the last king of Troy, was slain by
Pyrrhus, the son of Achilles, the same night on which Troy was taken.
[63] For this sense of "laus," cf. Catull. lxi. 102. Cicer. in Verr. § 47 B.
[64] So θανόντων οὐδὲν ἄλγος ἅπτεται. Soph. Œd. C. 955. B.

Trojans [were flying], while plumed Achilles, in his chariot, pressed on their rear. Not far from that scene, weeping, ho espies the tents of Rhesus,[65] with their snow-white veils; which, betrayed by the first sleep,[66] cruel Diomede plundered, drenched in much blood, and led away his fiery steeds to the [Grecian] camp, before they had tasted the pasture of Troy, or drank of Xanthus.[67] In another part, Troilus,[68] flying after the loss of his arms, ill-fated youth, and unequally matched with Achilles! is dragged by his horses, and from the empty chariot hangs supine, yet grasping the reins; his neck and hair trail along the ground, and the dusty plain is traced by the inverted spear. Meanwhile the Trojan matrons were marching to the temple of adverse Pallas, with their hair dishevelled, and were bearing the robe, suppliantly mournful, and beating their bosoms with their hands. The goddess turned away, kept her eyes fixed on the ground. Thrice had Achilles dragged Hector round the walls of Troy, and was selling his breathless corpse for gold. Then, indeed, Æneas sent forth a deep groan from the bottom of his breast, when he saw the spoils, the chariot, and the very body of his friend, and Priam stretching forth his feeble hands. Himself too he recognised mingled with the Grecian leaders, and the Eastern bands, and the arms of swarthy Memnon.[69] Furious Penthesilea[70] leads on her troops of Amazons, with their crescent

---

[65] Rhesus, a warlike king of Thrace, who marched to the assistance of Priam. The oracle having foretold that Troy should never be taken if the horses of Rhesus drank the waters of Xanthus, and fed upon the grass of the Trojan plains; the Greeks, however, surprised him on the night of his arrival, slew him in his tent, and carried away his horses in triumph to their camp.

[66] "Primo somno, ut graviorem ostenderet somnum." SERVIUS. Sleep is poetically said to have betrayed him, because he was surprised while at rest. B.

[67] Xanthus, (Mendere,) a river of Troas, in Asia Minor, rising in Mount Ida, and falling into the sea at Sigæum. It is the same with the Scamander; according to Homer, it was called Xanthus by the gods, and Scamander by men.

[68] Troilus, a son of Priam and Hecuba, slain by Achilles.

[69] Memnon, a king of Ethiopia, son of Tithonus and Aurora. He came with a body of 10,000 men to assist his uncle Priam in the Trojan war, where he displayed great courage, and killed Antilochus, Nestor's son, but was himself afterwards slain by Achilles in single combat.

[70] Penthesilea, a queen of the Amazons, daughter of Mars, who assisted Priam, and was slain by Achilles.

shields, and burns amidst the thickest ranks. Below her exposed breast the heroine had girt a golden belt, and the virgin
warrior dares even to encounter with men.

These wondrous scenes while the Trojan prince surveys,
while he is lost in thought, and in one gaze stands unmoved ;
Queen Dido, of surpassing beauty, advanced to the temple,
attended by a numerous retinue of youth. As on the banks
of Eurotas, or on Mount Cynthus' top, Diana leads the circu-
lar dances, round whom a numerous train of mountain nymphs
play in rings; she bears her quiver on her shoulder, and
moving majestic, she towers above the other goddesses, while
silent raptures thrill Latona's [71] bosom; such Dido was, and
such, with cheerful grace, she passed amidst her train, urging
forward the labour and her future kingdom. Then at the
gate of the goddess, in the middle of the temple's dome, she
took her seat, surrounded with her guards, and raised aloft on
a throne. [Here] she dispensed justice and laws to her subjects, and, in equal portions, distributed their tasks, or settled them by lot ; when suddenly Æneas sees, advancing with
a vast concourse, Antheus, Sergestus, brave Cloanthus, and
other Trojans, whom a black storm had tossed up and down
the sea, and driven to other far-distant shores. At once he
was amazed, at once Achates was struck, and between joy and
fear both ardently longed to join hands ; but the uncertainty
of the event perplexes their minds. They carry on their disguise, and, shrouded under the bending cloud, watch to learn
the fortune of their friends; on what coast they left the fleet,
and on what errand they came: for a select number had come
from all the ships to sue for grace, and, with mingled voices,
approached the temple.

Having gained admission and liberty to speak in the presence,
Ilioneus their chief, with mind composed, thus began: O
queen, to whom Jove has granted to found this rising city
and to curb proud nations with just laws, we Trojans forlorn,
tossed by winds over every sea, implore thee : keep from our
ships the merciless flames; spare a pious race, and propitious-
ly regard our distresses. We are not come either to ravage with
the sword the Libyan abodes, or to seize and bear away the plunder to our ships. We have no such hostile intention, nor does
such pride of heart become the vanquished. There is a place

[71] Latona, the mother of Apollo and Diana.

called by the Greeks Hesperia,[72] an ancient land, renowned
for martial deeds and fruitful soil; the Œnotrians [73] possessed
it once: now fame is that their descendants call the nation
Italy, from their leader's name; hither our course was bent,
when suddenly tempestuous Orion [74] rising from the main,
drove us on hidden shallows, and with southern blasts fiercely
sporting, tossed us hither and thither over waves, and over
pathless rocks, overwhelmed by the briny deep: hither we few
have floated [75] to your coasts. What a race of men is this?
what country so barbarous to allow such manners? We are
denied the hospitality of the shore. In arms they rise, and
forbid our setting foot on the first verge of land. If you set
at nought the human kind, and the arms of mortals, yet know
the gods have a mindful regard to right and wrong. We had
for our king Æneas, than whom no one was more just in piety,
none more signalized in war and in martial achievements;
whom, if the Fates preserve, if he breathe the vital air, and
do not yet rest with the ruthless shades, neither shall we despair, nor you repent your having been the first in challenging
to acts of kindness. We have likewise cities and arms in Sicily, and the illustrious Acestes is of Trojan extraction. Permit us to bring to shore our wind-beaten fleet, and from your
woods to choose [trees for] planks, and to refit our oars; that,
if it be granted to bend our course to Italy, upon the recovery
of our prince and friends, we may joyfully set out thither, and
make the Latian shore. But if our safety has perished, and
thou, O father of the Trojans, the best of men! now liest
buried in the Libyan sea, and no further hope of Iülus remains,
we may at least repair to the straits of Sicily, and the settlement there prepared for us, (whence we were driven hither,)
and visit king Acestes. So spoke Ilioneus; at the same time,
the other Trojans murmured their consent.

[72] Hesperia, a name applied to Italy by the Greeks, and to Spain by
the Romans.
[73] Œnotrians, the inhabitants of Œnotria, or that part of Italy which
was afterwards called Lucania. Œnotria is sometimes applied to Italy
in general.
[74] Orion, one of the constellations, generally supposed to be accompanied at its rising (in March) with great storms and rains.
[75] "Adnavimus" is employed to show that they had a bare escape. So
"vix enatavimus," Apul. Met. li. p. 30; ἐξινηξάμεθα, Lucian, Ver. Hist.
li and de Merc. Cond. B.

Then Dido, with downcast looks, thus in brief replies:
Trojans, banish fear from your breasts, lay your cares aside.
My hard fate, and the infancy of my kingdom, force me to take
such measures and to secure my frontiers with guards around.
Who is stranger to the Æneian race, the city of Troy, her
heroes, and their valorous deeds, and to the devastations of so
renowned a war? We Carthaginians do not possess hearts
that are so obdurate and insensible, nor yokes the sun his
steeds so far away from our Tyrian city. Whether Hesperia
the greater, and the country where Saturn reigned, or ye
choose [to visit] Eryx'[76] coast and king Acestes, I will dismiss you safe with assistance, and support you with my wealth.
Or will you settle with me in this realm? The city which I
am building shall be yours:[77] draw your ships ashore; Trojan and Tyrian shall be treated by me with no distinction.[78]
And would that your prince Æneas too were here, driven by
the same wind! However, I will send trusty messengers
along the coasts, with order to search Libya's utmost bounds,
if he is thrown out to wander in some wood or city.

Animated by these words, brave Achates and father Æneas
had long impatiently desired to break from the cloud. Achates
first addressed Æneas: Goddess-born, what purpose now
arises in your mind? You see all is safe; your fleet and
friends restored. One alone is missing, whom we ourselves
beheld sunk in the midst of the waves: every thing else agrees
with your mother's prediction. He had scarcely spoken, when
suddenly the circumambient cloud splits asunder, and dissolves
into open air. Æneas stood forth, and in the clear light shone
conspicuous, in countenance and form resembling a god: for
Venus herself had breathed upon her son graceful locks, and
the radiant bloom of youth, and breathed a sprightly lustre
on his eyes: such beauty as the hand superadds to ivory,
or where silver or Parian marble is enchased with yellow
gold.

Then suddenly addressing the queen, he, to the surprise of

[76] Eryx, a king of Sicily, son of Butes and Venus; also a town and
mountain of Sicily, near Drepanum. On the summit of Mount Eryx
(Giuliano) stood a famous temple of Venus, who is hence called Erycina.
[77] A common construction. Cf. Ter. Eun. iv. 3, 11. Plaut. Epid. iii.
4. 12. B.
[78] Cf. Æn. x. 108, "Tros Tyriusve fuat, nullo discrimine habebo." B.

all,[79] thus begins: I, whom you seek, am present before you;
Trojan Æneas, snatched from the Libyan waves. O thou,
who alone hast commiserated Troy's unutterable calamities!
who in thy town and palace dost associate us, a remnant saved
from the Greeks, who have now been worn out by woes in
every shape, both by sea and land, and are in want of all
things! to repay thee due thanks, great queen, exceeds the
power not only of us, but of all the Dardan race,[80] wherever
dispersed over the world. The gods (if any powers divine
regard the pious, if justice any where exists, and a mind conscious of its own virtue) shall yield thee a just recompence.
What age was so happy as to produce thee? who were the
parents of so illustrious an offspring? While rivers run into
the sea, while shadows move round the convex mountains,
while heaven feeds the stars; your honour, name, and praise
[with me] shall ever live, to whatever climes I am called.
This said, he embraces his friend Ilioneus with his right hand,
and Serestus with his left: then the rest, the heroic Gyas, and
heroic Cloanthus.

Sidonian Dido stood astonished, first at the presence of the
hero, then at his signal sufferings, and thus her speech addressed: What hard fate, O goddess-born, pursues thee
through such mighty dangers! what power drives thee on
this barbarous coast? Are you that Æneas, whom, by
Phrygian Simois' stream, fair Venus bore to Trojan Anchises?
And now, indeed, I call to mind that Teucer, expelled from
his native country, came to Sidon in quest of a new kingdom,
by the aid of Belus. My father Belus then reaped the soil of
wealthy Cyprus,[81] and held it in subjection to his victorious
arms. Ever since that time I have been acquainted with the
fate of Troy, with your name, and the Grecian kings. The
enemy himself extolled the Trojans with distinguished praise,
and with pleasure traced his descent from the ancient Trojan
race. Come then, youths, enter our walls. Me, too, through
a series of labours tossed, a like fortune has at length

[79] Mamertinus Pan. Jul. vi. § 3, "In medio Illyrici sinus improvisus
apparuit." "Improvisus "—"de improviso," "unexpectedly." B.
[80] Dardan race; the Trojans, as descended from Dardanus, the son of
Jupiter and Electra, who fled to Asia Minor, where he built the city of
Dardania, and became the founder of the kingdom of Troy.
[81] Cyprus, a large and fertile island in the eastern part of the Mediterranean Sea, sacred to Venus, who had here two celebrated temples.

doomed to settle in this land. Not unacquainted with misfortune [in my own person], I have learned to succour the
distressed.

This said, she forthwith leads Æneas into the royal apartments, and at the same time ordains due honours for the temples of the gods. Meanwhile, with no less care, she sends
presents to his companións on the shore, twenty bulls, a hundred bristly backs of huge boars, a hundred fat lambs, with
the ewes, as gifts and pleasure for the day.[62] But the inner
rooms are splendidly furnished with regal pomp, and banquets
are prepared in the middle of the hall. Couch draperies
wrought with art, and of proud purple; massy silver plate on
the table, and, embossed in gold, the brave exploits of her
ancestors, a lengthened series of history traced down through
so many heroes, from the first founder of the ancient race.
Æneas (for paternal affection suffered not his mind to rest)
with speed sends on Achates to the ships, to bear those tidings
to Ascanius, and bring [the boy] himself to the city. All
the care of the fond parent centres in Ascanius. Besides, he
bids him bring presents, saved from the ruins of Troy, a
mantle ʽstiff with gold and figures, and a veil woven round
with saffron-coloured acanthus, the ornaments of Grecian
Helen,[63] which she had brought with her from Mycenæ, when
bound for Troy, and lawless nuptials; her mother Leda's
wondrous gift; a sceptre too, which once Ilione, Priam's eldest
daughter, bore, a necklace strung with pearl, and a crown
set with double rows of gems and gold. This message to
despatch, Achates directed his course to the ships.

But Venus revolves in her breast new plots, new designs;
that Cupid[64] should come in place of sweet Ascanius, assuming his mien and features, and by the gifts kindle in the queen
all the rage of love, and enwrap the flame in her very bones;
for she dreads the equivocating race, and the double-tongued

[62] The readings vary between "die," "dii," and "dei." See Servius.
I have, with Wagner, preferred "dii," which has the additional authority
of Gellius, ix. 14. B.

[63] Helen, the wife of Menelaus, king of Sparta, was the most beautiful
woman of her age. In the absence of her husband, Paris, son of king
Priam, carried her away, which was the cause of the ten years' war against
Troy, and the destruction of that celebrated city.

[64] Cupid, in the heathen mythology, was the god of love, and the son
of Venus.

Tyrians. Fell Juno torments her, and with the night her
care returns. To winged Love, therefore, she addresses these
words: O son, my strength, my mighty power; my son, who
alone defiest the Typhœan bolts of Jove supreme, to thee I
fly, and suppliant implore thy deity. 'Tis known to thee
how round all shores thy brother Æneas is tossed from sea to
sea, by the spite of partial Juno, and in my grief thou hast
often grieved. Him Phœnician Dido entertains, and amuses
with smooth speech; and I fear what may be the issue of
Juno's acts of hospitality: she will not be idle in so critical
a conjuncture; wherefore, I purpose to prevent the queen by
subtle means, and to beset her with the flames of love, that
no power may influence her to change, but that with me she
may be possessed by great fondness for Æneas. How this
thou mayest effect, now hear my plan. The royal boy, my
chief care, at his father's call, prepares to visit the Sidonian
city, bearing presents saved from the sea and flames of Troy.
Him having lulled to rest, I will lay down in some sacred
retreat on Cythera's tops, or above Idalium,[24] lest he should
discover the plot, or interfere with it. Do you artfully counterfeit his face but for one night, and, yourself a boy, assume
a boy's familiar looks; that when Dido shall take thee to her
bosom in the height of her joy, amidst the royal feasts, and
Bacchus' stream, when she shall give thee embraces, and im-
print sweet kisses, thou mayest breathe into her the secret
flame, and by stealth convey the poison. Love obeys the dictates of his dear mother, and lays aside his wings, and-joyful
trips along in the gait of Iülus. Meanwhile Venus pours the
dews of balmy sleep on Ascanius' limbs, and in her bosom
fondled, conveys him to Idalia's lofty groves, where soft mar-
joram, perfuming the air with flowers and fragrant shade,
clasps him round.

Now, in obedience to his instructions, Cupid went along,
and bore the royal presents to the Tyrians, pleased with
Achates for his guide. By the time he arrived, the queen
had placed herself on a golden couch, under a rich canopy,
and had taken her seat in the middle. Now father Æneas,
and now the Trojan youth, join the assembly, and couch themselves on the strawn purple. The attendants supply water

---

[24] Idalium, (Dalin,) a town of Cyprus, at the foot of Mount Idalur,
with a grove sacred to Venus, who was hence called Idalia.

for the hands, dispense the gifts of Ceres from baskets, and
furnish them with the smooth-shorn towels. Within are fifty
handmaids, whose task it was to prepare provisions in due
order, and do honour[56] to the household gods. A hundred
more, and as many servants of equal age, are employed to
load the boards with dishes, and place the cups. In like
manner the Tyrians, a numerous train, assembled in the joyful courts, invited to recline on the embroidered beds. They
view with wonder the presents of Æneas: nor with less
wonder do they view Iülus, the glowing aspect of the god,
his well-dissembled words, the mantle and veil figured with
leaves of the acanthus in saffron colours. Chiefly the unhappy queen, henceforth devoted to love's pestilential influence, cannot satisfy her feelings, and is inflamed with every
glance, and is equally moved by the boy and by his gifts. He
on Æneas' neck having hung with embraces, and having fully
gratified his fictitious father's ardent affections, makes for[57]
the queen. She clings to him with her eyes, her whole soul,
and sometimes fondles him in her lap, Dido not thinking what
a powerful god is settling on her, hapless one. Meanwhile
he, mindful of his Acidalian mother, begins insensibly to
efface the memory of Sichæus, and with a living flame tries
to prepossess her languid affections, and her heart, chilled by
long disuse.

Soon as the first banquet ended, and the viands were removed, they place large mixers, and crown the wines. A
bustling din arises through the hall, and they roll through
the ample courts the bounding voice. Down from the gold-
fretted ceilings[58] hang the flaming lamps, and torches over-
power the darkness of the night. Here the queen called for
a bowl, heavy with gems and gold, and with pure wine filled
it to the brim, which Belus,[59] and all her ancestors from Belus,
used; then, having enjoined silence through the palace, [she
thus began:] O Jove, (for by thee, it is said, the laws of hospitality were given,) grant this may be an auspicious day both

[56] "Adolere" = "augere," i. e. "to increase the power of the gods
who presided over the hearth, by due attention to culinary offices." See
Anthon. Davidson's note is founded upon an old mistake. B.

[57] i. e. "insidiatur." Servius. See Burm. on Petron. p. 490. B."

[58] So Sidon. Apoll. Ep. ix. 13, "laquearibus coruscis camerae in su-
pernis lychnus." B.

[59] Belus, a king of Tyre, from whom Dido was descended.

to the Tyrians and my Trojan guests, and may this day be
commemorated by our posterity. Bacchus, the giver of joy
and propitious Juno, be present here; and you, my Tyrians,
with good will, solemnize this meeting. She said, and on the
table poured an offering; and, after the libation, first gently
touched [the cup] with her lips, then gave it to Bitias [90] with
a challenge: he quickly drained the foaming bowl, and laved
himself with the brimming gold. After him the other lords
[drank]. Long-haired Iopas [next] tunes his golden lyre to
what the mighty Atlas taught. He sings of the wandering
moon, and the eclipses of the sun; whence the race of men
and beasts, whence showers and fiery meteors arise: of Arcturus, the rainy Hyades, and the two northern wains; why
winter suns make so much haste to set in the ocean, or what
retarding cause detains the slow [summer] nights. The Tyrians redouble their applauses, and the Trojans concur.

Meanwhile unhappy Dido, with varied converse, spun out
the night, and drank long draughts of love, questioning much
about Priam, much about Hector: now in what arms Aurora's
son had come; now what were the excellences of Diomede's
steeds; now how mighty was Achilles. Nay come, my guest,
she says; and from the first origin, relate to us the stratagems
of the Greeks, the adventures of your friends, and your own
wanderings; for now the seventh summer brings thee [to our
coasts], through wandering mazes roaming o'er every land
and sea.

BOOK II.

In the Second Book, Æneas, at the desire of Queen Dido, relates the fall of
Troy, and his escape, through the general conflagration, to Mount Ida. A
comparison with the poems of Petronius and Tryphiodorus will repay the
reader.

ALL became silent, and fixed their eyes upon him, eagerly attentive: then father Æneas thus from his lofty [1] couch began:

[90] Bitias and Iopas, African chiefs and suitors of Queen Dido.
[1] Anthon is wrong in supposing that "alto" has no positive meaning.
It was customary to pile up the cushions and draperies of the couches, in
order to form a favourable position for the speaker to be heard. Cf. Apol.
Met. ll. p. 27, "Aggeratis in tumulum stragulis, et effultis in cubitum,
aaberectisque in torum—infit Telephon." B.

Unutterable woes, O queen, you urge me to renew: to tell
how the Greeks overturned the power of Troy, and its deplorable realms; both what scenes of misery I myself beheld,
and those wherein I was a principal party. What Myrmidon,[2]
or Dolopian, or who of hardened Ulysses'[3] band, can, in the
very telling of such woes, refrain from tears? Besides, humid
night is hastening down the sky, and the setting stars invite
to sleep. But since you are so desirous of knowing our misfortunes, and briefly hearing the last effort of Troy, though my
soul shudders at the remembrance, and hath shrunk back with
grief, yet will I begin. The Grecian leaders, now disheartened
by the war, and baffled by the Fates, after a revolution of so
many years, [being assisted] by the divine skill of Pallas,
build a horse to the size of a mountain, and interweave its ribs
with planks of fir. This they pretend to be an offering, in
order to procure a safe return; which report spread. Hither
having secretly conveyed a select band, chosen by lot, they
shut them up into the dark sides, and fill its capacious caverns
and womb with armed soldiers. In sight [of Troy] lies Tenedos,[4] an island well known by fame, and flourishing while
Priam's kingdom stood: now only a bay, and a station unfaith-
ful for ships. Having made this island, they conceal themselves in that desolate shore. We imagined they were gone,
and that they had set sail for Mycenæ. In consequence of
[this], all Troy is released from its long distress: the gates
are thrown open; with joy we issue forth, and view the Grecian camp, the deserted plains, and the abandoned shore.
Here were the Dolopian bands, there stern Achilles had
pitched his tent; here were the ships drawn up, there they

---

[2] The Myrmidons and Dolopians inhabited Thessaly, and the borders
of Epirus.
[3] Ulysses, the son of Laertes and Anticlea, king of the islands of Ithaca
and Dulichium, and the husband of Penelope, was distinguished among
the Grecian chiefs for superior prudence and cunning. After the fall of
Troy, setting sail for his native country, he was exposed to incredible
dangers and misfortunes, and at last reached home, without a single companion, after an absence of twenty years. The adventures of Ulysses, in
his return to Ithaca from the Trojan war, are beautifully depicted by Homer, in the first twelve books of the Odyssey.
[4] Tenedos, a small but fertile island of the Ægean Sea, opposite Troy.
Here the Greeks concealed themselves, to make the Trojans believe that
they had abandoned the siege.

were wont to contend in array.[5] Some view with amazement that baleful offering of the virgin Minerva, and wonder at the stupendous bulk of the horse; and Thymœtes[6] first
advises that it be dragged within the walls and lodged in the
tower, whether with treacherous design, or that the destiny
of Troy now would have it so. But Capys, and all whose[7]
minds had wiser sentiments, strenuously urge either to throw
into the sea the treacherous snare and suspected oblation of the
Greeks; or by applying flames consume it to ashes; or to lay
open and ransack the recesses of the hollow womb. The fickle
populace is split into opposite inclinations. Upon this, Laocoon,[8] accompanied with a numerous troop, first before all, with
ardour hastens down from the top of the citadel; and while
yet a great way off, [cries out,] O wretched countrymen, what
desperate infatuation is this? Do you believe the enemy
gone? or think you any gifts of the Greeks can be free from
deceit? Is Ulysses thus known to you? Either the Greeks lie
concealed within this wood, or it is an engine framed against
our walls, to overlook our houses, and to come down upon our
city; or some mischievous design lurks beneath it. Trojans,
put no faith in this horse. Whatever it be, I dread the
Greeks, even when they bring gifts. Thus said, with valiant
strength he hurled his massy spear against the sides and belly
of the monster, where it swelled out with its jointed timbers;
the weapon stood quivering, and the womb being shaken, the
hollow caverns rang, and sent forth a groan. And had not the
decrees of heaven [been adverse], if our minds had not been
infatuated, he had prevailed on us to mutilate with the sword
this dark recess of the Greeks; and thou, Troy, should still
have stood,[9] and thou, lofty tower of Priam, now remained!

[5] "Acie." Some MSS. and Rufin. de Schem. lex. p. 33, have "acies."
Cf. Oudendorp on Frontin. ii. 2. B.

[6] Thymœtes, a Trojan prince, whose wife and son were put to death by
Priam; In revenge, he persuaded his countrymen to bring the wooden
horse into the city.

[7] On the ellipse of the pronoun, cf. Ondend. on Lucan, x. 347. B.

[8] Laocoon, a son of Priam and Hecuba, and priest of Apollo, who,
with his two sons, were destroyed by two enormous serpents, while he
was sacrificing to Neptune. The punishment was believed to be inflicted
upon him for his temerity in dissuading the Trojans to bring into the
city the fatal wooden horse, as also for his impiety in hurling a javelin
against its sides as it entered within the walls.

[9] But Wagner prefers "staret" It.

In the mean time, behold, Trojan shepherds, with loud acclamations, came dragging to the king a youth, whose hands were bound behind him ; who, to them a mere stranger, had voluntarily thrown himself in the way, to promote this same design, and open Troy to the Greeks ; a resolute soul, and prepared for either event, whether to execute his perfidious purpose, or submit to inevitable death. The Trojan youth pour tumultuously around from every quarter, from eagerness to see him, and they vie with one another in insulting the captive. Now learn the treachery of the Greeks, and from one crime take a specimen of the whole nation.[10] For as he stood among the gazing crowds perplexed, defenceless, and threw his eyes around the Trojan bands, Ah ! says he, what land, what seas can now receive me ? or to what further extremity can I, a forlorn wretch, be reduced, for whom there is no shelter any where among the Greeks ? and to complete my misery, the Trojans too, incensed against me, sue for satisfaction with my blood. By which mournful accents our affections at once were moved towards him, and all our resentment suppressed : we exhort him to say from what race he sprung, to declare what message he brings, what confidence we may repose in him, now that he is our prisoner. Then he, having at length laid aside fear, thus proceeds : I indeed, O king, will confess to you the whole truth, says he, be the event what will ; nor will I disown that I am of Grecian extraction : this I premise ; nor shall it be in the power of cruel fortune, though she has made Sinon [11] miserable, to make him also false and disingenuous. If accidentally, in the course of report, the name of Palamedes,[12] the descendant of Belus, and

[10] Literally, "from one of their tricks learn what they all are." B.

[11] Sinon, a crafty Greek, who prevailed on the Trojans to admit into the city the wooden horse, which was filled with armed Greeks.

[12] Palamedes was the son of Nauplius, king of Eubœa, descended from Belus, king of Africa, by his grandmother Amymone, the daughter of Danaus. The story here referred to, is briefly thus : When Ulysses, to be exempt from going to the Trojan war, under pretence of madness, was ploughing up the shore, and sowing it with salt, Palamedes laid down his son Telemachus in his way, and observing him to turn his plough aside, that he might not hurt the boy, by this stratagem discovered his madness to be counterfeit. For this Ulysses never could forgive him, and at last wrought his ruin, by accusing him of holding intelligence with the enemy : to support which charge he forged letters from Priam to Palamedes, which he pretended to have intercepted, and conveyed gold into his tent,

his illustrious renown, ever reached your ears (who, though innocent, the Greeks sent down to death, under a false accusation of treason, upon a villanous evidence, because he gave his opinion against the war; [but whom] now they mourn bereaved of the light); with him my poor father sent me in company to the war, from my earliest years, being his near relative. While he remained safe in the kingdom, and had weight in the counsels of the princes, I too bore some reputation and honour: [but] from the time that he, by the malice of the crafty Ulysses, (they are well-known truths I speak,) quitted the regions above, I distressed dragged out my life in obscurity and grief, and secretly repined at the fate of my innocent friend. Nor could I hold my peace, fool that I was, but vowed revenge, if fortune should any way give me the opportunity, if ever I should return victorious to my native Argos; and, by my words, I provoked bitter enmity. Hence arose the first symptom[13] of my misery; henceforth Ulysses was always terrifying me with new accusations; henceforth he began to spread ambiguous surmises among the vulgar, and, conscious [of his own guilt], sought the means of defence. Nor did he give over, till, by making Calchas[14] his tool—But why do I thus in vain unfold these disagreeables ? or why do I lose time ? If you place all the Greeks on the same footing, and your having heard that be enough [to undo me], this very instant strike the fatal blow: this the prince of Ithaca wishes, and the sons of Atreus would give large sums to purchase. Then, indeed, we grow impatient to know and to find out the causes, unacquainted with such consummate villany and Grecian artifice. He proceeds with palpitation, and speaks in the falsehood of his heart. After quitting Troy, the Greeks sought often to surmount the difficulties of their return, and, tired out with the length of the war, to be gone. And I wish

alleging it was the bribe given him for his treason. Upon this presumption Palamedes was condemned by a council of war, and stoned to death. Vide Ovid. Met. xiii. 56. That Palamedes was thus taken off through a stratagem of Ulysses, was a fact probably well known to the Trojans, though they might be ignorant of the colour for his being taken off. Sinon, therefore, to secure the attention and belief of his hearers, very artfully pretends that Palamedes was murdered, because he had dissuaded the Greeks from continuing the war against Troy.

[13] Literally, "plague-spot." B.

[14] Calchas, a famous soothsayer, who accompanied the Greeks to the Trojan war.

they had! Often did the rough tempest on the ocean bar
their flight, and the south wind deterred them in their setting
out. Especially when now this horse, framed of maple planks,
was reared, storms roared through all the regions of the air.
In perplexity we send Eurypylus[15] to consult the oracle of
Apollo; and from the sacred shrine he brings back this dismal response: Ye appeased the winds, O ye Greeks, with the
blood of a virgin slain,[16] when first you arrived on the Trojan
coast; by blood must your return be purchased, and atonement made by the life of a Greek. Which intimation no
sooner reached the ears of the multitude, than their minds
were stunned, and freezing horror thrilled through their very
bones; [anxious to know] whom the Fates destined, whom
Apollo demanded. Upon this Ulysses drags forth Calchas
the seer, with great bustle, into the midst of the crowd; im-
portunes him to say what that will of the gods may be; and,
by this time, many presaged[17] to me the cruel purpose of the
dissembler, and quietly foresaw the event. He, for twice five
days, is mute, and close shut up, refuses to give forth his declaration against any person, or doom him to death. At length,
with much ado, teased by the importunate clamours of Ulysses,
he breaks silence by concert, and destines me to the altar. All
assented, and were content to have what each dreaded for
himself, turned off to the ruin of one poor wretch. And now
the rueful day approached; for me the sacred rites were prepared, and the salted cakes, and fillets [to bind] about my temples. From death, I own, I made my escape, and broke my
bonds; and in a slimy fen all night I lurked obscure among
the weeds, till they should set sail, if by chance they should

---

[15] Eurypylus, also a soothsayer in the Grecian camp before Troy.

[16] When the Grecian army was arrived at Aulis, ready to sail over the
Hellespont to the siege of Troy, Diana, incensed against Agamemnon
for killing one of her favourite deer, withheld the wind. Calchas, having consulted the oracles, reported that Iphigenia, Agamemnon's daughter,
must fall a victim to appease Diana's wrath. Ulysses went and fetched
the innocent fair, from the tender embraces of her mother, under colour
of her being to be married to Achilles. She was brought to the altar,
and on the point of being sacrificed, when Calchas informed that Diana
was satisfied with this act of submission, and consented to have a deer
substituted in room of Iphigenia; but that she must be transported to
Tauris, there to serve the goddess for life in quality of priestess.

[17] Canebant. Cf. Westerhov. on Ter. Heut. ii. 3, 19, who remarks that
it is an augurial word. B.

do so. Nor have I now any hope of being blessed with the
sight of my ancient country, nor of my sweet children, and
my much-beloved sire; whom they, perhaps, will sue to
vengeance for my escape, and expiate this offence of mine
by the death of those unhappy innocents. But I conjure
you, by the powers above, by the gods who are conscious to
truth, by whatever remains of inviolable faith are any where
among mortals, compassionate such grievous afflictions, compassionate a soul suffering unworthy treatment.

At these tears we grant him his life, and pity him from our
hearts. Priam himself first gives orders that the manacles
and strait bonds be loosed from the man, then thus addresses
him in the language of a friend : Whoever you are, now henceforth forget the Greeks you have lost; ours you shall be : and
give me an ingenuous reply to these questions : To what
purpose raised they this stupendous bulk of a horse? who
was the contriver? or what do they intend? what was the
religious motive? or what warlike engine is it? he said. The
other, practised in fraud and Grecian artifice, lifted up to
heaven his hands, loosed from the bonds: To you, ye everlasting orbs of fire, he says, and your inviolable divinity; to
you, ye altars, and horrid swords, which I escaped; and ye
fillets of the gods, which I a victim wore; to you I appeal,
that I am free to violate all the sacred obligations I was under
to the Greeks; I am free to hold these men in abhorrence,
and to bring forth to light all their dark designs; nor am I
bound by any of the laws of my country. Only do thou, O
Troy, abide by thy promises, and, being preserved, preserve
thy faith; provided I disclose the truth, provided I make thee
large amends.

The whole hope of the Greeks, and their confidence in the
war begun, always depended on the aid of Pallas : but when
the sacrilegious Diomede, and Ulysses the contriver of wicked
designs, in their attempt to carry off by force from her holy
temple the fatal Palladium,[19] having slain the guards of her
high tower, seized her sacred image, and with bloody hands
dared to touch the virgin fillets of the goddess; from that day
the hope of the Greeks began to ebb, and, losing footing, to

[19] Palladium, a celebrated statue of Pallas, said to have fallen from
heaven upon Troy, and on the preservation of which depended the safety
of that city.

decline: their powers were weakened, the mind of the goddess alienated: nor did Tritonia [19] show these indications [of
her wrath] by dubious prodigies; for scarcely was the statue
set up in the camp, when bright flames flashed from her staring
eye-balls, and a briny sweat flowed over her limbs; and (wonderful to hear) she herself sprung thrice from the ground,
armed as she was, with her shield and quivering spear. Forthwith Calchas declares, that we must attempt the seas in flight,
and that Troy can never be razed by the Grecian sword, unless they repeat the omens at Argos, and carry back the goddess whom they had conveyed over the sea in their curved ships.
And now, that they have sailed for their native Mycenæ with
the wind, they are providing themselves with arms, and gods
to accompany them; and, having measured back the sea, they
will come upon you unexpected: so Calchas interprets the
omens. This figure, being warned, they reared in lieu of the
Palladium, in lieu of the violated goddess, in order to atone
for their direful crime. But Calchas commanded to build this
enormous mass, and raise it to the skies, that it might not be
admitted into the gates, or dragged into the city, nor protect
the people under their ancient religion. For [he declared
that] if your hands should violate this offering sacred to
Minerva, then signal ruin (which omen may the gods rather
turn on himself!) awaited Priam's empire and the Trojans.
But, if by your hands it mounted into the city, that Asia,
without further provocation given, would advance with a
formidable war to the very walls of Pelops, and our posterity
be doomed to the same fate. By such treachery and artifice
of perjured Sinon, the story was believed: and we, whom
neither Diomede, nor Larissæan [20] Achilles, nor [a siege of]
ten years, nor a thousand [21] ships, had subdued, were insnared
by guile and constrained tears. Here another greater scene,
and far more terrible, is presented to our wretched sight, and
disturbs our unexpecting breasts. Laocoon, ordained Neptune's priest by lot, was sacrificing a stately bullock at the

[19] Tritonia, a surname of Minerva, from Tritonis, a lake and river of
Africa, near which she had a temple.
[20] Larissæan, an epithet applied to Achilles, from Larissa, the capital
city of Thessaly.
[21] See the commentators on Æsch. Ag. 45. Virgil speaks in round
numbers, for the number of ships somewhat exceeded a thousand, but is
variously stated. B.

altars set apart for that solemnity; when, lo! from Tenedos
(I shudder at the relation) two serpents, with orbs immense,
bear along on the sea, and with equal motion shoot forward
to the shore; whose breasts erect amidst the waves, and
crests bedropped with blood, tower above the flood; their
other parts sweep the sea behind, and wind their spacious
backs in rolling spires. A loud noise is made by the briny
ocean foaming: and now they reached the shores, and, suffused with fire and blood as to their glaring eyes, with quivering tongues licked their hissing mouths. Half-dead with the
sight, we fly different ways. They, with resolute motion,
advance towards Laocoon; and first both serpents, with close
embraces, twine around the little bodies of his two sons,
and with their fangs mangle their wretched limbs. Next
they seize himself, as he is coming up with weapons to their
relief, and bind him fast in their mighty folds; and now
grasping him twice about the middle, twice winding their
scaly backs around his neck, they overtop him by the head
and lofty neck. He strains at once with his hands to tear
asunder their knotted spires, while his fillets are stained with
gore and black poison: at the same time he raises hideous
shrieks to heaven; such bellowing, as when a bull has fled
wounded from the altar, and has eluded with his neck the
missing axe. Meanwhile, the two serpents glide off to the
high temple, and repair to the fane of stern Tritonia, and are
sheltered under the feet of the goddess, and the orb of her
buckler. Then, indeed, new terror diffuses itself through the
quaking hearts of all; and they pronounce Laocoon to have
deservedly suffered for his crime, in having violated the sacred
wood with his pointed weapon, and hurled his profane spear
against its sides. They urge with general voice to convey
the statue to its proper seat, and implore the favour of the
goddess. We make a breach in the walls, and lay open the
bulwarks of the city. All keenly ply the work; and under
the feet apply smooth-rolling wheels; stretch hempen ropes
from the neck. The fatal machine passes over[77] our walls,
pregnant with arms; boys and unmarried virgins accompany

[77] As it were "scales" the walls. Thus Ennius in Macr. Sat. vi. 2,
"Nam maximo saltu superavit gravidus armatis equus." Cf. Stat. Silv.
i. 1, 11 sqq. I need scarcely remark that the whole description has been
copied by Tryphiodorus. B.

it with sacred hymns, and are glad to touch the rope with
their hand. It advances, and with menacing aspect slides
into the heart of the city. O country, O Ilium, the habitation
of gods, and ye walls of Troy by war renowned! Four times
it stopped in the very threshold of the gate, and four times
the arms resounded in its womb: yet we, heedless, and blind
with frantic zeal, urge on, and plant the baneful monster in
the sacred citadel. Then, too, Cassandra,[23] by the inspiration
of the god, opens her lips to our approaching doom, never believed by the Trojans. Unhappy we, to whom that day was
to be the last, adorn the temples of the gods throughout the
city with festive boughs. Meanwhile, the heavens change,[24]
and night advances rapidly from the ocean, wrapping in her
extended shade both earth and heaven, and the wiles of the
Myrmidons. The Trojans, dispersed about the walls, were
hushed: deep Sleep fast binds them weary in his embraces.
And now the Grecian host, in their equipped vessels, set out
from Tenedos, making towards the well-known shore, by the
friendly silence of the quiet moonshine, as soon as the royal
[galley] stern had exhibited the signal fire; and Sinon, preserved by the will of the adverse gods, in a stolen hour unlocks the wooden prison to the Greeks shut up in its womb:
the horse, from his expanded caverns, pours them forth to the
open air; and with joy issue from the hollow wood Thessan-
drus and Sthenelus the chiefs, and dire Ulysses, sliding down
by a suspended rope, with Athamas and Thoas, Neoptolemus,
the grandson of Peleus, and Machaon who led the way, with
Menelaus, and Epeus the very contriver of the trick. They
assault the city buried in sleep and wine. The sentinels are
beaten down; and with opened gates they receive all their
friends, and join the conscious bands. It was the time when
the first sleep invades languid mortals, and steals upon them,
by the gift of the gods, most sweet. In my sleep, lo! Hector,
extremely sad, seemed to stand before my eyes, and to shed
floods of tears; dragged, as formerly by the chariot, and black

[23] Cassandra, the daughter of Priam and Hecuba. According to the
poets, she had the gift of prophecy, while none believed her predictions.
[24] This is according to the astronomy of the ancients, who supposed
the heavens revolved round the earth, which remained stationary. On
the time in which Troy was taken, cf. Petron. 69, p. 435. Tryph. 452
sqq. B.

with gory dust, and his swollen feet bored through with
thongs. Ah me! in what piteous plight he was! how changed
from that Hector who returned clad in the armour of Achilles,
or darting Phrygian flames against the ships of Greece!
wearing a grisly beard, hair clotted with blood, and those
many wounds which he had received under his native walls.
I, methought, in tears addressed the hero first, and poured
forth these mournful accents: O light[25] of Troy, O Trojans'
firmest hope! what tedious causes have detained thee so
long? Whence comest thou, my long-looked-for Hector?
With what joy we behold thee after the many deaths of thy
friends, after the various disasters of men and city! What
unworthy cause has deformed the serenity of thy looks? or
why do I behold these wounds? He [said] not a word; nor
regards me, questioning of what nought availed; but heavily,
from the bottom of his heart, drawing a groan! Ah! fly,
thou goddess-born, he says, and snatch thyself from these
flames: the enemy is in possession of the walls; Troy falls
from its towering tops. To Priam, to my country, all duty
has been done. Could those walls have been saved by the
hand, by this same hand had they been saved. Troy commends to thee her sacred things, her gods: these take companions of thy fate; for these go in quest of a city, which, in
process of time, you shall erect, larger of size, after a wandering voyage. He said, and with his own hands brings forth,
from the inner temple, the fillets, the powerful Vesta, and the
fire which always burned.
Meanwhile the city is filled with mingled scenes of woe;
and though my father Anchises' house stood retired, and enclosed with trees, louder and louder the sounds rise on the ear,
and the horrid din of arms assails. I start from sleep, and,
by hasty steps, gain the highest battlement of the palace, and
stand with erect ears: as when a flame is driven by the furious south winds on standing corn; or as a torrent impetuously
bursting in a mountain-flood desolates the fields, desolates the
rich crops of corn, and the labours of the ox, and drags woods
headlong down: the unwary shepherd, struck with the sound

[25] A beautiful imitation of Ennius, as quoted by Macrob. Sat. vi. 2,
"O lux Trojæ, germane Hector. Quid ita cum tuo lacerato corpore
miser? Aut qui te sic respectantibus Tractavere nobis?" So Quintus
Calaber i. 12, calls Hector ἧμαρ πόλιων. B

from the top of a high rock, stands amazed. Then, indeed,
the truth is confirmed, and the treachery of the Greeks disclosed. Now Deiphobus'[26] spacious house tumbles down,
overpowered by the conflagration; now, next to him, Ucalegon[27] blazes: the straits of Sigæum[28] shine far and wide with
the flames. The shout of men and clangour of trumpets arise.
My arms I snatch in mad haste: nor is there in arms enough
of reason: but all my soul burns to collect a troop for the
war, and rush into the citadel with my fellows: fury and rage
hurry on my mind, and it occurs to me how glorious it is to
die in arms. Lo! then Pantheus, escaped from the sword of
the Greeks, Pantheus, the son of Othrys, priest of the citadel
and of Apollo, is hurrying away[29] with him the holy utensils,
the conquered gods, and his little grandchild, and makes for
the shore in distraction. How is it, Pantheus, with the main
affair? what fortress do we seize? I had scarcely spoken,
when, with a groan, he thus replies: Our last day is come,
and the inevitable doom of Troy: we are Trojans no more:
adieu to Ilium, and the high renown of Teucer's race: fierce
Jupiter hath transferred all to Argos: the Greeks bear rule
in the burning city. The towering horse, planted in the
midst of our streets, pours forth armed troops; and Sinon victorious, with insolent triumph scatters the flames. Others are
pressing at our wide-opened[30] gates, as many thousands as
ever came from populous Micenæ: others with arms have
blocked up the lanes to oppose our passage; the edged sword,
with glittering point, stands unsheathed, ready for dealing
death: hardly the foremost wardens of the gates make an
effort to fight, and resist in the blind encounter. By these
words of Pantheus, and by the impulse of the gods, I hurry

[26] Deiphobus, a son of Priam and Hecuba, eminently distinguished
himself in the Trojan war, and after the death of his brother Paris, married Helen.
[27] Ucalegon, a Trojan chief, praised for the soundness of his counsels,
and his good intentions, though accused by some of betraying his country
to the Greeks.
[28] Sigæum, a famous promontory of Troas, at the entrance of the Hellespont, where the Scamander fell into the sea. Here was the tomb of
Achilles, and near it were fought many of the battles between the Greeks
and the Trojans.
[29] But "trahere" is properly used of little children, who follow with
difficulty. Curt. iii. 13, 12. B.
[30] i. e. "having both valves open." B.

away into flames and arms; whither the grim Fury, whither the din and shrieks that rend the skies, urge me on. Ripheus,[21] and Iphitus mighty in arms, join me; Hypanis and Dymas coming up with us by the light of the moon, and closely adhere[22] to my side; and also young Corœbus,[23] Mygdon's son, who at that time had chanced to come to Troy, inflamed with a mad passion for Cassandra, and [in prospect, his] son-in-law, brought assistance to Priam and the Trojans. Ill-fated youth, who heeded not the admonitions of his raving spouse! Whom, close united, soon as I saw resolute to engage, to animate them the more I thus begin: " Youths, souls magnanimous in vain! if it is your determined purpose to follow me in this last attempt, you see what is the situation of our affairs. All the gods, by whom this empire stood, have deserted their shrines and altars abandoned [to the enemy]: you come to the relief of the city in flames: let us meet death, and rush[24] into the thickest of our armed foes. The only safety for the vanquished is to throw away all hopes of safety." Thus the courage of each youth is kindled into fury. Then, like ravenous wolves[25] in a gloomy fog, whom the fell rage of hunger hath driven forth, blind to danger, and whose whelps left behind long for their return with thirsting jaws; through arms, through enemies, we march up to imminent death, and advance through the middle of the city: sable Night hovers around us with her hollow shade. Who can describe in words the havoc, who the deaths of that night? or who can furnish tears equal to the disasters? Our ancient city, having borne sway for many years, falls to the ground: great numbers of sluggish carcasses are

[21] Ripheus was distinguished for his love of justice; having joined Æneas the night that Troy was burnt, he was, after a brave resistance, slain by the Greeks. Dymas: this brave Trojan also joined Æneas; but, being dressed in Grecian armour, was, through mistake, killed by his countrymen.

[22] i. e. "implicare." Nonius L. a. v. "agglomerare." B.

[23] Corœbus, a Phrygian, son of Mygdon, the brother of Hecuba. He assisted Priam in the Trojan war, with the hopes of being rewarded with the hand of Cassandra, who advised him in vain to retire from the war. He was slain by Peneleus.

[24] On the supposition that the gods deserted a captured city, cf. Æsch. Sept. c. Th. 204, ἀλλ' οὖν θεοὺς τοὺς τῆς ἁλούσης, πόλεος ἐκλείπειν λόγος. See the notes, and Northmore on Tryphiod. 508. B.

[25] ὕστερον πρότερον, as Servius rightly remarks. So in Eur. Hec. 50, τοῦτόν ποτ' ἴσιον κάρφορον ζώνης ὕπο. B.

strewn up and down, both in the streets, in the houses, and the
sacred thresholds of the gods. Nor do the Trojans alone pay
the penalty with their blood: the vanquished too at times resume courage in their hearts, and the victorious Grecians fall:
every where is cruel sorrow, every where terror and death in
thousand shapes.[86] Androgeos first comes up with us, accompanied by a numerous band of Greeks, unadvisedly imagining
that we were confederate troops; and he introduces himself to
us with this friendly address: Haste, men; what so tardy
sloth detains you? Others tear and plunder the blazing towers
of Troy: are you but just come from your lofty ships? He
said, and instantly perceived (for we returned him no very
trusty answer) that he had stumbled[87] into the midst of foes.
He was confounded, and with his words recalled his step. As
one who, in his walk, hath trodden upon a snake unseen in the
rough thorns, and in fearful haste hath started back from him,
while he is collecting all his rage, and swelling his azure
crest; just so Androgeos, terrified at the sight [of us], began
to withdraw. We rush in, and pour around with arms close
joined, and knock them down here and there, strangers as
they were to the place, and possessed with fear: fortune
smiles upon our first enterprise. Upon this Corœbus, exulting with success and courage, cried out, My fellows, where
fortune thus early points out our way to safety, and where
she shows herself propitious, let us follow. Let us exchange
shields, and fit to ourselves the badges of the Greeks: whether
stratagem or valour, who questions in an enemy? they themselves will supply us with arms. This said, he puts on the
crested helmet of Androgeos, and the rich ornament of his
shield, and buckles to his side a Grecian sword. The same
does Rhipheus, the same does Dymas too, and all the youth
well pleased: each arms himself with the recent spoils. We
march on, mingling with the Greeks, but not with heaven on
our side; and in many a skirmish we engage during the dark
night; many of the Greeks we send down to Hades. Some
fly to the ships, and hasten to the trusty shore; some, through
dishonest fear, scale once more the bulky horse, and lurk

---

[86] Thucyd. i. 81, πᾶσά τι ἰδία ξαριστῇ θανάτου. Cf. Tryphiodor.
573, sqq. B.

[87] For the construction compare Muret. on Catull. iv. 2, "Ait fuisse
navium celerrimus." Soph. Ant. 87. Trach. 5.

within the well-known womb. Alas! on nothing ought man
to presume, while the gods are against him! Lo! Cassandra,
Priam's virgin daughter, with her hair dishevelled, was
dragged along from the temple and shrine of Minerva, raising
to heaven her glaring eyes in vain; her eyes—for cords
bound her tender hands. Corœbus, in the madness of his
soul, could not bear this spectacle, and, resolved to perish,
threw himself into the midst of the band. We all follow, and
rush upon them in close array. Upon this we are first overpowered with the darts of our friends from the high summit
of the temple, and a most piteous slaughter ensues, through
the appearance of our arms, and the disguise of our Grecian
crests. Next the Greeks, through anguish and rage for the
rescue of the virgin, fall upon us in troops from every quarter;
Ajax, most fierce, both the sons of Atreus, and the whole
band of the Dolopes: as, at times, in a burst hurricane, opposite winds encounter, the west and south, and Eurus, proud
of his eastern steeds; the woods creak, foaming Nereus rages
with his trident, and rouses the seas from the lowest bottom.
They, too, whom, through the shades, in the dusky night, we
by stratagem had routed, and driven all over the city, make
their appearance; they are the first who discover our shield ·
and counterfeit arms, and mark our voices in sound discordant
with their own. In a moment we are overpowered by
numbers; and first Corœbus sinks in death by the hand of
Peneleus, at the altar of the warrior-goddess: Ripheus too
falls, the most just among the Trojans, and of the strictest
integrity: but to the gods it seemed otherwise.[28] Hypanis and
Dymas die by the cruel darts of their own friends, nor did thy
signal piety, nor the fillets of Apollo, save thee, Pantheus, in
thy dying hour. Ye ashes of Troy, ye expiring flames of my
country! witness, that in your fall I shunned neither darts nor
any deadly chances[29] of the Greeks; and, had it been fated that
I should fall, I deserved it by my hand. Thence we are forced
away, Iphitus, Pelias, and myself (of whom Iphitus was
now unwieldy through age, and Pelias disabled by a wound
from Ulysses,) forthwith to Priam's palace called by the
outcries. Here, indeed, [we beheld] a dreadful fight, as

[28] i. e. "contra," as explained by Donatus on Ter. Andr. Prol. 4.
There is an ellipse of, "such should have been his fate, but," &c. B.
[29] i. e. "pœnas," says Burm. on Propert. i. 13, 10. B.

though this had been the only seat of the war, as though none had been dying in all the city besides; with such ungoverned fury we see Mars raging and the Greeks rushing forward to the palace, and the gates besieged by an advancing testudo. Scaling ladders are fixed against the walls, and by their steps they mount to the very door-posts, and protecting themselves by their left arms, oppose their bucklers to the darts, [while] with their right hands they grasp the battlements. On the other hand, the Trojans tear down the turrets and roofs of their houses; with these weapons, since they see the extremity, they seek to defend themselves now in their last death-struggle, and tumble down the gilded rafters, those stately ornaments of their ancestors : others with drawn swords beset the gates below ; these they guard in a firm, compact body. Our ardour is restored to relieve the royal palace, support our friends with aid, and impart fresh strength to the vanquished. There was a passage, a secret entry, a free communication between the palaces of Priam, a neglected postern-gate, by which unfortunate Andromache,[40] while the kingdom stood, was often wont to resort to her parents-in-law without retinue, and to lead the boy Astyanax to his grand-sire. I mount up to the roof of the highest battlement, whence the distressed Trojans were hurling unavailing darts. With our swords assailing all around a turret, situated on a precipice, and shooting up its towering top to the stars, (whence we were wont to survey all Troy, the fleet of Greece, and all the Grecian camp,) where the topmost story made the joints more apt to give way,[41] we tear it from its deep foundation, and push it on [our foes]. Suddenly tumbling down, it brings thundering desolation with it, and falls with wide havoc on the Grecian troops. But others succeed: meanwhile, neither stones, nor any sort of missile weapons, cease to fly. Just before the vestibule, and at the outer gate, Pyrrhus exults, glittering in arms and gleamy brass; as when a snake [comes forth] to light, having fed on noxious herbs, whom, bloated [with poison], the frozen winter hid under the earth, now renewed, and sleek with youth, after casting his skin, with breast erect he rolls up his slippery back, reared to the sun, and brandishes a

---

[40] Andromache, the daughter of Ætion, king of Thebes, in Mysia, and the wife of Hector, by whom she had Astyanax.

[41] It must be remembered that this tower was of wood. See Anthon.

three-forked tongue in his mouth. At the same time bulky
Periphas and Automedon, charioteer to Achilles, [now Pyrrhus'] armour-bearer; at the same all the youth from Scyros
advance to the wall, and toss brands to the roof. Pyrrhus
himself in the front, snatching up a battle-axe, beats through
the stubborn gates, and labours to tear the brazen posts from
the hinges; and now, having hewn away the bars, he dug
through the firm boards, and made a large, wide-mouthed
breach. The palace within is exposed to view, and the long
galleries are discovered: the sacred recesses of Priam and the
ancient kings are exposed to view; and they see armed men
standing at the gate.

As for the inner palace, it is filled with mingled groans
and doleful uproar, and the hollow rooms all throughout howl
with female yells: their shrieks strike the golden stars. Then
the trembling matrons roam through the spacious halls, and
in embraces hug the door-posts, and cling to them with their
lips.[42] Pyrrhus[43] presses on with all his father's violence:
nor bolts, nor guards themselves, are able to sustain. The gate,
by repeated battering blows, gives way, and the door-posts,
torn from their hinges, tumble to the ground. The Greeks
make their way by force, burst a passage, and, being admitted,
butcher the first they meet, and fill the places all about with
their troops. Not with such fury a river pours on the fields
its heavy torrent, and sweeps away herds with their stalls over
all the plains, when foaming it has burst away from its broken
banks, and borne down opposing mounds with its whirling
current. I myself have beheld Neoptolemus raving with bloody
rage, and the two sons of Atreus at the gate: I have beheld
Hecuba, and her hundred daughters-in-law, and Priam at the
altar, defiling with his blood the fires which himself had consecrated.[44] Those fifty bed-chambers, so great hopes of descendants, those doors, that proudly shone with barbaric gold
and spoils, were levelled with the ground: where the flames
relent, the Greeks take place.

Perhaps, too, you are curious to hear what was Priam's

[42] Cf. Soph. Phil. 535, Ιωμιν, ὦ ταῖ, προσκύσαντι -ἡν ἴσω Ἄοικον
ἀσοίκησιν. B.
[43] Pyrrhus, also called Neoptolemus, was the son of Achilles and Dei-
damia daughter of King Lycomedes. His cruelty exceeded even that of
his father.
[44] Ennius in Cicer. T. Q. lii. in Scriver. Coll. p. 19, "Haec omnia vid.
hußammarl: Priamo vi vitam evitari. Jovis aram sanguine turpari." B.

fate. As soon as he beheld the catastrophe of the taken city,
and his palace gates broken down, and the enemy planted in
the middle of his private apartments, the aged monarch,
with unavailing aim, buckles on his shoulders (trembling with
years) arms long disused, girds himself with his useless sword,
and rushes into the thickest of the foes, resolute on death. In
the centre of the palace,[44] and under the bare canopy of heaven, stood a large altar, and an aged laurel near it, overhang-
ing the altar, and encircling the household gods with its
shade. Here Hecuba and her daughters (like pigeons flying
precipitantly from a blackening tempest) crowded together,
and embracing the shrines of the gods, vainly sat round the
altars. But as soon as she saw Priam clad in youthful arms,
unhappy spouse, she cries, What dire purpose has prompted
thee to brace on these arms ? or whither art thou hurrying ?
The present conjuncture hath no need of such aid, nor such
defence : though even my Hector himself were here [it would
not avail]. Hither repair, now that all hope is lost; this
altar will protect us all, or here you [and we] shall die together. Having thus said, she took the old man to her embraces, and placed him on the sacred seat. But lo! Polites,
one of Priam's sons, who had escaped from the sword of
Pyrrhus, through darts, through foes, flies along the long
galleries, and wounded traverses the waste halls. Pyrrhus,
all on fire, pursues him with the hostile weapon, is just
grasping him with his hand, and presses on him with the
spear. Soon as he at length got into the sight and presence
of his parents, he dropped down, and poured out his life with
a stream of blood. Upon this, Priam, though now held in the
very midst of death, yet did not forbear, nor spared his tongue
and passion: But[46] may the gods, he cries, if there be any
justice in heaven to regard such events, give ample retribu-
tion and due reward for this wickedness, for these thy audacious crimes, to thee who hast made me to witness[47] the death
of my own son, and defiled a father's eyes with the sight of

[44] The *impluvium* is meant, Priam's palace forming a square court.
Cf. Athen. v. 3, Ὁμηρὸς δὲ τὴν αὐλὴν ἀεὶ τάττει ἐπὶ τῶν ὑπαίθρων τόπων,
ἔνθα ἦν ὁ τοῦ Ἑρκείου Ζηνὸς βωμός. B.
[46] For this use of "at" in reproaches, cf. Ovid. Her. xii. 1, "At ubi
Colchorum (memini) regina vacavi." Catull. iii. 13, "At vobis male sit,
malæ tenebræ." B.
[47] "Cernere fecisti" is a Lucretian form of expression. Cf. Lucr. iii.
101; "faciat vivere," 302, vi. 261. B.

blood: yet he from whom you falsely claim your birth, even Achilles, was not thus barbarous to Priam,[48] though his enemy, but paid some reverence to the laws of nations, and a suppliant's right, restored my Hector's lifeless corpse to be buried, and sent me back into my kingdom. Thus spoke the old man, and, without any force, threw a feeble dart: which was instantly repelled by the hoarse brass, and hung on the highest boss of the buckler without any execution. To whom Pyrrhus replies, These tidings then yourself shall bear, and go with the message to my father, the son of Peleus: forget not to inform him of my cruel deeds, and of his degenerate son Neoptolemus: now die. With these words he dragged him to the very altar, trembling and sliding in the streaming gore of his son: and with his left hand grasped his twisted hair, and with his right unsheathed his glittering sword, and plunged it into his side up to the hilt. Such was the end of Priam's fate: this was the final doom allotted to him, having before his eyes Troy consumed, and its towers laid in ruins; once the proud monarch over so many nations and countries of Asia: now his mighty trunk lies extended on the shore, the head torn from the shoulders, and a nameless corpse.[49] Then, and not till then, fierce horror assailed me round: I stood aghast; the image of my dear father arose to my mind, when I saw the king, of equal age, breathing out his soul by a cruel wound; Creüsa,[50] forsaken, came into mind, my rifled house, and the fate of the little Iülus. I look about, and survey what troops were to stand by me. All had left me through despair, and flung their fainting bodies to the ground, or gave them to the flames. And thus now I remained all alone, when I espy Helen keeping watch in the temple of Vesta, and silently lurking in a secret corner: the bright flames give me light as I am roving on, and throwing my eyes around on every object. She, the common Fury of Troy and her country, dreading the Trojans, her deadly foes, upon account of their ruined country, and the vengeance of the Greeks, with

---

[48] "In hosts" is for "erga hostem." See Broukh. on Tibull. lii. 6, 19. B.

[49] See my note on Æsch. Choeph. 437. B.

[50] Creüsa, daughter of Priam, and the wife of Æneas, who was lost in the streets of Troy, when Æneas made his escape with his father Anchises and his son Ascanius.

L

the fierce resentment of her deserted lord, had hidden herself, and was sitting near the altars, an odious sight. Flames were kindled in my soul: rage possessed me to avenge my falling country, and take the vengeance her guilt deserved. Shall she then with impunity behold Sparta and her country Mycenæ, and go off a queen, after she has gained her triumph? shall she see her marriage-bed, her home, her fathers, her sons, accompanied with a retinue of Trojan dames and Phrygian women her slaves? shall Priam have fallen by the sword, shall Troy have burnt with the flame, shall the Trojan shore so often be drenched in blood? It must not be so: for though there be no memorable name in punishing a woman, nor any honour in such a victory, yet shall I be applauded for having extinguished a wicked wretch, and for inflicting on her the punishment she deserves: besides, it will be a pleasure to gratify my desire of burning revenge, and to give satisfaction to the ashes of my friends. Thus was I rapidly reflecting, and furiously agitated in my soul, when my benign mother presented herself to my view with such brightness as I had never seen before, and amidst the night shone forth in pure light, displaying all the goddess, with such dignity, such stature, as she is wont to show to the immortals: she restrained me fast held by the right hand, and besides, let fall these words from her rosy lips: My son, what high provocation kindles thy ungoverned rage? why art thou raving? or whither art thy regards to me fled? Will you not first see in what situation you have left your father Anchises, encumbered with age? whether your spouse Creüsa be in life, and the boy Ascanius, around whom the Grecian troops from every quarter reel? and, do not my care oppose, the flames will have already carried off, or the cruel sword imbibed their blood. Not the features of Lacedæmonian Helen, odious in your eyes, nor Paris blamed; but the gods, the unrelenting gods, overthrow this powerful realm, and level the towering tops of Troy with the ground. Turn your eyes; for I will dissipate every cloud which now, intercepting the view, bedims your mortal sight, and spreads a humid veil of mist around you: fear not you the commands of a parent, nor refuse to obey her orders. Here, where you see scattered ruins, and stones torn from stones, and smoke in waves ascending with mingled dust, Neptune shakes the walls and foundations loosened by his mighty trident, and overturns the whole city from its basis. Here Juno, extremely fierce, is posted in the front to guard the Scæan [51] gate, and, girt with the sword, with furious summons calls from the ships her social band. Tritonian Pallas (see!) hath now planted herself on a lofty turret, refulgent in a cloud, and with her Gorgon [52] terrible. The Sire himself supplies the Greeks with courage and strength for victory: himself stirs up the gods against the arms of Troy. Speed thy flight, my son, and put a period to thy toils. In every danger I will stand by you, and safe set you down in your father's palace. She said, and hid herself in the thick shades of night. Direful forms appear, and the mighty powers of the gods, adverse to Troy. Then, indeed, all Ilium seemed to me at once to sink in the flames, and Troy, built by Neptune, to be overturned from its lowest foundation: even as when with emulous keenness the swains labour to fell an ash that long hath stood on a high mountain, hewing it about with iron and many an axe, ever and anon it threatens, and waving its locks,[53] nods with its shaken top, till gradually by wounds subdued, it hath groaned its last, and torn from the ridge of the mountain, draws along with it ruin. Down I come, and under the conduct of the god, clear my way amidst flames and foes: the darts give place, and the flames retire. And now, when arrived at the gates of my paternal seat and ancient house, my father, whom I was desirous first to remove to the high mountains, and whom I first sought, obstinately refuses to prolong his life after the ruin of Troy, and to suffer exile. You, says he, who are full of youthful blood, and whose powers

[51] Scæan gate, one of the gates of Troy, where the tomb of Laomedon was seen.

[52] Gorgon, Medusa, whose head Perseus cut off and presented to Minerva, who placed it on her ægis, with which she turned into stone all such as fixed their eyes upon it. The Gorgons were the three daughters of Phorcys and Ceto; their hair, according to the ancients, was entwined with serpents. Medusa was the only one of them who was subject to mortality.

[53] Comam—nutat. Virgil, considering a tree in analogy to the human body, calls the extended boughs its arms, brachia, Georg. ii. 296, 368, and here its leaves, comam, hair, or locks. So also Milton, Paradise Lost, i. 1065,

———— while the winds
Blow moist and keen, shattering the graceful locks
Of those fair spreading trees——————

remain firm in all their strength, do you attempt your flight.
As for me, had the powers of heaven designed I should prolong my life, they had preserved to me this house: enough
, it is, and more than enough, that I have seen one catastrophe,
and outlived the taking of this city. Thus, oh leave me thus
with the last farewell to my body laid in its dying posture.
With this hand will I find death myself. The enemy will
pity me, and lust for my spoils. Trivial is the loss of sepulture. I have long since been lingering out a length of
years, hated by the gods, and useless from the time when the
father of gods, and sovereign of men, blasted me with the
winds of his thunder, and struck me with lightning.

Such purpose declaring, he persisted, and remained un-
alterable. On the other hand, I, my wife Creüsa, Ascanius,
and the whole family, bursting forth into tears, [besought] my
father not to involve all with himself, nor hasten our impending fate. He still refuses, and perseveres in his purpose, and
in the same settled position. Once more I fly to my arms,
and, in extremity of distress, long for death: for what expedient had I left, or what chance of hope? Could you hope, sire,
that I could stir one foot while you were left behind? could
such impiety drop from a parent's lips ? If it is the will of
the gods that nothing of this great city be preserved ; if this
be your settled purpose, and you will even involve yourself
and yours in the wreck of Troy ; the way lies open to that
death of which you are so fond. Forthwith Pyrrhus, [reck-
ing] from the effusion of Priam's blood, will be here, who
kills the son before the father's eyes, and then the father at
the altar. Was it for this, my benign mother, you saved me
through darts, through flames, to see the enemy in the midst
of these recesses, and to see Ascanius, my father, and Creüsa
by his side, butchered in one another's blood ? Arms, my
men, bring arms ; this day, which is our last, calls upon us,
vanquished as we are. Give me back to the Greeks : let me
visit once more the fight renewed : never shall we all die unrevenged this day.[64]

Thus I again gird on my sword : and I thrust my left hand
into my buckler, bracing it fitly on, and rushed out of the
palace. But lo ! my wife clung to me in the threshold, grasp-

[64] Donatus quotes this line to illustrate the threatening use of " hodie,"
on Ter. Andr. i. 2, 25; ii. 4, 7, &c. So Plaut. Curc. v. 3, 11. B.

ing my feet, and held out to his father the little Iülus : If,
[says she,] you go with a resolution to perish, snatch us with
you to share all : but if, from experience, you repose confidence in those arms you have assumed, let this house have
your first protection : To whom are you abandoning the tender Iülus, your sire, and me once called your wife ? Thus
loudly expostulating, she filled the whole palace with her
groans, when a sudden and wondrous prodigy arises : for amid
the embraces and parting words of his mourning parents, lo !
the fluttering tuft from the top of Iülus' head is seen to emit
light, and with gentle touch the lambent flame glides harmless
along his hair, and feeds around his temples. We, quaking,
trembled for fear, brush the blazing locks, and quench the
holy fire with fountain-water.   But father Anchises[55] joyful
raised his eyes to the stars, and stretched his hands to heaven
with his voice; Almighty Jove, if thou art moved with any
supplications, vouchsafe to regard us; we ask no more : and
O sire, if by our piety we deserve it, grant us then thy aid,
and ratify these omens.   Scarcely had my aged sire thus
said, when, with a sudden peal, it thundered on the left, and a
star, that fell from the skies, drawing a fiery train, shot
through the shade with a profusion of light.   We could see
it, gliding over the high tops of the palace, lose itself in the
woods of Mount Ida, full in our view, and marking out the
way : then all along its course an indented path shines, and
all the place, a great way round, smokes with sulphureous
steams.   And now my father, overcome, raises himself to
heaven, addresses the gods, and pays adoration to the holy star :
Now, now is no delay : I am all submission, and where you
lead the way I am with you.   Ye gods of my fathers, save
our family, save my grandson.   From you this omen came,
and Troy is at your disposal.   Now, son, I resign myself indeed, nor refuse to accompany you in your expedition. He said,
and now throughout the city the flames are more distinctly
heard, and the conflagration rolls the torrents of fire nearer.
Come then, dearest father, place yourself on my neck ; with
these shoulders will I support you, nor shall that burden op-
press me. However things fall out, we both shall share either

---

[55] Anchises, the son of Capys, by Themis, daughter of Ilus. His son
Æneas saved his life by carrying him on his shoulders through the flames,
when Troy was on fire.

one common danger or one preservation : let the boy Iülus be
my companion, and my wife may trace my steps at some distance. Ye servants, heedfully attend to what I say. In your
way from the city is a rising ground, and an ancient temple
of deserted Ceres;[56] and near it an aged cypress, preserved
for many years by the religious veneration of our forefathers.
To this one sent by several ways we will repair. Do you,
father, take in thy hand the sacred symbols, and the gods of
our country. For me, just come from war, from so fierce and
recent bloodshed, to touch them would be profanation, till I
have purified myself in the living stream. This said, I spread
a garment and a tawny. lion's hide over my broad shoulders
and submissive neck ; and stoop to the burthen : little Iülus
is linked in my right hand, and trips after his father with
unequal steps: my spouse comes up behind. We haste away
through the gloomy paths: and I, whom lately no showers of
darts could move, nor Greeks enclosing me in a hostile band,
am now terrified with every breath of wind;[57] every sound
alarms me anxious, and equally in dread for my companion
and my burthen. By this time I approached the gates, and
thought I had overpassed all the way, when suddenly a thick
sound of feet seems to invade my ears just at hand ; and my
father, stretching his eyes through the gloom, calls aloud,
Fly, fly, my son, they are upon you ; I see the burnished
shields and glittering brass. Here, in my consternation, some
unfriendly deity or other confounded and bereaved me of my
reason ; for while in my journey I trace the by-paths, and
forsake the known beaten tracks, alas ! I know not whether
my wife Creüsa was snatched from wretched me by cruel fate,
or lost her way, or through fatigue stopped short; nor did
these eyes ever see her more. Nor did I observe that she
was lost, or reflect with myself, till we were come to the rising
ground, and the sacred seat of ancient Ceres: here, at length,
when all were convened, she alone was wanting, and gave
disappointment to all our retinue, especially to her son and
husband. Whom did I frantic not accuse, of gods or men ?
or of what more cruel scene was I a spectator in all the
desolation of the city ? To my friends I commend Ascanius,

---

[56] I. e. neglected during the war. See Anthon. B.
[57] Silius vi. 58, " Sonus omnis et aura Exterrent, pennaque levi com.
mota volucris." B.

my father Anchises, with the gods of Troy, and lodge them
secretly in a winding valley.   I myself repair back to the
city, and brace on my shining armour.   I am resolved to renew every adventure, revisit all the quarters of Troy, and
expose my life once more to all dangers.   First of all, I return to the walls, and the dark entry of the gate by which I
had set out, and backward unravel my steps with care amidst
the darkness, and run them over with my eye.   Horror on all
sides, and at the same time the very silence affrights my soul.
Thence homeward I bent my way, lest by chance, by any
chance, she had moved thither: the Greeks had now rushed
in, and were masters of the whole house.   In a moment the
devouring conflagration is rolled up in sheets by the wind to
the lofty roof; the flames mount above; the fiery whirlwind
rages to the skies.   I advance, and revisit Priam's royal seat,
and the citadel.   And now in the desolate cloisters, Juno's
sanctuary, Phœnix and the execrable Ulysses, a chosen guard,
were watching the booty: hither, from all quarters, the precious Trojan moveables, saved from the conflagration of the
temples, the tables of the gods, the massy golden goblets,
and plundered vestments, are amassed: boys, and timorous
matrons, stand all around in a long train.   Now adventuring
even to dart my voice through the shades, I filled the streets
with outcry, and in anguish, with vain repetition, again and
again, called on Creüsa.   While I was in this search, and with
incessant fury ranging through all quarters of the town, the
mournful ghost and shade of my Creüsa's self appeared before my eyes, her figure larger than I had known it.   I stood
aghast! my hair rose on end, and my voice clung to my jaws.
Then thus she bespeaks me, and relieves my cares with these
words: My darling spouse, what pleasure have you thus to
indulge a grief which is but madness?   These events do not
occur without the·will of the gods.   It is not allowed you
to carry Creüsa hence to accompany you, nor is it permitted
by the great ruler of heaven supreme.   In long banishment
you must roam, and plough the vast expanse of the ocean: to
the land of Hesperia you shall come, where the Lydian [55]
Tiber, with his gentle current, glides through a rich land of

---

[55] Lydian Tiber; the epithet is applied to the Tiber, because it passes
along the borders of Etruria, whose inhabitants were once a Lydian
colony.

heroes. There, prosperous state, a crown, and royal spouse,
await you : dry up your tears for your beloved Creüsa. I, of
Dardanus' noble line, and the daughter-in-law of divine Venus,
shall not see the proud seats of the Myrmidons and Dolopes,
nor go to serve the Grecian dames ; but the great mother of
the gods detains me upon these coasts. And now farewell,
and preserve your affection to our common son.

With these words she left me in tears, ready to say many
things, and vanished into thin air. There thrice I attempted
to throw my arms around her neck; thrice the phantom,
grasped in vain, escaped my hold, swift as the winged winds,
and resembling most a fleeting dream. Thus having spent
the night, I at length revisit my associates. And here, to my
surprise, I found a great confluence of new companions : matrons, and men, and youths, drawn together to share our exile,
a piteous throng ! From all sides they convened, resolute [to
follow me] with their souls and fortunes, into whatever country I was inclined to conduct them over the sea. By this time,
the bright morning star was rising on the craggy tops of lofty
Ida, and ushered in the day : the Greeks held the entrance of
the gates blocked up ; nor had we any prospect of relief.
I gave way, and bearing up my father, made towards the
mountain.

BOOK III.

In the Third Book, Æneas continues his narration, by a minute account of
his voyage, the places he visited, and the perils he encountered, from the
time of leaving the shores of Troas, until he landed at Drepanum, in Sicily,
where he buried his father.—This Book, which comprehends a period of
about seven years, ends with the dreadful storm, with the description of
which the First Book opened.

AFTER it had seemed fit to the gods to overthrow the power
of Asia, and Priam's race, undeserving [of such a fate], and
stately Ilium fell, and while the whole of Troy, built by Neptune, smokes on the ground ; we are determined, by revelations
from the gods, to go in quest of distant retreats in exile, and
unpeopled lands; we fit out a fleet just under the walls of
Antandros [1] and the mountains of Phrygian Ida ; and draw
our forces together, uncertain whither the Fates point our way,
where it shall be given us to settle. Scarcely had the first

[1] Antandros, a city of Troas, in the Gulf of Adramyttium.

summer begun, when my father Anchises gave command to
hoist the sails, in accordance with the Fates. Then with tears
I leave the shores and ports of my country, and the plains
where Troy once stood : an exile I launch forth into the deep,
with my associates, my son, my household gods, and the great
gods [of my country].

At a distance lies a martial land, peopled throughout its
wide-extended plains, (the Thracians cultivate the soil,) over
which in former times fierce Lycurgus[1] reigned : an ancient
hospitable retreat for Troy, and whose gods were leagued with
ours, while fortune was with us. Hither I am carried, and
erect my first walls along the winding shore, entering with
Fates unkind; and from my own name I call the citizens
Æneades. I was performing sacred rites to my mother Venus,
and the gods, the patrons of my works begun ; and to the exalted king of the immortals I was sacrificing a sleek bull on
the shore. Near at hand there chanced to be a rising ground,
on whose top were young cornel-trees, and a myrtle rough
with thick spear-like branches. I came up to it, and attempting to tear from the earth the verdant wood, that I might
cover the altars with the leafy boughs, I observe a dreadful
prodigy, and wondrous to relate. For from that tree which
first is torn from the soil, its rooted fibres being burst asunder,
drops of black blood distil, and stain the ground with gore :
cold terror shakes my limbs, and my chill blood is congealed
with fear. I again essay to tear off a limber bough from another, and thoroughly explore the latent cause: and from the
rind of that other the purple blood descends. Raising in my
mind many an anxious thought, I with reverence besought the
rural nymphs, and father Mars, who presides over the Thracian territories, kindly to prosper the vision[2] and avert evil
from the omen. But when I attempted the boughs a third
time with a more vigorous effort, and on my knees struggled
against the opposing mould, (shall I speak, or shall I forbear ?)
a piteous groan is heard from the bottom of the rising ground,
and a voice sent forth reaches my ears: Æneas, why dost thou

---

[1] Lycurgus, a king of Thrace, son of Dryas, who, it is said, drove Bacchus out of his kingdom.
[2] For " visa," which is used in the same phrase by Silius, viii. 124.
Lucan. i. 635. On the myrtle-tomb of Polydore, compare Auson.
Epitaph. Her. xix.

tear an unhappy wretch? Spare me, now that I am in my
grave; forbear to pollute with guilt thy pious hands: Troy
brought me forth no stranger to you; nor is it from the trunk
this blood distils. Ah, fly this barbarous land, fly the ava-
ricious shore! For Polydore[4] am I: here an iron crop of
darts hath overwhelmed me, transfixed, and over me shot up
in pointed javelins. Then, indeed, depressed at heart with
perplexing fear, I was stunned; my hair stood on end, and
my voice clung to my jaws. This Polydore unhappy Priam
had formerly sent in secrecy with a great weight of gold to
be brought up by the king of Thrace, when he now began[5]
to distrust the arms of Troy, and saw the city with close siege
blocked up. He, as soon as the power of the Trojans were
crushed, and their fortune gone, espousing Agamemnon's
interest and victorious arms, breaks every sacred bond, assassinates Polydore, and by violence possesses his gold. Cursed
thirst of gold, to what dost thou not drive the hearts of men!
After fear left my bones, I report the portents of the gods to
our chosen leaders, and chiefly to my father, and demand
what their opinion is. All are unanimous to quit that accursed land, abandon the polluted society, and spread the sails
to the winds. Therefore we renew funeral ceremonies to
Polydore, and a large mound of earth is heaped up for the
tomb: an altar is reared to his manes, mournfully decked
with leaden-coloured wreaths and gloomy cypress; and
round it the Trojan matrons stand with hair dishevelled according to custom. We offer the sacrifices of the dead, bowls
foaming with warm milk, and goblets of the sacred blood: we
give the soul repose in the grave, and with loud voice address
to him the last farewell.[6]

[4] Polydorus, the youngest son of Priam and Hecuba, was assassinated
by Polymnestor, king of Thrace, who had been intrusted with the care
of the young prince.
[5] Eur. Hec. ii. ἵν', εἰ ποτ' Ἰλίου τείχη πέσοι. I need scarcely refer
the reader to the whole passage. B.
[6] I have illustrated this custom in my notes on Eurip. Alcest. 610.
Ausonius Parent. 159, 10, "Voce ciere animas funeris instar habet.
Gaudent compositi cineres sua nomina dici. . . . Nomine ter dicto pœno
sepultus erit." On the funeral offerings here described, see my notes on
Æsch. Pers. p. 83, ed. Bohn. Statius, Theb. vi. 209, "Spumantesque
mero pateras vertuntur, et atri Sanguinis, et rapti gratissima cymbia lac-
tis." Alcæus Mess. in Brunck. Annal. i. p. 490, καὶ τάφον ὑψώσαντο
γάλακτι δὲ ποιμένες αἰγῶν Ἑρράναν, ξανθῷ μιζάμενοι μέλιτι. B.

This done, when first we durst confide in the main, when
the winds present peaceful seas, and the south wind in soft
whispering gales invites us to the deep, my mates launch the
ships and crowd the shore. We are wafted from the port,
and the land and cities retreat.

Amidst the sea there lies a charming spot of land, sacred to
[Doris], (the mother of the Nereids,) and Ægean Neptune;
which once wandering about the coasts and shores, the pious
god who wields the bow fast bound with high Gyaros[1] and
Mycone, and fixed it so as to be habitable, and mock the
winds. Hither I am led: this most peaceful island receives
us to a safe port after our fatigue. At landing we pay veneration to the city of Apollo. King Anius,[2] both king of men
and priest of Phœbus, his temples bound with fillets and sacred laurel, comes up, and presently recognises his old friend
Anchises. We join right hands in amity, and come under his
roof. I venerated the temple of the god, a structure of ancient
stone, [and thus began]: Thymbræan Apollo, grant us, after
all our toils, some fixed mansion; grant us walls of defence,
offspring, and a permanent city: preserve those other towers
of Troy, a remnant left by the Greeks and merciless Achilles.
Whom are we to follow; or whither dost thou bid us go?
where fix our residence? Father, grant us a prophetic sign,
and glide into our minds. Scarcely had I thus said, when
suddenly all seemed to tremble, both the temple itself, and
laurel of the god; the whole mountain quaked around, and
the sanctuary being exposed to view, the tripod moaned. In
humble reverence we fall to the ground, and a voice reaches
our ears: Ye hardy sons of Dardanus, the same land which
first produced you from your forefather's stock, shall receive
you in its fertile bosom after all your dangers; search out
your ancient mother. There the family of Æneas shall rule
over every coast, and his children's children, and they who
from them shall spring.

Thus Phœbus. Emotions of great joy, with mingled tumult, arose; and all were seeking to know what city is designed; whither Phœbus calls us wandering, and wills us to

[1] Gyaros and Mycone, two of the islands called the Cyclades, in the
Ægean Sea.
[2] Anius, the son of Apollo and Rhea, was king of Delos, and father of
Andrus.

return. Then my father, revolving the historical records of ancient heroes, says, Ye leaders, give ear, and learn what you have to hope for. In the middle of the sea lies Crete, the island of mighty Jupiter, where is Mount Ida, and the nursery of our race. The Cretans inhabit a hundred mighty cities, most fertile realms: whence our mighty ancestor Teucrus, if I rightly remember the tradition, first arrived on the Rhœtean coasts,[9] and chose the seat of his kingdom. No Ilium then nor towers of Pergamus[10] were raised; in the deep vales they dwelt. Hence came mother Cybele, the patroness of the earth, and the brazen cymbals of the Corybantes,[11] and the Idæan grove; hence that faithful secrecy in her sacred rites; and harnessed lions were yoked in the chariot of their queen. Come, then, and, where the commands of the gods point out our way, let us follow; let us appease the winds, and seek the Gnossian realms. Nor lie they at the distance of a long voyage: provided Jove be with us, the third day will land our fleet on the Cretan coast.

This said, he offered the proper sacrifices on the altars, a bull to Neptune, a bull to thee, O fair Apollo: a black sheep to the Winter, and a white one to the propitious zephyrs. A report flies abroad, that leader Idomeneus[12] banished, hath quitted his paternal kingdom, and that the shore of Crete is deserted; that its mansions are free from the enemy, and palaces stand forsaken. We leave the port of Ortygia,[13] and scud along the sea: we cruise along Naxos, (on whose mountains the Bacchanals revel,) green Donysa,[14] Olearos, snowy Paros, and the Cyclades scattered up and down the main, and narrow seas thick-sown with clustered islands. With various

[9] Rhœtean coasts; Trojan coasts, from Rhœteum, a promontory of Troas, on the Hellespont, near which the body of Ajax was buried.

[10] Pergamus, the citadel of Troy, often used for Troy itself.

[11] Corybantes, the priests of Cybele.

[12] Idomeneus, king of Crete, the son of Deucalion. Having left Crete after his return from the Trojan war, he came to Italy, and founded the city of Salentum on the coast of Calabria.

[13] Ortygia, an ancient name of the island of Delos, where was a famous temple and oracle of Apollo. Naxos, a celebrated island of the Ægean Sea, the largest and most fertile of all the Cyclades.

[14] Donysa, one of the Cyclades famed for producing green marble, as Paros was for white marble. Olearos, (Antiparos,) one of the Cyclades, south-west of Paros. Cyclades, islands in the Ægean Sea, about fifty in number, encircling Delos.

emulation the seamen's shouts arise. The crew animate one
another: For Crete and our ancestors let us speed our course.
A wind springing up astern, accompanies us on our way, and
we at length skim along to the ancient seats of the Curetes.
Therefore, with eagerness, I raise the walls of the so-much-
wished for city, and call it the city of Pergamus; and I exhort my colony, pleased with the name, to love their hearths,
and erect turrets on their roofs. And now the ships were
mostly drawn up on the dry beach: the youth were engaged
in their nuptials and new settlements; I was beginning to
dispense laws and appropriate houses; when suddenly, from
the infection of the climate, a wasting and lamentable plague
seized our limbs, the trees, and corn; and the year was
pregnant with death. Men left their sweet lives, or dragged
along their sickly bodies: at the same time the dog-star
burned up the barren fields: the herbs were parched, and the
unwholesome grain denied us sustenance. My father advises, that, measuring back the sea, we again apply to the
oracle of Ortygia, and Apollo, and implore his grace, [to
know] what end he will bring to our forlorn state; whence
he will bid us attempt a redress of our calamities, whither
turn our course.

It was night, and sleep reigned over all the animal world.
The sacred images of the gods, and the tutelar deities of
Phrygia, whom I had brought with me from Troy and the
midst of the flames, were seen to stand before my eyes while
slumbering,[16] conspicuous by a glare of light, where the full
moon darted her beams through the inserted windows. Then
they thus [seemed to] address me, and dispel my cares with
these words: What Apollo would announce to you, were you
wafted to Ortygia, he here reveals, and lo! unasked, he sends
us to your dwelling. We, after Troy was consumed, followed
thee and thy arms; under thy conduct we have crossed the
swelling sea in ships: we too will exalt thy future race to
heaven, and give imperial power to thy city. Do thou prepare walls mighty for mighty inhabitants, and shrink not
from the long labours of thy voyage. You must change your
place of residence: these are not the shores that Delian Apollo
advises for you; nor was it in Crete he commanded you to

<hr>

⁴ I read "in somnis," not "insomnia." See Anthon. B.

settle. There is a place, (the Greeks call it Hesperia by name,)
an ancient country, powerful in arms and fertility of soil: the
Œnotrians peopled it once; now there is a report, that their
descendants have called the nation Italy, from the founder's
name. These are our proper settlements: hence Dardanus
sprang, and father Iasius,[16] from which prince our race is derived. Haste, arise, and with joy report to thy aged sire these
intimations of unquestionable credibility: search out Coritus [17]
and the Ausonian lands; Jupiter forbids thee the Cretan territories.

Astonished by this vision and declaration of the gods (nor
was that a sound sleep, but methought I clearly discerned their
aspect before me, their fillet-bound locks, and their forms full
in my view; then a cold sweat flowed over my whole body);
I snatch my frame from the couch, and lift up my hand supine
to heaven with my voice, and pour hallowed offerings on the
fires. Having finished the sacrifice, with joy I certify Anchises, and disclose the fact in order. He recognised the double stock, and the double founders [of the Trojan race], and
that he had been deceived by a modern mistake respecting
ancient countries; then he thus bespeaks me: My son, practised in woe by the fates of Troy, Cassandra alone predicted
to me that such was to be our fortune. Now I recollect that
she foretold this should be the destiny of our race, and
that she often spoke of Hesperia, often of the realms of Italy.
But who could believe that the Trojans were to come to the
Hesperian shore? or whom then did the prophetic Cassandra
influence? Let us resign ourselves to Phœbus, and, since
we are better advised, let us follow. He said; and, exulting,
we all obey his orders. This realm we likewise quit, and.
leaving a few behind, unfurl our sails, and bound over the
spacious sea in our hollow barks.

When the ships held possession of the deep, and no land is
any longer in view, sky all around, and ocean all around; then
an azure rain-cloud stood over my head, bringing on night and
wintry storm; the waves grew rough in the gloom;[18] the winds

[16] Iasius, a son of Jupiter and Electra, and brother to Dardanus; he
was one of the Atlantides, and reigned over part of Arcadia.
[17] Coritus, (Cortona,) a town and mountain of Etruria, so called from
Coritus, a king of Etruria, father to Iasius.
[18] Compare Pacuvius, "Inhorrescit mare, tenebræ conduplicantur, noc-
tisque et nubiûm occæcat nigror." B.

overturn the sea, and mighty surges rise : we are tossed to and
fro on the face of the boiling deep : clouds enwrapped the day,
and humid night snatched the heavens [from our view] ; from
the bursting clouds flashes of lightning redouble. We are
driven from our course, and wander in unknown waves. Palinurus [19] himself owns he is unable to distinguish day and
night by the sky, and that he has forgotten his course in the
mid sea. Thus for three days, that could hardly be distinguished by reason of the dark clouds, as many starless nights,
we wander up and down the ocean. At length, on the fourth
day, land was first seen to rise, to disclose the mountains from
afar, and roll up smoke : the sails are lowered, we ply hard
the oars ; instantly the seamen, with exerted vigour, toss up
the foam, and sweep the azure deep.

The shores of the Strophades [20] first receive me rescued from
the waves. The Strophades, so called by a Greek name, are
islands situated in the great Ionian Sea ; which direful Celæno [21]
and the other Harpies inhabit, from what time Phineus' palace
was closed against them, and they were frighted from his table,
which they formerly haunted. No monster more fell than they,
no plague and scourge of the gods more cruel, ever issued from
the Stygian waves. They are fowls with virgin faces, most
loathsome is their bodily discharge, hands hooked, and looks
ever pale with famine. Hither conveyed, as soon as we entered the port, lo ! we observe joyous herds of cattle roving
up and down the plains, and flocks of goats along the meadows
without a keeper. We rush upon them with our swords, and
invoke the gods and Jove himself to share the booty. Then
along the winding shore we raise the couches, and feast on the
rich repast. But suddenly, with direful swoop, the Harpies
are upon us from the mountains, shake their wings with loud
din, prey upon our banquet, and defile every thing with their

[19] Palinurus, a skilful pilot of the ship of Æneas. He fell overboard
while asleep, and after being three days exposed to the tempests, he
reached the shore near Velia, a town of Lucania, when he was murdered
by the inhabitants. A promontory, on which a monument was raised to
him, received the name of Palinurus.
[20] Strophades, (Stamphane,) two small islands in the Ionian Sea, south
of the island of Zacynthos (Zante).
[21] Celæno, one of the Harpies : these were fabulous monsters, with
wings, three in number, daughters of Neptune and Terra. They were
sent by Juno to plunder the tables of Phineus, king of Thrace, whence
they were driven to the Strophades, where Æneas found them.

touch: at the same time, together with a rank smell, hideous
screams arise. Again we spread our tables in a long recess,
under a shelving rock, enclosed around with trees and gloomy
shade; and once more we plant fire on the altar. Again the
noisy crowd, from a different quarter of the sky, and obscure
retreats, flutter around the prey with hooked claws, taint our
viands with their mouths. Then I enjoin my companions to
take arms, and wage war with the horrid race. They do no
otherwise than bidden, dispose their swords secretly among
the grass, and conceal their shields out of sight.[22] Therefore,
as soon as stooping down they raised their screaming voices
along the bending shores, Misenus[23] with his hollow trumpet
of brass gives the signal from a lofty place of observation: my
friends set upon them, and engage in a new kind of fight, to
employ the sword in destroying obscene sea-fowls. But they
neither suffer any violence on their plumes, nor wounds in
the body; and, mounting up in the air with rapid flight, leave
behind them their half-eaten prey, and the ugly prints of
their feet. Celæno alone alighted on a high rock, the prophetess of ill, and from her breast burst forth these words:
War too, ye sons of Laomedon, is it your purpose to make
war for our oxen which you have slain, for the havoc you
have made upon our bullocks, and to banish the innocent
Harpies from their hereditary kingdom? Lend them an ear,
and in your minds fix these my words: what the almighty
Sire revealed to Phœbus, Phœbus Apollo to me, I the chief
of the furies disclose to you. To Italy you steer your course,
and Italy you shall reach after repeated invocations to the
winds, and you shall be permitted to enter the port: but you
shall not surround the given city with walls, till dire famine
and disaster, for shedding our blood, compel you first to gnaw
around and eat up your tables[24] with your teeth.

---

[22] Cf. Silius ix. 99, "condit membra occultata." B.

[23] Misenus was a son of Æolus, and the trumpeter of Hector, after
whose death he followed Æneas to Italy, and was drowned on the coast
of Campania, because he had challenged one of the Tritons.

[24] The sense of this prediction is seen from its accomplishment in the
Seventh Book, verse 116. This is not merely poetical invention, it was an
historical tradition, related by Dionysius and Strabo, that Æneas had received a response from an oracle, foretelling that, before he came to his
settlement in Italy, he should be reduced to the necessity of eating his
trenchers. Varro says he got it from the oracle of Dodona. Virgil puts

She said, and on her wings upborne flew into the wood. As for my companions, their blood, chilled with sudden fear, stagnated; their minds sunk: and now they are no longer for arms, but urge me to solicit peace by vows and prayers, whether they be goddesses, or cursed and inauspicious birds. My father Anchises, with hands spread forth from the shore, invokes the great gods, and enjoins due honours to be paid them: Ye gods, ward off these threatenings; ye gods, avert so great a calamity; and propitious save your pious votaries. Then he orders to tear the ropes from the shore, loose and disengage the cables. The south winds stretch our sails: we fly over the foaming waves, where the wind and pilots urged our course. Now amidst the waves appear woody Zacynthos,[25] Dulichium, Same, and Neritos, with its steep rocks. We shun the cliffs of Ithaca,[26] Laertes' realms, and curse the land that bred the cruel Ulysses. Soon after this the cloudy tops of Mount Leucate,[27] and [the temple of] Apollo, the dread of seamen, open to our view. Hither we steer our course oppressed with toil, and approach the little city. The anchor is thrown out from the prow: the ships are ranged on the shore. Thus at length possessed of wished-for land, we both perform a lustral sacrifice to Jupiter, and kindle the altars in order to perform our vows, and signalize the promontory of Actium[28] by celebrating the Trojan games. Our crew, having their naked limbs besmeared with slippery oil, exercise the wrestling matches of their country: it delights us to have escaped so many Grecian cities and pursued our voyage through the midst of our enemies.

Meanwhile the sun finishes the revolution of the great year, and frosty winter exasperates the waves with the north winds.

this prophecy in the mouth of the harpies, as being both suitable to their nature, and more apt to raise surprise when coming from them.

[25] Zacynthos, &c. These are islands in the Ionian Sea, on the western coast of Greece. Zacynthos is now called Zante. Dulichium was part of the kingdom of Ulysses. Same, now called Cephalonia, the inhabitants of which went with Ulysses to the Trojan war. Neritos, a mountain in the island of Ithaca, often applied to the whole island.

[26] Ithaca, an island in the Ionian Sea, where Ulysses reigned.

[27] Leucate, (Cape Ducato,) a high promontory of Leucadia, (St. Maura,) an island in the Ionian Sea, where was a famous temple of Apollo.

[28] Actium, (Azio,) a town, and (Cape Figalo) a promontory of Epirus, celebrated for the naval victory of Augustus over Antony and Cleopatra, .31.

M

On the front door-posts [of the temple] I set up a buckler of
hollow brass, which mighty Abas wore, and notify the action by
this verse: " These arms Æneas [won] from the victorious
Greeks." Then I ordered [our crew] to leave the port, and
take their seats on the benches. They with emulous ardour
lash the sea, and sweep the waves. In an instant we lose
sight of[29] the airy towers of the Phæacians, cruise along the
coast of Epirus, and enter the Chaonian port, and ascend the
lofty city of Buthrotus.[30] Here a report of facts scarce cre-
dible invades our ears, that Helenus,[31] Priam's son, was reigning over Grecian cities, possessed of the spouse and sceptre of
Pyrrhus, the grandchild of Æacus, and that Andromache had
again fallen to a lord of her own country. I was amazed, and
my bosom glowed with strange desire to greet the hero, and
learn so signal revolutions of fortune. I set forward from the
port, leaving the fleet and shore. Andromache, as it chanced,
was then offering to [Hector's] ashes her anniversary[32] feast
and mournful oblations before the city in a grove, near the
stream of the fictitious Simois, and invoked the manes at
Hector's tomb ; an empty tomb which she had consecrated of
green turf, and two altars, incentives to her grief. As soon
as she saw me coming up, and to her amazement beheld the
Trojan arms around me, terrified with a prodigy so great, she
stiffened at the very sight ; vital warmth forsook her limbs :
she sinks down, and at length, after a long interval, with fal-
tering accent speaks : Goddess-born, do you present yourself
to me a real form, a real messenger ? Do you live ? or, if
from you the benignant light has fled, where is Hector ? She
said, and shed a flood of tears, filling all the place with cries.
To her, in this transport, I with difficulty make even a brief
reply, and in great perturbation open my mouth in these few
broken words : I am alive indeed, and spin out life through
all extremes. Doubt not ; for all you see is real. Ah ! what
accidents of life have overtaken you, since you were thrown

---

[29] So κρύπτειν is elegantly used in Greek. Plat. Protag. 70, φεύγειν
εἰς τὸ πέλαγος, ἀποκρύψαντα γῆν.   See Herndorf's note.   B.

[30] Buthrotus, (Butrinto,) a sea-port town of Epirus, opposite Corfu.

[31] Helenus, a celebrated soothsayer, the only one of Priam's sons who
survived the ruin of his country; he was king of Chaonia when he received
Æneas on his way to Italy.

[32] So Servius.   In the same manner ἑορτὴ ἔτος ἕκαστον.   Thucyd. iii.
58.   B.

down from [the possession of] your illustrious lord ? or what fortune, some way suited to your merit, hath visited you once more ? Is then Hector's Andromache bound in wedlock to Pyrrhus ? Downward she cast her eyes, and thus in humble accents [spoke]: O happy, singularly happy, the fate of Priam's virgin-daughter, who, compelled to die at the enemy's tomb under the lofty walls of Troy, suffered not in having any lots cast for her, nor as a captive ever touched the bed of a victor lord ! We, after the burning of our country, being transported over various seas, have in thraldom borne with a mother's throes the insolence of Achilles' heir, and a haughty, imperious youth; who afterwards, attaching himself to Hermione,[33] the granddaughter of Leda, and a Lacedæmonian match, delivered me over a slave into the possession of a slave, Helenus. But Orestes,[34] inflamed by the violence of love to his betrothed snatched from him, and hurried on by the Furies of his crimes, surprises him in an unguarded hour, and assassinates him at his paternal altar. By the death of Neoptolemus, a part of his kingdom fell to Helenus ; who denominated the plains Chaonian, and the whole country Chaonia, from the Trojan Chaon, and built on the mountains [another] Pergamus and this Trojan fort. But what winds, what fates, have guided your course ? or what god hath landed you on our coasts without your knowledge ? What is become of the boy Ascanius ? Lives he still, and breathes the vital air ? whom to your care, when Troy was——Has the boy now any concern for the loss of his mother ? Is he incited, by both his father Æneas and his uncle Hector, to ancient valour and manly courage ?

Thus bathed in tears she spoke, and heaved long unavailing sobs ; when the hero Helenus, Priam's son, advances from the city with a numerous retinue, knows his friends, with joy conducts them to his palace, and sheds tears in abundance between each word. I set forward, and survey the little

---

[33] Hermione, the daughter of Menelaus and Helen, was married to Pyrrhus, (Neoptolemus,) the son of Achilles ; but having been previously promised to Orestes, Pyrrhus was assassinated, when she became the wife of Orestes.

[34] Orestes, the son of Agamemnon, and the faithful friend of Pylades. Having slain his mother Clytemnestra and her paramour Egisthus, because they had murdered his father, Orestes was tormented by the Furies, and exiled himself to Argos, the throne of which he afterwards filled.

Troy, the castle of Pergamus resembling the great original, and a scanty rivulet bearing the name of Xanthus; and I embrace the threshold of a Scæan gate. The Trojans too, at the same time, enjoy the friendly city. The king entertained them in his spacious galleries. In the midst of the court they quaffed brimmers of wine, while the banquet was served in gold, and each stood with a goblet in his hand.

And now one day, and a second, passed on, when the gales invite our sails, and the canvass bellies by the swelling south wind. In these words I accost the prophet, [Helenus,] and question him thus: Son of Troy, interpreter of the gods, who knowest the divine will of Phœbus, the tripods, the laurels of the Clarian[26] god; who knowest the stars, the ominous sounds of birds, and the prognostics of the swift wing,[26] come, declare (for [hitherto the omens of] religion have pronounced my whole voyage to be prosperous, and all the gods, by their divine will, have directed me to go in pursuit of Italy, and attempt a settlement in lands remote: the Harpy Celæno alone predicts a prodigy strange and horrible to relate, and denounces direful vengeance and foul famine) what are the principal dangers I am to shun? or by the pursuit of what means may I surmount toils so great? Upon this Helenus first solicits the peace of the gods by sacrificing bullocks in due form, then unbinds the fillets of his consecrated head, and himself leads me by the hand to thy temple, O Phœbus, anxious with great awe of the god; then the priest, from his lips divine, delivers these predictions: Goddess-born, (for that you steer through the deep under some higher auspices, is unquestionably evident; so the sovereign of the gods dispenses his decree; thus he fixes the series of revolving events; such a scheme of things is coming to its accomplishment,) that you may with greater safety cross the seas to which you are a

[26] Clarian god, a name of Apollo, from Claros, a city of Ionia, where he had a famous temple and oracle.

[26] Volucrum linguas, et præpetis omina pennæ. Some birds were subservient to divination by the sounds they uttered, and these were called "Oscines;" of which kind were the crows, ravens, &c. Hor. iii. Carm. Ode xxvii. 2,

Oscinem corvum prece suscitabo
Solis ad ortu.

Others, again, answered the same end by their manner of flying, and were called "Præpotes."

stranger, and settle in the Ausonian port, I will unfold to you
a few particulars of many; for the Destinies[37] prevent you
from knowing the rest, and Saturnian Juno forbids Helenus
to reveal it. First of all, a long intricate voyage, with a
length of lands, divides [you from] Italy, which you unwittingly deem already near, and whose ports you are preparing
to enter, as if just at hand. You must both ply the bending
oar in the Trinacrian wave, and visit with your fleet the
plains of the Ausonian Sea, the infernal lakes, and the isle of
Ææan Circe, before you can build a city in a quiet, peaceful
land. I will declare the signs to you: do you keep them
treasured up in your mind. When, thoughtfully musing by
the streams of the secret river, you shall find a large sow that
has brought forth a litter of thirty young, reclining on the
ground, under the holms that shade the banks, white [the
dam], the offspring white around her dugs: that shall be the
station of the city; there is the period fixed to thy labours.
Nor be disturbed at the future event of eating your tables:
the Fates will find out an expedient, and Apollo invoked will
befriend you. But shun those coasts, and those nearest limits
of the Italian shore, which are washed by the tide of our sea:
all those cities are inhabited by the mischievous Greeks. Here
the Narycian Locrians have raised their walls, and Cretan
Idomeneus with his troops has possessed the plains of Salentum: here stands that little city Petilia, defended by the walls
of Philoctetes[38] the Melibœan chief. [Remember] also (when
your fleet, having crossed the seas, shall come to a station,
and you shall pay your vows at the altar raised on the shore)
to cover your head, muffling yourself in a purple veil, lest
the face of an enemy, amidst the sacred fires in honour of the
gods, appear, and disturb the omens. This custom, in sacrifice, let your friends, this yourself observe; to this religious
institution let your pious descendants adhere. But when,
after setting out, the wind shall waft you to the Sicilian coast,

[37] The Destinies, or Fates, deities who presided over the birth and
the life of mankind. They were three in number, Clotho, Lachesis, and
Atropos, daughters of Nox and Erebus, or, according to others, of Jupiter
and Themis.

[38] Philoctetes, the son of Pœan, king of Melibœa in Thessaly. After
his return from the Trojan war, he settled in Italy, where he built the
town of Petilia (Strongoli) in Calabria.

and the straits of narrow Pelorus [39] shall open wider to the
eye, veer to the land on the left, and to the sea on the left, by
a long circuit; fly the right both sea and shore. These lands,
they say, once with violence and vast desolation convulsed,
(such revolutions a long course of time is able to produce,)
slipped asunder; when in continuity both lands were one, the
sea rushed impetuously between, and by its waves tore the
Italian side from that of Sicily; and with a narrow frith runs
between the fields and cities separated by the shores. Scylla
guards the right side, implacable Charybdis [40] the left, and thrice
with the deepest eddies of its gulf swallows up the vast billows,
headlong in, and again spouts them out by turns high into the
air, and lashes the stars with the waves. But Scylla a cave
confines within its dark recesses, reaching forth her jaws, and
sucking in vessels upon the rocks. First she presents a human
form, a lovely virgin down to the middle; her lower parts are
those of a hideous sea-monster, with the tails of dolphins
joined to the wombs of wolves. It is better with delay to
coast round the extremities of Sicilian Pachynus, [41] and steer
a long winding course, than once to behold the misshapen
Scylla under her capacious den, and those rocks that roar
with her sea-green dogs. Further, if Helenus has any skill,
if any credit is due to him as a prophet, if Apollo stores his
mind with truth, I will give you this one previous admonition,
this one, O goddess-born, above all the rest, and I will inculcate
it upon you again and again: Be sure you, in the first place,
with supplications worship great Juno's divinity; to Juno
cheerfully address your vows, and overcome the powerful queen
with humble offerings: thus, at length, leaving Trinacria,
you shall be dismissed victorious to the territories of Italy.
When, wafted thither, you reach the city Cumæ, the hallowed
lakes, and Avernus resounding through the woods, you will
see the raving prophetess, who, beneath a deep rock, reveals
the fates, and commits to the leaves of trees her characters
and words. Whatever verses the virgin has inscribed on the
leaves, she ranges in harmonious order, and leaves in the
cave enclosed by themselves: uncovered they remain in their

---

[39] Pelorus, (Cape Peloro,) one of the three principal promontories of
Sicily, separated from Italy by the straits of Messina.

[40] Charybdis, a dangerous whirlpool on the coast of Sicily, opposite
Scylla, on the coast of Italy.

[41] Pachynus, (Cape Passaro,) the south-eastern promontory of Sicily.

position, nor recede from their order. But when, upon
turning the hinge, a small breath of wind has blown upon
them, and the door [by opening] has discomposed the tender
leaves, she never afterwards cares to catch the verses as they
are fluttering in the hollow cave, nor to recover their situation,
or join them together. Men depart without a response, and
detest the Sibyl's [a] grot. Let not the loss of some time there
seem of such consequence to you, (though your friends chide,
and your voyage strongly invite your sails into the deep, and
you may have an opportunity to fill the bellying canvass with
a prosperous gale,) as to hinder you from visiting the prophetess, and earnestly entreating her to deliver the oracles
herself, and vouchsafe to open her lips in vocal accents. She
will declare to you the Italian nations, and your future wars,
and by what means you may shun or sustain each hardship ;
and, with reverence addressed, will give you a successful voyage. These are all the instructions I am at liberty to give
you. Go then, and by your achievements raise mighty Troy
to heaven. Which words when the prophet had thus with
friendly voice pronounced, he next orders presents to be
carried to the ships, heavy with gold and ivory ; and within
the sides of my vessel stows a large quantity of silver plate,
and caldrons of Dodonean brass, a mail thick set with rings,
and wrought in gold of triple tissue, together with the cone
and waving crest of a shining helmet, arms which belonged
to Neoptolemus : my father too has proper gifts conferred on
him. He gives us horses besides, and gives us guides. He
supplies us with rowers, and at the same time furnishes our
crew with arms. Meanwhile Anchises gave orders to equip
our fleet with sails, that we might not be late for the favouring gale. Whom the interpreter of Apollo accosts with much
respect : Anchises, honoured with the illustrious bed of Venus,
thou care of the gods, twice snatched from the ruins of Troy,
lo ! there the coast of Ausonia lies before you ; thither speed
your way with full sail : and yet you must needs steer your
course beyond. That part of Ausonia which Apollo opens lies
remote. Go, says he, happy in the pious duty of your son : why
do I further insist, and by my discourse retard the rising gales ?

[a] The Sibyls were certain women supposed to be inspired, who flourished in different parts of the world. According to Varro, the number of
the Sibyls was ten, of whom the most celebrated was that of Cumæ in
Italy.

In like manner Andromache, grieved at our final departure, brings forth for Ascanius vestments wrought in figures of gold, and a Phrygian cloak; nor falls short of his dignity:[43] she loads him also with presents of her labours in the loom, and thus addresses him, Take these too, my child, which may be memorials to you of my handywork, and testify the permanent affection of Andromache, the spouse of Hector: accept the last presents of thy friends. O image, which is all that I have now left of my Astyanax! just such eyes, such hands, such looks he showed; and now of equal age with you, would have been blooming into youth. I, with tears in my eyes, thus addressed them at parting: Live in felicity, ye whose fortune is now accomplished: we are summoned from fate to fate. To you tranquillity is secured; no expanse of sea have you to plough, or to pursue the ever-retreating lands of Ausonia. You behold the image of Xanthus, and the Troy which your own hands have built: Heaven grant it be with happier auspices, and be less obnoxious to the Greeks. If ever I shall enter the Tiber, and the lands that border on the Tiber, and view the walls allotted to my race, we will hereafter make of our kindred cities an allied people, [yours] in Epirus, [and mine] in Italy, who have both the same founder, Dardanus, and the same fortune; [we will, I say, make] of both one Troy, in good-will. Be this the future care of our posterity.

We pursue our voyage near the adjacent Ceraunian mountains; whence lies our way, and the shortest course by sea to Italy. Meanwhile the sun goes down, and the dusky mountains are wrapped up in shade. On the bosom of the wished-for earth we throw ourselves down by the waves, having distributed the oars by lot, and all along the dry beach we refresh our frames [with food]; sleep diffuses its dews over our weary limbs. Night, driven by the hours, had not yet reached her mid-way course, when Palinurus springs alert from his bed, examines every wind, and lends his ears to catch the breeze. He marks every star gliding in the silent sky, Arcturus, the rainy Hyades, and the two northern Bears, and throws his eyes round Orion armed with gold. After having

---

43 i. e. "her presents are such as his merits deserve." Scaurus, as we learn from Servius, read "honore," which certainly seems more simple. B.

seen all appearances of settled weather in the serene sky, he
gives the loud signal from the stern: we decamp, attempt our
voyage, and expand the wings of our sails. And now the
stars being chased away, blushing Aurora appeared, when far
off we espy the hills obscure, and lowly Italy. Italy! Achates
first called aloud; Italy the crew with joyous acclamations
hail. Then father Anchises decked a capacious bowl with a
garland, and filled it up with wine; and invoked the gods,
standing on the lofty stern: Ye gods who rule sea, and land,
and storms, grant us a prosperous voyage by the wind, and
breathe propitious. The wished-for gales begin to swell; and
now the port opens nearer to our view, and on a height appears the temple of Minerva. Our crew furl the sails, and
turn about their prows to the shore. Where the wave breaks
from the east, the port bends into an arch; the jutting cliffs
foam with the briny spray; [the port] itself lies hidden: two
turret-like rocks stretch out their arms in a double wall, and
the temple recedes from the shore. ´ Here, on the grassy
meadow, I saw, as our first omen, four snow-white steeds
grazing the plain at large. And father Anchises [calls out],
War, O hospitable land, thou betokenest; [44] for war steeds are
harnessed; war these cattle threaten: but yet, the same qua-
drupeds having long been used to submit to the chariot, and
in the yoke to bear the peaceful reins, there is hope, also, of
peace, he says. Then we address our prayers to the sacred
majesty of Pallas, with clashing arms arrayed, who first received us elated with joy; and before her altars we veiled our
heads with a Phrygian veil; and according to the instructions
of Helenus, on which he laid the greatest stress, in due form
we offer up to Argive Juno the honours enjoined. Without
delay, as soon as we had regularly fulfilled our vows, we turn
about the extremities of our sail-yards, and quit the abodes
and suspected territories of the sons of Greece. Next is seen
the bay of Tarentum, sacred to Hercules, if report be true;
and the Lacinian [45] goddess rears herself opposite: the towers
of Caulon [46] [also appear], and Scylaceum infamous for ship-

[44] Cf. Æn. iv. 840, "tristia omnia portans." Petron. § 124, "incendia
portat." See also Westerhov. on Ter. Andr. i. 1, 46. B.

[45] Lacinian goddess; that is, Juno Lacinia, who had a celebrated temple near Crotona, a city of Calabria in Italy.

[46] Caulon and Scylaceum, (Squillace,) both towns of Calabria, south
of Crotona.

wrecks. Then, far from the waves, is seen Trinacrian Ætna;
and from a distance we hear the loud growling of the ocean,
the heaten rocks, and the murmurs of breakers on the coast:
the deep [47] leaps up, and sands are mingled with the tide. And,
[says] father Anchises, Doubtless this is the famed Charyhdis;
these shelves, these hideous rocks Helenus foretold. Rescue
us, my friends, and with equal ardour rise on your oars. They
do no otherwise than bidden; and first Palinurus whirled
about the creaking prow to the left waters. The whole crew,
with oars and sails, bore to the left. We mount up to heaven
on the arched gulf, and down again we settle to the shades
below, the wave having retired. Thrice the rocks hellowed
amid their hollow caverns; thrice we saw the foam dashed
up, and the stars drenched with its dewy moisture.

Meanwhile the wind with the sun forsook us spent with
toil; and not knowing our course, we near the coasts of the
Cyclops. The port itself is ample, and undisturbed by the
access of the winds; but, near it, Ætna thunders with horrible ruins, and sometimes sends forth to the skies a black cloud,
ascending in a pitchy whirlwind of smoke and glowing embers; throws up halls of flame, and kisses the stars: sometimes, belching, hurls forth rocks and the shattered howels of
the mountain, and with a rumbling noise wreaths aloft the
molten rocks, and boils up from its lowest hottom. It is said
that the body of Enceladus, [48] half consumed with lightning, is
pressed down by this pile, and that cumbrous Ætna, laid
above him, spouts forth flames from its burst furnaces; and
that, as often as he shifts his weary side, all Trinacria, [49] with
a groan, inly trembles, and overshades the heavens with smoke.
Lying that night under the covert of the woods, we suffer
from those hideous prodigies; nor see what cause produced
the sound. For neither was there the light of the stars, nor
was the sky enlightened by the starry firmament; hut gloom
was over the dusky sky, and a night of extreme darkness
muffled up the moon in clouds.

And now the next day with the first dawn was rising, and

---

[47] "Vada" must not be rendered "shallows." See Heyne. B.
[48] Enceladus, the son of Titan and Terra, and the most powerful of all
the giants, who conspired against Jupiter. According to the poets, he was
struck with Jupiter's thunders, and overwhelmed under Mount Ætna.
[49] Trinacria, an ancient name of the island of Sicily, from its three
promontories.

Aurora had dissipated the humid shades from the sky; when suddenly a strange figure of a man unknown to us, emaciated to the last degree, and in a lamentable plight, stalks from the woods, and, with the air of a suppliant, stretches forth his hands to the shore. We look back: he was in horrid filth, his beard overgrown,[80] his garment tagged with thorns; but, in all besides, he was a Greek, and had formerly been sent to Troy accompanying the arms of his country. As soon as he descried our Trojan dress and arms, struck with terror at the sight, he paused a while, and stopped his progress: a moment after, rushed headlong to the shore with tears and prayers. I conjure you, [says he,] by the stars, by the powers above, by this celestial light of life, ye Trojans, snatch me hence; convey me to any climes whatever, I shall be satisfied. It is true, I am one who belonged to the Grecian fleet, and, I confess, I bore arms against the walls of Troy: for which, if the demerit of my crime be so heinous, scatter my limbs on the waves, and bury them in the vast ocean. If I die, I shall have the satisfaction of dying by the hands of men. He said, and clasping our knees, and wallowing [on the ground], clung to our knees. We urge him to tell who he is, of what family born; and next to declare what fortune pursues him. My father Anchises frankly gives the youth his right hand, and re-assures his mind by that kind pledge. At length, fear removed, he thus begins: I am a native of Ithaca; a companion of the unfortunate Ulysses, Achæmenides my name. I went to Troy, my father Adamastus being poor, but would that my state of life had remained as it was: Here, in the huge den of the Cyclop, my unmindful companions deserted me, while in consternation they fled from his cruel abodes. It is an abode of gore and bloody banquets, gloomy within, and vast; [the Cyclop] himself, of towering height, beats the stars on high, (ye gods, avert such a pest from the earth!) fiercely scowling in his aspect, and inaccessible to every mortal: he feeds on the entrails and purple blood of hapless wretches. I myself beheld, when, having grasped in his rapacious hand two of our number, as he lay stretched on his back in the middle of the cave, he dashed them against the stones, and the bespattered pavement floated with their blood: I beheld, when he ground

---

* Cf. Sisenna apud Non. ii. 471, "Complures menses barba immissa, et intonso capillo." B.

their members distilling black gore, and their throbbing limbs
quivered under his teeth.[51] Not with impunity, it is true; such
barbarity Ulysses suffered not [to pass unrevenged], nor was
the prince of Ithaca forgetful of himself in that critical hour.
For as soon as, glutted with his banquet, and buried in wine,
he reposed his reclined neck to rest, and lay at his enormous
length along the cave, disgorging blood in his sleep, and gob-
bets intermixed with gory wine; we, having implored the
great gods, and distributed our several parts by lot, pour in
upon him on all hands at once, and with our pointed javelins
bore out the huge single eye which was sunk under his lowering front, like a Grecian buckler, or the orb of Phœbe; and
at length we joyfully avenge the manes of our friends. But
fly, ah wretches! fly, and tear the cables from the shore. For
such and so vast Polyphemus[52] [is, who] pens in his hollow
cave the fleecy flocks, and drains their dugs, a hundred other
direful Cyclops commonly haunt these winding shores, and
roam on the lofty mountains. The horns of the moon are now
filling up with light for the third time, while in these woods,
among the desert dens and holds of wild beasts, I linger out
my life, and descry from the rock the vast Cyclops, and quake
at the sound of their feet and voice. The berries and the
stony cornels, which the branches supply, form my wretched
sustenance, and the herbs feed me with their plucked up roots.
Casting my eyes around on every object, this fleet I espied
first steering to the shore; to it I was resolved to give up myself, whatever it had been; it suffices me that I have escaped
from that horrid crew. Do you rather destroy this life by
any sort of death. Scarcely had he spoken this, when on
the summit of the mountain we observe the shepherd Polyphemus himself, stalking with his enormous bulk among his
flocks, and seeking the shore; his usual haunt; a horrible
monster, mis-shapen, vast, of sight deprived. The trunk of a
pine guides his hand, and makes firm his steps: his fleecy
sheep accompany him; this his sole delight, and the solace of
his distresses: [*from his neck his whistle hangs.* [53]] After

[51] The reader may compare Hom. Od. I. 288; Eur. Cycl. 379 sqq.;
Ovid Met. xiv. 205 sqq. B.

[52] Polyphemus, a son of Neptune, and king of the Cyclops. He is represented as a monster of great strength, with one eye in the middle of
the forehead, which Ulysses put out as he was asleep.

[53] A spurious attempt to fill up the verse. B.

he touched the deep floods, and arrived at the sea, he therewith
washes away the trickling gore from his quenched orb, gnashing his teeth with a groan: and now he stalks through the
midst of the sea, while the waves have not yet wetted his
gigantic sides. We, in consternation, hasten our flight far
from that shore, having received our suppliant, who thus
merited our favour; we silently cut the cable, and bending
forward, sweep the sea with struggling oars. He perceived,
and at the sound turned his steps. But when no opportunity
is afforded him to reach us with his eager grasp, and he is
unable in pursuing us to equal the Ionian waves, he raises a
prodigious yell, wherewith the sea and every wave deeply
trembled, and Italy, to its inmost bounds, was affrighted, and
Ætna bellowed through its winding caverns. Meanwhile the
race of the Cyclops, roused from the woods and lofty mountains, rush to the port, and crowd the shore. We perceive the
Ætnean brothers, standing side by side in vain, with lowering
eye, bearing their heads aloft to heaven; a horrid assembly :
as when aërial oaks, or cone-bearing cypresses, Jove's lofty
wood, or Diana's grove, together rear their towering tops.
Sharp fear impels our crew to tack about to any quarter whatever, and spread their sails to any favourable wind. On the
other hand, the commands of Helenus warn them not to continue their course between Scylla and Charybdis, a path which
borders on death on either hand: our resolution [therefore]
is, to sail backward.

And lo ! the north-wind sent from the narrow seat of Pelorus comes to our aid. I am wafted beyond the mouth of
l'antagia,[54] formed of natural rock, the bay of Megara, and
low-lying Tapsus. These Achæmenides, the associate of
accursed Ulysses, pointed out to us, as backward he cruised
along the scenes of his wanderings.

Before the Sicilian bay outstretched lies an island opposite
to rough Plemmyrium;[55] the ancients called its name Ortygia.[56] It is said, that Alpheus, a river of Elis, hath hither

[54] Pantagia, a small but rapid river on the eastern coast of Sicily, between Catana and Syracuse. Tapsus, a peninsula in the bay of Megara,
north of Syracuse.

[55] Plemmyrium, a promontory in the bay of Syracuse.

[56] Ortygia, a small island within the same bay, in which was the celebrated fountain Arethusa.

worked a secret channel under the sea ; which, by thy mouth, O Arethusa, is now blended with the Sicilian waves. We venerate the great divinities of the place, as commanded ; and thence I pass the too luxuriant soil of the overflowing Helorus.[57] Hence we skim along the high cliffs and prominent rocks of Pachynos ; and at a distance appears Camarina, by fate forbidden to be ever removed ; the Geloian plains and huge Gela, called by the name of the river. Next lofty Acragas[58] shows from far its stately walls, once the breeder of generous steeds. And thee, Selinus, fruitful in palms, I leave, by means of the given winds ; and I trace my way through the shallows of Lilybeum,[59] dangerous through its hidden rocks. Hence the port and joyless coast of Drepanum receive me. Here, alas ! after being tossed by so many storms at sea, I lose my sire Anchises, my solace in every care and suffering. Here thou, best of fathers, whom in vain, alas ! I saved from so great dangers, forsakest me spent with toils. Neither prophetic Helenus, when he gave me many fearful warnings, nor dire Celæno, predicted to me this mournful stroke. This was my finishing disaster, this the termination of my long tedious voyage. Parting hence, a god directed me to your coasts.

Thus father Æneas, while all sat attentive, alone recounted the destiny allotted to him by the gods, and gave a history of his voyage. He ceased at length, and, having here finished his relation, rested.

[57] Helorus, (Abisso,) a river of Sicily, south of Syracuse, which overflowed its banks at certain seasons. Camarina, a lake, and Gela, a city on the southern coast of Sicily.

[58] Acragas, called also Agrigentum, (Girgenti,) a celebrated city of Sicily, built on a mountain of the same name. Selinus, a city in the south-west of Sicily, the vicinity of which abounded with palm-trees.

[59] Lilybeum, (Cape Boœ,) one of the three famous promontories of Sicily. Drepanum, (Trapani,) a town on the western coast of Sicily near Mount Eryx, where Anchises died.

BOOK IV.

In the Fourth Book, Queen Dido becomes deeply enamoured of Æneas, to whom she proffers her hand and her crown; but, on finding him determined, in obedience to the command of the gods, to leave Carthage, rage and despair took possession of the unhappy queen. At last, the sudden departure of Æneas led to the fatal catastrophe of her death, by her own hand, on the funeral pile which she had erected.

BUT the queen, long since pierced with painful care, feeds the wound in her veins, and is consumed by unseen flames.[1] The many virtues of the hero, the many honours of his race, recur to her thoughts: his looks and words dwell fixed in her soul: nor does care allow calm rest to her limbs. Returning Aurora now illuminated the earth with the lamp of Phœbus, and had chased away the dewy shades from the sky, when she, half-frenzied, thus addresses her sympathizing sister: Sister Anna, what dreams terrify and distract my mind! What think you of[2] this wondrous guest who has come to our abodes? In mien how graceful he appears! in manly fortitude and warlike deeds how great! I am fully persuaded (nor is my belief groundless) that he is the offspring of the gods. Fear argues a degenerate mind. Ah! by what fatal disasters has he been tossed! what toils of war he sang, endured to the last![3] Had I not been fixed and stedfast in my resolution, never to join myself to any in the bonds of wedlock, since my first love by death mocked and disappointed me; had I not been thoroughly tired of the marriage-bed and nuptial torch, to this one frailty I might perhaps give way. Anna, (for I will own it,) since the decease of my unhappy spouse Sichæus, and since the household gods were stained with his blood shed by a brother, this [stranger] alone has warped my inclinations, and interested my wavering mind: I recognise the symptoms of my former flame. But sooner may earth from her lowest depths yawn for me, or the almighty Sire hurl me by his thunder to the shades, the pale shades of Erebus and deep night, than I violate thee, modesty, or break thy laws. He who first linked

---

[1] Cf. Aristenst. Ep. II. 5, ἱκβάσεται γὰρ μὴ τις ἀνερμήνευτος ὀδύνη. B.
[2] Davidson has better expressed the force of this Greek construction than Anthon. Cf. Soph. Ant. 7; El. 328; Æsch. Ch. 8. B.
[3] Literally, "drained to the dregs." Cf. Æn. x. 57. B.

me to himself hath borne away my affection; may he possess
it still, and retain it in his grave. This said, she filled her
bosom with trickling tears. Anna replies: O dearer to your
sister than the light, will you thus in mournful solitude waste
your bloom of youth, nor know the dear delights of children,
and rewards of love? Think you that ashes and the buried
dead care for that?[4] What though no lovers moved you before,
when your sorrows were green, either in Libya, or before in
Tyre? what though Iarbas[5] was slighted, and other princes
whom Afric, fertile in triumphs, maintains? Will you also resist a flame which you approve? Will you not reflect in whose
country you now reside? Here the Getulian[6] cities, a race
invincible in war, unrestrained Numidians, and inhospitable
quicksands, enclose you round; there, a region by thirst
turned into a desert, and the wide-raging Barcæans. Why
should I mention the kindling wars from Tyre, and the menaces of your brother? It was surely, I think, under the
auspices of the gods, and by the favour of Juno, that the Trojan ships steered their course to this our coast. O sister, how
flourishing shall you see this city, how potent your kingdom
rise from such a match! By what high exploits shall the Carthaginian glory be advanced, when the Trojan's arms join
them! Do thou but supplicate the favour of the gods, and,
having performed propitiating rites, indulge in hospitality,
and devise one pretence after another for detaining [your
guest], while winter's fury rages on the sea, and Orion charged
with rain; while his ships are shattered, and the sky is inclement.

By this speech she fanned the fire of love kindled in Dido's
breast, buoyed up her wavering mind with hope, and banished
her scruples. First to the temples they repair, and by sacrifice the peace of heaven implore: to Ceres the lawgiver, to
Phœbus, and to father Bacchus, they offer ewes of the age of
two years, according to custom; above all to Juno, whose
province is the nuptial tie. Dido herself, in all her beauty,

---

[4] Petron. § lli. "Id cineres, aut manes credis sepultos sentire?" B.

[5] Iarbas, a son of Jupiter and Garamantis, and king of Getulia, from
whom Dido bought land to build Carthage. He was a lover of the queen
at the time Æneas came to Carthage.

[6] Getulians, Numidians, &c., the inhabitants of countries in Northern
Africa, now Algiers, Barbary, &c.

holding in her right hand the cup, pours it between the horns
of a white heifer; or before the images of the gods in solemn
pomp around the rich-loaded altars walks, renews one offering
after another all the day long, and, gaping over the disclosed
breasts of the victims, consults their panting entrails. Alas!
how ignorant the minds of seers! what can prayers, what can
temples, avail a raging lover? The gentle flame preys all the
while upon her vitals, and the secret wound rankles in her
breast. Unhappy Dido burns, and frantic roves over all the
town; like a wounded deer, whom, off her guard, a shepherd
pursuing with his darts has pierced at a distance among the
Cretan woods, and unknowingly [in the wound] hath left the
winged steel: she flying bounds over the Dictæan woods and
glades: the fatal shaft sticks in her side. Now she conducts
Æneas through the midst of her fortifications; shows him both
the treasures brought from Tyre, and her new city: she begins to speak, and stops short in the middle of a word. When
day declines, she longs to have the same banquets renewed;
and, fond even to madness, begs again to hear the Trojan
disasters, and again hangs on the speaker's lips. Now, when
they had severally retired, while the fading moon in her alternate course withdraws her light, and the setting stars invite
sleep, she mourns alone in the desert hall, presses the couch
which he had left, and in fancy hears and sees the absent
hero; or, captivated with the father's image, hugs Ascanius
in her bosom, if possibly she may divert her unutterable love.
The towers which were begun cease to rise; her youth practise not their warlike exercises, nor prepare ports and bulwarks
for war; the works and the huge battlements on the walls,
and the engines that mate the skies, are discontinued.

Whom when Jove's beloved wife perceived to be thus possessed with the blighting passion, and that even sense of
honour could not resist its rage, Saturnia thus artfully addresses Venus: Distinguished praise, no doubt, and ample
spoils, you and your boy carry off, high and signal renown, if
one woman is overcome by the wiles of two deities. Nor am
I quite ignorant, that you apprehend danger from our walls,
and view the structures of lofty Carthage with a jealous eye.
But where will all this end? or what do we now propose by
such hot contention? Why do not we rather promote an eternal
peace, and nuptial contract? You have your whole soul's de-

N

airs; Dido burns with love, and has sucked the fury into her
very bones. Let us therefore rule this people in common,
and under equal sway: let Dido be at liberty to bind herself
in wedlock to a Trojan lord, and into thy hand deliver over
the Tyrians by way of dowry.

To whom Venus (for she perceived that she spoke with au
insincere mind, with a design to transfer the seat of empire
from Italy to the Libyan coasts) thus in her turn began:
Who can be so mad as to reject these terms, and rather choose
to engage in war with you, would fortune but concur with the
scheme which you mention? But I am driven to an uncertainty by the Fates, [not knowing] whether it be the will of
Jupiter that the Tyrians and Trojans should dwell in one city,
or if he will approve the union of the two nations, and the
joining of alliance. You are his consort: to you it belongs
by entreaty to work upon his mind. Lead you the way; I
will follow. Then imperial Juno thus replied: That task
be mine: meanwhile (mark my words) I will briefly show by
what means our present design may be accomplished. Æneas
and most unhappy Dido are preparing to hunt together in the
forest, soon as to-morrow's sun shall have brought forth the
early dawn,'and enlightened the world with his beams. While
the [bright-hued] plumage flutters,[7] and they enclose the
thickets with toils, I will pour on them from above a blackening storm of rain with mingled hail, and with peals of thunder
make heaven's whole frame to shake. Their retinue shall fly
different ways, and be covered with a dark night [of clouds].
Dido and the Trojan prince shall repair to the same cave:
there will I be present, and, if I have your firm consent, I will
join them in the lasting bonds of wedlock, and consecrate her
to be his for ever. The god of marriage[8] shall be there. Venus,
without any opposition, agreed to her proposal, and smiled at
the fraud she discovered.

Meanwhile Aurora rising left the ocean. Soon as the beams

---

[7] This is the proper meaning of "alæ." Cf. Ovid. Met. l. 106. In
ounting, nets were drawn around a considerable space, within which the
beasts were driven. In order to scare them thither, a number of bright-
coloured feathers were hung to strings at a little distance, called the
"formido." It was chiefly employed in hunting deer. Cf. Ulit. ou
Gratius Cyneg. 77 and 85.　B.

[8] Hymen, the god of marriage, was the son of Bacchus and Venus, or,
according to others, of Apollo and one of the Muses.

of day shot forth, the chosen youth issue through the gates:
the fine nets, the toils, the broad-pointed hunting spears, the
Massylian⁹ horsemen, and a pack of quick-scented hounds,
pour forth together. Before the palace-gate the Carthaginian
nobles await the queen lingering in her alcove: her steed,
richly caparisoned with purple and gold, ready stands, and
fiercely champs the foaming bit. At length she comes attended by a numerous retinue, attired in a Sidonian chlamys
with embroidered border: she has a quiver of gold; her
tresses are tied in a golden knot; a golden buckle binds up her
purple robe. The Trojan youth, too, and sprightly Iulus,
accompany the procession. Æneas himself, distinguished in
beauty above all the rest, mingles with the retinue, and adds
his train to hers: as when Apollo, leaving Lycia,¹⁰ his winter
seat, and the streams of Xanthus, revisits his mother's island
Delos, and renews the dances: the Cretans, Dryopes,¹¹ and
painted Agathyrsi,¹² mingle their acclamations around his
altars: he himself moves majestic on Cynthus' top, and ad-
justing his waving hair, crowns it with a soft wreath, and en-
folds it in gold; his arrows rattle on his shoulders. With no
less active grace Æneas moved: such comeliness shines forth
in his matchless mien. Soon as they reached the high mountains, and pathless lairs, lo! from the summit of the craggy
cliff the wild goats dislodged skip down the rocks: on the
other side the stags scour along the open plains, and gather
together in flight their dust-covered squadrons, and forsake
the mountains. Now the boy Ascanius delights in his
sprightly courser through the enclosed vales; and now these,

⁹ The Massylians, a warlike people of Mauritania in Africa, near Mount
Atlas: when they went on horseback, they never used saddles or bridles,
but only sticks.

¹⁰ As Dido is before compared to Diana, Æn. i. 498, so Æneas here to
Apollo, the brother of Diana. It was a common opinion, that the gods at
certain times of the year changed their places of residence; and Servius
says it was firmly believed, that Apollo gave responses at Patara, a city of
Lycia, during the six months of winter, and at Delos in the summer
months. Hence Apollo is called Delius and Patareus, Hor. Carm. ii.
4, 62.

——————— qui Lyciæ tenet
Dumeta, natalemque silvam,
Delius et Patareus Apollo.

¹¹ Dryopes, a people of Greece, in the vicinity of Mount Œta and
Parnassus.

¹² Agathyrsi, an effeminate nation of Scythia.

now those he outrides, and devoutly wishes that a foaming
boar would cross his way amidst the feeble flocks, or a tawny
lion descend from the mountain.

Meanwhile the air begins to be disturbed with loud murmur-
ings; a deluge of rain with mingled hail succeeds. And here
and there the Tyrian train, the Trojan youth, and Venus'
grandchild of Dardanian line, for fear sought different shelters
through the fields. Whole rivers from the mountains come
pouring down. Dido and the Trojan prince repair to the
same cave. [Then] first the Earth, and Juno who presides
over marriage, gave the signal: lightnings flashed, the sky
was a witness to the alliance, and the nymphs were heard to
shriek on the mountain tops. That day first proved the
source of death, the source of woes: for [now] Dido is neither
influenced by appearance nor character, nor is she now studious to carry on clandestine love: she calls it marriage: she
veils[13] her guilt under that name.

Forthwith Fame[14] through the populous city of Libya runs:
Fame, than whom no pest is more swift, by exerting her
agility grows more active, and acquires strength on her way:
small at first through fear; soon she shoots up into the skies,
and stalks along the ground, while she hides her head among the
clouds. Parent Earth, enraged by the vengeance of the gods,
produced her the youngest sister, it is said of Cœus, and
Enceladus, swift to move with feet and persevering wings: a
monster hideous, immense; who (wondrous to relate!) for as
many plumes as are in her body, numbers so many wakeful
eyes beneath, so many tongues, so many babbling mouths,
pricks up so many listening ears. By night, through the mid
region of the sky, and through the shades of earth, she flies
buzzing, nor inclines her eyes to balmy rest. Watchful by
day, she perches either on some high house-top, or on lofty
turrets, and fills mighty cities with dismay; as obstinately
bent on falsehood and iniquity as on reporting truth. She
then, delighted, with various rumours filled the people's ear,
and uttered facts and fictions indifferently; [namely,] that

---

[13] More literally, "she weaves over her fault with this title." D'Orville
on Chariton, p. 82, compares Ovid Her. v. 131, "vim licet appelles, et
culpam nomine veles." Aristoph. Plut. 159, ὀνόματι περιπλοῦσι τὴν
μοχθηρίαν.

[14] Fame was worshipped by the ancients as a powerful goddess, and
generally represented blowing a trumpet, &c.

Æneas, sprung from Trojan blood, had arrived, whom Dido, with all her charms, vouchsafed to wed; that now in revelling with each other they enjoyed the winter, throughout its length, unmindful of their kingdoms, and enslaved by a base passion.
With such news the foul goddess fills the mouths of the people. To king Iarbus straight she turns her course; inflames his soul by her rumours, and aggravates his rage. This Iarbus, the son of Ammon by the ravished nymph Garamantis, raised to Jove a hundred lofty temples within his extensive realms, a hundred altars; and there had he consecrated the wakeful fire, with a sacred watch to keep eternal guard, a piece of ground, fattened with victims' blood, and the gates adorned with wreaths of various flowers. He, maddened in soul, and inflamed by the bitter tidings, is said, before the altars, amid the very presence of the gods, to have [thus] importunately addressed Jupiter in suppliant form with uplifted hands: Almighty Jove, to whom the Maurusian race, that feast on painted couches, now honour thee with a libation of wine, seest thou these things? or do we vainly dread thee, when thou, O father! dartest thy thunder-bolts? and are those lightnings in the clouds that terrify our minds blind and fortuitous, and do they mingle mere idle sounds? A wandering woman, who hath built in our dominions a small city [on a spot] she purchased; to whom we assigned a tract of shore for tillage, and upon whom we imposed the laws of the country, hath rejected our proffered match, and hath taken Æneas into her kingdom for her lord: and now this other Paris,[16] with his unmanly[16] train, bound under the chin with a Lydian cap,[17] and with his locks bedewed [with odours],

[16] He calls Æneas Paris, both to denote him effeminate, and a ravisher, one who had carried off from him that princess whom he looked upon as his property, and thought he had a right to marry. In allusion to which rape, he says at the end of the sentence, rapto potitur.
[16] Is said in allusion to the manner of the Phrygians, who were great worshippers of the goddess Cybele, whose priests were eunuchs.
[17] Mæonian or Lydian mitre, a sort of bonnet worn by the Lydian and Phrygian women, a part of dress which would have been quite infamous in a man, especially when it had the redimicula or fillets, wherewith it was tied under the chin, mentum subnexus:

Vobis picta croco et fulgenti murice vestis;
Desidiæ cordi; juvat indulgere choreis;
Et tunicæ manicas et habent redimicula nitræ:
O vere Phrygiæ, neque enim Phryges! Æn. ix. 14.

enjoys the ravished prize: [this we have deserved forsooth,]
because we bring offerings to thy temples, and cherish an
idle glory.[18]

While in such terms he addressed his prayer, and grasped
the altar, the almighty heard, and turned his eyes towards
the royal towers [of Carthage], and the lovers regardless of
their better fame. Then thus he bespeaks Mercury, and gives
him these instructions: Fly quick, my son, call the zephyrs,
and on thy pinions glide: and to the Trojan prince, who now
loiters in Tyrian Carthage, nor regards the cities allotted him
by the Fates, address yourself; and bear [this] my message
swiftly through the skies. Not such a one did his fairest
mother promise us, nor was it for this she saved him twice
from the Grecian sword: but that he should be one who
should rule Italy, big with [future] empire, and fierce in war,
who should evince his descent from Teucer's noble blood, and
bring the whole world under his sway. If he is not fired
by the glory of such deeds, nor will himself attempt any
laborious enterprise for his own renown, will he, the father,
envy Ascanius Rome's imperial towers? What does he propose? or with what prospect lingers he so long among an
unfriendly race, nor regards his Ausonian offspring, and
Lavinian fields? Bid him set sail. No more: be this our
message.

He said: Mercury prepared to obey his mighty father's
will: and first to his feet he binds his golden sandals, which
by their wings waft him aloft, whether over sea or land, swift
as the rapid gales. Next he takes his wand; with this he
calls from hell the pale ghosts, despatches others down to sad
Tartarus, gives sleep, or takes it away, and unseals the eyes
from death.[19] Aided by this, he drives along the winds, and
breasts the troubled clouds. And now in his flight he espies
the top and lofty sides of hardy Atlas,[20] who with his summit

---

[18] i. e. of being thy descendants. B.
[19] This explanation is neatly supported in Anthon's note. B.
[20] Atlas, one of the Titans, son of Japetus and Clymene. He was king
of Mauritania, and upon Perseus showing him the head of Medusa, was
changed into the mountain which bears his name. Mount Atlas runs
across the deserts of Africa, east and west, and is so high that the ancients
imagined that the heavens rested on its top, and that Atlas supported the
world on his shoulders.

supports the sky; Atlas, whose head, crowned with pines, is always encircled with black clouds, and lashed by wind and rain: large sheets of snow enwrap his shoulders; from his aged chin torrents headlong roll, and his grisly beard is stiff with icicles. Here first Cyllenius,[21] poising himself on even wings, alighted; hence with the weight of his whole body he flings himself headlong to the floods; like the fowl, which [hovering] about the shores, about the fishy rocks, flies low near the surface of the seas: just so Maia's son, shooting down from his maternal grandsire between heaven and earth, [skimmed along] the sandy shore of Libya, and cut the winds.[22] As soon as he touched the cottages [of Afric] with his winged feet, he views Æneas founding towers, and raising new structures; and at his side he wore a sword studded with yellow jasper, and a cloak, hanging down from his shoulders, glowed with Tyrian purple; presents which wealthy Dido had given, and had interwoven the stuff with threads of gold. Forthwith he accosts him: Is it for you now to be laying the foundations of stately Carthage, and, the fond slave of a wife, be raising a city [for her], regardless, alas! of your kingdom and nearest concerns? The sovereign of the gods, who governs heaven and earth by his nod, himself sends me down to you from bright Olympus. The same commanded me to bear these his instructions swiftly through the air. What dost thou propose, or with what prospect dost thou waste thy peaceful hours in the territories of Libya? If no glory from such deeds moves thee, and thou wilt attempt no laborious enterprise for thy own renown; have some regard [at least] to the rising Ascanius, and the hopes of thine heir Iülus, for whom the kingdom of Italy and the Roman territories are destined. When Cyllenius had spoken thus, he left mortal vision in the very midst of the conference, and far beyond sight vanished into thin air.

Meanwhile Æneas, entranced by the vision, was struck dumb; his hair with horror stood erect, and his tongue cleaved to his jaws. He burns to be gone in flight, and leave the darling land, awed by the message and dread command of

---

[21] Cyllenius, a name of Mercury, from Cyllene, a mountain of Arcadia, where he was born.

[22] This whole passage is probably spurious. See Anthon. The zeugma in the last line is intolerable. B.

the gods. Ah! what can he do? in what terms can he now presume to solicit the consent of the [29] raving queen? With what words shall he introduce the subject? And now this way, now that, he swiftly turns his wavering mind, snatches various purposes by starts, and roams uncertain through all. Thus fluctuating, he fixed on this resolution as the best: he calls to him Mnestheus,[34] Sergestus, and the brave Cloanthus; [and bids them] with silent care equip the fleet, summon their social bands to the shore, prepare their arms, and artfully conceal the cause of this sudden change: [adding,] that he himself, in the mean time, while generous Dido was in ignorance, and had no apprehension that their so great loves could be dissolved, would try the avenues [to her heart], what may be the softest moments of address, what means might be most favourable to their design. With joyful speed they all obey the commands, and put his orders in execution.

But the queen (who can deceive a lover?) was beforehand in perceiving the fraud, and the first who conjectured their future motions, dreading even where all seemed to be safe: the same malignant fame conveyed the news to her frantic, that the fleet was being equipped, and preparing to set sail. She rages even to madness, and inflamed, she wildly roams through all the city: like a Bacchanal wrought up into enthusiastic fury in celebrating the sacred [mysteries of her god], when the triennial orgies stimulate her, at hearing the name of Bacchus, and the nocturnal howlings on Mount Citheron invite her. At length, in these words she first accosts Æneas: And didst thou hope, too, perfidious one, to be able to conceal from me so wicked a purpose, and to steal away in silence from my coasts? Can neither our love, nor thy once plighted faith, nor Dido resolved to die by a cruel death, detain thee? Nay, you prepare your fleet even in the wintry season, and haste to launch into the deep amidst northern blasts! Cruel one! suppose you were not bound for a foreign land and settlements unknown, and old Troy was still remaining; should you set sail for Troy on this tem-

---

[29] Literally, "to get around." ANTHON.

[34] Mnestheus, a Trojan, descended from Assaracus: he obtained a prize at the funeral games of Anchises, and was the progenitor of the Memmii at Rome. Sergestus, a sailor in the fleet of Æneas, from whom the family of the Sergii at Rome were descended. Cloanthus, one of the companions of Æneas, the ancestor of the Cluentii family at Rome.

pestuous sea? Wilt thou fly from me? By these[25] tears, by
that right hand, (since I have left nothing else to myself now,
a wretch forlorn,) by our nuptial rites, by our conjugal loves
begun; if I have deserved any thanks at thy hand, or if ever
you saw any charms in me, take pity, I implore thee, on a
falling race, and, if yet there is any room for prayers, lay
aside your resolution. For thy sake have I incurred the
hatred of the Libyan nations, of the Numidian princes, and
made the Tyrians my enemies; for thy sake have I sacrificed
my shame, and, what alone raised me to the stars, my former
fame: to whom dost thou abandon Dido, soon about to die,
my guest! since, instead of a husband's name, only this remains?[26] What wait I for? is it till my brother Pygmalion
lay this city of mine in ashes, or Iarbas, the Getulian, carry
me away his captive? Had I but enjoyed offspring by thee
before thy flight; did a young Æneas play in my hall, were
it but to give me thy image in his features, I should not indeed
have thought myself quite a captive and forlorn.

She said. He, by the commands of Jove, held his eyes
unmoved, and with hard struggles suppressed the anxious
care in his heart. At length he briefly replies, That you, O
queen, have laid on me numerous obligations, which you may
recount at large, I never shall disown; and I shall always remember Elisa with pleasure, while I have any remembrance
of myself, while I have a soul to actuate these limbs. But to
the point in debate I shall briefly speak: believe me, I neither
thought by stealth to have concealed this my flight, nor did I
ever pretend a lawful union, or enter into such a contract.
Had the Fates left me free to conduct my life by my own direction, and ease my cares according to my own choice; my
first regards had been shown to Troy and the dear relics of
my country; Priam's lofty palace should [now] remain, and
with this hand I would have repaired for the conquered the
walls of Pergamus, raised again from ruin. But now to great
Italy Grynæan Apollo, to Italy the Lycian oracles have com-

[25] For this collocation of words, compare Eur. Andr. 892, πρὸς εἰ τῶν
δὲ γουνάτων. Hipp. 601, πρὸς σὲ τῆς σῆς δίξιᾶς. Æn. x. 369. Ter.
Andr. iii. 3, 6. Tibull. L 5, 7. B.

[26] Valpy well remarks, that, as Æneas disowns the nuptial tie, Dido
addresses him by the title of guest, which he cannot reject. Seneca has
expressed the same idea, Herc. Fur. 1, " Soror Tonantis, hoc enim
solum mihi nomen relictum est." B.

manded me to repair. This is the object of my love, this my
country. If the towers of Carthage and the sight of a
Libyan city engross you, a Phœnician born, why should you
be dissatisfied that we Trojans settle in the land of Ausonia?
Let us too have the privilege to go in quest of foreign realms.
Whenever the night overspreads the earth with humid shades,
as often as the fiery stars arise, the troubled ghost of my
father Anchises visits me in my dreams, and with dreadful
summons urges [my departure]: my son Ascanius [calls] me
[hence], and the injury done to one so dear, whom I defraud
of the Hesperian crown, and his destined dominions.   Now [77]
also the messenger of the gods, despatched from Jove himself,
(I call them both to witness!) swift gliding through the air,
bore to me his high commands: myself beheld the god in conspicuous brightness entering your walls, and with these ears
I received his voice.   Cease to torment yourself and me by
your complaints: the Italian coasts I pursue, not out of
choice. [78]
     Thus while he speaks, she views him all along from the
beginning with averted looks, rolling her eyes hither and
thither, and with silent glances surveys his whole person, then
thus inflamed with wrath breaks forth: Nor goddess gave
thee birth, perfidious one! nor is Dardanus the founder of
thy race, but frightful Caucasus on flinty cliffs brought thee
forth, and Hyrcanian tigers gave thee suck.   For why should
I dissemble? or for what greater injuries can I be reserved?
Did he so much as sigh at my distress? did he once move his
eyes? Did he, overcome, shed a tear, or compassionate me in
my love? Where shall I begin my complaint? Now neither
mighty Juno nor the Saturnian sire, considers these things
with impartial eyes.   Firm faith no where subsists.   An
outcast on my shores, an indigent wretch, I received him, and
fool that I was, settled him in partnership of my crown; his
wrecked fleet [I renewed], his companions from death I saved.
Ah! I am all on fire, I am distracted with fury! "Now [79] the
prophetic voice of Apollo; now the Lycian lots; and now the

____

[77] This sophistical defence of Æneas has been partly copied by Silius,
viii. 109 sqq. B.
[78] On this abruptly finished passage, see Weichart, de vers spur. p.
71. B.
[79] Dido ironically repeats his words.

messenger of the gods, despatched from Jove himself, through the air conveys the horrid mandate." A worthy employment, forsooth, for the powers above, a weighty concern to disturb them ·in their peaceful state! I neither detain you, nor argue against what you have said. Go, speed your way for Italy with the winds, pursue this kingdom of yours, over the waves. I hope, however, (if the just gods have any power,) thou mayest suffer punishment amid the rocks, and often [vainly] call on Dido's name. I, though absent, will pursue thee with black flames: and, when cold death shall have separated these limbs from my soul, as a shade will I haunt[80] thee in every place: Wretch! thou shalt make atonement: I shall hear it; even in the deep shades these tidings will reach me. With these words she breaks off in the middle of the conference, and sickening shuns the light: she turns about, and flings away out of his sight, leaving him greatly perplexed through fear, and preparing to say a thousand things. Her maids raise her up, bear her fainting limbs into her marble bed-chamber, and gently lay her on a couch.

Meanwhile pious Æneas, though by solacing means he desires to ease her grief, and by words to divert her anguish, heaving many a sigh, and staggered in his mind by mighty love, yet gives obedience to the commands of the gods, and revisits his fleet. Then, indeed, the Trojans intensely ply their work, and launch the ships all along the shore. The pitchy keel floats; through eager haste to sail, they bring from the woods oars not cleared of leaves, and unfashioned timber. You might have seen them removing, and pouring from all quarters of the town, as when ants, mindful of winter, plunder a large granary of corn, and hoard it up in their cell; the black battalion marches over the plains, and along the narrow track they convey their booty through the meadows; some, shoving with their shoulders, push forward the cumbrous grain; some rally the [straggling] bands, and chastise those that lag: the path all glows with the work.

Dido, how wast thou then affected with so sad a prospect? What groans didst thou utter, when from thy lofty tower thou beheldest the shore in its wide extent glowing [with bustle],

---

* Ovid, Ibis, 146. "Tum quoque factorum veniam memor umbra tuorum, Insequar et vultus omnes forma tuos. Quæ vis Deorum est omnium." B.

‹

and didst also observe, full in thy view, the whole watery
plain resounding with such mingled shouts ? Unrelenting
love, how irresistible is thy sway over the mind of mortals !
She is constrained once more to have recourse to tears, once
more to assail him by prayers, and suppliant to subject the
powers of her soul to love, lest, by leaving any means unattempted, she, should throw away her life rashly, and without
cause. Anna, thou seest over all the shore how they are
hastening: the whole bands are drawn together, the canvass
now invites the gales; and the joyful mariners have crowned
their sterns with garlands. O sister, since I was able to foresee this so sad a blow, I shall be able to bear it. Yet, Anna,
perform this one request for your wretched sister: for that
perfidious man made you the sole object of his esteem, even
intrusted you with the secrets of his soul, you alone knew the
occasions and soft approaches to his heart. Go, sister, and in
suppliant terms bespeak the haughty foe: I never conspired
with the Greeks at Aulis[31] to extirpate the Trojan race, or
sent a fleet to Troy; nor did I disturb the ashes and manes
of his father Anchises. Why does he stop his unrelenting
ears to my words? whither does he fly ? Let him grant but
this last favour to his unhappy lover; to defer his flight till it
be safe, and till the winds blow fair.[32] I plead no more for
that old-promised wedlock, which he has betrayed; nor that
he should deprive himself of fair Latium, and relinquish a
kingdom. I ask a trifling moment; a respite and interval
from distracting pain, till, subdued by fortune, I learn to sustain my woes. This favour I implore as the last, (pity thy
sister!) which, when he has granted, I shall send him away
completely happy in my death.

To this effect she prayed; and her sister, deeply distressed,
bears once and again this mournful message to Æneas; but by
none of her mournful messages is he moved, nor listens with
calm regard to any words. The Fates stand in his way; and
heaven renders his ears deaf to compassion. And as the
Alpine north winds by their blasts, now on this side, now on

---

[31] Aulis, a sea-port town of Bœtia, in Greece, where the Grecian forces
assembled in the expedition against Troy.

[32] Ventosque ferentes, i. e. Ventosque secundos, as in Seneca de B. V
c. 21, Navigantem secundus et ferens ventus exhilarat. So Pliny in his
panegyric, Venti ferentes et brevus cursus optentur.

that, strive with joint force to overturn a sturdy ancient oak ;
a loud howling goes forth, and the leaves strew the ground in
heaps, while the trunk is shaken ; the tree itself cleaves fast to
the rocks ; and as high as it shoots up to the top in the ethereal
regions, so deep it descends with its root towards Tartarus:
just so the hero on this side and that side is plied with importunate remonstrances, and feels deep pangs in his mighty soul ;
his mind remains unmoved ; unavailing tears are shed.

Then, indeed, unhappy Dido, struck to the heart by her
fate, longs for death ; she sickens of beholding the canopy of
heaven. The more to prompt her to execute her purpose,
and to part with the light, while she was presenting her
offerings upon the altar that smoked with incense, she beheld,
horrid to relate ! the sacred liquors grow black, and the outpoured wine turn into inauspicious blood. This vision she
revealed to none, not even to her sister. Besides, there was in
the palace a marble shrine in honour of her former husband,
to which she paid extraordinary veneration, [having] it encircled with snowy fillets of wool and festal garlands. Hence
voices, and the words of her husband calling her, seemed to
be heard,[33] when dim night shrouded the earth ; and on the
house-tops the solitary owl often complained in doleful ditty,
and spun out his long notes in a mournful strain. Besides,
many predictions of pious prophets terrify her with dreadful
forebodings. Æneas himself, now stern and cruel, disturbs
her raving in her sleep ; and still she seems to be abandoned
in solitude, still to be going a long tedious journey, with no
attendance, and to be in quest of her Tyrians in some desert
country: as frantic Pentheus[34] sees troops of Furies, two
suns, and Thebes appear double ; or like Orestes, Agamemnon's son, with distraction hurried on the stage, when he flies
from his mother armed with firebrands[35] and black snakes
and the avenged Furies are planted at the gate.[36]

[33] Compare Silius, viii. 122 sqq., and Ovid, Her. vii. 100 sqq. Such
prodigies are great favourites with the Greek romancists. Thus in
Heliodor. ii. 70, ἐκ μυχῶν τοῦ σπηλαίου, φωνῆς τις ἦχος ἐξηκούετο,
θιάγινις, καλούσης. And Chariton, i. p. 12, ψόφος οὐκ ἐστίν, ἀλλὰ φωνή
καλούντων με τῶν ὑποχθονίων πρὸς αὑτούς. B.

[34] Pentheus, son of Echion and Agave, was king of Thebes in Bœotia.
In consequence of his refusal to acknowledge the divinity of Bacchus, he
was torn to pieces by the bacchanals.

[35] There is an evident reference to the stage costume of the Furies. B

[36] According to Servius, Virgil follows a tragedy of Pacuvius, in which

When, therefore, overpowered with grief, she had taken the Furies[37] into her breast, and determined to die, she ponders the time and manner with herself; and thus accosting her sister, the partner of her grief, covers her intention in her looks, and puts on a serene air of hope. Rejoice, O sister, with thy sister ! I have found an expedient, which will restore him to me, or set my love-sick soul at liberty from him. Near the extremity of the ocean and the setting sun, the utmost boundary of Æthiopia lies, where mighty Atlas on his shoulder whirls about the globe, spangled with refulgent stars : hence appeared to me a priestess of the Massylian nation, the guardian of the temple of the Hesperides,[38] who supplied the dragon with food, and watched the sacred branches on the tree, infusing liquid honey and the sleepy poppy. She undertakes, by charms, to release any souls, whom she will, [from the power of love,] and to entail on others irksome cares: to stop the course of rivers, and turn the stars backward : she summons up the ghosts by night. You shall see the earth bellow under her feet, and the wild ashes descend from the mountains. My dear sister, I call the gods, and you, and that dear person of thine, to witness, that it is against my will I set about these magic arts. Do you in secrecy erect a funeral pile in the inner court, under the open air, and lay upon it his arms, which he, impiously base, left fixed in my bed-chamber, with all his clothes, and the nuptial bed in which I was undone. The priestess orders and directs me to destroy every monument of that execrable man. Having thus said, she ceases: at the same time, paleness overcasts her whole complexion. Yet Anna imagines not that her sister aimed at death under pretext of these unusual rites; nor once suspects that she had formed such a desperate purpose,

---

Orestes was represented taking refuge in the temple of Apollo, while the Furies kept watch for him at the gate. For the more usual stage arrangement, see my notes on Æsch. Eum. p. 180, note 4, ed. Bohn. B.

[37] The Furies, daughters of Acheron and Nox: they were three in number, Tisiphone, Megara, and Alecto, and were supposed to be the ministers of the vengeance of the gods.

[38] Hesperides, three celebrated nymphs, daughters of Hesperus: they presided over the garden which contained the golden apples that Juno gave to Jupiter on the day of their nuptials. This garden, according to the ancients, was situated near Mount Atlas, in Africa, and the tree bearing the golden apples was guarded by a huge dragon.

nor dreads any thing worse than had happened at the death of Sichæus. Therefore she makes the desired preparations.

But the queen, as soon as the vast pile was erected under the open air in the inner court, with torches and faggots of oak, encircles the ground with garlands, and crowns it with funeral boughs: upon the bed she lays his clothes, the sword he left, and his image, well knowing of the future. Altars are raised around; and the priestess, her hair dishevelled, with thundering voice, invokes three hundred gods, and Erebus, and Chaos, and threefold Hecate,[39] virgin Diana's triple form. She sprinkled also water counterfeiting that of the lake Avernus:[40] full-grown herbs, cut by moonlight with brazen sickles, are searched out, together with the juice of black poison: the [mother's] love,[41] too, torn from the forehead of a new-foaled colt, and snatched away from the dam, is sought out. The queen herself, now resolute on death, having one foot bare, her robe ungirt, standing by the altars, with the salt cake and pious hands, makes her appeal to the gods, and to the stars conscious of her fate: then, if any deity, both just and mindful, regards lovers unequally yoked, him she invokes.

It was night, and weary bodies over the earth were enjoying a peaceful repose: the woods and raging seas were still; when the stars roll in the middle of their gliding course; when every field is hushed: the beasts, and speckled birds, both those that far and wide haunt the liquid lakes, and those that possess the fields with rough bushes overgrown, all stretched under the silent night, allayed their cares with sleep, and every heart forgot its toil. But not so the soul-distressed queen; not one moment is she lulled to rest, nor enjoys the night with eyes or mind. Her cares redouble; and love, again arising, rages afresh, and fluctuates with a high tide of passions. Thus then she persists, and revolves these secret reflections in her breast: Lo! what shall I do? Baffled as I am, shall I, in my turn, apply to my former suitors? shall I humbly sue for a match with one of the Numidians, whom I

[39] Hecate, the daughter of Perses and Asteria, or rather of Jupiter and Latona: she was called Luna in heaven, Diana on earth, and Hecate, or Proserpine, in hell.
[40] "Avernales aquas." Hor. Ep. v. 15.   Cf. Macrob. iii. 1. B
[41] On the "hippomanes," here meant, see Anthon. B.

have so often disdained as lords? Shall I then attend the fleet
of Ilium, and submit to the basest commands of the Trojans?
and that, because I am well rewarded for having lent them my
assistance, and in their grateful hearts a just sense of my
former kindness remains? But, suppose I had the will, who
will put it in my power, or receive into their proud ships me,
the object of their hate? Ah! lost one, art thou unacquainted
with, art thou still to learn, the perfidiousness of Laomedon's
race? What then? Shall I steal away by myself to accompany the triumphant crew? or, attended by my Tyrians, and
all my people in a body, shall I pursue them, and again lead
out to sea, and order those to spread their sails to the winds,
whom, with much ado, I forced from Tyre? Nay, rather die,
as you deserve, and end your woes with the sword. You,
sister, subdued by my tears, you first oppressed my distracted
mind with these woes, and exposed me to the enemy. Might
I not have led an innocent unwedded life, like a savage of the
field, and have avoided such cares? I have violated the faith
I plighted to the manes of Sichæus.

Such heavy complaints she poured forth from her heart.
Æneas, determined to depart, was enjoying sleep in the lofty
stern, all things being now in readiness. The form of the god,
returning with the same aspect, appeared to him in his sleep,
and thus again seemed to admonish him; in every thing resembling Mercury, in voice, complexion, golden locks, and
comely youthful limbs: "Goddess-born, can you indulge in
sleep at this conjuncture? Infatuated, not to see what dangers
in a moment may beset you, nor listen to the breathing of the
friendly zephyrs! She, bent on death, is revolving guileful
purposes and horrid wickedness in her breast, and fluctuates
with a tide of angry passions. Will you not fly hence with
precipitation, while thus to fly is in your power? Forthwith
you shall behold the sea in commotion with her oars, and
torches fiercely blaze; forthwith the shore lighted up with
flames, if the morning reach you lingering on these coasts.
Come then, quick, break off delay: woman is a fickle and
ever changeable creature." This said, he mingled with the
sable night.

Then, indeed, Æneas, in consternation at this sudden apparition, snatches his frame from the couch, and rouses his
companions: Awake, my mates, in haste, and plant your-

selves on the benches; instantly unfurl the sails. A god, despatched from the high heavens, once more prompts me to hasten my departure, and cut the twisted cables. We follow thee, O holy power, whoever thou art, and once more with joy obey thy commands. Ah! be present, lend us thy propitious·aid, and light up friendly stars in the heavens. He said, and snatches his keen flashing sword from the sheath, and cuts the halsers with the drawn steel. The same eagerness at once seizes them all: they hale, they hurry away: they have quitted the shore; the sea lies hidden under the fleet; they with exerted vigour upturn the foaming billows, and sweep the azure deep.

And now Aurora, leaving Tithonus' saffron bed, first sowed the earth with new-born light: soon as the queen from her watch-towers marked the dawn whitening, and the fleet setting forward with balanced sails, and perceived the shore and vacant port without a rower; thrice and four times smiting her fair bosom, and tearing her golden locks: O Jupiter! shall he go? she says: and shall this stranger mock my kingdom? Will they not make ready arms, and pursue from all the city? and will not others tear my ships from the docks? Run quick, fetch flames, unfurl the sails, ply the oars. What am I saying? or where am I? what madness turns my brain? Unhappy Dido! art thou then at length stung with the sense of his foul impious deeds?[a] Then it had become thee so to act, when thou impartedst [to him] thy sceptre. Is this the honour, the faith! this [the man] who, they say, carries with him his country's gods! who bore on his shoulders his father spent with age! Might I not have torn in pieces his mangled body, and strewn it on the waves? might I not with the sword have destroyed his friends, Ascanius himself, and served him up for a banquet at his father's table? But the fortune of the fight was doubtful. Grant it had been so: thus resolute on death, whom had I to fear? I might have hurled fire-brands into his camp, filled the hatches with flames, extirpated the son, the sire, with the whole race, and flung myself upon the pile. Thou Sun, who with thy flaming beams surveyest all works on earth, and thou, Juno, the author[b] and witness of these my cares; Hecate, with howlings invoked through

---

[a] "facta," not "fata." B.

[b] "in·erpres," i. e. "media et conciliatrix." Servius. B.

the cities in the crossways by night; and ye avenging Furies,
and gods of dying Elisa! receive these my words; in justice
to my wrongs, turn to me your divine regard, and hearken to
my prayers. If it must be, and Jove's decrees so require, if
this be his determination, that the execrable traitor reach the
port, and get safe to land: yet harassed, at least, by war, and
the hostilities of an audacious people, expelled from his own
territories, torn from the embraces of Iülus, may he sue to
others for relief, and see the ignominious deaths of his friends;
and, after he shall have submitted to the terms of a disadvantageous peace, let him neither enjoy his crown, nor the wished-
for light, but die before his time, and [lie] unburied in the
midst of the sandy shore. These are my prayers; " these the
last words I pour forth with my blood. You, too, O Tyrians,
with irreconcilable enmity, pursue his offspring and all his
future race, and present these offerings to my shade: let no
amity or leagues between the two nations subsist. Arise some
avenger " from my ashes, who may persecute those Trojan
fugitives with fire and sword, now, hereafter, at whatever time
power shall be given. Let them take this curse from me,"
that their shores, their waves, their arms, and ours, may still
be opposed to one another; and may their posterity too [and
ours] be still in war engaged.

She said, and every way turned her shifting soul, seeking,
as soon as possible, to bereave herself of the hated light.
Then briefly thus she bespoke Barce, the nurse of Sichæus

" Respecting their mythical fulfilment, see Servius, and the satisfac-
tory notes of Anthon.   B.
  " Such as Hannibal proved.   B.
  " It was an opinion very prevailing among the ancients, that the prayers of the dying were generally heard, and that their last words were prophetic. Thus Virgil makes Dido imprecate upon Æneas a series of
misfortunes, which actually had their accomplishment in his own person,
or in his posterity. 1. He was harassed with war in Italy by Turnus
2. He was necessitated to abandon his son, and go into Etruria to beg for
assistance, Æn. viii. 80. 3. He saw his friends cruelly slain in battle,
especially Pallas, Æn. x. 489. 4. He died before his time, being slain
by Mezentius, according to the most authentic tradition, and was left unburied on the banks of the Numicus, by whose waters his body was at
length carried off, and never more appeared. 5. The Romans and Carthaginians were irreconcilable enemies to one another, and no leagues,
no ties of religion, could ever bind the two nations to peace. 6. Hannibal
was Dido's avenger, who arose afterwards to be the scourge of the
Romans, and carried fire and sword into Italy.

(for the dark grave lodged her own in her native country): Dear nurse, call hither to me my sister Anna; bid her make haste to sprinkle her body with running water, and bring with her the victims and the things for expiation of which I told her: thus let her come; and you yourself cover your temples with a holy fillet. I have a mind to finish the sacrifice begun with proper rites, which I have prepared for Jupiter Stygius,[47] to put a period to my miseries, and to commit to the flames the pile of the Trojan. She said: the other quickened her pace with an old woman's officiousness.[48]

But Dido, trembling with agitation, and maddened on account of her horrid purpose, rolling her blood-red eye-balls, her throbbing cheeks suffused with spots, and all pale with approaching death, burst into the gate of the inner palace, and frantic mounts the lofty pile, and unsheaths the Trojan sword; a present not provided for such purposes as these.[49] Here, after she had viewed the Trojan vestments and the conscious bed, having wept and mused awhile, she threw herself on the bed, and spoke her last words: Ye dear remains, while god and the fates permitted, receive this soul, and free me from these cares. I have lived, and finished the race which fortune gave me. And now my ghost shall descend illustrious to the shades below: I have raised a glorious city, have seen the walls of my own building, have avenged my husband, punished an unnatural brother; happy, ah! too happy, had but the Trojan ships never touched my shores! She said, and pressing her lips to the bed, Shall I die unrevenged? But let me die,[50] she says: thus, thus with pleasure I descend to the shades below. Let the cruel Trojan from the sea feed his eyes with these flames, and bear with him the omens of my death. She said; and while she spoke, her attendants perceive her fallen on the sword, and the weapon stained with foaming gore, and her hands besmeared. The outcry reaches the lofty palace; fame wildly flies through the alarmed city;

[47] i. e. Pluto. Cf. Macrob. Sat. ili. 3. Æsch. Suppl. 164, Ζῆνα τῶν κεκμηκότων. B.

[48] With Anthon, I prefer "anili" to "anilem." B.

[49] i. e. "quæsitum in pignus amoris," as Silius, viii. 50, says, with an evident reference to this passage. Cf. Ovid Her. vii. 195. B.

[50] Happily imitated by Propert. ii. 7, 79:

"Sic igitur prima moriere ætate, Properti?
Sed morere, interitu gaudeat illa tuo." B.

the houses ring with lamentations, groans, and female yells,[61]
and the sky resounds with loud shrieks: just as if all Carthage, or ancient Tyre, in the hands of the invading enemy,
were falling to the ground, and the furious flames were rolling
over the tops of houses and temples.

Her sister was breathless at the news, and with trembling
haste, all aghast, tearing her face with her nails, and [beating]
her bosom with her hands, rushes through the midst of the
crowd, and calls her dying [sister] by name: O sister, was
this your meaning? did you practise thus to deceive me? was
this what I had to expect from that pile, those fires and altars?
Abandoned! where shall I begin to complain? Did you disdain a sister for your companion in death? Had you invited
me to the same fate, one distress and one hour had snatched
us both away by the sword. Did I raise [that pile] with
these very hands, and with my voice invoke our country's
gods, that I should cruelly absent myself from you, thus
stretched upon it. Ah sister! you have involved yourself
and me, your people, your Tyrian nobles, and your city, in
one common ruin. Let me bathe her wounds with water,[62]
and catch with my lips, if there be yet any straggling remains
of breath.[63] This said, she mounted the high steps, and in
her bosom embracing, cherished her expiring sister with
sighs, and dried up the black blood with her robe. She
essaying to lift her heavy eyes, again sinks down. The wound
deep fixed in her breast, emits a bubbling noise. Thrice
leaning on her elbow, she made an effort to raise herself up;
thrice she fell back on the bed, and with swimming eyes
sought the light of heaven, and having found it, heaved a
groan.

Then all-powerful Juno, in pity to her lingering pain and
uneasy death, sent down Iris[54] from heaven, to release the

---

[61] Synes. Ep. p. 164, C. ἀνδρῶν οἰμωγή, γυναικῶν ὀλολυγή.   B.
[62] I read " date, [i. e. " aquam,"] vulnera."   See Anthon, who renders,
" give me it, I will wash."   B.
[63] This was the ancient custom.   Cf. Bion. l. 47, ἄχρις ἀπὸ ψυχῆς ἐς
ἐμὸν στόμα εἰς ἱμὸν ἦπαρ πνεῦμα τεὸν ῥεύσῃ.   B.
[54] Iris, daughter of Thaumas and Electra, was one of the Oceanides,
and messenger of the gods, more particularly of Juno.   Her office was
to cut the thread which seemed to detain the soul in the body of those
that were expiring.   She is represented with all the variegated and beautiful colours of the rainbow

struggling soul and the tie that bound it to the body: for, since she neither fell by fate, nor by a deserved death, but unhappily before her time, and maddened with sudden rage, Proserpina had not yet cropped the yellow hair from the crown of her head, and condemned her to Stygian Pluto. Therefore dewy Iris, drawing a thousand various colours from the opposite sun, shoots downward through the sky on saffron wings, and alighted on her head: I, by command, bear away this lock sacred to Pluto, and disengage you from that body. She said, and cut the lock with her right hand: at once all the vital heat was extinguished, and life vanished into air.

BOOK V.

In the Fifth Book, Æneas sails from Carthage for Italy, but is forced by a storm to revisit Drepanum in Sicily, where he celebrates the anniversary of his father's death by various games and feats at arms. Here the Trojan women set fire to the fleet, which is saved by the interposition of Jupiter, with the loss of four ships. After this event, Æneas pursues his voyage to Italy.

MEANWHILE, Æneas, in direct course, was now fairly on his route with the fleet,[1] and was cutting the black billows before the wind, looking back to the walls which now glare with the flames of unfortunate Elisa. What cause may have kindled such a blaze is unknown; but the thought of those cruel agonies that arise from violent love when injured, and the knowledge of what frantic woman can do, led the minds of the Trojans through dismal forebodings.

As soon as their ships held the main, and no more land appears, sky all around, and ocean all around; a dark lead-coloured watery cloud stood over his head, bringing on night, and storm; and the waves became horrid in the gloom. The pilot Palinurus himself from the lofty stern [exclaims]: Ah! why have such threatening clouds begirt the sky? or what, O father Neptune, hast thou in view? Thus having spoken, he next commands to furl the sails, and ply the sturdy oars; the bellying canvass he turns askance to the wind, and thus speaks: Magnanimous Æneas, should Jupiter on his authority assure me, I could not hope to reach Italy in this weather. The winds changed roar across our path, and arise thick from

---

[1] See Anthon, whom I have closely followed. B.

the darkening west, and the air is condensed into cloud. We
are neither able to make head against [the storm], nor even
to withstand it: since fortune overpowers us, let us follow
her, and turn our course where she invites us: the trusty
shores of your brother Eryx, and the Sicilian ports, I deem
not far off, if I but rightly remembering review the stars I
observed before. Then the pious Æneas [said], I indeed
have observed long ago that the winds urge us to this, and
that your contrary efforts are in vain. Shift your course by
the sails. Can any land be more welcome to me, or where I
would sooner choose to put in my weather-beaten ships, than
that which preserves for me Trojan Acestes, and in its womb
contains the bones of my father Anchises? This said, they
make towards the port, and the prosperous zephyrs stretch the
sails: the fleet swiftly rides on the flood; and at length the
joyous crew are wafted to the well-known strand. But
Acestes, from a mountain's lofty summit, struck with the distant prospect of their arrival, and at the friendly ships, comes
up to them, all rough with javelins,[1] and the hide of an
African bear: whom, begotten by the river Crinisius,[2] a Trojan mother bore. He, not unmindful of his origin, congratu-
lates them on their safe arrival, and cheerfully entertains them
with rude magnificence, and refreshes them fatigued with
friendly cheer.

When with the early dawn the ensuing bright day had
chased away the stars, Æneas summons to council his followers from all the shore, and from the summit of a rising ground
addresses them: Illustrious Trojans, whose descent is from
the exalted blood of the gods, the annual circle is completed,
by the fulfilment of months, since we lodged in the earth the
relics and bones of my godlike sire, and consecrated to him
the altars of mourning. And now the day, if I mistake not,
is at hand, which I shall always account a day of sorrow, always a day to be honoured: such, ye gods, has been your
pleasure. Were I to pass this day in exile among the Syrtes

---

[1] It is strange that Heyne should have found any difficulty in this
phrase. The preposition is merely redundant. Cf. Val. Flacc. i. 641,
"sublitus in hasta." Lucan, i. 423, "leves in armis." See Wagner, and
Weichart on Val. Flacc. viii. 136.

[2] Crinisius, a river on the western side of the island of Sicily, near the
city Segesta.

of Getulia, or overtaken [by it] on the Grecian Sea, or in the city of Mycene, yet would I regularly perform my annual vows, and the solemn funeral processions, and heap the altars with their proper offerings. Now, without premeditated design, though not, I judge, without the will or the influence of the gods, we are come to the ashes and bones of my own father, and are wafted to the friendly port which we are now entering. Come then, and let us all celebrate the joyous rites. Let us pray for [prosperous] winds, and that, when our city is built, he will permit me to offer to him these rites annually in temples consecrated to his honour. Acestes, a son of Troy, gives you two oxen for each ship: invite to the feast your household and country gods, and those whom our host Acestes worships. Further, if the ninth morning shall bring forth the day fair and serene to mortals, and brighten up the world with its beams, I will propose to the Trojans the first trial of skill to be with the swiftest of their ships. And whoever excels in running, in strength who boldly dares, or moves superior in the javelin,[4] and the light arrows, or who has courage to encounter with the bloody cestus; let all such be ready at hand, and expect prizes of victory suitable to their merit. Do ye all keep religious guard over your lips, and encircle your temples with boughs.

This said, he crowns his temples with his mother's myrtle. The same does Elymus;[5] the same Acestes ripened in years; the same the boy Ascanius, whose example the other youths follow. He went from the assembly to the tomb with many thousands, in the centre of a numerous retinue attending. Here in due form, by way of libation, he pours on the ground to Bacchus two bowls of wine, two of new milk, two of sacred blood; then scatters blooming flowers, and thus speaks: Hail, holy sire! once more hail, ye ashes revisited in vain! ye ghosts and shades of my father! Heaven would not allow us to go together in quest of the bounds of Italy, and of the lands allotted to me by fate, or the Ausonian Tiber, whatever river that is. He said; when from the bottom of the shrine a huge slippery snake trailed along, seven circling spires, seven folds, gently

---

[4] Wyttenbach on Julian, p. 161, condemns this as corrupt. I do not see any substantial grounds of objection. B.

[5] Elymus, a youth at the court of Acestes, who engaged in the foot-races at the tomb of Anchises.

twining round the tomb, and gliding over the altars; whose
back azure streaks, and whose scales drops of burnished gold
brightened up; as the bow in the clouds draws a thousand
various colours from the opposite sun. Æneas stood amazed
at the sight. At length the reptile, creeping with his long
train between the bowls and smooth-polished goblets, gently
tasted the banquet, and harmless retired again into the bottom
of the tomb, and left the altars on which he had fed. Æneas
with the more zeal pursues the sacrifice begun in honour of his
father, in doubt whether to think it the genius of the place, or
the attendant of his parent. He sacrificed five ewes, two years
old, according to custom; as many sows, as many bullocks
with sable backs: and he poured out wine from the goblets,
and invoked the soul of great Anchises, and his ghost from
Acheron released. In like manner his companions offer gifts
with joy, each according to his ability; they load the altars,
and sacrifice bullocks. Others place the brazen caldrons in
order, and, stretched along the grass, apply burning coals
under the spits, and roast the flesh.[6]

Now the wished-for day approached, and the steeds of the
sun ushering in the ninth morning with serene sky; fame,
and the renown of illustrious Acestes, had drawn together the
neighbourhood. They filled the shores with joyous crowd,
some to see the Trojans, some too prepared to try their skill.
The prizes first are set before their eyes in the midst of the
circus; sacred tripods, green garlands, and palms, the reward
of the conquerors; arms, and vestments of purple dye, two
talents. one of gold and one silver: and the trumpet from
the midst of the rising ground gives the signal that the games
are begun.

Four ships selected from the whole fleet, equally matched
with ponderous oars, first enter the lists. Mnestheus manages
the swift-sailing Pristis, with stout rowers, [destined] soon
[to be] the Italian Mnestheus, from which name the family
of Memmius is derived; Gyas,[7] the huge Chimera of stupendous bulk, a work like a city, which with a triple tier the Trojan youth impel; the oars rise together in a triple row. Ser-

---

[6] " Viscera," i. e. all that is contained in the skin of the animal. See
Anthon, on Æn. i. 211. So "visceratio" is "a distribution of meat." B.
[7] Gyas, one of the companions of Æneas, who distinguished himself at
the naval games exhibited by Æneas in honour of his father Anchises.
Gyas commanded the ship Chimera, of which Menœtes was the pilot.

gestus, from whom the Sergian family has its name, rides in
the bulky Centaur; and Cloanthus in the sea-green Scylla,
from whom, O Roman Cluentius, is thy descent.   Far in the
sea there lies a rock opposite to the foaming shore, which
sometimes overwhelmed is buffeted by the swelling surges,⁸
when the wintry north-west winds overcloud the stars: in a
calm it lies hushed, and rises above the still wave as a plain,
and a delightful station for the cormorants basking in the sun.
Here father Æneas erected a verdant goal of branching oak
for a signal to the mariners; whence they might know to turn
back, and whence to wind about the long circuits.   Then they
choose their places by lot; and on the poops the leaders,
adorned with gold and purple, shine from afar with distinguished lustre.   The rest of the youth are crowned with poplar wreaths, and glitter, having their naked shoulders besmeared with oil.   They sit down side by side on the benches,
and their arms are stretched to the oars: with eager attention
they wait the signal, and their throbbing hearts beat heavily
with the impulse of fear, and the generous thirst of praise.
Then, as soon as the loud trumpet gave the signal, all (there
is no delay) started from their barrier: the seamen's clamour
strikes the skies; and the seas, upturned by their in-bent
arms, foam.   At once they plough the watery furrows; and
the whole deep opens, convulsed with oars and trident beaks.
Not with such violent speed the coursers in the two-yoked
chariot-race spring to the field, and start with full career from
the goal; nor with such ardour do the charioteers shake the
waving⁹ reins over the flying steeds, and, bending forward,
hang to [give] the lash.¹⁰   Then, with the applause and uproar of the seamen, and the eager acclamations of the favouring crowd, every grove resounds: the bounded shores roll the
voices on; the lashed hills re-echo the sound.   Amidst the
bustle and uproar, Gyas flies out before the rest, and scuds
away the foremost on the waves: whom next Cloanthus follows, a more skilful rower, but the vessel, sluggish through its
bulk, retards him.   After these, at equal distance, the Pristis

---

⁸ The reading quoted by Agrœtius de Serm. Lat. p. 1346, "tumidis
quod fluctibus olim Tunditur," is far more harmonious than the usual arrangement. B.

⁹ Cf. Tryphiod. 67, ἱπικυμαίνουσα μετήορος αὐχένι εὐρτῷ. H.

¹⁰ For this construction, cf. Sil. viii. 283, "trepida pendens in verbera
planta." B.

and Centaur strive to gain the foremost place. And now the
Pristis has the advantage, now the huge Centaur gets before
her vanquished [antagonist]; anon both advance together
with united fronts, and with their long keels plough the briny
waves. And now they were approaching the rock, and had
reached the goal, when Gyas the foremost, and [hitherto] victorious, thus in mid-sea accosts Menœtes, the pilot of his ship:
Whither, I pray, are you going so far to the right? this way
steer your course; keep to the shore, and let the oar graze
upon the rocks to the left: let others stand out to sea. He
said: but Menœtes, dreading the hidden rocks, turns out his
prow towards the waves. Gyas with loud voice called to him
again, Menœtes, whither are you steering opposite? once
more, I say, keep to the rocks: And lo! he espies Cloanthus
pressing on his rear, and keeping a nearer compass. He, between Gyas' ship and the roaring rocks, brushes along the
left-hand path on the inside, and suddenly gets a-head of him
who was before, and leaving the goal, gains the safe seas.
Then indeed severe grief blazed up in the inmost vitals of the
youth: nor were his cheeks free from tears; and regardless
both of his own dignity and the safety of his friends, he hurls[11]
dastardly Menœtes headlong from the lofty stern into the sea.
Himself succeeds to the helm both as pilot and commander;
encourages his men, and turns his rudder to the shore. But
when encumbered Menœtes with difficulty at length had risen
from the deep bottom, being now in years, and languid by
reason of his wet garments, he crawls up to the summit of the
rock, and sat down on the dry cliff. The Trojans laughed
both to see him fall, and to see him swimming; and they renew their laughter when from his breast he vomits up the
briny wave. Here Sergestus and Mnestheus, the two last,
were fired with joyous hope to outstrip Gyas lagging behind.
Sergestus gets the start, and makes up to the rock, nor yet
had he the advantage by the whole length of the ship, only by
a part: the rival Pristis partly presses him with her beak.
But Mnestheus on the mid-deck walking among his crew animates them: My Hectorean[12] bands, whom I chose associates
in Troy's last fatal hour, now, now with keenness ply your

[11] "Deturbare, dejicere, demovere." Nonius ii. p. 540, ed. Gothof. B.
[12] Instead of "Hectorei socii," Rufinianus, § 35, p. 221, ed. Ruhuk.
reads, "hortor vos socii." B.

oars; now exert that vigour, now that soul of which you
were masters in the quicksands of Getulia, in the Ionian Sea,
and on Malea's [13] coast, where waves succeeding waves pursued us. Your Mnestheus aspires not now to the foremost
place, nor contends for the victory: though would to heaven!
but may those conquer to whom thou, O Neptune, hast given
that boon. Let us be ashamed to come in the last. Surmount,
my countrymen, and repel that criminal disgrace. They
bend to the oar with the greatest emulation: the brazen-
beaked galley trembles with the vast strokes, and the [watery]
surface flies from under them. Then thick panting shakes
their limbs and parched jaws: sweat flows from every pore
in rivulets. Mere chance procured the men the wished-for
honour: for while Sergestus, between Mnestheus and the goal,
in his furious career, is pressing up the head of the ship to the
rocks, and steers in a disadvantageous place, he unluckily stuck
among the jutting rocks. The cliffs are shaken, and on a
sharp reef the struggling oars were loudly snapped, and the
prow dashed against [the rocks] stood suspended. The mariners arise together, and with great clamour desist; and apply
stakes shod with iron, and poles with sharpened points, and
gather up their shattered oars on the stream. Meanwhile
Mnestheus rejoiced, and more animated by this same success,
with the nimble march of the oars, and winds called to his
aid, cuts the easy waves, and scuds away on the open sea. As
a pigeon, whose nest and darling young are in some harbouring rock, suddenly scared from her covert, flies away into the
fields, and, starting in a fright, gives a loud flapping with her
wings against the nest; then, shooting through the calm still
air, skims [14] along the liquid way, nor moves her noble
pinions: thus Mnestheus, thus the Pristis herself in her
career, cuts the utmost boundary of the watery plain; thus
the mere vehemence of her motion carries her forward in her
flying course. And first she leaves behind her Sergestus
struggling against the high rocks and scanty shallows, in vain
imploring aid, and trying to row on with shattered oars. Then
he overtakes Gyas, and Chimera's self of mighty bulk: she
yields, because she is deprived of her pilot. And now, in the
very end of the course, Cloanthus alone is before him; whom

[13] Malea, a promontory of Peloponnesus, on the southern coast of Laconia, dangerous to navigators.
[14] λιαρὸν οἶμον αἰθέρος ψαίρει πτεροῖς. Æsch. Prom. 394. B.

he endeavours to reach, and, straining with the utmost vigour,
pursues. Then, indeed, the shouts redouble, and all, with
hearty applauses, stimulate him in the pursuit, and the sky
resounds with roaring acclamations. These are fired with indignation, lest they should lose their possession of glory and
the honour they have won; and they are willing to barter life
for renown. Those success cherishes; they are able because
they seem to be able. And, perhaps, they had both gained
the prize with equalled beaks,[15] had not Cloanthus, stretching
out his hands to the sea, poured forth prayers and invoked the
gods to his vows: Ye gods, to whom belongs the empire of
the main, over whose seas I sail, I, bound by vow,[16] will
joyously present before your altars a snow-white bull on this
shore, and cast forth the entrails on the briny wave [as an
offering to you], and make a libation of pure wine. He said;
and the whole choir of the Nereids and Phorcus,[17] and the
virgin Panopea, heard him from the bottom of the waves; and
father Portunus[18] himself, with his mighty hand, pushed on
the galley in her course. She flies to land swifter than the
south wind, and the winged arrow, and lodged herself in the
harbour's deep recess. Then Anchises' son, having assembled
all in form, proclaims Cloanthus conqueror, by the loud voice
of the herald, and crowns his temples with verdant laurel;
allows him the choice of three bullocks as presents for the
galleys, and gives him wine and a great talent of silver to
carry away. On the leaders themselves he confers peculiar
honours: to the conqueror he presents a mantle embroidered
with gold, round which a thick fringe of Melibean purple ran
in a double maze, and where the royal boy [Ganymede] inwoven pursues, with darts and full career, the fleet stags on
woody Ida, eager, seeming to pant for breath; whom Jove's
swift armour-bearer, with his crooked talons, snatched aloft
from Ida. The aged keepers in vain stretch out their hands
to the stars, and the baying of the hounds rages to the skies.
To him who by his merit won the second place, he gives to

---

[15] I. e. "they would have both come in together." B.
[16] He is said to be reus voti who has undertaken a vow on a certain
condition; and when that condition is fulfilled, then he is damnatus voti,
or votis, i. e. the gods condemn and sentence him to pay his vow.
[17] Phorcus, a sea-deity, son of Pontus and Terra, and father of the
Gorgons.
[18] Portunus, a name of Melicerta.

wear a coat of mail, thick set with polished rings, and wrought
in gold with a triple tissue, which he himself victorious had
torn from Demoleus by rapid Simoïs under lofty Ilium: to be
his ornament and defence in war.   The servants, Phegeus
and Sagaris, with united force, scarcely bore the cumbrous
[armour] on their shoulders: but Demoleus, formerly clad
therein, used to chase before him the straggling Trojans. For
the third present he bestows two caldrons of brass, and silver
bowls of finished work, and rough with figures.   And thus
now all rewarded, and elated with their wealth, were moving
along, having their temples bound with scarlet fillets, when
Sergestus brought up his hooted galley without honour, hardly
with much art disentangled from the cruel rock, with the loss
of her oars, and in one tier quite disabled.   As often a serpent surprised in the highway, (which a brazen wheel hath
gone athwart, or a traveller, coming heavy with a blow, hath
left half dead and mangled by a stone,) attempting in vain to
fly, shoots his body in long wreaths; in one part fierce, darting fire from his eyes, and rearing aloft his hissing neck; the
other part, maimed with the wound, retards him, twisting [his
body] in knots, and winding himself up on his own limbs:
with such kind of steerage the ship slowly moved along: her
sails, however, she expands, and enters the port with full sail.
Æneas gladly confers on Sergestus the promised reward for
preserving the vessel, and bringing the crew safe back.   To
him is given a female slave, not unskilful in the works of
Minerva, Pholoe, a Cretan by extraction, with her two children on the breast.

   This game being over, pious Æneas advances to a grassy
plain, which woods on winding hills enclosed around; and in
the mid valley was the circuit of a theatre, whither the hero,
in the midst of many thousands, repaired, and took a high
seat.   Here he offers inviting rewards to those who chanced
to be inclined to enter the lists in the rapid race, and exhibits
the prizes.   The Trojans and Sicilians, in mingled throngs,
convene from every quarter: Nisus and Euryalus[19] the first:

   [19] Nisus and Euryalus, two Trojans who accompanied Æneas to Italy,
and immortalized themselves by their mutual friendship.   They fought
with great bravery against the Rutulians, but at last Nisus perished in
attempting the rescue of his friend Euryalus, who had fallen into the
enemy's hands.

Euryalus, distinguished by his lovely form and blooming
youth; Nisus, by his true affection for the boy: whom next
Diores followed, a royal youth of Priam's illustrious line.
After him Salius, and with him Patron; of whom the one
was an Acarnanian, the other from Arcadia, of the blood of
the Tegæan race. Next two Sicilian youths, Elymus and
Panopes, trained to the woods, the companions of aged
Acestes; and many more besides, whom fame hath buried in
obscurity. In the midst of whom thus Æneas spoke: Mark
these my words, and attend with joy: none of this throng
shall go unrewarded by me. Two bright Gnossian [20] darts of
polished steel, and a carved battle-axe of silver, I will give
[each man] to bear away. This honour shall be conferred
equally on all. The first three shall receive prizes, and shall
have their heads bound with swarthy olive. Let the first conqueror have a steed adorned with rich trappings; the second
an Amazonian [21] quiver full of Thracian arrows, which a broad
belt of gold around embraces, and a buckle clasps with a
tapering gem: and let the third content himself with this
Grecian helmet. When he had thus said, they take their respective places, and upon hearing the signal, start in a trice,
and quit the barrier, darting forward like a tempest: at the
same time they mark the goal. Nisus gets the start, and
springs away far before the rest, outflying the winds and
winged lightning. Next to him, but next by a long interval,
follows Salius: then after him Euryalus, with some space left
[between them]; and Elymus follows Euryalus; close by
whose side, lo! next Diores flies, and now jostles heel with
heel, pressing on his shoulder; and, had more stages remained,
he had skipped away before him, or left the victory dubious.
And now they were almost in the utmost bound, and, exhausted, were approaching towards the very goal; when unhappy Nisus slides in a slippery puddle of blood, as by chance
it had been shed on the ground from victims slain, and soaked
the verdant grass. Here the youth, already flushed with the
joy of victory, could not support his tottering steps on the
ground he trod, but fell headlong amidst the noisome filth and

---

[20] Gnosian darts, i. e. Cretan darts, from Cnossus, or Gnossus, a city
of Crete.

[21] Amazonian quivers: the Amazons were a warlike nation of women,
who lived near the river Thermodon in Pontus.

sacred gore. He, however, was not then forgetful of Euryalus, nor of their mutual affection; for, as he rose from the
slippery mire, he opposed himself to Salius: he again, tumbling backward, lay prostrate on the clammy sand. Euryalus
springs forward, and victorious by the kindness of his friend,
holds the foremost place, and flies with favouring applause
and acclamation. Elymus comes in next; and Diores, now
[entitled to] the third prize. Here Salius fills the whole assembly of the ample pit, and the front seats of the fathers,
with loud outcries, and demands the prize to be given to him
self, from whom it was snatched away by unfair means. The
favour [of the spectators] befriends Euryalus, and his graceful tears, and merit that appears more lovely in a comely person. Diores aids him, and exclaims with bawling voice; who
succeeded to a prize, and had a claim to the last reward in
vain, if the first honours be given to Salius. Then father
Æneas said: Your rewards, youths, stand fixed, and none
shall turn the prize out of its due course: give me leave to
compassionate the disaster of my innocent friend. This said,
he gives to Salius the huge hide of a Getulian lion, ponderous
with shaggy fur and gilt claws. Upon this Nisus says, If to
the vanquished such rewards be given, and your pity be extended to those that fell, what gifts are due to Nisus? [to
me,] who by my merit won the first prize, had not the same
unkind fortune which bore Salius down overpowered me.
And with these words he at the same time showed his face
and limbs besmeared with oozy filth. The excellent father
smiled on his plight, and ordered the buckler to be produced,
Didymaon's ingenious work, torn down by the Greeks from
the sacred posts of Neptune's temple. With this signal present he rewards the illustrious youth.

Next, when the race was finished, and the prizes were distributed: Now, [says he,] whoever he may be in whose breast
courage and resolution dwell, let him stand forth, and raise
aloft his arms, having his hands bound [with the cestus].. He
said, and proposes a double prize for the combat: to the conqueror a bullock decked with gold and fillets; a sword and
shining helm, the solace of the vanquished. Without delay,
Dares shows his face with strength prodigious, and rears himself amidst the loud murmurs of the spectators; he who alone
was wont to enter the lists with Paris; the same at the tomb

where mighty Hector lies, struck down victorious Butes[22] of
mighty frame, who boasted his descent from the race of
Amycus, king of Bebrycia, and stretched him gasping on the
tawny sand. Such Dares uprears his lofty head first in the
lists, and presents his broad shoulders, and in alternate throws
brandishes his arms around, and beats the air with his fists.
For him a match is sought; nor dares one of all that numerous crowd encounter him, and draw the gauntlets on his hands.
Elated, therefore, and imagining that all had quitted preten-
sion to the prize, he stood before Æneas' feet: and then, without further delay, with his left hand he seizes the bull by the
horns, and thus speaks: Goddess-born, if no one will dare to
trust himself to the combat, where will be the end of hanging
on? how long must I be detained? Order the presents to
be brought. At the same time all the Trojans murmured their
consent, and ordered the promised prizes to be delivered to
him. Then venerable Acestes thus chides Entellus, as he sat
beside him on the verdant grassy couch: Entellus, in vain
[reputed] the stoutest of champions once, will you then suffer
so great prizes to be carried off without any contest? Where
is now that god of ours, Eryx, whom you in vain gave out to
be your master? where is your fame through all Trinacria?
where the spoils that used to hang from your roof? He to this
immediately [replies]: It is not that my thirst of praise is
gone, or my glory has departed, driven away by fear: but my
frozen blood languishes through enfeebling age, and the strength
worn out in my body is benumbed. Did I but now enjoy that
youth which once I had, and wherein that varlet triumphs
with vain confidence, then would I have taken the field; not
indeed induced by the prize of this fair bullock, for I regard
not rewards. Thus having spoken, he then throws into the
midst a pair of gauntlets[23] of huge weight; wherewith fierce

---

[22] Butes, a descendant of Amycus, king of Bebrycia, (Bithynia,) killed
by Dares at the tomb of Hector. At the funeral games of Anchises in
Sicily, Dares was overcome at the combat of the cestus, by Entellus, a
friend of Acestes.

[23] Cestus. The cestus was a sort of leathern guards for the hands,
composed of thongs, and commonly filled with lead or iron, to add force
and weight to the blow: though others, indeed, will have them to have
been a kind of whirlbats or bludgeons of wood, with lead at one end.
But the description Virgil gives of these weapons, particularly when he
calls them immensa volumina vinclorum, 408, and sa· ·, 425, .

Eryx was wont to engage in the fight, and to brace his arms
with the stubborn hide. Amazement seized their minds. Seven
huge thongs of such vast oxen lay stiffening with lead and iron
sewed within. Above all Dares himself stands aghast, and
utterly declines the combat: and the magnanimous son of
Anchises this way and that way poises the weight and the
complicated folds of the gauntlets. Then the aged champion
thus spake from his soul: What if any [of you] had seen the
gauntlet and arms of Hercules himself, and the bloody [24] combat on this very shore? These arms your brother Eryx formerly wore. You see them yet stained with blood and shattered brains. With these he stood against great Alcides: with
these I was wont [to combat], while better blood supplied me
with strength, nor envious age as yet had scattered grey hairs
over my temples. But if Trojan Dares decline our
arms, and if the pious Æneas be so determined, and Acestes,
who prompts me [to the fight], approve, let us be equally
matched: To oblige you, I lay aside the weapons of Eryx;
dismiss your fears, and do you put off your Trojan gauntlets.
This said, he flung from his shoulders his double vest, and
bared his huge limbs, his big bones and sinewy arms, and
stood forth of mighty frame in the middle of the field. Then
the sire, sprung from Anchises, brought forth equal gauntlets,
and bound both their hands with equal arms. Forthwith
each on his tiptoes stood erect, and undaunted raised his arms
aloft in the air. Far from the blow they backward withdrew
their towering heads: now hand to hand they join in close
encounter, and provoke the fight; the one having the advan-

Et paribus palmas amborum innexuit armis,
agrees to the former idea, but by no means to the latter. They were tied
about the arm as high as the elbow, both as a guard to the arm, and to
keep them from sliding off. Some derive the name from κεστος, a girdle;
others from cædo, to kill; which last answers well enough to the nature
of the combat, which was so cruel and bloody, that Lycurgus made a law
forbidding the Lacedæmonians to practise it.

[24] The combat is called tristis, woeful, or bloody, because Eryx was
slain in it by Hercules. The occasion of the combat is thus related.
Hercules having put to death Geryon, king of Spain, was returning with
his booty, which was a herd of fine oxen: and having visited Sicily in his
way, received a challenge from Eryx, king of the island, to fight him with
the gauntlet. If the victory fell to Eryx, he was to have Hercules's
oxen; but if he was vanquished, then the whole island of Sicily was to be
Hercules's property. Thus Eryx lost both his life and his crown.

P

tago in agility of foot, and relying on his youth; the other
surpassing in limbs and bulk; but his feeble knees sunk under
his trembling body: his difficult breathing shakes his vast
frame. The heroes deal many blows to one another with
erring aim, and many on the hollow sides redouble; from
their breasts [the thumps] resound aloud, and round their
ears and temples thick strokes at random fly; their jaws
crackle under the heavy blow. Entellus stands stiff and unmoved in the same firm posture, only with his body and
watchful eyes evades the strokes. The other, as one who
besieges a lofty city with batteries, or under arms besets a
mountain fortress, explores now these, now those approaches,
and artfully traverses the whole ground, and pursues his
attack with various assaults, still baffled. Entellus, rising on
tiptoe, extended his right arm, and lifted it on high: the
other nimbly foresaw the blow descending from above, and
with agility of body shifting, slipped from under it. Entellus spent his strength on the wind; and, both by the force of
his own natural weight, and the violence of the motion, falls
to the ground of himself with his heavy bulk; as sometimes,
on Erymanthus[23] or spacious Ida, a hollow pine torn from the
roots tumbles down at once. The Trojan and Sicilian youth
rise together with eager feelings: their acclamations pierce
the skies; and Acestes first advances in haste, and in pity
raises from the ground his friend of equal age. But the hero,
not disabled nor daunted by his fall, returns to the combat
more fierce, and indignation rouses his spirit: then shame and
conscious worth set all the powers of his soul on fire; and
inflamed he drives Dares headlong over the whole plain, re-
doubling blows on blows, sometimes with the right hand,
sometimes with the left. No stop, no stay: as thick showers
of hail come rattling down on the house-tops, so with thick
repeated blows, the hero thumps Dares with each hand, and
tosses him hither and thither. Then father Æneas suffered not their fury longer to exert itself, nor Entellus to
rage with such fierce animosity; but put an end to the combat, and rescued Dares quite overpowered, soothing him with
words, and bespeaks him in these terms: Unhappy! what
strong infatuation possessed your mind? Are you not sensible

---

* Erymanthus, a mountain of Arcadia, where Hercules slew the famous
Erymanthian boar.

of [his having] foreign assistance, and that the gods have changed sides ? Yield to the deity. He said, and by his word put an end to the combat. As for Dares, his trusty companions conduct him to the ships, dragging his feeble limbs, and tossing his head to either side, disgorging from his throat clotted gore, and teeth mingled with his blood ; and, at Æneas' call, they take the helmet and sword, leave the palm and bull to Entellus. At this the conqueror, in soul elated, and proud of the bull, says : Goddess-born, and ye Trojans, hence know both what strength I have had in my youthful limbs, and from what death you have saved Dares. He said, and stood against the front of the opposite bull that was set for the prize of the combat, and rearing himself up, with his right hand drawn back, levelled the cruel gauntlets directly between the horns, and, battering the skull, drove through the bones. Down drops the ox, and, in the pangs of death, falls sprawling to the ground. Over him he utters these words : This life, more acceptable, O Eryx, I give thee in exchange for Dares' death ; here, victorious, I lay down the gauntlets with my art.

Æneas forthwith invites such as may be willing to try their skill with the swift arrow, and sets prizes : and with his mighty hand raises a mast taken from Sercstus' ship, and from the high mast hangs a fluttering dove by a rope thrust through at which they may aim their shafts. The competitors assemble ; and a brazen helmet received the shuffled lots. The lot of Hippocoön,[26] the son of Hyrtacus, comes out first of all with favouring shouts ; whom follows Mnestheus, lately victor in the naval strife, Mnestheus, crowned with green olive. The third is Eurytion, the brother, illustrious Pandarus, of thee, who, once urged to violate the treaty, didst first hurl thy dart into the midst of the Greeks. Acestes remained the last, and in the bottom of the helmet ; he too adventuring with his [aged] hand to essay the feats of youth. Then with stout force they bend their pliant bows, each man according to his ability, and draw forth their arrows from their quivers. And first the arrow of young Hyrtacus' son, shot through the sky from the whizzing string, cleaves the fleeting air, both reaches [the mark], and fixes in the wood of the opposite mast. The

* Hippocoön was brother to Nisus, and the friend of Æneas. Eurytion and Pandarus were sons of Lycaon ; the latter was slain by Diomedu, in the Trojan war.

mast quivered; and the frighted bird, by its wings, showed
signs of fear; and all quarters rang with loud applause. Next
keen Mnestheus stood with his bow close drawn,[77] aiming on
high, and directed his eye and arrow both together. But it
was his misfortune not to be able to hit the bird itself with his
shaft; he burst the cords and hempen ligaments to which it
hung tied by the foot from the high mast. She with winged
speed shot into the air and dusky clouds. Then Eurytion in
eager haste, having his arrow long before extended on the
ready bow, poured forth a vow to his brother [Pandarus], as
he now beheld the joyful dove in the void sky, and pierced
her under a dark cloud as she was clapping her wings. She
dropped down dead, and left her life among the stars of heaven;
and, falling to the ground, brings back the arrow fastened
[in the wound]. Acestes alone remained after the prize was
lost; who, notwithstanding, discharged his shaft into the
aërial regions, the sire displaying both his address and twang-
ing bow.[28] Here is unexpectedly presented to view a prodigy,
designed to be of high portent; this the important event afterwards declared, and the alarming soothsayers predicted the
omens late. For the arrow, flying among the watery clouds,
took fire, and with the flames marked out a path, till, being
quite consumed, it vanished into thin air; as often stars loosened from the firmament shoot across, and flying draw [after
them] a train of light. The Sicilians and Trojans stood fixed
in astonishment, and besought the gods; nor does mighty
Æneas reject the omen, but, embracing Acestes overjoyed,
loads him with ample rewards, and thus bespeaks him: Accept these, O sire, for the great king of heaven, by these
omens, has signified his will, that you receive the honour [of
the victory, though] out of course. This gift, which belonged
to aged Anchises' self, you shall possess; a bowl embossed
with figures, which Thracian Cisseus formerly gave for a
magnificent present to my sire, as a monument and pledge of
his love. This said, he crowns his temples with verdant
laurel, and in view of all pronounces Acestes the first conqueror. Nor does good Eurytion envy him the preference in
honour, though he alone struck down the bird from the ex-

---

[77] This is the force of "adducto," denoting that the bow was fully
drawn. Cf. Sil. i. 334. Ovid. Met. i. 435. B.
[28] i. e. having lost the mark, he showed to what height he could shoot.

alted sky. He next comes in for a prize, who broke the cords; the last is he who pierced the mast with his winged shaft.

But father Æneas, the games not being yet ended, calls to him the son of Epytus, young Iülus' guardian and companion, and thus whispers in his trusty ear : Go quick, says he, desire Ascanius (if he has now gotten ready with him his company of boys, and has arranged the movements of the horses) to bring up his troops, and show himself in arms in honour of his grandsire. He himself orders the crowd to remove from the extended circus, and the field to be cleared. The boys advance in procession, and uniformly shine on the bridled steeds full in their parents' sight ; in admiration of whom, as they career along, the whole Trojan and Trinacrian youth join in acclamations. All in due form had their hair pressed with a trim garland. They bear two cornel spears pointed with steel ; some have polished quivers on their shoulders. A pliant circle of wreathed gold goes from the upper part of their breasts about their necks. Three troops of horsemen, and three leaders, range over the plain: twelve striplings following each, shine in a separate body, and with commanders equally matched. One band of youths young Priam, bearing his grandsire's name, leads triumphant; thy illustrious offspring, O Polites,[29] who shall one day do honour to the Italians, whom a Thracian courser bears, dappled with white spots ; the fetlocks of his foremost feet are white, and, tossing his head aloft, he displays a white front. The second is Atys,[30] from whom the Attii of Rome have derived their origin ; little Atys, a boy beloved by the boy Iülus. Iülus the last, and in beauty distinguished from all the rest, rode on a Sidonian steed which fair Dido had given him as a monument and pledge of her love. The rest of the youths ride on Trinacrian horses of aged Acestes. The Trojans with shouts of applause receive them anxious [for honour],[31] and are well-pleased with the sight, and recognise the features of the aged sires. Now when the joyous youths had paraded on horseback round

---

[29] Polites, a son of Priam and Hecuba, whose son, also named Priam, accompanied Æneas to Italy, and was one of the friends of young Ascanius.

[30] Atys, who also accompanied Æneas, is supposed to have been the progenitor of the family of the Attii at Rome.

[31] i. e. "eager with excitement." So Servius, "gloriæ cupiditato illicitor." B.

the whole ring, and full in their parents' view, Epytus' son,
from afar, gave a signal to them by a shout, as they stood
ready, and clanked with the lash. They broke away in parted
order, keeping the same front, and broke up the troops into
separate bands by threes; and again, upon summons given,
they wheeled about, and bore their hostile spears [on one
another].[92] Then they again advance, and again retreat in
their opposite grounds, and alternately involve intricate circles
within circles, and call up the representation of a fight in
arms. And now flying they expose their defenceless backs;
now in hostile manner turn their darts [on each other]: now,
peace being made up, they are borne along together. As of
old in lofty Crete was a labyrinth famed for having had an
alley formed by dark intricate walls, and a puzzling maze
with a thousand avenues, where a [single] mistake, unob-
served, but not to be retraced, frustrated the marks for guiding
one on the way ; in just such course the sons of the Trojans
involve their motions, and with intricate movement represent
fighting and flying in sport; like dolphins, that, swimming
through the watery deep, cut the Carpathian or Libyan Sea,
and gambol amid the waves. This manner of tilting, and
those mock fights, Ascanius first renewed, and taught the
ancient Latins to celebrate, when he was enclosing Alba
Longa with walls: as he himself, when a boy, as the Trojan
youth with him [had practised them], so the Albans taught
their posterity ; hence, in after times, imperial Rome received
them, and preserved the same in honour of her ancestors: and
at this day it is called [the game of] Troy,[93] and the boys
'that perform it], the Trojan band.
   Thus far the trials of skill were exhibited [by Æneas in

   [92] I have followed Anthon. The student will find an excellent explanation of the manœuvres in his notes. B.
   [93] This game, commonly known by the name of the Lusus Trojæ, is
purely of Virgil's own invention, he had no hint of it from Homer. This
he has substituted in the room of three of his, the wrestling, the single
combat, and the discus, and, in the opinion of a very judicious modern,
it is worth all those three in Homer. This game Virgil added to please
Augustus, who had at that time renewed the same. Suetonius tells us,
Trojæ ludum edidit (Augustus) frequentissime, majorum minorumve
puerorum delectu : prisci decorique moris existimans, claræ stirpis indo-
lem sic innotescere, &c. Suet. in August. cap. 43. Julius Cæsar had
also exhibited the same before, as we learn from the same author, Trojam
lusit turma duplex, majorum minorumve puerorum. In Jul. cap. 30.

honour] of his sanctified sire. Here shifting Fortune, changing,
first altered her faith. While they are celebrating the anniversary festival at the tomb with various games, Saturnian
Juno despatched Iris from heaven to the Trojan fleet, and with
the fanning winds speeds her on her way, forming many plots,
and having not yet glutted her old revenge. The virgin goddess accelerating her way, seen by none, amidst the bow with
a thousand colours, shoots down the path with nimble motion.
She descries the vast concourse; then, surveying the shore,
sees the port deserted, and the fleet deserted. But at a distance the Trojan dames apart were mourning the loss of Anchises on the desolate shore, and all of them with tears in
their eyes viewed the deep ocean: Ah! that so many shoals,
such a length of sea should still remain for us after all our
toils! was the sole complaint of all. They pray for a city,
are sick of enduring the hardships of the main. Therefore
she, not unpractised in mischief, throws herself into the midst
of them, and lays aside the mien and vesture of a goddess.
She assumes the figure of Beroe, the aged wife of Thracian
Doryclus,[34] who was of noble birth, and once had renown, and
offspring. And thus she joins in discourse with the Trojan
matrons: Ah! unhappy we, who were not dragged forth to
death in the war by the Grecian host under our native walls!
Ill-fated race! for what miserable doom does fortune reserve
you? The seventh summer since the destruction of Troy is
already rolled away, while we, having measured all lands and
seas, so many inhospitable rocks and barbarous climes, are
driven about; while along the wide ocean we pursue an ever-
fleeing Italy, and are tossed on the waves. Here are the
realms of his brother Eryx, and his friend Acestes: who prevents our founding walls, and giving our citizens a city? Ah,
my country, and our gods in vain saved from the enemy!
shall a city never more arise to be named from Troy? Shall I
never see the Hectorean rivers, Xanthus and Simois? Nay,
rather come, and burn with me our cursed ships. For in my
sleep the ghost of the prophetess Cassandra seemed to present me with flaming brands: Here, says she, seek for Troy,
here is your fixed residence. Now is the time for action.

---

[34] Doryclus, a brother of Phineus, king of Thrace, and the husband of
Beroe, whose form was assumed by Iris, when she advised the Trojan
women to burn the fleet of Æneas in Sicily.'

Nor let there be delay after such signs from heaven. Lo!
here are four altars to Neptune: the god himself supplies us
with fire-brands, and with courage [for the attempt]. With
these words, she violently snatches the destroying fire, and,
lifting up her right hand with exerted force, waves it at a
distance, throws it. Roused are the minds and stunned the
hearts of the Trojan matrons. Then one of the number,
Pyrgo,[25] the most advanced in years, the royal nurse to
Priam's numerous sons, [said,] Matrons, this is not Beroe
whom you have here, it is not she from Rhœteum, the wife of
Doryclus: mark the characters of divine beauty, eyes bright
and sparkling; what breath, what looks; or the accents of
her voice, or her gait as she moves. Myself lately, as I came
hither, left Beroe sick, in great anguish that she alone was cut
off from such a solemnity, and was not to pay the honours due
to Anchises. She said. But the matrons first began to view
the ships with malignant eyes, dubious and wavering between
their wretched fondness for the present land, and the realms
that summoned them by the Fates; when on equal poised
wings the goddess mounted into the sky, and in her flight cut
the spacious bow beneath the clouds. Then, indeed, confounded at the prodigy, and driven by madness, they shriek
out together, and snatch the flame from the inmost hearths.[26]
Some rifle the altars, and fling boughs, and saplings, and
brands together; the conflagration rages with loose reins
amidst the rowers' seats, and oars, and painted sterns of fir.
Eumelus conveys the tidings to Anchises' tomb, and to the
benches of the theatre, that the ships were burned; and they
themselves behold the sparks of fire flying up in a pitchy
cloud. And first, Ascanius, as joyous he led the cavalcade,
just as he was, with full speed rode up to the troubled camp;
nor was it in the power of his guardians, half-dead for fear, to
check him. What strange frenzy this? whither, he cries, ah !
my wretched countrywomen, whither would you now? It is
not the enemy, or the hostile camp of the Greeks, but your
own hopes ye burn. Here am I, your own Ascanius. He
threw at their feet the empty helmet, which he wore while

---

[25] Pyrgo, the nurse of Priam's children, who followed Æneas in his
flight from Troy.
[26] i. e. from the neighbouring dwellings. The fire on the altars was
not sufficient. B.

calling forth the images of war in sport. At the same time
Æneas and the bands of the Trojans came up in haste. But
the matrons for fear fly different ways up and down the shore,
and skulking repair to the woods and hollow rocks wherever
there are any. They loathe the deed, the light, and penitent
recognise their friends; and Juno is dislodged from their
breasts. But the flames and conflagration did not therefore
abate their ungovernable fury. The tow lives under the
moistened boards, disgorging languid smoke; the smothered
fire gradually consumes the keel, and the contagious ruin
spreads through the whole body of the vessel. Neither the
efforts of the heroes, nor outpoured streams, avail. Then
pious Æneas tore his robe from his shoulders, and invoked
the gods to his aid, and stretched out his hands: Almighty
Jove, if thou dost not yet abhor all the Trojans to a man, if
thy ancient goodness regards human disasters with commiser-
ation, grant now, O father, that our fleet may escape from
these flames, and save from desolation the humbled state of
the Trojans. Or, to complete thy vengeance, hurl me down
to the death with thy vindictive thunder, if I so deserve, and
crush me here with thy right hand. Scarce had he spoken
these words, when a black tempest of bursting rain rages with
uncommon fury: both hills[37] and valleys quake with thunder;
the shower in turbid rain, and condensed into pitchy darkness by the thick-beating south winds, pours down from the
whole atmosphere. The ships are filled from above; the
half-burned boards are drenched, till the whole smoke is extinguished, and all the ships, with the loss of four, are saved
from the pest.

But father Æneas, struck with the bitter misfortune, turned
his anxious thoughts now this way, now that, pondering with
himself whether she should settle in the territories of Sicily,
regardless of the Fates, or steer his course to the Italian
coast. Then aged Nautes,[38] whom above others Tritonian
Pallas taught, and rendered illustrious for deep science, gave
forth these responses, what either the great displeasure of the

[37] More literally, "the steeps of land." Cf. Symmach. Epist. vii. 69,
"ardua clivi." Apul. Met. i., "ardua montium." Varro, R. R. ii. 10,
"montium arduitatem." Hieron. Epist. 22, "aspera montium." D.
[38] Nautes, a Trojan soothsayer, who consoled Æneas when his fleet
had been burnt in Sicily. He was the progenitor of the Nautii, at Rome,
a family to whom the Palladium of Troy was afterwards intrusted.

gods portended, or what the series of the Fates required.
And, thus, solacing Æneas, he begins: Goddess-born, let us
follow the Fates, whether they invite us backward or forward:
come what will, every fortune is to be surmounted by pa-
tience. You have Trojan Acestes of divine origin : admit
him the partner of your counsels, and unite yourself to him
your willing friend : to him deliver up such as are supernu-
merary, now that you have lost some ships ; choose out those
who are sick of the great enterprise, and of your fortunes ;
the old with length of years oppressed, and the matrons fatigued with the voyage ; select the feeble part of your company, and such as dread the danger, and, since they are tired
out, let them have a settlement in these territories : they shall
call the city Acesta[39] by a licensed name.

   Then indeed Æneas, fired by these words of his aged friend,
is distracted in his mind amidst a thousand cares. Now sable
Night, mounted on her chariot with two horses, held the skies,
when the form of his father Anchises, gliding down from the
skies, suddenly seemed to pour forth these words : Son, once
dearer to me than life, while life remained ; my son, severely
tried by the fates of Troy ; hither I come by the command of
Jove, who averted the fire from your fleet, and at length
showed pity from the high heaven. Comply with the excellent counsel which aged Nautes now offers : carry with you
to Italy the choice of the youths, the stoutest hearts. In
Latium you have to subdue a hardy race, rugged in manners.
But first, my son, visit Pluto's infernal mansions, and, in
quest of an interview with me, cross the deep floods of Avernus : for not accursed Tartarus, nor the dreary ghosts, have
me in their possession ; but I inhabit the delightful seats of
the blest, and Elysium.[40] Hither the chaste Sibyl shall conduct thee after shedding profusely the blood of black victims.
Then you shall learn your whole progeny, and what walls are
assigned to you. And now farewell : humid Night wheels
about her mid course,[41] and the dawning light, which fiercely
summons me away, hath breathed upon me with panting steeds.

   [39] Acesta, or Segesta, a city of Sicily, built by Æneas in honour of
king Acestes.
   [40] Elysium, a place in the infernal regions, where, according to the
mythology of the ancients, the souls of the virtuous were placed after
death. The Elysian fields, according to Virgil, were situated in Italy
   [41] The reader will call to mind the words of the ghost in " Hamlet." B.

He said; and vanished like smoke into the fleeting air.
Whither so precipitant? says then Æneas; whither dost thou
whirl away? whom fliest thou? or who debars me from my
embraces? So saying, he awakes the embers and dormant fire,
and suppliant pays veneration to his Trojan domestic god, and
the shrine of hoary Vesta, with a holy cake and full censer.
Forthwith he calls his followers, and first of all Acestes, and
informs them of Jove's command, and the instructions of his
beloved sire, and of the present settled purpose of his soul.
No obstruction is given to his plans; nor is Acestes averse
to the proposals made. They enrol[41] the matrons for the city,
and set on shore as many of the people as were willing, souls
that had no desire of high renown. Themselves renew the
benches, and repair the timbers half consumed by the flames;
fit oars and cables to the ships; in number small, but of animated valour for war.

Meanwhile Æneas marked out a city with the plough, and
assigns the houses by lot: here he orders a [second] Ilium
to arise, and these places to be called after those of Troy.
Trojan Acestes rejoices in his kingdom; institutes a court of
justice; and having assembled his senators, dispenses laws.
Then on the top of Mount Eryx a temple approaching the
stars is raised to Idalian Venus;[43] and a priest is assigned to
the tomb of Anchises, with a grove hallowed far and wide.
And now the whole people had kept the festival for nine days,
and sacrifices had been offered on the altars, peaceful breezes
have smoothed the seas, and the south wind in repeated gales
invites into the deep. Loud lamentations along the winding
shores arise: in mutual embraces they linger out both night
and day. Even the matrons, and those to whom the face of the
sea lately seemed horrid, and its divinity[44] intolerably severe,
would willingly go, and submit to all the toil of the voyage;
whom good Æneas solaces in friendly terms, and, weeping,
commends to his kinsman Acestes. Then he orders to sacrifice to Eryx three calves, and a female lamb to the tempests,
and to weigh anchor after the due rites were performed. He
himself, having his head bound with a trim garland of olive

[41] " Transcribere" is a word properly used of colonizing. See Servius
Cf. Seneca, Epist. 4, " te in viros philosophia transcripseris." B.
[43] So called from Mount Ida.
[44] But " nomen " seems simpler. See Anthon. B.

leaves, standing on the extremity of the prow, holds the cup,
and casts forth the entrails on the briny waves, and pours the
limpid wine. A wind arising from the stern accompanies them
in their course. The crew, with emulous vigour, lash the sea
and brush its smooth surface.

Meanwhile Venus, harassed with cares, addresses Neptune,
and pours forth these complaints from her breast: The heavy
resentment and insatiable passion of Juno compel me, O Neptune, to descend to all entreaties; Juno, whom neither length
of time or any piety softens; and who is not quelled and subdued even by Jove's imperial sway, or by the Fates. It is not
enough for her to have effaced the city from among the Phrygian race by her unhallowed hate, nor to have dragged its relics through all sorts of suffering; she persecutes the ashes and
bones of ruined Troy. The causes of such furious resentment
are to her best known. Yourself can witness for me what a
heaving tempest she suddenly raised of late on the Libyan
waves. The whole sea she blended in confusion with the sky,
vainly relying on Æolus' storms; this presuming [even] in
your realms. Lo also (O wickedness!) by acting upon the
Trojan matrons, she hath shamefully burned the ships, and
forced their friends, now that they have lost their fleet, to
abandon them in an unknown land. As to what remains, may
they be allowed, I pray, to sail over the waves secure by thy
protection: may they be allowed to reach Laurentian Tiber;[45]
if I ask what may be granted, if the Destinies assign those settlements. Then the Saturnian ruler of the deep ocean thus
replied: Cytherea,[46] it is perfectly just that you confide in my
realms, whence you derive your birth: besides, I have a just
claim; [for] often have I checked the furious rage and maddening tumult of sea and sky. Nor was I less careful of your
Æneas on earth (I call Xanthus and Simois to witness).
When Achilles, pursuing the breathless troops of Troy, dashed
them against their walls, gave many thousands to death, and
the choked rivers groaned, and Xanthus could not find his
way, nor disembogue himself into the sea; then in a hollow
cloud I snatched away Æneas, while encountering the mighty
Achilles with strength and gods unequal; though I was de-

[45] Laurentian Tiber, so called from Laurentum, (Paterno,) the capital
of Latium in the reign of Latinus.
[46] Cytherea. A surname of Venus.

sirous of overthrowing from the lowest foundation the walls
of perjured Troy, reared by my hands. And still I am of the
same disposition: banish your fear; he shall arrive safe at tho
port of Avernus, which you desire. One only, lost in the deep,
shall he seek for: one life shall be given for many.[47] The sire,
having by these words soothed and cheered the heart of the
goddess, yokes his steeds to his golden car, puts the foaming
bit into their fierce mouths, and throws out all the reins.
Along the surface of the seas he nimbly glides in his azure
car. The waves subside, and the swelling ocean smooths its
liquid pavement under the thundering axle: the clouds fly off
the face of the expanded sky. Then [appear] the various forms
of his retinue, unwieldy whales,[48] and the aged train of Glaucus,
and Palemon,[49] Ino's son, the swift Tritons, and the whole
band of Phorcus. On the left are Thetis, Melite, and the virgin
Panopœ, Nesœe, Spio, Thalia, and Cymodoce. Upon this,
soft joys in their turn diffuse themselves through the anxious
soul of father Æneas. Forthwith he orders all the masts to
be set up, and the yards to be stretched along the sails. At
once they all tacked together, and together let go sometimes
the left-hand sheets, sometimes the right: at once they turn
and turn back the lofty end of the sail-yards: friendly gales
waft the fleet forward. Palinurus, the master-pilot, led the
closely-united squadron: towards him the rest were ordered
to steer their course.

And now the dewy night had almost reached the middle of
her course; the weary sailors, stretched along the hard benches
under the oars, relaxed their limbs[50] in peaceful repose; when
the god of sleep, gliding down from the ethereal stars, parted
the dusky air, and dispelled the shades; to you, O Palinurus,
directing his course, visiting you, though innocent, with dismal
dreams: and the god took his seat on the lofty stern, in the
similitude of Phorbas,[51] and poured forth these words from

[47] i. e. Palinurus. Cf. Eur. Electr. 1026, ἱστᾶνι πολλῶν μίαν ὑπέρ. B.
[48] i. e. fish of large size. Nonius, v. "cetarii," remarks—"cela in mari
majora sunt piscium genera." B.
[49] Palemon, the same with Melicerta and Portumnus. See note 59,
Georgics, B. I. page 46. Tritons, &c., sea-deities. The name Tritons was
generally applied to those only who were half men and half fishes.
[50] Cf. Homer's λυσιμελὴς ὕπνος, Od. ⲯ. 342. Orph. in Somn. 5. B.
[51] Phorbas, a son of Priam, killed in the Trojan war by Menelaus.
The god Somnus, by assuming his shape, deceived Palinurus, and threw
him into the sea.

his lips: Palinurus, son of Iasius, the seas themselves carry
forward the fleet; the gales blow fair and steady, the hour for
rest is given. Recline your head, and steal your weary eyes
from labour. Myself awhile will discharge your duty.   To
whom Palinurus, with difficulty lifting up his eyes, answers:
Do you then bid me be a stranger to the aspect of the calm
sea and its quiet waves? Shall I confide in this extraordinary apparition? Why should I trust Æneas to the mercy of
the fallacious winds,[52] after having been so often deceived by
the treacherous aspect of a serene sky? These words he
uttered, while fixed and clinging he did not part with the
rudder, and held his eyes directed to the stars; when, lo! the
god shakes over both his temples a branch drenched in the
dew of Lethe, and impregnated with soporific Stygian influence; and, while he is struggling against sleep, dissolves his
swimming eyes. Scarcely had unexpected slumber begun to
relax his limbs, when the god, leaning on him, with part of
the stern broke off, together with the helm, plunged him headlong into the limpid waves, often calling on his friends in
vain: taking flight, raised himself on his wings aloft into the
thin air. Meanwhile, the fleet runs its watery course on the
plain with equal security, and fearless is conducted by father
Neptune's promises. And now wafted forward, it was even
coming up to the rocks of the Sirens,[53] once of difficult access, and white with the bones[54] of many (at that time the
hoarse rocks resounded far by the continual buffeting of the
briny waves); when father Æneas perceived the fluctuating
galley to reel, having lost its pilot; and he himself steered her
through the darkened waves, deeply affected and wounded in
his soul for the misfortune of his friend. Ah, Palinurus,
[says he,] who has too much confided in the fair aspect of
the skies and sea! naked wilt thou lie on unknown sands!

[52] On this general use of "austri," cf. Æn. i. 51, 536; ii. 304; v.
396, &c. B.
[53] Sirens; these were three fabulous sisters who usually resided in a
small island near Cape Pelorus in Sicily, and by their melodious voices
decoyed mariners to their destruction on the fatal coast. Ulysses having,
by an artifice, escaped their fascination, the disappointed Sirens threw
themselves into the sea, and perished.
[54] Statius Silv. ii. 7, 65, "albus ossibus Italis Philippos." Senec. Œd.
914. Cf. Pric. on Apul. p. 436. B.

BOOK VI.

In the Sixth Book, Æneas, on reaching the coast of Italy, visits, as he had been forewarned, the Sibyl of Cumæ, who attends him in his descent into the infernal regions, and conducts him to his father Anchises, from whom he learns the fate that awaited him and his descendants the Romans. The book closes with the well-known beautiful panegyric on the younger Marcellus, who was prematurely cut off in the flower of his youth.

Thus he speaks with tears, and gives his ship full sail,[1] and at length he reaches the Eubœan coast[2] of Cumæ. They turn their prows out to the sea: then the anchor with its tenacious fluke moored the ships, and the bending sterns fringe[3] the margin of the shore. The youthful crew spring forth with ardour on the Hesperian strand: some seek for the seeds of fire latent in the veins of flint; some plunder the copses, the close retreat of wild beasts, and point out rivers newly discovered. But the pious Æneas repairs to the towers over which Apollo presides on high, and to the spacious cave, the cell of the Sibyl awful at a distance; into whom the prophetic god of Delos breathes an enlarged mind and spirit, and discloses to her the future. Now they enter Diana's groves, and [Apollo's] golden roofs. Dædalus,[4] as is famed, flying the realms of Minos, adventuring to trust himself to the sky on nimble wings, sailed through an untried path to the cold regions of the north, and at length gently alighted on the tower of Chalcia. Having landed first on those coasts, to thee, O Phœbus, he consecrated his hoary wings, and reared a spacious temple. On the gates the death of Androgeos[5] [was represented]: then the Athenians, doomed, as an atonement

[1] Literally, "gives a loose rein." Cf. Ritterh. on Oppian, Hal. 229. B.
[2] Eubœan coast, applied to Cumæ in Italy, as having been built by a colony from Chalcis, a city of Eubœa, (Negropont,) an island in the Archipelago.
[3] i. e. with the "aplustria." See Anthon. B.
[4] Dædalus, a most ingenious artist of Athens, who, with his son Icarus, fled, by the help of wings, from Crete, to escape the resentment of Minos; but Icarus fell into that part of the Ægean Sea which bears his name.
[5] Androgeos, the son of Minos and Pasiphae, famous for his skill in wrestling, was put to death by Ægeus, king of Athens, who became jealous of him; to revenge his death, Minos made war upon the Athenians, and at last grant them peace, on condition that they sent yearly seven youths and seven virgins, from Athens to Crete, to be devoured by the Minotaur, a fabulous monster, half a man and half a bull.

(a piteous case!) to pay yearly the bodies of their children by sevens: there stands the urn whence the lots were drawn. In counterview answers the land of Crete raised above sea; here Pasiphae's fierce passion for the bull is seen, and she [is introduced] by artifice humbled [to his embrace], with the Minotaur, that mingled birth, and two-formed offsprings, monuments of execrable lust. Here [are seen] the laboured work of the Labyrinth, and the inextricable mazes. But Dædalus, pitying the violent love of queen [Ariadne], unravels [to Theseus][6] the intricacies and windings of the structure, himself guiding his dark mazy steps by a thread. You too, O Icarus, should have borne a considerable part in that great work, had [thy father's] grief permitted. Twice he essayed to figure the disastrous story in gold; twice the parent's hand misgave him. And now [the Trojans] would survey the whole work in order, were not Achates, who had been sent on, just at hand, and with him the priestess of Phœbus and Diana, Deiphobe,[7] Glaucus' daughter, who thus bespeaks the king: This hour requires not such amusements. At present it will be more suitable to sacrifice seven bullocks from a herd unyoked, and as many chosen ewes, with usual rites. The priestess having thus addressed Æneas, (nor are they backward to obey her sacred orders,) calls the Trojans into the lofty temple. The huge side of an Eubœan rock is cut out into a cave, whither a hundred broad avenues lead, a hundred doors; whence rush forth as many voices, the responses of the Sibyl. They had come to the threshold,[8] when thus the virgin exclaims: Now is the time to consult your fate: the god, lo the god! While thus before the gate she speaks, on a sudden her looks change, her colour comes and goes, her locks are dishevelled, her breast heaves, and her fierce heart swells with enthusiastic rage; she appears in a larger form, her voice speaking her not a mortal, now that she is inspired with the nearer influence of the god. Do you delay,[9] Trojan Æneas, she says, do you delay with thy vows

[6] Theseus, king of Athens, and son of Ægeus, was, next to Hercules, the most celebrated of the heroes of antiquity. He slew the Minotaur, and escaped from the Labyrinth of Crete, by means of a clue of thread given to him by Ariadne, daughter of Minos.

[7] Deiphobe, the Cumæan Sibyl, daughter of Glaucus, who conducted Æneas into the infernal regions.

[8] i. e. to the entrance nearest Cumæ. B.

[9] On this construction, see Markland on Stat. Silv. 1. 2, 195 B.

and prayers? [Instantly begin]: for not till then shall the
ample gates of this awe-stricken mansion unfold to the view.
And having thus said, she ceased. Chill horror ran thrilling
cold through the bones of the Trojans; and their king poured
forth these prayers from the bottom of his heart: Apollo, who
hast ever pitied the troubles of Troy, who guidedst the Trojan
darts and the hand of Paris to the body of Achilles; under
thy conduct I have entered so many seas encompassing coun
tries, and the Massylian nations far remote, and regions vast
stretched in front by the Syrtes. Now at length we grasp of
the coast of Italy that flies from us. Let it suffice that the
fortune of Troy has persecuted us thus far. Now it is just
that you too spare the Trojan race, ye gods and goddesses, all,
to whom Ilium and the high renown of Dardania were obnoxious. And thou too, most holy prophetess, skilled in futurity, grant (I ask no realms but what are destined to me
by fate) that the Trojans, their wandering gods, and the persecuted deities of Troy, may settle in Latium. Then will I
appoint to Phœbus and Diana a temple of solid marble, and
festal days, called by the name of Apollo. Thee too a spacious
sanctuary awaits in our realms: for there, benignant one, I
will deposit thy oracles, and the secret fates declared to my
nation, and will consecrate chosen men. Only commit not thy
verses to leaves, lest they fly about in disorder, the sport of
the rapid winds: I beg you yourself will pronounce them. He
ended his address.
  But the prophetess, as yet not suffering the influence of
Phœbus, raves with wild outrage in the cave, struggling if
possible to disburden her soul of the mighty god: so much
the more he wearies her foaming lips, subduing her ferocious
heart, and, by bearing down her opposition, moulds her to his
will. And now the hundred spacious gates of the abode were
opened of their own accord, and pour forth the responses of
the prophetess into the open air: O thou who hast at length
overpassed the vast perils of the ocean! yet more afflicting
trials by land await thee. The Trojans shall come to the
realms of Lavinium, (dismiss that concern from thy breast,)
but they shall wish too they had never come. Wars, horrid
wars, I foresee, and Tiber foaming with a deluge of blood.
Nor Simois nor Xanthus, nor Grecian camps, shall be wanting
to you there. Another Achilles is prepared in Latium: he

Q

too the son of a goddess. Nor shall Juno, added to the Trojans
[as their scourge], leave them wherever they are: while in
your distress, which of the Italian states, which of its cities,
shall you not humbly supplicate for aid ? Once more shall a
consort, a hostess, once more shall a foreign match, be the
cause of so great calamity to the Trojans. Yield not under
your sufferings, but encounter them with greater boldness
than your fortune shall permit.[10] What you least expect,
your first means of deliverance shall be unfolded from a Grecian city. Thus from her holy cell the Cumæan Sibyl delivers her mysterious oracles, and, wrapping up truth in
obscurity, bellows in her cave: Such reins Apollo shakes
over her as she rages, and deep in her breast he plies the
goads.

As soon as her fury ceased, and her raving tongue was silent,
the hero Æneas begins : To me, O virgin, no shape of sufferings
can arise new or unexpected; I have anticipated all things,
and acted them over beforehand in my mind: My sole request is, (since here the gate of the infernal king is said to
be, and the darksome lake [formed] from the overflowing
Acheron,) that it may be my lot to come into the sight and
presence of my dear father; that you would show the way,
and open to me the sacred portals. On these shoulders I
rescued him, through flames and a thousand darts pursuing,
and saved him from the midst of the enemy. He accompanied
my path, attended me in all my voyages, and, though infirm,
bore all the terrors both of the sea and sky, beyond the power
and condition of old age. Nay more, he it was who earnestly
requested and enjoined me to come to thee a suppliant, and
visit thy temple. Benignant one, pity, I pray, the son and
the sire ; for thou canst do all things ; nor hath Hecate in vain
given thee charge of the Avernian groves. If Orpheus had
power to recall his consort's ghost, relying on his Thracian
harp and harmonious strings ; if Pollux[11] redeemed his brother

---

* I prefer "quam" with Wagner, notwithstanding Anthon's defence
of " qua." B.

[11] Pollux and Castor were twin brothers; according to ancient mythology, Pollux was the son of Jupiter, and so tenderly attached to his
brother Castor, that he entreated Jupiter he might share his immortality,
which being granted, they alternately lived and died every day. They
were made constellations under the name of Gemini, which never appear
together, but when one rises the other sets.

by alternate death, and goes and comes this way so often : [I hope I may also be allowed to go and return :] why need I mention Theseus, or great Alcides ? I too derive my birth from Jove supreme.

In such terms he prayed, and held the altar, when thus the prophetess began to speak: Offspring of the gods, thou Trojan son of Anchises, easy is the path that leads down to hell ; grim Pluto's gate stands open night and day : but to retrace one's steps, and escape to the upper regions, this is a work, this is a task. Some few, whom favouring Jove loved, or illustrious virtue advanced to heaven, the sons of the gods, have effected it. Woods cover all the intervening space, and Cocytus gliding with his black winding flood surrounds it. But if your soul be possessed with so strong a passion, so ardent a desire, twice to swim the Stygian lake, twice to visit gloomy Tartarus, and you will needs fondly pursue the desperate enterprise, learn what first is to be done. On a tree of deep shade there lies concealed a bough, with leaves and limber twigs of gold, pronounced sacred to infernal Juno: this the whole grove covers, and shades in dark valleys enclose. But to none is it given to enter the hidden recesses of the earth, till from the tree he pluck the bough with its golden locks. Fair Proserpine hath ordained this to be presented to her as her peculiar present. When the first is torn off, a second of gold soon succeeds ; and a twig shoots forth leaves of the same metal. Therefore search out for it on high with thine eyes, and when found, pluck it with the hand in a proper manner ; for, if the Fates invite you, itself will come away willing and easy ; otherwise you will not be able to master it by any strength, or to lop it off by the stubborn steel. Besides, the body of your friend lies breathless, (whereof you, alas ! are not aware,) and pollutes the whole fleet with death, while you are seeking counsel, and hang lingering at my gate. First convey him to his place of rest, and bury him in the grave. Bring black cattle : let these first be the sacrifices of expiation. So at length you shall have a view of the Stygian groves, realms inaccessible to the living. She said, and closing her lips, was silent.

Æneas, his eyes fixed on the ground with sorrowing looks, takes his way, leaving the cave, and muses the dark event in his mind ; whom faithful Achates accompanies, and steps on with equal concern. Many doubts they started between them in the variety of their conversation; who was the lifeless friend designed by the prophetess, what corpse was to be interred. And as they came, they saw Misenus[11] on the dry beach, slain by an unworthy death; Misenus, son of Æolus, whom none excelled in rousing warriors by the brazen trump, and kindling the rage of war by its blast. He had been the companion of great Hector, and about Hector he fought, distinguished both for the clarion and spear. After victorious Achilles had bereaved Hector of life, the valiant hero associated with Dardanian Æneas, following no inferior chief. But at that time, while madly presumptuous he makes the seas resound with his hollow trump, and with bold notes challenges the gods to a trial of skill, Triton, jealous, (if the story be worthy of credit,) having inveigled him between two rocks, had overwhelmed him in the foaming billows. Therefore all murmured their lamentations around him with loud noise, especially pious Æneas; then forthwith weeping they set about the Sibyl's orders, and are emulous to heap up the altar of the funeral pile with trees, and raise it towards heaven They repair to an ancient wood, the deep lairs of the savage kind: down drop the firs: the holm crashes, felled by the axes; and the ashen logs and yielding oak are cleft by wedges; down from the mountains they roll the huge wild ashes. Æneas, too, chief amidst these labours, animates his followers, and is equipped with like implements.

Meanwhile he thus ruminates in his distressed breast, surveying the spacious wood, and thus prays aloud: O if that golden branch on the tree now present itself to our view amid this ample forest; since, Misenus, all that the prophetess declared of thee, is true, alas! too true. Scarcely had he spoken these words, when it chanced that two pigeons, in their airy flight, came directly into the hero's view, and alighted on the verdant ground. Then the mighty hero knows his mother's birds, and rejoicing prays: Oh! be the guides of the way, if any way there is, and steer your course through the air into the groves, where the precious branch overshades the fertile soil. And thou, my goddess-mother, oh be not wanting to me in this my perplexity! Thus having said, he paused, ob-

---

[11] Misenus, a son of Æolus, the trumpeter of Hector, after whose death as followed Æneas to Italy, and was drowned on the coast of Campania

serving what indications they offer, whither they bend their
way. They, feeding and flying by turns, advanced before
only as far as the eyes of the followers could trace them with
their ken. Then, having come to the mouth of noisome[13]
Avernus, they mount up swiftly, and, gliding through the
clear air, both alight on the wished-for place, on that tree
from whence the gleam of the gold, of different hue, shone
through the boughs. As in the woods the mistletoe, which
springs not from the tree from whence it grows, is wont to
bloom with new leaves in the cold of winter, and to twine
around the tapering trunk with its yellow offspring; such was
the appearance of the gold sprouting forth on the shady holm:
in like manner the metallic leaf tinkled with the gentle gale.
Forthwith Æneas grasps, and eagerly tears off the lingering
branch, and bears it to the grotto of the prophetic Sibyl.

Meanwhile the Trojans were no less assiduously employed
in mourning Misenus on the shore, and in paying the last
duties to his senseless[14] ashes. First they rear a vast pile
unctuous with pines and split oak, whose sides they interweave with black boughs, and place in the front deadly
cypresses, and deck it above with glittering arms. Some get
ready warm water, and caldrons bubbling from the flames;
and wash and anoint his cold limbs. The groan is raised:
they then lay the bewailed body on a couch, and throw over
it the purple robes, his wonted apparel. Others bore up the
cumbrous bier, a mournful office; and with their faces turned
away, after the manner of their ancestors, under it they held
the torch. Amassed together, blaze offerings of incense,
viands, whole goblets of oil poured [on the pile]. After the
ashes had sunk down, and the flames relented, they drenched
the relics and soaking embers in wine; and Chorinæus enclosed the collected bones in a brazen urn. Thrice too he
made the circuit of the company with holy water, sprinkling
them with the light spray, and a branch of the prolific olive;
and he purified them, and pronounced the last farewell. But

[13] Nonius, l. 46, quoting these verses, observes, "Avernus iccirco ap-
pellatus est, quia est odor ejus avibus infestissimus." This is probably a
mistaken etymology. For the expression, compare Georg. iv. 270,
"grave olentia Centaurea." B.

[14] "Ingrato, gratiam non sentienti," is Servius's last and correct explanation. Cf. Copa, vs. 35, (in Anth. Lat. T. l. p. 74,) "Quid cineri
ingrato servas bene olentia serta." B.

pious Æneas erects a spacious tomb for the hero, with his arms upon it, and an oar and trumpet, beneath a lofty mountain, which now from him is called Misenus, and retains a name eternal through ages.

This done, he speedily executes the Sibyl's injunctions. There was a cave profound and hideous with wide yawning mouth, stony, fenced by a black lake, and the gloom of woods; over which none of the flying kind were able to wing their way unhurt: such exhalations, issuing from its grim jaws, ascended to the vaulted skies: [for which reason the Greeks called the place by the name of Aornus.][15] Here first the priestess places four bullocks with backs of swarthy hue, and pours[16] wine on their foreheads, and cropping the topmost hairs between the horns, lays them on the sacred flames as the first offerings, by voice invoking Hecate whose power extends both to heaven and hell. Others employ the knives,[17] and receive the tepid blood in bowls. Æneas himself smites with his sword a ewe-lamb of sable fleece in honour of the mother of the Furies, and her great sister, and in honour of thee, Proserpina, a barren heifer. Then he sets about the nocturnal sacrifices to the Stygian king, and lays on the flames the solid carcasses of bulls, pouring fat oil on the broiling entrails. Lo now, at the early beams and rising of the sun, the ground beneath their feet began to rumble, the wooded heights to quake, and dogs were seen to howl through the shade of the woods, at the approach of the goddess. Hence, far hence, O ye profane, exclaims the prophetess, and begone from all the grove: and do you, Æneas, boldly march forward, and snatch your sword from its sheath: now is the time for fortitude, now for firmness of resolution. This said, she raving plunged into the open cave. He, with intrepid steps, keeps close by his guide as she leads the way.

Ye gods, to whom the empire of ghosts belong, and ye silent shades, and Chaos, and Phlegethon, places where silence reigns around in night I permit me to utter the secrets I have

---

[15] This line is probably the work of a grammarian. B.

[16] Literally, "tilts the vessel," the verb properly meaning the action of bending the cup as the liquid is poured out. So Lucret. v. 1007, "Illi imprudentes ipsi sibi sæpe venenum Vergebant." Cf. Gronov. Obs. ii. 7. B.

[17] i. e. cut the throats of the victims. B.

heard; may I by your divine will disclose things buried in
deep earth and darkness. They moved along amid the gloom
under the solitary night through the shade,[18] and through the
desolate halls and empty realms of Pluto; such as is a journey
in woods beneath the unsteady moon, under a faint, glimmer
ing light, when Jupiter hath wrapped the heavens in shade,
. and sable night hath stripped objects of colour.

Before the vestibule itself, and in the first jaws of hell,
Grief and vengeful Cares have placed their couches, and pale
Diseases dwell, and disconsolate Old Age, and Fear, and the
. evil counsellor Famine, and vile deformed Indigence, forms
ghastly to the sight! and Death, and Toil; then Sleep, akin
to Death, and criminal Joys of the mind; and in the opposite
threshold murderous War, and the iron bed-chambers of the
Furies, and frantic Discord, having her viperous locks bound
with bloody fillets.

In the midst a gloomy elm displays its boughs and aged
arms, which seat vain Dreams are commonly said to haunt,
and under every leaf they dwell. Many monstrous savages,
moreover, of various forms, stable in the gates, the Centaurs
and double-formed Scyllas, and Briareus[19] with his hundred
hands, and the enormous snake of Lerna[20] hissing dreadful,
and Chimæra armed with flames; Gorgons, Harpies, and the
form of Geryon's three-bodied ghost. Here Æneas, discon-
certed with sudden fear, grasps his sword, and presents the
naked point to each approaching shade: and had not his skilful guide put him in mind that they were airy unbodied phantoms, fluttering about under an empty form, he had rushed in,
and with his sword struck at the ghosts in vain.

Hence is a path, which leads to the floods of Tartarean
Acheron: here a gulf turbid and impure boils up with mire
and vast whirlpools, and disgorges all its sand into Cocytus.

---

[18] Observe the accumulation of epithets, all denoting the excessive
darkness; "obscuri "—" sola nocte "—" per umbram." B.

[19] Briareus, a famous giant, son of Coelus and Terra. The poets feigned
he had one hundred arms and fifty heads, and was thrown under Mount
Ætna for having assisted the giants against the gods.

[20] Lerna, a lake of Argolis in Greece, where Hercules killed the
famous hydra. Chimæra, a fabulous monster, represented with three
heads, that of a lion, of a goat, and of a dragon. Geryon, a celebrated
monster, whom Hercules slew. He was represented by the poets as
having three bodies and three heads.

A grim ferryman guards these floods and rivers, Charon,[31] o.
frightful slovenliness; on whose chin a load of grey hair neglected lies; his eyes are flame: his vestments hung from his
shoulders by a knot, with filth overgrown. Himself thrusts
on the barge with a pole, and tends the sails, and wafts over
the bodies in his iron-coloured boat, now in years: but the
god is of fresh and green old age. Hither the whole tribe in
swarms came pouring to the banks, matrons and men, the
souls of magnanimous heroes who had gone through life, boys
and unmarried maids, and young men who had been stretched
on the funeral pile before the eyes of their parents; as numerous as withered leaves fall in the woods with the first cold of
autumn, or as numerous as birds flock to land from deep ocean,
when the chilling year[32] drives them beyond sea, and sends
them to sunny climes. They stood praying to cross the flood
the first, and were stretching forth their hands with fond desire to gain the further bank: but the sullen boatman admits
sometimes these, sometimes those: whilst others, to a great
distance removed, he debars from the banks.

Æneas (for he was amazed and moved with the tumult)
thus speaks: O virgin, say what means that flocking to the
river? what do the ghosts desire? or by what distinction must
these recede from the banks, those sweep with oars the livid
flood? To him the aged priestess thus briefly replied: Son
of Anchises, undoubted offspring of the gods, you see the deep
pools of Cocytus, and the Stygian lake, by whose divinity the
gods dread to swear and violate [their oath]. All that crowd,
which you see, consists of naked and unburied persons: that
ferryman is Charon: these, whom the stream carries, are interred; for it is not permitted to transport them over the
horrid banks, and hoarse waves, before their bones are quietly
lodged in a final abode. They wander a hundred years, and
flutter about these shores: then at length admitted, they visit
the wished-for lakes.

The offspring of Anchises paused and repressed his steps,
deeply musing, and pitying from his soul their unkind lot.
There he espies Leucaspis,[33] and Orontes, the commander of

---

[31] Charon, a god of hell, son of Erebus and Nox, who conducted the
souls of the dead in a boat over the river Styx to the infernal regions.

[32] i. e. "season." See Broukh. on Tibull. l. 1, 17. B.

[33] Leucaspis, one of Æneas' companions, lost during a storm in the
Tyrrhene Sea.

the Lycian fleet, mournful, and bereaved of the honours of
the dead: whom, as they sailed from Troy, over the stormy
seas, the south wind sunk together, whelming both ship and
crew in the waves. Lo! the pilot Palinurus slowly advanced,
who lately in his Libyan voyage, while he was observing the
stars, had fallen from the stern, plunged in the midst of the
waves. When with difficulty, by reason of the thick shade,
Æneas knew him in this mournful mood, he thus first accosts
him: What god, O Palinurus, snatched you from us, and
overwhelmed you in the middle of the ocean? Come tell me.
For Apollo, whom I never before found false, in this one response deceived my mind, declaring that you should be safe
on the sea, and arrive at the Ausonian coasts: Is this the
amount of his plighted faith?

But he [answers]: Neither the oracle of Phœbus beguiled
you, prince of the line of Anchises, nor a god plunged me in
the sea; for, falling headlong, I drew along with me the helm,
which I chanced with great violence to tear away, as I clung
to it, and steered our course, being appointed pilot. By the
rough seas I swear, that I was not so seriously apprehensive
for myself, as that thy ship, despoiled of her rudder, dispossessed of her pilot, might sink while such high billows were
rising. The south wind drove me violently on the water over
the spacious sea, three wintry nights: on the fourth day I descried Italy from the high ridge of a wave [whereon I was]
raised aloft. I was swimming gradually towards land, and should
have been out of danger, had not the cruel people fallen upon
me with the sword, (encumbered with my wet garment, and
grasping with crooked hands the rugged tops of a mountain,)
and ignorantly taking me for a rich prey. Now the waves
possess me,[14] and the winds toss me about the shore. But by
the pleasant light of heaven, and by the vital air, by him who
gave thee birth, by the hope of rising Iülus, I thee implore,
invincible one, release me from these woes: either throw on
me some earth, (for thou canst do so,) and seek out the Veline
port; or, if there be any means, if thy goddess mother point
out any, (for thou dost not, I presume, without the will of the
gods, attempt to cross such mighty rivers and the Stygian
lake,) lend your hand to an unhappy wretch, and bear me

* I. e. "my body." So αὐτὸς is used by Hom. Il. A. 4. Cf. below,
vi. 507. B.

with you over the waves, that in death at least I may rest in peaceful seats.

Thus he spoke, when thus the prophetess began : Whence, O Palinurus, rises in thee this so impious desire ? Shall you unburied behold the Stygian floods, and the grim river of the Furies, or reach the bank against the command [of heaven] ? Cease to hope that the decrees of the gods are to be altered by prayers ; but mindful take these predictions as the solace of your hard fate. For the neighbouring people,[25] compelled by portentous plagues from heaven, shall through their several cities far and wide offer atonement to thy ashes, erect a tomb, and stated anniversary offerings on that tomb present ; and the place shall for ever retain the name of Palinurus. By these words his cares were removed, and grief was for a time banished from his disconsolate heart : he rejoices in the land that is to bear his name.

They therefore accomplish their journey begun, and approach the river : whom when the boatman soon from the Stygian wave beheld advancing through the silent grove, and stepping forward to the bank, thus he first accosts them in words, and chides them unprovoked : Whoever thou mayest be, who art now advancing armed to our rivers, say quick for what end thou comest ; and from that very spot repress thy step. This is the region of Ghosts, of Sleep, and drowsy Night : to waft over the bodies of the living in my Stygian boat is not permitted. Nor indeed was it joy to me that I received Alcides on the lake when he came, or Theseus and Pirithous,[26] though they were the offspring of the gods, and invincible in might. One with his hand put the keeper of Tartarus in chains, and dragged him trembling from the throne of our king himself ; the others attempted to carry off our queen from Pluto's bed-chamber.

In answer to which, the Amphrysian prophetess spoke : No such plots are here, be not disturbed, nor do these weapons bring violence : the huge porter may bay in his den for ever, terrifying the incorporeal shades : chaste Proserpine may re-

---

[25] This befell the Lucanians. See Servius. B.

[26] Pirithous, a son of Ixion, and king of the Lapithæ, whose friendship with Theseus, king of Athens, was proverbial. According to the poets, the two friends descended into the infernal regions to carry away Proserpine, but Pluto, who was apprized of their intention, bound Pirithous to his father's wheel, and Theseus to a huge stone.

ᴍain in her uncle's palace. Trojan Æneas, illustrious for piety
and arms, descends to the deep shades of Erebus to his sire.
If the image of such piety makes no impression on you, own
a regard at least to this branch (she shows the branch that was
concealed under her robe). Then his heart from swelling rage
is stilled : nor passed more words than these. He with wonder
gazing on the hallowed present of the fatal branch, beheld
after a long season, turns towards them his lead-coloured
barge, and approaches the bank. Thence he dislodges the
other souls that sat on the long benches, and clears the
hatches ; at the same time, receives into the hold the mighty
Æneas. The boat of sewn hide[77] groaned under the weight,
and, being leaky, took in much water from the lake. At
length he lands the hero and the prophetess safe on the other
side of the river, on the foul slimy strand and sea-green weed.
Huge Cerberus makes these realms to resound with barking
from his triple jaws, stretched at his enormous length in a den
that fronts the gate. To whom the prophetess, seeing his
neck now bristle with horrid snakes, flings a soporific cake of
honey and medicated grain. He, in the mad rage of hunger,
opening his three mouths, snatches the offered morsel, and,
spread on the ground, relaxes his monstrous limbs, and is extended at vast length over all the cave. Æneas, now that the
keeper [of hell] is buried [in sleep], seizes the passage, and
swift overpasses the bank of that flood whence there is no
return.

Forthwith are heard voices, loud wailings, and weeping
ghosts of infants, in the first opening of the gate ; whom, bereaved of sweet life out of the course of nature, and snatched
from the breast, a black day cut off, and buried in an untimely grave.

Next to those, are such as had been condemned to death by
false accusations. Nor yet were those seats assigned them
without a trial, without a judge. Minos,[28] as inquisitor,
shakes the urn: he convokes the council of the silent, and
examines their lives and crimes.

The next places in order those mournful ones possess,

---

[77] I. e. formed of hides sewn across wicker ribs. See Anthon. B.
[28] Minos, a celebrated king and lawgiver of Crete, son of Jupiter and
Europa. He was rewarded for his equity, after death, with the office of
judge in the infernal regions, with Æacus and Rhadamanthus.

who, though free from crime, procured death to themselves
with their own hands, and, sick of the light, threw away their
lives. How gladly would they now endure poverty and painful toils in the upper regions! Fate opposes, and the hateful lake imprisons them with its dreary waves, and Styx, nine
times rolling between, confines them.

Not far from this part, extended on every side, are shown
the fields of mourning: so they call them by name. Here by-
paths remote conceal, and myrtle-groves cover those around,
whom unrelenting love, with his cruel venom, consumed
away. Their cares leave them not in death itself. In these
places he sees Phædra[29] and Procris,[30] and disconsolate Eriphyle pointing to the wounds she had received from her cruel
son; Evadne[31] also, and Pasiphae: these Laodamia accompanies, and Cæneus, once a youth, now a woman, and again
by fate transformed into his pristine shape. Amongst whom
Phœnician Dido, fresh from her wound, was wandering in a
spacious wood; whom as soon as the Trojan hero approached,
and discovered faintly through the shades, (in like manner as
one sees, or thinks he sees, the moon rising through the clouds
in the beginning of her monthly course,) he dropped tears,
and addressed her in love's sweet accents: Hapless Dido, was
it then a true report I had of your being dead, and that you
had finished your own destiny by the sword? Was I, alas!
the cause of your death? I swear by the stars, by the powers
above, and by whatever faith may be under the deep earth,
that against my will, O queen, I departed from thy coast.

---

[29] Phædra, a daughter of Minos and Pasiphaæ, who married Theseus;
her criminal passion for Hippolytus, and the tragical end of that young
prince, by his chariot being overturned and dragged among rocks, so
stung her with remorse, that she hanged herself.

[30] Procris, a daughter of Erechtheus, king of Athens,' and wife of
Cephalus. Eriphyle, a sister of Adrastus, king of Argos, and the wife of
Amphiaraus: she was murdered by her son Alcmæon, for having discovered where Amphiaraus was concealed, that he might not accompany
the Argives in their expedition against Thebes.

[31] Evadne, the wife of Capaneus, one of the seven chiefs who went
against Thebes; she threw herself on his funeral pile, and perished in
the flames. Laodamia, a daughter of Acastus, and the wife of Protesi-
laus, whose departure for the Trojan war, and subsequent fall by the
hand of Hector, caused her death from excessive grief. Cæneus, a Thessalian woman, feigned by the poets to have had the power of changing
her sex.

But tho mandates of the gods, which now compel me to travel through these shades, through noisome dreary regions and deep night, drove me from you by their authority; nor could I believe that I should bring upon you such deep anguish by my departure. Stay your steps, and withdraw not thyself from my sight. Whom dost thou fly? This is the last time fate allows me to address you. With these words Æneas thought to soothe her soul inflamed, and eyeing him with stern regard, and provoked his tears to flow. She, turned away, kept her eyes fixed on the ground; nor alters her looks more, in consequence of the conversation he had begun, than if she were fixed immovable like a stubborn flint or rock of Parian marble. At length, she abruptly retired, and in detestation fled into a shady grove, where Sichæus[22] her first lord answers her with [amorous] cares, and returns her love for love. Æneas, nevertheless, in commotion for her disastrous fate, with weeping eyes, pursues her far, and pities her, as she goes.

Hence he holds on his destined way; and now they had reached the last fields, which by themselves apart renowned warriors frequent. Here Tydeus[23] appears to him, here Parthenopœus illustrious in arms, and the ghost of pale Adrastus. Here [appear] those Trojans who had died in the field of battle, much lamented in the upper world: whom when he beheld all together in a numerous body, he inwardly groaned: Glaucus,[24] Medon, Thersilochus, the three sons of Antenor, and Polybœtes devoted to Ceres, and Idæus still handling his chariot, still his armour. The ghosts in crowds around him stand on the right and left: nor are they satisfied with seeing him once; they wish to detain him long, to come into close conference with him, and learn the reasons of his

---

[22] Sichæus, the husband of Dido, and the priest of Hercules, whom Pygmalion, his brother-in-law, murdered, to obtain his riches.

[23] Tydeus, the son of Œneus, king of Calydon, was one of the seven chiefs of the army of Adrastus, king of Argos, in the Theban war, where he behaved with great courage, but was slain by Melanippus. He was father to Diomedes, who was therefore called Tydides. Parthenopœus, a son of Meleager and Atalanta, was also one of the seven chiefs who accompanied Adrastus in his expedition against Thebes.

[24] Glaucus, a son of Hippolochus, and grandson of Bellerophon. He assisted Priam in the Trojan war, and was slain by Ajax. Thersilochus, a son of Antenor, and leader of the Pæonians, was slain by Achilles.

visit. But as soon as the Grecian chiefs and Agamemnon's [58] battalions saw the hero, and his arms gleaming through the shades, they quaked with dire dismay: some turned their backs, as when they fled once to their ships; some raise their slender voices; the scream begun dies in their gasping throats.[56]

And here he espies Deiphobus, the son of Priam, mangled in every limb, his face, his face and both his hands cruelly torn, his temples bereft of the ears cropped off, and his nostrils slit with a hideously deformed wound. Thus he hardly knew him quaking for agitation, and seeking to hide the marks of his dreadful punishment; and he firsts accosts him with well-known accents: Deiphobus, great in arms, sprung from Teucer's noble blood, who could choose to inflict such cruelties? Or who was allowed to exercise such power over you? To me, in that last night, a report was brought that you, tired with the vast slaughter of the Greeks, had fallen at last on a heap of mingled carcasses. Then, with my own hands, I raised to you an empty tomb on the Rhœtean shore, and thrice with loud voice I invoked your manes. Your name and arms possess the place. Your body, my friend, I could not find, or, at my departure, deposit in thy native land. And upon this the son of Priam said: Nothing, my friend, has been omitted by you; you have discharged every duty to Deiphobus, and to the shadow of a corpse. But my own fate, and the cursed wickedness of Helen, plunged me in these woes: she hath left me these monuments [of her love]. For how we passed that last night amidst ill-grounded joys you know, and must remember but too well, when the fatal horse came bounding over our lofty walls, and pregnant brought armed infantry in its womb. She, pretending a dance, led her train of Phrygian matrons yelling around the orgies: herself in the midst held a large flaming torch, and called to the Greeks from the lofty tower. I, being at that time oppressed with care, and over-powered with sleep, was lodged in my unfortunate bed-chamber: rest, balmy, profound, and the perfect image of a calm, peaceful death, pressed me as I lay. Meanwhile my incomparable spouse removes all arms from my palace, and had

---

[58] Agamemnon was king of Mycenæ and Argos. He was chosen commander-in-chief of the Greeks in the Trojan war.

[56] Literally, " fails them as they open their mouths to utter it." B.

withdrawn my trusty sword from my head: she calls Menelaus[57] into the palace, and throws open the gates; hoping, no
doubt, that would be a mighty favour to her amorous husband,
and that thus the infamy of her former wicked deeds might
be extinguished. In short, they burst into my chamber: that
traitor of the race of Æolus,[58] the promoter of villany, is
joined in company with them. Ye gods, requite these cruelties to.the Greeks, if I supplicate vengeance with pious lips !
But come now, in thy turn, say what adventure hath brought
thee hither alive. .Dost thou come driven by the casualties
of the main, or by the direction of the gods? or what fortune
compels thee to visit these dreary mansions, troubled regions,
where the sun never shines?

In this conversation the sun in his rosy chariot had now
passed the meridian in his ethereal course; and they perhaps
would in this manner have passed the whole time assigned
them; but the Sibyl, his companion, put him in mind, and
thus briefly spoke: Æneas, the night comes on apace, while
we waste the hours in lamentations. This is the place where
the path divides itself in two: the right is what leads beneath
great Pluto's walls; by this our way to Elysium lies: but the
left carries on the punishments of the wicked, and conveys to
cursed Tartarus. On the other hand, Deiphobus [said]: Be
not incensed, great priestess; I shall be gone; I will fill up
the number [of the ghosts] and be rendered back to darkness. Go, go, thou glory of our nation; mayest thou find
fates more kind ! This only he spoke, and at the word turned
his steps.

Æneas on a sudden looks back, and under a rock on the
left sees vast prisons enclosed with a triple wall, which Tartarean Phlegethon's rapid flood environs with torrents of
flame, and whirls roaring rocks along. Fronting is a huge
gate, with columns of solid adamant, that no strength of men,
nor the gods themselves, can with steel demolish. An iron
tower rises aloft; and there wakeful Tisiphone, with her

---

[57] Menelaus, the brother of Agamemnon, and the husband of Helen,
the daughter of Tyndarus, with whom he received the crown of Sparta.
This, however, he had enjoyed only a short time, when Helen was carried away by Paris, the son of Priam, which laid the foundation of the
Trojan war, where Menelaus behaved with great spirit and courage.

[58] Race of Æolus; Ulysses is here meant, Sisyphus, the on of Æolus,
being, according to some his father.

bloody robe tucked up around her, sits to watch the vestibule
both night and day. Hence groans are heard; the cruel
lashes resound; the grating too of iron, and clank of dragging chains. Æneas stopped short, and starting, listened to
the din. What scenes of guilt are these? O virgin, say; or
with what pains are they chastised? what hideous yelling
[ascends] to the skies! Then thus the prophetess began:
Renowned leader of the Trojans, no holy person is allowed to
tread the accursed threshold: but Hecate, when she set me
over the groves of Avernus, herself taught me the punishments appointed by the gods, and led me through every part.
Cretan Rhadamanthus [39] possesses these most ruthless realms;
examines and punishes frauds; and forces every one to confess what crimes committed in the upper world he had left
[unatoned] till the late hour of death, hugging himself in
secret crime of no avail. Forthwith avenging Tisiphone,
armed with her whip, scourges the guilty with cruel insult,
and in her left hand shaking over them her grim snakes, calls
the fierce troops of her sister Furies.

Then at length the accursed gates, grating on their dreadful-sounding hinges, are thrown open. See you what kind
of watch sits in the entry? what figure guards the gate? An
overgrown Hydra, [40] more fell [than any Fury], with fifty
black gaping mouths, has her seat within. Then Tartarus
itself sinks deep down, and extends towards the shades twice
as far as is the prospect upwards to the ethereal throne of
heaven. Here Earth's ancient progeny, the Titanian youth,
hurled down with thunderbolts, welter in the profound abyss.
Here too I saw the two sons of Aloeus, [41] gigantic bodies, who
attempted with their might to overturn the spacious heavens,
and thrust down Jove from his exalted kingdom. Salmoneus [42]

---

[39] Rhadamanthus, a son of Jupiter and Europa, who reigned over the
Cyclades and many of the Greek cities in Asia, and for his justice and
equity was made one of the judges of hell.

[40] Hydra, a fabulous monster of the serpent tribe; that which infested
the neighbourhood of the lake Lerna, in Peloponnesus, was killed by
Hercules.

[41] Two sons of Aloeus, the giants Otus and Ephialtes, who made war
against the gods, and were killed by Apollo and Diana.

[42] Salmoneus, a king of Elis, who for his impiety in imitating the thunder of Jupiter, was feigned to have been struck by a thunderbolt, and
placed in the infernal regions, near his brother Sisyphus.

likewise I beheld suffering severe punishment, for having imitated Jove's flaming bolts, and the sounds of heaven. He,
.drawn in his chariot by four horses, and brandishing a torch,
rode triumphant among the nations of Greece, and in the
midst of the city Elis, and claimed to himself the honour of
the gods: infatuate! who, with brazen car, and the prancing
of his horn-hoofed steeds, would needs counterfeit the storms
and inimitable thunder. But the almighty Sire amidst the
thick clouds threw a bolt, (not firebrands he, nor smoky light
from torches,) and hurled him down headlong in a vast whirlwind. Here too you might have seen Tityus,[49] the foster-
child of all-bearing Earth: whose body is extended over nine
whole acres; and a huge vulture, with her hooked beak, peck-
ing at his immortal liver, and his bowels, the fruitful source
of punishment, both searches them for her banquet, and dwells
in the deep recesses of his breast; nor is any respite given to
his fibres still springing up afresh. Why should I mention
the Lapithæ, Ixion, and Pirithous, over whom hangs a black
flinty rock, every moment threatening to tumble down, and
seeming to be actually falling? Golden pillars [supporting]
lofty genial couches shine, and full in their view are banquets
furnished out with regal magnificence; the chief of the Furies
sits by them, and debars them from touching the provisions
with their hands; and starts up, lifting her torch on high,
and thunders over them with her voice. Here are those[44]
who, while life remained, had been at enmity with their brothers, had beaten a parent, or wrought deceit against a client;
or who alone brooded over their acquired wealth, nor assigned
a portion to their own; which class is the most numerous:
those too who were slain for adultery, who joined in impious
wars, and did not scruple to violate the faith they had plighted
to their masters: shut up, they await their punishment. But
what kind of punishment seek not to be informed, in what
shape [of misery], or in what state they are involved. Some
roll a huge stone, and hang fast bound to the spokes of wheels.
There sits, and to eternity shall sit, the unhappy Theseus:

---

* Tityus, a celebrated giant, son of Terra, or, according to others, of
Jupiter and Elara.
44 Cf. Aristoph. Ran. 146, and my notes on Æsch. Eum. p. 188, n. 2,
ed. Bohn. B.

and Phlegyas[43] most wretched is a monitor to all, and with loud voice proclaims through the shades: " Warned [by example], learn righteousness, and not to contemn the gods." One sold his country for gold, and imposed on it a domineering tyrant; made and unmade laws for money. Another invaded his daughter's bed, and an unlawful wedlock: all of them dared some heinous crime, and accomplished what they dared. Had I a hundred tongues, and a hundred mouths, a voice of iron, I could not comprehend all the species of their crimes, nor enumerate the names of all their punishments.

When the aged priestess of Phœbus had uttered these words, she adds, But come now, set forward, and finish the task you have undertaken; let us haste on: I see the walls [of Pluto], wrought in the forges of the Cyclops, and the gates with their arch full in our view, where our instructions enjoin us to deposit this our offering. She said; and with equal pace advancing through the gloomy path, they speedily traverse the intermediate space, and approach the gates. Æneas springs forward to the entry, sprinkles his body with fresh water, and fixes the bough in the fronting portal.

Having finished these rites, and performed the offering to the goddess, they came at length to the regions of joy, delightful green retreats, and blessed abodes in groves, where happiness abounds. A freer[46] and purer sky here clothes the fields with sheeny light: they know their own sun, their own stars. Some exercise their limbs on the grassy green, in sports contend, and wrestle on the tawny sand: some strike the ground with their feet in the dance, and sing hymns. [Orpheus,] too, the Thracian priest, in his long robe, replies[47] in melodious numbers to the seven distinguished notes; and now strikes the same with his fingers, now with his ivory quill. Here may be seen Teucer's ancient race, a most illustrious line, magnanimous heroes, born in happier times, Ilus,[48] Assaracus,

---

[43] Phlegyas, a son of Mars, king of the Lapithæ in Thessaly, who plundered and burnt the temple of Apollo at Delphi; for this impiety he was killed by Apollo, who placed him in hell, where a huge stone was suspended over his head, which kept him in continual alarms.

[46] Compare Anthon's note. B.

[47] See Anthon. B.

[48] Ilus, the fourth king of Troy, was son of Tros and Callirhoe, and father of Themis and Laomedon.

and Dardanus, the founder of Troy. From afar, [Æneas] views with wonder the arms and empty chariots of the chiefs. Their spears stand fixed in the ground, and up and down their horses feed at large through the plain. The same fondness they had when alive for chariots and arms, the same concern for training up shining steeds, follow them when deposited beneath the earth.

Lo! he beholds others on the right and left feasting upon the grass, and singing the joyful pæan to Apollo in concert, amidst a fragrant grove of laurel; whence from on high the river Eridanus rolls in copious streams through the wood. Here is a band of those who sustained wounds in fighting for their country; priests who preserved themselves pure and holy, while life remained; pious poets, who sung in strains worthy of Apollo; those who improved life by the invention of arts, and who by their worthy deeds made others remember them: all these have their temples crowned with a snow-white fillet. Whom, gathered around, the Sibyl thus addressed, Musæus [49] chiefly; for a numerous crowd had him in their centre, and looked up with reverence to him raised above them by the height of his shoulders: Say, blest souls, and thou, best of poets, what region, what place contains Anchises? on his account we have come, and crossed the great rivers of hell. And thus the hero briefly returned her an answer: None of us have a fixed abode; in shady groves we dwell, or lie on couches all along the banks, and on meadows fresh with rivulets: but do you, if so your heart's inclination leads, overpass this eminence, and I will set you in the easy path. He said, and advanced his steps on before, and shows them from a rising ground the shining plains; then they descend from the summit of the mountain. But father Anchises, deep in a verdant dale, was surveying with studious cares the souls there enclosed, who were to revisit the light above; and happened to be reviewing the whole number of his race, his dear descendants, their fates and fortunes, their manners and achievements. As soon as he beheld Æneas advancing towards him across the meads, he joyfully stretched out both his hands, and tears poured down his cheeks, and these words dropped

* Musæus, an ancient Greek poet, supposed to have been the son or disciple of Linus or Orpheus, and to have lived about 1410 years B. C.

from his mouth : Are you come at length, and has that piety,
experienced by your sire, surmounted the arduous journey?
Am I permitted, my son, to see thy face, to hear and return
the well-known accents? So indeed I concluded in my mind,
and reckoned it would happen, computing the time: nor have
my anxious hopes deceived me.   Over what lands, O son,
and over what immense seas, have you, I hear, been tossed !
with what dangers harassed ! how I dreaded lest you had
sustained harm from Libya's realms ! But he [said], Your
ghost, your sorrowing ghost, my sire, oftentimes appearing,
compelled me to set forward to these thresholds. My fleet
rides in the Tyrrhene Sea. Permit me, father, to join my
right hand [with thine]; and withdraw not thyself from my
embrace. So saying, he at the same time bedewed his cheeks
with a flood of tears. There thrice he attempted to throw his
arms around his neck; thrice the phantom, grasped in vain,
escaped his hold, like the fleet gales, or resembling most a
fugitive dream.

Meanwhile Æneas sees in the retired vale, a grove situate
by itself, shrubs rustling in the woods, and the river Lethe
which glides by those peaceful dwellings. Around this un-
numbered tribes and nations of ghosts were fluttering; as in
meadows on a serene summer's day, when the bees sit on the
various blossoms, and swarm around the snow-white lilies, all
the plain buzzes with their humming noise.   Æneas, confounded, shudders at the unexpected sight, and asks the causes,
what are those rivers in the distance, or what ghosts have in
such crowds filled the banks ?   Then father Anchises [said],
Those souls, for whom other bodies are destined by fate, at
the streams of Lethe's flood quaff care-expelling draughts and
lasting oblivion. Long indeed have I wished to give you a
detail of these, and to point them out before you, and enumerate this my future race, that you may rejoice the more
with me in the discovery of Italy. O father, is it to be
imagined that any souls of an exalted nature will go hence to
the world above, and enter again into inactive bodies? What
direful love of the light possesses the miserable beings? I,
indeed, replies Anchises, will inform you, my son, nor hold
you longer in suspense: and thus he unfolds each particular
in order.

In the first place, the spirit within nourishes the heavens,
the earth, and watery plains,[50] the moon's enlightened orb, and
the Titanian stars;[51] and the mind, diffused through all the
members, actuates the whole frame, and mingles with the vast
body [of the universe]. Thence the race of men and beasts,
the vital principles of the flying kind, and the monsters which
the ocean breeds under its smooth plain. These principles
have the active force of fire, and are of a heavenly original,
so far as they are not clogged by noxious bodies, blunted by
earth-born limbs and dying members. Hence they fear and
desire, grieve and rejoice; and, shut up in darkness and a
gloomy prison, lose sight of their native skies.[52] Even when
with the last beams of light their life is gone, yet not every
ill, nor all corporeal stains, are quite removed from the unhappy beings; and it is absolutely necessary that many im-
perfections which have long been joined to the soul, should be
in marvellous ways increased and riveted therein. Therefore
are they afflicted with punishments, and pay the penalties of
their former ills. Some, hung on high, are spread out to the
empty winds; in others the guilt not done away is washed
out in a vast watery abyss, or burned away in fire. We each
endure his own manes,[53] thence are we conveyed along the
spacious Elysium, and we, the happy few, possess the fields
of bliss; till length of time, after the fixed period is elapsed,
hath done away the inherent stain, and hath left the pure
celestial reason, and the fiery energy of the simple spirit.
All these, after they have rolled away a thousand years, are
summoned forth by the god in a great body to the river
Lethe; to the intent that, losing memory [of the past], they
may revisit the vaulted realms above, and again become willing to return into bodies. Anchises thus spoke, and leads his
son, together with the Sibyl, into the midst of the assembly
and noisy throng; thence chooses a rising ground, whence he
may survey them all as they stand opposite to him in a long
row, and discern their looks as they approach.

[50] i. e. "maris." Servius. Cf. Ovid. Met. i. 315, "campos aqua-
rum." B.
[51] The sun is particularly meant, "Sol, quem et supra unum fuisse de
Titanibus diximus." Servius.
[52] i. e. of their proper nature. Cf. Plato Phædon. § 24 and 25. B.
[53] See Servius, and Anthon's note. B.

Now come, I will explain to you what glory shall henceforth attend the Trojan race, what descendants await them of
the Italian nation, distinguished souls, and who shall succeed
to our name; yourself too I will instruct in your particular
fate. See you that youth who leans on his pointless spear?
He by destiny holds a station nearest to the light; he shall
ascend to the upper world the first [of your race] who shall
have a mixture of Italian blood in his veins, Sylvius,[54] an
Alban name, your last issue; whom late your consort Lavinia
shall in the woods bring forth to you in your advanced age,
himself a king, and the father of kings; in whom our line
shall reign over Alba Longa.[55] The next is Procas[56] the
glory of the Trojan nation; then Capys and Numitor follow,
and Æneas Sylvius, who shall represent thee in name, equally
distinguished for piety and arms, if ever he receive the crown
of Alba. See what youths are these, what manly force they
show! and bear their temples shaded with civic oak; these to
thy honour shall build Nomentum,[57] Gabii, and the city Fidena; these on the mountains shall raise the Collatine towers,[58]
Pometia, the fort of Inuus, Bola, and Cora. These shall then
be famous names; now they are lands without names. Further, martial Romulus, whom Ilia of the line Assaracus shall
bear, shall add himself as companion to his grandsire [Numi-
tor]. See you not how the double plumes stands on his head
erect, and how the father of the gods himself already marks

[54] Sylvius, a son of Æneas by Lavinia, from whom afterwards the
kings of Alba were called Sylvii. Lavinia, the daughter of Latinus and
Amata, who was betrothed to her relation, king Turnus, but was after his
death given to Æneas.
[55] Alba Longa, a city of Latium, built by Ascanius.
[56] Procas, a king of Alba, father of Numitor and Amulius. Numitor,
the father of Rhea Silvia, and grandfather of Romulus and Remus, who
restored him to his throne, from which he had been expelled by Amulius,
his younger brother.
[57] Nomentum, (La Mentana,) a town of the Sabines in Italy. Cabii,
a city of the Volsci, between Rome and Præneste, where Juno was worshipped, who was hence called Gabina. Fidena, a town of the Sabines,
on the Tiber, north of Rome.
[58] Collatine towers: Collatia, a town of the Sabines on the river Anio,
built on an eminence. Pometia, a town of the Volsci, which was totally
destroyed by the Romans because it had revolted. Inuus, a town of
Latium, on the shores of the Tyrrhene Sea. Bola, a city between Tibur
and Præneste. Cora, a town of Latium, on the confines of the Volsci,
built by a colony of Dardanians before the foundation of Rome.

him out with his distinguished honours! Lo, my son, under his auspicious influence Rome, that city of renown, shall measure her dominion by the earth, and her valour by the skies, and that one city shall for herself wall around seven strong hills, happy in a race of heroes; like mother Berecynthia, when, crowned with turrets, she rides in her chariot through the Phrygian towns, joyful in a progeny of gods, embracing a hundred grandchildren, all inhabitants of heaven, all seated in the high celestial abodes. This way now bend both your eyes; view this lineage, and your own Romans. This is Cæsar, and these are the whole race of Iülus,[68] who shall one day rise to the spacious axle of the sky. This, this is the man whom you have often heard promised to you, Augustus Cæsar, the offspring of a god ; who once more shall establish the golden age in Latium, through those lands where Saturn reigned of old, and shall extend his empire over the Garamantes and Indians: their land lies without the signs [of the zodiac], beyond the sun's annual course, where Atlas, supporting heaven on his shoulders, turns the axle studded with flaming stars. Against his approach even now both the Caspian[60] realms and the land about the Palus Mæotis are dreadfully dismayed at the responses of the gods, and the quaking mouths of seven-fold Nile hurry on their troubled waves. Even Hercules did not run over so many countries, though he transfixed the brazen-footed hind, quelled the forests of Erymanthus, and made Lerna tremble with his bow: nor Bacchus, who in triumph drives his car with reins wrapped about with vine leaves, driving the tigers from Nyssa's[61] lofty top. And doubt we yet to extend our glory by our deeds? or is fear a bar to our settling in the Ausonian land?

But who is he at a distance, distinguished by the olive boughs, bearing the sacred utensils? I know the locks and hoary beard of the Roman king, who first shall establish this city by laws, sent from little Cures[62] and a poor estate to vast

[58] Iülus, a name given to Ascanius.
[60] Caspian realms, the Scythian nations inhabiting the borders of the Caspian Sea. Palus Mæotis, Sea of Asoph.
[61] Nyssa, the name of several cities in various quarters of the world, sacred to Bacchus.
[62] Cures, a town of the Sabines: it was the birth-place of Numa Pompilius, the second king of Rome, a monarch distinguished by his love of peace. Numa was succeeded by Tullus Hostilius, who was of a warlike

empire. Whom Tullus shall next succeed, who shall break
the peace of his country, and rouse to arms his inactive subjects, and troops now unused to triumphs. Whom follows
next vain-glorious Ancus, even now too much rejoicing in the
breath of popular applause. Will you also see the Tarquin
kings, and the haughty soul of Brutus,[63] the avenger [of his
country's wrongs], and the recovered fasces?[64] He first shall
receive the consular power, and the axe of justice inflexibly
severe; and the sire shall, for the sake of glorious liberty,
summon to death his own sons, raising an unknown[65] kind of
war. Unhappy he! however posterity shall interpret that
action, love to his country, and the unbounded desire of
praise, will [prevail over paternal affection].[66] See besides at
some distance the Decii, Drusi,[67] Torquatus,[68] inflexibly severe with the axe,[69] and Camillus recovering the standards.
But those [two] ghosts whom you observe to shine in equal
arms, in perfect friendship now, and while they remain shut
up in night, ah! what war, what battles and havoc will they
between them raise, if once they have attained to the light of
life! the father-in-law descending from the Alpine hills, and
the tower of Monœcus;[70] the son-in-law furnished with the

disposition. Ancus Martius, the grandson of Numa, was the fourth king
of Rome after the death of Tullus: he inherited the valour of Romulus
with the moderation of Numa, and after a reign of twenty-four years, was
succeeded by Tarquin the elder.

[63] Brutus (L. Junius), son of M. Junius and Tarquinia, second daughter of Tarquin Priscus. He was the chief instrument in expelling the
Tarquins from Rome, thus avenging Lucretia's violated honour, to which
he had sworn.

[64] i. e. the government. B.

[65] Civil war being previously unknown in Rome. B.

[66] Alluding to the punishment of his sons for attempting the restoration
of Tarquin.

[67] Drusus, the surname of the Roman family of the Livii, of which was
Livia Drusilla, the wife of Augustus.

[68] Torquatus, a surname of Titus Manlius, a celebrated Roman, whose
severity in putting to death his son, because he had engaged the enemy
without his permission, though he had gained an honourable victory, has
been deservedly censured.

[69] i. e. strict in exacting justice. B.

[70] Monœcus, a maritime town on the south-west coast of Liguria,
where Hercules had a temple. The two warriors here referred to are
Julius Cæsar and his son-in-law, Pompey the Great. The civil war between Cæsar and Pompey, which terminated with the battle of Pharsalia,
A. C. 48, led to the overthrow of the Roman republic.

troops of the east to oppose him. Make not, my sons, make
not such [unnatural] wars familiar to your minds; nor turn
the powerful strength of your country against its bowels.
And thou, '[Cæsar,] first forbear, thou who derivest thy origin from heaven; fling those arms out of thy hand, O thou,
my own blood! That one, having triumphed over Corinth,[71]
shall drive his chariot victorious to the lofty Capitol, illustrious from the slaughter of Greeks. The other shall overthrow Argos, and Mycenæ, Agamemnon's seat, and Eacides[72]
himself, the descendant of valorous Achilles; avenging his
Trojan ancestors, and the violated temple of Minerva. Who
can in silence pass over thee, great Cato,[73] or thee, Cossus?[74]
who the family of Gracchus,[75] or both the Scipios,[76] those two
thunderbolts of war, the bane of Africa, and Fabricius in low
fortune exalted?[77] or thee, Serranus,[78] sowing in the furrow
[which thy own hands had made]? Whither, ye Fabii,[79] do
you hurry me tired? Thou art that [Fabius justly styled]
the Greatest, who alone shall repair our state by delay.

[71] Corinth, the capital of Achaia in Greece, was situated on the isthmus
between the Corinthian and Saronic gulfs. This famous city was totally
destroyed by L. Mummius the Roman consul, B. C. 146.

[72] Æacides is here applied to Perseus, king of Macedon, who was descended from Achilles, the grandson of Æacus. Perseus was totally defeated and taken prisoner by Paulus Æmilius, the Roman consul, in the
battle of Pydna, B. C. 168. Soon after this period, the whole of Greece
fell under the Roman power.

[73] Cato, surnamed Uticensis, great-grandson of Cato the censor, was
distinguished for his integrity and justice. To prevent his falling into
the hands of Cæsar, he stabbed himself, after he had read Plato's treatise
on the Immortality of the Soul, at Utica, in Africa, whither he had fled,
B. C. 46.

[74] Cossus, a military tribune, who killed Tolumnus, king of Veii, in
battle, and was the second who obtained the spolia opima, which he
offered to Jupiter.

[75] Gracchus, T. Sempronius, was distinguished both in the senate and
the field; he was the father of Tiberius and Caius Gracchus.

[76] Scipios; both the father and son are meant.

[77] Fabricius, C. L., a celebrated Roman, the conqueror of Pyrrhus,
king of Epirus, was remarkable for the great simplicity of his manners,
and contempt of luxury and riches. DAVIDSON. Cf. Lucan, x. 151, "et
nomina pauperis ævi Fabricios Curiosque graves." B.

[78] Serranus, a surname given to Cincinnatus, who was found sowing
his fields when informed that the senate had chosen him dictator.

[79] Fabii, a noble and powerful family at Rome, of whom sprung Quintus Fabius, the opponent of Hannibal.

Others, I grant indeed, shall with more delicacy mould the
breathing brass; from marble draw the features to the life;
plead causes better; describe with the rod the courses of the
heavens, and explain the rising stars: to rule the nations with
imperial sway be thy care, O Romans; these shall be thy
arts; to impose terms of peace, to spare the humbled, and
crush the proud.

Thus father Anchises, and, as they are wondering, subjoins: Behold how adorned with triumphal spoils Marcellus[80]
stalks along, and shines victor above the heroes all! He,
mounted on his steed, shall prop the Roman state in the rage
of a formidable insurrection; the Carthaginians he shall humble, and the rebellious Gaul, and dedicate to father Quirinus
the third spoils. And upon this Æneas [says]; for he beheld
marching with him a youth distinguished by his beauty and
shining arms, but his countenance of little joy, and his eyes
sunk and dejected: What youth is he, O father, who thus
accompanies the hero as he walks? is he a son, or one of the
illustrious line of his descendants? What bustling noise or
attendants round him! How great resemblance in him [to
the other]! but sable Night with her dreary shade hovers
around his head. Then father Anchises, while tears gushed
forth, began: Seek not, my son, [to know] the deep disaster
of thy kindred; him the Fates shall just show on earth, nor
suffer long to exist. Ye gods, Rome's sons had seemed too
powerful in your eyes, had these your gifts been permanent.
What groans of heroes shall that field near the imperial city
of Mars send forth! what funeral pomp shall you, O Tiberinus, see, when you glide by his recent tomb! Neither shall
any youth of the Trojan line in hope exalt the Latin fathers
so high; nor shall the land of Romulus ever glory so much
in any of her sons. Ah piety! oh that faith of ancient
times! and that right hand invincible in war! none with
impunity had encountered him in arms, either when on foot
he rushed upon the foe, or when he pierced with his spur his
foaming courser's flanks. Ah youth, meet subject for pity!.

---

[80] Marcellus, Marcus Claudius, a famous Roman general, signalized
himself against the Gauls, having obtained the spolia opima, by killing
with his own hand their king, Viridomarus. After achieving the conquest of Syracuse, he was opposed in the field to Hannibal, but perished
in an ambuscade.

if by any means thou canst burst rigorous fate, thou shalt be
a Marcellus.[81]   Give me lilies in handfuls; let me strew the
blooming flowers; these offerings at least let me heap upon
my descendant's shade, and discharge this unavailing duty.
Thus up and down they roam through all the [Elysian] regions in spacious airy fields, and survey every object: through
each of whom when Anchises had conducted his son, and
fired his soul with the love of coming fame, he next recounts
to the hero what wars he must hereafter wage, informs him
of the Laurentine people, and of the city of Latinus,[82] and
by what means he may shun or surmount every toil.

Two gates there are of Sleep, whereof the one is said to
be of horn; by which an easy egress is given to true visions;
the other shining, wrought of white ivory; but [through it]
the infernal gods send up false dreams to the upper world.
When Anchises had addressed this discourse to his son and
the Sibyl together, and dismissed them by the ivory gate,[83]
the hero speeds his way to the ships, and revisits his friends;
then steers directly along the coast for the port of Caieta:[84]
where, [when he had arrived,] the anchor is thrown out from
the forecastle, the sterns rest upon the shore.

BOOK VII.

In the Seventh Book, Æneas reaches the destined land of Latium, and concludes a treaty with the king Latinus, who promises him his only daughter
Lavinia in marriage; the treaty is, however, soon broken by the inter-
ference of Juno, whose resentment still pursues the Trojans. The goddess excites Turnus to war, who calls to his aid the neighbouring princes;
and the book concludes with an animated description of the enemy's forces,
and their respective chiefs.

Thou, too, Caieta, nurse to Æneas, gavest to our coasts
immortal fame by thy death; and now thy honour here re-

[81] Marcellus, the son of Octavia, the sister of Augustus. He married
Julia, the emperor's daughter, and was intended for his successor, but
died suddenly at the early age of eighteen. Virgil procured himself great
favours by celebrating the virtues of this amiable prince.
[82] City of Latinus; Laurentum, (Paterno,) which was the capital of
Latium in the reign of Latinus.
[83] Hence Warburton concluded that Virgil meant the whole episode
to be regarded only as a dream of the initiated. Too much ingenuity has
been wasted on the subject.   B.
[84] Caieta, (Gæta,) a sea-port town of Latium in Italy.

sides,[1] and thy name marks thy remains [interred] in Hesperia
the great, if that be any title to renown. And now that her
funeral obsequies in due form were paid, and the mound of
the tomb raised, pious Æneas, soon as the swelling seas were
hushed, sails on his course, and leaves the port. The gales
breathe fair towards the approach of night; nor does the silver
moon oppose his voyage; under her trembling light the ocean
shines. They skim along the coasts adjacent to Circe's[2] land:
where with incessant song the wealthy daughter of the Sun
makes her inaccessible groves resound, and in her proud palace burns fragrant cedar for nocturnal lights, running over
the slender web with her shrill-sounding shuttle. Hence were
distinctly heard groans, the rage of lions reluctant to their
chains, and roaring at the late midnight hour: bristly boars
and bears were raging in their stalls, and wolves of prodigious
form howled; whom Circe, cruel goddess, had by her powerful herbs transformed from human shape into the features
and limbs of wild beasts: which monstrous changes that the
pious Trojans might not undergo, if carried to that port, nor
land on those accursed shores, Neptune filled their sails with
favouring winds, and sped their flight, and wafted them beyond the boiling shoals. And now the sea began to redden
with the beams of the sun, and from the lofty sky the saffron-
coloured morn shone in her rosy car, when on a sudden the
winds grew still, every breath of air died away, and the oars[3]
struggle on the smooth surface of the lazy main. And here, from
the deep, Æneas espies a spacious grove. Through this Tiberinus, [god] of the pleasant river Tiber, with rapid whirls and
vast quantities of yellow sand discoloured, bursts forward into
the sea. All around, and over-head, various birds, accustomed
to the banks and channel of the river, charmed the skies with
their songs, and fluttered up and down the grove. [Hither
Æneas] commands his mates to bend their course, and turn
their prows towards land; and with joy he enters the shady
river.

[1] Literally, "thy honour preserves its abiding place." Others take
"sedens" as equivalent to "sepulchrum." B.
[2] Quos hominum ex facie. Circe is said to have transformed men into
wild beasts, by means of certain herbs, and a magical wand, with which
she touched them. The fable is taken from Homer, Odyss. x. 135.
[3] "tonsæ," scil. "arbores," used for oars. B.

Come now, Erato;[4] I will unfold, who were the kings, what the complexion[5] of the times, what the state of things in ancient Latium, when this foreign army first landed their fleet on the Ausonian coasts; and trace back the original of the rising war. Do thou, O goddess, do thou instruct thy poet. I will sing of horrid wars, and kings by their fierce passions driven to destruction, the Tuscan troops, and all Hesperia in arms combined. A greater series of incident rises to my view; in a more arduous task I engage. King Latinus,[6] now full of days, ruled the country and its cities quiet in a lasting peace. This prince, as we traditionally receive, was the offspring of Faunus and Marica, a Laurentine nymph. Faunus had Picus[7] for his sire; and he, O Saturn, claims thee for his: thou art the remotest author of the line. To him, (Latinus,) by the appointment of the gods, no son, no male issue remained; but one, just as he grew up, was snatched away in the opening bloom of youth. An only daughter was to preserve his line, and so large possessions, now arrived at maturity, and fully ripe for marriage. Many from wide Latium, and throughout Ausonia, sought her hand: Turnus[8] makes his addresses, in charms far surpassing all the rest, and powerful in ancestors for many generations; whom the royal consort, with wonderful eagerness, urged to have united to the family as her son-in-law: but prodigies from heaven, with various circumstances of terror, oppose. In the centre of the palace, within the deep recesses of the inner court, stood a laurel, with sacred locks, and for many years preserved with awe: which king Latinus having discovered when he was raising the first towers of his palace, was said to have conse-

Erato, one of the Muses, who presided over lyric, tender, and amatory poetry.

[5] "tempora" refers to the condition of the different states in their mutual relations; "status" to the independent condition of each respectively. B.

[6] Latinus, the son of Faunus, and king of the aborigines in Italy, who from him were called Latins. He was succeeded on the throne of Latium by Æneas, who married his daughter Lavinia.

[7] Picus, a son of Saturn, and father of Faunus, reigned in Latium, and was feigned to have been changed by Circe into a woodpecker.

[8] Turnus, son of Daunus and Venilia, and king of the Rutuli, in Italy. He made war against Æneas, who was his rival for the hand of Lavinia, daughter of king Latinus, but was defeated, and at last slain by Æneas in single combat.

crated to Phœbus, and from it to have given the name of
Laurentines to the inhabitants. On the high summit of this
tree thick clustering bees, strange to hear, wafted athwart the
liquid sky with a great humming noise, planted themselves;
and, having linked their feet together by a mutual hold, the
swarm hung in a surprising manner from the leafy bough.
Forthwith the prophet said, We behold a foreign hero hither
advancing, and an army making towards the same parts
[where the bees alight], from the same parts [whence they
came], and bearing sway in the lofty palace. Again, while
with holy torches the virgin Lavinia kindles the altars, and is
standing by her sire, she seemed, O horrid! to catch the fire
in her long flowing hair, and to have her whole attire consumed in the crackling flames, all in a blaze both as to her
royal locks and crown rich with gems: then in clouds of
smoke, [she seemed] to be involved in ruddy light, and to
spread the conflagration over the whole palace. As to this, it
was reputed terrible, and of astonishing aspect: for [the
soothsayers] foretold, that Lavinia herself would be illustrious,
both in fame and fortune, but threatened her people with a
great war.

But the king, anxious at these portentous signs, repairs to
the oracle of prophetic Faunus, his sire, and consults his
grove beneath lofty Albunea,[2] which, of woods the chief, resounds with a sacred fountain, and from its dark retreats sends
forth a pernicious stream. Hence the Italian nations, and the
whole land of Œnotria, seek responses when in perplexity.
Hither when the priest had brought offerings, and in the deep
silence of night laid himself down on the outspread skins of
slain sheep, and disposed himself to sleep; he observes
many visionary forms fluttering about in a wondrous manner,
hears various sounds, and enjoys interviews with the gods,
and converses with the manes in the infernal regions. Here
even father Latinus himself, being then in quest of a response, with due rites sacrificed an hundred fleecy ewes, and
lay supported on their skins and outspread fleeces. From the
deep grove a sudden voice was delivered: Seek not, my son,
to join thy daughter in Latin wedlock, nor rest thy hopes on
the match now designed. A foreigner comes, thy [future]

---

[2] Albunea, a wood near the city Tibur and the river Anio, sacred to
the Muses.

son-in-law, who, by his blood, shall exalt our name to the stars, and from whose race our descendants springing, shall see all things reduced under their feet, and ruled by their sway, where the revolving sun visits either ocean.

These responses of father Faunus, and intimations given in the silence of night, Latinus himself shuts not up within his lips: but fame, fluttering all around, had now wafted the tidings through the Ausonian cities, when Laomedon's sons had moored their fleet to[10] the grassy rising bank. Æneas, the chief leaders, and blooming Iülus, recline their bodies at ease under the branches of a tall tree; prepare the repast, and under their banquet spread cakes of fine wheat along the grass, (so Jove himself admonished,) and load the wheaten board with woodland fruits. Here, as it chanced, having consumed their other provisions, as want of food compelled them to turn their teeth to the scanty cake, and violate with hands and daring jaws the orb of the fated bread, nor spare its broad quarters: What I Iülus says, are we eating up tables too? nor carried his pleasantry further. No sooner was this remark heard than it announced the termination of their toils; and instantly from the speaker's mouth his father snatched the word, and transported with admiration at the fulfilment of the oracle, mused awhile. Forthwith he spoke: Hail, O land, destined to me by the Fates! and hail, ye gods, ye faithful tutelar gods of Troy! This is our home, this our country. My sire Anchises (for now I recollect) bequeathed to me these secrets of Fate: When famine shall compel thee, my son, wafted to an unknown shore, to eat up your tables after your provisions fail, then be sure you hope for a settlement after your toils, and there with your own hand found your first city, and fortify it with a rampart. This was that hunger [to which he alluded]: these our last calamities awaited us, which are to put a period to our woes. Come then, and with the sun's first light let us joyously explore what places are these, or what men are the inhabitants, or where are the cities of the race; and from the port let us pursue different ways. At present pour forth bowls in libation to Jove, and by prayers

---

[10] We must observe that the preposition "ab" is used in reference to the place whence the fastening proceeds. It is omitted in Ovid Met. 13, 439, "Litore Threicio classem religarat Atrides." In Greek the construction is with a dative, as Apoll. Rh. ii. 177, γαίη πείσματ' ανηψαν. B.

invoke my father Anchises, and replace[11] tho wine profusely on the boards.

Thus having said, he binds his temples next with a verdant bough, and supplicates the Genius of the place, and Earth, the eldest of the gods, together with the nymphs and rivers yet unknown;[12] then Night, and the night's rising constellations, and Idæan Jove, and Phrygian mother Cybele, he invokes in due form, and both his parents, the one in heaven, and the other in Erebus.[13] Upon this the almighty Sire thrice from the lofty heavens thundered aloud, and from the sky displays a cloud refulgent with beams of golden light, brandishing it in his hand.

Here suddenly the rumour spreads through the Trojan bands, that the day was arrived whereon they were to build the destined city. With emulation they renew the banquet, and, rejoicing in the mighty omen, place the bowls, and crown the wines. Soon as the next day arisen had enlightened the earth with its first beams, by different ways they explore the city, the boundaries and the coasts of the nation: [they learn that] these are the standing waters of the fountain Numicus,[14] this the river Tiber, that here the valiant Latins dwell. Then the son of Anchises orders a hundred ambassadors, selected from every rank,[15] to repair to the imperial palace of the king, all of them decked[16] with Minerva's boughs; and carry gifts to the hero, and implore his peace towards the Trojans. Forthwith, commanded, they hasten and set forward with quick pace. Æneas himself marks out the walls with a low trench, and builds upon the spot, and encloses the first settlement on the shore, in the form of a camp, with a parapet and rampart. And now the youths, having measured out their way, beheld the towers, and lofty structures of the Latins, and approached the wall. Before the city, boys and youths in the bloom of early life are exercised on horseback, and

---

[11] I. e. "renew the banquet." ANTHON.

[12] So Silius, vi. 171, "Inuramus tamen, et nymphas numenque precamur Gurgitis ignoti." B.

[13] i. e. Venus and Anchises. B.

[14] Now the Stagno di Levante. We must not understand the river Numicus near Lavinium. B.

[15] Not "from all the people." See Anthon. B.

[16] Compare the Greek ἱἱστεμμίνοι The garlands were carried in the hand. B.

tame the yoked steeds on the dusty plain; or bend the stiff
bows, or, with the exerted strength of their arms, hurl the
quivering dart, and challenge one another in the race or to
pugilism: when a messenger riding before, bears the news to
the aged king, that men of huge dimensions, in a strange garb,
were arrived. He orders them to be invited into the palace,
and seated himself in the midst on his ancient throne. On
the highest part of the city stood a magnificent capacious
structure, raised aloft on a hundred columns, the palace of
Picus of Laurentum, awful for its sacred woods, and the religious veneration of ancestors. It was [considered] a good
omen for the kings here to receive the sceptre, and raise the
first badges of royalty; this temple was their senate-house,
this their apartment allotted for sacred banquets: here, after
the sacrifice of a ram, the fathers were wont to take their seats
together at the long tables. Besides, in the vestibule, according to their order, the statues of their ancestors in antique
cedar stood; Italus,[17] and father Sabinus, and old Saturn,[18]
the planter of the vine, holding a crooked scythe under his
figure, and the image of double-faced Janus;[19] and other
monarchs from the origin [of the race], who sustained martial
wounds in fighting for their country. Besides, on the sacred
door-posts many arms, captive chariots, and crooked scimeters,
are suspended, helmet-crests, and massy bars of gates, and
darts and shields, and beaks torn from ships. Picus himself,
the breaker of steeds, sat with his augural wand,[20] dressed in

---

[17] Italus, an Arcadian prince, who is said to have established a kingdom in Italy, which received its name from him. Sabinus, from whom
the Sabines were named. He received divine honours after death, and
was one of those deities whom Æneas invoked when he entered Italy.

[18] Saturn, the son of Cœlus and Terra, married his sister Ops, who is
also called Rhea and Cybele. He was dethroned and imprisoned by his
brother Titan, but was restored to liberty and to his throne, by his son
Jupiter, who, however, afterwards banished him from his kingdom, which
he divided with his brothers Neptune and Pluto. Saturn fled to Italy,
where his reign was so mild, that mankind have called it the golden age.

[19] Janus, the most ancient king of Italy, was a native of Thessaly, and,
according to some, the son of Apollo; after death he was ranked among
the gods, and is represented with two faces. His temple at Rome, where
he was chiefly worshipped, was always shut in time of peace, and open in
time of war.

[20] This is the ablative of manner. Gellius, however, v. 8, supposes an
ellipse; others regard "succinctus lituo" as a zeugma. B.

s

his scanty tucked-up robe, and in his left hand wielded a little target; whom Circe, his concubine, stung with desire, having struck with her golden rod, and by her spells transformed, made a bird, and interspersed his wings with colours.

Within such a temple of the gods, and on his ancestral throne, Latinus, seated, called to him the Trojans into the palace; to whom, when they had entered, he, in mild accent, first these words addressed: Say, ye sons of Dardanus, (for we are not unacquainted with your city or with your race, nor hither have you steered your course unheard of,) what seek ye? what cause, or pressing exigency, has wafted your fleet to the Ausonian coast, over such an extent of azure seas? Whether you have entered the banks of our river, and stationed yourself in our port, by wandering from your way, or driven by stress of weather, (such things as in many shapes seamen suffer in the deep,) decline not hospitality, nor remain strangers to the Latins, Saturn's race, who practise equity, not by constraint or laws, but from spontaneous choice, and regulating themselves by the conduct of that ancient god. And, indeed, I call to mind, (the tradition is somewhat obscure through length of time,) that the old Aurunci [21] thus reported; how Dardanus, a native of this country, reached the Idæan cities of Phrygia, and Thracian Samos, which now is called Samothracia.[22] Hence he had set out from his Tuscan seat in Corythus; now enthroned, he sits in the golden palace of the starry heavens, and adds to the number of the altars of the gods.

He said; and Ilioneus made the following reply: O king, illustrious offspring of Faunus, neither a grim storm forced us, by billows harassed, to enter your realms; nor did the stars or the coast mislead us from the course of our voyage. We all with design, and willing minds, are brought to this city; expelled from a kingdom, once the most powerful which the sun coursing from the extremity of heaven surveyed. From Jove is the origin of our race; the sons of Dardanus rejoice in Jove their ancestor. Our king himself, Æneas the Trojan, sprung from Jove's exalted line, sent us to your courts. What a terrible storm, bursting from cruel Mycenæ, hath

---

[21] Aurunci, an ancient people of Latium, south-east of the Volsci.

[22] Samothracia, an island in the Archipelago, off the coast of Thrace.

overrun the plains of Ida, under the influence of what fates both worlds of Europe and Asia engaged; even those have heard, if such there are, whom earth's extremity removes afar, the expanded ocean intervening; and those, if such there are, whom the regions of the intemperate sun, extended in the midst of the other four, divides [from the rest of mankind]. From that deluge borne over so many vast oceans, we beg for our country's gods a small settlement, and a harmless shore, and water and air, which are open to all. We shall be no dishonour to your realm; nor shall trivial fame redound to you, or our grateful sense of so generous an action ever be effaced; nor shall the Ausonians repent that they received Troy into their bosom. I swear by the fates of Æneas, and by his right hand that excels, whether any one has experienced it in faith, or in war and martial deeds; many people, many nations, (contemn us not, because of ourselves we bring in our hands the wreaths, and [in our mouths] the words of suppliants,) have not only been willing, but courted us to associate with them. But the destiny of the gods, by their commanding influence, compelled us to go in quest of your territories. Dardanus, who sprang from this country, hither redemands his offspring; and Apollo, by his mighty summons, urges us to the Tuscan Tiber, and the sacred streams of the fountain Numicus.[20] Æneas offers you, besides, some small presents, remnants of his former fortune, saved from the flames of Troy. From this golden bowl father Anchises performed libations at the altar: this was borne by Priam, when he gave laws in form to the assembled people, the sceptre, and sacred diadem, and the robes, the work of the Trojan dames.

At these words of Ilioneus, Latinus keeps his countenance fixed in steady regard, and remains unmoved on the ground, rolling his eyes intent. Neither the embroidered purple, nor Priam's sceptre, move him so much, as he muses on his daughter's nuptials, and deep in his breast revolves the oracles of ancient Faunus; [concluding] that this is he who, come from foreign parts, by the Fates was ordained his son-in-law, and called to the regal power with equal sway: that from him a race would come in valour eminent, and who, by their power, should master the whole world. At length, with joy, he says: May the gods crown with success our enterprise and

their own presage. Trojan, what you demand shall be given:
nor do I reject your present. While Latinus is king, not the
fatness of a luxuriant soil, nor the opulence of Troy, shall be
wanting to you. Only let Æneas come in person, if he has so
great affection to us, if he longs to be joined with us in hospitable league, and to be called our ally; nor let him dread our
friendly presence. To me it will be an advance towards
peace to touch the hand of your prince. Do you now, on your
part, report these my instructions to your king: I have a
daughter, whom neither the oracles from my father's shrine,
nor numerous prodigies from heaven, permit me to match with
a husband of our own nation; they foretell that this destiny
awaits Latium, that its sons-in-law shall come from foreign
coasts, who, in their descendants, shall to the stars exalt our
name. That this is he whom the Fates ordain I both judge,
and (if aught of truth my mind divines) I wish it too.

This said, the sire chooses out steeds from his whole number: in lofty stalls, three hundred of them stood in sleek appearance. Forthwith for all the Trojans he commands the
winged coursers, caparisoned with purple and embroidered
trappings, to be led forth in order. Golden poitrels hang low
down from their breasts; arrayed in gold, they champ the
yellow gold under their teeth. For the absent hero, [he or-
ders] a chariot, and a pair of harnessed steeds of ethereal
breed, from their nostrils snorting fire, of the race of those
whom crafty Circe produced, when, having stolen [horses]
from her father [the Sun], she raised up a spurious breed by
a substituted mare. With these presents and speeches from
Latinus, the Trojans, mounted on their steeds, return, and
bring back peace.

But lo! the unrelenting wife of Jove was on her return
from Inachian Argos,[24] and, wafted in her chariot, possessed
the aërial regions; and, from on high, at the distance of
Sicilian Pachynus, far off she spied Æneas full joyous, and
the Trojan fleet. She sees [the Trojans] already labouring
on the buildings, already settled in the land, and that they
have abandoned their ships. Pierced with sharp grief she
stood; then tossing her head, she poured forth these words

---

[24] Inachian Argos, the capital of Argolis, in Peloponnesus, was so
called from Inachus, a son of Oceanus and Tethys, who founded the kingdom of Argos.

from her breast : Ah ! race detested, and Fates of Troy opposed to ours ! Was it in the compass of my power to overthrow them to the plains of Sigæum ?[25] made captives, could they be kept in captivity ? when Troy was burned to ashes, were they consumed? through the midst of armies, through the midst of flames, have they then found their way? But, I suppose, the power of my divinity, tired out now, lies inactive; or glutted [with full revenge], I have dropped my resentment. Yet, with hostile intention, I dared to pursue them over the waves, when they had been driven out of their country, and on the vast wide ocean to oppose myself to the exiles. The powers of heaven and sea have been spent on the Trojans. Of what avail to me were the Syrtes, or Scylla, or the vast Charybdis? In Tiber's wished-for channel they are lodged, secure against the seas and me. Mars was able to destroy the gigantic race of the Lapithæ; the father of the gods himself gave up his beloved Calydon[26] to Diana's resentment : what crime, either of the Lapithæ, or of Calydon, had deserved such severe punishment? But I, the great consort of Jove, who had power to leave no means untried, who had recourse to all expedients, unhappy I am vanquished by Æneas. But if my own divinity is not powerful enough, surely I need not hesitate to implore whatever deity any where subsists: if I cannot move the powers above, I will solicit those of hell. Grant I be not permitted to bar him from the kingdom of Latium, and Lavinia be unalterably destined his spouse by fate; yet I may protract, and throw obstacles in the way of those mighty events ; yet I may cut off the subjects of both kings. With this costly price of their people's blood, let the father and son-in-law unite. Thy dowry, virgin, shall be paid in Trojan and Rutulian blood ; and Bellona[27] waits thee for thy bride's-maid : nor did teem-

[25] Sigæum, see note [2], Æneid, Book II. p. 138.
[26] Calydon, a city of Ætolia in Greece, where Œneus, the father of Meleager, reigned. The king having neglected to pay homage to Diana, the goddess sent a wild boar to ravage the country, which at last was killed by Meleager. All the princes of the age assembled to hunt this boar, which event is greatly celebrated by the poets, under the name of the Chase of Calydon, or of the Calydonian Boar.
[27] Bellona, the goddess of war, daughter of Phorcys and Ceto, and, according to some, the sister and wife of Mars.   .—

ing Hecuba [28] alone, impregnated with a firebrand, bring forth
a blazing nuptial torch; to Venus too this production of hers
shall prove the same, even a second Paris, and a firebrand
fatal to Troy again tottering to its fall.

Having uttered these words, dreadful down to earth she
plunged. From the mansions of the dire sisters, and the infernal glooms, she calls up baleful Alecto; whose heart's delight are rueful wars, strifes, and deceits, and noxious crimes.
Her even her father, Pluto's self, abhors, her hellish sisters
abhor the monster; into so many shapes she turns herself, so
hideous are her forms, with so many snakes the grim Fury
sprouts up. Whom Juno stimulates with these words, and
thus addresses: Virgin, offspring of Night, perform me this
task, this service, your own peculiar province; that our honour and wounded fame be not quite baffled, nor the Ænean
race be able fawningly to circumvent Latinus by this match,
or take possession of the Italian territories. Thou canst arm
to war the most cordial brothers, and by animosities embroil
families : thou canst introduce into houses scourges and fire-
brands of death; with thee are a thousand specious pretexts,
a thousand arts of doing mischief: ransack thy fruitful bosom,
unhinge the established peace, sow crimes that lead to war ;
let the youth incline to, and at once demand and snatch up
arms.

Forthwith Alecto, infected with Gorgonian poisons, repairs
first to Latium, and the lofty palace of the Laurentine monarch, and took possession of Amata's [29] silent gate; in whose
inflamed breast female cares and angry commotions kept dis-
quieting [30] on account of the arrival of the Trojans, and the
match with Turnus. At her the goddess flings from her dark
locks one of her snakes, and plunges it deep in her bosom
down to its inmost recesses, that, by the monster, driven to
fury, she may embroil the whole family. He, sliding between
her robes and smooth breast, rolls on with imperceptible touch,

---

[28] Hecuba, daughter of Dymas, a Phrygian prince, or, according to
others, of Cisseus, a Thracian king, was the second wife of Priam king
of Troy, and the mother of Paris.

[29] Amata, the wife of king Latinus : she zealously favoured the interest
of Turnus against Æneas.

[30] So " coquit " is used in Ennius apud Cic. de Sen. i. " curamve la-
vasso, Quæ nunc te coquit." B.

and, in the transport of her rage, steals on her unawares, infusing into her a viperish soul: the huge snake becomes a chain of wreathed gold around her neck, he becomes a long winding fillet, and entwines her hair, and in slippery mazes creeps over her limbs. And while the first infection, downward gliding, with its humid poison attacks her senses, and blends the mingling fire with her bones; and while her mind has not yet felt the flame throughout her bosom; she spoke with softer accents, and in the wonted manner of mothers, making many a heavy lamentation about her daughter and the Phrygian match: And is Lavinia given in marriage to Trojan exiles? and have you, her father, no pity on your daughter, or on yourself, or on her mother, whom with the first fair wind[n] the perfidious pirate will abandon, and return to sea, carrying off the virgin? And did not the Phrygian shepherd thus steal into Lacedæmon, and bear away Leda's daughter, Helen, to the Trojan city? What becomes of your solemnly plighted faith, your ancient regard for your people, and your right hand so often plighted to your kinsman Turnus? If the Latins must have a son-in-law from a foreign nation, and this be determined, and the commands of your father Faunus press you, for my part I reckon every land foreign, which, independent, is disjointed from our dominion, and that thus the gods intend. And (if the first origin of his family be traced back) Turnus has Inachus and Acrisius[n] for his progenitors, and Mycenæ, the heart [of Greece, for his country].

When, having tried him by these words in vain, she finds Latinus resolutely fixed against her, and the serpent's infuriated poison had now sunk deep into her bowels, and crept through all her frame; then, indeed, in wretched disorder, startled by hideous monsters, she rages frantic with unexampled fury through the ample bounds of the city: as at times a whip-top whirling under the twisted lash, which boys intent on their sport drive in a large circuit round some empty court; the engine driven about by the scourge is hurried round and round in circling courses; the unpractised throng and beardless band are lost in admiration of the voluble box-wood:

[n] The north wind would be favourable to a departure from Italy. B.
[n] Acrisius, king of Argos, was descended from Inachus, its founder, and was one of Turnus' ancestors. He was accidentally slain by his grandson Perseus.

they lend their souls to the stroke. With no less impetuous career is the queen driven through the midst of cities, and among crowds all in fierce commotion. Aiming even at a more atrocious deed, and ushering in a higher scene of madness, having counterfeited the enthusiasm of Bacchus, she flies out into the forest, and conceals her daughter in the woody mountains, that from the Trojans she may wrest the match, and retard the nuptials: exclaiming, Evoe Bacchus, and bawling out, that thou alone art worthy of the virgin; for that, in honour of thee, she wields the tender ivy-wands, round thee she moves in the dance, for thee she feeds her sacred locks. The rumour flies; and the same enthusiasm at once actuates all the matrons, inflamed by the furies in their breasts, to seek new habitations: they instantly abandon their homes; to the winds they expose their necks and hair. Others again fill the skies with tremulous yells, and, wrapped in skins, wield their vine-dressed spears. She herself, in the midst of them, all on fire sustains a blazing pine, and sings the nuptial song for her daughter and Turnus, whirling her bloody eyeballs round; and suddenly, with a stern air, she cries, Io I ye Latin matrons, hear, whatever you may chance to be: if any affection for unhappy Amata dwells in your humane souls, if concern for a mother's right touches you to the quick, unbind the fillets of your hair, with me take up the orgies. In this manner among the woods, among the deserts of wild beasts, Alecto, with the stimulating fury of Bacchus, all around goads on the queen.

After she seemed sufficiently to have kindled the first transports of rage, and embroiled the counsel and the whole family of Latinus; forthwith the baleful goddess hence is borne on dusky wings lo the walls of the bold Rutulian; which city Danaë,[13] wafted by the impetuous south wind, is said to have founded for her Acrisian colony. The place was formerly called Ardea by the ancient inhabitants, and now Ardea it remains, an illustrious name:[14] but its fortune has departed. Here, in his lofty palace, was Turnus enjoying repose at the black hour of midnight. Alecto lays aside her hideous aspect, and Fury's limbs; she transforms herself into the shape of an

---

[13] Danaë, the daughter of Acrisius, king of Argos: she fled to Italy, and founded the city of Ardea, the capital of the Rutuli.

[14] i. e. "a name and nothing more." See Drakenb. on Silius i. 293. B.

old hag, ploughs with wrinkles her loathsome front, assumes
grey hairs with a fillet, and binds on them an olive bough:
she takes the form of Calybe, the aged priestess of Juno's
temple, and with these words presents herself to the youth full
in his view: O Turnus, will you suffer so many toils to be lost
and thrown away, and your sceptre to be transferred[25] to a
Trojan colony? The king absolutely refuses you the match
and dowry you have purchased with your blood; and a
foreigner is sought to inherit his kingdom. Go now, thus
baffled, expose yourself to thankless dangers; go, overthrow
the Tuscan armies; in peace protect the Latins. And now,
in these very terms, the all-powerful queen of heaven herself
commanded me plainly to address you, reclining in the still
silent night. Wherefore despatch, and with alacrity order the
youth to be armed, and march forth to war; in flames consume both the Phrygian leaders, who are stationed in the fair
river, and their painted vessels. So the awful majesty of
heaven commands. Let king Latinus himself, unless he con-
sents to grant the match, and stand to his word, know, and at
length experience Turnus in arms.

Upon this the youth, deriding the prophetess, thus in his
turn replies: The intelligence has not escaped my ears, as
you imagine, that a fleet is arrived in the Tiber's channel.
Forge not to me such grounds of fear: for of us imperial Juno
is not unmindful. But old age, O dame, oppressed with
dotage, and barren of the truth, in vain harasses thee with
cares; and with false alarms deludes thee a prophetess, amid
the warlike affairs of kings. Your province is to guard the
statues and temples of the gods: let men have the management
of peace and war, by whom war ought to be managed.

By these words Alecto kindled into rage. As for the
youth, while yet speaking, a sudden trembling seized his
limbs; his eyes stiffened: with so many snakes the Fury hisses,
and a shape so horrid discloses itself: then, as he hesitates,
and purposes more to say, rolling her fiery eyeballs, she repelled [his words], and reared the double snakes in her hair,
clanked her whip, and thus further spoke in outrageous
accent: Lo, here am I oppressed with dotage, whom old age,
barren of the truth, deludes with false alarms amid the arms

---

* Cf. Æn. v. 750, and the note. B

of kings. Turn thy eyes to these signs: I came from the
abode of the dire sisters; wars and death in my hand I bear.
Thus having spoken, she flung a firebrand at the youth, and
deep in his breast fixed the torch smoking with grim light.
Excessive terror broke his rest, and sweat bursting from every
pore drenched his bones and limbs. Frantic for arms he
raves, for arms he searches the bed and the palace: a passion
for the sword, a cursed madness after war, and indignation
besides rage [in his breast]. As when with loud crackling a
fire of twigs is applied to the sides of a bubbling caldron, and
by the heat the water dances; within, the violence of the
water rages, and high the smoky fluid in foam overflows; nor
can the wave now contain itself; in pitchy steam it flies all
abroad. Therefore, now that the peace is profanely violated,
he enjoins the chief of the youth to repair to king Latinus, and
orders arms to be prepared to defend Italy, to expel the
enemy from their territories: [adding,] that he is a sufficient
match for Trojans and Latins both. When he had thus
spoken, and in vows had addressed the gods, the Rutulians
with emulous ardour animate one another to arms. One is
incited by his distinguished gracefulness of form and youth;
another by his regal ancestors; a third by his right hand, with
its glorious deeds.

While Turnus inspires the Rutulians with courageous souls,
Alecto on Stygian wings against the Trojans speeds her flight:
having with fresh artifice espied the place where on the shore
fair Iülus was by snares and chase pursuing beasts of prey.
Here the virgin of hell throws on his hounds a sudden madness, and affects their nostrils with the well-known scent, with
keen ardour to pursue a stag; which was the first source of
calamities, and inflamed the rustic minds to war. The stag
was of exquisite beauty, and large horns; which, snatched
from its mother's dugs, the sons of Tyrrhus nursed up, and
Tyrrhus, the father, to whom the royal herds are in subjection, and the charge of the fields all around intrusted. The
animal, trained to discipline, their sister Sylvia[36] with her
utmost care was wont to deck, interweaving his horns with
soft garlands; she combed and washed him in the clear stream.

[36] Sylvia, the daughter of Tyrrhus, shepherd of king Latinus, whose
favourite stag was killed by Ascanius, which was the cause of war between
Æneas and the Latins.

He, patient of the touch, and accustomed to his master's board, would range in the woods; and again at night, however late, to his home, his familiar retreat, of himself repaired. Him at a distance, while roving, the mad hounds of the huntsman Iülus roused, when by chance he was floating down with the stream, and on the verdant bank was allaying his heat. Ascanius himself too, fired with the love of distinguished praise, from his bended bow aimed arrows [at him]; nor was the god unaiding to his erring hand ;[57] and with a loud [whizzing] sound the shaft impelled, pierced his belly and his flanks. The wounded animal fled homeward to his own habitation, and groaning entered his stall; and all bloody, and like one imploring [pity], filled the house with moans. Sylvia, the sister, first, beating her arms with her palms, implores aid, and calls together the hardy swains. They (for the fierce fiend lurks in the secret woods) suddenly appear; one armed with a brand hardened in the fire, one with a sturdy knotted club; whatever by each in rummaging was found, his rage makes a weapon. Tyrrhus, as by chance with driven wedges he was cleaving an oak in four, breathing fury, snatches up his axe, and summons his rustic bands. But the savage goddess, having from her place of observation found the opportunity of executing her mischievous plot, mounts the high roof of the stall, and from the lofty summit sounds the shepherd's signal, and in the winding horn strains her hellish voice; with which every grove forthwith quaked and the deep woods inly trembled. Even the lake of Diana heard it from afar; the Nar,[58] white with sulphureous water, heard it, as well as the springs of Velinus; and frightened mothers pressed their infants to their breasts. Then, indeed, wherever the cornet direful gave the alarm, the wild unpolished swains, snatching up arms, hasten in concert from every quarter; and, in like manner, from their open tents the Trojan youth pour forth supplies to Ascanius. They ranged their battalions. Nor now in rustic skirmish are they engaged with hardened clubs, and stakes burned at the point; but with the doubtful

---

[57] i. e. "his hand which would otherwise have erred." See Anthon. B.

[58] Nar, (Nera,) a river of Italy, rises in the Apennines, and forming a junction with the Velino, flows with great rapidity, and falls into the Tiber. Its waters are celebrated for their sulphureous properties. Velino also rises in the Apennines, and, by its stagnant waters, forms a lake near the town of Reate, and falls into the Nar, near Spoletium

steel[39] they encounter, and a hideous crop of drawn swords
shoot up with horrid aspect, far and wide, and the arms of
brass struck with the sunbeams glitter, and dart their radi-
ance to the clouds: as when with the first breath of wind the
wave begins to whiten, the sea rises by degrees, and higher
and higher heaves its billows, then from the lowest bottom
swells up together to the skies. Here, before the foremost
line of battle, young Almon, the eldest of the sons of Tyrrhus,
is by a whizzing arrow slain; for deep in his throat the
wounding weapon stuck fast, and with the blood choked up
the passage of the humid voice[40] and slender breath of life.
Round him many bodies of heroes fall, and aged Galæsus,
while he is offering to mediate peace; a man who was of all
others the most upright, and formerly the richest in Ausonian
lands. Five flocks of bleating sheep with five herds of cattle
returned home [from his pastures];[41] and with a hundred
ploughs he turned the soil.

Now whilst through the plains these actions are going on
with equal fury, the goddess, having accomplished her promise, when she had drenched the field of war in blood, and
began the havoc of the first encounter, leaves Hesperia, and
turning away through the aërial sky in triumph, addresses
Juno with haughty speech: See discord brought for you to its
consummation by baleful war! Bid them combine in friendship, and contract alliances, since I have imbrued the Trojans
with Ausonian blood! To these will I add this also; if I be
assured of your consent, the neighbouring towns by rumours
will I urge on to the war, and inflame their minds with the
passion of furious Mars, that from all hands they may come
as auxiliaries; war will I spread over all the country. Then
Juno [said] in return: Of terrors and fraud there is enough:
fixed are the causes of the war; in arms they combat hand to
hand; those arms, which chance first gave, recent blood hath
stained. Such espousals and such nuptial rites let Venus'
peerless offspring and king Latinus himself celebrate. Father

---

[39] Referring to the equality of forces on both sides. So "dubia cus-
pide," Silius iv. 188. B.

[40] Cf. Silius iv. 171, "Hæsit barbaricum sub anhelo gutture telum:
Et clausit raucum letali vulnere murmur." B.

[41] Davidson prefers taking "redeo" in its sense "of being one's in-
come, stock or revenue." B.

Jove, the great ruler of heaven supreme, permits you not to
roam with farther licence in the higher regions. Retire from
these places. Whatever turn of fortune our labours may
· henceforth take, myself will manage. These words Saturnia
uttered. At which the Fury lifts up her wings hissing with
snakes, and hies to the mansion of Cocytus, leaving the high
places in this upper world. In the centre of Italy, under lofty
mountains, lies a place of high renown, and celebrated by fame
in many regions, the valley of Amsanctus :[42] the side of a
grove, gloomy with thick boughs, hems it in on either hand,
and in the midst a torrent, in hoarse murmurs and with whirling eddies, roars along the rocks. Here are shown a horrible
cave and the breathing-holes[43] of grisly Pluto; and a vast
gulf, having burst hell's barriers, expands his pestilential jaws :
into which the Fury, abhorred demon, having plunged out of
sight, disburthened heaven and earth.

Not less active meanwhile is the imperial daughter of Saturn, in putting the last hand to the war begun. The whole
body of the shepherds rush from the field of battle into the
city; and bring back their slain, the young Almon, and the
corpse of Galæsus with ghastly wounds dishonoured: they
implore the gods, and call Latinus to witness. Turnus too
comes up, and in the midst of the charge of fire and sword,
aggravates the terror; [complains] that the Trojans are invited to share the crown, and the Phrygian race incorporated
[with the Latins], and he himself driven from the threshold.
Then those, whose mothers, struck with Bacchanal fury,
bound over the pathless groves in choirs, collected from every
quarter combine, and importunately urge the war; for not
inconsiderable is the influence of Amata's name. All these
forthwith against the omens, against the decrees of the gods,
in defiance of the thwarting power of heaven, crave the impious war. Emulously they beset the palace of king Latinus.
He, like a rock in the sea unmoved, withstands them: like a
rock in the sea, which, when the mighty shock comes on, while
numerous waves around it roar, supports itself by its own
huge weight; in vain the cliffs and foamy rocks rage around,
and the sea-weed dashed against its sides is driven back. But

---

Amsanctus, a pestilential lake near Capua, in Italy, supposed, by the
poets, to be the entrance to the infernal regions.
[43] i. e. the vents, through which the mephitic vapour exhales. B.

when no means avail to defeat their blind resolution, and
things go on by the direction of fierce Juno, the aged monarch,
having poured forth many protestations to the gods and skies
in vain, exclaims, Alas! by the Fates are we overpowered,
and borne down by the storm. Yourselves, O wretches! with
your sacrilegious blood shall pay the atonement; and thee, O
Turnus, the impious promoter of this war, thee dire vengeance
shall in time overtake; and thou shalt supplicate the gods by
vows too late. For, as to me, my rest is provided, and all my
security is near [44] at hand: I am only deprived of a happy end.
Nor more he said, but shut himself up in his palace, and quitted
the reins of government.

In Hesperian Latium it was a custom, which the Alban
cities all along have observed as sacred, and which Rome, the
mistress of the world, now religiously observes, when first they
rouse Mars to battle; whether with the Getes [45] they intend
to wage the disastrous war, or with the Hyrcanians, or the
Arabs, or to march against the Indians, and pursue the morning, and from the Parthians redemand the standards. There
are two gates of War (for so they are called) deemed sacred
from religious association, and the dread of cruel Mars: a
hundred brazen bolts, and the eternal strength of iron, shut
them fast; and guardian Janus stirs not from the threshold.
When the fathers have fixed the firm sentence of war, the
consul himself, distinguished by his royal robe and Gabine
cincture, unlocks the jarring portals; himself rouses the combat: then all the youth follow, and the brazen cornets with
hoarse assent conspire. In this fashion Latinus then too was
urged to declare war against the Trojans, and unfold the
dreary gates. The aged prince refrained from touching them,
and with abhorrence shrunk from the shocking office, and shut
himself up in the dark shades. Then Saturnia, the queen of
the gods, shooting from the sky, herself with her own hand
pushed the lingering doors, and, turning the hinge, burst the
brazen portals of war.

Ausonia, before at rest and unmoved, is all on fire. Some
prepare to take the field on foot; some, mounted on lofty
steeds, amidst clouds of dust, rush with fury [to the war]: all

[44] Literally, "my port is wholly in view." B.
[45] The Getes were a people of European Scythia, inhabiting that part
of Dacia near the mouth of the Danube.

are importunate for arms. Some with fat lard cleanse their smooth bucklers and glittering spears, and on the whetstone grind their axes; well pleased to bear the standards, and hear the trumpets sound. Moreover, five great cities renew their arms, on anvils raised, namely, the powerful Atina,[46] and proud Tivoli, Ardea, and Crustumeri, and Antemnæ, with turrets crowned. - They hollow trusty coverings for their heads, and bend the osier hurdles for the bosses of their bucklers: others hammer out the brazen corselets, or from ductile silver mould the smooth greaves. To this all regard of the share and scythe, for this all love for the plough gave way. In furnaces they forge their fathers' swords anew. And now the trumpets sound: the watchword, the signal for the war, is issued forth. One in eager haste snatches a helmet from the roof; another joins his neighing steeds to the yoke, and braces on his buckler and habergeon wrought in gold of triple texture, and girds himself with his trusty sword.

Now open Helicon,[47] ye goddesses, and inspire me while I sing: what kings were incited to the war; what troops following each leader filled the plain; with what heroes the auspicious land of Italy flourished even in those early days, with what arms it blazed. For you, O goddesses, both remember, and can record: to us a slight breath of fame scarcely glides.

First enters on the war, fierce from the Tuscan coasts, Mezentius,[48] the contemner of the gods, and arms his troops. Next to him Lausus his son, to whom no one was more graceful, except the person of Laurentine Turnus. Lausus, the breaker of horses, and a mighty huntsman, leads from the city Agylla a thousand followers in vain:[49] worthy to have had more joy in [obeying] a father's commands, and to whom

[46] Atina, a city of the Volsci. Tivoli, the ancient Tibur, a city of the Sabines, about sixteen miles north-east of Rome, delightfully situated on the banks of the Anio: it was the favourite country residence of the Romans. Ardea, the capital of the Rutuli. Crustumerium and Antemnæ, towns of the Sabines: the latter was situated near the confluence of the Anio and Tiber.

[47] Helicon, a celebrated mountain of Bœotia, sacred to Apollo and the Muses, from which issued the fountains Hippocrene and Aganippe.

[48] Mezentius, king of the Tyrrhenians, was expelled by his subjects on account of his cruelties, when he fled to Turnus, who employed him in his war against the Trojans. He and his son Lausus were slain by Æneas.

[49] Because he was never to return. B.

Mezentius ought not to have been the father. Next to these
fair Aventinus, sprung from renowned Hercules,[50] proudly
displays upon the grassy plain his chariot distinguished by the
palm, and his victorious steeds; and on his buckler wears his
paternal ensign, a hundred snakes, and a hydra environed
with serpents: whom in a wood on the Aventine hill the
priestess Rhea brought forth, her furtive offspring, into the regions of light, a woman mixing with a god; at the time when
the victorious Tirynthian[51] hero, having slain Geryon, reached
the Laurentine fields, and washed his Iberian heifers in the
Tuscan river [Tiber]. Javelins in their hands, and cruel pikes,
they bear into the field of war; and fight with the tapering point
of the Sabine spike-dart. Himself [appeared] on foot, shaking
a lion's enormous hide, shaggy with fearful bristles, its white
tusks displayed, having it thrown over his head: thus he entered the royal palace, a horrid figure, and his shoulders man-
tled with the attire of Hercules. Two brothers next, Catillus[52]
and fierce Coras, Argive youths, forsake the walls of Tibur, its
people called by their brother Tiburtus' name; and before the
van, amidst thick flying darts, are hurried along: as when two
cloud-born Centaurs from the high mountain's top descend,
with impetuous career, leaving Omole[53] and snowy Othrys; the
spacious wood gives way to them as they move, and the shrubs
with loud rustling noise give way. Nor did the founder of
the city Præneste[54] absent himself: king Cæculus, whom
every age believed to have been begotten by Vulcan amidst
the rural herds, and to have been found near the fire. Him
a rustic band accompanies from all the neighbourhood around:
both those who inhabit high Præneste, and those who cultivate the fields of Gabine Juno, or the cool Anio, and the
mountainous towns of the Hernicians,[55] dewed with rills;

[50] Anthon's version is, "Aventinus, of heroic mien, sprung from Hercules, type of heroic beauty." B.
[51] Tirynthian hero, a name of Hercules, from Tirynthus, a town of
Argolis in Peloponnesus, where he generally resided.
[52] Catillus, a son of Amphiaraus, who, with his brothers Coras and Tiburtus, assisted Turnus against Æneas.
[53] Omole and Othrys, two lofty mountains in Thessaly, once the residence of the Centaurs.
[54] Præneste, (Palestrina,) a city of Latium, about twenty-four miles east
from Rome, supposed to have been built by Cæculus, the son of Vulcan.
[55] Hernicians, a people of Campania, who were inveterate enemies of

whom thou, rich Anagnia, whom thou, father Amasenus,
feedest. These are not all supplied with rattling arms, or
shields, or cars: the greatest part sling balls of livid lead:
some wield two javelins in the hand, and for covering to their
heads wear tawny beavers of the fur of wolves: with the left
foot naked they tread the ground; a shoe of unwrought
leather covers the other. Messapus[56] next, a gallant horseman, Neptune's offspring, whom none had power to prostrate
by fire or steel, suddenly calls to arms his peopl long sunk in
indolence, and his troops disused to war, and handles the
sword once more. These command the Fescennine troops,
and the Falisci[57] famed for equity; those possess the strengths
of Soracte,[58] and the Flavinian land, and the lake and mountain of Ciminus, and Capena's groves. Uniformly they moved
in harmonious order, and sang the praises of their king: as
when at times the snow-white swans through the liquid sky
are homeward borne from pasture, and through their long
necks pour melodious notes; the river [Cayster] and the
Asian lake, struck from far, return the sound. Nor would
any one have taken them for armed troops of such a vast body
promiscuously joined, but for an airy cloud of hoarse-voiced
fowls driven to the shore from the deep abyss. Lo! Clausus,[59]
of the ancient blood of the Sabines, [came,] leading a mighty
host; [Clausus,] from whom the Claudian tribe and clan are
now through Latium diffused, since Rome has been shared
with the Sabines. With them Amiterna's[60] numerous bands,
and the ancient Quirites,[61] the whole power of Eretum, and
olive-bearing Mutuscæ: those who inhabit the city Nomen-

the Romans. Anagnia, a city of the Hernici. Amasanus, (La Toppia,)
a river of Latium, falling into the Tyrrhene Sea.
[56] Messapus, a son of Neptune, who left Bœotia, and came to settle in
Italy, where he assisted Turnus against Æneas.
[57] Falisci, a people of Etruria, originally a Macedonian colony. Fes-
cennia, also a town of Etruria.
[58] Soracte, (M. S. Oreste,) a mountain of Etruria, about 26 miles north
of Rome, sacred to Apollo. Flavinia and Copena, towns of Etruria.
Ciminus, a mountain and lake of Etruria.
[59] Clausus, king of the Sabines, who assisted Turnus against Æneas;
he was the progenitor of Ap. Claudius, the founder of the Claudian family.
[60] Amiterna, Eretum, and Mutuscæ, towns of the Sabines.
[61] Quirites; the Sabines were so called from the town of Cures, which
they inhabited; the name was also given to the citizens of Rome, after
their union with the Sabines.

z

turn, and the dewy fields of Velino, the horrid rocks of Tetrica,[62] and Mount Severus, Casperia, and Foruli, and the river
of Himella:[63] those who drink the Tiber and the Fabaris;
those whom cold Nursia sent, the Hortine squadrons, and the
Latin nations; and those whom Allia,[64] an inauspicious name,
dividing runs between: in such numbers as the billows are
rolled on the surface of the Libyan main, when surly Orion
sets in the wintry waves; or as numerous as are the thick
ears of corn, scorched by the first heat of the [summer's] sun,
either on the plain of Hermus, or in Lycia's yellow fields.
Their bucklers ring, and earth, struck with the trampling of
their feet, trembles.   Next Halesus,[65] of Agamemnon's race,
foe to the Trojan name, yokes his steeds in the chariot, and
hurries to Turnus' aid a thousand fierce tribes; those who
with harrows turn the soil of Massicus fertile in vines, and
whom the Auruncan fathers sent from their lofty hills, and
the adjacent plains of Sidicinum;[66] those who march from
Cales, and who border on the fordable river Vulturnus; together with the hardy inhabitants of Saticula,[67] and the troops
of the Osci. Short tapering darts are their weapons; but
their fashion is to fit them with a limber thong. A short
target covers their left arms; and hand to hand [they fight
with] crooked falchions. Nor shall you, Œbalus,[68] be in my
numbers left unnamed, whom Telon is said to have begotten
from the nymph Sebethis, when, now advanced in years, he

[62] Tetrica and Severus, mountains in the country of the Sabines, near
the river Fabaris. Casperia and Foruli, towns of the Sabines.

[63] Himella and Fabaris, (Farfa,) rivers of the Sabines; the former falls
into the Tiber below Cures. Nursia and Hortu, towns of the Sabines.

[64] Allia, (Aia,) a river of Italy falling into the Tiber. On its banks
the Romans were defeated with great slaughter by the Gauls under Brennus, b. c. 387. Hence it was deemed inauspicious.

[65] Halesus, a son of Agamemnon and Briseis or Clytemnestra. Having
been driven from home, he came to Italy, where he settled on Mount
Massicus, in Campania, and was killed by Pallas in the war between
Turnus and Æneas.

[66] Sidicinum and Cales, towns of Campania, in Italy. Vulturnus, a
river of Campania, rising in the Apennines, and falling into the Tyrrhene
Sea, after passing near the city of Capua.

[67] Saticola, a town of the Samnites, in Italy, east of Capua. Osci, a
people between Campania and the country of the Volsci.

[68] Œbalus, a son of Telon, king of the Teleboans, a people of Ætolia,
in Greece, and the nymph Sebethis. The Teleboans under Œbalus settled in Capreæ, (Capri,) an island on the coast of Campania in Italy.

possessed Capreæ, the realms of the Teleboans; and the son likewise, not content with his paternal lands, even then extended his dominion far and wide over the Sarrastes,[69] and the plains which Sarnus waters. Those also who inhabit Rufæ and Batulum, and the fields of Celenna, and those whom the walls of fruit-bearing Abella overlook; who, after the Teutonic fashion, are wont to sling the Cateian darts,[70] whose helmets are the rind torn from the cork-tree, and whose half-moon shields and swords are formed of glittering brass. And thee too, Ufens,[71] mountainous Nursæ sent forth to battle, signalized by fame and happy feats of arms: whose subjects are the Æquicolæ, a race peculiarly rough, bred in a hardened soil, and inured to frequent hunting in the woods. In arms they harass the earth, and ever take delight to carry off fresh spoils, and live by plunder. And Umbro[72] too, of singular fortitude, came by permission from his prince Archippus, priest of the Marrubian nation, his helmet decked with a wreath of the auspicious olive; who by enchantment and dexterity was wont to sprinkle sleep on the viper's race, and the noxious-breathing hydras; their fury he assuaged, and by his art their stings he healed. But to cure the hurt of pointed Dardanian steel surpassed his power and skill; nor soporific charms, nor herbs gathered on the Marsian mountains, availed him aught against those wounds. For thee, Angitia's grove, for thee, Fucinus, with his crystal flood, for thee the glassy lakes did mourn. Virbius,[73] too, the beauteous offspring of Hippolytus, marched to the war; whom his mother Aricia[74]

---

[69] Sarrastes, a people of Campania on the river Sarnus, which divides that country from the Picentini, and falls into the Bay of Naples. Rufæ, &c., towns of Campania.

[70] Perhaps resembling the "aclydes" in vs. 730. See Anthon. B.

[71] Ufens, a river of Latium, falling into the Tyrrhene Sea near Tarracina. Nursæ, a town of Umbria in Italy. Æquicoli, a people of Latium near Tibur.

[72] Umbro, a general of the Marsi, whose capital, Marrubium, was situated on the banks of the lake Fucinus. Angitia, a wood in the country of the Marsi, between Alba and the lake Fucinus (L. di Celano).

[73] Virbius, a name given to Hippolytus after he had been restored to life by Æsculapius at the instance of Diana, who pitied his unfortunate end. Virgil makes him the son of Hippolytus.

[74] Aricia, an Athenian, whom Hippolytus married, after he had been restored to life by Æsculapius. Egeria, a nymph of Aricia in Italy where Diana was particularly worshipped

sont forth illustriously accomplished, having been educated in
the groves of Egeria, near the humid shores, where, rich
with offerings], and not implacable, Diana's altar stands.
For they report that Hippolytus, when by his step-dame's art
he had fallen, and with his blood had satiated his father's
vengeance, having been torn in pieces by his frighted steeds,
again visited the ethereal stars, and the superior regions of
this world, recalled [to life] by medicinal herbs, and Diana's
love. Then the almighty father, incensed that any mortal
should rise to the light of life from the infernal shades, himself with thunder hurled down to the Stygian floods Apollo's
offspring, the inventor of such medicine and art. But propitious Diana conceals Hippolytus in a secret recess, and
consigns him to the nymph of the Egerian grove; where in
solitude and obscurity he passed his life in the Italian woods,
and changing his name was called Virbius: whence too from
Trivia's[75] temple and sacred groves horn-hoofed steeds are
debarred, because, frightened by sea-monsters, they overturned
the chariot and the youth on the shore. Yet not the less
eagerly his son managed his fiery steeds on the level plain,
and in his chariot rushed on to the war. Turnus himself, a
comely personage, moves on in the van, wielding his arms,
and by a full head overtops the rest; whose towering helmet,
plumed with a triple crest of hair, sustains a Chimæra breathing from her jaws Ætnean fires. The more outrageous was
she, and tremendous with baleful flames, in proportion as with
the effusion of blood the combat grows more fierce. An Io,
wrought in gold with horns erect, adorned his polished steel;
Io, now overgrown with fur, now a heifer, (a mighty device,)
and Argus[76] the virgin's keeper, and Inachus her sire, pouring
the river from his embossed urn. A cloud[77] of infantry succeeds, and shielded battalions in condensed array overspread
the whole plain; the Argive youth, the Ausonian bands, the
Rutuli, and ancient Sicanians, the Sacranian hosts, and the
Labici with their painted bucklers: those, Tiberinus, who
cultivate thy glades, and the sacred banks of Numicus, and

---

[75] Trivia, a name given to Diana, because she presided over all places
where three roads met.
[76] Argus, feigned to have a hundred eyes, of which only two were
asleep at once. Juno sent him to watch Io.
[77] Cf. Hom. Il. Δ. 274. Apoll. Rh. iv. 397, δυσμενέων ἀνδρῶν νέφος. B·

with the ploughshare labour the Rutulian hills and Circe's
mount; over which fields presides Jupiter of Anxur,[78] and Feronia rejoicing in her verdant grove, where lie Saturn's gloomy
fen, and where chill Ufens through deep valleys seeks his way,
and sinks into the sea. Besides these came Camilla[79] of the
Volscian nation, leading a squadron of horse, and troops gorge-
ously arrayed in brass; a virgin-warrior. Not to the distaff
or the work-baskets of Minerva had she accustomed her female hands; but, though a virgin, [was inured] to bear the
hardships of war, and in swiftness of foot to outstrip the
winds. Even over the topmost stalks of standing corn she
could have lightly skimmed, nor once had hurt the tender
ears in her career; or along the main, suspended on the heaving surge, could glide, nor in the liquid plain dip her nimble
feet. Her all the youth, pouring from city and country, and
the crowd of matrons, view with wonder, and gaze after her
as she goes, gaping with minds aghast to see how the regal
ornament of purple mantles her smooth neck; how the buckle
interlaces her hair in gold; with what grace she bears her
Lycian quiver, and her pastoral myrtle-spear tipped with
steel.

BOOK VIII.

In the Eighth Book, Æneas forms an alliance with Evander, who sends to
his assistance a chosen body of men under his son Pallas. Venus presents
Æneas with a suit of armour, fabricated by Vulcan; on the shield are
represented the future glory and triumph of the Romans.

SOON as from the citadel of Laurentum Turnus had displayed the signal, and with hoarse clangour the trumpets rattled; soon as he roused the sprightly coursers, and clashed
the arms; forthwith their minds are driven to high commotion; all Latium at once with hurrying tumultuous haste combine, and the frantic youth burn with fury. The chief leaders,
Messapus and Ufens, and that contemner of the gods, Mezen-

[78] Anxur, a city of the Volsci in Latium, sacred to Jupiter. Feronia,
a Roman goddess, the mother of Herilus; she had the care of woods and
orchards.
[79] Camilla, queen of the Volsci, was the daughter of Metabus and Casmilla. She assisted Turnus in the war against Æneas, and signalised
herself by undaunted bravery.

tius, draw together their succours from every quarter, and
of their labourers depopulate the lands around. Venulus[1]
too is sent to the city of great Diomede to crave a supply,
and to bear word, that the Trojans were settled in Latium;
that Æneas was arrived with a fleet, and was introducing
his conquered gods, and gave out that he was designed by
Fate to be the king [of Latium]; that many nations joined
themselves to the Trojan, and his fame began to be spread
abroad all through Latium. What he proposes by these
measures, what result of the war he longs to bring about, (if
fortune attend him,) appear more obvious to [Diomede] himself than to king Turnus, or king Latinus.

Such in Latium was the state of affairs: all which the Trojan hero perceiving, fluctuates with a high tide of anxious
care; and now this way, now that, he swiftly turns his wavering mind, snatches various purposes by starts, and shifts
himself every way: as when in brazen caldrons[2] of water the
tremulous light, reflected from the sun,[3] or from the image of
the radiant moon, swiftly glances over every place around, and
now is darted up on high, and strikes the ceiling of the lofty
roof. It was night, and profound sleep held fast the wearied
animals, the cattle and flying kind over all the earth; when on
the bank, and beneath the axis of the chill sky, father Æneas,
disturbed in mind with the thought of disastrous war, laid
himself down, and indulged his weary limbs in late repose.
To his view Tiberinus himself, the old god of the place, from
his smooth gliding stream, was seen to lift up his head among
the poplar boughs: a fine robe of lawn enwrapped his limbs
in its sea-green folds, and shady reeds covered his locks.
Then thus he addressed [Æneas], and with these words eased
him of his cares: O thou, sprung from the race of gods, who
to us bringest home Troy saved from its foes, and preservest
Pergamus, destined to stand for ever, an expected [guest] to
the Laurentine soil and lands of Latium; here is thy sure
abode, thy sure dwelling-place: flinch not, nor be dismayed
by the threats of war. All indignation and anger of the gods

---

[1] Venulus, an ambassador sent by Turnus to demand the assistance of
Diomedes.
[2] Literally, "the lips of the caldrons." B.
[3] By "sole" I think is to be understood the image of the sun reflected in
the water, as in the next words, the image of the moon.

are overpast. And now that you may not imagine sleep forms these as visionary images, under the elms on the banks of the river you will find a sow lying, that has farrowed a litter of thirty young, white the dam, reclining on the ground, her offspring white around her dugs. That place shall be the station for your city, a sure rest from your toils; in consequence of which, after a revolution of thrice ten years, Ascanius shall build the city Alba of illustrious name. Events I foretell not uncertain. Now attend; I will briefly show by what means you may accomplish with success the work in hand. On these coasts the Arcadians, a race from Pallas descended, (who, hither accompanying their king Evander and his standard, have chosen their place [of residence], and in the mountains built a city [called] Pallanteum,[4] from the name of their ancestor Pallas,) perpetually carry on war with the Latin nation: admit them as confederates of your camp, and with them join league. Myself will conduct you along my banks and river straight on your way, that borne up [by my aid] you may with oars surmount the adverse stream. Arise, bestir yourself, O goddess-born, and with the first-setting stars offer prayers to Juno in due form, and by suppliant vows overcome her resentment and threats. To me you shall pay honour when victorious. I am he whom you behold gliding along the banks with my full stream, and dividing the fertile lands; the azure Tiber, a river highly favoured by heaven. Here is my spacious mansion; near lofty cities my fountain springs. He said, then in the deep pool the river-god plunged, diving to the bottom: from Æneas night and sleep departed. He started up, and viewing the rising beams of the ethereal sun, in his hollow palms with pious form he raised water from the river, and poured forth to heaven these words: Ye nymphs, ye Laurentine nymphs, whence rivers have their origin! and thou, O father Tiber, with thy sacred river! receive Æneas, and defend him at length from dangers. In whatever source thy lake contains thee compassionate to our

---

[4] Evander, an Arcadian, and the grandson of Pallas, left his native city, Pallanteum, probably in consequence of parricide, committed at the instigation of his mother Nicostrata, or Carmentis, (Servius on vii. 51,) and founded a city in Latium, called after the mother state. Dionys. Hal. i. p. 25, ed. Sylb. Aurel. Victor de or. Rom. Gent. v. 3. Afterwards the Romans called it the Palatium. It was the most sacred and hallowed part of Rome, as Mamertinus remarks, Paneg. Vell. i. B

misfortunes, from whatever soil thou springest forth most beauteous. Horn-bearing river, monarch of the Italian streams, ever shalt thou be honoured with my veneration,[5] ever with my offerings: Oh grant us by thy present aid, and by nearer aid confirm thy divine oracles. Thus he speaks; and from his fleet singles out two galleys, and furnishes them with implements for rowing; at the same time supplies his friends with arms. But lo! a prodigy sudden and strange to sight, a milk-white sow of similar colour with her white young, lay along the wood, and was seen on the verdant bank; which to thee, O sovereign Juno, even to thee, pious Æneas devotes as an offering, and presents before thy altar with her offspring. The Tiber, all that night long, calmed his swelling river, and refluent with a silent stream subsided to such a degree, that, like a mild pool and peaceful lake, he smoothed his watery plain, that there might be no need of struggling with the oar. Therefore with auspicious cheers they speed their commenced voyage: the well-pitched fir glides along the stream; the waves admire, the woods, unaccustomed to the sight, survey with wonder the far-gleaming shields of heroes, and the painted keels floating on the river. Their steerage night and day they labouring ply, overpass the long windings [of the river], are screened with various trees,[6] and cut the green woods, as they move along the smooth glassy plain.

The scorching sun had ascended the mid region of the sky, when at a distance they descry the walls, the fort, and the roofs of houses here and there, which now the Roman power hath raised to heaven: Evander then possessed the scanty domains. They turn their prows to land without delay, and approach the city. On that day the Arcadian king chanced to be offering a solemn sacrifice before the city in a grove to the great [Hercules], Amphitryon's son,[7] and to the gods. At the same time his son Pallas,[8] and with him all the

---

[5] "Honor" refers to acts of worship, "donis" to offerings made therein. So Liv. viii. 33, "arae sacrificiis fument, honore, donis cumulentur." B.

[6] Which overhung the banks on both sides. B.

[7] i. e. reputed son, being really the son of Jove. B.

Pallas, the son of Evander, was sent with a body of troops to assist Æneas, and, after performing many gallant deeds, was killed by Turnus.

youth of quality, and the poor[9] senate, were offering incense; and the tepid blood smoked at the altars. Soon as they observe the tall vessels gliding towards them amidst the shady grove, and that [the crew] were bending to the silent oars, they are startled at the sudden sight, and leaving their banquets, all rise up at once; whom Pallas boldly forbids to interrupt the sacred rites, and snatching up a javelin flies himself to meet them, and at a distance speaks from a rising ground: Youths, what motives have induced you to attempt an unknown way? whither are you bound? who are you by descent? whence came you? peace bring you hither or war? Then father Æneas thus from the lofty deck replies, and in his hand before him extends a branch of peaceful olive: The sons of Troy you see, and arms hostile to the Latins, who have exiled and driven us out by haughty war. To Evander we repair. Bear him these tidings, and say, Dardania's chosen chiefs are come, imploring his confederate arms. Pallas, struck with so great a name, stood amazed: Land, he says, whoever thou art, address my father in person, and come under our roof as a guest. Then he grasped him by the hand, and clung closely to his right hand. Advancing, they enter the grove, and leave the river. Then with courteous accents Æneas addresses the king: Worthiest of the sons of Greece, to whom fortune hath led me to make my supplication, and to spread forth these boughs, with suppliant wreaths adorned; I truly had no apprehension from your being a Grecian leader and an Arcadian, or from your being originally allied to the two sons of Atreus; but my own uprightness, the holy oracles of the gods, the affinity of our ancestors, and your fame propagated over the earth, have bound you to me in friendship, and by fate urged me hither a willing guest. Dardanus, the first father and founder of the city Ilium,[10] born of Electra, the daughter of Atlas, as the Greeks record, to the Trojans steered his course: the mighty Atlas, who on his shoulder props the celestial orbs, gave to the world Electra. Your father is Mercury, whom bright Maia having conceived, on Cyllene's

---

[9] This phrase elegantly expresses the humble resources of the times. The observation of Servius deserves notice, " libri veterum tradunt a majoribus sacrificando parsimoniam observatam esse." B.

[10] Ilium, the citadel of Troy, generally taken for the city itself, so named from Ilus, one of the Trojan kings.

frozen top brought forth. But Atlas, if we may give any
credit to tradition, the same Atlas who supports the stars of
heaven, begot Maia. Thus from one stock both our stems
divide. Relying on these circumstances, I had not recourse
to embassies, nor artfully employed preliminary means of
sounding your inclination: myself and my own life I have
exposed, and am come a suppliant to your threshold. The
same Daunian nation,[11] which pursues you with cruel war,
if they once expel us, nothing they presume will hinder them
from entirely reducing all Hesperia under their yoke, and
from being masters of the sea, both that above, and that which
washes it below.[12] Take, and give pledges of faith. With
us are stout hearts for war, with us are valiant souls, and youth
tried and approved in action.

Æneas said. Evander had all along with attention surveyed his mouth and eyes, and whole body as he spoke. Then
thus he briefly replies: Most gallant of the Trojan race, how
gladly do I receive and recognise you! how well I recollect
the words, the voice, and features of your great sire Anchises!
For I remember, that Priam, Laomedon's son, in his way to
Salamis[13] to visit the realms of his sister Hesione, [continuing
his progress] forward, visited likewise Arcadia's frozen coasts.
Then manhood first shaded my cheek with down: I admired
the Trojan chiefs; Laomedon's son in particular[14] I admired;
but Anchises walked more majestic than all of them: my soul
burned with youthful desire to accost the hero, and join hand
in hand. I came up and fondly led him to the walls of Phe-
neus.[15] He at departing gave me a splendid quiver, and
Lycian arrows, a mantle interwoven with gold, and two
bridles with golden bosses, of which my son Pallas is now
possessed. Therefore I both join my right hand with you in

[11] Daunian nation: Daunus, a son of Pilumnus and Danae, and father
of Turnus, came from Illyricum into Apulia, where he reigned over part
of the country, from him called Daunia.

[12] i. e. the Adriatic and Tyrrhenian Seas. B.

[13] Salamis, (Coulouri,) an island of Greece in the Saronic Gulf, near
the coast of Attica. Hesione, a daughter of Laomedon, king of Troy,
and sister to Priam. Hercules, having delivered her from a sea-monster
to which she was exposed, gave her in marriage to Telamon, king of
Salamis.

[14] " Ipsum " is emphatic, in opposition to " duces Teucros." B.

[15] Phenæus, (Phonia,) a town of Arcadia, near Mount Cyllene.

league as you desire; and, when first the morrow's light shall to earth return, I will dismiss you joyful with supplies, and aid you with my power. Meanwhile, since hither you are come as our friends, with willing minds celebrate with us this anniversary festival, which to defer is impiety, and even now accustom yourselves to the banquets of your allies. Thus having said, he orders the dishes and cups which had been removed, to be replaced, and himself plants the heroes on the grassy seat: and Æneas in chief he compliments with a couch and the fur of a shaggy lion, and invites him to share his maple throne. Then with earnestness the chosen youths and priest of the altar bring forward the roasted joints of the bullocks, heap in canisters the gifts of laboured Ceres,[16] and dispense the joys of Bacchus. Æneas, and at the same time the Trojan youth, feast on the chine and hallowed entrails of an entire ox.

As soon as hunger was assuaged, and the lust of eating stayed, king Evander says: Not superstition vain, and ignorant of the ancient gods, hath imposed on us these solemn rites, these banquets in due form, this altar to so great a deity · from cruel dangers saved, my Trojan guest, we perform these rites,[17] and renew merited honours. Now first observe this rock suspended on crags; how the huge piles are scattered far abroad, and the mountainous abode stands desolate, and the cliffs have dragged down mighty ruin [in their fall]. Here, in a vast recess, far removed from sight, was a cave, which the hideous figure of the but half-human Cacus[18] possessed, inaccessible to the sunbeams; and ever with recent bloodshed the pavement smoked; and affixed to the haughty entrance hung the heads of men all pale with piteous gore. Vulcan was this monster's father; whose sooty flames belching from his mouth, he stalked with bulk enormous. Time at length to us also brought the wished-for aid and presence of a god: for Hercules, the illustrious avenger, seasonably arrived, proud from the death and spoils of three-bodied Geryon; and victorious drove his stately bulls this way: and

---

[16] l. e. "of Ceres wrought for use," a periphrasis for "bread." B.

[17] Anthon renders: "we do all this." But it seems better to give "facimus" its sacrificial sense. B.

[18] Cacus, the son of Vulcan and Medusa, a notorious robber, slain by Hercules.

the heifers possessed the valley and the river.   But the mind
of Cacus, maddened by the Furies, lest any villany or fraudu-
lent practice might be undevised or unattempted, he abstracts
from their stalls four bullocks of exquisite make, and as many
heifers of form surpassing: and these, lest there should be
any prints of their feet direct, having dragged towards the
cave by the tail, and hurried along with the traces of their
way reversed, he concealed in his gloomy den.   No signs[19]
led the searcher to the cave.   Meanwhile, when now the hero
was moving from their stalls his full-fed herds, and preparing
to be gone, the heifers, at parting, began to low, the whole
grove was filled with their plaintive notes, and the hills with
clamorous din were left. One of the heifers returned the sound,
and pent up in the spacious cave rebellowed, and frustrated the
hope of Cacus. Then, indeed, from his black gall the hero's indignation kindled into fury: in his hand he snatches up arms,
and his oak ponderous with knots, and with speed seeks the
summit of the airy mountain. Then first our men beheld Cacus
dismayed, and by his eyes betraying confusion.   Instantly he
flies swifter than the east wind, and seeks the cave: fear
added wings to his feet. Soon as he had shut himself in, and,
bursting the chains in haste, let down the enormous rock,
which, by iron[20] wrought by his father's art, was suspended,
and on bolts relying made fast the gates; lo! the Tirynthian
hero transported with fury was upon him, and, examining
every passage, hither and thither rolled his eyes, gnashing
with his teeth.   Boiling with ire, he thrice surveys the whole
Aventine mount; thrice in vain essays the gates of rock;
thrice in the vale fatigued he sat down to rest. A sharp flinty
rock stood forth, with broken cliffs in the points around; on
the ridge of the cave rose, towering to the sight, a convenient
shelter for the nests of inauspicious birds.   This, where,
bending forward with its brow, it overhung the river on the
left, [the hero,] opposite to it on the right, with strained effort
shook, and from the deep roots uptorn disjoined; then on a
sudden impelled it: with which impulse the sky in its wide
extent resounds, the banks leap hither and thither, and the
affrighted river runs back.   And now the den and spacious
hall of Cacus, bared of covering, appeared, and his gloomy

[19] Because the foot-prints pointed the wrong way. B.
[20] I consider this as an hendiadys. B.

caverns in their inmost recesses were laid open; just as if by
some violence the earth, in her deep recesses yawning wide,
should unlock the infernal mansions, and disclose those pale
realms abhorred by the gods, and from above the hideous gulf
be seen, and the ghosts be terrified at the light[21] darted in
upon them. Him, therefore, suddenly surprised in the unexpected light, imprisoned in his excavated rock, and in strange
manner braying, Alcides from above galls with darts, calls
every weapon to his aid, and plies him with boughs of trees
and ponderous stones.[22] But he (for now no refuge from the
danger remains) from his jaws vomits up vast quantities of
smoke, wondrous to tell! and involves the cave in pitchy
vapour, snatching all power of sight from the eye; and deep
in his cave shoots up in wreaths a night of smoke, inter-
mingling fire with darkness. Alcides in his rage could not
endure this, but with an impetuous spring threw himself
amidst the flame, where the smoke drives its waves thickest,
and the capacious den fluctuates with pitchy vapour. Here,
in his darkened cell, he seizes Cacus disgorging unavailing
flames, grasping him like a knot; then, griping fast, keeps
choking him until his eyes start from their sockets, and his
throat is drained of blood. Forthwith, the doors being
wrenched, the grim mansion is laid open; the heifers that had
been filched away, and the stolen effects abjured,[23] are exposed
to the sky; and the deformed carcass is dragged forth by the
feet. They are unable to satiate their curiosity with gazing
on his haggard eyes, his countenance, and the breast of the
half-savage shaggy with bristly hair, and the extinguished
fires in his throat. From that time the honours [of the hero]
have been celebrated, and posterity with joy have observed
the day: and Potitius,[24] the first founder, and the Pinarian
family, the guardian of this institution sacred to Hercules,
erected this altar in the grove, which shall both be styled by
us the Great, and the Great shall be for ever.[25] Wherefore

[21] Compare Silius v. 618, "Mansæque profundi Antiquum expavere
diem." B.
[22] Literally, "millstones." B.
[23] i. e. which he had denied the possession of, on oath. B.
[24] Potitius and Pinarius, Arcadians who came with Evander to Italy,
and were intrusted with the sacrifices of Hercules.
[25] Concerning this altar Livy puts the following words in the mouth of
Evander, addressing himself to Hercules: "Jove nate, Hercules salve,

come, O youths, in celebrating virtue so illustrious, encircle
your locks with a garland, and stretch forth your goblets in
your hands, invoke our common god, and offer the wine with
good will. He said; when with its Herculean shade the
poplar of varying hue both decked his locks, and with its leaves
entwined hung down; and a sacred goblet filled his right
hand. Quickly all with joy pour libations on the table, and
supplicate the gods. Meanwhile the sphere of day declining,
evening draws nearer on; and now the priests, and Potitius
at their head, marched in procession, clad in skins, according
to custom, and bore flaming torches. They renew the feast,
and introduce the grateful offerings of the second service,[26]
and heap the altars with loaded chargers. Then round the
altars smoking with perfumes, the Salii[27] amidst songs advance, having their temples bound with poplar boughs; [in
two bands they divide,] the one a choir of youths, the other of
aged men; who celebrate the praises of Hercules and his
deeds in verse: how with his hand he slew the first [sent]
monsters of his step-mother [Juno], and squeezing strangled
her two snakes; how in war the same hero overthrew illustrious cities, both Troy and Œchalia;[28] how, under king Eurystheus,[29] by the destination of unfriendly Juno, he endured a
thousand grievous toils. Thou, invincible, dost with thy arm
[subdue] the cloud-born, double-membered Centaurs, Hylæus
and Pholus; thou subduest Cretan monsters, and the huge
overgrown lion under the rock of Nemea.[30] For fear of thee

te mihi mater veridica interpres Deûm aucturum cœlestium numerum
cecinit, tibique aram hic dicatum iri, quam opulentissima in terris gens
maximam vocet, tuoque ritu colat." The reason of the name is given by
Dionysius, that this being the altar whereon Hercules himself offered the
tithes of his spoils, it became on that account the object of chief veneration,
and was called Maxima to distinguish it from the numerous other altars
which that hero had in Italy.

[26] i. e. the evening repast, as shown by Weichart. The other had taken
place at mid-day. B.

[27] Salii, an order of priests at Rome, who had the charge of the sacred
shields called Ancilia, which they carried every year, on the first of
March, in a solemn procession round the walls of Rome, dancing and
singing praises to the god Mars.

[28] Œchalia, a country of Laconia in Peloponnesus, with a town of the
same name, where Eurytus reigned, and which was destroyed by Hercules.

[29] Eurystheus, the brother and task-master of Hercules.

[30] Nemea, a town of Argolis in Peloponnesus, near which Hercules per
formed his first labour by killing the celebrated Nemean lion.

the Stygian lakes, for fear of thee the porter of hell did tremble, cowering down in his bloody den upon his half-gnawed
bones: nor did any forms throw thee into consternation ; not
Typhœus[81] himself, of towering height, with arms in hand:
thee, not perplexed, the Lernæan snake, many-headed monster,
around beset. Hail, undoubted offspring of Jove, added to
the gods as a glory: visit both us and these thy sacred rites
with thy auspicious presence. Such deeds they celebrate in
song: above all, they subjoin the den of Cacus, and himself
breathing flames. The whole grove rings with the din, and
the hills resound.

Then, having finished the divine service, all hie back to the
city. The king, oppressed with age, set forward; and, as he
walked along, had Æneas to accompany him, and his son by
his side, and with various discourse relieved [the tediousness
of] the way. Æneas admires, and turns his rolling[82] eyes
around on every object; is charmed with the different places;
and inquires and learns the several monuments of the men of
antiquity.

Then king Evander, the founder of the Roman power, [thus
began]: These groves the native Fauns and Nymphs possessed, and a race of men sprung from the trunks of trees and
stubborn oak ; who had neither laws nor refinement; knew
neither to yoke the steer, nor to gather wealth, nor to use their
acquisitions with moderation; but the branches, and hunting,
a rough source of sustenance, supplied them with food. From
the ethereal sky Saturn first came, flying from the arms of
Jove, and an exile dispossessed of his realms. He formed
into society a race undisciplined and dispersed among the high
mountains, and introduced laws; and chose to have the country named Latium, because in these regions he had lurked secure. Under his reign was the golden age which they
celebrate: in such undisturbed tranquillity he ruled his subjects ; till by degrees an age more depraved, and of an inferior

---

[81] Typhœus, a famous giant, son of Tartarus and Terra, said to have
had a hundred heads like those of a serpent or a dragon. He made war
upon the gods, but Jupiter put him to flight with his thunderbolts, and
crushed him under Mount Ætna, in Sicily, or, according to some, under
the island Inarime (Ischia).
[82] "faciles," i. e. easily bending and turning in all directions. B

hue, and the fury of war, and love of gain,[33] succeeded. Then came the Ausonian bands, and the Sicilian nations; and the Saturnian land often changed its name. Then [came a succession of] kings, and fierce Tybris of gigantic make, from whom we Italians in after times named the river Tiber; ancient Albula lost its true name. Me, from my country driven, and tracing the remote tracks of the sea, almighty fortune and uncontrollable destiny fixed in these regions: and the awful predictions of my mother, the nymph Carmentis,[34] and the god Apollo by his authority urged me [hither].

Scarcely had he spoken, when setting forward he shows him next both the altar, and the gate filled by a Roman[35] name Carmentalis, which they record to be the ancient memorial in honour of the prophetic nymph Carmentis, who first foretold the future grandeur of the Ænean race, and the renown of Pallanteum. Next he points out the spacious grove which Romulus reduced into a sanctuary, and under a cold rock the Lupercal,[36] so called, according to the Arcadian manner, from Lycæan Pan. He likewise shows the grove of Argiletum,[37] sacred [to Argus]; and calls the place to witness his innocence, and relates the death of Argus his guest. He leads him next to the Tarpeian Rock and the Capitol, now of gold, once rough and horrid with wild bushes. Even then the religious horrors of the place awed the minds of the timorous swains; even then they revered the wood and rock. This grove, says he, this wood-topped hill, a god inhabits, but what god is uncertain: the Arcadians believe they have seen Jove himself, when often with his right hand he shook the blackening ægis, and roused the clouds of thunder. Farther, [says he,] yon two towns you see with their walls demolished, the remains and monuments of ancient heroes: this city father Janus, that

[33] Literally, "of having," as in Hor. Ep. i. 7, 85. So "habendi fames," Pacatus Paneg. 25; "finis habendi," Prudent. Hamart. 255. B.

[34] Carmentis, a prophetess of Arcadia, mother of Evander, with whom she came to Italy. One of the gates of Rome was named after her.

[35] But Wagner and Anthon read "Romani," I think, with little reason. B.

[36] Lupercal, a place at the foot of Mount Aventine, sacred to Pan, whose festivals, called Lupercalia, were celebrated annually.

[37] Argiletum, a place at Rome near the Palatium, where tradesmen had their shops.

Saturnus built; the one was named Janiculum,[38] the other
Saturnia. In such mutual talk they came up to the palace
of poor Evander; and in [that place where now are] the
Roman forum and magnificent streets, they beheld around
herds of cattle lowing. Soon as they reached his abode,
This threshold, he says, the victorious[39] Alcides entered;
him this palace received: dare then, my guest, to under-
value magnificence, and do you too mould yourself [into a
temper] becoming a god, and come not disgusted with these
our mean accommodations. He said, and under the roof of
his narrow mansion conducted the magnanimous Æneas, and
set him down to rest on a bed of leaves, and the fur of a Libyan bear.

Night comes on apace, and with her dusky wings mantles
the earth. Meanwhile Venus, the parent-goddess, not without
cause alarmed in mind, and disturbed both by the threats
and fierce uproar of the Laurentines, addresses Vulcan,[40] and
in her husband's golden bedchamber thus begins, and by
her accents breathes into him love divine: While the Grecian
kings by war were bringing fated Troy to desolation, and its
towers doomed to fall by hostile flames, not any succour to the
wretches, nor arms of thy art and power, I craved ; nor, my
dearest spouse, was I willing to employ you or your labours
in vain; though I both owed much to the sons of Priam, and
often mourned the severe sufferings of Æneas. Now, by
Jove's command, he hath settled on the coast of the Rutulians:
therefore I the self-same [fond wife] appear as a suppliant,
and implore arms from thy divinity to me adorable, a mother
for a son. Thee the daughter of Nereus, thee the wife of Ti-

---

[38] Janiculum, one of the seven hills at Rome, on which Janus built a
town of the same name. Saturnia, an ancient town of Italy, supposed to
have been built by Saturn on the Tarpeian Rock.

[39] From this circumstance Hercules probably derived his surname of
"Victor," having been received into "parva regia, sed summa religione,"
as Mamertinus says, Pan. 1. See Macrob. Sat. iii. 6.   B.

[40] Vulcan, the son of Jupiter and Juno, or of Juno alone, and the husband of Venus, was the god of fire, and the patron of all artists who
worked in iron and metals. He is said to have been cast down from
heaven, and by his fall in the island of Lemnos, to have broke his leg, and
ever after remained lame of one foot. The Cyclops in Sicily were his
workmen, and with him they fabricated, in his forges, which were supposed to be under Mount Ætna, not only the thunderbolts of Jupiter,
but also arms for the gods and the most celebrated heroes.

U

thonus, by tears could persuade. See what nations combine,
what towns, having shut up their gates, whet their swords
against me, and for the extirpation of my people! The goddess said, and, [throwing] her snowy arms around him,
in soft embrace caresses him, hesitating: suddenly he caught
the wonted flame; and the accustomed warmth pierced his
marrow, and ran thrilling through his trembling bones: just
as when at times, with forked thunder burst, a chinky stream .
of fire in flashy lightning shoots athwart the skies. This his
spouse, well pleased with her wiles, and conscious of her
charms, perceived.

Then father [Vulcan], fast bound in eternal love, thus
speaks: Why hast thou recourse to far-fetched reasons? whither, goddess, hath thy confidence in me fled? Hadst thou
been under the like concern before, then too it had been a
righteous thing in me, [at thy desire,] to arm the Trojans.
Nor did almighty father Jove, or the Fates,[41] forbid that
Troy should stand, or Priam survive for ten years more.
And now if war you meditate, and this be your resolution;
whatever zeal in my art I can promise; whatever can be
done by steel or liquid electrum,[42] as far as the power of fire
and breathing engines reach, [you may depend on me;] forbear by solicitation to bring your power in question. Having spoken these words, he gave her the wished embrace, and,
on the bosom of his spouse dissolved away, courted soft repose
to every limb.

Then, soon as the first [interval of] rest, now that the mid-
career of night had rolled away, had chased away sleep [from
his eyes]; what time the housewife, whose chief concern it is
to earn her living by the distaff and poor handiwork,[43] awakes
the heaped-up embers and the dormant fires, adding night to
her labour, and by the lighted tapers employs her maids in
their long tasks, that chaste she may preserve her husband's
bed, and bring up her little ones: not otherwise, nor at that
time less industrious, the mighty god of fire rises from the soft
couch to his mechanic labours.

<hr/>

41 The ancients supposed that the will of the Fates could not be ulti-
mately overcome, but that its execution might be delayed. See Servius. B.

42 A mixture of gold and silver. B.

43 " The loom yielding but a scanty reward." ANTHON. B.

Near the side of Sicily and Æolian Lipari[44] an island is
upraised of steep ascent, with smoking rocks ; under which a
den, and the caves of Ætna, eaten out by the forges of the
Cyclops, thunder, and from the anvils the sturdy strokes in
echoing groans resound, the bars of steel hiss in the caverns,
and the fire pants in the furnaces: Vulcan's habitation, and the
land Vulcanium called. Hither then he of fiery power descended from the lofty sky. The Cyclops in their capacious
cave were working the steel, Brontes, and Steropes, and
naked-limbed Pyracmon. In their hands half-formed, with one
part already polished, was a thunderbolt, [such as those] which
in profusion the eternal father from all quarters of the sky
hurls on the earth: the other part unfinished remained.
Three shafts they had added of the wreathed hail, three of
watery cloud, three of glaring fire and winged wind. Now
they were mingling in the work alarming flashes, noise and
terror, and the wrath of heaven with its vengeful flames. In
another part they were hastening forward a chariot and nimble
wheels of Mars, by which he uprouses men and cities ; and
were polishing again the tremendous ægis, the armour of enraged Pallas, with serpent's scales of gold, and the snakes in
mutual folds entwined, and (to be worn on the breast of the
goddess) the Gorgon's self, rolling her eyes[45] after decapi-
tation.

Away with all, he says, ye Ætnean Cyclops, and set aside
your begun labours, and hither turn your minds. Arms for a
valiant hero must be forged; now it is requisite to ply your
strength, now your nimble hands, now all your masterly skill.
Shake off all delay. Nor more he said, and all instantly begun to work, and equally the labour shared. Brass and mines
of gold in rivulets flow; and wounding steel in the capacious
furnace melts. They mark out the form of a spacious shield,
alone sufficient against all the weapons of the Latins, and orbs
in orbs seven-fold involve. Some with the puffing bellows
receive and explode the air by turns ; others dip the sputtering metals in the trough ; the cave groans with the incumbent

[44] Lipari, anciently the Æolian Islands, on the northern coast of Sicily :
they are evidently of volcanic origin.
[45] The eyes moved by a mechanical contrivance, according to Wagner.
But I should simply understand the expression of the eye as meant. B.

anvils. They with vast force alternately lift their arms in
equal time, and with the griping pincers turn the mass.

While in the Æolian regions the Lemnian sire is urging on
these works, the cheering light, and the morning songs of
birds under his roof, rouse Evander from his humble mansion.
The veteran arises, and in his tunic clothes his limbs, and
binds the Tuscan sandals round his feet ; then to his side and
shoulders girds his Arcadian sword, doubling back [on the
right shoulder] a panther's skin that hung down from his left.
Two guardian-dogs too from the lofty gate march forth, and
accompany their master's steps. The hero, mindful of their
conversation, and the service he had promised, hies to the
apartment and recess of his guest Æneas. [Meanwhile]
Æneas no less early was on his way. With the one his son
Pallas, with the other Achates came in company. At meeting
they join hands, seat themselves in the midst of the court, and
at length enjoy unrestrained conversation. The king thus
first [begins]: Most mighty leader of the Trojans, during
whose life I truly will never admit that the power and realms
of Troy are overthrown; small are our abilities to support the
war in proportion to so great a name: on the one hand we
are bounded by the Tuscan river [Tiber] ; on the other hand
the Rutulians press upon us, and beset our walls around with
clashing arms. But I intend to join with you mighty nations
and camps rich and royally magnificent, which saving relief
unexpected fortune opens to our view: hither you come invited by the Fates. Not far from this spot stands inhabited
the city of Agylla,[46] of ancient foundation, where heretofore
the Lydian nation, illustrious in war, planted a settlement on
the Tuscan mountains. This city, having flourished for many
years, Mezentius at last came to rule with imperious sway and
cruel arms. Why should I mention his unutterable barbari-
ties ? or why the tyrant's horrid deeds ? May the gods re-
compense them on his own head, and on his race ! He even
bound to the living the bodies of the dead, joining together
hands to hands, and face to face, a kind of torture : and [the
victims] pining away with gore and putrefaction in this
loathed embrace, he thus with lingering death destroyed. But
at length his subjects, weary [of his cruelties], in arms around

---

" Agylla, afterwards called Cære, a town of Etruria.

beset both the tyrant himself raging past utterance, and all
his house: they assassinate his adherents, hurl flames against
his roof. He, amidst the massacre making his escape, flies
for shelter to the territories of the Rutulians, and finds protection from the arms of Turnus, his hospitable friend.
Therefore all Etruria ros with just fury; and the people by
present war redemand their king for punishment. Over these
thousands, Æneas, I will assign you leader. For all along
the shore the vessels ranged in thick array resound with
clamour; and crave to urge on the banners. Them an aged
soothsayer restrains, this oracle in prophetic strains deliver-
ing: Ye chosen youths of Lydia, the flower and excellence of
ancient heroes, whom just indignation urges against the foe,
and Mezentius fires with due resentment; no native of Italy
is destined to subdue that powerful nation: make choice of
foreign leaders. Then, overawed by the declaration of the
gods, the Tuscan army, respiting their fury, encamped on
this plain. Tarchon[47] himself hath sent ambassadors with
the royal crown and sceptre, and to me commends these ensigns; [imploring me] to repair to the camp, and assume the
Tuscan administration. But life with frozen blood benumbed,
and worn out with years, and my capacity for heroic deeds
superannuated, deny me empire. My son I would urge to it
were it not that, being of mixed race by reason of a Sabine
mother, he derived a portion of his country from this land. Do
you, most gallant leader of the Trojans and Italians, to whose
years and lineage also fate is indulgent, you whom the oracles
invite, enter upon the task. Him too, my hope and solace,
Pallas, to thee I will join; under thee his master let him practise to endure warfare, and the laborious service of Mars, be
spectator of thy deeds, and from his earliest years make thee
the object of his admiration. To him I will give two hundred Arcadian horsemen, the chosen strength of the youth;
and as many more will Pallas give thee in his own name.

Thus he had scarcely spoke, when Æneas, the offspring of
Anchises, and trusty Achates, held their eyes fixed on the
ground, and with heavy hearts began to revolve many hard
thoughts,[48] had not Cytherea displayed a sign in the open air:

---

[47] Tarchon, an Etrurian chief, who assisted Æneas against the Rutulians.
[48] Cf. Propert. i. 15, 1, "Sæpe ego multa tuæ levitatis dura time-
bam." B.

for unexpectedly a flash of lightning, darted from the sky, came with a peal;[49] and suddenly all things seemed to threaten ruin, and the blast of the Tuscan trumpet rattled through the skies. Upwards they gaze : again and again in dreadful peals it thunders ; in a serene quarter of the heavens, among the clouds they observe arms blaze athwart the clear expanse, and clashed peal with thunder. The rest were astounded with amazement; but the Trojan hero knew the sound and promised signs of his goddess-mother. Then [to Evander] he addressed his speech : By no means, my hospitable friend, by no means be anxious to explore what crisis these prodigies portend : I am called by heaven. My divine parent foretold that she was to send this signal, if war should assail me, and that she would bring Vulcan-wrought arms through the aërial regions to my aid. Ah! what havoc awaits the hapless Laurentines! what ample satisfaction shalt thou, O Turnus, give me! what numerous shields, and helmets, and bodies of gallant heroes, shalt thou, father Tiber, roll down thy streams! Let them challenge our armies, and violate their leagues.

Having said these words, he raised himself from his lofty throne; and first of all he wakes the dormant altars with fires in honour of Hercules, and visits with joy the Lar,[50] whom yesterday he had first worshipped, and the little household gods : with accustomed rites he offers a sacrifice of chosen ewes; in like manner Evander, in like manner the Trojan youth. After this he repairs to the ships, and revisits his friends ; from whose number he chooses out such as excelled in valour, to accompany him to the war: the rest by the descending stream are borne along, and without effort glide down with the current of the river, to bring Ascanius tidings of his father, and of the affairs in hand. The Trojans, repairing to the Tuscan territories, are supplied with steeds : for Æneas they led forth one distinguished from the rest, which a lion's tawny hide, shining before with gilded claws, completely covers.

Suddenly through the little city, the rumour, made public,

* D'Orville, Critic. Vann. p. 594, compares Quintus Cal. xiv. 457, αἰον ὅτι στεροπῆσιν ἐπιβρίμει ἀστετος αἰθήρ. B.

50 Lar : the Lares were two in number, sons of Mercury and Lara, one of the Naiads. The Romans paid them divine honours, and they presided over houses and families.

flies, that a band of horse were swiftly marching to the court of
the Tuscan king. Through fear the matrons redouble their
vows; and the nearer to the danger, the more the terror grows,
and the image of Mars appears enlarged. Then father Evander,
grasping the hand [of his son] as he was going away, clings
to him, weeping beyond measure, and utters these words : Oh
that Jupiter would recall my past years! [or that I were now]
what I was when, under the very walls of Præneste, I mowed
down the foremost ranks, and victorious set heaps of shields
on fire, and with this right hand sent king Herilus[51] down to
Tartarus ; to whom at his birth, dreadful to relate, his mother
Feronia had given three lives, and triple arms to wield ; thrice
by death was he to be overthrown: whom nevertheless this
right hand then bereft of all these lives, and stripped of as
many suits of armour! nothing now, my son, should part me
from your loved embrace: nor had ever our neighbour Mezentius, insulting over this person of mine, by the sword effected
so many cruel deaths, bereaved the city of so many inhabitants.
But, O ye powers, and thou Jupiter, great ruler of the gods,
compassionate, I pray, an Arcadian king, and hear a father's
prayers ; if your providence divine, if the Fates reserve Pallas for me in safety, if I live destined to see him again, and
to have a meeting with him, I pray for life ; I will submit to
endure any hardship whatever. · But if, O fortune, thou
threatenest him with some disaster not to be named, now, oh !
now, let me break off my cruel life, while my cares are hovering in suspense, while I have hope of the future, [however]
uncertain ; while thee, dear boy, my late, my only joy, I hold
in my embrace: lest more mournful tidings wound my ears.
These words the father poured forth at the final parting : his
attendants bear him to the palace fainting away.

And now the horse had gone forth by the expanded gates :
among the foremost Æneas and his faithful Achates ; then
other peers of Troy. Pallas himself, in the centre of his
troop, appears conspicuous in his mantling robe and painted
arms ; such as when, bathed in the ocean's waves, Lucifer,
whom Venus loves beyond the other starry lights, hath displayed his holy visage in the heaven, and dispersed the dark-

---

[51] Herilus, king of Præneste, was son of Feronia, the goddess of woods
and orchards : as he is said to have received three lives from his mother,
he was killed three times by Evander.

ness. On the walls the timorous matrons stand, and follow
with their eyes the dusty cloud, and troops gleaming with
brass. Through the thickets, where nearest lies the boundary
of their way, they march in arms. Their acclamations rise;
and, a squadron formed, the hoof beats with the trampling
din the mouldering plain.

Near the cold river of Cære[51] is a spacious grove, sacred
all around by the religion of the fathers; hollow hills on
every side have enclosed, and encompass the grove with
gloomy fir. There is a tradition, that to Sylvanus, god of
the fields and flocks, the ancient Pelasgi,[52] who were once the
first possessors of the Latin territories, consecrated this grove
and a festival-day. Not far from this, Tarcho and the Tuscans kept their camp, defended by the ground; and now from
the hill the whole legion could be surveyed, and had pitched
their tents upon the spacious plains. Hither father Æneas
and his youthful band, chosen for the war, advance, and
fatigued they tend their horses and themselves.

Meanwhile the goddess Venus in bright beauty among the
ethereal clouds, drew nigh, bearing her gifts; and soon as at
a distance she espied her son in a recluse valley, apart by
the cold river, she voluntarily presented herself, and addressed
him in these words: Behold, my son, the presents finished by
my consort's promised skill; that so this instant you need not
demur to challenge either the insolent Laurentines or fierce
Turnus to the combat. Cytherea said, and rushed into the
embraces of her son: under an oak, full in his view, she
placed the radiant arms. He, overjoyed with the presents of
the goddess, and such signal honour, gazes on them with insatiable fondness, and rolls his eyes over them one by one; he
admires, and in his hands or arms shifts about the helmet
terrible with its crest and shooting flames, and the sword
fraught with death, the corslet stiff with brass, immense, of
sanguine hue; as when the azure cloud by the sunbeams grows
more and more inflamed, and shines afar; then the polished
greaves of electrum and gold refined, the spear and the texture of the shield beyond expression. There the god of fiery

---

[51] Cære, anciently Agylla, a city of Etruria, once the capital of the
whole country, situated on a small river east of Rome.

[52] Pelasgi, the ancient inhabitants of Greece, supposed to be one of the
most ancient people in the world.

power, not unskilled of prophecies, or ignorant of futurity, had
represented the Italian history and triumphs of the Romans;
there all the descendants of the future race from Ascanius,
and their battles fought in order. There, too, he had figured
the fostering wolf lying in the verdant cave of Mars: the twin
boys, hanging about her dugs, to play, and fearless suck their
dam; while she, with tapering neck reclined, fondly licked
them by turns, and moulded their bodies with her tongue.
Not far from this he had added Rome, and the Sabine virgins
lawlessly ravished from the assembly of the circus at the great
Circensian[54] games, and suddenly a new war bursting upon
the sons of Rome, and aged Tatius,[55] and the rigid Cures.
Next the same princes, now that mutual hostilities are laid
aside, sheathed in armour, and with the goblets in their hands,
stood before Jove's altars, and, having sacrificed a sow, struck
a league. Not far from thence rapid chariots had torn Metius[56]
limb from limb asunder, (but thou, Alban, shouldst have ad-
hered to thy stipulations,) and Tullus was dragging the
traitor's entrails through the wood; and the bushes, sprinkled
with his blood, were dripping wet. Here, too, Porsenna[57]
was commanding [the Romans] to receive expelled Tarquini-
us, and invested the city with close siege. The Romans in
defence of liberty were rushing on the sword. Him [Por-
senna] you might have seen like one enraged, and like one
breathing threats, because Cocles had dared to beat down the
bridge, and Clœlia,[58] having burst her chains, swam across

[54] Circensian games were first established by Romulus, and performed
in the circus at Rome. The Romans, having invited their neighbours
the Sabines to the celebration of these games, forcibly carried away all
their females who had attended.

[55] Tatius, king of Cures among the Sabines, made war against the
Romans after the rape of the Sabine women. Peace having been made
between the two nations, Tatius shared the royal authority with Romulus.

[56] Metius, dictator of Alba in the reign of Tullus Hostilius. He became subject to the Romans by the combat of the Horatii and Curiatii,
but afterwards proving faithless, Tullus put him to death by placing him
between two chariots, which were drawn by four horses different ways.

[57] Porsenna, king of Etruria, who made war upon the Romans in
favour of Tarquin, and attempted in vain to replace him on the throne.
Cocles, (Pub. Horat.) a noble Roman, who greatly signalized himself by
alone opposing for a time the whole army of Porsenna.

[58] Clœlia, a Roman virgin, who having been given with other maidens
as hostages to Porsenna, escaped from her confinement, and swam across
the Tiber to Rome.

the river. On the summit [of the shield] Manlius,[59] guardian
of the Tarpeian tower, before the temple stood, and defended
the lofty Capitol; and the palace, as newly thatched with
Romulean straw, appeared rough. And here a goose in silver,
fluttering athwart the gilded galleries, gave warning that the
Gauls were just at hand: the Gauls were advancing along the
thickets, and were seizing the fort, protected by the darkness
and benefit of dusky night. Of gold their tresses were, and
of gold their vestments; in striped mantelets they shine; then
their milk-white necks are girt with gold: two Alpine javelins
each in his hand brandishes, having their bodies protected with
long bucklers. Here he had embossed the dancing Salii, and
the naked priests of Pan, the caps tufted with wool, and the
shields that fell from heaven: chaste matrons in soft carriages
were conducting the sacred pageants through the city. To
these in remoter prospect he likewise adds the Tartarean mansions, Pluto's profound realms, the sufferings of the damned;
and thee, Catiline,[60] suspended from a threatening rock, and
trembling at the faces of the Furies; and the good apart [from
the wicked, with] Cato[61] dispensing laws to them. Amidst
these scenes the image of the swelling ocean was widely diffused in gold; but the seas foamed with hoary waves, and all
around conspicuous in silver the wheeling dolphins swept the
seas with their tails, and cut the tide. In the midst were
to be seen fleets with brazen prows, the fight of Actium;[62]
and you could discern Leucate all in a ferment with the
marshalled war, and the billows brightly displayed in gold.
On one side is Augustus Cæsar conducting the Italians to the
engagement, with the senators and people, the domestic deities, and the great gods, standing on the lofty stern; whose
auspicious temples dart forth two flames, and on whose crest
his father's star is displayed. In another part Agrippa,[63]

---

[59] Manlius, (Marcus,) a celebrated Roman, surnamed Capitolinus, for
his gallant defence of the Capitol against the Gauls under Brennus.
Manlius was afterwards accused of ambitious designs, and having been
condemned, he was thrown down from the Tarpeian Rock.

[60] Catiline, a noble Roman, but cruel, and of the most depraved habits.
He conspired against the liberties of his country, and perished in battle,
B. C. 63.

[61] Cato the major is meant.

[62] Actium, the seat of the final victory of Augustus.

[63] Agrippa, a celebrated Roman, who favoured the interest of Augustus

with winds and gods propitious, stands aloft[64] leading his
squadron; for whom, proud badge of warfare, his brows are
adorned with a naval crown's refulgent beak. On the other
side victorious Antony,[65] with barbarian supplies and various
troops, brings up with him, from the nations of the morning,
and the coasts of the Red Sea, Egypt,[66] the strength of the
east, and Bactra, the boundary of his empire; and him follows, oh foul disgrace ! his Egyptian spouse Cleopatra.[67] All
are rushing on together, and the whole watery plain foams
convulsed with the labouring oars and trident-beaks.   They
make for the deep: you would have imagined, that the Cyclades uptorn were floating on the main, or lofty mountains
encountering mountains: with such force the warriors in their
turreted ships urge on the attack. From their hands flaming
balls of tow, and from missile engines the winged steel is
flung: Neptune's fields redden with the first slaughter. In
the midst the queen rouses her squadrons with her country's
sistrum; nor as yet regards the two snakes behind her.[68] Her
monstrous gods of every form, and barking Anubis,[69] opposed
to Neptune, Venus, and Minerva, are wielding their weapons.
In the midst of the combat Mars sculptured in iron storms,
and the grim Furies from the sky; and Discord with her
mantle rent stalks well pleased, whom Bellona follows with
her bloody scourge. Apollo of Actium, viewing these things
from above, was bending his bow: with the terror thereof all
Egypt and the Indians, the Arabs and Sabæans, all were

at the battles of Actium and Philippi, where he behaved with great
valour.

[64] " arduus " refers to his position on the stern of his ship.   B.

[65] Mark Antony, the Roman triumvir. After his defeat in the battle of
Actium, he fled to Alexandria in Egypt, where he stabbed himself,
в. c. 30.

[66] Egypt, a celebrated country of Africa, watered by the Nile; bounded
by the Red Sea (Arabian Gulf) on the east, and by Libya on the west.

[67] Cleopatra, queen of Egypt, daughter of Ptolemy Auletes, was celebrated for her beauty and mental acquirements, as also for her intrigues
and licentious life. Cleopatra supported the cause of her favourite Antony against Augustus at the battle of Actium, but by flying with sixty
sail, contributed to his defeat; she then retired to Egypt, where, to avoid
falling into the hands of Augustus, she destroyed herself by the bite of an
an asp, в. c. 30. At her death Egypt became a Roman province.

[68] i. e. she does not foresee her end.   B.

[69] Anubis, an Egyptian god, represented with the head of a dog.

turning their backs. The queen herself, invoking the winds,
seemed to sail, and with eager haste to be letting loose the
uncoiled cables. Her the god of fire had represented amidst
the slaughter, driven along by waves and winds, pale with the
[terrors of] approaching death; and opposite, [he had sculp-
tured] the Nile with his gigantic form in deep distress, expanding his skirts, and with all his robe displayed, calling the
vanquished into his azure bosom and sheltering streams.
Cæsar again, having in triple triumph entered the walls of
Rome, was consecrating through all the city three hundred
stately temples, his immortal vow to the Italian gods. The
streets rung with joy, and games, and acclamations. In all
the temples are choirs of matrons; and in all the temples altars. Before the altars the sacrificed bullocks cover the
ground. Augustus himself, seated in the snow-white porch
of shining Phœbus, reviews the offerings of the people, and
fits them to the stately pillars. In long orderly procession
the vanquished nations march, as various in the fashion of their
garb and arms as in their language. Here Mulciber had
figured the Numidian race, and the Africans loose in their
attire; here the Leleges,[70] the Carians, and Geloni armed with
arrows. Euphrates now flowed with gentler streams; the
Morini,[71] remotest of the human race, [appeared,] and the
two-horned Rhine, the untamed Dahæ, and the Araxes,[72] that
disdained a bridge.

Such scenes on Vulcan's shield, the present of his parent-
goddess, the hero views with wonder, and [though] a stranger
to the events, rejoices in their representation, and on his
shoulder bears aloft the fame and fortune of his descendants.

[70] Leleges, a wandering people who originally inhabited Caria, in Asia
Minor, and who fought in the Trojan war under their king Altes.
[71] Morini, a people of Belgic Gaul, on the shores of the British Ocean.
[72] Araxes, (Arras,) a large river of Asia, falling into the Caspian Sea;
it swept away a bridge which Alexander the Great built over it.

BOOK IX.

In the Ninth Book, Turnus, availing himself of Æneas' absence, makes a furious assault upon his camp. The Trojans, reduced to the utmost extremity, despatch to Æneas, Nisus and Euryalus, whose immortal friendship, in this perilous adventure, is painted in the most glowing language. Turnus attacks the city, but is forced, after making a great slaughter, to save himself by swimming the Tiber.

AND while these transactions were carrying on in a far different quarter, Saturnian Juno sent Iris from heaven to daring Turnus. Turnus then by chance was sitting at rest in the grove of his progenitor Pilumnus, in a consecrated vale; whom thus the daughter of Thaumas [1] with rosy lips bespoke: What none of the gods, O Turnus, could dare to promise to thy wishes, lo ! revolving time hath of itself brought about ! Æneas, having abandoned his city, his friends, and fleet, hath repaired to the realms and abode of Palantine Evander. And, not content with that, he hath penetrated to the remotest cities of Corythus,[2] and arms a band of Lydians, rustics, whom he has drawn together. Why do you demur? now is the time to call for your steeds, now your chariots. Break off all delay, and seize his camp while in disorder. She said, and on poised wings raised herself to heaven, and in her flight cut the spacious bow beneath the clouds. The youth knew [the goddess], and, stretching forth both hands to heaven, with these accents pursued her flying : Iris, thou glory of heaven, who sent thee down to me on earth shot from the clouds? whence arises, on a sudden, this so bright a sky ? I see heaven in the midst cleave asunder,[3] and stars wandering athwart the firmament. Signs so illustrious will I obey, whoever thou art who summonest me to arms. And thus having said, he repaired to the river, and from the surface of the stream drew water, invoking the gods at large ; and loaded heaven with vows.

And now on the open plains his whole army marched, rich in steeds, rich in embroidered vests and gold. Messapus

[1] Thaumas, a son of Neptune and Terra, who married Electra, one of the Oceanides, by whom he had Iris, the Harpies, &c.

[2] The mythic founder of Cortona, here put for the city itself. B.

[3] "Discedere" is a customary term in describing this prodigy, as in Cicer. de Div. l. 43. Jul. Obseq. de Prod. p. 60. Compare Plutarch. Timol. p. 239, ἔδοξεν αἰφνιδίως ῥαγῆναι τὸν οὐρανὸν ὑπὲρ τῆς νεὼς ἐσχίαι πολὺ καὶ περιφανὲς τὸ πῦρ. R.

commands the van, the sons of Tyrrhus in the rear; in the centre king Turnus moves along, wielding his arms, and overtops the rest by the whole head.[1] As the deep Ganges, fed with seven peaceful rivers, in silence [flows]; or, as the Nile, with its fertilizing waters, when from 'the plains he has retired, and now lodges himself within his channel. Here the Trojans descry a sudden cloud condensed in wreaths of blackening dust, and darkness rising on the plains. Caïcus first from the opposite rampart calls forth: What numerous bands, O citizens, are hither rolling in a black cloud of dust? Quick, bring arms, give darts, mount the walls: haste, the foe is at hand. With loud outcry the Trojans block themselves up within all their gates, and man the walls: for thus Æneas, most accomplished in arms, at departing had ordered; that, if any accident should befall in the interim, they would not venture to set their army in array, nor trust to the field; only guard their camp and walls secured by a rampart. Therefore, though shame and indignation prompt them to engage, yet they barricade their gates against [the foe], execute the orders [of their chief], and in arms expect the enemy within their holy turrets.

Turnus, flying out before, had got the start of his sturdy band, accompanied with twenty chosen horse, and unexpected comes upon the city; whom a Thracian steed with white spots bears, and a golden helmet with crimson crest defends. Which of you youths first will join me to attack the foe? See here, he cries, and brandishing his javelin, darts it into the air, the prelude of the fight; and mounted aloft he rushes to the field. With shouts his friends second the motion, and follow with dreadful-sounding din: they wonder at the faint-heartedness of the Trojans, that they venture not themselves in the equal field, nor oppose arms [to arms], but lie loitering in the camp. Turbulent with ire, hither and thither on his steed he surveys the walls, and by every pathless pass explores access. As when a wolf, in ambush for a full cot of sheep, lies growling at the folds, enduring winds and rains at midnight; under their dams the lambkins in safely bleat; he, fierce and ruthless with ire, rages against the absent prey: his ravenous hunger by length of time contracted, and his blood-thirsty jaws, pinch him incessantly: just so the Rutulian's anger

---

[1] This line is a spurious repetition from Æn. vii. 784. B.

kindles, while he views the walls and camp ; and within his hard bones anguish burns, [exploring] by what means he may tempt access, and now force the enclosed Trojans from their entrenchment, and pour them forth into the plain. Their fleet, which, adjoining the side of their camp, lay concealed, fenced around with ramparts and the streams of the river, he assails; loudly calls for flames from his triumphing followers; and ardent fills his hand with a blazing pine. Then indeed they exert themselves strenuously : the presence of Turnus urges them on, and the whole youth are armed with black torches. They pillage the hearths : the smoky brand sends up a pitchy light, and the flames hurl mingled ashes to the stars.

Ye muses, say, what god averted from the Trojans so fierce a conflagration? who from the ships repelled such mighty flames? Ancient is the testimony of the fact, but immortal is its fame.

At the time when Æneas first formed his fleet on Phrygian Ida, and prepared to launch into the deep, Berecynthia* herself, the mother of the gods, is said to have addressed great Jove in these words : At my request, O son, bestow what thy dear parent from thee craves, now that Olympus is subdued. On a lofty mountain stood a piny wood by me many years beloved, shaded with gloomy firs, and the maples' boughs, whither they brought me sacred offerings : these trees I with pleasure gave to the young Trojan hero, when he wanted a fleet: now anxious dread [on their account] presses my unquiet mind. Dissipate my fears, and let a parent by her prayers obtain, that by no voyage they may be shattered, or by whirling blast of wind subdued : let it avail them that from our mountains they sprung. To her in reply her son, who rolls the stars of the universe, said : Whither, my parent-goddess, art thou urging destiny ? or what is thy aim in this request ? Shall vessels built by mortal hands enjoy an immortal privilege, and Æneas, insured of safety, run the round of dubious peril ? in what god is so great power lodged ? However, when, having finished their course, they shall reach the goal and the Ausonian ports, whichever of them hereafter shall have escaped the waves, and carried the Dardanian chief to the Laurentian fields, I will divest them

* Berecynthia, a name of Cybele, from Mount Berecynthus in Phrygia, where she was worshipped.

of their mortal form, and command to be goddesses of the
spacious ocean; such as the daughters of Nereus, Doto, and
Galatea, who cut with their breasts the foaming deep. He
said: and in sign of its being ratified by the rivers of his
Stygian brother, by those banks that roll with torrents of
pitch and black whirlpools, nods his head; and with that nod
he made heaven's whole frame to tremble.

The promised day was therefore come, and the Fates had
filled up the destined periods of time, when the outrage of
Turnus called on the mother [of the gods] to repel the fire-
brands from her sacred ships. Here first an unusual light
flashed forth on the eyes [of the Trojans], and from the east
a vast refulgent cloud was seen to shoot athwart the sky, and
[in it] her choirs of priests;[6] then through the air a tremendous voice drops from above, and fills the hosts both of Trojans and Rutulians: Be in no hurry,[7] ye Trojans, to protect
my ships, nor arm your hands; sooner to Turnus it shall be
given to burn up the seas than those sacred pines. Glide on
at your liberty, glide ye on, goddesses of the main; the parent
[of the gods] commands. And forthwith from the banks the
ships break each away her halsers, and dolphin-like diving
with their beaks plunge to the bottom of the sea. Thence,
wondrous prodigy, so many virgin-forms rise up, and ride
along the main, as brazen prows had before stood ranged
along the shore. The Rutulians stoop astonished in their
minds; Messapus himself, his steeds being startled, is seized
with consternation; the river too makes a pause, resounding
hoarsely, and Tiberinus recalls his current[8] from the deep.

But the confidence of daring Turnus abated not; he briskly
raises their spirits with his words, and briskly chides [their
fears]: Against the Trojans are these portents aimed; from
them even Jove himself hath withdrawn his wonted aid;
[their ships] wait not the darts or fires of the Rutulians.
Therefore the seas are inaccessible to the Trojans, nor have
they any hopes of flight; from one half of the globe they are
cut off; and the land [the other half] is in our hands; so
many armed thousands the Italian nations bring to our aid.
To me the fatal responses of the gods, whatever they are do

[6] i. e. the Corybantes, Curetes, and the Idæi Dactyli. B.
[7] "trepidate" is explained as equivalent to "festinate" by Nonius i. 7. B.
[8] Literally, "his foot." B.

which the Phrygians pretend, give no concern. To the Fates
and Venus enough is given, that the Trojans have reached
the lands of fruitful Ausonia. I too, on the other hand, have
my destiny, to extirpate with the sword the accursed race,
being robbed of my spouse: nor does the painful sense of
that indignity move only the sons of Atreus,[*] nor to Mycenæ
alone is licence given to take up arms [in such a cause].
But [perhaps] it is enough that they fell once : [doubtless,]
had they thought it enough to commit the same crime but
once before, having conceived almost a total aversion towards
the whole race of women. They whom this confidence in
their intervening rampart, whom the temporary defences of
their trenches, narrow partitions from death, inspire with so
much courage; have they not seen the walls of Troy, built by
the hand of Neptune, sink down in flames ? But, my chosen
warriors, who prepares to storm their rampart sword in hand,
and with me invades their disordered camp? To me there
is no need of Vulcan-wrought armour, or of a thousand ships
against the Trojans. Let all the Tuscans this instant con-
nect themselves with them in alliance : they need not fear the
night, and the dastardly theft of the Palladium, slaying the
guards of [Minerva's] lofty tower ;[10] nor will we hide ourselves in the dark womb of a horse ; we are resolved openly by
day to surround their walls with fire. I shall make them
sensible that they have not to do with Greeks and Argive
striplings, whom Hector kept at bay till the tenth year. Now
then, since the better part of the day is past, for what remains,
my men, as things have [thus far] succeeded well, cheerfully
refresh your bodies, and prepared expect the fight. Meanwhile to Messapus is assigned the charge to beset their gates
with sentinels, and enclose their ramparts with watch-fires.
Twice seven Rutulians are chosen out to guard the walls ;
and those are followed each by a hundred youths waving their
purple plumes, and glittering with gold : they patrole around,
and mount guard by turns, and by turns stretched along the
grass they indulge the wine, and drain[11] the brazen bowls.
The fires together shine ; in play the guards spend the sleep-

[*] Alluding to the abduction of Helen. B.
[10] Turnus sneers at the conduct of Ulysses and Diomede. See Æn. ii.
164 sqq. B.
[11] Compare Virgil's use of "vergere." B.

x

less night. These things the Trojans above from the ramparts survey, and in arms guard their high posts ; their gates
too in hurrying consternation they strictly watch, and with
bridges join the outworks : they stand to their arms. Mnestheus and fierce Serestus urge them on ; whom father Æneas
appointed directors of the youthful bands, and managers of
affairs, if at any time cross accidents should call them. The
whole legion, having shared the danger, by lot keep guard
along the walls, and perform the alternate duties of the post
which each has assigned him to maintain.[17]

Nisus, the son of Hyrtacus, in arms most fierce, stood sentinel of the gate ; whom Ida, famed for hunting, sent the attendant of Æneas, nimble at the javelin and fleet arrows : and
by his side his companion Euryalus, than whom of all the
followers of Æneas no one was more comely, and none [more
graceful] wore the arms of Troy ; a stripling whose cheeks
were streaked with the first bloom of youth. Their love was
one, and with equal eagerness they rushed to the war : then
too they were posted in common to guard the gate. Nisus
says, Do the gods, Euryalus, infuse this ardour into our
minds ? or is each one's earnest inclination his god ?[18] Long
has my mind been instigating me either to attempt the fight,
or some great enterprise ; for it is not content with peaceful
inaction. You see what confidence in the state of their
affairs possess the Rutulians ; their lights twinkle here and
there ; buried in sleep and wine they have laid themselves
down ; the places all around are hushed in silence. Learn
further what my doubting thoughts suggest, and the purpose
which now rises in my soul. That Æneas should be invited
home, all, both the people and the higher orders, importunately crave ; and that messengers be despatched to inform
him of the true state of our affairs. If to thee they will promise
what I demand, (for, to myself the glory of the exploit is
enough,) I think I can find a way under the brow of yon hill
to the walls and fortifications of Pallanteum. Euryalus,
stung with violent desire of praise, stood astonished ; at the
same time he thus addresses his ardent friend : Do you then,
Nisus, decline to admit me as your companion in those high

[17] Literally, " take turns as to what is to be defended."   B.
[18] " Diine nostris mentibus cupiditates injiciunt et desideria ? An deus
sit ipse mentis cupiditas ?"   SERVIUS.   B.

enterprises? Shall I send you away alone on such perilous
adventures? It was not thus my warlike father Opheltes
instructed me, bred up amidst the alarms of Greece and the
disasters of Troy; nor have I acted such a part in your
company, following the magnanimous Æneas and his fortune in all extremities. This soul, this soul of mine, con-
temns the light, and deems that honour, to which you aspire,
well bought, even at the expense of life itself. To this Nisus
[replied]: Believe me, I had no such apprehensions of you;
nor have I reason. No, so may great Jove, or whatever god
with a favouring eye regards what we are about, return me
to you triumphant. But if any chance, (as many such you
see in an enterprise of this hazardous nature,) or deity hurry
me on to adverse fate, I wish that you may survive: your age
has a juster claim to life. Let me leave one who may deposit
me in the earth among the dead, snatched from the field, or
redeemed by ransom; or who (if any fortune shall stand in
the way of this) may pay funeral obsequies to my absent
corpse, and honour me with an empty tomb: nor let me be
the cause of such deep anguish to thy wretched mother, who,
my boy, of many mothers alone adventurous follows thee, nor
minds the walls[14] of the great Acestes. But he rejoined: In
vain you weave fruitless remonstrances, nor is my resolution
now staggered from its first position: let us despatch: at the
same time he awakes the guard. They succeed, and take
their turns of duty: having resigned his post, he sets forward
in company with Nisus, and they seek the king.

All other creatures over the whole earth with sleep relaxed
their cares, and lost their toils in sweet oblivion. But the
Trojan chiefs and select youth were holding consultation about
the important concerns of the state; what they ought to do,
or who should be the messenger to Æneas. Leaning on their
long spears they stand, wielding their targets, in the centre
of the camp and plain. Then Nisus, and with him Euryalus,
with prompt alacrity, beg to be admitted; [alleging] that
their business was important, and would compensate the delay.[15] In this their hurry and trepidation Iülus first received them, and ordered Nisus to speak. Then thus Hyrta-

[14] i. e. nor cares to tarry at Segesta with the other matrons. B.
[15] i. e. the delay of their councils. D.

n 2

cides [16] [spoke]: Ye followers of Æneas, listen with unbiassed minds; nor be these our proposals judged of by our years. The Rutulians, buried in sleep and wine, have composed themselves to rest; we ourselves have observed a place fit for our secret design, that lies obvious in the double way from the gate which is nearest the sea. Their fires are dying away, and a pitchy smoke ascends to heaven. If you give us leave to embrace the fortunate occasion, you shall soon see Æneas, in quest of whom we go to the walls of Pallanteum, here present with spoils, and after vast havoc made: nor set we out strangers to the way; often in the shady vales at hunting have we seen the skirts of the town, and have surveyed the whole river.

At this, Alethes, loaded with years and matured in judgment, [said:] Ye gods of my country, under whose divine protection Troy always is, [though you have been angry with us for a time,] yet you do not intend utterly to destroy the Trojans, since you have produced such souls, and such resolute hearts in our youth. So saying, he grasped the shoulders and hands of both, and with tears his face and cheeks bedewed. What rewards, brave youths, what rewards of worth proportioned to such enterprises can I judge possible to be conferred upon you? the fairest shall the gods in the first place and your own virtues give; then the rest the pious Æneas shall anon bestow, and Ascanius, in his prime of life, who never will forget so high an obligation.

But, subjoins Ascanius, I, whose sole happiness depends on my father's safe return, conjure you, Nisus, by our great domestic gods, by the tutelar deity of Assaracus, and the shrines of hoary Vesta, (whatever fortune or confident hope [17] I have, I rest in your own bosoms,) recall my parent, give back his presence; at his return all our sorrows will disappear. Two goblets of silver will I give of finished work, and rough with embossed figures, which my father won from sacked Arisba; [18] and a pair of tripods, two great talents of gold, a bowl of an-

---

[16] Hyrtacides, Nisus and Hippocoon are so styled, from their father Hyrtacus, who was a Trojan of Mount Ida.

[17] i. e. of my father's safety. B.

[18] Arisba, a colony of the Mityleneans in Troas, destroyed by the Trojans.

tique cast, which Sidonian Dido gave me. But if it shall be
my fortune to be victorious, possess myself of Italy, enjoy the
crown, and divide the spoils by lot; saw you on what steed,
in what arms Turnus rolled all in gold? that very shield and
crimson-crested helmet I will choose out from the lot; prizes,
O Nisus, which are already your own. Besides the persons
of twelve select matrons my sire shall give, and as many captives of the other sex, and the arms that to them all belong;
besides these, that ground which king Latinus himself possesses. And as for you, idolized boy, whom my age follows
in the nearer stages of life, I now receive you with my whole
soul, and embrace you for my companion in all events. Without thee no glory shall be sought by my exploits, whether I
am engaged in peace or war; to thee chiefly I will intrust
my acts and counsels. To whom Euryalus thus replies: No
day shall evince me unfit for enterprises so heroic; let fortune
fall out prosperous or adverse. But one thing above all favours I of thee implore: I have a mother of Priam's ancient
race, whom unhappy neither the land of Ilium, nor the city of
king Acestes, could withhold from going along with me. Her
now I leave a stranger to this perilous adventure, whatever it
is, and without taking farewell; night, and this right hand of
thine, be witness [for me, that it was not for want of duty,
but] that I cannot bear a mother's tears: but comfort her forlorn, I beg, and succour her in her desolation. Let me bear away
this hope from thee; so shall I go with greater intrepidity on
all adventures. The Trojans with minds deeply affected shed
tears; above all, comely Iülus; and the image of parental
affection touched his soul to the quick. Then thus he addresses
[Euryalus]: Expect all that is due to your glorious under-
takings. For that mother of thine shall be mine, and only the
name Creüsa shall be wanting; nor small gratitude awaits
her for giving birth to such a son, whatever fortune may attend the deed. I swear by this head of mine, by which my
father before me was wont to [swear], whatever I promise to
yourself, if you return in safety, and the event be prosperous,
the same shall be made good to your mother and kindred.
Thus weeping over him he speaks; at the same time divests
his shoulder of his gilded sword, which Cretan Lycaon with
marvellous art had made, and dexterously fitted to the ivory
sheath. On Nisus, Mnestheus bestows the skin and spoil of

a grim shaggy lion; trusty Alethes exchanges with him his
helmet. Forthwith they march thus armed; whom the whole
body of the nobles, both young and old, with ardent prayers
accompany in their way to the gates; and the comely Iülus
too, endued with a soul and manly concern beyond his years,
gave them many instructions to carry to his sire; but the
winds disperse them all, and fruitless give them to the clouds
away.[19]

Having set out, they overpass the trenches, and amidst the
shades of night advance to the hostile camps; destined, however, first to be[20] the death of many. In loose disorder they
beheld bodies under the influence of wine and sleep, stretched
along the grass, chariots with their poles erect[21] along the
banks, men between the traces and the wheels; arms together
lying, together wine. First the son of Hyrtacus thus spoke:
The right hand, Euryalus, must be boldly exerted; now the occasion itself invites us. Here lies our way: watch you, and keep
guard that no hand be able to lift itself against us from behind.
These fields I will render waste, and lead thee along a broad
pathway. This said, he suppresses his speech; at the same
time with his sword attacks proud Rhamnes; who, as it
chanced, raised high on lofty carpets, was snoring forth sleep
from his whole breast; at once a king himself, and an augur
in highest favour with king Turnus: but not by his augur's
art could he ward off the stroke of death. Three servants by
his side lying at random among the arms, and the armour-
bearer of Remus, and (whom he found beneath the very horses'
feet) the charioteer he stabs, and with his sword cuts off their
reclining necks; then from the master himself takes off the
head, and leaves the trunk gulping with blood; in purple
gore the reeking earth and beds are drenched. Add to these
Lamyrus, Lamus, and young Serranus, who, of distinguished
beauty, had been much engaged that night in play, and was
lying overpowered in every limb with the fulness of the god;
happy if without intermission he had equalled that play with
the night, and lengthened it out till day. As a famished lion

<hr>

[19] Because both the messengers perished by the way. B.
[20] "Destined to be." This sense of "futurus," and similar participles,
is very common in Virgil. "Inimica" seems to contain the notion that
the camps would prove fatal to themselves. B.
[21] The horses being unharnessed. B.

making wild havoc amidst a sheep-fold, (for ravenous hunger prompts him on,) grinds and tears the flock, feeble and dumb with fear, and gnashes his bloody jaws : nor less was the carnage made by Euryalus : he too all on fire rages throughout, and in the middle falls upon a vulgar nameless throng. Fadus and Hebesus, Rhœtus and Abaris, not dreaming of their fate ; Rhœtus broad awake, and viewing all ; but who, for fear, was hiding himself behind a capacious jar ; in whose opposed breast now close at hand he plunges the whole blade as he rises, and withdrew it amidst abundant death. He vomits up the purple stream of life, and in death renders back his wine mingled with blood. The other, with ardour at [the success of his] stratagem, presses on, and now was advancing towards the social bands of Messapus, where he saw the fire just in its extremity dying away, and the horses in order tied cropping the grass ; when Nisus thus briefly says, (for he perceived that they were hurried on by too eager love of slaughter,) Let us desist ; for the unfriendly light approaches. We have glutted ourselves with vengeance to the full : a passage is made through our foes. Many arms of the heroes [slain], of solid silver elaborately wrought, they leave behind, and, together with them, goblets and beautiful carpets. Euryalus [seized] the rich trappings of Rhamnes, and the belts with golden bosses ; presents which opulent Cædicus of old had sent to Tiburtine Remulus,[22] when in absence he plighted with him a league of hospitality (he at death bequeaths the same to his grandson to possess ; and after his death the Rutulians, masters of the field and booty):[23] these he seizes, and adjusts to his valiant shoulders, but in vain.[24] Then he puts on the well-fitting helmet of Messapus, with plumes adorned. They quit the camp, and take possession of safe ground.

Meanwhile three hundred horse, all shielded, with Volscens[25]

---

[22] Remulus, a chief of Tibur, whose arms were seized by the Rutulians, and became part of the plunder which Euryalus obtained.

[23] We must understand, "gave them to Rhamnes." Wagner with reason considers this line spurious. B.

[24] " Nequidquam " must be joined with " aptat," not with " fortibus," as is remarked by Servius. Compare ver. 312 sq. B.

[25] Volscens, a Latin chief, who attacked Nisus and Euryalus as they returned from the plunder of the Rutulians. He killed Euryalus, but was himself immediately slain by Nisus.

at their head, despatched before from the city of Latinus,
(while the rest of the legion in battle-array slowly on the plains
advance,) were marching up, and bore an answer to king
Turnus. And 'now they were approaching the camp, and
just entering the rampart, when at a distance they espy them
turning away on the left-hand path; and in the glimmering
shade of night the helmet betrayed the unwary Euryalus, and
opposed to the beams of the moon, shot a gleamy light. Scarcely was the object seen, Volscens from the troop exclaims
aloud: Stand, fellows; what motive brings you hither? or
who are ye thus in armour? or whither are ye bound? They
aimed not at making a reply; but hastened their flight into
the woods, and trusted to the night. On each side the horsemen plant themselves at the known passes, and encircle every
avenue with a guard. There was a wood wide overgrown
with stiff underwood and gloomy holms, which thick brambles had choked up on every side; here and there a path led
through hidden tracks. The thick shade of boughs and cumbrous booty embarrass Euryalus, and fear misleads him from
the straight way. Nisus retires; and now unawares had
escaped from the foe, and from the lakes which in after times
were called Albanian from Alba's name: then king Latinus
had there his lofty stables. Soon as he stopped, and for his
absent friend looked back in vain, [he exclaimed:] Unfortunate Euryalus, in what quarter have I left thee? or whither
shall I follow thee? Again measuring back the whole perplexed path of the mazy wood, he at once with accurate survey retraces his steps, and ranges over the silent thickets: he
hears the steeds, he hears the bustling noise, and signals of the
pursuers. Nor long time intervened, when a shout assails
his ears, and he sees Euryalus, whom the whole band are
now dragging along with sudden tumultuous uproar, betrayed
and intercepted by the treachery of the place and night, and
struggling hard in vain. What shall he do? by what power,
by what arm shall he attempt the youth to rescue? shall he,
resolute on death, fling himself into the midst of his foes, and
through wounds open a quick passage to a glorious death?
Straight with his contracted arm brandishing a javelin, thus
to the moon on high with eyes upturned he addresses his
prayer: Do thou, O goddess, do thou propitious aid my enter-

prise, thou glory of the stars,[36] and daughter of Latona, guardian of the groves: if ever my father Hyrtacus for me brought
offerings to thy altars; if ever I added to the number by my
sylvan spoils, or suspended any in thy vaulted ceiling, or affixed to thy sacred roof; suffer me to confound this congre-
gated rout, and guide my weapons through the air. He said,
and straining at once with his whole body, hurls the steel.
The flying spear cuts the shades of night, and lights on the
back of Sulmo, who stood opposite to him; and there is
shivered, and with the splintered wood pierces through his
vitals. Down he falls cold [in death], discharging from his
breast the warm stream of life, and with long sobs beats his
flanks. They throw their eyes around different ways. Lo,
he, animated the more with this, poised from the tip of his
ear[37] another weapon, while they are bustling about. The
whizzing spear pierced through both the temples of Tagus,
and warmed in his transfixed brain stuck fast. Volscens
furious storms, nor any where discerns the owner of the weapon, or one on whom in his burning rage he may wreak his
vengeance. But you, meanwhile, he says, with your warm
blood, shall pay the forfeit of both: at the same time with
sword unsheathed he rushed on Euryalus. Then indeed in
terrible agony Nisus frantic screams aloud; nor longer was
able to conceal himself in darkness, or to support such deep
distress: On me, on me, here am I who did the deed, O turn
your swords on me, Rutulians: mine is all the offence: he
neither durst nor could do aught: this heaven and conscious
stars I call to witness: only he loved his unhappy friend too
much. Thus he spoke: but the sword with force driven
home pierces through his sides, and bursts his snow-white
breast. Euryalus is overwhelmed in death, the blood flows
down his beauteous limbs, and on his shoulders the drooping
neck reclines: as when a purple flower, cut down by the
plough, pines away in death, or the poppies on their weary
necks drop down their heads, when with rain they chance to
be overcharged. But Nisus rushes into the midst of them,
and seeks Volscens alone through all: on Volscens alone he
fixes his attention; whom (Nisus) the foes encircling close,

---

[36] So Hor. Carm. Sec. 1, " Phœbe, lucidum cœli decus." Moschus,
vii. 2, ευανιας ιερον φλι νυκτος αγαλμα. B.
[37] Virgil expresses the παρά χαίραν ρίψαι of Eurip. Hippol. 220. B.

this way and that way drive off. He not less keenly presses on, and whirls his flashing sword, till he plunged it into the mouth, full opposite, of the bawling Rutulian, and dying, bereft his foe of life. Then covered with wounds, he flung himself on his lifeless friend, and there at length in peaceful death reposed. Happy pair! if my verses can aught avail, no day shall ever erase you from the records of time; while the race of Æneas shall inhabit the immovable Capitoline rock, and a Roman monarch hold the empire [of the world].

The victorious Rutulians, masters of the prey and spoils, in mournful procession bore lifeless Volscens to the camp. Nor in the camp was, the mourning less, when they found Rhamnes pale in death, and so many chiefs slain by one slaughter, and Serranus, and Numa. There is a great concourse about the bodies, about the expiring warriors, the ground recent with warm slaughter, and rivulets full of foaming blood. They recognise the spoils, and among themselves Messapus' shining helmet, and the trappings with much sweat regained.

And now early Aurora, leaving Tithonus' saffron-coloured bed, sprinkled the earth with new-born light; the sun having now shed his beams [on the world], and objects by his light being again revealed; Turnus rouses his men to arms, himself with arms begirt around, and each leader rallies to the battle his troops arrayed in brass; and by various rumours they stimulate their martial rage. Even the heads of Nisus and Euryalus, a piteous spectacle, on spears erect they in the front affix, and with vast acclamation follow. On the left side of the walls the hardy Trojans opposed to them their host (for the right is bounded by the river); and they maintain their ample trenches, and on their lofty turrets mournful stand, as soon as the heads of the youths fixed up to view, but too well known to the unhappy spectators, distilling black gore, excited [their grief].

Meanwhile the winged messenger Fame, flying through the affrighted city, rushes along, and glides to the ears of the mother of Euryalus; then suddenly, with misery overwhelmed, the vital warmth forsook her bones. The weaving instruments dropt from her hands, and her labours were unravelled. The hapless woman flies out, and with female shrieks, tearing her hair, frantic takes her way with speed to the walls and nearest bands. Not of men, or of darts, or of danger, is she heedful: then with these complaints she fills the sky: Is this you[28] I see, Euryalus? art thou that late solace for my old age? Cruel one! couldst thou leave me all alone? and to thy wretched mother didst thou not allow access to address to thee her last farewell, when on such perilous adventures sent? Alas! in a strange land, given a prey to Latian dogs and fowls, thou liest! nor I, thy own mother, laid thee out for thy funeral obsequies, nor closed thy eyes, nor bathed thy wounds, covering thee with the robe, which for thee in haste I forwarded both night and day, and with the loom solaced my aged cares. Whither shall I go in pursuit of thee? or what land now holds thy limbs, thy mangled members, and lacerated corse? Is this all of thee, my son, thou bringest me back? is this what I have followed both by land and sea? Pierce me, O Rutulians, (if you have any tenderness,) at me hurl all your darts; me first cut off with the sword: or thou, great father of the gods, compassionate me, and with thy bolts thrust down to Tartarus this detested head, since I can by no other means shake off cruel life. By these doleful lamentations the minds [of the Trojans] are deeply struck, and a sorrowful groan is heaved from every breast; quite broken and benumbed are all their powers for battle. Idæus and Actor, by the direction of Ilioneus and deeply afflicted Iulus, seize her while she is thus inflaming the general grief, and in their arms bear her back to her dwelling.

Meanwhile the trumpet from afar, with its shrill-sounding brass, chided with dreadful peal.[29] Shouts follow, and heaven echoes back the sound. The Volscians with uniformity advance, a testudo being formed.[30] They prepare both to fill up the trenches and demolish the rampart. Some explore access, and by scaling-ladders [seek] to mount the walls, where the troops are but thin, and where, not so thick of men, the circling band is seen through. On the other hand, the Trojans, practised by long war to defend their walls, poured on them every kind of missile weapons, and pushed them down with

---

[28] "Hunc" is used for "talem." See Pierius. B.

[29] "Increpuit" is elegantly used. Servius well explains it thus: "et insonuit, et segnitiam increpuit." B.

[30] Cf. Sallust, Jug. 94, "tum vero cohortatus milites, et ipse extra vallum egressus, testudine acta, succedere." D.

sturdy poles. They rolled down rocks too of destructive
weight, trying whether they could break through their fenced
battalion: while [the Rutulians] notwithstanding, under the
close fence of their shields, are willing to sustain all dangers.
Nor now are they able to stand the shock ; for, where thick
embodied ranks press on the attack, the Trojans roll and hurl
down an enormous pile, which made wide havoc among the
Rutulians, and broke the fence-works of their shields. Nor
care the bold Rutulians longer to contend in covered fight, but
by missile weapons strive to beat them from the rampart. In
another quarter Mezentius, horrid to be seen, brandished a
Tuscan pine, and hurls smoky firebrands. Again, Messapus,
a horseman brave, the progeny of Neptune, makes a breach
in the rampart, and calls for ladders against the walls.

Ye [sacred Nine, and thou], Calliope, [in chief,][31] aid me
while I sing what desolations, what deaths there Turnus then
with the sword effected, what hero each sent down to Pluto ;
and trace with me the vast outlines of the war : for ye, O
goddesses, both remember, and can rehearse them.

Of height prodigious, and with lofty communications,[32]
there stood a tower, commodious in its situation, which with
their utmost efforts all the Latins strove to storm, and with
the full extent of their resources to overthrow : the Trojans,
on the other hand, defended it with stones, and flung darts in
thick volleys through the hollow loop-holes. Turnus in the
foremost tossed a blazing brand, and to the sides [of the tower]
fixed the flame, which by the wind diffusely spread, seized the
boards, and to the pillars clung until they were consumed.[33]
[The Trojans,] all aghast, raised a fearful bustle within, and
shelter from the disaster sought in vain. While they crowd
together, and retreat into that part which is free from the contagious ruin, then suddenly the tower, with the weight [over-
burthened], tumbled town, and with the crash all heaven thunders : down to the ground half dead they come, an immense
pile of ruins following, pierced with their own weapons, and

---

[31] I have retained Davidson's translation of this bold syllepsis, for which,
as Servius remarks, correct language would require, " vos Musæ, aut tu,
Calliope." B.

[32] i. e. from the walls.

[33] Anthon renders "partially consumed." But the other sense seems
borne out by Silius i. 363, " pluteis Vulcanus exercet adesis." B.

their breasts transfixed with the iron-pointed wood. Helenor
alone and Lycus with great difficulty escaped: whereof the
elder Helenor (whom the slave Licymnia by a stolen embrace
had borne to the Lydian king, and sent to Troy in forbidden
arms) was lightly armed with a naked sword, and inglorious
with his escutcheon blank. And as soon as he saw himself
amidst Turnus' thousands, and on either hand around him
ranged the Latin troops; as a beast of chase, which, hemmed
in by a thick band of huntsmen, rages against their darts, wil-
fully flings herself on death, and with a bound springs on the
hunters' spears; just so the youth, certain to die, rushes on
his foes, and where he sees the darts thickest, advances. But
Lycus, far more swift of foot, through foes and through arms,
by flight reaches the walls, and strives with his hand to grasp
their high summits, and reach the arms of his friends: whom
victorious Turnus at once with swift career and dart pursuing,
thus upbraids: Fool, didst thou hope thou wouldst be able to
escape our hands? At the same time he gripes him hanging,
and with a great fragment of the wall pulls him down: as
when Jove's armour-bearer, soaring on high, hath in his
crooked talons raised aloft either a hare, or snow-white swan;
or, sacred to Mars, the wolf hath snatched from the folds a
lambkin, by the dam with many a bleating sought. The shout
from every quarter rises. They fall on, and with heaps of
earth fill up the trenches; others to the battlements toss the
blazing brands. With a rock, and vast fragment of a mountain, Ilioneus overthrows Lucetius, approaching to the gate,
and armed with flames; Liger Emathion, Asylas Chorinæus,
the one skilled in the javelin, the other in the far-deceiving
arrow; Cæneus [overthrows] Ortygius, Turnus the victorious
Cæneus; with Itys, Clonius, Dioxippus, Promulus, Sagaris,
and Idas standing in defence of the lofty turrets: Capys
Privernus. Him the spear of Themilla at first had grazed;
[on which he,] infatuate, throwing away his shield, applied
his hand to the wound; up to him then the arrow glides on
its wings, and to the left side his hand was nailed: and deep
lodged within, with a deadly wound, it burst the breathing
engines[34] of the soul. In arms illustrious the son of Arcens[35]

---

[34] "Definitio pulmonum, qui dicuntur a spirando." SERVIUS. B.
[35] Arcens, a Sicilian, who permitted his son to accompany Æneas into
Italy, where he was killed by Mezentius

stood, clad in an embroidered chlamys, and shining in Iberian
purple, of distinguished form; whom his father Arcens sent,
in the grove of Mars bred up about the streams of Simæthus,[36]
where, fat [with offerings] and placable, the altar of Palicus[37]
stands. Mezentius himself, having laid aside his arms, thrice
whirling around his head the thong, discharged a hissing
sling, and with the half-melted lead clove his temples asunder
as he stood full opposite to him, and stretched him at his full
length on a large space of the sandy plain. Then for the first
time in war Ascanius is said to have directed a fleet arrow,
having been wont before only to fright the fugitive beasts of
chase, and by his hand to have prostrated brave Numanus,
whose surname was Remulus, and who had to wife the
younger sister of Turnus, in wedlock lately joined. Before
the van, bawling aloud [whatever first occurred, whether]
decent or indecent to hear, and in heart puffed up with his new
regal honour, he stalked, and thus with vast clamour made
his vaunt: Ye Phrygians, twice enslaved, are you not ashamed
to be a second time shut up by blockade and entrenchments,
and to screen yourselves from death within your walls? Lo,
these are they, who by force of arms claim to themselves our
brides! What god, what madness drove you to Italy? They
are not the sons of Atreus you have here, nor the crafty-
tongued Ulysses; but a race hardy from their original. Our
infants soon as born to the rivers we first convey, and in the
rigid icy stream we harden. In the chase our boys are keen,
and harass[38] the woods: their pastime is to manage steeds, and
dart the arrow from the bow. Our youth again of labour
patient, and to frugality inured, either by the harrow subdue
the ground, or batter towns in war. Our whole lifetime is
worn out in arms, and with the inverted spear we goad the
backs of our steers; nor does slow age impair our strength of
mind, or alter our vigour. Our grey hairs we with the helmet

---

[36] Simæthus, (Giaretti,) a river of Sicily which falls into the sea between Catana and Leontini. In its neighbourhood the gods Palici were
born, and particularly worshipped.

[37] As the Palici (sons of Jove by the nymph Ætna, or the muse Thalia) were two in number, we should perhaps read "Palicûm" with
Cerda. I myself prefer "Palicis," which might be more easily corrupted
from ignorance of this use of the dative. B.

[38] For this use of "fatigare," compare Val. Flacc. iii. 26. So "fatigat
llebrum," Silius ii. 74.

press; and still 'tis our delight to sweep together fresh booty,
and to live on plunder. Your very dress is embroidered with
saffron-hues and gaudy purple; indolence is your heart's delight; to indulge in dances you love; your vests have sleeves,
and your mitres ribands. O Phrygian women, surely, for
Phrygian men you cannot be! go range along the lofty tops of
Dindymus,[39] where the pipe sounds the discordant[40] note to
you accustomed. The timbrels and Berecynthian flute[41] of
the Idæan mother Cybele invite you: leave arms to men, and
from the sword refrain. Him blustering thus in words, and
proclaiming horrid indignities, Ascanius could not bear; and,
fronting him full, on the horse-hair string extended his arrow,
and drawing both his arms to a wide distance, paused, first
suppliant addressing Jove in vows: Almighty Jove, assist my
daring enterprise. So to thy temples will I bring thee solemn
offerings, and before thy altars present a bullock with a gilded
forehead of snowy whiteness, and bearing his head of equal
stature with his dam, who already butts with his horn, and
spurns the sand with his feet. The sire gave ear, and from a
serene quarter of the sky thundered on the left. At the same
time twangs the deadly bow; and whizzing dreadful flies the
drawn-back arrow, and passes through the head of the Rutulian, and with the steel point transfixes his hollow temples.
Go, insult valour in haughty terms. To the Rutulians your
twice subdued Phrygians send back this answer. Ascanius
·said no more. The Trojans second him with acclamation,
ring with joyous applauses, and extol his valour to the stars.
    In the ethereal region fair-haired Apollo was then by
chance surveying from above the Ausonian troops and city,
seated on a cloud, and thus he bespeaks victorious Iülus: Go
on, increase in early valour, O boy! Such is the pathway to
the stars, O descendant of the gods, and from whom gods are
to descend. Under the line of Assaracus all wars by fate ordained in justice shall subside; nor is Troy capable of containing thee. At the same time, having pronounced these

---

[39] Dindymus, a mountain of Galatia in Asia Minor, where Cybele was
worshipped.
[40] Literally, "its twofold tone." "Biforis" simply means that it had
but two perforations. B.
[41] These flutes were formed of box. B.

words, he throws himself from the lofty sky, divides the whispering gales, and seeks Ascanius; then in the features of his face he is transformed into aged Butes. To Dardanian Anchises this man had formerly been armour-bearer, and faithful guardian at the gate: then father Æneas assigned him the companion of Ascanius. Thus marched Apollo, in every thing resembling the aged sire, both in voice and complexion, in silver locks, and arms fierce with rattling din: and in these words he addresses the ardent Iülus: Offspring of Æneas, let it suffice that by thy shafts Numanus hath fallen, thyself unhurt: to thee this first glory great Apollo vouchsafes, and envies not thy similar feats of arms. For what remains, O .oy, abstain [42] from fight. This said, Apollo dropped his human appearance, in the midst of the interview, and into thin air far vanished out of sight. The Dardanian chiefs knew the god and his divine shafts, and in his flight perceived his rattling quiver. Therefore, by the mandate and divine authority of Phœbus, they restrain Ascanius greedy for the fight: themselves once more to the combat advance, and on apparent dangers throw their lives. Along the battlements round the whole compass of the walls their acclamations run; they bend the rapid bows, and whirl the slings. All the ground is strewn with darts; then shields and hollow helmets in the conflict ring: a fierce engagement ensues: with such fury as a shower by the influence of the rainy Kids [43] arising from the west lashes the ground; or as thick as storms of hail come down headlong into the floods, when Jupiter in the south wind tremendous hurls down a watery tempest, and bursts the hollow clouds in the sky.

Pandarus and Bitias, sprung from Alcanor of Mount Ida, whom sylvan Hiera trained up in Jupiter's sacred grove, youths tall as their native firs and mountains, on their arms relying, throw open the gate which by their general's command was intrusted to their charge, and from the ramparts voluntarily challenge the foe. Themselves within, on right and left, before the turrets stand, armed with steel, and their towering heads with plumes adorned: as about the crystal

---

[42] Homer Il. A. 422, πολίμου δ' ἀποπαύεο πάμπαν. B.

[43] These stars rise in October, and are always attended with rain. They are seated in the constellation Auriga. See Servius. B.

streams, whether on the banks of Po, or by the pleasant
Adige,[44] two aërial oaks together rise, and shoot up to heaven
their unshorn heads, and nod with their towering tops. The
Rutulians, soon as they saw a passage opened, rush in.
Forthwith Quercens, Aquicolus graceful in arms, and Tmarus
in mind precipitant, and martial Hæmon, with all their troops,
either routed turned their backs, or at the very threshold of
the gate laid down their lives. Then the hostile minds
[within] grow more fierce with rage; and thither now the
Trojans flock in thick embodied troops, and dare to encounter
hand to hand, and make sallies[45] [on the foe]. To Turnus the
leader, in a different quarter raving, and throwing the troops
into disorder, intelligence is brought that the enemy rages
with fresh slaughter, and had set the gates wide open. He
quits his present enterprise, and stirred with hideous rage,
rushes forward to the Trojan gate, and the haughty brothers;
and first Antiphates, (for he presented himself the first,) the
spurious issue of noble Sarpedon by a Theban mother, with a
javelin hurled he overthrows. The Italian shaft[46] flies
through the thin air, and, piercing the stomach, sinks deep
into his breast; the gaping aperture of the wound emits a
foamy tide of black blood, and in his transfixed lungs the steel
is warmed. Then Merops, Erymas, and Aphidnus with his
hand he stretches on the plain; next Bitias, flashing fire from
his eyes, and in soul outrageous; not by a javelin, for to the
javelin he would not have resigned his life; but a brandished
fiery dart loud hissing flew, like a bolt of thunder shot, which
neither the two bulls' hides [which formed his shield], nor his
trusty corslet with double scales of gold, were able to sustain: his enormous limbs fall prostrate on the ground. Earth
gives a groan, and over him his buckler thunders loud. As on
Baia's[47] Euboean shore there falls at times a rocky pile, which
before built of enormous bulk they in the ocean place; thus
tumbling headlong it draws ruin with it, and dashed against the
shallows, sinks to its rest quite down: the seas are all embroiled,

[44] Adige, the ancient Athesis, a river of Cisalpine Gaul; it rises in the
Rhœtian A.ps, and falls into the Adriatic.
[45] Such is the sense of "procurrere." See Drakenb. on Silius, vii.
566. B.
[46] Literally "cornel-wood." B.
[47] Baia, a city of Campania, on a small bay west of Naples, and opposite Puteoli, said to have been founded by Baius, a companion of Ulysses

and the black sands are heaved on high; then at the roaring
noise high Prochyta[a] trembles, and Inarime's hard bed, thrown
on Typhœus by Jove's command. Here Mars potent in arms
inspired the Latins with additional courage and prowess, and
deep in their breast plies his sharp goad; and on the Trojans
he threw flight and grim terror. [The Latins] from every
quarter gather, now that opportunity of a battle is offered,
and the warrior god hath fallen upon their minds. Pandarus,
soon as he perceives his brother stretched at his length, in
what situation their fortune stands, and what an unexpected
turn is given to their affairs, hurls the gate with vast force on
the turned hinge, shoving it along with his broad shoulders, and
leaves many of his friends shut out from the city in the hard
combat; but others with himself he encloses, and admits them as
they pour forward: infatuate! who did not mark the Rutulian
prince amidst the troops rushing upon him, or eagerly confined him within the city, as a hideous tiger among the feeble
flocks. Instantly an unusual light flashed from his eyes, and
his arms sounded dreadful; his flaming crests tremble on his
head, and from his shield he gleamy lightnings darts. The
Trojans suddenly discover his detested face and hideous limbs,
and are confounded. Then mighty Pandarus springs out,
and, inflamed with rage for his brother's death, addresses him
aloud: Not Amata's palace thy promised dowry this, nor is it
the heart of Ardea that contains Turnus within his native
walls. The hostile camps you see; there is no possibility of
your escaping hence. Turnus with mind sedate smiling on
him [says]: Begin, if any courage be in thy soul, and hand
to hand with me engage; to Priam you shall report that here
too you found an Achilles. He said. The other, exerting
his utmost force, hurls at him a spear rough with knots and
the green rind. The air received the wound; Saturnian
Juno interposing turned it aside, and the spear fixes in the
gate. But not so this weapon, which my right hand wields
with might, shall you escape; for not [so feeble is [b]] he who

[a] Prochyta, (Procida,) an island of Campania, between the island of
Inarime and the coast. Inarime, (Ischia,) an island near the coast of
Campania, with a mountain, under which Jupiter is feigned to have con-
fined the giant Typhœus.

[b] "Is" is here used for "talis," as "hunc" for "talem" in
Æn. B.

owns the weapon, or who inflicts the wound. Thus he said;
and rises to his sword lifted high, and in the middle between
the temples, his forehead with the blade cleaves asunder, and
[pierces] his beardless cheeks with a hideous wound. A sound
ensues; with his mighty weight earth receives a shock. In
death he stretches on the ground his stiffening limbs, and
arms bespattered with blood and brains; and on this side and
that side his head in equal parts from either shoulder hung.
In tumultuous consternation the Trojans, turning their backs,
fly hither and thither; and had the conqueror immediately
conceived the thought of tearing away the bolts with his
hands, and admitting his comrades by the gates, that day
both to the war and ['Trojan] race had been the last: but
fury and mad desire of slaughter drove him on the foes now
full in his view. First Phalaris and Gyges (having smitten
on the ham)[50] he catches up; then seizing their spears, darts
them into the backs of the fugitives: Juno supplies him with
force and courage. He joins Halys their companion [in death],
and Phegeus, having transfixed his shield; next Alcander and
Halius, Noemon and Prytanis on the walls, unapprized [of his
admission], and rousing the martial spirit [of their friends].
Lynceus advancing against him, and calling on his friends,
he from the rampart dexterously with his glittering sword
assails, straining every nerve: his head, together with the
helmet, at one close blow struck off, was laid far off; the next
[attacks and kills] Amycus, that destroyer of the savage kind,
than whom no one was more skilful to anoint[51] the dart, and
arm the steel with poison; and Clytius, a son of Æolus, and
Creteus, a friend to the Muses; Creteus, the Muses' companion, who in the song and lyre still took delight, and to
adapt poetic numbers to the strings: of steeds, and arms, and
combats of heroes he for ever sang.

At length the Trojan leaders, Mnestheus and fierce Serestus, apprized of the slaughter of their troops, assemble;
and perceive their friends dispersed and the enemy within the
city. And Mnestheus calls: Whither, whither next bend ye

[50] The nature of this wound shows that he was flying with the rest, as
Anthon observes. Cf. Ovid. Met. viii. 364, "succiso liquerunt poplite
acrvi." B.
[51] i. e. to poison. So "ungere" is used in Hor. Od. ii. 1. Lucan
fi. 266. B.

your flight? what other walls, what other fortifications have
you now beyond this? Shall one man, O citizens, by ramparts
every way hemmed in, spread such vast havoc through the
city with impunity? shall he despatch to Pluto so many of
the most illustrious of our youths? Can neither shame nor
pity towards your unhappy country, your ancient gods, and
great Æneas, touch your recreant breasts? Fired by these
words they are fortified [with courage], and in a close body
stand firm. Turnus begins by slow degrees to retreat from
the fight, and make towards the river, and that part [of the
wall] which is bounded by the stream. So much the more
keenly the Trojans press upon him with loud acclaim, and
form a clustering band: as with annoying darts a troop [of
hunters] press on after a fierce lion; while the appalled savage,
surly, louring stern, flinches back; nor rage, nor courage,
suffer him to fly; nor can he, for darts and men, (though fain
indeed he would,) make head against them; just so Turnus
hovering in suspense backward withdraws his lingering steps;
and his soul with rage tumultuous boils. Even then twice
had he attacked the enemy in the centre; twice along the
walls he chased the troops in confusion routed. But [issuing]
from the camp in haste, the whole host against him alone
combine; nor dares Saturnian Juno supply him with strength
against them, for Jupiter sent down from heaven aërial Iris,
bearing no mild mandates to his sister, unless Turnus quit the
lofty walls of the Trojans. Therefore, neither with his shield
nor arm is the youth able to withstand so great a shock: he is
so overwhelmed on all hands with showers of darts. With
incessant clang the helmet round his hollow temples rings,
and the solid arms of brass are riven with battering stones;
from his head the plumes are struck off; nor is his buckler's
boss sufficient to support the blows: The Trojans, and thundering Mnestheus himself at their head, with spears redouble
thrust on thrust. Then all over his body the sweat comes
trickling down, and pours a black clammy tide; nor has he
power to breathe; languid, panting heave his weary limbs.
Then at length in all his arms with a bound he flung himself
headlong into the river. He, expanding his yellow bosom,
received him at coming up, and upbore him on his peaceful
streams; and, having washed away his stains of blood, returned him joyous to his friends.

BOOK X.

In the Tenth Book, Jupiter calls a council of the gods, and attempts in vain a reconciliation between Juno and Venus, who favour the opposite parties. The fight is renewed. Æneas returns and joins battle with the Latins, when Pallas is killed by Turnus, who is saved from the avenging hand of Æneas by the interposition of Juno.

MEANWHILE the palace of all-powerful heaven is opened, and the parent of the gods, the sovereign of men, summons a council into the starry mansion, whence, from aloft, he views all lands, the Trojan camp, and Latin nations. In the abode with its two-valved gates, they take their seats; Jove himself begins: Ye high celestials, why is your purpose backward turned; and why so fiercely do ye with hostile minds contend? It was my will that with the Trojans Italy should not engage in war: what means this dissension against my prohibition? what jealousy hath prompted these or those to pursue hostilities, and rouse the sword? The just time for fight will come, (anticipate it not,) when hereafter fierce Carthage shall on Roman towers pour down mighty ruin, and the opened Alps: then shall leave be given you to fight with mutual animosities, then to plunder.[1] At present forbear, and cheerfully ratify the destined league. Thus Jupiter briefly said; but bright Venus on the other hand not briefly replies: O Sire, O eternal power of gods and men! (for what other subsists whom now we can implore?) seest thou how the Rutulians insult, and how Turnus on his steed conspicuous is hurried through the ranks, and swollen with successful war pours along? now not even their fenced bulwarks protect the Trojans; even within the gates, and on the very turrets of the walls, they join battle, and the trenches are deluged with blood. Æneas unwittingly is absent. Will you never suffer them from blockade to be relieved? Once more our enemies, another army too, are hovering over the walls of Troy just rising anew into life; and once more Tydides from Ætolian Arpi[2] rises

---

[1] i. e. to carry on war after the early fashion. Servius well refers this to the "clarigatio," or public challenge offered by the Feciales, (see Dict. Antiq.,) observing that "Cædere" was equivalent to "res rapere," "satisfacere" to "res reddere." B.

[2] Arpi, called also Argyripa, a city of Apulia in Italy, built by Diomede after the Trojan war.

against the Trojans. I truly believe new wounds are reserved
for me;[1] and I, your own progeny, await a contest with a
mortal. If without thy permission, and in defiance of thy
will, the Trojans have come to Italy, let them atone for their
offence; and do not support them with thy aid: but if [they
came] in pursuance of so many responses, which powers celestial and infernal both delivered, why now has any one the
power to pervert thy commands, or to frame new schemes of
fate? What need have I to recall to mind the firing of their
fleet on the Sicilian shore? or why the king of storms and his
furious winds raised from Æolia, or Iris sent down from the
clouds? Now, even to the powers of hell (that quarter
of the universe [alone] unsolicited remained) she has recourse; and Alecto, suddenly let loose upon the upper world,
infuriate hath roamed through the midst of the Italian
cities. For empire I am no further solicitous; these hopes we
entertained while fortune was ours; let those prevail whom
thou wilt rather have prevail. If there be no spot on earth
which thy rigid spouse will vouchsafe to the Trojans, thee
I conjure, O father, by the smoking ruins of demolished Troy,
permit me to dismiss Ascanius safe from arms; permit my
grandchild to survive. For Æneas, truly let him on seas
unknown be tossed, and pursue whatever course fortune shall
give him: let me but have power to protect the boy, and
rescue him from the horrid fray. Amathus is mine: lofty
Paphos, and Cythera, and the mansion of Idalia, are mine:
here, laying arms aside, let him inglorious spend his days.
Command Carthage to rule Ausonia with powerful sway;
from him no opposition shall arise to the Tyrian cities. What
hath it availed Æneas to escape the ravages of war, and to
have fled through the midst of Grecian flames; and to have
drained to the dregs so many dangers both by sea and land
immense, while the Trojans are in quest of Latium, and of
another Pergamus again tottering to its fall? Would it not
have been better for them to settle on the last ashes of their
country, and the soil where Troy once was? Give back, I
pray, to the hapless ones their Xanthus and Simois; and,
further, permit the Trojans to struggle once more with the
disasters of Troy. Then imperial Juno, stung with fierce rage,
thus spoke: Why do you compel me to break my profound

[1] Venus had been previously wounded by Diomede. B.

silence, and by words proclaim my smothered grief? Did any
of the gods or human race constrain Æneas to pursue war, and
present himself as a foe to king Latinus? He set out for Italy,
by the authority of the Fates: I grant it; impelled by Cassandra's mad predictions.   Did we advise him to abandon his
camp, or to commit his life to the winds? or to trust a boy
with the chief administration of the war, or with the city;
or [to solicit] the protection of the Tuscan monarch, and
embroil nations that were at peace? What god, or what rigid
power of mine, urged him to these guileful measures? Where
was Juno on this occasion, or Iris, who, [you tell us,] has
been despatched from above? A high indignity, [no doubt,]
it is, that the Latins should surround your infant Troy with
flames, and that Turnus should settle in his native land; he
whose grandsire is Pilumnus,[4] whose mother is the goddess
Venilia.[5]   What is it then for the Trojans to assault the
Latins with the gloomy brand, or to enthral kingdoms not
their own, and bear away the plunder? What is it for them to
suborn fathers-in-law, and carry off betrothed spouses from
the bosoms [of their plighted lords]? What is it for them to
sue for peace like suppliants, while on their ships they displayed the ensigns of war? You can privately convey Æneas
from the hands of the Greeks, and in his stead spread before
their eyes a misty cloud and empty air: you too can transform his ships into so many nymphs; for us to have aided the
Rutulians against him ever so little is a heinous crime. Æneas,
[you say,] in ignorance is absent: and absent let him remain
in ignorance. Paphos is yours, Idalium also, and lofty Cythera;
why then do you solicit a city big with war, and hearts is
rough mould? Do we attempt to overturn from its foundation
thy frail Phrygian state? is it we? or rather he who to the
Greeks exposed the wretched Trojans? Who[6] was the cause
that Europe and Asia rose together in arms, and by a perfidious crime violated their league? Was it under my conduct that
the Trojan adulterer stormed Sparta? or did I supply him
with arms, or foment the war by lust? Then it became you to

----

[4] Pilumnus, a deity worshipped at Rome, from whom Turnus boasted
of being lineally descended.

[5] Venilia, a nymph, sister to Amata, and mother of Turnus by Daunus.

[6] "Quæ" must not be joined with "causa," but taken independently,
as is evident from the imitation of Propert. ii. 2, 45, "Olim mirabar, quæ
unti ad Pergama belli Europæ atque Asiæ causa puella fuit."   B.

bo in fear for your minions: now too late you rise with un-
just complaints, and throw out reproaches of no avail. Thos
Juno pleaded her cause; and all the celestials murmured out
various assent; as when the rising gales, pent in the woods,
begin to mutter, and roll along soft whispers, that to mariners
betoken approaching winds.

Then the almighty Sire, whose is the chief command of the
universe, begins. While he speaks, the sublime mansion of
the gods is hushed, and earth from its foundation trembles;
the lofty sky is silent; then the zephyrs are still; the sea levels
its peaceful surface. Listen, therefore, and fix in your minds
these my words: since it is not permitted that with the Trojans the Ausonians be joined in league, and your dissensions
receive no end; whatever fortune to-day is for each, whatever
hope each cuts out for himself, be he Trojan or Rutulian, I
will regard them both without distinction; whether the camp
[of the Trojans] be now besieged by the Latins, through the
decrees of fate, or in consequence of Troy's fatal error, and
inauspicious presages.[1] Nor do I exempt the Rutulians. To
each his own enterprise shall procure disaster or success.
Sovereign Jove shall be to all the same. The Fates shall take
their course. Bowing his head, he confirmed the promise by
the streams of his Stygian brother, by the banks that roll
with torrents of pitch and black whirlpools, and by his nod
made heaven's whole frame to tremble. Here the consultation ended: then Jupiter rises from his golden throne, whom
in their centre the celestial powers conduct to his palace.

Meanwhile the Rutulians at all the gates are keenly employed in slaughtering the troops, and encompassing the walls
with flames. On the other hand, the host of the Trojans
within their ramparts are closely shut up; nor have they any
hope of escape. Forlorn they stand on the lofty turrets to no
purpose, and with thin bands beset the walls. Asius, the son
of Imbracus, and Thymœtes, the son of Hicetaon, the two
Assaracci, and aged Tybris, with Castor, lead the van: those
both the brothers of Sarpedon and Clarus, and Hæmon, from
lofty Lycia, accompany. Acmon of Lyrnessus, inferior
neither to his father Clytius, nor to his brother Mnestheus,

---

[1] i. e. "or through their wrongly interpreting the uncertain presages
which had been sent as a warning." Servius refers the remark to
"Cassandræ impulsus furiis" in vs. 68. B

straining with his whole body, bears a huge rock, no inconsiderable portion of a mountain. Some with darts, some with rocks, strive to defend [the town]; others hurl firebrands, and fit their arrows to the string. Lo, in the midst, Venus' most worthy care, the young prince of Troy, with his comely head uncovered, sparkles like the diamond which divides the yellow gold, an ornament either for the neck or for the head: or as shines the ivory by art enchased in boxwood, or Orician ebony;[8] whose spreading locks his milk-white neck receives, and a circle of ductile gold upbinds. Thee too, O Ismarus, the magnanimous nations saw aiming wounds, and arming thy shafts with poison; [Ismarus,] descended from a noble Lydian family, where the swains till, and Pactolus[9] waters with his golden streams, rich fertile lands. Mnestheus too lent his aid, whom his former glory of having beaten Turnus from the bastion greatly exults: and Capys: from him the name of the Campanian city[10] is derived. They were mutually engaged in the combats of rugged war: Æneas at midnight was ploughing the waves. For soon as having left Evander, entering the Tuscan camp, he repairs to the king, and lays before him his name and nation; informs him what is his demand, what proposals he brings; what troops Mezentius is procuring for himself; the outrageous temper of Turnus; reminds him how little confidence there is in human affairs, and intermixes prayers: no delay ensues. Tarchon joins his forces, and strikes a league. Then the Lydian nation, disengaged from the restraint of fate, enter the fleet, by order of the gods put under the conduct of a foreign leader. Æneas' galley leads the way, under whose beak are Phrygian lions yoked: Ida towers above, most grateful to the Trojan exiles. Here great Æneas sits, and revolves with himself the various events of war; and Pallas attached to his left side, now questions him of the stars, their path amid the darksome night; now of the sufferings he sustained both by land and sea.

---

[8] Orician ebony, from Oricum, a town of Epirus in Greece, on the Adriatic.

[9] Pactolus, a river of Lydia in Asia Minor, issuing from Mount Tmolus, and falling into the Hermus below Sardes. The sands of the Pactolus, like those of the Hermus, were mingled with gold.

[10] i.e. Capua. B.

Now open Helicon, ye goddesses, and me inspire to sing;
what troops meanwhile accompany Æneas from the Tuscan
coasts, man his ships, and are borne on the main.

First Massicus in the brazen-beaked Tigris ploughs the
waves, under whom is a band of a thousand youths, who left
the walls of Cláusium,[11] and who the city Cosæ;[12] whose
weapons are arrows and light quivers on their shoulders, and
the deadly bow.   With him stern Abas goes: his whole
squadron with burnished arms, and his stern with a gilded
Apollo shone.   To him Populonia, his mother-city, had given
six hundred youths expert in arms; but Ilva,[13] an island ennobled by inexhaustible mines of steel, three hundred.   The
third, Asylas, the famed interpreter of gods and men, to whom
the fibres of victims, to whom the stars of heaven, are in subjection, and the languages of birds, and the flashes of presaging
thunder, pours along his thousand close-ranged in battle-
array, and with erect spears.   These Pisa,[14] a Tuscan city in
its territory, Alphean in origin, to him put in subjection.
Astur follows, a most comely hero, Astur confiding in his
steed and parti-coloured arms.   Those who in Cære,[15] who in
the plains of Minio[16] dwell, and ancient Pyrgi, and unwholesome Graviscæ, join [with him] three hundred (all have one
resolution to follow).   Thee, Cycnus,[17] chief of the Lugurians,
most valorous in war, I cannot pass over; nor thee, Cupavo,
by few troops accompanied, on whose crest a swan's plumes
arise, (your crime was love,) the ensign of your father's trans-

[11] Clausium, the ancient Clusium, a town of Etruria, on the banks of the Clanis, where Porsenna was buried.

[12] Cosæ and Populonia, maritime towns of Etruria.

[13] Ilva, (Elba,) an island of the Tyrrhene Sea, between Italy and Cor-sica; it was famous for its iron mines. DAVIDSON. Compare Rutil. [Itin. i. 351, "Chalybum memorabilis Ilva metallis." B.

[14] Pisa, a town of Etruria, at the mouth of the Arnus, built by a colony from Pisa in Elis.

[15] Cære, a city of Etruria, of which Mezentius was king when Æneas came to Italy.

[16] Minio, (Mignone,) a river of Etruria, falling into the Tyrrhene Sea. Pyrgi and Graviscæ, maritime towns of Etruria.

[17] Cycnus, a son of Sthenelus, king of Liguria, who was deeply af-fected at the death of his friend Phaëton, and was metamorphosed into a swan.   Phaëton, the son of Phœbus and Clymene, according to the poets, was intrusted by his father with the chariot of the sun for one day, when, by his unskilful driving, he nearly set the world on fire, upon which Jupi-ter struck him with a thunderbolt, and he fell into the river Po.

formation.[18] For they tell us that Cyonus, while for grief of
his beloved Phaëton he sings among the poplar boughs, his
sisters' shade, and with music soothes his disconsolate love,
[by transformation clothed] with downy plumes, brought upon
himself[19] hoary age, leaving the earth, and soaring to the stars
with his song. The son, in the fleet accompanying his coëval
troops, with oars impels the bulky Centaur: the monster stands
on the flood, and reared high threatens the waves with an
enormous rock, and with his long keel ploughs the deep seas.
The famed Ocnus[20] too leads on a squadron from his native
coasts, son of the prophetic Manto and the Tuscan river
[Tiber], who gave thee walls, O Mantua, and his mother's
name; Mantua rich in ancestors:[21] but they are not all of
one lineage. Three clans to her belong: under each clan are
four communities; of those communities she herself is the
capital city. The strength [of her inhabitants are] of Tuscan
blood. Hence too Mezentius arms five hundred against himself, whom Mincius, sprung from the parent-lake Benacus,
crowned with azure reed, conveyed to the sea in hostile ships
of pine. The stern Aulestes advances, and, rising [to the
stroke], lashes the wave with a hundred oars: the surface
overturned, the billows foam. The enormous Triton bears
him with his shell-trumpet affrighting the azure floods: whose
hairy front, as he swims along, displays a human form down
to the waist, his belly terminates in a pristis, under his half-
savage breast the foamy surges murmur. So many chosen
chiefs in thirty vessels went to the aid of Troy, and ploughed
with prows of brass the briny plains.

And now day had withdrawn from the heavens, and auspicious Phœbe in her night-wandering car was shaking the
mid-region of the sky. Æneas (for anxiety gives not sleep
to his limbs) himself, seated at the helm, both steers and manages the sails. And, lo! in his mid-course there came up to
him a choir of those who were his attendants before, nymphs

[18] Put a comma after "pennæ," taking the words "crimen amor ves-
trum" in a parenthesis. See Wagner. B.

[19] I have followed Heyne. The whiteness of his plumage made him
appear like an aged person. B.

[20] Ocnus, the son of Tiber and Manto, who assisted Æneas against
Turnus. He built a town which he called Mantua, after his mother's
name.

[21] So Statius Theb. L. 391, "Adrastus dives avis." B.

whom propitious Cybele had appointed to enjoy divinity in
the sea, and from ships to become nymphs: with equal motion
they swam along,[22] and cut the waves; as numerous as the
brazen-beaked vessels which had before been drawn up on
the shore. Their king at a distance they descry, and in
circling dances him surround: of whom the most accomplished
speaker, Cymodocea, following, with her right hand grasps
the stern, while with her back she rises [above the flood], and
with her left hand gently rows her way along the silent waves.
Then him unknowing she thus addresses: Wakest thou,
Æneas, offspring of the gods? awake and give your ship full
sails. We are the pines of Ida, from that mountain's sacred
top, [once] thy fleet, now nymphs of the sea. When the perfidious Rutulian pressed us with fire and sword till we were
on the brink of ruin, constrained we burst thy cables, and go
in quest of thee through the ocean. The mother [of the
gods] in pity new-fashioned in form, and permitted us to become goddesses, and to pass our life under the waves. But
[know that] the boy Ascanius is blocked up in the wall and
trenches, amidst darts, and amidst the Latins arrayed in all
the terrors of Mars. Now the Arcadian horse, united with
the valiant Tuscans, have reached the place appointed: It is
the determined resolution of Turnus to intercept their march
with his troops, that they may not join the camp. Come,
arise, and at the approach of morn first command thy troops
to arms; and take thy shield, which, of unconquerable might,
the god of fire gave to thee, and encircled its borders with
gold. To-morrow's sun (if you deem not my words vain)
shall behold vast heaps of Rutulian slaughter. She said; and
parting, with her right hand shoved forward the lofty stern,
not unskilful in the art: the vessel flies along the waves
swifter than the javelin, and the arrow that keeps pace with
the winds. The rest then speed their course. The Trojan
son of Anchises, himself not knowing [the cause], is lost in
wonder, yet by the omen raises the spirits of his men. Then
surveying the high vault of heaven, he briefly prays: Bounteous parent of the gods, Idæan Cybele, whose dear delight is
Dindymus, and turret-bearing cities, and lions yoked in pairs

---

[22] So Oppian Hal. i. 565, Ἴασυτο θάσσον ὀιστοῦ. v. 477, διλφὶς δ' ὥυτ'
ὀιστος—κραικνά θίων. " Modo " refers to the keeping the ship properly
poised, while the impulse was given, as is remarked by Anthon. B.

under thy reins, be thou now my leader in the fight; do thou, O goddess, in due form render the omen propitious, and with thy propitious influence aid the Trojans.

This only he said, and meanwhile the day revolved, was now with perfect light advanced, and had chased away the night. First he enjoins his troops to observe the signal, and to dispose their minds for arms, and prepare themselves for the combat. And now he has the Trojans and his camp in view, standing on his lofty deck. Then next on his left arm he raised aloft his flaming buckler. The Trojans from their walls raise acclamations to the stars. Additional hope rouses up their fury. Darts from their hands they hurl: as under the gloomy clouds Strymonian cranes give the signal, and swim along the skies with din, and from the south winds with joyous clamour fly. But to the Rutulian prince and Ausonian leaders this seemed amazing; till looking back they observed the fleet turned towards the shore, and the whole channel of the river gliding along with vessels. The tufted helmet on his head blazes, and from the top of his crest a flame is poured forth, and the golden boss of his buckler darts copious fires; just as when in a clear night the sanguine comets baleful glare; or, as Sirius, that blazing star, when he brings droughts and diseases on sickly mortals, rises and saddens the sky with inauspicious light. Yet daring Turnus dropped not his bold purpose to preoccupy the shore, and, as they approached, beat them from the land. Then eagerly addressing his men, he raises their courage, and briskly chides their fears:[23] That which you ardently wished is come, by dint of valour to crush [the foe]; Mars himself, brave men, is in your power.[24] Now each man be mindful of his wife and home; now let him reflect on the mighty deeds, the glory of his ancestors. Let us of ourselves make head against them by the stream, while they are in disorder, and their first steps at landing stagger. Fortune assists the daring. He said, and ponders within himself whom to lead against [the enemy], or to whom he may intrust the siege of the town.

Meanwhile Æneas by bridges lands his troops from their lofty ships. Many watched the retreat of the ebbing sea, and

[23] There seems little doubt that this line is a spurious introduction from: Æn. ix. 127. B.

[24] i. e. you can bring them to an open fight. B.

with a spring committed themselves to the shallows; others row themselves ashore. Tarchon having surveyed the strand where there is no surf,[25] and where no dashing wave remurmurs, but the sea unbroken glides along with the swelling tide, suddenly turns hither his prow, and addresses his associates: Now, my select band, ply the sturdy oars; push briskly, urge on your vessels; cleave with your beaks this hostile soil, and let the keel plough a way for itself. Nor shall I refuse to dash my ship in pieces in such a port, if we but once seize the land. Which as soon as Tarchon thus had said, his mates rose to their oars at once. And full on the Latin coast their foaming galleys bear, till the beaks rest on the dry dock, and all the keels without harm are moved: but not so thy vessel, Tarchon; for while against the shallows dashed she hangs on the fatal ridge, long balanced in suspense, and tires the waves, she is staved, and exposes the crew in the midst of the waves; whom fragments of oars and floating benches embarrass, while the tide retreating draws back their steps.

Then no supine delay withholds Turnus; but impetuous he hurries on his whole host against the Trojans, and on the shore ranges them full opposite. They sound the alarm. Æneas first attacked the rustic troops, an omen[26] of the fight; and routed the Latins, having slain Theron, their giant chief, who boldly makes up to Æneas: through the brazen texture [of his buckler], and through his tunic rough[27] with gold, he with the sword drains[28] his transfixed side. Next he smites Lycas, who was cut out of his mother when dead, and to thee, O Phœbus, devoted, because in infancy he was permitted to escape the perilous chances of steel.[29] Not far onward be

---

[25] But others read "sperat" for "spirant." B.

[26] Servius observes: "omen, quia, sicut nunc, sic ubique vincet Æneas." B.

[27] Or "dull to the view." ANTHON. But I prefer the explanation of Gellius II. 6, "significat copiam densitatemque auri in summarum speciem intexti." B.

[28] i. e. "drinks the blood from his side." But it may also be taken as equivalent to "transfodit." Servius observes: "cum enim a latere quis aliquem adortus gladio occidit, hausit illum dicunt." So Ovid Met. v. 126, "Herenti latus haurit Abas." Silius i. 392, "Et rapto nudum clypeo latus haurit Hiberi." B.

[29] Such children were consecrated to Apollo. See Servius. B.

overthrows in death hardy Cisseus, and gigantic Gyas, as they were felling the troops with clubs. Neither the weapons of Hercules, nor their strength of arm, aught availed them; nor did they profit by having Melampus for their father, the companion of Alcides, as long as earth supplied him with toilsome labours. Lo, at Pharus hurling a javelin, he fixes it full in his bawling mouth, while he vaunts dastardly speeches. Thou, too, Cydon, (while thou hapless art pursuing Clytius, thy new charmer, shading his cheeks with the first yellow down,) overthrown by the Trojan arm, regardless of those loves which thou ever didst entertain for boys, hadst lain an object of compassion, had not a band of brothers, the progeny of Phorcus, in close array made head against him: seven in number, and seven darts they fling; part from his helm and shield ineffectual rebound; part just grazing on his skin indulgent Venus turned aside. Æneas thus bespeaks his trusty Achates: Supply me with darts, (not one against the Rutulians shall my right hand hurl in vain,) [of those] which on the Trojan plains once stood in the bodies of the Greeks.[20]   Then he grasps at once and tosses a mighty spear; it flying pierces through the brazen plates of Mæon's shield, and his cuirass together with his breast transfixes. To him comes up his brother Alcanor, and with his right hand sustains his falling brother; piercing whose arm, the darted spear flies straitly on, and drenched in blood, holds on its course; and from the shoulder by the nerves the arm hung lifeless. Then Numitor, from his brother's body having snatched a javelin, aims it at Æneas: but to him it is not permitted in his turn to transfix [the hero], and it grazed on the thigh of great Achates. Here Clausus of Cures, confiding in his youthful person, comes up, and wounds Dryops at a distance with a rigid spear, under his chin with force driven home; and, transfixing his throat while the word is in his mouth, at once of speech and life bereaves him: but he with his front beats the ground, and at his mouth disgorges clotted blood. Three Thracians, too, of Boreas' exalted line, and three whom their father Idas and Ismara their parent soil sent, by various fate he overthrows. Halæsus runs up, and the Auruncian bands; Messapus, too, the son of Neptune, with his steeds conspicuous comes up: now these, now those,

[20] Which had been plucked from the bodies of the slain. N.

strive to beat off each other. In the very confines of Ausonia
the contest rages. As in the spacious sky jarring winds with
equal rage and force raise war; nor they to one another, nor
clouds, nor sea, [on either side] give way: long is the combat dubious; all things stand struggling against each other:
just so the Trojan and the Latin hosts encounter: foot to foot
is fixed, and man to man closely joined. But in another quarter, where the torrent had far and wide dispersed whirling
stones, and thickets uptorn from the banks, as soon as Pallas
saw the Arcadians, unused to combat on foot, turning their
backs to Latium fierce in the pursuit, since the rugged nature
of the ground induced them to let go their steeds ; now with
entreaty, now with bitter expostulation, (the sole expedient left
in this distress,) he rouses their valour: Whither, my fellow-
soldiers, do you fly? By yourselves and your own gallant
deeds, by the name of Evander your chief, by the battles you
have won, and by my hopes, which now, emulating my father's
glory, trust not to your heels. With the sword you must
burst a passage through your foes, where that globe of men in
thickest array press on us: this way your ennobled country
calls you and Pallas your leader. They are not gods who
pursue us: mortal ourselves, by a mortal foe are we urged:
to us as many souls, as many hands, [as to them] belong.
Lo! the ocean with his immense barrier of sea hems us in:
now land too is wanting for us to fly to: whither, into the
deep, or for Troy, shall we bend our course? He said, and
into the midst of thick-embodied foes bursts a way. Him
Lagus first opposes impelled by his inauspicious fate; him,
while he is tugging a stone of enormous weight, he transfixes
with a whirled lance, where along the middle [of the back]
the spine divided the ribs; and forces away the spear fast
sticking in the bones: whom, [while thus employed,] Hisbon
fails in striking from above, though this, indeed, he hoped;
for, as he rushes on unguarded, while, by the cruel death of
his companion, he is driven to madness, Pallas surprises him
first, and buries the sword in his swollen lungs. Next Sthenelus he attacks, and, of the ancient race of Rhœtus, Anche-
molus, who dared to violate, by incest, his step-dame's bed.
In the Rutulian plains, likewise, you twin-brothers fell, Laridus and Thymber, Daucus' exactly similar offspring, undistinguished by your own parents, and [the objects of] their

pleasing error. But now Pallas on you fixed cruel marks of
distinction; for from thee, O Thymbras, the Evandrian blade
lopped off the head; and thy dismembered hand, O Laridus,
seeks for thee its owner; the dying fingers quiver, and gripe
once more the steel. Against their foes mixed indignation
and shame arm the Arcadians fired by this warning, and viewing the hero's glorious deeds. Then Pallas transfixes Rhœteus
flying across [him] in his chariot. This gave Ilus space [to
live], and just so long respite: for at Ilus he had aimed from
far the sturdy spear; which Rhœtcus coming between inter-
cepts, as thee he flies, most valiant Teuthras, and thy brother
Tyres; and, rolled from his chariot, half-dead, he spurns the
Rutulian fields. And as in summer, the winds having risen
to his wish, the shepherd lets loose scattered fires among the
woods; in a trice Vulcan's squadrons, having seized the intermediate trees, are at once extended in horrid array over all
the spacious plains; victorious he sits viewing the triumphant
flames: just so the whole valour of thy troops in one com-
bines, and supports thee, O Pallas. But Halæsus, fierce in
war, advances against the hostile bands, and within the covert
of his arms himself collects. Ladon, Pheres, and Demodocus
he knocks down; from Strymonius with his shining blade he
strikes off the right hand raised against his throat; with a
rock he batters Thoas' front, and scatters the bones mingled
with bloody brains. His father in the woods had concealed
Halæsus, presaging his fate. Soon as the aged sire in death
relaxed his aged eyes, the Destinies laid hands on him, and
devoted him to the arms of Evander, whom Pallas approaches,
first addressing his prayer thus: Grant now, O father Tiber,
to this missile steel I poise, success, and a passage through the
breast of stern Halæsus; so shall thy oak possess these arms
and spoils of the hero. To this address the god gave ear;
while Halæsus screened Imaon, in an unhappy hour he exposes his defenceless breast to the Arcadian dart. But Lausus, no small portion of the war, suffers not his troops to be
dispirited by the vast havoc which the hero made. First
Abas to him opposed he kills, the knot and stay[21] of the battle. Down drop Arcadia's sons, down drop the Tuscans, and

n "Nodum" is a metaphor derived from the difficulty with which
knots are unfastened. On "mora" compare Silius i. 479, "Romani
belli mora." So Senec. Ag. 211. Troad. 124. Phœn. 458. B.

z

you, ye Trojans, frames undestroyed by the Greeks. Both
hosts in encounter join, with leaders and with forces equal;
those in the rear press on the ranks before; nor does the
throng leave room to wield their hands or weapons. Here
Pallas drives on and urges the attack; there, in opposition to
him, Lausus; nor is there great difference in their ages; in
comeliness they are distinguished; but their return to their
country fortune had denied. Yet he who reigns in heaven
supreme permitted not that with each other they should engage; their destiny awaits them soon from a superior foe.

Meanwhile Turnus, who through the midst of the host in
his fleet chariot cuts his way, his gentle sister warns to fly to
Lausus' relief. Soon as his friends he viewed, [he exclaimed,]
It is time to desist from battle: against Pallas I alone am
bound: to me alone is Pallas doomed: would to heaven his
sire himself were spectator. He said; and from the plain the
troops at his command retired. But the youth, struck with
the retreat of the Rutulians, and the imperious orders, gazes
on Turnus with astonishment; over his huge body he rolls his
eyes, and with ferocious visage all the man aloof surveys.
Then with these words in return to the tyrant's speech moves
up: Now, or by bearing away triumphal spoils, or by illustrious death, shall I be signalized. For either chance my sire
is equal. Away with your threatenings. This said, he advances
into the middle of the plain. Round the Arcadian hearts the
cold blood congeals. Down from his chariot Turnus sprang;
on foot prepares to meet him hand to hand. And as a lion,
when from his lofty place of observation he hath espied a bull
standing on the plains aloof, meditating the fight, flies up to
him; such is the image of Turnus rushing [to the combat].
Soon as Pallas supposed him to be within reach of the darted
lance, he makes the first advance with strength unequal,
[trying] if fortune by any means will aid his bold enterprise;
and thus to the lofty heavens himself addresses: By my father's
hospitality, and those boards which thou his guest didst visit,
Alcides, aid, I thee implore, my arduous attempt: may the
dying eyes of Turnus behold me strip him expiring of his
bloody armour, and let his dying eyes endure the sight of a
victorious foe. Alcides heard the youth, and deep in the bottom
of his heart a heavy groan suppresses, and pours forth unavailing tears. Then the Sire with these kind words his son be-

speaks : To every one his day is fixed : a short and irretrievable term of life is given to all : but by deeds to lengthen out fame, this is virtue's task.   Under the lofty walls of Troy so many sons of gods have fallen : with them even Sarpedon, my own offspring, fell ; Turnus too his destiny calls, and to the utmost verge of life he is arrived.   He said ; and from the fields of the Rutulians he averts his eye.

But Pallas with mighty force hurls the spear, and from the hollow scabbard tears his shining blade.   The weapon flying lighted where the armour rises high on the shoulder, and, opening a way through the extremity of the shield, at length too on the great body of Turnus grazed.   At this Turnus, long poising a javelin tipped with sharpened steel, darts it at Pallas, and thus speaks : See whether ours be not the more penetrating dart.   He said ; and with a quivering stroke the point pierces through the mid-shield, through so many plates of iron, so many of brass, while the bull's hide so many times encompasses it, and through the corslet's cumbrous folds transfixes his breast with a hideous gash.[32]   He in vain wrenches out the reeking weapon from the wound : at one and the same passage the blood and soul issue forth.   Down on his wound he falls : over him his armour gave a clang ; and in death with bloody jaws he bites the hostile ground.   Whom Turnus bestriding, says, Ye Arcadians, to Evander faithfully these my words record : in such plight as he deserved I send his Pallas back. Whatever honour is in a tomb, whatever solace is in interment, I freely give him.   His league of friendship with Æneas shall cost him not a little.   And thus having spoken, he pressed with his left foot the breathless corpse, tearing away his belt's enormous weight, and the horrid story with which it was embossed, (in one nuptial night a band of youths barbarously murdered, and their bridal beds bathed in blood,)[33] which Clonus, Eurytion's son, had carved in abundant gold : in which spoil Turnus now triumphs, and exults in the possession.   How blind is the mind of men to fate and future events ! how unwilling to practise moderation, and how with prosperity elated ! the time will come when Turnus shall wish that it had been purchased at a dear price, that Pallas had not been touched, and when these spoils and this day he shall detest.   But Pallas

<hr>

[32] Servius, and I think more correctly, refers " ingens " to " cuspis." B

[33] i.e. the story of the daughters of Danaus.   B.

stretched on his shield, a numerous retinue of his friends, with many a groan and tear, back convey. O thou that art about to return to thy parent, his grief and ample glory both ! This day first gave thee to the war, the same snatches thee away ; yet after thou hast left vast heaps of Rutulians.

And now not mere rumour, but an unquestionable voucher of so great disaster flies to Æneas; that his friends were on the verge of utter ruin, that it was high time to succour the flying Trojans. With his sword he mows down whatever was near him, and with the steel impetuous forces a wide passage through the host, in quest of thee, O Turnus, proud of thy recent slaughter. Pallas, Evander, all are full before his eyes ; the first banquets in which then a guest he joined, and their plighted right hands. Here four youths, the progeny of Sulmo, and as many more whom Ufens bred, alive he snatches ; whom as victims he may offer to the shade [of Pallas], and drench with their captive blood the flames of his funeral pile. Next, when at Magus he aimed from afar his hostile lance, he artfully stoops, and over his head the quivering javelin flies ; and embracing his knees, him suppliant he thus addresses : By my father's manes, and the hopes of thy rising son Iülus, I implore thee, spare this life,[34] both for a son and for a father's sake. A stately mansion I possess ; talents of silver embossed lie deep-lodged under ground ; masses of wrought and unwrought gold I have; it is not upon this that the victory of the Trojans turns : one life will not so great a difference make. He said; to whom Æneas thus, on the other hand, replies : Those many talents of gold and silver you mention, reserve for your sons : those mutual stipulations of war Turnus first cancelled from the moment Pallas was slain. So [thinks] the manes of my sire Anchises, so thinks Iülus. This said, he grasps his helmet with his left hand, and bowing back his neck, as he begged for mercy, plunged [in his throat] his sword up to the hilt. Not far on Æmonides, the priest of Phœbus and Diana, whose temples a mitre with holy fillets bound, in his robe and burnished armour all refulgent: him encountering he drives along the plain, and standing over him fallen, offers him a victim, and covers him with the deep shades [of death]. Serestus, gathering up his arms, bears them on

[34] A Greek expression. Herodot. viii. 118. Ἰσασι βασιλῆος τὴν ψυχήν So Juvenal vi. 653, " Morte viri cupient animam servare catellæ."   B.

his shoulders as a trophy to thee, king Mars. Cæculus, born
of Vulcan's race, and Umbro, who came from the Marsian
mountains, renew the fight. The Trojan prince burns with
fury against them. Anxur's left arm and his buckler's whole
circumference he with his sword had struck off. Some mighty
spell he had pronounced, and imagined there would be virtue
in the word; perhaps he was exalting his soul to heaven with
vain hopes, and had proposed himself grey hairs and length
of years. On the other hand, Tarquitus, whom to sylvan
Faunus the nymph Dryope bore, in his refulgent arms exulting, to the incensed hero himself opposed. He, darting a
spear with full force, renders his corslet and buckler's vast
bulk useless for defence: then strikes down to the ground
his head as he begs in vain, and seeks to plead much; and,
tumbling the warm trunk, over it pronounces these words
from his hostile breast: There now, thou dreaded one, lie.
Thee in the earth no dearest mother shall lodge, nor in thy
native soil load thy limbs with a grave; to birds of prey thou
shalt be left; or sunk in the deep, the waves shall bear thee
down, and hungry fishes suck thy wounds. Forthwith Antæus
and Lycas, Turnus' foremost leaders, he pursues, and valiant
Numa, and Camera of yellow locks, from magnanimous Volscens sprung; who of all Ausonia's sons was richest in land
estate, and over Amyclæ, the city of silence,[35] reigned. As
Ægæon who, they say, had a hundred arms and a hundred
hands, and flashed fire from fifty mouths and breasts; when
against the thunderbolts of Jove he on so many equal bucklers
clashed, unsheathed so many swords: just so the victorious
Æneas wreaked his fury all over the plain, when once his
pointed steel was warmed [with blood], even against the four
harnessed steeds of Niphæus and their chests opposed he advances: but, as soon as from far they saw him marching up,
and breathing dire revenge, with affright wheeling about, and
rushing back, they tumble out the chief, and whirl the chariot
to the shore. Meanwhile Lucagus, in his chariot drawn by two
white steeds, flings himself into the midst, as also his brother
Liger: but with the reins his brother guides the steeds: fierce
Lucagus flourishes the naked sword. Æneas could not pati-

[35] It had been deserted by the inhabitants, in consequence of the serpents that infested it. So Wagner. Heyne refers the epithet to its
Laconian extraction. See Servius. B.

rutly see them raging with such impetuosity: on he rushed, and majestic stood before them with his lance opposed. To whom Liger [said], You see not here the steeds of Diomede, nor the chariot of Achilles, or the plains of Troy: now on this ground shall a period to the war and thy life be given. Such words from raving Liger fly: but somewhat instead of words the Trojan hero in return prepares; for against his foe a javelin he hurls. As Lucagus stooping forward to the lash with a dart urged his yoked steeds, while with his left foot thrown out before he prepares himself for the fight; the spear passes through the lowest border of his shining buckler, then pierces his left groin: tossed from the chariot in the pangs of death he wallows; whom pious Æneas in bitter terms addresses: Lucagus, it is not the slowness of thy steeds in flight thy chariot hath betrayed, nor have empty shadows turned them from the foe: thyself springing from the wheels, desertest the chariot. Thus having said, he seized the steeds. His hapless brother, leaping down from the same car, stretched forth his defenceless hands: By thy own self, O Trojan hero, by the parents who begot thee thus illustrious, spare this life, and pity a wretch who begs for mercy. To whom, pleading at greater length, Æneas: It was not language like this you lately uttered: die, and brother desert not brother. Then with the pointed steel he discloses his breast, the latent seat of the soul.[36] Such havoc made the Trojan chief over the field, raging like an impetuous flood or gloomy whirlwind. At length the boy Ascanius and the youth, in vain blocked up, sally forth and quit the camp.

Meanwhile Jupiter, of his own free motion, thus addresses Juno: My sister, and my dearest consort both! it is Venus, as you alleged, who supports the Trojan powers: nor does your judgment deceive you; no active hands for war have the men themselves, no souls courageous or patient of danger. To whom Juno, all submission, [says,] My spouse, in whom all beauty dwells, why dost thou tease me oppressed with anguish, and dreading thy severe mandates? Had I that influence over your affection which once I had, and which it became me to have, thou the Omnipotent couldst not surely refuse me this; that I might have it in my power both to res-

* Davidson has happily anticipated the explanation of Jacobs, regard-ing "latebras animæ" as in apposition with "pectus," not vice versa. B

cue Turnus from the fight, and preserve him in safety for his father Daunus. Now let him die, and glut the vengeance of the Trojans with his pious blood; yet from our stock he derives his name, and Pilumnus is his father in the fourth degree: and often with liberal hand and many offerings has he heaped thy courts. To whom the sovereign of the ethereal heaven thus briefly speaks: If you plead for a respite from present death, and a breathing-time to the short-lived youth, and if it be thy will that I should settle it thus; bear off Turnus by flight, and save him from impending fate. Thus far to indulge thee is allowed. But if any higher favour be couched under these petitions, and you imagine that the whole face of the war is to be shifted or reversed, you feed yourself with empty hopes. To whom Juno [replies] with tears: What if thou shouldst grant with thy heart what in words thou declinest, and this life to Turnus were to be continued fixed? Now a woeful end awaits the guiltless youth, or vain are my pretensions to the truth: but oh that I may rather be with groundless fears misled, and that thou, to whom the power belongs, mayest alter thy purposes for the better!

When she had pronounced these words, forthwith she shot down from the lofty sky arrayed in a cloud, driving storm and tempest through the air; and sought the Trojan army and Latin camp. Then of a hollow cloud, strange monster to behold! the goddess, in the shape of Æneas, dresses up in Trojan armour an airy powerless phantom, and imitates to the life both his shield and the crested helmet of his divine head; gives it empty words, and gives it sound without sense, and counterfeits his gait as he walks; such as those forms which after death are said to flutter about, or those dreams which mock the slumbering senses. But the phantom frisky exults before the foremost ranks, and the hero with darts provokes, and with the tongue defies: on whom Turnus presses, and at a distance hurls a hissing spear: the spectre, wheeling about, turned its steps. But then, as soon as Turnus imagined that Æneas with his back turned was giving ground, and boisterous in soul drunk in vain hope, [he cried out,] Æneas, whither dost thou fly? Desert not thy plighted nuptials: by this right hand shall the settlement be given you in quest of which you have traversed the seas. Thus vociferating, he pursues him, and brandishes his naked sword; nor sees that the winds bear his joys away.

By chance there stood a ship adjoining to the margin of a
steep rock with extended ladders, and a bridge prepared, in
which king Osinius had been wafted from the Clusian shores.
Hither in fearful haste the image of Æneas flying throws itself into a hiding-place: and Turnus with no less speed pursues; surmounts all obstacles, and overleaps the lofty bridges.
Scarcely had he reached the prow, when Saturnia bursts the
cable, and over the rolling waves hurries the vessel torn away
from the shore. But him absent Æneas with impatience to
the combat seeks; and many a hero whom he meets on the
way he despatches to the shades below. Then the fleeting
image now no further concealment seeks, but soaring aloft
blended itself with a dusky cloud; when in the mean time the
whirlwind drives Turnus on the mid-ocean. Back he casts
his eyes quite at a loss, and thankless for his preservation, and
both hands to heaven he raises with his voice: Almighty Father, couldst thou judge me worthy of such criminal shame,
and appoint me to suffer such punishment? Whither am I
borne? Whence am I come? What ignominious flight carries
me off, and in what disgrace will it bring me back? Shall I
again venture to behold the walls of Laurentum, or the Ausonian camp? What will that band of warriors [say], who followed me and my arms, and whom, O soul impiety! I abandoned in horrible death? And now I see them straggling, and
hear the groans of the falling. What can I do? or what
earth will now yawn deep enough for me? Or rather, on me,
ye winds, have pity; on rocks, on crags (I Turnus heartily
entreat you) drive my vessel, and fling it on the cruel shelves
of quicksands, whither neither the Rutulians nor conscious
fame may follow me. So saying, now hither, now thither, he
fluctuates in his soul, whether frantic he shall sheathe the
pointed steel in his bosom on account of such a flagrant disgrace, and through his sides drive home the cruel sword, or
throw himself into the midst of the waves, by swimming seek
the winding shore, and rush again amidst the Trojan arms.
Thrice he essayed either expedient: thrice mightiest Juno
restrained, and pitying him from her soul checked the youth.
He glides away, cutting the deep, with prosperous wind and
tide, and is wafted to the ancient city of his father Daunus.
  Meanwhile, by Jove's suggestion, furious Mezentius succeeds [him] in the fight, and assaults the Trojans flushed with
success. The Tuscan troops rush on him at once, and with

all their rage and darts following press on him, on him alone.
He [stands firm] as a rock that projects into the vast ocean,
obnoxious to the fury of the winds, and exposed to the main,
and endures all the violence and threatenings of the sky and
sea, itself remaining unmoved. He stretches on the ground
Hebrus, the son of Dolicaon, with him Latagus and fugitive
Palmus; but to Latagus with a rock and vast fragment of a
mountain he gives a preventing blow on his jaws and adverse
face : Palmus hamstrung he suffers to roll inactive ; and gives
Lausus [37] to wear his armour on his shoulders, and on his helmet's top to fix his plumes. Evas the Phrygian too [he over-
throws], and Mimas, the companion of Paris, and his equal
in age ; whom Theano brought forth to his father Amycus in
the same night that queen Hecuba, the daughter of Cisseus,
pregnant with a firebrand, bore Paris: he in his native
city buried lies, while the Laurentine coast possesses Mimas
unknown. And as a huge [38] boar by baying hounds pursued
from the high mountains, (while pine-bearing Vesulus [39] had
sheltered for many years, and the lake of Laurentum,) that in
the reedy wood had fed, makes a stand soon as he has arrived
among the toils, ferocious roars aloud, and bristles up his
shoulders : nor has any one the courage to venture boldly
or approach near him, but aloof they ply him with darts and
shouts secure from harm : [40] undaunted, however, he resists
their attacks on every side, gnashing his tusks, and shakes the
lances from his back : in the same manner, of those whom just
rage against Mezentius fires, not one has spirit to encounter
him with the naked sword; at a distance they gall him with
missile weapons and loud clamour. From the ancient coasts
of Corytus had Acron come, a Grecian, who deserted [to
Æneas], leaving his nuptials unconsummated : him when from
far Mezentius saw breaking through the midst of the ranks,
gaily arrayed in the plumes and purple favours of his be-

[37] Lausus, a son of king Mezentius, killed by Æneas. Mimas, a Trojan, son of Amycus and Theano, and the intimate friend of Paris. He
accompanied Æneas to Italy, and was slain by Mezentius.

[38] "Antiqui *ille*, vel magnitudini, vel nobilitati adsignabant." SERVIUS.
See, however, Anthon's note. B.

[39] Vesulus, (Viso,) a large mountain in the range of the Alps, between
Liguria and Gaul, where the Po takes its rise.

[40] Compare Silius v. 442, " propioremque addere Martem Haud ausum
cuiquam, laxo ceu bellua campo Incessebatur tutis ex agmine telis." B.

trotbed spouse; as a famished lion that often ranges over the lofty stalls, (for maddening hunger prompts him,) if by chance he espies a timorous goat, or stag conspicuous for stately horns, exults yawning hideously, rears his hair on end, and couching down over [his prey], fast to the entrails clings, black gore laves his ravenous jaws: thus Mezentius rushes with alacrity on the embodied foes. Ill-fated Acron is overthrown, and expiring spurns with his heels the tawny ground, and with his blood besmears the broken lance. The same deigned not to cut off Orodes as he fled, or with the darted spear to give him a wound unseen: but, overtaking him, he confronted face to face, and encountered man to man; superior not in stratagem, but valiant arms. Then, trampling on him overthrown, and resting on his lance, [he says]: Friends, stately Orodes lies no mean portion of the war. His associates in acclamation join, repeating the joyful pæan. But he expiring [says]: Whoever thou art, not over me unrevenged, nor long shalt thou victorious rejoice; thee too like destiny awaits, and soon shalt thou on these same fields be stretched. To whom Mezentius, smiling with a mixture of indignation, [replied]: Now die; but of me let the father of gods and king of men dispose. So saying, he from the body outdrew the dart. Cruel slumbers and the iron sleep of death press down his eyes; his eyes are sealed in everlasting night.[41] Cædicus slays Alcathous, Sacrator, Hydaspes, Rapo Parthenius, and Orses extremely robust in strength; Messapus [kills] Clonius, and Ericetes the Lycaonian; the one by a fall from his unruly steed thrown on the ground; the other on foot himself on foot [assailed: against him] Lycian Agis too had stepped forth; but him Valerius, not lacking of the valour of his ancestors, overthrows: Anthronius by Salius falls, and Salius by Nealces, skilled in the javelin and far-deceiving arrow. Now stern Mars equalled the distresses and mutual deaths: the victors and the vanquished equally slew, and equally fell: nor these, nor those, know what it is to fly. In the courts of Jove the gods compassionate the fruitless rage of both, and [seem to lament] that such toils are appointed to mortals. On the one side Venus, on the other Saturnian Juno sits spectator. Pale Tisiphone in the midst of thousands wreaks her fury.

[41] I almost prefer the ablative, as in Ovid Ep. x. 113. See Burm. on Propert. ii. 10, 17. B.

But now Mezentius all turbulent and boisterous advances in the field, brandishing his massy spear; as huge Orion, when on foot he marches, cutting his way through the vast watery fields of the mid-ocean, with his shoulder overtops the waves; or, conveying an aged ash from the high mountains, stalks on the ground, and hides his head among the clouds; just so Mezentius in vast armour strides along. Him on the other hand Æneas, having descried him in the long battalion, prepares to encounter. He unterrified remains expecting his magnanimous foe, and stands firm in his own vast mass of frame; and, measuring with his eye as much space as his javelin could reach, [says,] Now let this right hand, my god, and the missile weapon [42] which I poise, be my aid; I vow that you, my own Lausus, shall be clad in the spoils torn from the pirate's body, the trophy of Æneas. He said, and hurled from afar the hissing dart: but the winged dart is by the shield flung off, and deep pierces illustrious Antores between the side and flank; Antores, the attendant of Hercules, who from Argos sent had joined Evander, and settled in his Italian city. He falls, unhappy, by another's wound, looks up to heaven, and in death remembers his beloved Argos. Then pious Æneas darts his spear: through the concave orb of triple brass, through the linen folds, and the work with three bulls' hides [43] inwoven, it made way, and settled low down in the groin; but had spent its force. Instantly Æneas, overjoyed at seeing the Tuscan blood, snatches his sword from his thigh, and darts impetuous on his confused foe. Lausus, soon as he saw it, heaved a deep groan in fond pity to his beloved sire, and the tears came trickling down his cheeks. Here be assured I shall not pass in silence either thee, praiseworthy youth, or the catastrophe of thy piteous death, or thy deeds, thou best of sons, if any future age will give credit to an act so noble. The father, drawing back his steps, quite disabled and encumbered, gave ground, and in his buckler trailed the hostile spear. The youth sprang forward, and flung himself amidst the armed troops; and stood under the

---

[42] See my note on Æsch. Sept; c. Th. p. 51, ed. Bohn. B.

[43] Observe the metaphor by which the animal itself is put for its hide. Lucan iv. 133, " cæsoque induta juvenco." Statius Theb. " clipeum vestiæe juvenco." B.

point of Æneas' sword, just as he was rising with his arm,
and fetching the stroke; and keeping him awhile at bay, sustained the shock. His friends second him with loud acclamation, till, by the target of the son protected, the father withdrew; fling showers of darts, and at a distance repel the foe
with missile weapons. Æneas storms, and keeps himself
under covert [of his shield]. And as, if at times the clouds
in a drift of hail rush down, every labouring hind flies from
the fields away, and every swain, and the traveller lurks in
some secure retreat, either on the banks of a river, or in the·
cleft of a high rock, the shower be overblown, that on the
earth, when the sun returns, they may be able to pursue the
labours of the day: just so Æneas, with darts from every
quarter overwhelmed, sustains the whole storm of war, till
the thunder spends its rage; and chides Lausus, and threatens
him thus: Whither dost thou rush to thy own destruction, .
and why dost thou attempt what exceeds thy strength? Thy
pious duty blindfolds thee unguarded. He infatuated still
braves [the hero] no less. And now the fierce wrath of the
Trojan leader rises to a greater height, and the Destinies to
Lausus collect the last threads [of life]; for Æneas through
the middle of his body plunges his mighty sword into the
youth, and buries it to the hilt.[44] The pointed steel pierced
both through the thin shield, the light armour of the vaunting
youth, and the vest, which with soft thread of gold his mother
had spun; and the blood filled his bosom: then to the shades
his soul fled mourning through the air, and left the body. But
soon as the offspring of Anchises saw his visage and dying
looks, his looks wondrously pale, in pity he drew a heavy
groan, and stretched forth his hand; and the image of his
filial piety touched his soul. Lamented youth, what recompence for those virtues, what honour becoming so great excellence, shall pious Æneas on thee now confer? Thy arms,
wherein thou rejoiced, still retain: and to the manes and
ashes of thy parents, if that be any object of thy care, I resign thee. Yet, hapless one, with this thou shalt solace thy
wretched death; by the hand of great Æneas thou fallest.[45]

[44] "Totum" seems equivalent to "capulo tenns." ʙ.
[45] Compare Ovid Met. viii. 7, "Magnaque dat nobis tantus solatia
victor." ʙ.

Then straight he chides his lingering followers, and from the
ground raises up the youth, with his blood marring his locks
in comely order dressed.

Meanwhile the father at the stream of the river Tiber
stanched his wounds with water,[46] and gave a more easy posture to his body, leaning on the trunk of a tree. From the
boughs apart his brazen helmet hangs, and his unwieldy arms
rest on the mead. Chosen youths around him stand; himself
faint, panting for breath, eases his drooping neck, having
spread on his breast a length of waving beard. Of Lausus he
incessantly inquires, and many messengers he sends again and
again to recall him [from the fight], and bear to him the
orders of his afflicted father. But his weeping friends were
carrying lifeless Lausus on their arms, a mighty corpse, and
with mighty wound overthrown.[47]

The ill-boding mind [of Mezentius] at a distance understood their groans. His hoary locks with vile dust he deforms, to heaven stretches both his hands, and fast to the body
clings: O my son, was I with such fond desire of life possessed, to suffer him whom I begot to substitute himself for
me to the foe's right hand? by these wounds of thine am I
thy father saved, living by thy death? Alas! now at length
on wretched me my exile heavy lies, now a wound is driven
deep home. I too, my son, the same have by my guilt sullied
thy fame, for odious misdeeds driven from my throne and paternal sceptre. It is I that to my country owed satisfaction,
and to the odium of my subjects ought to have forfeited my
guilty life by every kind of death. And still I live: nor yet
from men and light withdraw: but I will withdraw. Then
with these words he raises himself on his maimed thigh; and,
though the violent smart of the deep wound retards him, yet,
not cast down, he orders his courser to be brought. This was
his glory, this his solace; by this he came off victorious in all
his wars. The sympathizing animal he bespeaks, and thus
begins: Long, Rhœbus, have we lived, if aught can be said
to subsist long with mortals. To-day you shall either victorious bear away the head of Æneas, and those spoils all

---

[46] That this was the customary treatment, we learn from Celsus v. 26.
Athenæus ii. 4. B.

[47] So Silius v. 524, "Interea exanimem mœstl super arma Sychæum
Portabant Pœni, corpusque in castra ferebant." B.

bathed in his blood, and with me avenge the griefs of Lausus; or, if no efforts open a way, you shall fall with me: for never, I presume, wilt thou, most generous, deign to bear the commands of another, and a Trojan lord. He said; and received on his back, placed his limbs on the accustomed seat, and with pointed javelins loaded each hand, his head gleaming with brass, and roughly garnished with a crest of horse-hair. Thus with rapid speed he drove into the midst. Deep in his heart boils overwhelming shame: and frantic rage, with intermingled grief, and love racked with furious despair, and conscious worth: and here thrice with loud voice he called Æneas. Æneas knew him well; and, pleased [with the challenge, thus] his prayer addresses: So may that great father of the gods, so may exalted Apollo influence thee to begin the combat. This only he said, and with his menacing spear advances against him. But he [exclaimed], Most barbarous man, why thinkest thou to affright me, now that my son is snatched from me? This was the only way whereby thou couldst destroy me. I neither fear death, nor any of your gods regard. Forbear threats: now I am come to die, but first to thee these gifts I bring. He said, and hurled a dart against the foe; then after that another and another he fixes fast, and flies around in a spacious circuit; but the golden boss sustains the shock. Thrice round Æneas, as he stood against him, he rode in circles to the left, throwing javelins with his hand; thrice the Trojan hero, [wheeling as he wheels,] bears about with him in his brazen shield a frightful grove [of spears]. And now when he is tired with spinning out so long delays, and drawing out so many darts, and when he is severely harassed, being engaged in an unequal fight, revolving many thoughts in his mind, at length he springs forth, and between the hollow temples of the warrior-steed darts his lance. The horse raises himself upright, then with his heels buffets the air, and falling upon his dismounted rider, keeps him down, and falling forward, overlays his prostrate shoulder. The Trojans and Latins both with acclamations rend the sky. Æneas flies to him, and snatches his sword from the scabbard, and over him these [words pronounces]: Where is now the stern Mezentius? where is that wild impetuosity of soul? On the other hand, the Tuscan, as soon as lifting up his eyes to heaven he began to breathe the

air, and recover his senses, [said,] Despiteful foe, why insult-
est thou and threatenest death? There is no crime in shedding my blood; nor engaged I in the combat on such terms
[that you should spare my life], nor did my Lausus make
such a contract with you on my behalf. One thing I implore,
by that grace, if any grace to a vanquished foe belongs, suffer
my body to be covered with earth. I know the cruel resentment of my subjects besets me round;[48] defend me, I pray
you, from this outrage, and to a grave consign me in partnership with my son. He said, and in his throat, not unpre-
pared, receives the blade, and pours forth life in the blood
streaming on his armour.

BOOK XI.

In the Eleventh Book, the funeral of Pallas is solemnized. Latinus, in
council, attempts a reconciliation with Æneas, which is prevented by Turnus, and by the hostile approach of the Trojan army. Camilla greatly
signalizes herself, but is at last slain, when night puts an end to the
combat.

MEANWHILE Aurora rising left the ocean. Æneas, though
both his cares strongly urge him to allot time for interring
his friends, and his mind is disturbed by the death [of Pallas],
yet, in consequence of his victory, paid to the gods his vows
soon as the dawn appeared.[1] A huge oak, with its boughs
on every side lopped off, he erected on a rising ground, and
adorned it with shining arms, the spoils of king Mezentius:
to thee a trophy, thou great warrior-god! He fits [to the
trunk] his crest dripping with blood, and the hero's shattered
arms, and his breastplate in twice six places dented and transfixed; and to the left arm he fastens his target of brass, and
from the neck suspends his ivory-hilted sword. Then thus
beginning he encourages his joyous friends (for all the chiefs
in a crowded body enclosed him): Warriors, our most important work is done: henceforth all fear be banished. For
what remains, these are the spoils, the first-fruits of victory

---

[48] He feared that they would deprive him of sepulture. B.

[1] Servius well remarks that those who were polluted by a funeral could
not make offerings to the gods, until they had been purified. If, however, as in the present case, a man was bound to the performance of both
duties, he first made his offering, and then engaged in the funeral rites.

won from that insolent tyrant; and to this state Mezentius is
by my arm reduced. Now to the king and the walls of Latium our way lies open: make ready your arms, and with
stout hearts and hopes anticipate the war, that obstacles may
not detain you unawares, or deliberation, resulting from fear,
retard you, slow of movement, when first the gods permit us
to pluck up the standard, and to lead forth the youth from
the camp. Meanwhile let us commit to earth the unburied
corpses of our friends; which is the sole honour in deep Acheron. Go, he says, with the last duties grace those illustrious
souls who for us have won this country with their blood; and
first to the mourning city of Evander let Pallas be conveyed,
whom, not deficient in prowess, a gloomy inauspicious day cut
off, and sank in an untimely death. Thus weeping he speaks,
and to the threshold takes his way, where aged Acœtes
watched the corpse of lifeless Pallas laid out: Acœtes, who
formerly was armour-bearer to Arcadian Evander, and now
with less auspicious omens came [to the war], appointed
guardian to his darling foster-son. The whole retinue of his
servants stood around, a band of Trojans and mourning dames
of Ilium, with tresses in usual form dishevelled. But soon as
Æneas entered the lofty gates, beating their breasts they
raise to heaven a mighty groan, and the palace rings with
mournful lamentation. When he himself beheld the bolstered
head and face of Pallas, white and cold as snow, and in his
smooth breast the gaping wound of the Ausonian spear, he
thus with gushing tears begins: Lamented youth, how envious
was Fortune, just when she began to smile, to snatch thee
from me, that thou shouldst not see my kingdom, nor be borne
victorious to thy paternal dwelling! Not such things of thee
I at parting promised to thy sire Evander, when taking leave
of me with embraces, he sent me against a mighty empire,
and trembling warned me that the enemy were fierce, and
that the battle would be with a sturdy nation. And now he
indeed, highly possessed with empty hope, is, perhaps, both
making vows, and loading the altars with offerings; while we
in grief with unavailing pomp attend the youth, a lifeless
corpse, and now released from his allegiance to the powers
above. Ill-fated sire, thou shalt see the dismal funeral of thy
own son! Is it thus we return? are these our hoped-for triumphs? this my boasted confidence? Yet, Evander, thou

shalt not see him with inglorious wounds repulsed; nor on thy son, thus saved, shalt thou, in spite of paternal affection, imprecate an accursed death. Ah me, how glorious a protector thou, Ausonia, and thou, Iülus, [in him] hast lost!

When he had thus vented his grief, he orders them to bear away the woeful corpse, and sends a thousand men, selected from the whole army, to accompany these last honours, and bear a part in the parent's tears; small consolation for such mighty woe, but due to the unhappy sire! others with forward zeal weave hurdles, and a pliant bier of arbute rods and oaken twigs, and with a covering of boughs shade the bed high raised. Here on the rural couch aloft they raise the youth: like a flower, either of the tender violet or drooping hyacinth, cropped by a virgin's hand,[2] from which not the gay bloom, or its own fair form, hath yet departed; the parent soil no longer feeds it, or supplies it with strength. Then two vests, stiff with embroidery of gold and purple, Æneas brought forth; which formerly Sidonian Dido, pleased with the task, with her own hands for him had wrought, and striped the stuff with slender threads of gold. In one of these, the last ornament, he sorrowful arrays the youth, and muffles up in a veil his hair devoted to the flames. Besides, he piles up many prizes of the Laurentine war, and orders the booty to be led in long procession. He adds the steeds and arms whereof he despoiled the foe. And to their backs he had bound the hands of those whom to his shade as offering he would send, to sprinkle with their shed blood the flame; and the chiefs themselves he commands to bear trunks of trees decked with hostile arms, and the names of the enemies to be inscribed upon them. Unhappy Acœtes, worn out with age, is led, now with his fists tearing his breasts, now with his nails his face; and bending forward with his whole body, he lies prostrate on the ground. His chariots too they lead besmeared with Rutulian blood. Next his warrior-horse, Æthon, his trappings laid aside, moves on weeping, and with the big drops bedews his cheeks. Others bear his spear and helmet: for of the rest victorious Turnus is possessed. Then in mournful plight, the phalanx, the Trojan and the Tuscan leaders follow, and the Arcadians with inverted arms. After

[2] Propert. i. 20, 39, "Quæ modo decerpens tenero pueriliter ungui Proposito florem prætulit officio." B.

the whole body of attendants had advanced before in long procession, Æneas paused, and with a deep groan subjoined these words: We to other scenes of woe, by the same horrid fate of war, are summoned hence. Farewell for ever, illustrious Pallas, and adieu for ever. This said, he bent his course to the high walls, and directed his steps back to the camp.

And now from the city of king Latinus ambassadors came bearing olive boughs, supplicating grace [from Æneas]; that he would deliver to them the bodies [of their dead], which by the sword lay scattered over the field, and permit them to be entombed in the earth; [alleging] that with the vanquished and the lifeless war is at an end; [and hoping] that he would spare a people to whose hospitality and alliance he was once invited.

Whom, not unreasonable in their demands, the courteous Æneas receives with grace, and adds these words: What undeserved fate, ye Latins, hath involved you in so disastrous a war, who thus decline us your friends? Is it for the dead, and the slain by the chance of war, you implore peace? I truly would grant it to the living too. I should not have come hither unless the Fates had here assigned my settlement and place of residence; nor with the [Latin] nation wage I war. With us your king renounced hospitality, and rather trusted himself to the arms of Turnus. More just had it been for Turnus to expose himself to this death. If to terminate the war by personal valour, if to expel the Trojans, he intends, me in these arms he ought to have encountered: he [of us two] had lived, to whom God or his own right hand had given life. Now go, and under your unfortunate countrymen apply the funeral fire. Æneas said. They in silence stood astonished, and turning held their eyes and faces to each other.

Then aged Drances,[*] who still by calumny and invectives vented his animosity on young Turnus, thus replies in turn: Trojan hero, mighty in fame, but mightier still in arms, by what praises shall I exalt thee to heaven? which shall I most admire, thy justice or thy achievements in war? We truly with grateful hearts will bear this answer back to our city; and, if any fortune shall open the way, will associate thee to king Latinus: let Turnus seek alliances for himself. We will even with

---

[*] Drances, a friend of king Latinus, remarkable for his eloquence and weakness.

pleasure rear up the fabric of your destined walls, and on our shoulders bear the stones of Troy.

He said; and all with one voice murmured their assent. They settled a truce for twice six days: and during the intermediate[4] peace, Trojans and Latins promiscuous without hostility ranged the woods along the mountains. Felled by the two-edged steel the ash crashes; pines shot up to the stars they overthrow; they neither cease to cleave with wedges the oaken planks and fragrant cedar, nor to convey in groaning waggons the mountain-ashes.

And now flying fame, the harbinger of so great woe, fills Evander and Evander's palace and city; fame, which just now to Latium bore the news that Pallas was victorious. The Arcadians rush to the gates, and, as the ancient manner was, snatched up funeral torches. With a long train of flames the path all shines, and far and wide illuminates[5] the fields. The band of Trojans advancing opposite to them join the lamenting troops; whom, soon as the matrons beheld approaching the walls, they inflame the mourning city with their shrieks. But no force can restrain Evander from rushing through the midst. The bier being laid down, on Pallas he falls prostrate, and with sobs and groans clings to [the corpse]; and at length with much ado for grief is a passage opened to these words: These, O Pallas, are not the promises thou gavest thy parent, that with more caution thou wouldst trust thyself to the savage combat. I was not ignorant how far rising glory in arms, and the bewitching renown of the first action, might carry you. Ah! fatal to the youth his first essays, hard his probation in early war! Alas! my vows and prayers by none of the gods regarded! Thou most holy partner of my bed, happy in thy death, and not to this woe reserved; whilst I by living on have overpassed my natural bounds to remain a childless father.[6] When I followed the confederate arms of Troy, the Rutulians should have overwhelmed me with their darts: my life I had resigned, and me, not Pallas, this pomp had home con-

[4] "*Media*: namque *sequester* est aut medius inter duos altercantes; aut ad quem aliquid ad tempus seponitur." Servius. B.

[5] Literally, "renders distinguishable." B.

[6] Literally, "surviving [my own son]." This was thought a severe misfortune. So Plautus, "Ita ut tuum vis unicum gnatum tua superesse vitae, suspitem et superstitem." B.

veyed. Nor you, ye Trojans, will I accuse, nor your alliance, nor those right hands we joined in hospitable league : this stroke of fortune was destined for my old age. However, if untimely death awaited my son, it will be some satisfaction, that ushering the Trojans into Latium he fell, having first slain thousands of the Volscians. And now with no other funeral obsequies, O Pallas, can I grace thee, than what pious Æneas, and the noble Trojans, the Tuscan leaders, and whole army of the Tuscans, [have given thee]. Thy illustrious trophies they bear, those whom to death thy right hand offered. Thou too, O Turnus, shouldst have stood [among them] a huge trunk in arms, had my age been equal, and my strength from years the same. But why do I, hapless one, detain the Trojans from the war ? Go, and faithfully bear back these mandates to your king : If I linger out a hated life, after Pallas is slain, it is in consequence of thy [avenging] right hand ; from which you see Turnus is justly due to a son and sire. This post [of honour] is alone reserved for thee and thy fortune. It is not joy in life I seek, nor is it fit I should ; but I wish to bear the tidings to my son down to the shades below.

Meanwhile to wretched mortals Aurora had brought forth the benignant light, renewing the works and labours [of the day].[1] Now father Æneas, now Tarchon, on the winding shore erected funeral piles. Hither they conveyed, each after the manner of his ancestors, the bodies of their dead ; and the sad[1] fires being applied under them, the lofty sky with smoke is hidden in darkness. Thrice round the blazing piles they ran, clad in shining armour ; thrice they encompassed the mournful funeral fire on horseback, and sent forth doleful yells. With their tears is the earth bedewed, bedewed are their arms. The shrieks of men and clang of trumpets pierce through the sky. Next into the fire some throw the spoils torn from the Latins slain, helmets, and gleaming swords, bits, and glowing wheels : some, well-known gifts, their own bucklers and unsuccessful darts. Many heads of oxen all around are offered

---

[1] Cf. Quintus Calab. vi. 4, τοὶ δ' εἰς ἔργα τράποντο βροτοὶ μετά φθινύθοντες. B.

[1] This is the usual interpretation of "atris ignibus," but I think it is far more natural to understand, "dark, pitchy flames." So Eur. Troad. 550, δόμοις δὲ παμφαῖς σἴλας πυρὸς μέλαιναν αἴγλαν Ἔδωκεν. B.

victims to death ; and over the flames they stab bristly boars,
and sheep snatched from all the fields : then along the whole
shore they view their burning friends, and watch their half-
consumed piles : nor can they be torn from them, before humid
night inverts the face of heaven, bespangled with shining
stars.

Nor with less care the sorrowing Latins in a different quarter reared numberless piles ; and they partly bury in the earth
many bodies of their heroes, and part carried off they to the
neighbouring fields convey, and send back to the city. The
rest, and a vast heap of promiscuous slaughter, without number and without honour, they burn : then on all sides the spacious fields, as rivalling each other, blaze together with frequent
fires. The third day's light had from the sky removed the
chill shades : when in sadness they huddled together on the
hearths the heaped-up ashes and bones mingled in confusion,
and loaded them with a warm mound of earth. But now in
the courts of opulent Latinus, and in the city, is the chief uproar, and by far the deepest scene of mourning. Here mothers
and hapless brides, here tender-hearted sisters in deep anguish,
and striplings of their sires bereft, curse the rueful war, and
the nuptials of Turnus ; and himself they urge by arms, himself by the sword, to decide the quarrel, since for himself alone
he claims the crown of Italy and the first honours. These the
malicious Drances aggravates, and protests that Turnus alone
is called, alone is challenged to the combat. On the other side
the votes of many, in various speech, are given for Turnus,
and him the queen's illustrious name protects ; and his own
distinguished fame, for trophies justly won, supports the hero.

Amidst these commotions, in the heat of this raging tumult,
lo ! to complete the distress, the ambassadors, from Diomede's
imperial city [returning] sorrowful, bring their answer ; that
nothing was effected by all the expense of so great labour :
that neither the gifts, nor gold, nor importunate prayers, had
aught availed ; that the Latins must have recourse to other
arms, or sue for peace from the Trojan prince. With great
grief king Latinus himself faints away. The wrath of the
gods, and the recent tombs before his face, declare that
Æneas, the messenger of fate, is led on by a manifest divine
impulse.

Therefore within the lofty palace he assembles his great

council, and the peers of his realm, summoned by his imperial
order. They meet together, and flock to the royal apartments
along the crowded ways. In the centre, with unjoyous aspect, sits Latinus, both most advanced in age, and first in
sway And here he orders the ambassadors now returned
from the Ætolian city, to say what message they bring back,
and demands each particular answer in its order. Then silence sat on every tongue; and Venulus thus, in obedience to
command, begins: We have seen, O citizens, Diomede and
the Argive camp, and measuring a length of way, have overpassed a thousand dangers, and touched that hand by which
Troy's kingdom fell. He victorious was raising in the plains
of Apulian Garganus⁹ the city Argyripa,¹⁰ from the name of
his native country. After we were admitted, and had permission given to speak in the presence, we first present our
gifts; declare our name and country; who made war upon
us; what errand drew us to Arpi. Our message heard, he
thus with mild accent replied: O happy nations, once Saturn's
realm, ancient Ausonians, what fortune disturbs you peaceful,
and prompts you to rouse unusual wars? As many of us as
with the sword violated the lands of Ilium, (I wave those extremities which in fighting under its lofty walls we sustained,
what illustrious heroes that Simois of theirs swept away,) have
borne unutterable sufferings over the world, and all punishments for our crime; a band whom even Priam would pity.
Minerva's disastrous constellation knows, and the Eubœan
rocks, and vengeful Caphareus.¹¹ Ever since that expedition,
have we on different coasts been driven; Menelaus, the son
of Atreus, is exiled as far as the pillars of Proteus;¹² Ulysses
hath seen the Cyclops of Ætna. Shall I mention [the tragic
fate of] Neoptolemus' realms, and the overthrow of Idomeneus'
settlement, or the [dispersion of the] Locri who inhabit Libya's coast? The prince of Mycenæ¹³ himself, the leader of

⁹ Garganus (St. Angelo,) a lofty mountain of Apulia, projecting in the
form of a promontory into the Adriatic Sea.
¹⁰ Argyripa, or Arpi.
¹¹ Caphareus, (Cape D'Oro,) a lofty promontory on the south-east coast
of Eubœa, an island in the Ægean Sea.
¹² Proteus, a king of Egypt, on whose coasts Menelaus, in his return
from the Trojan war, was forced by stress of weather.
¹³ Prince of Mycenæ, Agamemnon, who was chosen chief commander
of the Grecian forces in the war against Troy. After the destruction of

the illustrious Greeks, fell by the hand of his unnatural[14]
spouse, in the first entrance to his palace; and his adulterous
assassin by traitorous means lay in wait for the conqueror of
Asia.[16] [Or shall I mention] how the envious gods forbade
that I myself, restored to my native country, should see my
much-loved spouse, and lovely Calydon? Even now prodigies
of horrid aspect pursue me; my lost associates, into the aërial
regions have winged their way, and, to birds transformed,
wander along the rivers, (ah, dire vengeance on my friends!)
and fill the rocks with doleful notes. And indeed I had reason to expect these calamities ever since that time, when with
the sword I madly assaulted the celestial beings, and violated
the hand of Venus with a wound. But urge me not, urge not
me to fights like these: neither with the Trojans wage I any
war, now that Troy is overthrown; nor remember I with joy
their former woes. Those gifts, which to me you brought
from your native coasts, transfer to Æneas. We against his
keen darts have stood, and engaged him hand to hand; trust
me, who by experience know how stern he rises to his shield,
with what a whirl[16] he throws his lance. Had Ida's land
produced two such heroes more, the Trojans had first advanced to the cities of Inachus, and Greece by a reverse of
fate would have mourned. Whatever obstruction was given
at the walls of stubborn Troy, the victory of the Greeks was
suspended by the hand of Hector and Æneas, and was retarded till the tenth year. Both for valour are distinguished,
both for noble feats of arms; this man in piety excels. Let
your right hands be joined in league, by whatever means it is
permitted; but beware of opposing arms to arms. Thus, best
of kings, you have at once both heard his answer, and his resolution on this important war. Scarcely had the deputies
spoken, when through Ausonia's troubled sons a various noise
ran; as, when rocks retard a river's rapid course, from the
pent-up flood a murmur arises, and with the beating waves
the neighbouring banks resound.

that city, Agamemnon returned to Argos, where he was murdered by his
wife Clytemnestra and her paramour Ægisthus.
[14] For "infandæ," Macrobius, Sat. iv. 4, reads "infandum!" which is
approved by Burmann on Anthol. Lat. T. i. p. 196. B.
[15] See Anthon. The readings vary, since the time of Servius. D.
[16] So "ballistæ turbine," Lucan. iii. 465; "directo turbine robur,"
Silic. iv. 542. B.

Soon as their minds were calmed, and their tumultuous tongues were hushed, the king, having first addressed the gods, from his lofty throne begins: I indeed could wish, ye Latins, and it had been better, that we had before determined on the common cause, and not to call a council at such a juncture,[17] when the foe lays siege to our walls. Incommodious war, O citizens, we wage with a nation of gods and heroes invincible, whom no battles tire out, and who, when vanquished, cannot lay down the sword. What hope you entertained from the invited arms of the Ætolians, now dismiss: each must be his own hope: but how feeble this is, you see. In what ruin the rest of our affairs are involved, all is by yourselves both seen and felt. Nor yet accuse I any: what the highest pitch of valour could, has been achieved; with the whole strength of the realm we have struggled. Now then, (lend your attention,) I will unfold, and briefly show what purpose rises in my doubtful soul. To me an ancient tract of land belongs, near the Tuscan river, in length extended to the west, even beyond Sicania's[18] bounds: the Auruncians and Rutulians sow, and harass with the share the stubborn hills, and turn to pasture their most rugged parts. Let this whole region, and the lofty mountain's piny tracts, be given away to the friendship of the Trojans; and let us pronounce equal terms of peace, and, as our allies, invite them into our realms. Let them settle, if they have such strong desire, and build cities. But if they have a mind to take possession of other territories and another country, and if from our land they can withdraw, let us build twice ten ships of Italian timber, or more, if they are able to man them: all the materials lie along the river; let themselves order the number and fashion of the vessels; let us with money, men, and naval stores supply them. Besides, our pleasure is, that a hundred ambassadors of the first rank from Latium go to bear our instructions, and confirm the alliance, and in their hands extend the boughs of peace, bearing presents of ivory, and sums of gold, a chair of state, and royal robe, the ensigns of our crown. Advise for the common good,[19] and relieve a distressed state.

[17] This is the proper meaning. See Drakenb. on Sil. viii. 112. B.

[18] Sicania, an ancient name of Sicily, which it received from the Sicani, a people of Spain, who first passed into Italy, and afterwards into Sicily, where they established themselves.

[19] So "in commune" is used, as in Tacit. Agr. § 12. Sueton. Ner. § 15. B.

Then the same hostile Drances rises, (whom the glory of
Turnus inflamed with oblique envy [20] and malignant stings ;
abounding in wealth, and more in tongue, but a cold champion
in war, yet deemed of no mean authority in consultations ; in
faction powerful ; him his mother's quality inspired with the
pride of noble blood, but by the father's side he was of birth
obscure,[21]) and loads Turnus with these invectives, and aggravates animosity : Gracious sovereign, you ask counsel in an
affair which to none is obscure, nor requires our debate. All
must own that they well know what the weal of the nation
demands; but they hesitate to speak their mind. Let him
allow that freedom of speech, and moderate his vaunts, for
whose inauspicious influence and perverse conduct (for my
part I will speak out, even though he should threaten me with
hostility and death) we have seen so many illustrious chiefs
perish, and the whole city sit in mourning; while he tempts
the Trojan camp trusting to flight, and defies heaven with his
arm. To those numerous gifts which you order to be sent and
delivered to the Trojans, this one, this one more, O best of
sovereigns, add ; nor let any one's violent remonstrances deter
thee from giving away your daughter, by a father's right, to
an illustrious son-in-law, (a worthy match,) and from confirm-
ing this peace by a perpetual alliance. And if such dread [of
Turnus] haunts our minds and souls, him let us implore, and
from him sue for grace; that to his sovereign he may resign,
and to his country give up his proper right. Why dost thou
so often expose thy wretched citizens to open dangers? O
thou, the source and origin of these ills to Latium! no safety
[is for us] in war : to thee, O Turnus, we all sue for peace,
at the same time for the sole inviolable pledge of peace.[22] I
the first, (whom as your malicious foe you image to yourself,
nor am I concerned to disprove the charge,) lo! I come thy
suppliant: have pity on thy own ; lay aside thy fierceness,
and baffled quit the field. Full many deaths have we with
loss of victory seen, and brought the extended fields to desolation. Or, if fame have influence, if in your breast such fortitude you lodge, and if your heart be so much set on a palace

---

[20] "Qui non ex aperto impugnabat Turnum ; sed eum reipublicæ
simulata defensione lacerabat." SERVIUS. B.
[21] Literally, "he bore himself] uncertain on the father's side." B.
[22] i. e. Lavinia. B.

for your dowry; dare it, and bravely expose your breast adverse to the foe. Forsooth, that Turnus may be blessed with a
royal consort, we, abject souls, may be strewn on the field, an
unburied and unwept throng. And now, if you have any
spirit, if you have aught of your country's Mars, look him in
the face who gives you the challenge. With these invectives
the fierce mind of Turnus was inflamed: he groans, and from
the bottom of his breast forces out these accents: Drances, I
own, you have always a rich profusion of words at the time
when wars call for action; and when the fathers are convened,
you are there the foremost: but this is not a time to fill the
court with words which fly in big torrents from thee in safety,
while the bulwarks of our walls keep off the foe, and the
trenches float not with blood. Wherefore thunder on in noisy
eloquence, as thou art wont, and arraign me of cowardice,
thou [the valiant] Drances, since thy right hand hath raised
so many heaps of slaughtered Trojans, and every where thou
deckest the fields with trophies. You may, however, put that
animated valour of yours to the proof; for not far have we to
seek our foes; they all around beset our walls. March we
against the adversary? why do you demur? will your prowess
always lie in your blustering tongue, and in those feet only
swift to fly? Am I routed? or will any one, thou most abject
wretch, justly tax me with being routed, who shall view the
swollen Tiber rise with Trojan blood, and Evander's whole
family with his race stretched on the ground, and the Arcadians stripped of their armour? Not so Bitias and bulky
Pandarus me proved, nor those thousands whom, in one day,
I victorious sent down to Tartarus, enclosed within the walls,
and shut up by the rampart of the foe. No safety, [you say,]
is in war. Go, madman, vent such language to the Dardanian
chief, and thy own party. Wherefore cease not to embroil
all with dreadful alarms, to extol the strength of the twice
vanquished race, and on the other hand to depress the arms
of Latinus. Now the Myrmidonian[23] chiefs tremble at the
Phrygian arms! now Diomede and Larissæan Achilles! and
the river Aufidus[24] flies back from the Adriatic waves; even
when the wicked dissembler feigns himself under terror of

---

[23] All this is spoken ironically. B.
[24] Aufidus, (Ofanto,) a river of Apulia in Italy, falling into the Adriatic. The battle of Cannæ was fought on the banks of the Aufidus.

my menaces, and by his own fear aggravates the charge against
me. Cease from being disturbed; never shalt thou lose such
a soul as thine by this right hand: let it dwell with thee, and
rest in that ignoble breast. Now I return to thee, sire, and
to thy important debates. If in our arms you repose no further
confidence; if we are so desolate, and utterly undone by our
army being once defeated, and our fortune is capable of no
redress; let us sue for peace, and let us extend our hands unarmed. Yet oh! did any of our wonted worth remain, that
man were happy in my judgment beyond all others, in his
toils, and heroic in soul, who, that he might not see aught like
this, fell once for all, and dying bit the ground. But if we
both have resources, and youthful troops still fresh, and Italian
cities and nations left to our aid; if the Trojans purchase their
honour with much blood; if they too have their funerals, and
the storm [of war has raged] through all with equal fury;
why faint we dishonourably in the first entrance [to the
war]? why does trembling seize our limbs, before the trumpet
[sounds]? Length of days, and the various labour of change-
ful time, have reduced many things to a better state: fortune,
that visits alternately [with good and ill], hath baffled many,
and again placed them on a firm basis. The Ætolian prince,
[it seems,] and Arpi, will not support us; but Messapus will,
and the fortunate Tolumnius,[20] and those leaders whom so
many nations have sent: nor shall small glory attend the select troops from Latium and the Laurentine fields. With us
too is Camilla,[21] of the illustrious race of the Volscians, who
leads a squadron of horse, and troops gaily glittering with
brass. But if the Trojans demand me alone to the fight, and
if this be your pleasure, and I so much obstruct your common good; victory has not hitherto with so much hate abandoned my right hand, as for me to decline any enterprise for
so glorious a prospect. I will advance against [Æneas] with
confidence, though he should even approve himself a great
Achilles, and sheathe himself in similar armour forged by
Vulcan's hands. To you, and to Latinus, my [promised]
father-in-law, I, Turnus, not inferior in valour to any of the

---

[20] Tolumnius, an augur in the army of Turnus against Æneas, who
violated the league between the Rutulians and Trojans, and was afterwards slain.

[21] Camilla, the virago female warrior.

ancient heroes, have this life devoted. Does Æneas challenge
me alone? Heaven grant he may. Nor let Drances rather,
if either this be the angry resolve of the gods, by death make
the atonement; or, if an opportunity of glory and valour, let
him bear away [the prize].

They in mutual contention were debating on the perplexed
state of their affairs, Æneas was advancing his camp and army
[towards the city of Laurentum]. Lo, in great hurry, a messenger rushes through the court, and fills the city with dreadful alarms; that, from the Tiber's stream, the Trojans, arranged in battle-array, and the Tuscan host, were marching
down over all the plains. Forthwith their minds were seized
with perturbation, the hearts of the populace are stunned, and
their rage with keen impulse is roused. In hurry they call
for arms in hand; for arms, the storming youth exclaim: the
fathers in sadness mourn and repine in low accents.[27] Here,
from every quarter, the loud clamour ascends with various
discordant notes to the skies: just as when by chance in some
tall grove flocks of birds alight, or in Padusa's[28] fishy streams,
hoarse swans raise a clattering din through the loquacious
floods. Citizens, says Turnus, seizing the opportunity, convene your council, and seated harangue in praise of peace,
whilst they rush into our kingdom in arms. This said, he
instantly put himself in motion, and quick from the lofty hall
withdrew. You, Volusus, he says, command to arms the
Volscian troops, and lead on the Rutulians; ye, Messapus, and
Coras[29] with your brother, pour abroad the armed horsemen
over the extended plains; let some secure the passes to the
city, and man the towers; the rest employ their arms with me
where I shall command. Instant to the walls they flock from
all quarters of the town. The sire, Latinus himself, quits the
council and his great designs [of peace], and distracted with
the dismal conjuncture, adjourns; himself he much accuses,
that he had not directly received the Trojan hero, and to the
city admitted him as his son-in-law. Others dig trenches
before the gates, or heave up to them rocks and palisades;
the hoarse trumpet sounds the bloody signal for the war:

---

[27] This is the proper force of "mussant." B.
[28] Padusa, the most southern mouth of the Po, from which there was
a cut to the town of Ravenna.
[29] Coras, a brother of Catillus and Tiburtus, who fought against Ænec-

then in various circling bands, matrons and boys crowned the ramparts: the extremity of distress calls every one. Meanwhile the queen, with a great retinue of matrons, is borne aloft to the temple and high towers of Pallas, carrying offerings; and by her side attends the virgin Lavinia, the cause of so great woe, fixing on the ground her beauteous eyes. The matrons follow, and with incense fume the temple, and from the lofty threshold pour forth their doleful prayers: Patroness of war, powerful in arms, Tritonian virgin, crush with thine arm the Phrygian pirate's lance, and stretch himself prostrate on the ground, and overthrow him under our lofty gates.

Turnus himself, with emulous ardour raging, is armed for battle; and now, clad in his Rutulian corslet, was rough with brazen scales, and had sheathed his legs in gold, his temples yet naked; to his side he had buckled on his sword, and from the high fort speeding his way shone all in gold; with spirit he exults, and already in hope anticipates the foe: as when the courser, having burst his bonds, flies from the stall, at length at liberty, and possessed of the open plain; either to the pastures and herds of mares he bends his way, or accustomed to be laved in the well-known flood, springs forth, and rearing up his crest on high, neighs with wanton pride; and his mane plays on his neck and shoulders. Whom full in the face, Camilla, attended by her Volscian squadron, meets, and under the very gates the queen leaps down from her horse; after whose example the whole troop, quitting their steeds, slid down to earth. Then thus she speaks: Turnus, if justly in themselves the brave may aught confide, I dare, and promise to stand the shock of the Trojan host, and singly to make head against the Tuscan horse. Suffer me with this arm to tempt the first dangers of the war: near the walls stay you behind on foot, and guard the city. To this Turnus, with eyes fixed on the formidable maiden, [replies]: O heroine, glory of Italy, what thanks can I prepare to express, or what return can I make to thee? But now since that soul of thine is superior to all things, share with me the toil. Æneas, as fame and the scouts we sent bring sure advice, with wicked purpose hath sent on light-armed horse to scour the plains: himself along the desert height of the mountains, hastening down its brow, marches against the city. A stratagem of war I devise, in a winding path of the wood to beset the twofold defile with an armed band. Do you in close fight engage the Tuscan horse. The brave Messapus will be with you, and the Latin troops, and the Tiburtine band: and do thou also assume the general's charge. He said, and in like terms animates Messapus and the confederate chiefs to the fight, and marches on against the foe. In a mazy winding tract a valley lies, commodious for ambush and the wiles of war; which a gloomy flank of wood encloses with thick boughs: whither leads a scanty path, narrow defiles and malignant passes guide. Over this, in the mountain's heights and lofty summit, lie a concealed plain and safe retreats; whether from right or left you wish to attack an enemy, or from the ridge to harass him, and tumble on him ponderous rocks. Hither young Turnus repairs along the path's well-known track; he with expedition seized the post, and in the dangerous thickets insidiously lay.

Meanwhile Diana in the superior mansions addressed swift Opis,[20] one of her virgin train and sacred retinue, and with sad accent pronounced these words: O nymph, Camilla to cruel war sets out, and is with our arms in vain arrayed, she who is dear to me above her fellows: nor is this a new passion that rises in Diana, and with a sudden fondness moves my soul. When Metabus,[31] expelled from his kingdom for invidious measures, and insolent abuse of power, quitted his ancient city Privernum, flying amidst the contests of war, he carried off the infant his companion in exile, and from her mother's name Casmilla, with small variation, called her Camilla. He, in his bosom bearing her before him, to the remote mountains and solitary groves took his way; cruel darts pursued him on all sides, and the Volscians hovered about with troops around him spread. Lo, in the midst of his flight, Amasenus overflowing foamed over his highest banks; such a torrent of rain had burst from the clouds: he, preparing to swim, is retarded by his tenderness for the child, and fears for his darling charge. As he was pondering every expedient within himself, suddenly this resolution with reluctance settled [in his breast]. An enormous javelin, which in his strong hand the warrior chanced to wield, solid with

---

[20] Opis, a nymph among Diana's attendants, who avenged the death of Camilla by shooting Aruns, by whose hand the queen had fallen.

[31] Metabus, king of Privernum, a city of the Volsci in Latium, and father of Camilla.

knots and well-seasoned oak; to this he fastens the babe wrapped up in bark and sylvan cork, and with dexterity binds her about the middle of the dart; which poising in his vast hand, he thus addresses himself to heaven: To thee, virgin daughter of Latona, auspicious inmate of the woods, this child, thy handmaid, I in a father's right devote: wielding thy weapons first she flies through the air, thy suppliant, from the foe: O goddess, I implore thee, receive thy own, who now is committed to the uncertain winds. He said, and with inbent arm flung the whirled lance; the waves resound; over the rapid stream ill-fated Camilla on the whizzing javelin flies. But Metabus, a numerous troop now pursuing him more closely, flings himself into the flood, and, master of his wish, plucks from the grassy turf the spear, with the virgin, Diana's gift. Him no cities, houses, or walls received; nor, by reason of his savage nature, would he have condescended [so to live]: but in the lonely mountains he led a shepherd's life. There among the brakes and horrid lairs, he nurtured his child from the dugs of a brood-mare, and with animal milk, milking the teats into her tender lips. And soon as the infant with the first prints of her feet had marked the ground, he loaded her hands with the pointed javelin, and from the shoulders of the little girl hung a bow and arrows. Instead of ornaments of gold for the hair, instead of being arrayed in a long trailing robe, a tiger's hide hangs over her back down from her head. Even then with tender hand she flung childish darts, and whirled round her head a smooth-thonged sling, and struck down a Strymonian crane or white swan. Many matrons through the Tuscan towns in vain wished her for their daughter-in-law. She with Diana alone content, a spotless maid, cherishes the perpetual love of darts and virginity. Would she had never been in love with war like this, nor attempted to assault the Trojans! My favourite, and one of my retinue, she might now have been. But come, O nymph, since it is so determined by cruel fates, glide down from the sky, and visit the Latin coast, where with inauspicious omens the woeful fight is ushered in. Take these [weapons], and from thy quiver draw forth a vengeful arrow: by this, whoever with a wound shall violate her sacred body, whether Trojan or Italian, let him to me without distinction pay the forfeit with his blood. Then in a hollow cloud will I into a

tomb convey the corpse and uncaptured arms of my lamented
maid, and restore her to her native land. She said : but Opis,
shooting down through the light airy regions of the sky, rattled along, her body wrapped around in a black whirlwind.

But the Trojan host meanwhile approach the walls, and the
Tuscan chiefs and the whole army of horsemen in order were
ranged in troops. The prancing courser neighs aloud over
all the plain, and battles with the tightened reins, this way and
that way wheeling about: then far and wide an iron field of
spears bristles to the view, and the plains shoot a fiery glare
with arms raised aloft. Again on the other side opposed to
these appear in the field Messapus, and the swift Latins, and
Coras with his brother, and virgin Camilla's wing : and with
right hands drawn back stretch forth their spears far before
them, and brandish their darts : the advance of the heroes and
neighing of the steeds appear more and more fierce. And
now each army, advancing within a javelin's throw, make a
halt: with a sudden shout they spring forth, and cheer on
their sprightly steeds: at once from all quarters they pour
thick showers of darts, like snow, and with their shade the
face of heaven is screened. Forthwith Tyrrhenus and fierce
Aconteus, exerting their whole force, rush on each other
with lance to lance opposed, and first with mighty noise give
the first shock, and with violent contact dash their horses'
breasts against each other. Aconteus, tossed [from his steed]
after the manner of a thunderbolt, or weight shot from an
engine, is flung headlong to a distance, and disperses his
life in air. Instantly the lines are thrown into disorder; and
the Latins put to flight, cast their shields behind, and turn the
horses to the city. The Trojans pursue: Asylas chief leads
on the troops. And now they approached the gates: when
the Latins again raise a shout, and wheel about the pliant
necks [of their steeds]; the others fly, and, giving their horses
full reins, retreat: as when the sea rolling with alternate
tides now rushes on the land, and foaming throws over the
rocks its waves, and with its skirts overflows the extremity of
the strand: now back with rapid motion, and sucking in
again the stones rolled . backwards with the tide, it retreats,
and with the ebbing current leaves the shore. Twice the
Tuscans drove the flying Rutulians to their walls: twice the
repulsed [Rutulians] face about on their foes, who, with their

targets defend their backs. But, after joining battle the third
time, they mingled their whole armies in close fight, and man
singles out his man; then are dying groans; and arms, and
bodies, and expiring steeds, mingled with slaughtered heaps
of men, roll in deep blood: a furious combat ensues. Orsilochus against the horse of Remulus, when he dreaded to encounter the rider himself, hurled a lance, and left the steel
beneath his ear: with which blow the courser rages bounding
high, and, impatient of the wound, tosses his legs aloft, rearing up his breast. His lord dismounted, falls to the ground.
Catillus overthrows Iolas, and Herminius, formidable for
courage, for size, and arms; whose yellow locks [waved] on
his bare head, and whose shoulders were also uncovered.
Wounds dismay him not: so mighty he stands to arms opposed. The spear, driven through his broad shoulders, trembles, and, transfixing the warrior, doubles him down with
pain. Black gore is poured forth all around: vying with each
other, they deal destruction with the sword, and by wounds
seek glorious death. But amidst heaps of slain the Amazon
Camilla, armed with a quiver, proudly prances over the field,
with one breast bared for the fight; and now with her hand
in showers tough javelins she throws, now with unwearied
arm she snatches her sturdy halberd. From her shoulder rat-
tles her golden bow, and the arms of Diana. Even if at any
time repulsed she gave ground, still turned [against the foe]
she aimed the winged shafts from her bow. Around her were
her select retinue, the virgin Larina, Tulla, and Tarpeia brandishing her brazen axe, Italian nymphs; whom sacred Camilla
herself had chosen for her glory, and as trusty assistants in
war and peace: like Thracian Amazons, when they beat the
banks of Thermodon,[32] and war with particoloured arms,
either round Hippolyte,[33] or about Penthesilea, when that
martial lady in her chariot returns; and with loud yelling uproar the female troops with half-moon[34] shields exult. Whom
first, whom last, didst thou, fierce virgin, with thy shafts

[32] Thermodon, (Thermeh,) a river of Pontus, in Asia Minor, in the
country of the Amazons, falling into the Euxine Sea near Themiscyra.
[33] Hippolyte, queen of the Amazons, given in marriage to Theseus, by
Hercules, who had conquered her.
[34] So called from their form. Cf. Quintus Calab. i. 146, ἀνγ ἴθατ' ἀσ-
πίδα θᾶν ἀλίγειον ἀντυγι μήνης.   B.

2 s

overthrow ? or how many bodies didst thou stretch gasping
on the ground ? First Eumenius, the son of Clytius, whose
exposed breast, as he stood right against her, she transfixes
with the long spear of fir. He, vomiting up torrents of blood,
falls and bites the bloody ground, and dying writhes on his
own wound. Then Liris and Pagasus besides ; of whom the
one tumbling backward from his horse wounded under him
while he gathers up the reins, the other, as he comes up, and
reaches his unavailing hand to his falling friend, both fall
headlong and at once. To these she joins Amastrus, the son
of Hippotas ; and at distance keenly plying with darts pursues Tereas, Harpalycus, Demophoon, and Chromis ; and
as many shafts as shot from her hand the virgin hurled, so
many Trojan heroes fell. Afar the hunter Ornytus in strange
arms rides on his Iapygian[n] steed ; his broad shoulders a
hide torn from a fierce bullock overspreads ; his head a wolf's
vast yawning mouth and jaws with white teeth cover, and a
rustic lance[38] arms his hand. In the midst of the troops he
moves about, and overtops the rest by a full head. Him intercepted (nor hard was the task, now that she had put his
troop to flight) she transfixes, and over him these words with
hostile heart pronounces : Tuscan, didst thou fancy that thou
wast hunting beasts of chase in the woods ? The day is come,
that by a female arm confutes your vaunts : yet to the manes
of thy fathers this no trifling honour shalt thou bear, that
thou didst fall by the weapon of Camilla. In order next Orsilochus and Butes, the two most bulky bodies of the Trojans,
[she assaults] : but Butes right against her with the pointed
lance she transfixes, between the corslet and the helmet, where,
as he sits [upon the horse], the shining neck appears, and
where down from his left arm the buckler hangs: Orsilochus
she mocks with [dissembled] flight, and wheeling round in a
spacious orb, turns short upon him in a narrower circle, and
pursues the pursuer. Then rising high, with redoubled
strokes she drives her sturdy axe through his arms, and
through his bones, while he prays and earnestly begs his life :
with his warm brains the wound besmears his face. The
warrior son of Aunus, the Apennine mountaineer, casually

encountered her, and startled' with the sudden sight stopped
short ; not the last of the Ligurians, while the Fates suffered
him to practise fraud. Soon as he perceives that now by no
flight he can evade the combat, nor avert the queen who
presses him close, with policy and craft attempting to execute
his wishes, he thus begins: What mighty courage, female, if
on a warlike steed you rely ? throw away the means of flight,
and trust thyself with me hand to hand on equal ground, and
prepare for the combat on foot: soon shalt thou know to
which of us his vain-glorious boasting will bring harm.[57] He
said; but she, breathing fury, and stung with fierce resentment, delivers her steed to an attendant, and confronts him in
equal arms with the naked sword on foot, and with her device-
less shield undaunted. But the youth, presuming that he had
overcome by artifice, instantly flies off, and, turning about his
horse's head, is borne away with precipitation, and tires his
fleet courser with the iron spur. Fond Ligurian, [says she,]
flushed with unavailing pride of soul, in vain hast thou perfidious tried thy country's slippery arts ; nor shall all thy artifice bring thee off safe to cheating Aunus. Thus the virgin
said, and with nimble foot, all on fire, outruns his courser's
speed, and, grasping the reins, engages him face to face, and
takes vengeance on his hostile blood ; with the same ease as
from a lofty rock the falcon, sacred bird [of Mars], with
winged speed overtakes a dove aloft among the clouds, and
seizing gripes her fast, and scoops out the bowels with his
hooked talons : then from the sky her blood and torn plumes
drop down.

But not with inattentive eyes the Sire of gods and men
these scenes surveying, on high Olympus exalted sits. The
Sire rouses Tuscan Tarchon to bloody battles, and with no
mild incentives inflames his rage. Therefore, amidst the
scenes of slaughter and flying squadrons, Tarchon is hurried
on by his steed, and with various remonstrances animates the
wings, calling each man[58] by his name ; and rallies the broken
troops to battle. Oh never to be moved with just indignation! Oh still dastardly faint-hearted Tuscans, what fear,

---

[57] "Fraudem" seems to have been always regarded as the correct
reading. See Servius. B.
[58] So Furius apud Macrob. Sat. vi. 1, "nomine quemque ciet." Silius
l. 454, "Cunctosque ciebat nomine." B.

what cowardice so base has seized your souls? Does a woman
drive you straggling, and put these squadrons to flight?
What avails the sword? or why wield we in our hands these
useless weapons? But not so slothful are ye in the service of
Venus and her nocturnal wars,[39] or when the bent pipe of
Bacchus hath summoned the choirs to wait for the banquets
and bowls at the sumptuous board. This is your delight,
this your ambition, while the auspicious augur declares the
sacred rites, and the fat victim invites you to the deep groves.
This said, he spurs on his steed into the midst, he too bent on
death, and in furious perturbation advances directly against
Venulus; and with his right hand grasps the foe torn off his
steed, and precipitant with huge violence bears him off before
him. A shout is raised to heaven; and all the Latins turned
their eyes. Fiery Tarchon flies over the plain, bearing both
the warrior and his arms: then from the top of his lance he
breaks off the steel, and explores the open chinks where he
may inflict the mortal wound. He, on the other hand, struggling against him, wards off his hand from his throat, and
force by force evades. And as when the tawny eagle soaring
high bears off a serpent whom she hath seized, hath fixed in
him her feet, and with her talons griped him fast; but the
wounded serpent writhes his curving volumes, and with
erected scales is stiff, and hisses with his mouth, rising high
against [his foe]: she not the less with hooked beak squeezes
him struggling, at the same time flaps the air with her wings;
just so, from the army of the Tiburtines Tarchon in triumph bears off his prey. The Tuscans, following the example and fortune of their leader, rush on. Then Aruns [40]
to death devoted, with his javelin and much artifice, first
courses round the swift Camilla, and watches what most
favourable opportunity may occur. Wherever amidst the
troops the furious maid drove on, there Aruns follows, and
silently surveys her steps. Wherever she victorious returns,
and from the foe withdraws her steps, that way the youth
secretly winds about the reins with speed. Now these, now
those approaches, and the whole circuit he traverses, and with
mischievous purpose shakes his unerring lance. By chance

---

[39] Virgil expresses the Greek νυκτομαχεῖν (cf. Aristænet. i. 10). B.
[40] Aruns, a Trojan, who slew Camilla, and was killed by a dart of
Diana.

Chloreus,[41] sacred to Cybele, and formerly her priest, at distance shone conspicuous in Phrygian arms, and spurred on his foaming courser; which a hide compact with gilt scaly plates of brass in form of plumes, covered. He himself, gaudy in barbaric purple of darkened hue, shot Cretan arrows from his Lycian bow. Of gold the bow hung rattling from his shoulders, and of gold was the helmet of the priest : then in a knot with a clasp of yellow gold he had collected his saffron chlamys, and its rustling plaits of lawn, having his Phrygian tunic embroidered with needle-work. Him the virgin, whether that she might fix Trojan arms in the front of the temple, or show herself at the chase in captive gold, of all the warring chiefs alone blindly pursued ; and through the whole host, from a woman's longing for the prey and spoils, with heedless ardour roamed : when at length Aruns, snatching the occasion, from his covert throws a dart, and thus to the powers above addresses his prayer : Apollo, greatest of gods, guardian of holy Soracte, whom we chiefly adore ; for whom the fire of pine [42] with heaps [of fuel] is fed ; and in whose honour, through the midst of the flames,[43] we thy votaries, relying on our piety, walk over a length of burning coals ; grant, almighty Sire, that by our arms this infamy may be blotted out. Not pillage or trophy, or any spoils of a vanquished maid, I seek : to me my other exploits will bear renown. If, smitten by a wound from me, this rueful pest shall fall, I to my native city shall [willingly] return inglorious. Phœbus heard, and with himself ordained that part of the vow should be fulfilled ; part in fleet air he dispersed. By sudden death to overthrow Camilla off her guard, he granted to his suppliant ; that his illustrious country should see him safely return he denied, and that petition the tempests turned adrift among the winds. Therefore, soon as sent from his hand the spear gave a whizzing sound through the air, the armies turned their attention,

[41] Chloreus, a priest of Cybele, who came with Æneas into Italy, and was killed by Turnus.

[42] But this may also mean "the pitchy flame," as in Soph. Antig. 124, πιπάιν θ' ᾿Ηφαιστον. So Tryphiodorus, 214, πιεσήιντος ἀνασχόμενοι πυρὸς ὁρμήν. Compare Heins. on Silius v. 179. B.

[43] This is illustrated from a historical passage in Pliny, lib. vii. cap. 2. Haud procul urbe Româ, in Faliscorum agro, familiæ sunt paucæ, quæ vocantur Hirpiæ: quæ sacrificio annuo, quod fit ad montem Soractem Apollini, super ambustam ligni struem ambulantes non aduruntur.

and all the Volscians on the queen their eyes directed. Neither
air nor whizzing sound did she heed, or the weapon flying
from the sky, till plunged beneath her naked breast the spear
stuck fast, and driven home drank deep her virgin blood.
Her attendants in trembling haste pour in together, and lift
up their falling queen. Above all, Aruns, stunned with joy
and mingled fear, flies ; and now no longer dares trust to his
spear, or make head against the weapons of the virgin. And
as some fierce [*] wolf, after he has slain a shepherd or lusty
bullock, conscious of his daring deed, forthwith by some un-
beaten path hath to the lofty mountains made his retreat,
before the hostile darts pursue him ; and cowering hides his
cowardly tail under him, and hastens to the woods : just so
Aruns in hurrying perturbation from sight withdrew, and
pleased with his flight mixed among the armed troops. She
dying wrenches out the weapon with her hand ; but between
the bones in her side the steel point stands fixed with a deep
wound. Down she sinks lifeless ; down sink her cold eyes in
death ; her once blooming hue hath forsaken her face. Then
thus, breathing her last, she addresses Acca, one of her com-
peers, who, beyond the rest, was singularly trusty to Camilla,
with whom she used to divide her cares ; and thus these words
she speaks : So far, O sister Acca, have I held out ; now a
cruel wound undoes me, and all objects around put on a
face of darkness. Fly quick, and bear these, my last commands, to Turnus : let him advance to the combat, and repel
the Trojans from the city. And now farewell. At the same
time with these words she dropped the reins, sinking to the
ground involuntarily : then of vital heat bereft, she disengages
herself from the whole body by degrees ; and reclined her
drooping neck, and head subdued by death, leaving her arms ;
and with a groan her life indignant fled to the shades. Then
indeed a prodigious outcry arising strikes the golden stars.
The combat grows more bloody, now that Camilla is overthrown. At once in thick array rush on the whole strength
of the Trojans, the Tuscan chiefs, and the wings of Arcadian
Evander.

But Opis, appointed by Diana to watch [the fair], a long
while had sat aloft on the high mountains, and fearless viewed

[*] See, however, Anthon on Æn. x. 707. B.

the combat.   And soon as from far she espied Camilla by a
lamontable death overthrown amidst the bustle of the infuriated youths, she inly groaned, and from the bottom of her
breast uttered these words: Ah virgin, too, too cruel punishment hast thou sustained, for offering to defy the Trojans in
war! nor hath it aught availed thee that lonely in the woods
thou wast a votary to Diana, and on thy shoulder didst bear
our quivers: yet not without honour has thy queen forsaken
thee now in death's extremity, nor shall this thy death be un-
recorded amongst the nations, nor shalt thou bear the infamy
of being unrevenged : for whoever with a wound hath violated
thy body, shall by just death his crime atone.   Under the
lofty mountain stood the stately tomb[45] of Dercennua, the
ancient king of Laurentum, formed of a mount of earth, and
shaded with gloomy holm.   Here first the goddess, pre-emi-
nent in beauty, with a rapid effort [of her wings] alights, and
Aruns from the high eminence surveys.   Soon as she saw him
shining in armour, and vainly swelling, she said, Why dost
thou move off that way? hither direct thy course, hither come
to meet thy doom, that from Camilla thou mayest receive thy
due reward.   Shalt thou, too, have the honour to die by Diana's shafts?   She said, and from her gilded quiver the Thracian nymph drew forth a winged arrow, and wrathful bent
her bow, and stretched it to its length, till the crooked points
together met, and now with both hands alike she touched,
with the left the steel point, and with the right and bow-string
her breast.   Forthwith Aruns heard at once the hissing of
the shaft and sounding air, and in his body the steel stuck
fast.   Him, expiring and groaning his last, his regardless
friends abandon in the dusty plain unknown: Opis to the
ethereal sky on wings is borne away.

First fly the warriors of Camilla's left-armed wing, now
that their queen is lost; the Rutulians in confusion fly; valiant Atinas flies; the discomfited leaders, and the desolate
companies, both seek safe retreats, and turning their backs, on
coursers bend their way towards the town.   Nor is any one
able with arms to sustain, or stand against the Trojans pressing on, and dispensing death ; but on their languid shoulders
they bear off their bows unbent, and with swift career tho

---

[45] "Bustum" is, properly, the place where a corpse has been burnt.   D.

courser's hoof beats the mouldering plain. Dust, in thick
clouds of black vapour, is rolled towards the walls; and from
the towers the matrons beating their breast raise the female
shriek to the stars of heaven. On those who first with speed
burst within the expanded gates a hostile throng in a mingled
body presses; nor escape they deplorable death, but in the
very entrance, under their native walls, and amidst the shelter
of the houses, transfixed together they breathe out their souls.
Some shut the gates, nor dare to open a passage to their
friends, or within the walls to receive them imploring: and a
most lamentable slaughter ensues of such as guarded with
their arms the passes, and such as rushed on those arms. The
excluded, before the eyes and faces of their grieving parents,
partly tumble headlong into the deep trenches, ruin closely
pursuing. Some giving loose reins, blindfold and with rapid
speed batter against the gates, and the firmly barricaded posts.
Even the trembling matrons, soon as from the walls they
espied the corpse of Camilla, with the greatest eagerness (since
affection to their country prompts them) cast darts with their
hands, and, rushing precipitant with hardened oaks, stakes,
and poles burnt at the point, imitate iron weapons, and are
ambitious to die the first before the walls. Meanwhile this
horrid intelligence fills [the ears of] Turnus [as he lies am-
bushed] in the woods, and to the youth Acca reports the
dreadful disorder; that the troops of the Volscians were cut
in pieces, Camilla had fallen, the vengeful foes were making a
furious onset, and by a successful battle had made themselves
masters of all; that the consternation was now propagated to
the city. He furious (for so the inflexible decrees of Jove
require) quits the hills he had beset, forsakes the rugged woods.
Scarcely had he gone out of sight, and possessed the plain,
when father Æneas, entering the open lawns, overpasses the
mountain's ridge, and safe through the gloomy wood takes his
way. Thus both impetuous, and with their whole army, towards the city advance; nor are they many paces distant from
each other. And at once Æneas at a distance espied the plain
smoking with dust, and saw the Laurentine bands; and Turnus descried Æneas fierce in arms, and heard the tread of feet,
and the snorting of the steeds. Forthwith they would engage
in fight, and essay the combat, did not rosy Phœbus now dip
his tired steeds in the western ocean, and, day declining,

bring back the night.   In their camps before the town they rest, and entrench the walls.

BOOK XII.

In the Twelfth Book, Juno prevents the single combat agreed upon by Turnus and Æneas. The Trojans are defeated in the absence of their king, who had retired wounded, but is miraculously cured by Venus. On his return, he again challenges Turnus to the combat, with whose death the poem concludes.

As soon as Turnus saw that the Latins, broken with unsuccessful war, had lost heart; that now his promise was claimed, himself marked out by the eyes [of all]; he burns with voluntary determination not to yield,[1] and raises his martial spirit. As in the fields of Carthage, a lion, whose breast is pierced by the hunters with a smart wound, then at length prepares for battle, and delights in shaking the brawny muscles of his shaggy neck, and undaunted breaks the inflxed weapon of the hunter and roars with bloody jaws: just so in Turnus' inflamed breast violence rises,[2] then thus he addresses the king, and thus in perturbation begins: In Turnus is no delay; the dastardly Trojans have no handle to retract their challenge, or to decline what they have agreed to. I enter the lists: order thou, O sire, the sacred rites, and ratify the truce. Either I with this right hand shall despatch to Tartarus the Trojan, the renegado of Asia, (let the Latins sit still and look on,) and alone shall with the sword repel the common charge; or let him rule us vanquished, let Lavinia be resigned his spouse. To him with mind composed Latinus replied: O youth surpassing in soul, the more you excel in fierce valour, the more solicitously it concerns me to consult [your safety], and with fearful caution to weigh the danger. You are heir to the kingdom of your father Daunus, many cities have been won by your valour, wealth also, and a high spirit, belong to Latinus. There are other virgins unwedded in Latium and

[1] I have been compelled to use a circumlocution in translating "ultro implacabilis ardet." Servius well observes: "bene ducis dignitatem servavit, ut non ideo faceret, quia quidam reposcebant; sed sua sponto accenderetur in prœlium." B.
[2] "Gliscit" rather means "increases, grows vehement." So Lucret. i. 475, "Ignis Alexandri Phrygio sub pectore gliscens." iv. 1062, "Inquo dies gliscit furor." B.

tho territories of Laurentum, not ignoblo in their birth.
Give me leave to lay before you without guile these truths, not
pleasant to be spoken; at the same time, imbibe them with deep
attention. It was decreed that I should wed my daughter to
none of her former suitors; and this both gods and men unanimous pronounced. Overpowered by my affection for thee, overpowered by the ties of kindred blood, and by the tears of my
afflicted consort, I broke through all restraints; wrested my
daughter from the son-in-law to whom she was promised;
took up impious[3] arms [against him.] From that time, Turnus,
you see what calamities, what wars pursue me; what disasters
you in chief endure. In two great battles routed, with difficulty we defend our hopes of Italy in this city: the streams
of Tiber still run warm with our blood, and the spacious
fields are white with the bones [of our slain]. Whither am I
so often driven back? what infatuation changes my mind?
If, upon Turnus' death, I am resolved to invite [the Trojans
to be] my allies, why not rather put an end to all dissensions
while he lives? What will my kinsmen the Rutulians, what
will the rest of Italy say, if to death (Heaven disappoint my
fears!) I betray you, who court my daughter and alliance by
marriage? Consider the various chances of war: pity your
aged sire, whom now disconsolate his native Ardea separates
far from you. By these remonstrances the rage of Turnus is
by no means checked: he swells up the more, and by medicine
grows more distempered. As soon as he was able to speak,
he thus began in words: Whatever care for me you entertain,
most excellent prince, I beseech you, for my sake, lay aside,
and suffer me to purchase death in exchange for glory. We
too, O sire, can fling[4] the dart and spear with no feeble arm,
and blood is wont to flow from the wounds which we inflict.
Nought shall his goddess-mother him avail,[5] who in a female
cloud screens the fugitive, and conceals herself in delusivo
shades. But the queen, terribly alarmed with the new state
of the fight, wept, and ready to die [with grief], grasped her

---

[3] Not only because Æneas was destined by the gods to be his son-in-
law, but because the war was between persons who had formed a truce. B.

[4] Literally, scatter. So Silius vii. 635, "spargentem in vulnera sævus
Fraude fugæ calamos." ix. 390, "spargere tela manu." B.

[5] Such is the force of "longe," as illustrated by Gronov. on Sen. Hippol. 974; Drakenb. on Sil. xvii. 80. B.

raging son-in-law: Turnus, by these tears, by whatever regard
for Amata touches your soul: thou art now the only hope.
the only solace of my wretched old age; on thee depends the
glory and power of Latinus; on thee our whole family now in
its decline relies; this one request I make, forbear to engage
with the Trojans. Whatever fortune awaits thee in that combat, Turnus, awaits me also; with you will I quit this hated
light, nor captive will I see Æneas my son-in-law. Lavinia,
bathing her glowing checks in tears, listens to the words of
her mother; [Lavinia,] in whom profound modesty kindled
up a burning flush,[6] and diffused itself over her blushing
visage. As if one had stained the Indian ivory with ruddy
purple; or as white lilies mingled with copious roses blush;
such colours the virgin in her visage showed. Love raises
a tumult in his soul, and fixes his looks upon the maid.
He burns for arms the more, and briefly thus addresses
Amata: O mother, do not, I beseech thee, do not with
tears, do not with so inauspicious an omen, send me from
you, now that I am on my way to the combat of rigid wars;
for Turnus is not at liberty to retard his death! Idmon,
my herald, report from me this no pleasing message to the
Phrygian tyrant: when first the ensuing morn, borne in her
crimson car, shall blush in the sky, let him not lead his
Trojans against the Rutulians; let the arms of Trojans and
Rutulians rest; by our blood be the war decided; in that field
let Lavinia be won as a bride. When he had pronounced
these words, and with great speed retired into the palace, he
calls for his steeds, and exults to see them neighing in his
presence; which steeds Orithyia[7] gave (a royal present) to
Pilumnus, such as in whiteness might surpass the snow, in
speed the winds. The active grooms stand around, and with
their hollow hands cheer their stroked chests, and comb their
waving manes. Then he himself wraps about his shoulders
his corslet, rough with gold and pale orichalchum: at the
same time fits for use his sword and buckler, and the horns of
his flaming crest; the sword which the god of fire himself had
forged for his father Daunus, and plunged, when glowing, in

---

[6] More literally, "unto whom a deep blush kindled up the hot current
within, and overspread her burning visage." Anthon.

[7] Orithyia, a daughter of Erechtheus, king of Athens, and wife of
Boreas, king of Thrace.

the Stygian wave. Next with force he grasps his strong
spear, which in the middle of the palace stood resting on a
mighty column, Auruncian Actor's spoil, and brandishes it
quivering, exclaiming: Now, O spear, that never baulked my
call, the time is now at hand. Thee, heroic Actor, thee the
right hand of Turnus now wields: grant that I may stretch
his body on the ground, and with my strong hand rend the
corslet torn from the Phrygian eunuch, and soil in the dust
his locks frizzled with hot irons and dripping with myrrh.
With such furies is he driven, and from the whole face of the
inflamed warrior sparks incessant fly: from his fierce eyes the
fire flashes: as when a bull to usher in the fight raises
hideous bellowings, and essays his rage for a combat with
horns, goring against the trunk of a tree; with blows he beats
the air, and preludes to the fight by spurning the sand.
Meanwhile Æneas, fierce in the arms given by his mother, no
less whets his martial fury, and kindles up his rage, pleased
that the war was to be decided on the proffered terms. Then
he solaces his friends and the fears of sorrowing Iülus, teaching them the fates; and orders the messengers to carry back
his positive answer to king Latinus, and prescribe the terms
of peace.

The next day arisen had scarcely sprinkled the tops of the
mountains with light, when first from the deep gulf the horses
of the sun lift up their heads, and from their erected nostrils
breathe forth day. Under the walls of the spacious city both
the Rutulians and Trojans, having measured the ground, prepared it for the combat; and in the centre [raised] hearths
and altars of turf to their common gods: others attired in
linen veils,[b] and having their temples bound with vervain,
bore fountain-water, and fire. The Ausonian legion advances, and the armed squadrons pour forth at the crowded
gates: on the other side the whole Trojan and Tuscan army
with various arms rush [to the field], no otherwise arranged
in battle-array, with sword in hand, than if summoned to the

___

[b] Servius writes that the priests and sacred ministers among the Romans, by whom the laws of peace and war were confirmed, were prohibited
to wear any thing of linen; and that Virgil designedly clothes the Feciales
in linen veils on this occasion, to give us to know beforehand that the
league was to be broken, since it was ushered in with unlawful rites.
Others for *lino* read *limo*, a kind of garment or apron worn by the priests
in sacrifice, that reached down from the navel to the feet.

fierce combat of Mars. The leaders, too, in gold and purple
decked, amidst the thousands scamper [over the plain];
Mnestheus, the offspring of Assaracus, and brave Asylas; and
Messapus, a renowned horseman, Neptune's son. And soon
as, upon the signal given, each man to his station retired, they
fix down their spears in the ground, and rest their shields.
Then, with eagerness [to see the combat], matrons in crowds,
the populace unarmed, and feeble old men, occupy the towers
and roofs of houses; others stand near the lofty gates. But
from the summit of the hill, which is now called Alban, (then
the mount had neither name, nor honour, nor glory,) Juno,
stretching her view, surveyed the field and both armies of
Laurentines and Trojans, and the city of Latinus. Forthwith
she thus addressed the sister of Turnus, a goddess to the deity
who over pools and sounding streams presides; on her this
sacred honour Jove, the high sovereign of the sky, for her
ravished virginity conferred: O nymph, the glory of rivers,
dearest to my soul, thou knowest how thee in chief, to all the
maids of Latium who mounted[9] the ungrateful bed of mighty
Jove, I have preferred, and willingly settled thee partner of
the skies: learn now, Juturna,[10] lest you should accuse me,
your sad disaster. As far as fortune seemed to suffer, and the
Fates permitted the state of Latium to prosper, Turnus and
your city I protected: now I see the youth engaging with
unequal fates: the day and unfriendly power of the Destinies
approach. With these eyes I am not able to behold this combat, or this league. If aught thou darest more ready for a
brother, proceed: it becomes thee; perhaps better fortune
will attend the wretched [Latins]. Scarcely had she spoken,
when from her eyes Juturna poured forth tears, and thrice
and four times with her hand smote her comely breast. This
is no time for tears, Saturnian Juno says; despatch, and if
there be any means, rescue your brother from death: or
kindle now the war anew, and dissolve the concerted league.
I authorize you in the daring attempt. Having thus advised, she left her perplexed, and distracted with a sad
wound of soul.

---

[9] Virgil expresses Æsch. Suppl. 37, ἐπιβῆναι λέκτρων. So also Eurip.
Hel. 376. B.

[10] Juturna, the sister of king Turnus, changed into a fountain of the
same name, the waters of which were used in the sacrifices of Vesta.

Meanwhile the kings, [and in particular] [11] Latinus of ample frame, rides in a chariot by four horses drawn, whose refulgent temples twelve golden rays encompass, the emblem of his ancestor the sun: [12] Turnus moves in a car drawn by two white steeds, brandishing in his hand two javelins tipped with broad steel. On the other side, father Æneas, the founder of the Roman race, blazing with his starry shield and arms divine, and Ascanius by his side, the other hope of mighty Rome, advance from the camp: in a pure vestment the priest brought up the youngling of a bristly sow, and an unshorn ewe-lamb, [13] and presented the victims at the blazing altars. They, turning their eyes towards the rising sun, sprinkle with their hands the salt cakes, and mark with the sword the top of the victims' foreheads, and from the sacred goblets pour libations on the altars. Then pious Æneas, having unsheathed his sword, thus prays: Thou, O sun, be witness now to my prayer, and this land, for whose sake I have been able to sustain such grievous toils; and thou, almighty father, and thou, Saturnian Juno, now goddess, now more propitious, I pray: and thou, glorious father Mars, who by thy sovereign will disposest the fate of all battles: the fountains and rivers I invoke, and whatever objects of religion are in the heavens above, and the deities that dwell in the azure ocean. If the victory should chance to fall to Ausonian Turnus, it is agreed that the vanquished [Trojans] shall to Evander's city retire: Iülus shall quit these territories: nor in future shall the Æneades, violating the peace, make war again to harass these realms with the sword. But if victory shall declare Mars on our side, (as I rather presume, and rather may the gods confirm by their divine will,) never shall I compel the Italians to be subject to the Trojans, nor aim I at empire for myself: let both nations

[11] I have followed Anthon's construing. B.

[12] Latinus was the grandson of Picus, who took Circe, the daughter of the sun, to be his wife or concubine, and by her had Faunus, the father of Latinus, who consequently was the grandchild of the sun.

[13] Rumus observes, that the ewe was offered for Æneas, after the manner of the Greeks, who commonly ratified a league with the sacrifice of a sheep or lamb, as we see in Homer, Il. iii. 103. The sow again is for Latinus, after the Roman or Italian fashion, which Livy intimates to have been of very great antiquity, lib. i. 24, where he gives the form of ratifying a league between the Romans and Albans, in the reign of Tullus Hostilius: "Audi Jupiter, &c.—Si prior defexit, tu illo die Jupiter populum Romanum sic ferito, ut ego hunc porcum hic hodie feriam."

unsubdued submit on equal terms to an everlasting league. I shall ordain the sacred rites and the gods:[14] let my father-in-law Latinus enjoy the control of the war, his wonted sovereign rule: to me my Trojans shall raise a city, and to that city Lavinia shall give the name. Thus Æneas first [said]: then thus Latinus, raising his eyes to heaven, succeeds, and to the stars stretches forth his right hand: By those same powers, Æneas, by the earth, the sea, the stars, I swear, by Latona's double offspring, and two-faced Janus, by the majesty of the gods infernal, and the sanctuary of inexorable Pluto. These oaths let the Sire hear, who by his thunder ratifies our leagues. On the altars I lay my hand; and the fires here placed in the midst of them, and the gods I call to witness: no day shall ever violate this peace, this treaty, on the part of the Italians, whatever way the event shall fall out: nor shall any power make me swerve from them with my will, even though it should wash away the earth into the waves, blending it with the flood, and dissolve heaven into hell. As this sceptre (for a sceptre in his hand he chanced to wield) shall never sprout forth with light leaves, twigs, or shady boughs, since once lopped in the wood from the low stem it was severed from its mother-tree, and by the axe laid down its locks and branching arms; once a tree, now the artist's hand hath enchased it in beauteous brass, and fashioned it for the Latin kings to wield. By such asseverations they mutually confirmed the league full in the view of the chiefs: then over the flames they stab[15] the victims consecrated in due form, and tear out their entrails from them yet alive, and heap up the altars with loaded chargers.

But to the Rutulians the match had long seemed unequal, and their breasts were agitated with various mixed emotions; but then the more, as they discern more nearly that the contest is one of unequal strength. Turnus advancing with a silent gait, and in suppliant form with downcast eyes venerating the altars, his wan cheeks, and the paleness over his youthful form, aggravate their fears; which surmises soon as his sister Juturna observed to be spread abroad, and that the drooping hearts of the populace were wavering; into the midst of the troops, personating the form of Camertus, (who

14 L. e. the Latins are to receive those of the Trojans. B.
15 "Jugulare" properly means "to cut the throat." B.

was of a noble ancient line, and from his father's valour derived an illustrious name, himself too most valiant in arms,)
Into the midst of the troops she throws herself, not unskilled
in expedients, sows various rumours [among the ranks], and
thus harangues them: Are you not ashamed, O Rutulians! to
expose one life for all who are such?[16] are we not equal in
numbers and in strength? Lo Trojans and Arcadians both,
and the fatal band, Etruria, inveterate to Turnus, all are here:
yet should but every second man of us engage, we hardly have
a foe. He, [Turnus,] it is true, by fame shall be advanced to
the gods, at whose altars he devotes himself, and in the mouths
[of men] shall ever live; we who now are seated idle on the
plain, shall, after having lost our country, be constrained to
submit to haughty lords.

By these words the resolution of the youths was now more
and more inflamed, and through the troops the murmur glides.
Even the Laurentines are changed, and those very Latins,
who were recently promising themselves repose from war,
and prosperity to the state, now are to arms inclined, wish the
league unmade, and pity the hard fate of Turnus. To these
incentives Juturna adds another yet stronger, and gives a
sign from high heaven, than which none more effectually disturbed the minds of the Italians, and misled them by its portent. For in the ruddy sky the tawny bird of Jove with
winged speed pursued some water-fowl, and a noisy tribe of
the feathered kind; when suddenly swooping down to the
waves, cruelly rapacious, he snatched up in his crooked
pounces a goodly swan. The Italians roused their attention:
and all the fowls with screaming noise turn their flight,
amazing to see! and darken the sky with their wings, and
forming a cloud, pursue[17] their foe through the air; till, by
the force [of their attacks], and the very encumbrance of his
burthen, overpowered, the bird gave way, and from his talons
dropped his prey into the river, and flew far into the clouds.
Then indeed with acclamation the Rutulians salute the omen,
and make ready their troops: and first Tolumnius the augur
says, This is what with prayers I often sought: I welcome

[16] i. e. "who are equal in valour to Turnus." ANTHON. B.
[17] Literally, "press on." Silius v. 281, "ceu tigride cerva Hyrcana
cum pressa tremit. x. 125, "Haud secus ac Libyca fetam telluro lea-
nam Venator premit obsesso cum Maurus in antro." B.

[the omen], and own [the interposition of] the gods; myself, myself at your head, snatch up the steel, O Rutulians, whom this injurious foreigner like weak fowls with war dismays, and by violence ravages your coasts. He shall betake himself to flight, and set sail far into the deep. Do ye with one accord close your squadrons, and from the combat save your king, whom they would ravish from you.[14]

He said, and rushing forth, hurled a dart full in the face of the enemy : the whizzing cornel-shaft gives a twang, and with unerring aim cuts the air. At once it is done, at once a loud shout arises, and the whole ranks are disturbed, and their hearts inflamed with tumultuous rage. The flying javelin, as against it stood nine brothers, (most comely personages, whom one faithful consort of Tuscan blood had borne to Arcadian Gilippus,) one of those, a youth distinguished by his mien and shining arms, just in the middle, where the stitched belt is worn by the waist, and a clasp confines the joints of the sides : it penetrates the ribs, and stretches him on the yellow sand. But the brothers, a resolute band, and stung with grief, some draw their swords, some snatch the missile steel, and rush blindfold ; against whom the troops of Laurentum spring forth : then in close array Trojans, and Tuscans, and Arca-dians with painted arms, again stream forth. One common ardour so strongly possesses all to decide the strife by dint of sword. They rifled the very altars ; a thick tempest of darts flies through all the air, and an iron shower pours down amain ; and they bear away the hearths and goblets.[19] Latinus himself, the league now broken, flies, bearing off his baffled gods. Some rein their chariots, or with a bound vault on their steeds, and with drawn swords are ready. Messapus, eager to violate the truce, gives a terrible shock to the Tuscan Aules-tes, a king, and bearing the ensigns of a king, by jostling against him with his horse : he retreating falls, and unhappily among the altars planted behind him tumbles on his head and shoulders. But Messapus fierce flies up with his lance, and with the beamy weapon from on high, raising himself on his steed, smites him heavily, earnestly imploring [his life], and

---

[14] "Raptum" is used proleptically. B.

[19] The priests and ministers bear away the utensils which had been employed in pledging the truce. B.

2 c

thus speaks: He has got it,[20] this victim is given to the great
gods as a more grateful offering. The Italians flock toward
him, and strip his limbs, yet warm. From the altar Chorinæus snatches a burning brand, and confronting Ebusus, as
he is coming up and aiming a blow, prevents him, by dashing
the flames full in his face. His bushy beard blazed, and singed
all over, diffused a smell. The other, pursuing the blow, with
his left hand grasps the hair of his confounded foe, and with
exerted force, pressing his knee against him, nails him fast to
the ground; in this posture he plunges the cruel sword into
his side. Podalirius with naked sword pursuing the shepherd
Alsus, as in the front of the battle he rushes through the darts,
presses close upon him: he (Alsus) drawing back his axe,
cleaves asunder in the middle the forehead and chin of his opponent, and with the bespattered blood besmears his arms.
Cruel slumbers and the iron sleep [of death] press down his
eyes; closed are their orbs in everlasting night.

But pious Æneas, with his head uncovered, stretched forth
his unarmed hand [in sign of truce], and with loud acclamation called to his men: Whither rush you? what sudden discord has thus arisen? O restrain your rage! the league is
now struck up, and all the articles are settled: I alone have
a right to engage; permit me, and banish your fears: this hand
of mine shall make the league firm: those sacred rites give me
security for Turnus. Amidst these words, amidst such ex-
postulations, lo! a hissing arrow with winged speed alighted
on the hero: by whose hand shot, by whose whirling force
impelled, who acquired such glory to the Rutulians, whether a
god or chance, is uncertain: smothered was the fame of the
illustrious action; nor did any one vaunt himself on [having
inflicted] a wound on Æneas.

Soon as Turnus saw Æneas retiring from the army, and
the leaders all in disorder, with sudden hope impetuous he
burns: for his steeds and arms at once he calls, and proudly
springs into the chariot with a bound, and with his own
hands guides the reins. Flying along, he gives to death many
gallant frames of men; many half dead he rolls along, or with
his chariot tramples down the troops, or plies their flying

---

[20] i. e. "he has received his *coup de grace*," a gladiatorial phrase. Cf
Ter. Andr. i. 8, 56. B.

backs with darts caught up.[11] As when by the streams of the
cold Hebrus bloody Mars with fierce commotion clashes with
his shield, and kindling war, lets loose his furious steeds; they
over the plain outfly the south winds and zephyr; Thrace to
its utmost bounds groans beneath the trampling of their feet,
and the features of grim Terror, Rage, and Stratagem, the retinue of the god, stalk around: with like fury Turnus through
the midst of the embattled plain exulting drives his steeds
steaming with sweat, prancing over his miserably slaughtered
foes: their rapid hoofs scatter the dewy drops of blood, and gore
with mingled sand is spurned up. And now to death he gave
Sthenelus, and Thamyris, and Pholus, encountering the two last
hand to hand, the other at a distance; at a distance also both
the sons of Imbrasus, Glaucus and Lades, whom in Lycia Imbrasus had bred, and furnished with equal skill in arms, either
to fight hand to hand, or on horseback to outfly the wind. In
another quarter Eumedes rushes into the midst of the field,
the warlike son of the ancient Dolon,[22] representing his grandsire in name, in soul and action his sire; who once, sent as a
spy to visit the Grecian camp, durst claim for his reward the
chariot of Achilles. Him Tydides for so audacious an attempt
honoured with a very different reward; and no more he
aspires [now] to the steeds of Achilles. Him as soon as Turnus at a distance espied on the open plain, having first sent
after him a fleet arrow through the extended void, he stops
his harnessed steeds, down from the chariot springs, and flies
up to him expiring and prostrate; and, pressing his foot on
his neck, wrests the sword from his hand, and deep in his
throat plunged the shining blade, and withal added these
words: Lo! Trojan, stretched at your length measure the
lands, and that Hesperia which by war you sought: these
rewards they reap who dare attack me with the sword; thus
they build their walls. Hurling his lance he sends Butes to
bear him company: and Chloreus, and Sybaris, Darea, and
Thersilochus, and Thymœtes, who had fallen from the neck
of his plunging[23] steed. And as, when the blast of Thracian

---

[11] Snatched up from his own chariot, or from the bodies of the slain. B.

[22] Dolon, a Trojan remarkable for his swiftness, having been sent as a
spy to the Grecian camp, he was seized and put to death by Diomedes.

[23] So Silius uses "sternax," i. 261, "correpti sternacem ad prælia
frænis Frangere equum." Servius interprets it, "qui facile sternit au-
dentem." B.

Boreas roars on the Ægean Sea, and to the shore pursues the
waves, wherever the winds exert their incumbent force, the
clouds fly through the air: just so before Turnus, wherever
he cuts his way, the troops give way, and the routed squadrons
fly: his impetuous ardour bears him on, and the wind, blowing
right against his chariot, shakes his fluttering crest. Him thus
bearing all before him, and bellowing with mad rage, Phegeus
could not endure; he opposed himself to the chariot, and, with
his right hand, twisted the mouths of the steeds as they are
hurried along, foaming with the bit. While he is dragged
along, and bangs upon the pole, [Turnus'] broad lance reaches
him undefended, and piercing bursts his double-tissued coat
of mail, and with a wound grazes the surface of his body.
But he, with shield opposed turning on the foe, advanced,
and from his unsheathed sword [24] sought assistance; when
the wheel, and the axle accelerated in its career, hurled him
headlong, and stretched him on the ground; and Turnus following, with his sword struck off his head, between the lower
extremity of the helmet and the upper border of the corslet,
and left him on the sand a [headless] trunk.

Now while in the field victorious Turnus makes such havoc,
in the interim Mnestheus, and trusty Achates, and Ascanius,
accompanying, placed in the camp Æneas bleeding [from his
wound, and] on a long spear propping his alternate steps. [25]
He storms, and, having broken off the shaft, struggles to
wrench out the dart, and demands the speediest means of aid;
bids them make an incision with the broad sword, and quite
lay open the weapon's recess, and send him back to the war.
And now came to his aid Iapyx, [26] the son of Iasius, by Phœbus above others beloved; upon whom Apollo himself, captivated with a violent passion for him, heretofore had offered
to bestow his arts, his own gifts, his skill in augury, the lyre
and winged shafts. He, to prolong his dying father's fate,
chose to understand the powers of herbs and use of medicine,
and inglorious to practise those silent arts. [27]   Raving vio-

---

[24] I may as well remark, that "mucro" generally means a short,
broad weapon. B.
[25] So Silius vi. 68, "Saucius—fractæ innitens hastæ." B.
[26] Iapyx, a Trojan, the son of Iasius, and a favourite of Apollo, who
instructed him in medicine.
[27] Because unheralded by fame. ANTHON. B.

lently Æneas stood, leaning on his massy spear, unmoved, amidst the vast confluence, either by the tears of the youths or of grieving Iülus. The sage, in his robe doubled back, girt up [28] after the physician's fashion, with anxious trepidation makes many efforts in vain with his healing hand, and the potent herbs of Phœbus; in vain with his right hand tugs the dart, and with tenacious pincers grips the steel. No success attends the means; his patron Apollo lends no aid; and the fierce terror of the field spreads more and more, and the mischief is nearer. Now they see the air stand thick with dust: [Turnus'] cavalry are advancing, and thick showers of darts fall in the midst of the camp: to heaven ascend the dismal shouts of youth, some fighting, and some falling under cruel Mars.

Here the parent-goddess Venus, deeply affected with the undeserved suffering of her son, from Cretan Ida crops a stalk of dittany, all blooming with downy leaves and purple flowers: to the wild goats those herbs are not unknown; [for from them they seek relief,] when in their backs the winged shafts have stuck. This Venus, her face muffled in a dim cloud, conveyed; with this she tinctures the water poured in the shining vase, secretly medicating it; and injects the juice of healing ambrosia, and fragrant panacea. With this liquor aged Iapyx, not knowing [its communicated virtue], fomented the wound; and suddenly (for all the pain fled from his body, and all the blood in the deep wound was stanched; and now the arrow, following the hand, without any compulsion dropped out, and to his pristine state his vigour returned anew) Iapyx exclaims, Quick fly for the hero's arms; why do you stand? thus he first kindles their courage against the foe. [He adds,] Not from human aid, or from the masterly art [of man], proceeds this cure, nor, Æneas, is it my right hand that saves thee: a god more powerful is the agent, and releases thee for enterprises of greater moment. He, panting for the combat, had incased his legs in gold, is impatient of delay, and brandishes his lance. When his shield was fitted to his side, and the corslet to his back, within his armed folds he embraces Ascanius, and, through his helmet, gently touching his lips, thus addresses him: From me, my son, learn valour and true

---

[28] In order to be less encumbered in his operations. So Silius v. 367, "intortos de more adstrictus amictus, Mulcebat lympha purgatum sanguine vulnus." D.

fortitude; thy fortune [learn] from others. Now shall my
hand by war set thee in safety, and lead thee to the glorious
fruits of victory. Be sure you this remember, when ere long
your age shall reach maturity; and, calling often to mind the
examples of your ancestors, let your father Æneas, and uncle
Hector, spur you on.

Soon as he uttered these words, from the gates he issued
forth majestic; in his hand brandishing a ponderous javelin:
at the same time in a thick body rush forth Antheus and
Mnestheus, and all the troops from the abandoned camp pour
along. Then with mingled clouds of blinding dust the plain
is overspread, and the earth, shaking by the trampling of their
feet, trembles. Them marching Turnus saw from an opposite hill; the Ausonians saw, and cold fear ran through their
inmost bones. Before all the Latins Juturna first heard and
recognised the sound, and in consternation fled. The hero
(Æneas) speeds his way, and along the open plain drives his
fiery squadron. As when under some stormy[20] constellation
a tempest moves athwart the mid ocean towards the land;
ah! how the hearts of the desponding swains, presaging from
afar, shudder! it will bring ruin on the trees, and desolation
on the fields of corn, it will lay all waste around: the winds
before it fly, and waft hoarse murmurs to the shore: with such
fury the Trojan chief leads on his squadron against the opposing foes: in the thick array they crowd upon each other,
closing their serried files. Thymbræus with the sword smites
down the stern Osiris, Mnestheus beats down Archetius,
Achates kills Epulo, and Gyas Ufens. The augur's self Tolumnius falls, who first had hurled his lance against the adverse foes. To heaven a shout is raised; and the Rutulians,
routed in their turn, show their backs all dusty over the field.
Æneas himself neither deigns to put the fugitives to death,
nor does he pursue those who engage in close fight, or who
[at a distance] throw the javelin: Turnus alone, with accurate survey, he searches out, amidst the thick clouds of dust:
him alone he demands to the combat.

With dread of this the warlike maid Juturna, struck to the
heart, overthrows Metiscus,[30] Turnus' charioteer, between the •

---

[20] Literally, "when [the influence of] some constellation has burst
forth." B.
[30] Metiscus, the charioteer of Turnus, whose form was assumed by
Juturna, the sister of Turnus.

harness, and leaves him far behind fallen from the beam. Herself succeeds, and with her hand guides the waving reins, assuming all, the voice, the person, and arms of Metiscus. As when throughout the spacious mansions of some wealthy lord the sable swallow flutters, and on the wing traverses the lofty courts, picking up her scanty fare, and food for her loquacious young; and now in the empty cloisters, now about the liquid pools chatters: in like manner through the midst of the foes Juturna rides, and flying in her rapid chariot, circuits all: and now here, now there, exhibits her brother in triumph; nor suffers him to engage [in single combat]; but far [from Æneas] devious flies.

Æneas, with no less eagerness, pursues mazy orbs, in order to intercept him, traces out the warrior, and with a loud voice calls after him through the broken troops. As often as he casts his eyes on the foe, and by his agility attempted the winged courser's speed; so often Juturna wheeled about the chariot, turning it from him. Alas, what can he do? in vain, be fluctuates with a varying tide, and different cares urge his mind to opposite schemes. At him Messapus, as in his swift career he chanced in the left hand to wield two javelins pointed with steel, levels one of them, hurling it with a well-aimed blow. Æneas stopped short, and shrunk himself up behind his buckler, stooping on his knee; yet the impetuous dart bore away the tufted top of the helmet, and from his head struck off the towering crest. Then indeed his rage swells; and, driven on by the deceitful arts [of his foe], when he perceived that the steeds and chariot were driven back in a different career, he makes large protestations to Jove, and the altars of the broken league. At length he rushes into the midst of the lines, and under the auspicious influence of Mars, arrayed in terrors, ushers in a hideous undistinguished slaughter, and gives loose reins to all his fury.

What god in song can now to me unfold so many disastrous scenes, what god [can tell] the various havoc and death of the chiefs, whom by turns now Turnus chases over all the plain, and now the Trojan hero? Was it thy pleasure, Jove, that nations, which were [one day] to be joined in everlasting peace, should with such commotion engage? Æneas, not losing time, full in the side smote Sucro the Rutulian, (this combat first checked the Trojans in their career,) and, where death is

speediest, through the ribs and wattled fences of his breast
drives home the cruel blade.   Turnus on foot encountering
Amycus from his horse overthrown, and his brother Diores,
smites the one with his long spear as he comes up, the other
with his sword; and, having cut off the heads of both, suspends them on his chariot, and bears them along bedewed with
blood.   The other despatches Talos, Tanais, and stout Cethe-
gus, all three at one assault, and dejected Onytes, of Theban
extraction, the son of Perida.   Turnus [again overthrows]
the brothers sent from Lycia and Apollo's lands, and Menœtes,
an Arcadian youth, in vain to war averse; whose art and poor
abode had been about the streams of Lerna, abounding in
fishes; nor were the employments of the great known to him,
while in farmed land his father sowed.   And as two fires rage,
let loose from different quarters upon a withered copse, and
crackling laurel groves; or as with impetuous fall from the
steep mountains two foaming rivers roar along and roll to the
sea, each laying his passage waste: with no less impetuosity
Æneas and Turnus both rush through the embattled plain;
now, now their rage boils up within; their invincible breasts
are ready to burst with fury; now with full career they drive
into the midst of wounds.   The one (Æneas) with a rock and
the whirling force of a huge stone, overthrows headlong, and
at his length stretches on the ground, Murranus, vaunting loud
his ancestry, and the ancient names of his forefathers, and his
whole line through the Latin kings derived: him beneath the
harness and yoke the wheels dragged along, and with rap on
rap the hurrying hoofs of his steeds, regardless of their master, trample upon him.   The other (Turnus) encounters Ilus
rushing on, and storming hideous with ire, and against his
gilded temples hurls a javelin; through his helmet transfixing
his brain, the spear stood still.   Nor could thy right hand, O
Creteus, bravest of Greeks, save thee from Turnus; nor did
his own gods protect Cupencus from the assault of Æneas.
The sword found easy access to his heart: nor did the resistance of the brazen shield aught avail its hapless owner.   Laurentum's fields, O Æolus, saw thee too fall, and [stretched] on
thy back widely cover the earth.   Thou, whom neither the
Grecian squadrons could prostrate, nor Achilles, who overthrew Priam's empire, meetest thy doom.   Here were the
boundaries of thy life: under Mount Ida thy stately palace,

in Lyrnessus thy stately palace; [here] a grave in Laurentine ground. Thus now both hosts are [on each other] turned, both Latins and Trojans all: Mnestheus, and stern Serestus, and Messapus, a horseman renowned, and gallant Asylas, the Tuscan phalanx, and Arcadian Evander's cavalry, the warriors each to his power their utmost efforts exert.[31] No stop, no stay; with vast emulation they strain their utmost.

Here his lovely parent inspired Æneas with the resolution to march to the walls, and forthwith advance his army against the city, and with an unexpected blow confound the Latins. While through the various ranks in quest of Turnus he rolled his eyes hither and thither around, he sees the city exempt from the disastrous war, and in safety undisturbed. Instantly the image of a more decisive battle inflames his soul: he calls the chiefs, Mnestheus, Sergestus, and brave Serestus, and takes a rising ground, where the rest of the Trojan army assemble in thick array,[32] nor lay their targets or darts aside. He in the centre, posted on the eminence, addresses them: Let no obstruction be given to my proposal: Jove stands by us: nor, because the design is sudden, let any one be the more backward. The city, the cause of the war, the empire itself of Latinus, unless the people consent to receive our yoke, and vanquished to submit, this day will I overturn, and lay their smoking towers level with the ground. Am I forsooth to wait till Turnus deign to accept our offered challenge, and [so often] beaten, be again disposed to take the field? This is the source, my friends, this the great hinge of the execrable war. Quickly bring brands, and with fire re-assert the league. He said; and all at once with emulous ardour form the wedged battalion, and to the walls in a dense body move. Suddenly the scaling ladders, and unexpected flames appear. Some fly to the gates, and butcher the first they meet; others hurl the steel, and darken the sky with darts. Æneas himself among the foremost beneath the walls extends his hand, and with a loud voice accuses Latinus; the gods he calls to witness, that he is a second time compelled to the fight; that the Italians are now twice become his foes, and this the second league they

---

[31] This seems like an imitation of Plautus, Amphit. l. 1, 76, "Pro se quisque, id quod quisque potest et valet." Cf. Ter. Heaut. i. 1, 74. Ovid Met. iii. 642. B.

[32] "Densi" refers to "milites," which is implied in "legio." B.

broke. Among the trembling citizens dissension arises ; some press to dismantle the town, and open the gates to the Trojans, and drag the king himself to the ramparts. Others take up arms, and march on to defend the walls. As when a shepherd hath traced out a swarm of bees enclosed in some harbouring cleft, and filled [their cells] with bitter smoke ; they within, alarmed for their affairs, in trepidation run hither and thither through the waxen camp, and with loud buzzing whet their rage : through their cells the black stench is rolled ; then with faint murmur the caverns within resound ; to the empty regions of air the smoke ascends.

This disaster too befell the distressed Latins, which with woe shook the whole city to the foundation. The queen, soon as she saw the enemy advancing to the town, the walls assaulted, the flames flying up to the roofs ; no where the Rutulian bands, no troops of Turnus ; had the misfortune to believe the youth slain in the heat of battle, and, with sudden grief distracted, cries, that she had been the cause, the criminal author, and source of ills ; and frantic in her raving anguish, pouring forth many exclamations, with her hands in despair asunder tears her purple robes, and from a lofty beam ties the noose of her unseemly [83] death. Which disaster when it reached the unhappy Latin dames, first her daughter Lavinia tore her golden tresses and rosy cheeks with her hands ; then all the rest run raving about. With shrieks the palace far and wide resounds. Hence the doleful intelligence is blazed through the town. Their souls despond. Latinus, thunderstruck with the destiny of his queen, and the ruin of his city, goes about tearing his robe, deforming his hoary locks, sprinkled over with sordid ashes ; and much himself accuses, for not having before received Trojan Æneas, and cordially admitted him as his son-in-law.

Meanwhile the warrior Turnus in the extremity of the field pursues a few straggling troops, now more languid, and less elated with the speed of his horses. The wind wafted to him this outcry mingled with unseen terrors ; the din and unjoyous murmurs of the distracted city struck his listening ears. Ah me ! why with such woe are our walls disturbed ? What

---

[83] Either referring to the supposed treatment of those who had committed suicide, in the other world, or to the disgracefulness of a death by hanging. See Servius. B.

alarming shouts burst from the various quarters of the town?
He said, and, pulling in the reins, stood still, in amazement
lost.   Then his sister, now that she was transformed into the
figure of the charioteer Metiscus, and guided the chariot, the
horses, and the reins, in these words replies: This way, Turnus, let us pursue the sons of Troy, where our first conquest
opens the way.   Others there are who by their prowess can
defend the walls: Æneas assails the Italians, and [with them]
joins battle.   Let us too, by exerting our activity, dispense
death to the Trojans without pity; nor shall you quit the field
inferior to him in the number [of the slain], or in the honour
of the fight.   To this Turnus [replied]: O sister; I knew
you long ago, when first by artifice you broke the truce, and
engaged yourself in these wars; and now, though a goddess,
in vain you wear disguise.   But what god commissioned you
to quit the skies in order to sustain such toils? [are you
come] to be witness of your unhappy brother's cruel death?
For what can I do? or what success now can fortune promise?   Myself before my eyes saw Murranus, than whom
there survives not one to me more dear; [I saw him] fall as
he called on me with his [expiring] breath, mighty the man,
and with a mighty wound subdued.   Ill-fated Ufens fell, that
he might not be a spectator of my disgrace: The Trojans are
in possession of his corpse and arms.   Shall I suffer our city
to be razed, the only thing that was wanting to our distress—
nor by this right hand refute the calumnies of Drances?
Shall I turn my back? and shall this earth see Turnus fly?
Is it then so grievous a misfortune to die? Oh infernal powers,
befriend me, since the will of the powers above is hostile!   To
you I shall descend a spotless soul, from that imputation clear,
and at no time degenerate from my great ancestors.

  Scarcely had he said, when lo! Sages, hurried by his foaming steed, flies through the midst of the foes, wounded with
an arrow athwart the face, and imploring Turnus by name he
rushes forward: Turnus, on thee our last relief depends;
have pity on thy own.   Æneas thunders in arms, and threatens to overthrow the stately towers of Latium, and raze them
to the ground: and now to our roofs the fire-brands fly.   On
thee their eyes, on thee their whole regard the Latins turn:
king Latinus himself demurs, whom to call his son-in-law, or
to which alliance to incline.   Besides, the queen, most faith-

ful to your interest, has fallen by her own hand, and, abandoned to despair, has fled from life. Before the gates Messapus and brave Atinas alone sustain the fight. Around those on each side the battalions stand in thick array, and an iron crop of naked swords shoot a horrid glare: [yet, during these public alarms,] you are wheeling your chariot along the desert field.

Confounded with the varied aspect of affairs, Turnus was stunned, and stood in silent gaze. Deep in his breast boils overwhelming shame, also frantic rage with intermingled grief, and love racked with fury, and conscious worth. Soon as the clouds were dispelled, and light to his mind restored, towards the walls he rolled his flaming eye-balls in turbulence of soul, and from his car surveyed the spacious city. When lo! a torrent of flames whirling amid the different stories, in rolling waves ascended to heaven, and had seized the tower; the tower which himself of jointed beams had reared, and under it wheels applied, and with lofty bridges overlaid. Sister, [he cries,] now, now, destiny prevails; forbear to stop me; let us follow whither god and rigid fortune calls. I am resolved to enter the lists with Æneas; whatever bitterness is in death, I am resolved to bear it: nor, sister, shall you see me longer in disgrace. Permit me first, I pray, to give vent to this fury.

He said, and instantly from his chariot sprang with a bound upon the plain; through foes, through darts he rushes, and leaves his mourning sister, and with rapid course bursts through the middle ranks. And as when a rock tumbles precipitately down from a mountain's top, torn by the winds, whether furious rains have washed it away, or undermining time by length of years hath loosened it; down the precipice abrupt the pertinacious mass of mountain with vast impulse is hurried, and bounds over the ground, sweeping away with it woods, flocks, and men: just so through the broken troops Turnus rushes to the walls of the city, where to a vast extent the earth is drenched in streaming blood, and the air hisses with javelins. With his hand he makes a sign, and at the same time thus with a loud voice begins: Now, Rutulians, forbear, and, ye Latins, withhold your darts; whatever fortune of the war remains is mine: it is more equitable that I alone expiate the [violated] league in your stead, and by the sword decide the strife. All the troops retired from between them, and made room.

But father Æneas, having heard Turnus' name, forsakes the walls, and forsakes the lofty towers, and spurns at all delays: all his enterprises he breaks off, exulting with joy, and thunders dreadful in arms; as mighty as Athos, as mighty as Eryx, or mighty as the parent [mountain] Apenninus[34] himself, when with his waving oaks he roars, and rejoices in his snowy top, exalting himself to the skies. And now both Rutulians, and Trojans, and all the Italians, eagerly turned their eyes; both those who on high guarded the battlements, and those who with the ram battered the walls below: their arms they laid down from their shoulders. Latinus himself with amazement views the mighty heroes, born in distant quarters of the globe, encountering each other, and deciding their quarrel with the sword. They, soon as the lists in the spacious plain were cleared, having with rapid onset flung their javelins from afar, rush to the combat with shields and arms of brass resounding. Earth gives a groan; then stroke on stroke they redouble. Chance and courage are blended together. And as in Sila's[35] spacious grove, or on lofty Taburnus,[36] when two bulls with butting fronts rush to the hostile combat, the shepherds in consternation have fled; all the herd stand dumb with fear, the heifers faintly low, dubious which shall rule the herd, whom the whole drove are to obey: they with great force deal promiscuous wounds to each other, and struggling keenly infix their horns, and with profusion of blood lave their necks and shoulders: the whole grove re-bellows with their groans. Just so Trojan Æneas, and the Daunian hero, with shields against each other tilting, rush forward: loud clashing fills the skies. Great Jove sustains two equally-poised scales, and puts into them the different fates of both; whom the toilsome combat destines to victory, and in which scale death sinks down. Here Turnus, presuming he might with safety, springs forth, and on his tiptoes rises with his whole body to his uplifted sword and aims a blow. The Trojans and trembling Latins shriek aloud, and

[34] Apenninus, a ridge of high mountains, running through the middle of Italy.
[35] Sila, a large wood in Lucania, abounding with pitch.
[36] Taburnus, a mountain of Campania. B.

both armies are fixed in suspense. But the treacherous sword
breaks short, and in the middle of the stroke leaves the inflamed chief [at the mercy of his foe], unless flight should
succeed to his relief. Swifter than the east wind he flies, soon
as he saw the unknown hilt,[77] and his right hand disarmed.
There is a report that in his headlong haste, when he mounted
his yoked steeds for the first onset, while he was in hurried
trepidation, he snatched the sword of his charioteer Metiscus,
leaving his father's [heavenly tempered] steel behind: and
long that served his purpose, while the Trojans offered their
flying backs; but, when it came to Vulcan's arms divine,[78]
the mortal blade, like brittle ice, in shivers flew with the
stroke; along the yellow sands its splinters shine.   Therefore
Turnus, in frantic flight, traverses the several quarters of the
field, and now hither, then thither, wheels in uncertain mazes.
For on every hand the Trojans in close circling bands enclosed him; and on this side a vast morass, on that steep
mountains environ him.   Nor less eagerly Æneas, though, disabled by the shaft, his knees sometimes check and oppose his
speed, pursues, and fervent presses close upon the heels of his
trembling foe.   As a hound, when he has found a stag enclosed by a river, or hedged around by the terror of the crimson plumes,[29] pursues him with speed and full cry; he, meanwhile, scared by the toils and steep bank, backward and
forward flies a thousand ways: but the staunch Umbrian dog
closes upon him, with open mouth, is just in act to gripe [his
prey] and, as if now he griped him, chides with his jaws, and
with delusive bite is mocked: then shouts arise, the banks
and lakes around re-echo, and the whole sky thunders with
uproar.   At once he (Turnus) flies, at once chides the Rutulians all, calling on each by name, and importunately
craves his well-known sword.   Æneas, on the other hand, denounces death and present destruction, if any one should approach; and overawes the trembling troops, threatening to
raze the city, and, wounded as he was, presses on.   Five rounds
they finish in their career, and trace back as many more, this
way and that.   For no slight or frivolous prize is sought; but
for the life and blood of Turnus they strive.

[77] He struck with the sword of Metiscus, not his own.   B.
[78] i. e. those of Æneas.   B.
[80] On the "formido," see my note on Æn. iv. 120.   B.

Sacred to Faunus [40] here chanced to stand a wild olive with
its bitter leaves, a tree long revered by seamen; where saved
from the waves they used to fix their offerings to the Laurentine god, and suspend their garments vowed. But the Trojans without distinction had cut down the sacred stock, that
they might combat in a clear field. Here stood the spear of
Æneas: here fixed the hurling force [of his right hand] had
conveyed it, and riveted it in the tough root. The Trojan
stooped, and attempted with his hand to wrench out the steel,
that with the missile weapon he might pursue him, whom by
speed he could not overtake. Then Turnus, with fear distracted, cries: O Faunus, pity, I pray; and thou, propitious
Earth, detain the weapon, if I have always held your honours
sacred, which, on the contrary, the sons of Troy have by war
profaned. He said, and invoked the aid of the god by vows
not vain. For Æneas, long struggling, after loss of time in
essaying the tenacious root, was unable, by his utmost efforts,
to disengage the firm hold of the wood. While he keenly
strains and presses, the Daunian goddess, again transformed
into the shape of the charioteer Metiscus, runs forward, and
restores to her brother the sword. Venus, indignant that
such licence should be given to the audacious nymph, approached, and from the deep root tore up the spear. The
towering chiefs, in arms and courage renewed, the one relying
on his trusty sword, the other stern and majestic with his
spear, stand opposed, breathless in the martial combat.

Meanwhile the sovereign of all-powerful Olympus addresses
Juno, as from a yellow cloud she viewed the fight: Consort,
when shall this strife be at an end? what further remains?
You yourself know, and own you are not ignorant, that
Æneas is destined to be a denizen of the sky, and by the
Fates is to be advanced to the stars. What then do you propose, or with what view are you hovering in the chill clouds?
Was it seemly for a god [elect] to be violated by a wound
from a mortal? or that Turnus (for without you what power
had Juturna?) should have his wrested sword restored, and to
the vanquished new strength accrue? Now at length desist,
and be swayed by my entreaty: nor let such discontent prey
upon you in silence; nor let gloomy cares so often meet me

---

[40] Faunus, the son of Picus, who is said to have reigned in Italy about
500 B. C.

from those sweet lips. Now affairs are come to a crisis: you
have been empowered to harass the Trojans by sea and land,
to kindle a nameless war, entail dishonour on the house [of
Latinus], and blend sorrows with these nuptials [of Æneas
and his daughter]; further to attempt I forbid you. Thus
Jupiter spoke: thus on the other hand the Saturnian goddess
with downcast look [rejoined]: I own, great Jove, it was
because I knew this to be your will, that I, against my inclination, from Turnus and the earth withdrew. Nor had you
seen me else now sitting alone in this airy recess, enduring
things worthy, unworthy;[41] but, girt with flames, I had been
planted in the very field of battle, drawing the Trojans on to
adverse fight. I confess that I advised Juturna to relieve her
unhappy brother, and I approved that for his life she should
make higher attempts; yet not that she should [throw] a dart
or bend a bow; I swear by the inexorable source of the Stygian lake, which is set forth the sole object of religious dread
to the gods above. And now for my part I yield, and loath-
ing renounce combats. This, which by no law of fate is with-
holden, I implore of thee in behalf of Latium, and for the
honour of [its princes], thy own blood; that when by this
auspicious match (so be it) they shall establish peace, when
they shall unite in laws and leagues, you will not command
the natives of Latium to change their ancient name, or become
Trojans, and be called Teucri, or to change[42] their language
or alter their dress. Let Latium subsist; let the kings of
Alba subsist through ages; let the sons of Rome rise to
imperial power by means of the Italian valour: Troy hath
perished, and suffer it to perish with its name for ever. To
her the founder of men and things thus smiling [spoke]:
Sister of Jove, and Saturn's other offspring, do you still roll
in your breast such tides of passion? But come and quell the
fury indulged in vain. I grant what you desire; [by your
prayers] I am subdued, and willingly myself resign. Their
native language and customs the Ausonians shall retain; and,
as it now is, the name shall be: only incorporated with them
the Trojans shall settle [in Latium]; the institutions and

---

[41] A proverbial phrase, equivalent to "suffering every thing." So
"æqua, iniqua;" "fanda, infanda." B.

[42] I think "viros" is somewhat emphatic, thus: "nor compel such
men, as they are, to wear the *effeminate* Trojan costume." B.

ceremonials of religion I will add, and make them all Latins
of one speech.   Hence a race mingled with Ausonian blood
shall rise, which by its piety you shall see exalted above men,
above gods; nor shall any nation with equal zeal celebrate
your honour.   To these words Juno assents, and, filled with
complacency, gave her mind a contrary bias.   Meanwhile she
quitted the sky, and from the cloud withdrew.

This done, the Sire revolves another purpose with himself,
and meditates to dismiss Juturna from [aiding] her brother's
arms.   Two pests there are, the dire sisters called ; whom,
with hellish Megæra,[a] joyless Night at one and the same
birth brought forth, and bound with equal spires of serpents,
and added to them wings swift as the wind.   These at the
throne of Jove, and at the court of the incensed sovereign
present themselves, and sharpen terror in the minds of feeble
mortals, what time the king of gods prepares baleful death and
diseases, or terrifies guilty cities with war.   Of these Jove
sends down one in haste from the lofty æther, and bids her
stand before Juturna as a fatal sign.   She flies and in a rapid
whirlwind to earth is borne: just as through a cloudy sky an
arrow shot from the string, which tinged with the bitterness
of malignant poison a Parthian (a Parthian or Cydonian) hath
hurled an incurable dart, flies hissing and unseen athwart the
fleeting shades; in like manner the offspring of Night shot
away and hied to the earth.   Soon as she perceives the Trojan battalions and the troops of Turnus, she suddenly shrinks
up into the form of the little fowl, which at times sitting by
night on tombs or desolate towers, late inauspicious hoots
amidst the shades: into this shape transformed, the fiend in
sight of Turnus flies backward and forward screaming, and
flaps on his buckler with her wings.   Unusual numbness relaxed
his limbs with fear, his hair with horror stood on end, and his
speech clove to his jaws.   But, when his sister Juturna at a
distance knew the shrill noise and the Fury's wings, in deep
distress she tears her dishevelled tresses, mangling her face
with her nails, and her breasts with blows : Turnus ! what
can thy sister now avail thee ? wretch that I am, what expedient have I now left ? by what art can I prolong thy life ? so
rueful a portent can I withstand ? Now, now I quit the field.

---

a Megæra, one of the Furies, daughter of Nox and Acheron.

2 D

Add not terror to my fear, ye inauspicious fowls: the beating
of your wings, your deadly screams I know; nor am I a stranger to the stern mandates of imperious Jove. Are these the
returns he makes for my virginity? Why gave he me immortal life? why was I exempt from the law of mortality? surely
now I might have put an end to such oppressive woes, and
accompanied my wretched brother through the shades below.
I immortal! or can I, brother, relish aught of my enjoyments
without thee? Oh, what earth to me will yawn full deep, and
despatch a goddess to the shades below? This said, the goddess muffled up her head in a sea-green veil, drawing many a
groan, and plunged herself into the deep river.

On the other hand, Æneas urges the attack, majestic waves
his massy spear, and thus with wrathful soul bespeaks [his
foe]: What means this delay now after all? or why, O
Turnus, do you now decline the combat? It is not in running
that we must try our skill, but in close fight with cruel arms.
Turn thee into all shapes, collect whatever assistance you can,
whether from valour or from artifice: wish to reach on wings
the lofty stars, or shut up within the hollow earth to lie concealed. He, shaking his head, [replies]: Not thy boisterous
words, insulting foe, cause my fears: the gods, and adverse
Jove, intimidate me. Nor more he said, but casts his eye on
a huge stone, a stone antique, of huge dimensions, which in
the field by chance was lying, set for a land-mark, to distinguish the controverted bounds of the fields.[44] Scarcely
would twelve chosen men support it on their shoulders, such
frames of men as earth now produces. The hero snatched it
up with hurrying hand; raising himself aloft, and rushing on
with speed, he hurled it against his foe. But he knows not
himself, either while running or going, nor when he lifts up
with his hand, or wields the enormous stone.[45] His knees
sink under him: his chill blood with shuddering terror
is congealed. Then the stone itself, rolled through the
empty air, neither reached the hero's whole length, nor
bore home the intended blow. And as in dreams by night,
when languid sleep hath closed our eyes, we seem in vain to
make effort to prolong a race on which we are intent, and in
midst of our efforts sink down faint; nor power is in the

---

[44] Literally, "to determine some dispute respecting the fields." B.
[45] i. e. he feels the loss of his wonted strength. B.

tongue, nor in the body competency of wonted strength,
nor voice nor words obey [the dictates of our will]; just so
from Turnus the cursed fiend withholds success, by whatever
efforts of valour he sought the way. Then various thoughts
are rolling in his breast. Now he turns his eyes on the Rutulians, now on the city [of Laurentum], now stands hovering in dread, and trembles for the approach of the dart. Nor
[perceives he] whither he can fly, nor how he may make
head against his foe, nor sees he any where the chariot or his
sister charioteer. In this perplexity Æneas brandishes against
him the dart of fate, having with his eye marked out the destined wound, and with the whole force of his body hurls it
from afar. Never did stones shot from a battering engine
roar so loud, nor from the thunder burst such mighty peals.
Like a black whirlwind flies the javelin winged with dire destruction; it opens a passage through his corslet's border, and
the utmost orb of his seven-fold shield; then hissing passes
through his mid thigh. Down to earth the mighty Turnus
wounded sinks on his doubled knee.

Up rise the Rutulians together with a groan, and the whole
mountain around rebellows, and the deep groves far and near
return the sound. He, humble and suppliant, stretching his
eyes and imploring hand, says, I have indeed deserved, nor
do I deprecate : improve thy fortune. If any regard to a
wretched father can move thee, (thou too hadst such a sire,
Anchises,) have compassion, I pray thee, on the age of Daunus ;
and me, or, if you rather choose, this body, despoiled of life,
unto my friends restore. You have overcome, and the Ausonians have seen thy vanquished foe stretch forth his [suppliant]
hands : Lavinia is thy bride. Persist not further in thy hate.
Æneas, fierce as he was from the heat of action, stood rolling
his eyes, and repressed his hand : and still more and more the
speech had begun to move his wavering mind, when on the
high shoulder [of his foe] the inauspicious belt appeared, and
with its well-known bosses, the girdle of youthful Pallas shone,
whom vanquished, Turnus with a wound had slain, and on
his shoulders wore the hostile badge. Soon as the hero espied
the memorials of his cruel grief and the spoils [of his friend],
inflamed with fury and terribly enraged, [he exclaimed, And]
shalt thou from me hence escape clad in the spoils of my

friends? Thee Pallas, Pallas, with this wound a victim-devotes, and takes vengeance on thy accursed blood. With these words deep in his opposed bosom he furious plunged the sword. But with the chill of death are his limbs relaxed, and with a groan the indignant soul hurries down to the shades.

THE END.

550299

Longfellow's Poetical Works. *Twenty-four page Engravings, by Birket Foster and others, and a new Portrait.*

—— ; or, without the illustrations, 3s. 6d.

—— Prose Works, complete. *Sixteen page Engravings by Birket Foster and others.*

Loudon's (Mrs.) Entertaining Naturalist. New Edition. Revised by W. S. DALLAS, F.L.S. *With nearly 500 Engravings.* 7s.

Marryat's Masterman Ready; or, The Wreck of the Pacific. *93 Engravings.*

—— Mission; or, Scenes in Africa. (Written for Young People.) *Illustrated by Gilbert and Dalziel.*

—— Pirate; and Three Cutters. New Edition, with a Memoir of the Author. *With 20 Steel Engravings, from Drawings by Clarkson Stanfield, R.A.*

—— Privateer's-Man One Hundred Years Ago. *Eight Engravings on Steel, after Stothard.*

—— Settlers in Canada. New Edition. *Ten fine Engravings by Gilbert and Dalziel.*

Maxwell's Victories of Wellington and the British Armies. *Illustrations on Steel.*

Michael Angelo and Raphael, their Lives and Works. By DUPPA and QUATREMERE DE QUINCY. *With 13 highly-finished Engravings on Steel.*

Miller's History of the Anglo-Saxons. Written in a popular style, on the basis of Sharon Turner. *Portrait of Alfred, Map of Saxon Britain, and 12 elaborate Engravings on Steel.*

Milton's Poetical Works. With a Memoir by JAMES MONTGOMERY, Todd's Verbal Index to all the Poems, and Explanatory Notes. *With 120 Engravings by Thompson and others, from Drawings by W. Harvey.* 2 vols.
Vol. 1. Paradise Lost, complete, with Memoir, Notes, and Index.
Vol. 2. Paradise Regained, and other Poems, with Verbal Index to all the Poems.

Mudie's British Birds. Revised by W. C. L. MARTIN. *Fifty-two Figures and 7 Plates of Eggs.* In 2 vols.

—— ; or, with the plates coloured, 7s. 6d. per vol.

Naval and Military Heroes of Great Britain; or, Calendar of Victory. Being a Record of British Valour and Conquest by Sea and Land, on every day in the year, from the time of William the Conqueror to the Battle of Inkermann. By Major JOHNS, R.M., and Lieutenant P. H. NICOLAS, R.M. *Twenty-four Portraits.* 6s.

Niccolini's History of the Jesuits: their Origin, Progress, Doctrines, and Designs. *Fine Portraits of Loyola, Lainez, Xavier, Borgia, Acquaviva, Père la Chaise, and Pope Ganganelli.*

Norway and its Scenery. Comprising Price's Journal, with large Additions, and a Road-Book. Edited by T. FORESTER. *Twenty-two Illustrations.*

Paris and its Environs, including Versailles, St. Cloud, and Excursions into the Champagne Districts. An Illustrated Handbook for Travellers. Edited by T. FORESTER. *Twenty-eight beautiful Engravings.*

Petrarch's Sonnets, and other Poems. Translated into English Verse. By various hands. With a Life of the Poet, by THOMAS CAMPBELL. *With 16 Engravings.*

Pickering's History of the Races of Man, with an Analytical Synopsis of the Natural History of Man. By Dr. HALL. *Illustrated by numerous Portraits.*

—— ; or, with the plates coloured, 7s. 6d.

*** An excellent Edition of a work originally published at 3l. 3s. by the American Government.

Pictorial Handbook of Modern Geography, on a Popular Plan. 3s. 6d. *Illustrated by 150 Engravings and 51 Maps.* 6s.

—— ; or, with the maps coloured, 7s. 6d.

Pope's Poetical Works. Edited by ROBERT CARRUTHERS. *Numerous Engravings.* 2 vols.

—— Homer's Iliad. With Introduction and Notes by J. S. WATSON, M.A. *Illustrated by the entire Series of Flaxman's Designs, beautifully engraved by Moses (in the full 8vo. size).*

—— Homer's Odyssey, Hymns, &c., by other translators, including Chapman, and Introduction and Notes by J. S. WATSON, M.A. *Flaxman's Designs beautifully engraved by Moses.*

Pope's Life. Including many of his Letters. By ROBERT CARRUTHERS. New Edition, revised and enlarged. *Illustrations.*

The preceding 5 vols. make a complete and elegant edition of Pope's Poetical Works and Translations for 25s.

Pottery and Porcelain, and other Objects of Vertu (a Guide to the Knowledge of). To which is added an Engraved List of all the known Marks and Monograms. By HENRY G. BOHN. *Numerous Engravings.*

———; or, *coloured.* 10s. 6d.

Prout's (Father) Reliques. New Edition, revised and largely augmented. *Twenty-one spirited Etchings by Maclise.* Two volumes in one. 7s. 6d.

Recreations in Shooting. By "CRAVEN." New Edition, revised and enlarged. 62 *Engravings on Wood, after Harvey, and 9 Engravings on Steel, chiefly after A. Cooper, R.A.*

Redding's History and Descriptions of Wines, Ancient and Modern. *Twenty beautiful Woodcuts.*

Rennie's Insect Architecture. New Edition. Revised by the Rev. J. G. WOOD, M.A.

Robinson Crusoe. With Illustrations by STOTHARD and HARVEY. Twelve beautiful Engravings on Steel, and 74 on Wood.

———; or, without the Steel Illustrations. 3s. 6d.
The prettiest Edition extant.

Rome in the Nineteenth Century. New Edition. Revised by the Author. *Illustrated by 34 fine Steel Engravings.* 2 vols.

Southey's Life of Nelson. With Additional Notes. *Illustrated with 64 Engravings.*

Starling's (Miss) Noble Deeds of Women; or, Examples of Female Courage, Fortitude, and Virtue. *Fourteen beautiful Illustrations.*

Stuart and Revett's Antiquities of Athens, and other Monuments of Greece. *Illustrated in 71 Steel Plates, and numerous Woodcuts.*

Tales of the Genii; or, the Delightful Lessons of Horam. *Numerous Woodcuts, and 9 Steel Engravings, after Stothard.*

Tasso's Jerusalem Delivered. Translated into English Spenserian Verse, with a Life of the Author. By J. H. WIFFEN. *Eight Engravings on Steel, and 24 on Wood, by Thurston.*

Walker's Manly Exercises. Containing Skating, Riding, Driving, Hunting, Shooting, Sailing, Rowing, Swimming, &c. New Edition, revised by "CRAVEN." *Forty-four Steel Plates, and numerous Woodcuts.*

Walton's Complete Angler. Edited by EDWARD JESSE, Esq. To which is added an Account of Fishing Stations, &c. by H. G. BOHN. *Upwards of 203 Engravings.*

———; or, *with 26 additional page Illustrations on Steel.* 7s. 6d.

Wellington, Life of. By AN OLD SOLDIER, from the materials of Maxwell. *Eighteen Engravings.*

White's Natural History of Selborne. With Notes by Sir WILLIAM JARDINE and EDWARD JESSE, Esq. *Illustrated by 40 highly-finished Engravings.*

———; or, *with the plates coloured,* 7s. 6d.

Young, The, Lady's Book. A Manual of Elegant Recreations, Arts, Sciences, and Accomplishments; including Geology, Mineralogy, Conchology, Botany, Entomology, Ornithology, Costume, Embroidery, the Escritoire, Archery, Riding, Music (instrumental and vocal), Dancing, Exercises, Painting, Photography, &c., &c. Edited by distinguished Professors. *Twelve Hundred Woodcut Illustrations, and several fine Engravings on Steel.* 7s. 6d.

———; or, *cloth gilt, gilt edges,* 9s.

II.

Bohn's Classical Library.

5s. per Volume, excepting those marked otherwise.

Æschylus. Literally Translated into English Prose by an Oxonian. 3s. 6d.

———, Appendix to. Containing the New Readings given in Hermann's posthumous Edition of Æschylus. By GEORGE BURGES, M.A. 3s. 6d.

Ammianus Marcellinus. History of Rome from Constantine to Valens. Translated by C. D. YONGE, B.A. Dble. vol. 7s. 6d.

Antoninus. The Thoughts of the Emperor Marcus Aurelius. Translated by GEO. LONG, M.A. 3s. 6d.

Apuleius, the Golden Ass; Death of Socrates; Florida; and Discourse on Magic. To which is added a Metrical Version of Cupid and Psyche; and Mrs. Tighe's Psyche. *Frontispiece.*

Lucan's Pharsalia. Translated, with Notes, by H. T. Riley.

Lucretius. Literally Translated, with Notes, by the Rev. J. S. Watson, M.A. And the Metrical Version by J. M. Good.

Martial's Epigrams, complete. Literally Translated. Each accompanied by one or more Verse Translations selected from the Works of English Poets, and other sources. With a copious Index. Double volume (660 pages). 7s. 6d.

Ovid's Works, complete. Literally Translated. 3 vols.
Vol. 1. Fasti, Tristia, Epistles, &c.
Vol. 2. Metamorphoses.
Vol. 3. Heroides, Art of Love, &c.

Pindar. Literally Translated, by Dawson W. Turner, and the Metrical Version by Abraham Moore.

Plato's Works. Translated by the Rev. H. Cary and others. In 6 vols.
Vol. 1. The Apology of Socrates, Crito, Phædo, Gorgias, Protagoras, Phædrus, Theætetus, Euthyphron, Lysis.
Vol. 2. The Republic, Timæus, & Critias.
Vol. 3. Meno, Euthydemus, The Sophist, Statesman, Cratylus, Parmenides, and the Banquet.
Vol. 4. Philebus, Charmides, Laches, The Two Alcibiades, and Ten other Dialogues.
Vol. 5. The Laws.
Vol. 6. The Doubtful Works. With General Index.

——— **Dialogues, an Analysis and** Index to. With References to the Translation in Bohn's Classical Library. By Dr. Day.

Plautus's Comedies. Literally Translated, with Notes, by H. T. Riley, B.A. In 2 vols.

Pliny's Natural History. Translated, with Copious Notes, by the late John Bostock, M.D., F.R.S., and H. T. Riley, B.A. In 6 vols.

Propertius, Petronius, and Johannes Secundus. Literally Translated, and accompanied by Poetical Versions, from various sources.

Quintilian's Institutes of Oratory. Literally Translated, with Notes, &c., by J. S. Watson, M.A. In 2 vols.

Sallust, Florus, and Velleius Paterculus. With Copious Notes, Biographical Notices, and Index, by J. S. Watson.

Sophocles. The Oxford Translation revised.

Standard Library Atlas of Classical Geography. *Twenty-two large coloured Maps according to the latest authorities.* With a complete Index (accentuated), giving the latitude and longitude of every place named in the Maps. Imp. 8vo. 7s. 6d.

Strabo's Geography. Translated, with Copious Notes, by W. Falconer, M.A., and H. C. Hamilton, Esq. With Index, giving the Ancient and Modern Names. In 3 vols.

Suetonius' Lives of the Twelve Cæsars, and other Works. Thomson's Translation, revised, with Notes, by T. Forester.

Tacitus. Literally Translated, with Notes. In 2 vols.
Vol. 1. The Annals.
Vol. 2. The History, Germania, Agricola, &c. With Index.

Terence and Phædrus. By H. T. Riley, B.A.

Theocritus, Bion, Moschus, and Tyrtæus. By J. Banks, M.A. With the Metrical Versions of Chapman.

Thucydides. Literally Translated by Rev. H. Dale. In 2 vols. 3s. 6d. each.

Virgil. Literally Translated by Davidson. New Edition, carefully revised. 3s. 6d.

Xenophon's Works. In 3 Vols.
Vol. 1. The Anabasis and Memorabilia. Translated, with Notes, by J. S. Watson, M.A. And a Geographical Commentary, by W. F. Ainsworth, F.S.A., F.R.G.S., &c.
Vol. 2. Cyropædia and Hellenica. By J. S. Watson, M.A. and the Rev. H. Dale.
Vol. 3. The Minor Works. By J. S. Watson, M.A.

XII.
Bohn's Scientific Library.
5s. per Volume, excepting those marked otherwise.

Agassiz and Gould's Comparative Physiology. Enlarged by Dr. Wright. *Upwards of 400 Engravings.*

Bacon's Novum Organum and Advancement of Learning. Complete, with Notes, by J. Devey, M.A.

Blair's Chronological Tables, Revised and Enlarged. Comprehending the Chronology and History of the World, from

the earliest times. By J. Willoughby Rosse. Double Volume. 10s.; or, halfbound, 10s. 6d.

Index of Dates. Comprehending the principal Facts in the Chronology and History of the World, from the earliest to the present time, alphabetically arranged. By J. W. Rosse. Double volume, 10s. or, half-bound, 10s. 6d.

Bolley's Manual of Technical Analysis. A Guide for the Testing of Natural and Artificial Substances. By B. H. PAUL. 100 Wood Engravings.

BRIDGEWATER TREATISES.—

—— **Bell on the Hand.** Its Mechanism and Vital Endowments as evincing Design. Seventh Edition Revised.

—— **Kirby on the History, Habits,** and Instincts of Animals. Edited, with Notes, by T. RYMER JONES. Numerous Engravings, many of which are additional. In 2 vols.

—— **Kidd on the Adaptation of** External Nature to the Physical Condition of Man. 3s. 6d.

—— **Whewell's Astronomy and** General Physics, considered with reference to Natural Theology. 3s. 6d.

—— **Chalmers on the Adaptation** of External Nature to the Moral and Intellectual Constitution of Man. 5s.

—— **Prout's Treatise on Chemistry,** Meteorology, and Digestion. Edited by Dr. J. W. GRIFFITH.

—— **Buckland's Geology and** Mineralogy. 2 vols. 15s.

—— **Roget's Animal and Vegetable Physiology.** Illustrated. In 2 vols. 6s. each.

Carpenter's (Dr. W. B.) Zoology. A Systematic View of the Structure, Habits, Instincts, and Uses, of the principal Families of the Animal Kingdom, and of the chief forms of Fossil Remains. New edition, revised to the present time, under arrangement with the Author, by W. S. DALLAS, F.L.S. Illustrated with many hundred fine Wood Engravings. In 2 vols. 6s. each.

—— **Mechanical Philosophy, Astronomy,** and Horology. A Popular Exposition. 181 Illustrations.

—— **Vegetable Physiology and** Systematic Botany. A complete Introduction to the Knowledge of Plants. New Edition, revised, under arrangement with the Author, by E. LANKESTER, M.D., &c. Several hundred Illustrations on Wood. 6s.

—— **Animal Physiology.** New Edition, thoroughly revised, and in part re-written by the Author. Upwards of 300 capital Illustrations. 6s.

Chess Congress of 1862. A Collection of the Games played, and a Selection of the Problems sent in for the Competition. Edited by J. LÖWENTHAL, Manager. With an Account of the Proceedings, and a Memoir of the British Chess Association, by J. W. MEDLEY, Hon. Sec. 7s.

Chevreul on Colour. Containing the Principles of Harmony and Contrast of Colours, and their application to the Arts. Translated from the French by CHARLES MARTEL. Only complete Edition. Several Plates. Or, with an additional series of 16 Plates in Colours. 7s. 6d.

Clark's (Hugh) Introduction to Heraldry. With nearly 1000 Illustrations. 18th Edition. Revised and enlarged by J. R. PLANCHÉ, Rouge Croix. Or, with all the Illustrations coloured, 15s.

Comte's Philosophy of the Sciences. By G. H. LEWES. 5s.

Ennemoser's History of Magic. Translated by WILLIAM HOWITT. With an Appendix of the most remarkable and best authenticated Stories of Apparitions, Dreams, Table-Turning, and Spirit-Rapping, &c. In 2 vols.

Handbook of Domestic Medicine. Popularly arranged. By DR. HENRY DAVIES. 700 pages. With complete Index.

Handbook of Games. By various Amateurs and Professors. Comprising treatises on all the principal Games of chance, skill, and manual dexterity. In all, above 40 games (the Whist, Draughts, and Billiards being especially comprehensive). Edited by H. G. BOHN. Illustrated by numerous Diagrams.

Hogg's (Jabez) Elements of Experimental and Natural Philosophy. Containing Mechanics, Pneumatics, Hydrostatics, Hydraulics, Acoustics, Optics, Caloric, Electricity, Voltaism, and Magnetism. New Edition, enlarged. Upwards of 400 Woodcuts.

Hind's Introduction to Astronomy. With a Vocabulary, containing an Explanation of all the Terms in present use. New Edition, enlarged. Numerous Engravings. 3s. 6d.

Humboldt's Cosmos; or Sketch of a Physical Description of the Universe. Translated by E. C. Otté and W. S. DALLAS, F.L.S. Fine Portrait. In five vols. 3s. 6d. each; excepting Vol. V., 5s.
  . In this edition the notes are placed beneath the text, Humboldt's analytical Summaries and the passages hitherto suppressed are included, and new and comprehensive Indices are added.

—— **Travels in America.** In 3 vols.

—— **Views of Nature; or, Contemplations** of the Sublime Phenomena of Creation. Translated by E. C. Otté and H. G. BOHN. A fac-simile letter from the Author to the Publisher; translations of the quotations, and a complete Index.

Humphry's Coin Collector's Manual. A popular Introduction to the Study of Coins. Highly finished Engravings. In 2 vols.

13

Hunt's (Robert) Poetry of Science; or, Studies of the Physical Phenomena of Nature. By Professor Hunt. New Edition, enlarged.

Index of Dates. See Blair's Tables.

Joyce's Scientific Dialogues. Completed to the present state of Knowledge, by Dr. Griffith. Numerous Woodcuts.

Knight's (Chas.) Knowledge is Power. A Popular Manual of Political Economy.

Lectures on Painting. By the Royal Academicians. With Introductory Essay, and Notes by R. Wornum, Esq. Portraits.

Mantell's (Dr.) Geological Excursions through the Isle of Wight and Dorsetshire. New Edition, by T. Rupert Jones, Esq. Numerous beautifully executed Woodcuts, and a Geological Map.

—— **Medals of Creation;** or, First Lessons in Geology and the Study of Organic Remains; including Geological Excursions. New Edition, revised. Coloured Plates, and several hundred beautiful Woodcuts. In 2 vols. 7s. 6d. each.

—— **Petrifactions and their Teaching.** An Illustrated Handbook to the Organic Remains in the British Museum. Numerous Engravings. 6s.

—— **Wonders of Geology;** or, a Familiar Exposition of Geological Phenomena. New Edition, augmented by T. Rupert Jones, F.G.S. Coloured Geological Map of England, Plates, and nearly 200 beautiful Woodcuts. In 2 vols. 7s. 6d. each.

Morphy's Games of Chess. Being the Matches and best Games played by the American Champion, with Explanatory and Analytical Notes, by J. Löwenthal. Portrait and Memoir.

It contains by far the largest collection of games played by Mr. Morphy extant in any form, and has received his endorsement and co-operation.

Oarsted's Soul in Nature, &c. Portrait.

Richardson's Geology, including Mineralogy and Palæontology. Revised and enlarged, by Dr. T. Wright. Upwards of 400 Illustrations.

Schouw's Earth, Plants, and Man; and Kobell's Sketches from the Mineral Kingdom. Translated by A. Henfrey, F.R.S. Coloured Map of the Geography of Plants.

Smith's (Pye) Geology and Scripture; or, The Relation between the Holy Scriptures and Geological Science.

Stanley's Classified Synopsis of the Principal Painters of the Dutch and Flemish Schools.

Staunton's Chess-player's Handbook. Numerous Diagrams.

—— **Chess Praxis.** A Supplement to the Chess-player's Handbook. Containing all the most important modern improvements in the Openings. Illustrated by actual Games; a revised Code of Chess Laws; and a Selection of Mr. Morphy's Games in England and France. 6s.

—— **Chess-player's Companion.** Comprising a new Treatise on Odds, Collection of Match Games, and a Selection of Original Problems.

—— **Chess Tournament of 1851.** Numerous Illustrations.

Principles of Chemistry, exemplified in a series of simple experiments. Based upon the German work of Professor Stockhardt, and Edited by C. W. Heaton, Professor of Chemistry at Charing Cross Hospital. Upwards of 270 Illustrations.

Stockhardt's Agricultural Chemistry; or, Chemical Field Lectures. Addressed to Farmers. Translated, with Notes, by Professor Henfrey, F.R.S. To which is added, a Paper on Liquid Manure, by J. J. Mechi, Esq.

Ure's (Dr. A.) Cotton Manufacture of Great Britain, systematically investigated; with an introductory view of its comparative state in Foreign Countries. New Edition, revised and completed to the present time, by P. L. Simmonds. One hundred and fifty Illustrations. In 2 vols.

—— **Philosophy of Manufactures;** or, An Exposition of the Factory System of Great Britain. New Ed., continued to the present time, by P. L. Simmonds. 7s. 6d.

XIII.

Bohn's Cheap Series.

Boswell's Life of Johnson, and Johnsoniana. Including his Tour to the Hebrides, Tour in Wales, &c. Edited, with large additions and Notes, by the Right Hon. John Wilson Croker. The second and most complete Copyright Edition, re-arranged and revised according to the suggestions of Lord Macaulay, by the late John Wright, Esq., with further additions by Mr. Croker. Upwards of 80 fine Engravings on Steel. In 6 vols. cloth. 30s.

Carpenter's (Dr. W. B.) Physiology of Temperance and Total Abstinence, 1s.; on fine paper, cloth, 2s. 6d.

Dibdin's Sea Songs (Admiralty Edition). *Illustrations by Cruikshank.* 2s. 6d.

Emerson's Twenty Essays. 1s. 6d.

——— English Characteristics. 1s.

——— Orations and Lectures. 1s.

——— Representative Men. Complete. 1s. 6d.

Franklin's (Benjamin) Genuine Autobiography. From the Original Manuscript. By Jared Sparks. 1s.

Hawthorne's (Nathaniel) Twice Told Tales. First and Second Series. 2 vols. in one. 2s.

——— Snow Image & other Tales. 1s.

——— Scarlet Letter. 1s. 6d.

——— House with the Seven Gables. A Romance. 1s. 6d.

Hazlitt's Table Talk. Parts 1, 2, and 3. 1s. each.

——— Plain Speaker. Parts 1, 2, and 3. 1s. 6d. each.

——— Lectures on the English Comic Writers. 1s. 6d.

——— Lectures on the English Poets. 1s. 6d.

——— Lectures on the Literature of the Age of Elizabeth. 1s. 6d.

——— Lectures on the Characters of Shakespeare's Plays. 1s. 6d.

Irving's (Washington) Life of Mohammed. *Portrait.* 1s. 6d.

——— Successors of Mohammed. 1s. 6d.

——— Life of Goldsmith. 1s. 6d.

Irving's (Washington) Sketch Book. 1s. 6d.

——— Tales of a Traveller. 1s. 6d.

——— Tour on the Prairies. 1s.

——— Conquests of Granada and Spain. 2 vols. 1s. 6d. each.

——— Life of Columbus. 2 vols. 1s. 6d. each.

——— Companions of Columbus. 1s. 6d.

——— Adventures of Captain Bonneville. 1s. 6d.

——— Knickerbocker's New York. 1s. 6d.

——— Tales of the Alhambra. 1s. 6d.

——— Conquest of Florida. 1s. 6d.

——— Abbotsford and Newstead. 1s.

——— Salmagundi. 1s. 6d.

——— Bracebridge Hall. 1s. 6d.

——— Astoria. 2s.

——— Wolfert's Roost, and other Tales. 1s.; fine paper, 1s. 6d.

——— Life of Washington. Authorised Edition (uniform with the Works). *Fine Portrait, &c.* 5 parts, with General Index. 2s. 6d. each.

——— Life and Letters. By his Nephew, Pierre E. Irving. *Portrait.* In 4 parts. 2s. each.

*** For Washington Irving's Collected Works, see p. 5.

Lamb's (Charles) Essays of Elia. 1s.

——— Last Essays of Elia. 1s.

——— Eliana, with Biographical Sketch. 1s.